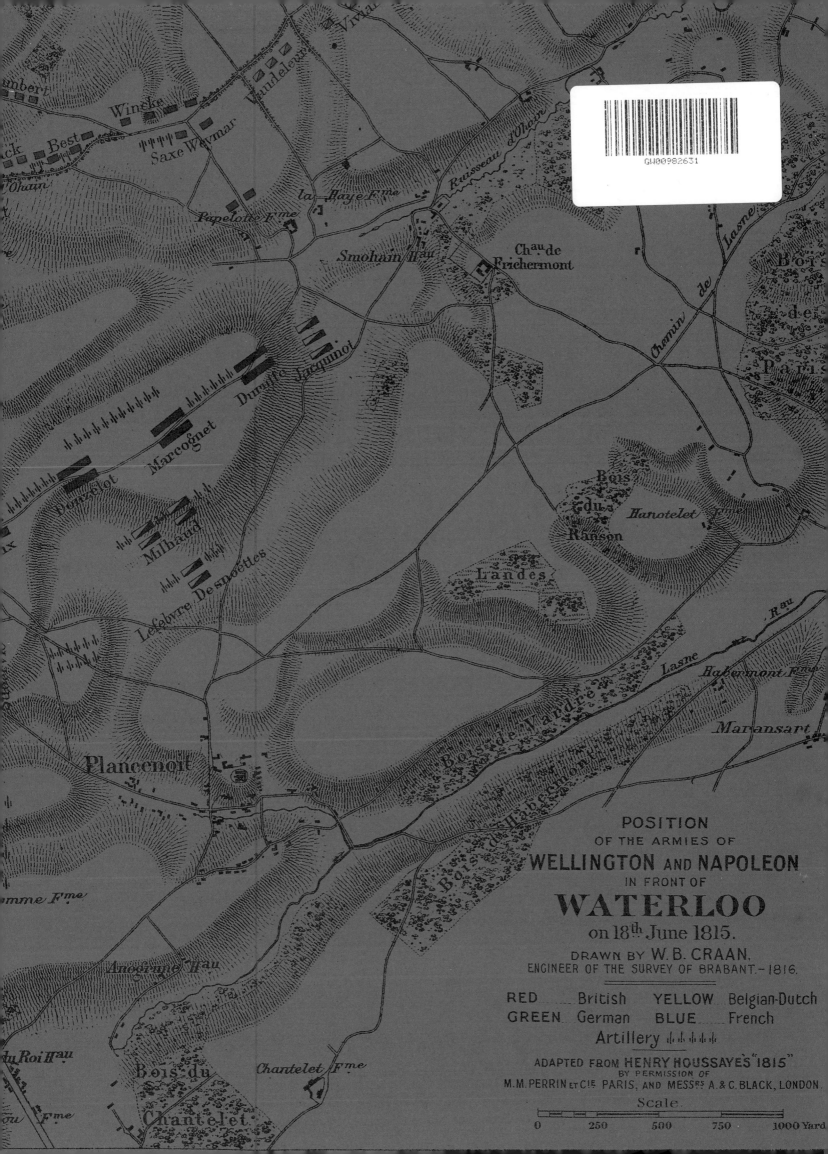

POSITION
OF THE ARMIES OF
WELLINGTON AND NAPOLEON
IN FRONT OF
WATERLOO
on 18th June 1815.
DRAWN BY W. B. CRAAN,
ENGINEER OF THE SURVEY OF BRABANT.—1816.

RED ___ British YELLOW ___ Belgian-Dutch
GREEN ___ German BLUE ___ French
Artillery ┥┝┥┝

ADAPTED FROM HENRY HOUSSAYES "1815"
BY PERMISSION OF
M.M. PERRIN ET CIE PARIS, AND MESSRS A. & C. BLACK, LONDON.

Scale.
0   250   500   750   1000 Yard

British Battles & Medals

The Charge of the Scots Greys at Waterloo
detail from the painting by Lady Butler

British Battles
& Medals

E. C. Joslin,   A. R. Litherland,   B. T. Simpkin

SPINK   *London 1988*

iv

Published by Spink & Son Ltd
5, 6 & 7 King Street, St James's
London SW1Y 6QS

British Battles and Medals.-6th ed.
1. Military forces, British.Medals.
I. Joslin, E.C. (Edward Charles), 1924-
II. Litherland, A.R. III. Simpkin, B.T.
IV. Gordon, L.L. (Lawrence Lee)
737'.223' 0941

ISBN 0-907605-25-7

Designed by Paul Sharp

Photoset by Grillford Ltd, Bletchley
Printed by Pardy & Son Printers Ltd, Ringwood

Contents

Preface

Over 40 years ago, Major L. L. Gordon produced his 1st Edition of *British Battles and Medals*. This was followed in 1949 by a 2nd and improved Edition, and in 1962 by the 3rd Edition. The 4th Edition was revised by Mr E. C. Joslin and was published by Spink & Son; likewise, the 5th Edition was also published by Spink's in 1979, again revised by Mr Joslin.

Each succeeding volume has been revised following advice and help from numerous collectors the world over. The opportunity has now been taken with this new edition to make major changes to the contents. With the advent of specialised books on the subject of medals, this edition is limited purely to campaign medals; good shooting and best shot medals have been omitted.

The entire text has been revised and many specialist articles from various sources have been taken into account to refine and polish the information now presented. It is obvious that in a general work on such a broad subject the minutiae cannot be given for every unit for every action, but with each succeeding edition of this now generally accepted classic work on campaign medals, the standard of accuracy and detail is improved.

The late Major Gordon performed an invaluable task when he first produced this book. He was stepping in the footsteps of those earlier pioneers—Hastings Irwin, J. H. Mayo and Dr Payne; that he had errors and omissions cannot be denied, but with each succeeding revision, helped by many collectors, these have been corrected, and none more so than in this latest work.

It must also be a matter of satisfaction that after the disappearance of the old established firm of Gale & Polden, the original publishers and printers of Major Gordon's book, that the enthusiasm engendered by the original author has been maintained by Spink.

J. M. A. TAMPLIN

Introduction

In producing this work we hope to satisfy the requirements of both the established collector and the historian, whilst at the same time encouraging the interest shown by newcomers to the hobby. Much consultation of existing reference works, learned articles and reports has taken place over many years in order to bring this work as up to date as possible. At the same time we have endeavoured to assure the accuracy of information demanded by today's collectors. This updating process has also involved much merciless pruning to keep the work down to a manageable size. In order to make the book more "workable" we have produced two indexes, one giving the name of the medal in alphabetical order and the other listing the bars, both alphabetically and by date.

The medals have been arranged in chronological order. The book has been completely redesigned and the illustrations for this publication, all of which are new, have been placed adjacent to the text making identification much easier. We have produced a completely new ribbon chart incorporating new material and which reproduces as accurately as possible the colours of the ribbons.

It is hoped that the newly compiled and updated regimental table will enable rapid translation of regimental numbers to present day titles.

All the medals are fully described numismatically, giving details of obverse, reverse, size, bars etc., and this information has been laid out in a much improved standardised form for ease of reference. This numismatic information is followed by much historical data and details of units present for each action.

In conclusion we would like to thank the many people who helped us in the production of this new work. It should be appreciated by all that in compiling such a work it is inevitable that errors will remain and we would welcome any corrections since it is, after all, a far better thing to correct than to criticise.

THE EDITORS

Acknowledgements

The Editors would like to acknowledge the following for their valued assistance and advice given during the preparation of this work:

G. Brown, Canadian Medals
Lt Col M.K. O'M. Dewar RGJ, Army General Service Medals
N. Dix, for assistance throughout
Mrs J. E. Doel
Capt K. J. Douglas-Morris, DL, RN, Naval Medals
B. W. Ellis, QSA Medals to Australians
G. R. Everson, South African Medals
D. Fearon, Medals prior to 1700
W. H. Fevyer
D. R. Forsyth, South African Medals
A. V. Hall, Naval Medals
A. Harrison, MGS Medals
M. G. Hibbard
M. Johnson and Members of the Indian Military Collector's Society
R. Kirch
Lt Col A. M. MacFarlane, RA, Artillery Units
Dr F. Mitchell
R. Perkins, South Atlantic Medal
D. H. Saville
J. M. A. Tamplin, TD
E. G. Ursual
J. W. Wilson

and also many members of the Orders and Medals Research Society who kindly responded to the editors' plea for help, along with contributions from collectors and historians worldwide.

We would like to thank R. J. Scarlett for providing the majority of the photographs, the copyright of which is held by J. B. Hayward & Son; also Paul Sharp for his imaginative design for this new edition.

British Battles & Medals

Elizabethan Naval Medals 1588-1590

These medals were probably instituted to commemorate the defeat of the Spanish Armada on 29th July 1588. They are the first issued for service against a foreign enemy, and are allegorical in that they depict on their reverses an ark undamaged or an island safe from the storms that surround them.

1 Naval Reward c 1588

Obverse	Bust of Queen Elizabeth to left, wearing a large ruff, legend around, 'ELIZABETH.D.G.ANGLIE.F.ET.HI.REG.'. (Translation: 'Elizabeth, by the grace of God, Queen of England, France and Ireland.').
Reverse	A completely closed in ark on a turbulent sea, above it a heavy cloud and the rays of the sun. Surrounding the whole is the legend, 'SEVAS:TRANQVILLA:PER:VNDAS.'. (Translation: 'Tranquil amid violent waves.').
Size	Oval, 51mm x 42mm
Metal	Silver
Suspension	The medals are cast with an integral loop for suspension.
Designer	Nicholas Hilliard

This medal has always traditionally been associated with the defeat of the Spanish Armada, though on it there are no specific allusions to the event. The ark is probably a symbolic representation of the Protestant Church, as well as to the *Ark Royal,* which was the flagship of Lord Howard. Sir Francis Drake, the second-in-command, flew his flag in the *Revenge,* whilst Admiral Hawkins was in the *Victory*—the first record of a ship bearing this famous name.

2 *The Dangers Averted Medal* c 1590

Obverse	Facing bust of Queen Elizabeth, crowned and wearing large ruff and a highly ornamented dress, she holds the orb and sceptre, legend around, 'DITIOR·IN·TOTO·NON·ALTER·CIRCVLVS·ORBE.'. (Translation: 'No other crown in the whole world more rich.').
Reverse	A flourishing bay tree standing on a small island surrounded by a rough sea, and undamaged by lightning and winds. Beneath the tree is the legend, in two lines, 'NON·IPSA·PERICVLA·TANGVNT.'. (Translation: 'Not even dangers affect it.').
Size	Oval, 57mm x 51mm
Metal	Gold, silver and copper
Suspension	The medals are cast with an integral loop for suspension
Designer	Nicholas Hilliard

'This medal was executed shortly after the destruction of the Armada, when the greatest dangers to Elizabeth I had ceased, and it was most probably a Naval Reward. Mary, Queen of Scots was dead, and the plots of which she had been the cause were at an end; James VI of Scotland had been conciliated; the Armada defeated; the Duke de Guise was dead; France and the Vatican were baffled. The legend of the obverse alludes to the Queen's crown (CIRCVLVS), the power and real wealth of which was fully established as that of any crown in Europe. The device of the reverse refers to the imputed virtues of the laurel or bay-tree, which was deemed incapable of injury from lightning, and also a preservation to the places where it grew, or to the persons who wore it.' (Medallic Illustrations).

2A *Second Type*
There is a variety of this medal which is smaller but has the added initials 'E.R.' to either side of the bay-tree.

Metal	Gold, silver and copper-gilt

2B *Third Type*
There is a variety of this medal where the portrait of the Queen on the obverse is replaced by the Royal arms, crowned, and within the Garter.

Metal	Gold, silver and silver-gilt

James I 1603-1625

3 *Badge or Naval Reward*

Obverse	Bust of the King, three-quarters right, wearing a large hat decorated with feathers, and the George suspended on a riband, legend, '+IACOBVS.D.G.MAG.BRITA.FR.ET.HI.REX.'
Reverse	The ark, on the sea with, above, bright rays bursting from the clouds, legend, '+STET.SALWS.IN.VNDIS.' (Translation: 'May it stand safe amid the waves.')
Size	Oval, 48mm x 41mm
Metal	Gold, and silver
Suspension	The medals are cast with an integral loop for suspension
Designer	Manner of Nicholas Hilliard

Although this medal may have been an honorary reward for service or bravery at sea, it was more probably intended as a complimentary present to Court favourites, the design symbolizing the state of the nation after the disturbances occasioned by the Reformation.

Civil War Medals 1643-1645

Royalist Medals of Charles I

The English Civil War saw the production of a great number of Royalist Badges or Medals, though it would seem that only a few were issued as actual Military Rewards, however the Royal Warrants for the 'Forlorn Hope' and the 'Welch Medal' still exist, and there is no doubt as to their purpose.

---

4 *Medal of Charles I and Henrietta Maria* c 1643

Obverse	Bust of the King to the right, crowned and wearing the robes, collar and George of the Order of the Garter, legend around, 'CAROLVS.D.G.MAG.BRITAN.FRAN.ET.HIB.REX.FI.D.'
Reverse	Bust of the Queen to the left, her hair drawn back through a small coronet, wearing a pearl necklace and pendant, and a brooch on her bodice, legend around, 'HENRIETTA.MARIA.D.G.MAG.BRITAN. FRAN.ET.HIB.REG.'
Edge	An integral wreath border surrounds the design
Size	Oval, 47mm x 39mm
Metal	Gold, silver and silver-gilt
Suspension	The medals are cast with an integral loop for suspension
Designer	Thomas Rawlins

This medal, with its two Royal portraits, is probably the grandest of the Royalist badges or medals. The quality of its execution shows that it was obviously intended as a high reward—if not actually a military award. It also emphasises the importance of Queen Henrietta Maria, who had arrived in Oxford on the 14th July 1643, where Rawlins, and the Mint, were established, and the medal was made. She was the self-styled, 'Her She Majesty Generalissima', and as such she would surely deserve to feature on the medals.

---

5 *The 'Forlorn Hope' Medal* 1643

Obverse	Bust of Charles I three-quarters right, his hair long and a lovelock on his left shoulder, a lace collar extends over his armour. Both obverse and reverse are without legend
Reverse	Bust of Prince Charles to left, hair long, and wearing a plain collar over richly decorated armour
Size	Oval, 42mm x 33mm
Metal	Silver-gilt
Suspension	The medal is cast with a small integral loop for suspension
Designer	Thomas Rawlins

The Forlorn-hope party was that which led in an attack, and it has been suggested that the word 'forlorn' has been derived in some way from the German word *foloren*, which means lost. Medals were issued in accordance with a Royal Warrant adddressed to Sir William Parkhurst and Thomas Bushell, Wardens of the Mint at Oxford, and dated on the 18th May 1643:

'Trusty and well beloved, we greet you well; Whereas we have received information that those soldiers which have been forward to serve us in the Forlorn-hope, are not looked upon according to their merited valour and loyal service. We do therefore require, that from henceforward the Commander-in-Chief, both of Horse and Foot, which lead up the Forlorn-hope, upon whom also we mean to bestow special tokens of our princely favour, do signify in writing the names of those soldiers whom they find most forward in serving us, their King and Country, that care may be taken to reward their deservings, and make them specially known to all our good subjects. For which end we have thought fit to require Sir William Parkhurst, Knight, and Thomas Bushell, Esquire, Wardens of our Mint, to provide from time to time certain Badges of silver, containing our Royal image, and that of our dearest son, Prince Charles, to be delivered to wear on the breast of every man who shall be certified under the hands of their Commanders-in-Chief to have done us faithful service in the Forlorn-hope. And we do, therefore, most straitly command, that no soldier at any time do sell, nor any of our subjects presume to buy, or wear, any of those said Badges, other than they to whom we shall give the same, and that under such pain and punishment as our Council of War shall think fit to inflict, if any shall presume to offend against this our Royal command. And we further require the said Commanders, and Wardens of our Mint, to keep several Registers of the names of those and of their country, for whom they shall give their certificate.'

The Warrant nowhere makes it clear that this is indeed the 'Forlorn Hope' medal, but the tradition is too strong for it to be robbed of its title of honour.

6 *The Welch Medal* 1643

Obverse	The conjoined busts of Charles I and Prince Charles to right, both in armour and wearing scarves and medals, legend around, '.CAR:REX.M:B:F:ET.H:CAR:PRINCEPS.'
Reverse	The Royal Standard, billowing to the right, the legend in two lines around, 'PER:REGALE MANDATV CAROLI:REGIS:HOC: ASSIGNAT^{VR} ROB:WELCH.MILITI.'. (Translation: 'By the Royal mandate of King Charles this medal is conferred upon Robert Welch, Knight.')
Size	Oval, 43mm x 38mm
Metal	Gold
Suspension	The medal is cast with a small integral loop for suspension
Designer	Thomas Rawlins

No original of this medal exists, however the Royal Warrant to Thomas Rawlins and dated at Oxford on the 1st June 1643, contains the following passage:

'Our will and pleasure is that you make a medal in gold for our trusty and well-beloved Sir Robert Welch, knight, with our own figure and that of our dearest sonne Prince Charles. And on the reverse thereof to insculp ye form of our Royal Banner used at the battail of Edge-hill, where he did us acceptable service and received the dignity of knighthood from us, and to inscribe it *Per Regale Mandatum Caroli Regis hoc assignatur Roberto Welch Militi.*'

Robert Welch served in a troop of horse—Wilmot's troop—at the battle of Edgehill on the 23rd October 1642, the first battle in the Civil War. He recovered the standards of the King's own regiment, and captured two pieces of cannon and the Earl of Essex's wagon. As an award for a particular act of gallantry it was the forerunner of many later medals. His companion in arms, John Smith, was also knighted and received a similar medal, now also lost. It was reported that both Smith and Welch wore their medal on a band of broad green watered silk across their shoulders, though Welch sometimes seems to have also worn his on a blue band. The scarves or ribbons that were donned for identification before the days of standard uniforms, therefore progressed logically into the coloured ribbons from which medals today are still suspended.

7 *Prince Rupert's Medal* 1645

Obverse	Bust of Prince Rupert three-quarters left, his hair long, a lace collar over armour; he holds a baton and wears a medal of King Charles. The medal is without legend
Reverse	The ornate arms of the Prince with helm and lion supporters, to either side, R. P. (Prince Rupert)
Size	Oval, 37mm x 31mm
Metal	Silver and silver-gilt
Suspension	The medal is cast with an integral loop for suspension
Designer	Possibly by Thomas Rawlins

The example in the Hunterian Museum is cast (in silver), with an integral wreath border.

> Prince Rupert, Count Palatine, was the younger son of Frederick, King of Bohemia and Elizabeth, daughter of James I. His appointment as General of the Horse at the age of twenty-three at the beginning of the Civil War was not popular with the older Royalist leaders, but he was bold and successful, though his failure at Marston Moor, and the loss of Bristol the following year were to be his downfall, and he left the country.
> It is of interest that he wears, like the King and Prince Charles on both the 'Forlorn Hope' medal and the Welch medal, a medal on his breast. It would seem that this medal was intended as a Military Reward that Prince Rupert could bestow on those under his command.

Parliamentary Medals

Several of the Parliamentary leaders feature on medals which, like those of Charles I, must have served as Military Rewards. Morale was often low during the early stages of the Civil War, and the medals, judging by their numbers, must have served to strengthen confidence. Most are attractive, well-worked pieces—Thomas Simon was one of the medallists who remained in London at the Mint.

8 *The Earl of Essex's Medal* c 1642

Obverse	Half-length figure of the Earl of Essex, almost full face, wearing armour and holding a sword, above the letters S.X. (Essex), the legend in two lines around, '*Should hear both houses of parliament for true Religion and fredom stand. Pro Religione.lege.Rege.et.Parliamento.*'. (Translation: 'For Religion, law, the King, and Parliament.')
Reverse	The two houses of Parliament, the Lords in the top half, with the King enthroned; the Commons below, with the Speaker before the woolsack
Edge	An integral wreath border surrounds the design—though examples are found without it.
Size	Oval, 44mm x 36mm
Metal	Gold, silver and silver-gilt
Suspension	The medals are cast with an integral loop for suspension
Designer	The reverse is Thomas Rawlin's design for the medal for *The Declaration of Parliament* (1642)

The medals were issued to persons of various ranks in Essex's army, as a token of loyalty and also as a Military Reward. Though it seems curious that the King should feature on a Parliamentary medal, it should be remembered that the Civil War was fought over his policies and, initially, was not an attack on the Monarchy.

Essex was appointed Commander-in-Chief of the Parliamentary forces in 1642, but was displaced in 1645, and died in the following year. For most of that time he had trouble in getting money and men for his army, and considering the shortages, it is obvious that medals were a priority. The legend on the obverse, also adapted from the medal for *The Declaration of Parliament*, reflects Essex's own oath that, 'I do promise in the sight of Almighty God, that I shall undertake nothing but what shall tend to the advancement of the true Protestant Religion, the security of his Majesty's royal person, the maintenance of the just privileges of Parliament and the liberty and property of the subject.'

8A   *Second Type*

Above the portrait of Essex, a sword brandished from clouds, and the legend, 'THE SWORD OF THE LORD AND OF GYDEON.'. The reverse is similar, but has a legend added, 'IN THE MVLTITVDE OF COVNCELLORS THERE IS PEACE'.

Metal   Silver and silver-gilt

9 *The Earl of Manchester's Medal* 1643

Obverse	Half-length bust of the Earl of Manchester, turned three-quarters left, a decorative lace collar falling over his armour, the legend around, *'Pro Religione Lege Rege et Parliamento.'*
Reverse	The two houses of Parliament, as on the Essex medal (No. 8)
Edge	An integral wreath border surrounds the design
Size	Oval, 43mm x 36mm
Metal	Silver and silver-gilt
Suspension	The medals are cast with an integral loop for suspension
Designer	Not known

This medal is remarkably similar to that of Essex, though perhaps the portrait is worked in finer detail. There is no doubt that it, too, was a Military Reward. Manchester had fought at the battle of Edgehill and was made General of the Eastern Association. In 1644 he was to play an important part at the battle of Marston Moor.

10 *Sir Thomas Fairfax's Medal* 1645

Obverse	Bust of Sir Thomas Fairfax to left, his hair long, a mantle fastened to the left shoulder of his armour, legend around, 'THO.FAIRFAX. MILES.MILIT:PARL:DVX.GEN.' (Translation: 'Thomas Fairfax, Knight, General-in-Chief of the Parliamentary Army.')
Reverse	Across the centre, 'MERVISTI.' (Translation: 'You have merited.'), and also around, 'POST.HAC.MELIORA.' (Translation: 'Better hereafter'). '1645'.
Size	Oval, 33mm x 28mm
Metal	Gold, silver and silver-gilt
Suspension	The medals are cast with a small integral loop for suspension
Designer	Thomas Simon

10A *Second Type*

A variety of this medal is somewhat smaller (26mm x 21mm), perhaps intended as a lesser award. The obverse is without legend, otherwise the medal is similar.

Metal   Gold, silver and silver-gilt

Sir Thomas Fairfax succeeded Essex as General-in-Chief of the Parliamentary forces. He fought with his father, Ferdinand, Lord Fairfax, but did not see much success early in the Civil War. He commanded the right wing of the cavalry at the battle of Marston Moor, but is best remembered for winning the battle of Naseby. The two medals described above are simpler in form than those of Essex or Manchester, though they were of no less importance as Military Rewards.

These medals were issued on Fairfax's appointment as General-in-Chief, bestowed by the authority of Parliament and the City of London. The warrants below show them to have been awarded in 1645 and 1647, but it would seem that they would have been first awarded after the battle of Marston Moor in 1644. The two warrants both relate to a single recipient, one John Sharpe, of Horton, near Bradford in Yorkshire:

'I do acknowledge that *John Sharpe* hath deservedly received a Medall from Parliament and Citty of *London*, in rembrance of his faithful Service under my Command, in the Year 1645. *Fairfax.*'
and:
'I do hereby acknowledge that Mr. *John Sharpe* hath deservdly

received a Medall from Parliament and Citty of *London*, in rembrance of his faithful Service under my Command. Given under my Hand and Seal at *Kingston*, the 30 Day of *August* 1647. *Fairfax.*'

Many more badges and medals were made during the early part of the Civil War, but those selected here demonstrate the military nature of them, and their obviously accepted status in both the Royalist and Parliamentarian armies. That no medal was ever made of John Pym, 'one of the great architects of Parliamentary government', and who, even though he died on the 8th December 1643, more than any other leader, was ultimately responsible for the death and defeat of the King—surely demonstrates the role of these medals as military rewards.

11 *Commonwealth Naval Medal* 1649-1650

Obverse   An anchor with two shields suspended from the beam, one with the cross of St. George for England, the other the Harp of Erin for Ireland, a cable encircles the whole, above, 'MERVISTI'
Reverse   The Parliament assembled in the House of Commons, with the Speaker
Size   Oval, 24mm x 21mm
Metal   Gold and silver
Suspension   Struck with an integral loop for suspension
Designer   Thomas Simon (signed T.S. on the anchor beam)

These medals were struck following an Act of Parliament of 1649, which decreed that one-tenth of all prize money should be set aside for the purpose of granting medals and rewards to officers and men who had performed 'Extraordinary Service'. They are obviously the first purely Naval medals awarded for particular acts of gallantry. In 1651 Scotland was incorporated in the Commonwealth, and new medals with a third shield were introduced in 1653 (see No. 14).

In 1648 there had been a revolt in the Parliamentary Navy and several ships had sailed to Holland, where Prince Rupert had organised them into a Royalist squadron and sent them to Ireland. Two ships remained and Parliament ordered the destruction of one of these, the *Antelope*, an old ship, built in 1618 for James I. This was achieved in April 1649, when Lieutenant Stephen Rose, on board the *Happy Entrance*, sailed into Helvoetsluys and burnt the *Antelope* as she lay at anchor.

The Council of State published the rewards for this exploit in October 1649:
Stephen Rose—£50, of which £2 was to be in the form of a gold medal.
James Tulley, Volunteer, and Thomas Tulley, Corporal—£10, and a gold medal of the value of £1.

12 *The Wyard Medal* 31st July-1st August, 1650

Obverse	An anchor with two shields suspended from the beam, one with the cross of St. George for England, the other the Harp of Erin for Ireland, a cable encircles the whole, above, 'MERUISTI'. (Translation: 'You have merited.')
Reverse	A ship engaged between two frigates, four others in the distance, legend in two lines, 'SERVICE.DON.AGAINST.SIX.SHIPS.JULY.Y.XXXI. & AVGVST.Y.I.1650.'
Size	Oval, 40mm x 34mm
Metal	Gold and silver
Suspension	Struck with an integral loop for suspension
Designer	Possibly by Thomas Simon

This medal was especially voted by Parliament to be given in gold to Captain Wyard of the *Adventure* (The present whereabouts of this specimen is not known), and in silver to his officers. The *Adventure* was a ship of 22 guns, and was protecting a convoy of vessels from Hull to London and Rotterdam, when they were intercepted by six Irish frigates of 26, 22, 20, 18 and two of 16 guns respectively. The engagement commenced at about ten o'clock on the night of 31st July, and after a sharp conflict was over by noon the following day.

13 *The Dunbar Medal* 3rd September, 1650

Obverse	The bust of Cromwell to left, a plain collar over armour, a scarf across his breast, in the distance the battle, legend above, 'THE LORD OF HOSTS', and in smaller lettering, 'WORD.AT.DVNBAR. SEPTEM: Y.3.1650.'
Reverse:	The Parliament assembled in the House of Commons, with the Speaker
Size	Oval, 34mm x 29mm
Metal	Gold, silver and bronze
Suspension	Struck with an integral suspension loop
Designer	Thomas Simon

13A *Second Type*

Another version of the medal was struck in a smaller size, the design was the same, though the medallist's signature on the truncation of the bust was shortened from THO.SIMON.FE. to T.SIMON.F.. The reverse is from the same die as the Commonwealth Naval Medal.

Size	25mm x 21mm
Metal	Gold, silver and bronze

The Scottish Presbyterian army of some 20,000 men commanded by David Leslie, threatened to invade England, whilst Fairfax, who commanded the smaller Parliamentary army of 16,000 men, refused to cross the border to attack them, though he would have led his army against them should they have invaded. Fairfax resigned his command, and Cromwell was named as Commander-in-Chief, or Lord General. Cromwell crossed the border into Scotland in June, but sickness in the ranks forced him to withdraw to the plain of Dunbar. Leslie expected him to withdraw to the supply ships and came down from his defensive position on the hills. Cromwell saw his chance and attacked. That night he wrote to Speaker Lenthall, 'The best of the enemy's horse being broken through and through in less than an hour's dispute, their whole army being put into confusion, it became a total rout: our men having the chase and execution of them nearly eight miles.'

On 7th September the Commons resolved 'that their special thanks be conveyed to the Lord-General for his eminent services at the great victory of Dunbar, and that his Excellency be desired to return their thanks also to the officers and soldiers of the army, and that a number of gold and silver medals be distributed amongst them' Cromwell suggested the design and Thomas Simon was specially ordered by Parliament to proceed to Scotland to take the 'effigies, portrait or statue of the Lord General to be placed on the medal.'

Original strikings in either size and in any metal are exceedingly rare, but the dies came to light in the early or mid-eighteenth century, and many restrikes were issued. The reverse die of the small medal was missing so these are always found uniface, with a slight die flaw above the head increasing in definition the later they were made. Both dies for the large medal survived, but a flaw developed on the reverse, running down across the medal from the top left. The Wyon family owned the dies in the nineteenth century and may well have been using them as late as the 1870's. Finally some completely new dies were cut and medals struck from these are simply restitutions.

14 *Commonwealth Naval Medals* 1653

Medals were awarded by Parliament in 1658 to be designed by Thomas Simon, for issue to Admirals, officers and men for services against the Dutch during 1653. The first encounter was on 8th February, off Cape la Hogue, when Admiral Blake, on board the *Triumph* defeated Admiral Tromp. Blake was wounded in this action and it was General George Monk, a military leader (and later Duke of Albermarle), who finally defeated Tromp in an action on 31st July, in which the Dutch Admiral was killed.

The medals come in three sizes, according to merit.

First Type

Obverse	An anchor, with the three shields of England, Scotland and Ireland, containing the crosses of St. George, St. Andrew and a harp, a cable encircles the whole design
Reverse	A naval engagement with, in the foreground, a ship sinking
Edge	The whole design is contained within a broad border of naval trophies including the shields of Holland and Zealand
Size	Oval, 56mm x 51mm
Metal	Gold
Suspension	Struck with an integral loop and with added ring for suspension
Designer	Thomas Simon (his signature T.S. is near the ring of the anchor on the obverse, on the stern of the sinking ship, SIMON, and on the prow of another, T.S.)

Four of these medals were ordered, Blake and Monk receiving theirs with gold chains to the value of £300, whilst Admirals Penn and Lawson received theirs with chains to the value of £100.

14A *Second Type*

The medal issued to the four flag officers was identical, except that the border was a narrower design of laurel leaves. They were awarded with gold chains to the value of £40. The recipients included a Captain Haddock.

Size	Oval, 50mm x 45mm
Metal	Gold

14B *Third Type*

The medal issued to the Captains of the vessels engaged was similar, but without any border, and was issued without any gold chain. To cover the expense of these smaller medals Parliament had to increase the amount of money alloted from £960 to £2,000.

Size	Oval, 41mm x 36mm
Metal	Gold

15 *The Triumph Medal* 1653

A variety of the previous medal was awarded to the crew of the *Triumph*, the flag-ship of Admiral Blake. During the action of the 31st July, 1653, the ship took fire and was abandoned by some of the crew. Others, who regarded the ship as a great favourite, disregarded the danger, and ultimately succeeded in saving her. The medal they were awarded has the added engraved inscription on the reverse, 'FOR EMINENT SERVICE IN SAVING Y TRIVMPH FIERED IN FIGHT W^H Y DVCH IN JVLY 1653'. Although a number of these medals must have been distributed, only a single example survives, in the National Collection at the British Museum.

Size	Oval, 41mm x 36mm
Metal	Gold

Charles II 1660-1685

16 *Naval Reward Medal* 1665

Obverse	Bust of Charles II to right, laureate, and with his hair short, a mantle over his shoulders, legend around, 'CAROLVS.SECVNDVS.D.G. MAG.BRI.FRAN.ET.HIB.REX.'
Reverse	The King dressed as a Roman General stands on a rock on the shore, watching a naval engagement, with one ship wrecked in the foreground, legend, 'PRO.TALIBVS.AVSIS.' (Translation: 'For such enterprises.')
Size	62mm
Metal	Gold, and silver
Suspension	Suspension loops attached at top (though most examples of this medal are found without them)
Designer	John Roettier

The medal is without date—the implication being that it could be used on future occasions. *Medallic Illustrations* suggests that this medal was an honorary award to officers of the rank of Captain and upwards, whereas another variety, showing the King with long hair, and known only in silver, was the 'Lesser' medal for persons under the rank of Captain.

The commercial treaties between England, France and Holland had not succeeded in restraining the hostilities between the English and Dutch merchants; the issue became a national one, and war was declared by the Dutch in January 1665. On 3rd June the English fleet, under the command of the Duke of York (later James II), Prince Rupert, and the Earl of Sandwich, engaged and defeated the Dutch in a decisive victory fought off Lowestoft. The Dutch Commander, Admiral Opdam, was killed, and nineteen of their ships were destroyed or captured.

17 *The Dominion of the Sea Medal* 3rd June, 1665

Obverse	Bust of Charles II left, his hair long, and wearing richly figured and ornamented armour, legend, 'CAROLVS.II.D;G;M;BR;FR;ET.H; REX.'
Reverse	An English ship in full sail to the right, the flag inscribed, 'C.R.', legend, 'NOS.PENES.IMPERIVM.' (Translation: 'The empire is with us.')
Size	Oval, 41mm x 38mm
Metal	Gold, and silver
Suspension	The medal is struck with an integral loop for suspension
Designer	Thomas Rawlins

The medal is supposed to have been struck after the victory off Lowestoft, on 3rd June, 1665, which gave to Charles the empire of the sea. It was probably given to officers who had distinguished themselves, to be worn as an award of merit, and honour.

William and Mary 1689-1694

18 *La Hogue Medal* 19th-24th May, 1692

Obverse	The conjoined busts of William and Mary to right, he in armour and she draped, legend, 'GVL:ET.MAR:D:G:M:B:F:ET.H:REX.ET. REGINA.'
Reverse	The naval action with *Le Soleil Royal,* flagship of the French Admiral de Tourville, in flames, legend, 'NOX NVLLA.SECVTA.EST.' (Translation: 'No night followed.'). In the exergue, 'PVGN:NAV: INT:ANG:ET.FR:21.MAY.1692.'. (Translation: 'Naval action between England and France, 21 May, 1692')
Size	49mm
Metal	Gold, and silver
Suspension	Usually found without any loops, etc, for suspension
Designer	James Roettier

In 1692 an Act of Parliament authorized the granting of medals to, 'Officers, Marines and Seamen who shall be found to have done any signal or extraordinary service.' The medals were uniface strikings in silver of the *La Hogue Medal,* the reverse being left plain so that they could be engraved with a description of the act for which they were awarded. They were fitted with a loop for suspension.

The battle of La Hogue was fought over six days, the 19th-24th, May, 1692, and the combined English and Dutch fleets, under the command of their respective Admirals, Russell and Almonde, defeated the French. Queen Mary ordered medals to be struck for presentation to Admiral Russell and his officers. William personally gave one of these medals and a 'massive' chain to Captain Tupper of Guernsey, who had given warning that the French fleet was in the Channel. Admiral Russell also received a gold metal and chain.

19 *The Toubocanti Medal* 8th February, 1700

Obverse   A fort besieged on all sides with, in the foreground, a Highlander, in ancient armour with sword and a shield decorated with a unicorn, legend on scroll above, 'QUID NON PRO PATRIA.' (Translation: 'What not for one's country.'). Legend in the exergue, 'TOUBOCANTI UBI 1600 HISPAN FUDIT DUX ALEXANDER CAMPBELL.MDCC. 8.FEBR.' (Translation: 'At Toubocan, where Captain Alexander Campbell put to flight 1,600 Spaniards, 8 Feb. 1700.').

Reverse   Armorial shield of the African and Indian Company of Scotland, helm and radiant sun above, an African and Indian as supporters, legend on scrolls above and below, 'QUA PANDITUR ORBIS.', and, 'VIS UNITA FORTIOR.' (Translation: 'To wherever the world extends.', and, 'Power stronger by union.').

Size   56mm
Metal   Gold, silver and silver-gilt
Designer   Martin Smeltzing

William III granted a charter to a Scotsman, William Paterson, to establish a colony on the Isthmus of Darien, in Central America, in the name of the African and Indian Company of Scotland. Two successive parties of some 1,200 persons each, had gone there to settle, but famine, disease and interference from the Spanish diminished their numbers. Captain Campbell arrived with a party from his own estate, whom he had commanded in Flanders, and straightway attacked a group of 1,600 Spanish troops that were encamped and waiting for the arrival of a squadron of eleven ships. His small group of 200 men attacked the Spanish entrenchments and drove them out, with many casualties; but he was unable to withstand the accumulated force of the Spanish and eventually capitulated on highly honourable terms.

On his return to Scotland the Company awarded Alexander Campbell a medal in gold for his services, his officers receiving theirs in silver.

William Paterson was also one of the founders of the corporation that became the Bank of England, which commenced to operate on 1st January, 1695.

20 *Vigo Bay Medal* 12th October, 1702

Obverse   Crowned bust of Queen Anne to left, legend, 'ANNA.DEI.GRA: MAG:BR:FRA:ET.HIB:REGINA.'

Reverse   A view of the harbour at Vigo, with some ships burning, and others in the narrow entrance, by a fort, legend around and in exergue, 'CAPTA.ET.INCENSA.GAL:ET.HISP:CLASSE. AD.VIGUM. XII.OCT.MDCCII.' (Translation: 'The French and Spanish fleets taken and burnt—at Vigo, 12 October, 1702.')

Size   37mm
Metal   Gold, silver and copper
Designer   John Croker

This medal was struck to commemorate the daring attack on Vigo Bay, by the combined English and Dutch fleets, where seventeen laden galleons from the West Indies were lying under the protection of French and Spanish warships. Sir George Rooke battered the forts guarding the harbour, and the *Torbay*, wearing the flag of Admiral Hopson, attacked the boom and in doing so was set on fire. Eventually all the fifteen French and three Spanish warships were either sunk or captured. Sir George Rooke entrusted Sir Cloudesley Shovel with the task of bringing home seventeen captured galleons, which were said to have contained over two and a half million pounds' worth of bullion and merchandise.

These medals must have been struck in large numbers, as three slightly differing pairs of dies were used. These same medals were issued in silver to the officers of the English fleet. Two gold medals were specially engraved for issue to the master and boatswain of the *Torbay*.

21 *Admiral Dilkes—Gold Medal for Service* 1703

In previous editions this medal has been listed as the LAMPRIÈRE GOLD MEDAL, on account of the name of the recipient, Captain James Lamprière, on the one recorded example of this medal.

Obverse	Crowned bust of Queen Anne to left, a lovelock on her left shoulder, wearing the collar, star and George of the Garter, legend, 'ANNA.DEI. GRATIA.MAG.BRITAN:FRA:ET.HIB:REGINA.'
Reverse	An engraved legend above the arms of the recipient, *'Her Maj^{ties} reward to . . . for his Zeal to her Service and Successful Conducting ye Squadron commanded by Rear Admiral Dilkes who destroyed a considerable number of ye Enemys Merchant Ships under Convoy of Men of War on their own coast'*
Size	70mm
Metal	Gold (said to have weighed approx 10.27 ozs.)
Suspension	A small loop and ring attached at top
Designer	John Croker

Between July 22nd and July 27th, Admiral Dilkes pursued a convoy of 43 merchant ships and three men of war, in and around Concalle Bay. Only four French vessels escaped destruction. Queen Anne ordered gold medals to be struck and presented to the Admiral and his officers, and as well as Captain James Lamprière, Sir Robert Fairfax also received one.

The obverse of the medal is from the same die as the undated medal, with the reverse of Queen Anne as Pallas, listed in *Medallic Illustrations* as commemorating the Union of England and Scotland in 1707, though van Loon lists it for the Queen's Accession. It would seem unlikely that the recipients would have had to wait some four years for their medals.

In *Milford Haven* a unique silver medal is recorded with an engraved inscription on the reverse of Croker's medal for the Peace of Utrecht, in 1713. The medal is set in a wreath border and the legend reads, *'Her Maj^{ties} reward to Robt. Taylor, Boy of y^e Mary Galley for his Zeal and Courage at y^e taking of y^e French Privateer Jacques La Bloude of Dunkirk.'* Both the engraving and the wording are very similar to the gold medal of 1703.

22 *Medal for the Capture of Gibraltar, and Naval Engagement off Malaga* 1704

Obverse	Bust of Queen Anne to left, a lovelock on her right shoulder, and her hair bound with pearls, legend, 'ANNA.D:G:MAG:BRI:FRA:ET.HIB: REG:'.
Reverse	Neptune, in a sea chariot, presents his trident to Britannia, who stands on the shore, legend, 'VICTORIA.NAVALES'. exergue, 'CALPE. EXPVG.ET.GALL.VICT.MDCCIV.' (Translation: 'Naval Victories—Gibraltar taken and the French defeated, 1704.')
Size	40mm.
Metal	Gold, silver and copper
Designer	John Croker

Earlier editions have stated that, 'A few of these medals were given for the capture of Gibraltar, which took place between July 21st and July 24th, 1704, and for its subsequent defence against various attempts to recapture it that were made by France and Spain in the remainder of that year and in 1705.' However the claim that these medals were issued as awards or rewards cannot be substantiated, and it would seem much more likely that the medal commemorates, as well as the capture of Gibraltar, the devastating engagement between the English fleet, under Sir George Rooke, and the French, under Prince Louis de Bourdon, Comte de Toulouse.

After the death of Charles II of Spain on 1st November, 1700, Europe became involved in what was known as 'The War of the Spanish Succession'.

There were three claimants—Philip of Anjou, grandson of Louis XIV; Joseph, Electoral Prince of Bavaria; and Archduke Charles, son of the Emperor Leopold of Austria.

Though Joseph was selected, he died suddenly and then the British favoured Charles owing to the political and territorial advantages his accession would have, compared with those of Philip. The Spaniards, however, favoured Philip and the war started.

On 12th Feburary, 1704, Admiral Sir George Rooke joined the Archduke Charles (son of Emperor Leopold of Austria) at Portsmouth and set sail for Lisbon and then to Barcelona, where he landed 2,000 men under the Prince of Hesse-Darmstadt. Finding that the populace was unsympathetic, he re-embarked the force and sailed to Lagos, where he was joined by Sir Cloudesley Shovel with more ships and men.

On 17th July, 1704, he called a council of war which decided to attack Gibraltar. With a fleet of sixty English and Dutch ships and an army of 1,800 men under the Prince of Hesse, he arrived off the Bay of Gibraltar on 21st July. As the Governor, Don Diego de Salinas, refused to surrender, the troops were disembarked on the isthmus. These consisted of the King's Own, East Lancashire, East Surrey Regiments, and the Duke of Cornwall's Light Infantry, which had accompanied the fleets as marines.

On the 22nd the fleet bombarded the forts and sent landing parties ashore from HMS *Lennox* (Captain Jumper), *Yarmouth* (Captain Hicks) and *Nottingham* (Captain Whitaker).

The Governor surrendered the fortress on 24th July, 1704. British troops remained in occupation. Admiral Rooke revictualled his fleet at Tetuan and awaited the attack of the French fleet under the Count of Toulouse. With forty-one English and eleven Dutch ships he defeated the French off Malaga on 13th August, 1704.

The Spaniards tried to recapture Gibraltar from the landward side, assisted by a French fleet under Admiral de Pointis. Admiral Sir John Leake was ordered by Admiral Rooke to sail from Lisbon to assist the garrison, which he did by surprising the blockading French Squadron and landing 400 marines, on 29th October, 1704.

On 18th December reinforcements consisting of a composite battalion of Grenadier and Coldstream Guards, a battalion of the Somerset Light Infantry and a battalion of the Royal Sussex Regiment arrived to increase the strength of the garrison to 3,000 men.

In 1705, the Spaniards, this time under the French Marshal de Tesse, again attacked the fortress, but Sir John Leake when on his way from Lisbon encountered and defeated the French fleet, driving a part of it, including the flagship, ashore.

After this Marshal de Tesse raised the seige. Gibraltar was ceded to Britain by the Treaty of Utrecht signed on 11th April, 1713.

It was again attacked by the Spanish in 1720 and 1727, but, so far as is known, no medals or Battle Honours were awarded for these operations.

The major credit for the capture of Gibraltar belongs to the Navy, who not only protected and transported the troops and acted as marines, but fired over 15,000 projectiles into the defensive works and then manned their small boats and captured the key positions.

It was to Sir George Rooke that the Governor surrendered.

Credit for the subsequent defence is shared by both services.

The military units present at the capture and defence of Gibraltar between 1704 and 1705 were: 1, 2 Foot Guards; 4, 13, 30, 31, 32 and 35 Foot.

---

23 *Callis Medal* 1742

Obverse	George II portrayed as a Roman Emperor standing, holding a baton in his left hand and with his right presents a medal to a kneeling officer, with the legend, 'PRO TALIBUS AUSIS' above. In the exergue in small lettering, 'T Pingo F.'
Reverse	A squadron of ships preparing to attack five galleys at anchor near the shore. In the exergue, 'OB.V. TRIREM. HISPAN. A.S. CALLIS. COMBVST. V. IVLII. MDCCXLII.'
Size	53mm diameter
Metal	Gold and silver
Designer	T. Pingo

A gold medal and chain was awarded by the King to Captain Smith Callis who, in his fireship the *Duke*, destroyed five Spanish galleys in the French port of St Tropez in June 1742. The medal in silver was given to officers commanding the other British ships engaged.

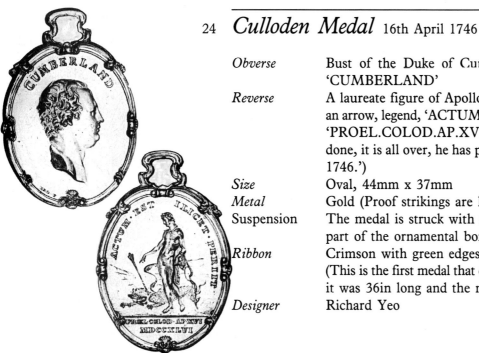

24 *Culloden Medal* 16th April 1746

Obverse	Bust of the Duke of Cumberland to right, his hair short, above, 'CUMBERLAND'
Reverse	A laureate figure of Apollo stands, pointing to a dragon wounded by an arrow, legend, 'ACTUM.EST.ILICET.PERIT.', and in the exergue, 'PROEL.COLOD.AP.XVI.MDCCXLVI.' (Translation: 'The deed is done, it is all over, he has perished—The Battle of Culloden, 16 April, 1746.')
Size	Oval, 44mm x 37mm
Metal	Gold (Proof strikings are known in silver and copper)
Suspension	The medal is struck with an integral loop for suspension, forming a part of the ornamental border
Ribbon	Crimson with green edges, 63mm. wide (This is the first medal that can be traced with a definite coloured ribbon; it was 36in long and the medal was worn suspended from the neck)
Designer	Richard Yeo

William, Duke of Cumberland, was the second son of George II, and the battle of Culloden was fought on the first day of his 26th year. On the day following the battle a Cumberland Society was formed by the senior officers who had fought at Culloden. The original membership was twenty-seven, and it is believed that George II sanctioned the wearing of the gold medals. In subsequent years further members were elected, the first being John, Marquess of Granby, and the last, in 1766, and bringing the membership to fifty-four, was Captain Ross, of General Oughton's Regiment.

One rule of the Cumberland Society stated that members 'shall wear their medals openly in battle and should they be lost in action with the enemy a new one, to the value of ten guineas, is to be replaced at the cost of the Society.'

There is only one entry in the original Minutes Book to show that this was ever done. It was dated 1758 and reads 'that a gold medal be granted to Captain William Sparkes, of Conway's Regiment, his having been lost at the Battle of Monongahela.' This action, sometimes referred to as 'Braddock's Defeat', was fought on the banks of the Monongahela river where it joins the Alleghany river to form the Ohio. The city of Pittsburgh, Pennsylvania, now stands on the site.

25 *Capture of Louisbourg* 27th July 1758

Obverse	Globe resting upon the prone figure of 'France'. On the globe are the words 'CANADA AMERICA'. Directly above is a scroll with the legend, 'PARITER·IN·BELLA'. Above this is the flying figure of victory and the Union Jack. To the right of the globe is a sailor with his hat raised in his left hand; to the left a soldier with a musket in his right hand.
Reverse	Representation of the bombardment of Louisbourg with the inscription above, 'LOVISBOVRG. TAKEN. MDCCLVIII'.
Size	44mm diameter
Metal	Gold, silver and copper
Ribbon	Half yellow, half blue
Designer	Thomas Pingo

Louisbourg, on Cape Breton Island, at the entrance to the St Lawrence River was first captured from the French in 1745 but was handed back again in 1748 under the Treaty of Aix-la-Chapelle.

As part of a multiple offensive during the later French and Indian wars a British expedition commanded by General Jeffrey Amherst supported by 40 ships under Admiral Edward Boscawen invested the French fortress. Brigadier General James Wolfe being amongst those present. The expedition landed on June 8th 1758 and after heavy fighting the garrison surrendered on the 27th July, 1758.

It was to be the first major victory of the war, followed by that of Wolfe's at Quebec, in 1759, which established British supremacy in Canada.

Known examples were awarded in gold to Sir Alexander Schomberg, Captain of the frigate *Diana*, Midshipman George Young, HMS *York* and Captain Buckler, Flag Captain to Admiral Boscawen. Others are known to have been issued.

Regiments present: RA, 1/1, 15, 17, 22, 28, 35, 40, 45, 47, 48, 58, 2/60, 3/60 and 78th Foot.

26 *Carib War* 1773

Obverse   George III in armour, facing right, with the legend, 'GEORGIVS III MB REX.'

Reverse   The helmeted and standing figure of Britannia offering an olive branch of peace to a defeated Carib. With the legend, 'PEACE AND PROSPERITY TO ST VINCENTS.' In the exergue is the date 'MDCCLXXIII'.

Size   56mm diameter

Metal   Silver and copper

Ribbon   Red

Suspension   Fitted with a ring for suspension. Worn around the neck.

Designer   Georg Michael Moser

This cast and chased medal was supposedly issued by the islanders of St Vincent to those who took part in the suppression of the native rising during the period 1772-73. A combined British and local force under the command of Major General Dalrymple, Commander-in-Chief of the West Indies campaigned against the Caribs who finally submitted on 20th February 1773.

Units present: 14th, 31st and 70th Foot, local militia and local volunteers.

27 *German Town Medal* 4th October 1777

Obverse   Within a wreath is the inscription embossed in three lines 'GERMAN/TOWN/OCT^R·4·1777'

Reverse   American troops attacking Chew's storehouse, two cannon in the foreground. In the exergue, 'I.MILTON.F'

Size   44.5mm diameter

Metal   Silver and bronze though the latter are very rare; also seen in gilt.

Ribbon   Dark blue

Suspension   A flattish loop is riveted through a hole at the top of the piece through which the ribbon is threaded.

Designer   Milton

Naming   The medals issued unnamed, some privately engraved

Three variations of this medal are known: (1) as above, (2) as above but with the obverse inscription in four lines, '40 REG/GERMAN/TOWN/OCT^R·4·1777'. (3) as (2) but reverse with 'Reward of Merit' in running script in the sky above Chew's storehouse. The '40 Reg' in (2) and (3) being engraved.

Version (2) was awarded to the defenders of Chew's storehouse, (3) was awarded as a regimental medal for merit.

During the War of American Independence, George Washington, after his defeat at Brandywine on 11th September, 1777 by General Howe, advanced to German Town, now part of Philadelphia.

By a surprise night attack the British troops were forced to withdraw. Lieutenant Colonel Musgrove, with six companies of the 40th Foot, held a large building known as Chew's storehouse until relieved.

The losses during the action were very heavy. The Americans said to have 1,000 and the British over 600 casualties.

To commemorate the action, Colonel Musgrove presented medals to the 40th Foot.

Defence of Gibraltar 21st June 1779-2nd February 1783

The two most common medals awarded for the Defence of Gibraltar* are the silver ones which were presented by Generals Picton and Eliott at their own expense. There were, however, other medals given for the same event.

28 *General Eliott's Medal for the Defence of Gibraltar*

Obverse	View of Gibraltar under siege. Above is the legend, 'PER TOT DISCRIMINA RERUM.' In the exergue is the date 'XIII. SEPT.MDCCLXXXII.'
Reverse	The names of four officers "REDEN LAMOTTE SYDOW ELIOTT", one underneath the other in the centre surrounded by a laurel wreath. In large letters almost around the circumference the word, 'BRUDERSCHAFT' (Brotherhood). At the bottom in small lettering is the designer's name L PINGO F.
Size	47mm diameter
Metal	Mostly silver, a few struck in gold.
Ribbon	The ribbon usually seen fitted to the piece is a dark blue although there does not appear to be any particular colour defined.
Suspension	On some, a loop 38mm wide is fitted to the top of the piece, whilst others have rings etc fitted.
Naming	The medals were issued un-named.
Designer	L. Pingo

The medal was presented by General Eliott to his Hanoverian troops. The defence was carried out by some 7,000 British and Hanovarian troops against French and Spanish forces. British troops appear to have gone unrewarded.

The 16th of June 1779 saw the entry of Spain into the War of the American Revolution on the side of France and the United States against Great Britain. This posed an immediate threat to British held Gibraltar and it's small garrison under the Governor, General George Augustus Eliott.

On the 21st of June 1779 the Spanish began a loose blockade marking the beginning of the siege. Troubled throughout by a lack of men and supplies, the garrison was initially replenished by Admiral Rodney and his fleet arriving in January 1780. (Rodney defeated a screening Spanish Squadron on January 16th—sinking one and capturing six enemy ships) Meanwhile, the Spanish had stepped up the blockade and were making active preparations to bombard the town and fortress.

A fleet under Admiral Darby again broke through to re-supply the garrison on 12th April 1781. On the same day, the Spanish began a bombardment that lasted, but for a few intermissions, until the siege's end.

Following the fall of Minorca (5th February 1782) the Duc de Crillon, with French and Spanish reinforcements, prepared to press the siege in earnest. Amassing 47 ships of the line, innumerable smaller vessels, 10 of the newly invented battery ships, over 200 pieces of land

based artillery and nearly 40,000 troops, he launched his major attack on the 7,000 strong garrison on 9th September 1782. Bombarding Gibraltar by land and sea, the battle came to a climax on 13th September when the new battery ships were moved into position. However, they proved unequal to the task of combatting the garrison's artillery and by noon of the following day all ten were destroyed.

The siege continued, with the fleet maintaining the blockade and land batteries the bombardment, finding the garrison determined but once again in dire need of men and supplies. Relief came when on 11th October 1782 a British fleet under Lord Howe evaded the blockaders and for a third time during the siege the garrison was re-supplied.

With the threat of starvation removed, the garrison held firm against the diminishing efforts of the besiegers until on 2nd February 1783, news of peace brought hostilities and the epic siege to an end.

Units present throughout: RA, RM, 12th, 39th, 56th, 58th, 72nd (Manchester Volunteers) Foot, Reden's, La Motte's and Hardenberg's Hanovarian Regiments
Arriving January 1780: 2/71st Foot, 97th (Stanton's) Foot
Arriving October 1782: 25th, 59th Foot

---

*In AD 711 the fortress was captured by the Saracens under Tarik, who called it Gibel-el-Tarik (Mountain, or Rock of Tarik), from whence it gets its present name of Gibraltar and its popular title The Rock.

29 *General Picton's Medal for the Defence of Gibraltar*

Obverse	View of Gibraltar and part of La Linea. On a scroll around the top is the legend 'BATTERING SHIPS DESTROYED'. At the bottom is the date 'SEPTEMBER XIII MDCCLXXXII'.
Reverse	An inscription, enclosed by a laurel wreath, which reads, 'BY A ZEALOUS EXERTION OF PATIENCE PERSEVERENCE AND INTREPIDITY AFTER CONTENDING WITH AN UNPARALLELED SUCCESSION OF DANGERS AND DIFFICULTIES IN THE DEFENCE OF GIBRALTAR DURING A BLOCKADE AND SIEGE OF ALMOST FOUR YEARS. THE GARRISON UNDER THE AUSPICES OF GEORGE III, TRIUMPHED OVER THE COMBINED POWERS OF FRANCE AND SPAIN.' Upon the exergue reclines the British Lion with an oval shield in it's paws picturing a castle and key. The dates of the siege are given in the exergue, thus: 'BLOCKADE COMMENCED JUNE XXI. MDCCLXXIX : SIEGE TERMINATED FEBRUARY II. MDCCLXXXIII'.
Size	58mm diameter
Metal	Silver

Tancred mentions a medal having the following inscription around the edge, 'To Ensign D. Latimer Tinling, 12th Regiment, from M General Picton, Colonel 12th Regiment Foot, 1783.'

30 *Red Hot Shot Medal* 13th September 1782

Obverse	A moored floating battery with three fire bombs landing on the roof. Below which inscribed in two lines, 'The *Pastora Batty Ship*/*Adml* Morino'. On a third line below is the recipients name.
Reverse	An active furnace with 'Fur' to the left of it and 'nace' to the right. Below, is the inscription in five lines, '*Spaniards defeated/by* RED hot SHOT *at*/GIBRALTAR/*Sept*^{ey}*13th*/1782'. Both obverse and reverse and suspender are edged with a cable border.
Size	38mm
Metal	Copper, one known in silver
Suspension	Flat suspender fitted to the top with a hole in the centre through which either cord or ribbon was threaded.

Named medals are known to T. Cole, T. Dodd, J. Hamilton, C. Hills, H. Hillson, H. Hobbs, J. Rogers, J. Shaw, J. Wells, J. Wheatley (silver).

The medals may have been available for purchase by individual soldiers as a souvenir of the event. Alternatively, Tancred, Payne and Milford Haven state the medals were awarded by officers to deserving soldiers.

> The grand attack, which started on 13th September, 1782, was opened by a cannonade from 200 pieces of heavy ordnance, followed by an assault of some 40,000 Frenchmen, under the Duc de Crillon, from the landward side.
> The Bay was crowded with the combined French and Spanish fleets composed of forty-seven line-of-battle ships, numerous frigates, small armed vessels and ten battery ships which their designer, the French engineer Jean Claude d'Arcon, states cost over half a million pounds apiece. They were converted line-of-battle ships from 600-1,400 tons,

Design variation

armed with from nine to twenty-one guns, with crews of from 250 to 760 men. The fronts of the batteries were protected by thick layers of square timber and covered with a sloping roof. The whole was lined with cordage and hides. In order to make them fireproof, a reservoir was installed in each battery from which, by means of hand pumps, hoses and buckets, every part of the fabric could be kept wet. Each battery had a single sail to enable it to take up its designed position, which was about four hundred yards offshore.

The fate of these batteries, in view of the high hopes that they raised, became comical. The wetting system was so efficient that not only did it keep the fabric wet but the powder as well, so that by the time the two leading and largest batteries, the *Talla Piedra* and *Pastora*, had got into position they were more like soaking targets than fireproof batteries.

During the first evening of the attack a red-hot shot became lodged in and set alight to the roof of the *Talla Piedra*, on which D'Arcon was serving, but as the British fire was so severe it could not be moved. The sight of this vaunted incombustible vessel burning furiously was too much and orders were given to destroy and abandon the others. Why the remainder, which were functioning quite well, should have been sacrificed, D'Arcon at the time could not understand.

These vessels are particularly interesting in that they were probably the first to be built purely as floating gun platforms with no consideration whatever as to quarters for the crews. Similar ships, but without the water systems, were used by the British on the Irrawaddy during the War in Ava, 1824-26, so that the rocket ships used during the second world war beach landings were only an improvement of an old idea.

---

31 *Deccan Medal* 1778-1784

Obverse	Britannia seated on a military trophy, her right arm extended, holding forth a laurel wreath towards a fort flying the Union Jack.
Reverse	Persian inscriptions: That in the centre reads—'As coins are current in the world, so shall be the bravery and exploits of those heroes by whom the name of the victorious English Nation was carried from Bengal to the Deccan.' The surrounding inscription reads—'Presented in AD 1784 (Hegira 1199) by the East India Company's Calcutta government'.
Size and Metal	Struck in two sizes: 40.5mm diameter in gold and silver, and 32mm diameter in silver.
Suspension	A ring affixed to the piece through which a cord of no specified colour is passed. A yellow or sand coloured cord is most frequently seen. The medal was worn around the neck.
Designer	The dies were prepared and medals struck by the firm of Young & Shepperd

This is an unusual medal as the edge is milled like that of a coin. It was issued to native troops only. Struck in two sizes, the large gold medal was given to Subadars, the large silver medal to Jemadars, and the small silver medal to other ranks.

The medal was the first issued by the Honourable East India Company and was given to native officers and men for service in Gujerat during the First Mahratta War 1778-1782, and for service in the Carnatic during the Second Mysore War 1780-83.

First Mahratta War

This was an inconclusive dispute with the Mahrattas, despite British success under Colonel Goddard in Baroda and Gujerat. An outstanding feat of the War was the capture of the Fortress of Gwalior by Captain Popham (3rd August 1780). Peace was eventually concluded on 17th May 1782 with Britain restoring her recent territorial gains. Governor-General Warren Hastings was then able to concentrate on the more dangerous contest with Haider Ali and the French in Mysore and the Carnatic.

Second Mysore War

Haider Ali's relations with Britain had remained strained since the First Mysore War of 1766-69. When hostilities commenced between Britain and France in June 1778 (War of the American Revolution) Haider Ali sided with France and in July 1780 invaded the Carnatic. On 10th September 1780, Haider Ali heavily defeated a small British force at Perambakum; in response, General Sir Eyre Coote was called upon to take command of all troops in the Carnatic. At Porto Novo (1st June 1781), Coote, with 8,000 men, defeated Haider Ali with 60,000 troops, a victory saving the beleaguered Madras Presidency. Further defeats were inflicted at Pollilur (27th August) and Sholinghur (27th September). In 1782 French aid materialized. A French squadron under Admiral Pierre de Suffren operated successfully along the Carnatic coast and captured Trincomalee in Ceylon (30th August 1782). Haider Ali died in December 1782 and was succeeded by his son Tippoo Sahib.

In 1783 Tippoo Sahib began operations against the tenuous British gains along the Canara coast of west Mysore—the British defence of Mangalore under Major John Campbell being the most notable action (20th May 1783—30th January 1784). Brigadier General James Stuart who had replaced the ailing Sir Eyre Coote began operations against the French stronghold at Cuddalore* (7th June 1783) with mixed results. News of peace with France by the Treaty of Versailles ended the operation (28th June) and official French participation in the war. In October 1783, Colonel Fullerton successfully invaded south Mysore, capturing Paighautcherry and Coimbatore. Finally, on 11th March 1784, a treaty of peace was signed ending the desultory and inconclusive war.

32 *Mysore Medal* 1790-1792

Obverse	A sepoy holding the Union Jack in his right hand and the flag of Mysore which is upside down in his left. In the background is the fortress of Seringapatam
Reverse	Within a laurel wreath, 'FOR SERVICES IN MYSORE AD 1791-1792'. Outside the wreath a Persian inscription (translation; 'A token of the bravery of the troops of the English Government in the war in Mysore, in the year of the Hegira, 1205-1206').
Size and Metal	Issued in gold, 43mm diameter, and silver, 43 and 38mm diameter
Suspension	A ring is affixed to the piece through which a cord of no specified colour is threaded. A yellow or sand coloured cord is most frequently seen. The medal was worn around the neck.
Designer	The dies were prepared by Mr Mair, a silversmith of Calcutta

Struck in two metals, the large gold medal was given to Subadars, the large silver medal was issued to Jemadars and Serangs, and the small, inferior quality silver medal was awarded to Havildars, Naiks, Tindals, Sepoys and Lascars.

The medal was awarded by the Honourable East India Company to native troops who served under Cornwallis, Abercromby and Medows in the defeat of Tippoo Sahib in the Third Mysore War (1790-92).

Early in 1790 Tippoo Sahib attacked the British allied State of Travancore thus causing the British to retaliate. General Medows reduced the south Mysore region of Coimbatore, whilst General Abercromby captured the west coast province of Malabar. However, Tippoo in turn invaded the British held Carnatic region.

The following year, the Governor-General, Lord Cornwallis took the field, launching a major offensive into the heart of Mysore. Capturing the town (7th March) and fortress (21st March, 1791) of Bangalore in the face of heavy opposition, Cornwallis then made for the Mysorean stronghold of Seringapatam. Defeating Tippoo at Arikera (15th May), Cornwallis arrived before Seringapatam, but a grave shortage of supplies and transport, coupled with heavy rains, compelled him to withdraw.

Later in 1791, Cornwallis again advanced and captured a series of strongly held fortresses between Bangalore and Seringapatam. Arriving before Seringapatam on 5th February, 1792, Cornwallis captured the town after a battle on the 6th and 7th of February. As a result Tippoo Sahib came to terms, signing a treaty (19th March) in which a substantial tract of land was ceded to Britain and her Mahratta allies and a war indemnity paid.

---

*One of the French prisoners captured during the course of this action was a certain Sgt Bernadotte—later a Marshal of France, then King of Sweden as Charles XIV.

33 *Isle of St Vincent Medal* 1795

Obverse	A winged figure of Britannia holding out a sword in her right hand. Behind her is the figure of a native lying down and supporting himself on his right elbow. Round the edge is written, 'ST VINCENT'S BLACK CORPS'.
Reverse	A native holding a musket and bayonet in his right hand. In the exergue is 'H.G.FEC.' Around the circumference is written 'BOLD LOYAL OBEDIENT'
Size	49mm diameter
Metal	Silver and bronze
Suspension	None
Designer	Although having HG in the exergue, no indication can be found as to who HG was

At the Treaty of Peace signed in Paris on 10th February, 1763, between Britain, France, Spain and Portugal, ending the Seven Years War, the island of St Vincent was ceded to Britain by the French. The majority of the Caribs were not kindly disposed to us, in 1779 the French assisted the Caribs to revolt, and again in 1795.

Given to Officers and Non-commissioned Officers of a Corps of Natives which numbered 500 men, which was raised in May, 1795, by Brigade Major Seton, from among the slaves, and was officered from the Militia, a serjeant being appointed to each company from the regulars. After useful and active service it was disbanded in 1799.

34 *Capture of Ceylon Medal* 1795-1796

Obverse	The legend, 'FOR SERVICES ON THE ISLAND OF CEYLON A.D. 1795/6'.
Reverse	A Persian inscription. (Translation: 'This medal was given by way of acknowledgement of services in Ceylon in the year of the Hegira 1209-1210')
Size	51mm diameter
Metal	Gold and in silver
Suspension	The medal was suspended from a cord of no specified colour worn round the neck. There is a loop riveted onto the piece through which the cord is threaded.

This medal was awarded in gold to Captains Barton and Clarke and in silver to 121 native gunners of the Bengal Artillery for their services during the capture of the Island from the Dutch. The dies were engraved and the medals struck at the Calcutta Mint. This medal must not be confused with another issued in 1818 as a meritorious service medal for the Kandy Rebellion.

35 *Bantry Garrison Medal* 1797

Obverse	A crown, with 'FRIENDLY ASSOCIATION' around and above with 'BANTRY GARRISON' below
Reverse	Ships in a storm, with the legend above and around 'AFFLAVIT DEUS ET DISSIPANTUR'. In the exergue 'JAN MDCCXCVII'
Size	38mm diameter
Metal	In silver and in copper
Ribbon	—
Suspension	—
Designer	W. Mossop

During the Wars of the French Revolution a French force under Vice-Admiral Morard de Galles and General Hoche left Brest on 15th December, 1796 to invade Ireland and give aid to the Irish Nationalists in their rebellion (United Irishmen Revolt 1795-97). The force consisted of 17 ships of the line, 13 frigates, 6 corvettes, 7 transports and a powder ship with some 18,000 troops. Fog, then storms plagued the fleet. A few ships managed to enter Bantry Bay (21st December 1796) but with continual bad weather made no attempt to land and returned to France. The cost of the ill-fated expedition was high; with 6 ships lost in the storms or battle, and another 7 captured by the British. (One of the French casualties being the *Droit de l'Homme*, see NGS Medal, bars Indefatigable 13 Jany 1797 and Amazon 13 Jany 1797).

Although no fighting took place on land, the garrison of Bantry had prepared itself well. As a reward for their efforts, the Friendly Association of Ireland struck a medal for distribution amongst the garrison.

Some officers and men of the Galway Militia who formed part of the garrison are known to have received the medal; in silver to officers and bronze to other ranks.

36 *Limerick Militia Medal for Coloony* 1798

Obverse	Crown surrounded by a laurel wreath with the legend, 'TO THE HEROES OF COLOONY 5TH SEPR 1798'
Reverse	A double turreted castle with a spire from which flies a flag. This partially enclosed by a laurel wreath, with the legend around, 'CORPORATION AND CITIZENS OF LIMERICK'
Size	38mm
Metal	Base silver
Ribbon	—
Suspension	Pierced for ring suspension
Engraver	J. Brush of Dublin
Naming	Issued un-named

Given by the Corporation of Limerick to the non-commissioned officers and men of the Limerick Militia under Colonel Charles Vereker, who fought a joint French/Irish army at Coloony, near Sligo, on 5th September 1798.

A French force of 1,200 men under General Joseph Amable Humbert landed at Killala, Sligo Bay, on 23rd August, 1798. Overpowering local opposition at Killala, Humbert, with additional Irish support, moved inland. At Castlebar on 27th August, he defeated an army of 1,700 militia and regulars under General Lake. He then moved towards Sligo hoping to secure the town and it's harbour. From the small garrison of Sligo, Colonel Vereker, with some 250 men of the Limerick Militia, 50 yeomanry, a troop of the 24th Light Dragoons and two curricle guns, defiantly marched out and took position across the French line of advance near Coloony.

In a short battle, on 5th September, Humbert forced Vereker's contingent to retreat. Casualties numbered 50 on both sides with 100 of Vereker's men taken prisoner.

Despite this victory, Humbert abandoned the attempt to capture Sligo. At Ballinamuck on 8th September, Humbert was defeated by an army of militia and regulars under Cornwallis, and surrendered with 843 men of his original army.

37 *Mr Davison's Nile Medal* 1st August 1798

Obverse	The figure of Pax with an olive branch in her right hand. Under her left arm she is supporting a large shield bearing the head and waist figure of Lord Nelson, with the inscription, 'EUROPE'S HOPE AND BRITAINS GLORY'. Around the circumference is the legend 'REAR-ADMIRAL LORD NELSON OF THE NILE'.
Reverse	A view of the fleet sailing into Aboukir Bay with the inscription, 'ALMIGHTY GOD HAS BLESSED HIS MAJESTY'S ARMS'. In the exergue is written 'VICTORY OF THE NILE AUGUST 1 1798'
Edge	Engraved in large capitals around the edge is the wording, 'A TRIBUTE OF REGARD FROM ALEX^R DAVISON ESQ. ST JAMES'S SQUARE'
Size	48mm diameter
Metal	Gold, silver, bronze-gilt, bronze
Ribbon	Dark blue
Suspension	Of no uniform style
Designer	C. H. Kuchler
Naming	Some are privately engraved on reverse field

This medal was a personal award from Nelson's prize agent Mr Davison, to the officers and men present. Admirals and Captains received it in gold, other officers in silver, petty officers in bronze-gilt, and the remainder in bronze. All the medals bore the name of the donor impressed on the edge, while the name of the recipient or his initials are sometimes found engraved on the face of the reverse. Many recipients appear to have left them as issued, that is, un-named. For further particulars concerning the action, see the appropriate bar of the Naval General Service Medal.

Many of these medals were found by Russian sailors scattered over the Island of Tenedos in 1807 after the explosion that took place on board the *Ajax* when that ship was burnt in the roads of Tenedos, 14th and 15th February, 1807.

38 *Seringapatam Medal* 4th May 1799

Obverse	A fine picture of a fight between the British Lion and Tippoo Sahib's Tiger, a pennon above bears the Union Flag and an Arabic inscription. (Translation: 'The Victorious Lion of God'). In the exergue is the date, 'IV MAY MDCCXCIX.'
Reverse	A scene of the attack on the fortress of Seringapatam showing a breach in the wall and a scaling party. Underneath is a Persian inscription. (Translation: 'Seringapatam God given 28th day of the month Zikadah, 1213 of the Hegira.')
Types	The English medals were 1.9 inches (48mm) in diameter and the Calcutta ones 1.8 inches (45mm). Five types of the medal were issued in England and two in Calcutta, as follows:

	Gold	Silver-gilt	Silver	Bronze	Pewter
English Medals	30	185	850	5,000	45,000
Calcutta Medals	83	Nil	2,786	Nil	Nil

Besides the size difference, the two strikings may be differentiated by the designer's initials which are found on the right immediately above

Suspension & *Ribbon*	the exergue. The medals struck at the Soho Mint, Birmingham, bear the initials C.H.K., while those struck by the Calcutta Mint have the initials in the wrong order and the letter 'K' reversed, thus C.Я.H. They were issued without means of suspension, but are found with various types added subsequently. Controversy has arisen over the correct ribbon for this medal. The correct one appears to be a pale watered orange colour 38mm wide, but it is found with the same ribbon as the Peninsular Gold Medal and also suspended from a yellow cord passing through a slightly tubular ring fitted to the medal by a pin. It would seem to have been the practice of General Officers to wear the medal round the neck whilst lower ranks wore it on the chest.
Designer	C. H. Kuchler
Naming	All were issued un-named, although some were engraved by the recipients
Bars issued	Nil, though some had bars added which were inscribed 'SERINGAPATAM'

The English strikings, made in 1801/02 were issued in 1808 to dignitaries and to the officers and men of the British and Company's (Madras and Bombay) forces engaged at Seringapatam on 4th May 1799.

Gold medals were given to:
His Majesty; The Rt Hon Lord Melville; The Governor-General in India at the time Marquis Cornwallis; The Nizam and his two Ministers; The Peishwab and his Minister; The Nabobs of Arcot and Oude; The Rajahs of Tanjore, Travancore, Mysore, Coorg and Berar; Dowlut Row of Scindia, the Commander-in-Chief; General Officers on the staff employed in the Service; The Oriental Museum.

Silver-gilt medals were given to:
The members of the Council at the three Presidencies; The Residents of Hyderabad and Poonah; The Field Officers; The General Staff.

Silver medals were given to Captains and Subalterns.

Bronze medals were given to:
British non-commissioned Officers, including Conductors and others of the General Staff considered as non-commissioned Officers; Sergeants, Drummers or Fifers, and Trumpeters of European Corps; Native commissioned and non-commissioned Officers as follows:
Subadars; Jemadars; Syrangs; 1st Tindals; Havildars; Trumpeters; Drummers and Fifers; Head Guides.

Pewter medals were given to:
British Corporals; Gunners and Privates.

Natives:
Naicks; Farriers; Native Doctors; Golundauze; Private Sepoys; Second Tindals; Lascars; Puckallies; Guides of the Native troops.

The inferior Calcutta strikings, based on the English model were issued in 1808 to native officers and men of the Bengal Presidency engaged at Seringapatam on 4th May 1799. The Presidency, apparently unaware of the above scale of awards, followed the precedent set by earlier issues and awarded gold medals to native officers and silver medals to native other ranks.

The Company's officers did not receive the Royal sanction to wear the medal until 1815. Officers of the British Army only received permission in 1851.

Fourth Mysore War 1799
Learning that Tippoo Sahib had entered into an alliance with France against Britain, Governor-General Lord Mornington (Richard Wellesley) ordered an army to be assembled under Lieutenant General G. Harris, with orders to march on Seringapatam. In February 1799 he began the advance into Mysore from the east, in conjunction with a subsidiary Hyderabad contingent under Colonel The Hon Arthur Wellesley—the Governor General's younger brother. A small Bombay force commanded by Lieutenant General J. Stuart entered Mysore from the west.
Attempts by Tippoo to halt the march of Harris and Stuart failed and on 17th April the siege of Seringapatam began. On 4th May 1799, the city was assaulted and captured with Tippoo Sahib amongst those killed in the fighting. With his death, the war ended and the state of Mysore was partitioned.

To those who have served in more recent wars, the most interesting fact to arise from Seringapatam was the prize money which came to over £1,140,000. It was distributed roughly as follows:

The Commander-in-Chief	£100,000
Generals	10,000
Colonels	4,300
Lieutenant Colonels	2,600
Majors	1,700
Captains	860
Lieutenants	430
Warrant Officers	150
Sergeants	14
Privates	7

It would have been interesting to have heard the Commander-in-Chief and one of his men comparing notes on the siege!

The following Regiments took part in the Campaign which led to the capture of the fortress:
EUROPEAN
19, 25, Light Dragoons; 12, 33, 57, 73, 74, 75, 77, 102, 103, Foot; The Scots Bde (94th); Regt de Meuron (Swiss mercenaries).

NATIVE
1, 2, 3, 4 Madras Cavalry; 3/1, 5/2, 1/3, 2/3 Bengal Art; Detachment Bombay Art; 1, 2 Madras Art; Coast Art; Madras Engrs; Pioneers; 1, 2, 3 Bn Bengal Native Volunteers 1/10, 2/10 Bengal NI; 1/1, 2/2, 2/3, 2/5, 1/6, 2/7, 1/8, 2/9, 1/11, 2/11, 1/12, 2/12 Madras NI; 1/2, 2/2, 1/3, 2/3, 1/4, 1/5 Bombay NI.

39 *Earl St Vincent's Medal* 1800

Obverse	Bust of the Earl facing left, enclosed by a wreath and legend, 'EARL ST VINCENT'S TESTIMONY OF APPROBATION 1800'
Reverse	A sailor and a marine shaking hands and the legend 'LOYAL AND TRUE'
Size	47.5mm diameter
Metal	Normally found in silver, though three or four are known in gold

These medals were given by the Earl to the crew of his ship, the *Ville de Paris,* which did not take part in the mutiny in the Mediterranean soon after the more serious one at the Nore in 1797. They were only given to Petty Officers and below.

40 *Honourable East India Company's Egypt Medal* 1801

Obverse	There is a Persian inscription in the exergue reading, 'This Medal has been presented in commemoration of the defeat of the French armies in the kingdom of Egypt by the great bravery of the victorious army of England.' Above, a sepoy supporting a union flag with an encampment in the background
Reverse	A Line-of-Battle ship in full sail towards the coast of Egypt, with an obelisk and four pyramids in the background. In the exergue, 'MDCCCI'
Size	48mm diameter
Metal	Gold and silver
Ribbon	Yellow silk cord
Suspension	Loop suspension through which the cord passes
Engraver	The dies were engraved and the medals struck at the Calcutta Mint

Granted by General Order issued by the Governor-General dated Fort William, July 31st, 1802, to the troops that composed the Expedition from India to Egypt under Major-General Sir David Baird, to assist Sir Ralph Abercromby's force against the French.

Those who had received this medal did not get the bar for Egypt which was subsequently (1850) awarded with the Military General Service Medal. The 61st Foot sailed from the Cape of Good Hope and joined the division on 17th May, 1801, but did not qualify for this medal. The eligible British recipients were members of the following regiments: One Troop 8 Light Dragoons; 10, 80, 86, 88 Foot; and 400 Artillerymen.

Given in gold and silver to the Bengal troops—16 gold and 760 silver—and in silver only to the troops from Bombay—1,439 silver to Officers and sepoys alike.

These medals do not appear to have been issued till nine years afterwards, as GOCC 13th May 1811, testified to their being ready for distribution.

A clasp for 'Egypt', 1801, was granted on 12th February, 1850, to be added to the 'War Medal', sanctioned by Her Majesty Queen Victoria, 1st June, 1847.

41 *The Sultan's Medal for Egypt* 1801

Obverse	Crescent and eight-pointed star with an ornamental border.
Reverse	Turkish script and the Sultan's cypher, (Sultan Selim III, The Peaceful), and the date 1801 below, with an ornamental border, as obverse.
Size and Metal	Four sizes of gold medals were issued: 2.1in, 54mm; 1.9in, 48mm; 1.7in, 43mm; and 1.4in 36mm diameter. Also issued in silver, 1.4in, 36mm diameter
Ribbon	Flame coloured for the Order, and 1st and 2nd class medals. Sand coloured for 3rd (1.7in) and 4th (1.4in) class medals.
Suspension	The plain gold medals were fitted with a chain and sharp pointed hook, although examples are found with replacement suspensions being worn from a ribbon.

Approximately four hundred and two gold medals made up from all four classes were available for naval officers as shown below.

Rank	Appointment of Officer	Class/Size		Totals
Captains RN	Commanding Officers, Flag Captains and 2nd Captains of Flag Ships.	1st Class (2.1")		36
Commanders	Commanding Officers, and when acting as Transport Agents.	2nd Class (1.9")	45	
Lts RN	Aboard 3rd Rate (74/80 Gun) Ships		45	92
Midshipmen	George Manson of HMS *Eurus*		1	
Snr Lts RN	Commanding Officers, & those aboard 4th Rate (64 Gun), 5th Rate/Frigates, Two Deck Troopships, Sloops, Frigate Troopships & when Transport Agents	3rd Class (1.7")	108	120
Actg Lts	Aboard 3rd Rate (74/80 Gun) Ships.		12	
Jnr Lts RN, Actg Lts, Master Mates & Midshipmen	Aboard any Type of Vessel at the landings on 8 March 1801. Selected from vessels above.	4th Class (1.4")		154
		TOTAL		402
Royal Marines				60

The above table has kindly been provided by Captain Douglas-Morris, RN, and is taken from his publication, 'Naval Medals 1793-1856'.

This medal is also referred to as The Order of the Crescent, which is incorrect as this Order was founded by Sultan Selim III in 1799 as a special reward to Lord Nelson for his victory in the Bay of Aboukir in 1798. The Order consists of two classes, and was only given to foreigners. The Badges of this Order were jewel studded and enamelled, being worn from a crimson ribbon. The Order was extended to officers who took part in the Nile Expedition in 1801 and they were also given gold or silver medals.

Although very scarce, examples of the Order are known to exist (see Whitaker, Gray and Payne collections).

42 *The Highland Society Medal* 1801

Obverse	Bust of Sir Ralph Abercromby facing right with the inscription, 'ABERCROMBIUS DUX IN EGYPTO CECIDIT VICTOR 28 MAR 1801'.
Reverse	Highlander with a raised sword capturing a standard from a French soldier, at their feet a crocodile, in the right background an obelisk. A raised border around the scene bears the inscription in Gaelic, 'NA FIR A CHOISIN BUAIDH SAN EPHAIT 21 MAR 1801'. (Translation: 'These are the heroes who achieved victory in Egypt.').
Rim	Inscription in Gaelic, 'On Chomun Ghaeleach don Fhreiceadan Dubh na XLII Rt'. (Translation: 'From the London Highland Society to the Black Watch or 42nd Regt.). Some examples are also found without this Gaelic inscription.
Size	49mm diameter
Metal	Gold, silver and bronze
Designer	The medal was designed by Benjamin West and engraved by G. F. Pidgeon.

This was struck by the Highland Society of London for possible award to The Prince Regent and General Sir Ralph Abercromby's sons. It is believed that some of the medals were presented by the Highland Society of London at a much later date as gifts to individuals who had served the Society, and these appear on the market from time to time.

43 *Mr Boulton's Trafalgar Medal* 1805

Obverse	Bust of Lord Nelson in uniform facing left, surrounded by the words, 'HORATIO VISCUNT NELSON. K. B. DUKE OF BRONTE. &.'.
Reverse	A scene of the battle with the legend, 'ENGLAND EXPECTS EVERY MAN WILL DO HIS DUTY'. In the exergue is 'TRAFALGAR OCT^R 21 1805'.
Edge	'From M. Boulton to the Heroes of Trafalgar'.
Size	48mm diameter
Metal	Silver and pewter
Ribbon	Dark blue
Suspension	Of no uniform style although often seen enclosed in a silver band and glazed with a ring suspension.
Designer	C. H. Kuchler
Naming	Privately engraved on reverse field.

This medal was given by Mr Boulton, a manufacturer of Birmingham, at his own expense, to all seamen who served on board the British Fleet on the 21st October.

The medal was awarded in silver to Captains and 1st Lieutenants, and in pewter to junior officers and men. Bronze medals are known, but these were not issued, being struck as proofs.

44 *Mr Davison's Trafalgar Medal* 1805

Obverse   A small bust of Lord Nelson surmounting a shield, the garter of which is inscribed 'TRIA JUNCTA IN UNO.' On a scroll beneath the shield is the inscription 'PALMAM QUI MERUIT FERAT.' The small letters H. F. appear under the ME of MERUIT. Under these, in three lines, is the inscription 'NATUS SEP. 29 1758, HOSTE DEVICTO REQUIEVIT, OCT 21 1805.' Around the top in large lettering is the wording 'ADMIRAL LORD NELSON D. OF BRONTE.' Under this is his famous signal in small lettering, 'ENGLAND EXPECTS EVERY MAN WILL DO HIS DUTY.'

Reverse   In the centre is a three-masted man-of-war facing to the right. Above is the inscription 'THE LORD IS A MAN OF WAR, EXODUS C.15.V.3.' Around the bottom half in four lines is the wording 'VICTORY OFF TRAFALGAR OVER THE COMBINED FLEETS OF FRANCE & SPAIN OCT 21 1805.'

Size   54mm diameter

Metal   The piece is of pewter and normally surrounded by a thin copper rim.

Ribbon   Dark blue

Suspension   A small loop is fitted to the copper rim through which there is a small ring. The ribbon passes through this ring.

Designer   Halliday

Naming   Issued un-named

This medal was struck to be given to the seamen of the *Victory*.

45 *Dr Turton's Trafalgar Medal* 1805

Obverse   Bust of Admiral Nelson in uniform facing left, surrounded by the legend above, 'NELSON ET BRONTI. VICTOR TRAFALGAR ET VICTIMA', below, 'PERIIT ET PERIIT. OCT. 21. 1805.'

Reverse   Within a laurel wreath, a bird's-eye view of the battle, with the British fleet in two columns on the point of breaking the Franco-Spanish line. Outside of the wreath, the legend, 'MEMORIAE CONSECRAVIT. GUL. TURTON M.D.F.L.S.' In the exergue, 'ESTO PERPETUA.'

Size   54mm diameter

Metal   Silver

A medal struck by Dr William Turton (1735-1806) as a tribute of his admiration for Admiral Nelson.

46 *Maida Gold Medal* 4th July, 1806

Obverse	Laureated head of George III and the inscription 'GEORGIVS TERTIVS REX.'
Reverse	The standing figure of Britannia facing left in the attitude of throwing a javelin. In her left hand she holds a shield bearing the Union banner. A small flying figure of Victory is crowning her with a laurel wreath. Behind Britannia is a trinacria and in front of her is inscribed in large letters in two lines 'MAI' and 'DA', whilst the date also occupies a further two lines, 'IVL.IV' and 'MDCCCVI'. In the exergue are crossed spears tied with a knot.
Size	39mm diameter
Ribbon	Red with blue edges, 39mm wide, fitted with a gold buckle.
Designer	G. F. Pidgeon

Medals were issued to officers of the rank of Lieutenant-Colonel and above,* whose names were usually engraved around the edge, however an un-named example is known to exist.

The battle of Maida was fought on the 4th July, 1806. The French had assembled a body of troops in Calabria, for the invasion of Sicily. Major General Stuart, who commanded the British troops in Sicily, formed the design of penetrating Calabria and attacking the French Division, under General Reynier. Disembarking at Saint Euphemia from the ships under the command of Admiral Sydney Smith, he advanced to the attack, and finally routed the enemy with great slaughter.

The French loss was estimated at over 2,000 men, while the British loss was only 1 officer and 44 men killed, and 11 officers and 271 men wounded. The heaviest casualties fell on the 78th and 81st Foot.

Major General Stuart received the thanks of Parliament, with £1,000 a year for life, was created a Knight of the Bath, and also Count of Maida by the King of Naples. The City of London voted him its freedom and a sword.

Lieutenant W. F. Carroll, RN, received the MGS medal with this bar.

The following regiments took part: 20 Light Dragoons; RA; RE; Sappers and Miners; Commissariat; Medical Staff; 20, 27, 35, 39 (1), 42 (1), 58, 61, 78, 81 Foot; Corsican Rangers; de Watteville's Regiment.

Recipients of the Gold Medal for Maida 1806
Sir John Stuart, KB, Maj Gen commanding; Hon. Sir G. L. Cole, KB, Brig Gen; W. P. Acland, Brig Gen; John Oswald, Col, commanding a brigade; James Kempt, Lt Col, commanding Light Infantry; Haviland Smith, Lt Col, commanding 27th Foot; Hon. R. W. O'Callaghan, Lt Col, commanding Grenadiers; †Robert Ross, Lt Col, commanding 20th Foot; George Johnson, Lt Col, commanding 58th Foot; Patrick McLeod, Lt Col, commanding 78th Foot; Louis de Watteville, Lt Col, commanding Regt de Watteville; David Stewart, Maj, commanding left bn 78th Foot; James Macdonnel, Maj, commanding 78th Foot; George D. Robertson, Maj, commanding 35th Foot; John M'Combe, Maj, commanding Royal Corsican Rangers; John Lemoine, Lt Col, commanding RA; H. E. Bunbury, Dep Quartermaster General.

---

*A silver medal was awarded to Lieutenant Pearce Lowen, 4 Foot, but the reason for this apparently unique award cannot be traced.

†Major General Robert Ross, 22nd Foot, Commander-in-Chief of the forces in the United States until his death by gunshot on 12th September, 1814, whilst making a reconnaissance before Baltimore, held a unique and fascinating combination of medals. These were the Maida Gold Medal, Small Army Gold Medal for Corunna 1809, the Army Gold Cross for Maida, Corunna, Vittoria and Pyrenees.

47 *Medal for Capture of Rodrigues, Isle of Bourbon and Isle of France* 1809-1810

Obverse	A Sepoy standing, holding in his right hand the Union Jack unfurled, and in his left a musket with fixed bayonet. His left foot rests upon the French Colours and Eagle; by his side a field gun, and in the background the British Fleet at anchor.
Reverse	Within a laurel wreath inscribed, in Persian, 'This Medal was conferred in commemoration of the bravery and accustomed fidelity exhibited by the Sepoys of the English company in the capture of the Mauritius Islands in the year of the Hegira, 1226.' Around the wreath in block lettering is inscribed, 'RODRIGUES VI JULY MDCCCIX. BOURBON VIII JULY & ISLE OF FRANCE III DEC. MDCCCX.'
Metal	Gold (45) and silver (2156)
Size	49mm diameter
Suspension	A flattened loop, pinned at base through which passes a cord of no specified colour
Engraver	The dies were engraved and the medals struck at the Calcutta Mint

The medals were given by the Honourable East India Company to native troops from Bombay and Bengal for their services in the capture of these three islands. The British troops present did not receive any medals. Re-strikes of this medal are to be found.

Rodrigues 6th July, 1809
A small force under Colonel Keatinge easily accomplished the capture of the Island.
Regiments present: 56 Foot (200 men), 2/2 Bombay Native Infantry (200 men).

Isle of Bourbon 8th July, 1810
This island, now known as Reunion, had already been invaded by Colonel Keatinge on 21st September, 1809. Owing to the small size of his force, he was unable to retain possession. A further attack became necessary, and so Colonel Keatinge was reinforced and, together with 236 seamen from the Squadron under Commodore Josias Rowley, of the *Raisonable*, a descent was made on 8th July, 1810.
Regiments present: 12, 33, 69, 86 Foot; 1/6, 2/22 Madras NI, 2/2 Bombay NI
HM Ships: *Nereide, Otter, Raisonable.*

Isle of France 3rd December, 1810
This island, now known as Mauritius, had for long been a nuisance, as it was the home of Corsairs who raided British merchantmen. A force 10,000 strong under General Sir John Abercromby was dispatched from India and together with a strong fleet, appeared off the island on 29th November, 1810. Several French ships were captured in the harbour of Port Louis, including the *Iphigenia*, which had recently been captured from the British Navy.
The British regiments present were the 22, 69 and 86 Foot.

48 *Portuguese Cayenne Medal* 1809

Obverse	High relief laureated head of the Prince Regent of Portugal facing left, with the legend, 'D: JOAM P:G:D:PRINC:REGEN:DE PORTUGAL &c 1809'. Below neck, 'Pidgeon F'.
Reverse	In the centre within a laurel wreath, '14 JAN 1809'. Around which the legend, 'CAYENNA TOMADA A: OS FRANCEZES'. (Cayenne taken from the French).
Size	51mm diameter
Metal	Silver-gilt and in bronze
Suspension	Issued without

Given by the Prince Regent of Portugal for the capture of the Island of Cayenne. Awarded to Captain (later Sir) James Lucas Yeo and eighty seamen and marines of HMS *Confiance* who assisted the Portuguese forces.

49 *Wooldridge Gold Medal* 1809

Obverse	A British fireship in flames in the act of breaking a boom, approaching French ships. Underneath, on a scroll, 'XI APRIL MDCCCIX.'
Reverse	An inscription, enclosed by a wreath of oak and laurel joined at the base by a scallop shell, 'CAPTAIN JAMES WOOLDRIDGE LED THE BRITISH FIRE SHIPS WHEN FOUR FRENCH SAIL OF THE LINE WERE BURNT UNDER THEIR OWN BATTERIES IN AIX ROADS.' The medal is surrounded by a cable border.
Size	43mm diameter
Metal	Gold
Suspension	Worn on a gold chain around the neck, attached by a ring suspension.
Manufacturer	R. W. Silvester

On the night of 11th April, 1809, an attempt was made to destroy the French squadron in Aix Roads by means of 12 fireships. Captain James Wooldridge, commanding the fireship *Mediator*, broke through the boom protecting the French ships and in remaining with his ship sustained severe injuries when she exploded.

French ships were burnt by this attack, although 13 of the 15 present ran aground in an effort to evade; such was the fear inspired.

The main action for which the 'Basque Roads' bar to the NGS medal was awarded, was fought the next day.

For his action, Wooldridge was awarded the gold medal and chain in 1812.

Provision for the bestowal of such a gold medal to successful fireship Captains dates from the 'Fighting Instructions' of 1665. Captain Wooldridge's medal is believed to be the last awarded.

50 *Spanish Medal for Bagur and Palamos* 10th & 14th September, 1810

Obverse	Crowned shields of Spain and Britain enfolded by their respective flags. The legend, 'ALIANZA ETERNA' below, the whole encircled by a wreath of laurel.
Reverse	In the centre, 'BAGUR *10 de Setiembre*, PALAMOS *14 de Setiembre 1810*'. Encircled by the legend, 'GRATITUD DE ESPANA A LA INTREPIDEZ BRITANICA'.
Size	48mm diameter
Metal	Issued in gold and in silver
Ribbon	Red with narrow yellow edges
Naming	Variable. A silver medal to W. Danials HMS *Cambrian* has the recipient's name engraved in script at the top of the reverse, with the name of the ship in capital letters at the bottom. Others are known with only the recipient's initials engraved upon the reverse.

Eight of the medals were issued in gold to senior officers, the remainder were in silver.

Awarded by the Spanish Government to the crews of HM Ships *Ajax* (74 guns), *Cambrian* (74 guns) and *Kent* (40 guns) for their part in expelling the French from Catalonia.

Although the records only mention personnel of the above three British ships as receiving medals, the sloops *Minstrel* and *Sparrowhawk* also took part.

51 *Java Medal* 26th August 1811

Obverse	A scene of the attack on Fort Cornelis; on a flag staff, the British Colours over the Dutch, and above the word 'CORNELIS'.
Reverse	A Persian inscription—'This medal was conferred in commemoration of the bravery and courage exhibited by the Sepoys of the English Company in the capture of the Kingdom of Java, in the year of Hegira 1228.' Around this, the inscription, 'JAVA CONQUERED XXVI AUGUST MDCCCXI.'
Size	51mm diameter
Metal	Gold (133) and silver (6,519).
Suspension	A flattened loop, pinned at the base through which passes a cord of no specified colour.
Engraver	The medals were engraved and struck at the Calcutta Mint.

This medal was issued by the HEIC to the native troops of 3rd, 4th, 5th and 6th Bengal Volunteers, Madras Pioneers and the Governor's Bodyguard. One hundred and thirty-three gold medals were issued; 5,761 natives received silver medals as well as about 750 Europeans. Only those in the service of the Company were allowed to wear their medals. For further particulars of the British troops and Naval ships present, the Military and Naval General Service Medals section should be referred to.

52 *Large Naval Gold Medal* 1794-1806 Given to Admirals

Obverse	A small figure of Victory standing on the prow of a galley is crowning Britannia with a wreath of laurel. Britannia's right foot is resting on a helmet and she is holding a spear in her left hand. Slightly behind her and to the right is an oval shield bearing the Union Jack.
Reverse	Engraved with the rank and name of the recipient, the event and date for which the medal was awarded, all surrounded by a wreath of oak and laurel.
Size	51mm diameter
Ribbon	45mm wide. White with 11mm wide dark blue borders.
Suspension	Medals are fitted with a gold ring through which the ribbon is threaded. Admirals wore their medals suspended around their necks.
Designer	R. Wood
Naming	The recipient's name and the action for which he received the award are engraved on the reverse.

The medals are mounted in gold frames, being glazed on both sides.
(For numbers awarded, see 'Small Naval Gold Medal' below.)

53 *Small Naval Gold Medal* 1794-1815 Given to Captains

Obverse	A small figure of Victory standing on the prow of a galley is crowning Britannia with a wreath of laurel. Britannia's right foot is resting on a helmet and she is holding a spear in her left hand. Slightly behind her and to the right is an oval shield bearing the Union Jack.
Reverse	Engraved with the rank and name of the recipient, the event and date for which the medal was awarded, but lacking the wreath found on the large medals.
Size	33mm diameter
Ribbon	38mm wide. White with 10mm wide dark blue borders.
Suspension	The medals are fitted with a small ring to which is attached a straight gold wire suspender through which the ribbon is threaded. Captains fastened their ribbons through the third or fourth buttonhole on the left side.
Designer	R. Wood
Naming	The recipient's name and the action for which he received the award are on the reverse.
Bars issued	Nil

The medals are mounted in gold frames, being glazed on both sides.

These medals were originally struck for presentation to the Admirals and Captains of Lord Howe's fleet in the victory over the French generally referred to as 'The Glorious First of June', which took place off Ushant on 1st June, 1794. Probably no victory has ever evoked such approbation from the Sovereign and the people, and awards, promotions and thanks were lavishly distributed by both Houses, Lloyd's, Trinity House, and citizens of all the large towns of Great Britain. It was also intended that these medals should be given to officers who especially distinguished themselves in the future, though the last one was awarded to Captain Hope of the *Endymion* for the capture of the *President* on 15th January, 1815. Only twenty-two of the large (including six with gold chains) and one hundred and seventeen of the smaller medals were awarded being issued for: 1st June, 1794 (17/8), St Vincent, 1797 (15/6);

Camperdown 1797 (15/2); Nile 1798 (14/1); Recapture of *Hermione* 1799 (1/-); Trafalgar 1805 (27/3); 4th November, 1805 (4/-); St. Domingo 1806 (8/2); Curacoa 1807 (4/-); Capture of *Thetis* 1808 (1/-); Capture of *Badere Zaffer* 1808 (1/-); Capture of *Rivoli* 1812 (1/-); Capture of *Chesapeake* 1813 (1/-); Capture of *L'Etoile* 1814 (1/-); *Endymion* with *President* 1815 (1/-).

Numbers in brackets indicate small and large medals awarded thus: Trafalgar 27 small and 3 large gold medals.

The Medal which would have been given to Lord Nelson was delivered to his family, and those of Captains John Cooke and George Duffall, for Trafalgar, to their respective widows in April, 1807. Five others would have received the small Medal had they not either been killed in action or died before they were distributed.

54 *Naval General Service Medal* 1793-1840

Obverse	The diademed head of Queen Victoria and legend 'VICTORIA REGINA' with the date '1848'.
Reverse	The figure of Britannia, holding a trident, seated sideways on a seahorse. The exergue is blank.
Size	36mm diameter
Ribbon	White with dark blue edges, 34mm wide.
Suspension	By a plain straight swivelling suspender.
Designer	W. Wyon, RA
Naming	Indented in Roman capitals. The recipient's rank is only given on medals to officers and warrant officers. The name of the ship is never given, but this can be traced by means of the medal rolls.
Bars issued	There were 231 bars sanctioned. One hundred and seventy-six of these were for actions fought by His or Her Majesty's warships, which will be dealt with first, and fifty-five for what were termed Boat Actions. For ten of these 231 bars there were no claimants. In addition to the above there was an unpublished bar for Boat Service, dated 6th May, 1814.
Number of medals issued	There were 15,577 medals issued with a single bar. A total of about 20,933 were issued altogether. The medal was not issued without a bar.

This medal which was originally intended to cover the period from 1793 to 1815, was later extended to cover that from the 1793 to 1840. It was not issued until 1849. A list was published in 1848 stating for which actions and boat services medals would be given. Those who considered themselves entitled to the medal had to give their names to the Staff Officer of Pensions in the district where they lived by 30th April, 1849. However in those days many could not read the papers or notices, which in any case would not have had a very wide circulation outside the towns. The medals previously issued, i.e. the medals given by Mr Davison for Trafalgar were, in many cases, thrown into the sea, so that there must have been a certain apathy towards medals. By 1849 many who would have been entitled to the medal must have died. These facts, together with the general illiteracy of the period probably account for the very few medals issued, and for the fact that there were no claimants at all for some of the awards sanctioned. The final date for submitting claims for the medal was extended to 1st May, 1851. Naval General Service Medals were awarded to the next-of-kin of applicants who died between the time of their application and the distribution. This statement must not be taken as meaning that medals were awarded to the next-of-kin of all the men who would have been entitled to them; this was not the case. It is worth noting that no boat action services were recognized after 1814, thirty-five years before the issue of the medal. It is thought that over 500 medals were issued after the original lists were closed for which there are no medal rolls. This factor should be noted if a medal is reported 'not on roll but appears to be perfect.'

The maximum number of bars issued with any one medal was seven. There are two such medals, which are confirmed as awarded to Captain James Alexander Gordon, RN, and Lieutenant John Hindmarsh, RN (later Rear Admiral and first Governor of South Australia 1836-38). Four medals were issued with six bars and fourteen with five.

Rear-Admiral Sir George Cockburn received a medal with six bars and in each case was in command at the action. His bars were: 14th March, 1795; Minerve, 19th December, 1796; St Vincent; Egypt; Martinique; Boat Service, 29th April, 1813. This officer escorted Napoleon to St Helena in HMS *Northumberland* and, it is believed, holds the record for *continuous* naval service—namely, sixty-eight years. He served fifty-six years afloat. His was the only medal indented to a Rear-Admiral.

Another interesting medal is that awarded to Stephen Laurie, who earned all his six bars whilst serving in HMS *Phoebe*. The dates of his bars show a period of apparently nearly seventeen years' continuous service in one ship—a truly remarkable record. His bars were as follows: Phoebe, 21 December, 1797 (as Boy); Phoebe, 19th February, 1801 (as Boy): Trafalgar (as Ableseaman). Off Tamatave, 20th May, 1811 (as Ableseaman); Java (as Ableseaman), Phoebe, 28th March, 1814 (as Captain of the Foretop).

During the battle of the Glorious First of June a son was born to Mrs McKenzie, who was on board HMS *Tremendous,* and he received the names of Daniel Tremendous and was duly awarded his medal and bar. As applications for the medal were not made until 1848, it must surely be unique for a man to apply fifty-four years later for a medal awarded for a battle fought on the day he was born. In these days, when we hear so much about the youthful age at which men go to war, we would do well to remember Daniel Tremendous McKenzie!

A unique rank is that of 'Passenger' which is mentioned for one of the medals awarded to HMS *Venerable* when she captured two French frigates off the Canary Islands on 16th January, 1814.

The first action in British history for which a clergyman received a medal is that of the Glorious First of June, 1794. The recipient was Thomas Morgan, who served on HMS *Alfred*. He also got the bar for Mars, 21st April, 1798.

There were about 126 military recipients of this medal—many of them for occasions when regiments served on board as marines. Some were awarded to artillery men and engineers who were co-opted for special services. (See tables).

Where the bar is particularly rare the names of the recipients are given.

There were a few recipients of two of these medals; for instance, Lieutenant William Parker, RN, received one with the bars for 14th March, 1795, St. Vincent and Nile, and another with the bar for Egypt. Incidentally, he also received the Sultan's Gold Medal. Ordinary Seaman Samuel Challis received a medal with the bar for 4th November, 1805, and another with that for Basque Roads. Clerk Thomas Bastin received a medal with a bar for Boat Service, 27th June, 1803, and another with those for Boat Service, 4th June, 1805; off Rota, 4th April, 1808; Grasshopper. 24th April, 1808.

Naval General Service Medals to Army Recipients

*The * denotes that he also received the Military General Service Medal and † denotes that he also received the Army Gold Medal*

A list of the officers, non-commissioned officers and men of the Army, present on board HM's ships on the occasions for which the medal was granted, and who received the same in accordance with the Gazettes of June 1st 1847 and June 8th 1848, showing the ships in which they were serving and the bars they received for those occasions.

Unattached
Lt Col T. C. Cradock, *afterwards* Lord
Howden *Asia* — Navarino
Lt Col E. Napier *Hydra* and *Hecate* — Syria
Received a duplicate
Lt Col Hugh Rose *Hecate* — Syria

Staff Corps
Capt C. Rochfort Scott *Hecate* — Syria

Cavalry and Infantry
3rd Dragoons
Lieut De Lacy Evans *Meteor* — 14 Dec, Boat Service, 1814

2nd Queen's
Lieut A. L. Pilkington *Royal George* — 1 June 1794
Sgt D. Wainwright *Russell* — 1 June 1794
Pte William Shaw *Royal George* — 1 June 1794

7th Royal Fusiliers
Capt Richard Wilbraham *Hecate* — Syria

11th Foot
Pte Samuel Hutson *Diadem* — St Vincent
Pte James Moorfield *Captain* — St Vincent

25th Foot
Pte Thomas Burchley *Gibraltar* — 1 June 1794
Pte Luke Thayyers *Gibraltar* — 1 June 1794
*Sgt J. Ward *St George* — 1 June 1794

29th Foot
*Lieut C. B. Egerton *Thunderer* — 1 June 1794
Ensn L. A. Northey *Alfred* — 1 June 1794
Pte Richard S. Bamford *Glory* — 1 June 1794
Pte Robert Cook *Alfred* — 1 June 1794
Pte James Kilgrove *Glory* — 1 June 1794
*Pte William Robinson *Thunderer* — 1 June 1794
*Pte Thomas Robson *Brunswick* — 1 June 1794
*Pte Thomas Smith *Alfred* — 1 June 1794

30th Foot
*Lieut David Maxwell *Princess Royal* — 14 March 1795

49th Foot
Pte John Smith *Blenheim* — St Vincent
*Capt Hon Hugh Arbuthnott *Ganges* — Copenhagen 1801
*Ensn John Armstrong *Ardent* — Copenhagen 1801
Capt William Bird Bleamire *Ganges* — Copenhagen 1801
Vol George Brock *Polyphemus* — Copenhagen 1801
Asst Surgn Robert Brown *Glatton* — Copenhagen 1801

*Pte W. Booth *Defiance*	Copenhagen 1801	Gnr Isaac Mowles	Syria
Sgt Joseph Coushay *Defiance*	Copenhagen 1801	Gnr John Mutlo	Syria
Pte William Donnelly *Defiance*	Copenhagen 1801	Bom Robert Pasley	Syria
*Pte Lawrence Dooley *Edgar*	Copenhagen 1801	Gnr John Peters	Syria
Dmr Chas. Hawker *Ramillies*	Copenhagen 1801	Gnr Joseph Preston	Syria
*Pte Andrew Jackson *Edgar*	Copenhagen 1801	Gnr George Riddle	Syria
Dmr Charles Knokes *Ramillies*	Copenhagen 1801	Gnr William Rouse	Syria
Lieut James Dennis *Monarch*	Copenhagen 1801	Gnr John Sheehan	Syria
*Vol Harry S. Ormond *Glatton*	Copenhagen 1801	Gnr John Shepheard	Syria
†Capt Chas. Plendeleath *Ardent*	Copenhagen 1801	Gnr John Short	Syria
Lt Col Roger H. Sheaffe *Bellona*	Copenhagen 1801	Gnr Andrew Smith	Syria
*Pte Edward Liston *Ganges*	Copenhagen 1801	Gnr Evan Williams	Syria
*Pte John Long *Saturn*	Copenhagen 1801	Gnr John Williams	Syria
*Pte Peter Plunkett *Defiance*	Copenhagen 1801		
Pte Reuben Potter *London*	Copenhagen 1801		
*Pte Dennis Slaynes *Edgar*	Copenhagen 1801		
*Pte Anthony Walsh *Bellona*	Copenhagen 1801		
*Pte Robert Young *Bellona*	Copenhagen 1801		

50th Foot

Pte John Milgrove *Diadem*   St Vincent

63rd Foot

*Lieut W. Cosby *Pompée*   Pompée, 17 June 1809

69th Foot

Capt Caleb Chute *Britannia*   St Vincent and
                                    14 March 1795
*Pte Samuel Chadwick *Britannia*   St Vincent
*Pte Benjamin Pratt *Otter*   Otter, 18 Sept. 1810

87th Foot

Capt Frederick H. Robe *Hecate*   Syria

95th Foot

Rfln Hugh Parsley *Isis*   Copenhagen, 1801
Rfln James Stiff *St George*   Copenhagen, 1801

Royal Artillery

Gnr Andrew Smith *Zebra*   Copenhagen, 1801
Lieut F. Robertson *Marlborough*   29 Ap., Boat
                                    Service, 1813
Capt Peter Faddy *Freija*   St Sebastian
Lieut J. T. Fuller, Rocket Bde *Minden*   Algiers
Sgt Edward Howe, Rocket Bde *Minden*   Algiers
Gnr Joseph Allen, H. A. *Granicus*   Algiers
*Gnr John Dickenson *Queen Charlotte*   Algiers
All the following serving in the *Hecate*,
excepting the two officers noted:
Capt and Bty Maj F. H. Colquhon   Syria
Lieut H. G. Ross   Syria
Maj T. G. Higgins *Thunderer*   Syria
Gnr Henry Bailey   Syria
Gnr William Bird   Syria
Gnr Samuel Chesney   Syria
Gnr John Dolby   Syria
Gnr Jesse Douch   Syria
Sgt William Dover   Syria
Gnr James Garrod   Syria
Cpl George Gurnett   Syria
Gnr Peter Guyte   Syria
Gnr William Hames   Syria
Gnr John Henry   Syria
Gnr Thomas Hill   Syria
Gnr Moses Johnston   Syria
Lieut W. S. Rowan *Pique and others*   Syria

Royal Engineers and Royal Sappers and Miners

Previous to 1856, the officers and men of
this Corps were differently denominated.
The officers were the Royal Engineers, but
the non-commissioned officers and men
were first known as the Soldier Artificer
Company and then as Military Artificers.
In 1812 they became the Royal Military
Artificers, or Sappers and Miners, and, in
the following year, the Royal Sappers and
Miners, which title they retained until
1856, when the whole Corps became Royal
Engineers.

†*Lt Col George Landermann *Milford*   23 Nov, Boat
                                        Service, 1810
Lieut George Hotham }   Algiers
*Lt Col Wm. Reid   } *Ship not mentioned*   Algiers
Lieut J. R. W. Whinyates *Impregnable*   Algiers
Spr James Bond *Queen Charlotte*   Algiers
Spr Thomas Fraser *Queen Charlotte*   Algiers
Spr Alexander McKenzie *Queen Charlotte*   Algiers
Sgt L. Melville *Queen Charlotte*   Algiers
Spr R. Parry *Impregnable*   Algiers
Spr Francis Rogers *Queen Charlotte*   Algiers
Dmr Alexander Smith *Impregnable*   Algiers
Spr William Stuart *Queen Charlotte*   Algiers
Lt Col R. C. Alderson *Hecate*   Syria
Lt Col Edward Aldrich *Military Secretary
Princess Charlotte*   Syria
*†Col Sir Chas. Smith *Princess Charlotte*   Syria
Lieut J. F. H. Symonds *Hecate*   Syria
Sgt Charles Beer *Princess Charlotte*   Syria
Spr William Black *Princess Charlotte*   Syria
Spr T. Edington *Gorgon*   Syria
Spr Robert Grant *Hecate*   Syria
Spr William Heathcote *Hecate*   Syria
Spr James Ireland *Hecate*   Syria
Spr Thomas Jorey *Implacable*   Syria
Spr John Moore *Pique and Stromboli*   Syria
Spr John Sleeman *Hecate*   Syria
Sgt Hugh Smith *Princess Charlotte*   Syria
Spr Philip Trevail *Hecate*   Syria

Medical Department

Hosp-Orderly William Caughlan (or
Cockland) *Minden*   Algiers

Storekeeper's Department

*Clerk of OS John Miller *in a Transport*   Algiers
Conductor of Stores E. Sargent *Minden*   Algiers

Colonial Regiment
Royal Newfoundland Regiment

Lieut Andrew Boulger (not given)   3 & 6 Sep., Boat
                                    Service, 1814

The following is also noted but no Corps
or Regiment given:
Soldier Andrew McKenzie *Barfleur*   23rd June 1795

Naval General Service Medals

Recent research has shown that all numbers given against bars should be considered as approximate. The information given to form a medal roll has been obtained from the clasp lists (now microfilm A.D.M. 171/1-3) which contain details of the recipient and his claim to a bar for his services. Upon inspection of the Muster Rolls, we find additional names but although these show services aboard a ship for an action, this does not mean that the bar was claimed. For these possible claims, we use the expression 'verified aboard not on roll' (VANOR). Numbers will therefore vary against bars depending on whether or not we include these additional names. For low issuance bars in particular, we have decided to exclude those 'VANORS' from the 'No of bars issued' and list them separately. We recommend that further information be drawn from both Hailes and Douglas-Morris Rolls.

In the list below dates in parenthesis are the dates of the actual action, which, in some cases, differ from those recorded on the bar.

The **approximate** number of medals issued to officers and ratings of individual ships for the major actions is indicated thus, 4/21 = 4 officers and 21 ratings.

	No of HM Ships Engaged	No of Bars Issued
Nymphe 18 June 1793	1	4
(19 June 1793)		

For the capture off Start Point, Devon by the *Nymphe*, 36 guns (Capt Ed. Pellew) of the French frigate *La Cléopatra*, 40 guns, which was afterwards added to the Royal Navy as HMS *Oiseau*.

Recipients: Qr Mr J. Gaze; Cpl J. Kelly, RM; Gnr's Crew J. Simpson; Captain's Servant J. Smart.

	No of HM Ships Engaged	No of Bars Issued
Crescent 20 Octr 1793	1	12
(20 October 1793)		

For the capture of the French frigate *La Réunion* by the *Crescent* (Captain J. Saumarez) off Cherbourg.

Recipients: Lieuts. G. Parker & Peter Rye, RN; Mstr's Mte J. Tancock; Mids T. Mansell, J. Marrett; Capt's Servant John Jones; Qtr Gnr William Madge; ABs John de Page, T. Handford, Richard Jeune, J. Kitt & John Soames.
An engraving was published on 20th January, 1794, the legend stating: 'The Submission of the French frigate *La Réunion* to H. Majesty's frigate *Crescent*, Captain Sir Jas. Saumarez, to whom and his officers, this print and its companion is most respectively inscribed by their obedt servt Robt. Dodd.' Beneath this is the interesting statement: 'It is singularly remarkable that tho' this action lasted two hours and twenty minutes there was not a man on board the *Crescent* either killed, wounded or hurt by the enemy, but the loss on their side was 120 killed and wounded, their vessel a complete wreck in hull, sails and rigging. Their national colours were shot away early in the action and their temporary one was also shot down three times and in token of submission they brought the remnants to the gangway, held them up and bowed over them to the gallant British Commander.'

The size of the forces engaged is quoted as: English force—*Crescent*, 36 guns, 250 men; French force—*La Réunion*, 36 guns, 320 men, and a cutter of 12 or 14 guns.

	No of HM Ships Engaged	No of Bars Issued
Zebra 17 March 1794	1	2
(20 March 1794)		

For the part played by the *Zebra* (Captain R. Faulknor) in the capture of Fort Royal, Martinique.
It seems extraordinary that this ship should be singled out for reward for her part in the capture of the island. She accompanied the boats from the other ships, manned by 1,250 men, only twenty-nine of whom received the bar for the Boat Action. However HMS *Zebra* accompanied HMS *Asia* in an attempt to break through the harbour boom. The latter failed to take up her position so that the task was performed by the *Zebra* alone.
The island was restored to the French under the Treaty of Amiens in 1802, and recaptured in 1809.
An interesting naval event is indirectly connected with this island off the south-east of which lies the Diamond Rock. This was taken by the Navy and commissioned and rated as a sloop in 1804 (see 'Anholt 27 March 1811' and 'BS 21 Jan. 1807'). It is now the custom for shore establishments to be rated as men-of-war, but one wonders whether this is not one of the earliest instances of a 'stone frigate'.

Recipients: Lieut Henry Hill, RN, and Joseph Bass, Carpenter's Crew.

	No of HM Ships Engaged	No of Bars Issued
Carysfort 29 May 1794	1	0
(28 May 1794)		

For the recapture of HMS *Castor* off Newfoundland by the *Carysfort* (Captain Francis Laforey). The *Castor* had been captured from the British on 10th May off Newfoundland.

No bars were issued.

	No of HM Ships Engaged	No of Bars Issued

1 June 1794

| | 37 | 540 |

(1 June 1794)

This was the date of the action known as the 'Glorious First of June'.

The French fleet of Admiral L. T. Villaret-Joyeuse had put to sea to cover the return of a large convoy of merchant ships, laden with foodstuffs from America. The British fleet of Admiral Lord Richard Howe intercepted Villaret and clashed several times in a running fight (28-31 May). On 1st June came the major battle, ending in a notable British victory. Of the 26 French ships-of-the-line in action, 1 was sunk and 6 captured.

Ships present: Lord Howe's flagship *Queen Charlotte* 4/21, and *Alfred* 4/22, *Aquilon* 1/5, *Audacious* 1/13, *Bellerophon* 2/17, *Barfleur* 1/15, *Brunswick* 1/18, *Caesar* 2/17, *Culloden* 6/19, *Defence* 4/15, *Gibraltar* 3/11, *Glory* 4/17, *Impregnable* 3/20, *Invincible* 2/14, *Kingfisher** 1/-, *Latona* -/9, *Leviathan* 1/16, *Majestic* 1/11, *Marlborough* 1/16, *Montagu* 2/16, *Niger* 1/4, *Orion* 1/12, *Pegasus* -/7, *Phaeton* 1/8, *Queen* 5/14, *Ramilles* 3/11, *Royal George* 4/35, *Royal Soveriegn* 4/22, *Russell* 1/16, *Southampton* 1/3, *Thunderer* 3/7, *Tremendous* -/21, *Valiant* 3/17, *Venus* -/5.

Sloops: *Ranger* 1/-, *Rattler* -/2.
Fireships: *Comet* 1/1, *Incendiary*.
Hospital ship: *Charon* 1/7.

Special Gold Medal: Admiral Lord Howe (*Queen Charlotte*) received a special gold medal suspended from the same chain as that given with the large gold medal.

Recipients of the Large Naval Gold Medal and Chain:
Vice-Admirals Graves (*Royal Sovereign*) and Hood (*Royal George*), Rear-Admirals Bowyer (*Barfleur*), Pasley (*Bellerophon*) and Gardner (*Queen*) and Captain of the Fleet Sir Roger Curtis (*Queen Charlotte*).
Rear-Admiral B. Caldwell, who was on board the *Impregnable*, did not receive a gold medal, and neither did Captain of the Fleet Sir Roger B. Westcott.
Small Gold Medal Recipients:
Capt Sir Andrew S. Douglas (*Queen Charlotte*), Capt W. Domett (*Royal George*), Capt Henry Nichols (*Royal Sovereign*), Capt Cuthbert Collingwood (*Barfleur*), Capt John Hutt (*Queen*), Capt John Elphinstone (*Glory*), Capt William Hope (*Bellerophon*), Capt James Pigott (*Tremendous*), Capt Thomas Pringle (*Valiant*), Capt Henry Harvey (*Ramillies*), Capt William Parker (*Audacious*), Capt John Bazeley (*Alfred*) Capt James Gambier (*Defence*), Capt Lord Hugh Seymour (*Leviathan*), Capt Hon Thomas Packenham (*Invincible*), Capt John T. Duckworth (*Orion*), Capt John W. Payne (*Russell*), Capt Hon G. C. Berkeley (*Marlborough*).

The roll gives the name of Thomas Morgan, Chaplain. This, therefore, is the first action in British history for which a clergyman received a medal. He also received the bar 'Mars, 21st April, 1798.'

The Queen's and the 1st Battalion The Worcestershire Regiment served with the fleet as Marines and carry a naval crown superscribed '1st JUNE 1794.' The King's Own Scottish Borderers were also serving in the fleet as Marines, but carry no distinction to commemorate the fact. The following members of the Army received the NGS Medal with this bar: 2nd Foot (Queen's Regt): Lieut A. Pilkington (HMS *Royal George*), Sgt D. Wainwright (HMS *Russell*).
25th Foot (KOSB): Pte Thomas Burchley, Pte Luke Thayyers (HMS *Gibraltar*).
29th Foot (The Worcestershire Regt): Lieut B. Egerton, Pte Wm Robinson (HMS *Thunderer*), Ensign L. A. Northey, Cpl R. Cook (*Alfred*), Pte T. Robson (HMS *Brunswick*)*, Pte T. Smith (HMS *Alfred*), Ptes S. R. Bamford and Jas Kilgrove (HMS *Glory*).

Romney 17 June 1794

| | 1 | 2 |

(17 June 1794)

For the capture of the French frigate *Sibylle*, which was at anchor in Mykonos Harbour (Captain The Hon Wm Paget).

Recipients: Midshipman Manly Dixon, and C. Woodley.

Blanche 4 Jany 1795

| | 1 | 5 |

(5 January 1795)

For the extremely fierce fight between the *Blanche* (Captain R. Faulknor, late of the *Zebra*) and the French frigate *Pique*, which was chased and captured off Grandeterre, Gaudaloupe. Captain Faulknor was killed in this action, and later a monument was erected to his memory in St Paul's Cathedral.

Recipients: Lieut Frederick Watkins, RN; Mid Thos L. Prescott; ABs Henry Greely and Thos Evans; Boy 3rd Class Joseph Clark.

Lively, 13 March 1795

| | 1 | 3 |

(13 March 1795)

For the capture of the French ship *Tourterelle* off Ushant by the *Lively* (Captain Geo Burlton).

Recipients: Mid J. Groves, Vol 1st Class B. Simpson, Boy 3rd Class, R. Wilcox. Verified aboard not on roll, ABs I. Buckmaster and T. Holland; Pte RM W. Laverton.

14 March 1795

| | 25 | 95 |

(14 March 1795)

Given for the defeat of the French fleet off Genoa by Admiral Hotham. Ships present: Admiral Hotham's flagship *Britannia* 1/4, and *Agamemnon* 1/-, *Bedford* 3/7, *Captain* 2/5, *Courageaux* -/2, *Diadem* 2/4, *Egmont* 1/3, *Fortitude* -/1, *Inconstant* 1/3, *Illustrious* 1/6, *Lowestoffe* 1/4, *Mediator*, *Meleager* 1/1, *Minerva*, *Moselle* 1/1, *Pilade*, *Poulette* -/1, *Princess Royal* 5/3, *Romulus* -/1, *Saint George* 4/10, *Tancredi*, *Terrible* 1/3, *Windsor Castle* 3/8. Brig: *Tarleton*. Cutter: *Fox*.

*HMS Kingfisher was incorrectly included by the Admiralty as a qualifying ship.

*Thos Robson also received the MGS Medal with bars for Roleia, Vimiera, Talavera and Albuhera.

	No of HM Ships Engaged	No of Bars Issued

The KOSB, E. Lancs, and 2nd Bn The Welch Regt were serving on board the fleet, and the following members of these regiments received the NGS Medal with this bar:
KOSB (25th Foot): Sgt J. Ward (HMS *St George*). E. Lancs (30th Foot): Lieut D. Maxwell (HMS *Princess Royal*). The Welch Regt (69th Foot); Capt Caleb Chute (HMS *Britannia*), who also received the bar for St Vincent.
The medal awarded to Captain Chute is probably unique, being the only NGS medal to the Army (69th Foot) carrying two bars (14 March 1795, St Vincent). J. G. Bussell, chaplain, received this bar.
VANOR (2).

Astraea 10 April 1795

	1	2

(10 April 1795)

For the capture of the French frigate *Gloire* off Brest by the *Astraea* (Captain Lord Henry Paulet).

Recipients: Lieut John Talbot, RN; Ord Wm Mainland.

Thetis 17 May 1795

	1	2

Hussar 17 May 1795

	1	1

(16 May 1795)

For the capture by HMS *Thetis* (Captain Hon A. Cochrane) and *Hussar* (Captain J. P. Beresford) of the French ships *Prevoyante* and *La Raison* off Cape Henry in Chesapeake Bay.

Recipients: HMS *Thetis*—Surgeon's 1st Mate R. Hume; Mid William George Maude. HMS *Hussar*—Vol 1st Class James Read.
VANOR. For *Thetis*. Lord Thomas Cochrane, later Earl of Dundonald.

Mosquito 9 June 1795

	1	0

(24 May 1795)

For the action which the *Mosquito* (Lieutenant Macarthy, RN) fought with a French privateer, as a result of which the *Mosquito* was lost with the entire crew. (As this fact must have been known to the committee which approved of the engagements for which bars were to be awarded, it seems particularly futile to have sanctioned a bar for this action.)

17 June 1795

	8	41

(17 June 1795)

This bar was given for Vice Admiral The Hon William Cornwallis's repulse of about thirty French ships off Ushant. Ships present: Cornwallis's flagship *Royal Sovereign* -/5, and *Bellerophon* 2/3, *Brunswick* -/2, *Kingfisher*, *Mars* -/13, *Pallas* -/4, *Phaeton* 1/4 and *Triumph* 1/7. (Master S. P. Pritchard of HMS *Royal Sovereign* later served as Captain of HMS *Blenheim* in China, 1842.) HMS *Kingfisher* left Spithead with Cornwallis's squadron, but must have been detached before the action or, alternatively, there may have been no claimants from her, as she does not appear on the rolls.
VANOR (8)

23rd June 1795

	32	177

(23 June 1795)

For the defeat of the French fleet by Admiral Bridport off the Isle de Groix. Ships present: Admiral Bridport's flagship *Royal George* 6/21, and *Aquilon* 2/4, *Astraea* -/1, *Babet* 1/2, *Barfleur* 1/5, *Boyne* -/1, *Colossus* -/8, *Galatea* 1/1, *Irresistible* -/8, *Leviathan* -/7, *London* 3/4, *Nymphe* -/2, *Orion* 4/9, *Pallas*, *Prince of Wales* 2/2, *Prince George* 1/4, *Queen* 1/12, *Queen Charlotte* 4/9, *Revolutionnaire* 2/2, *Robust* 2/9, *Russell* 4/5, *Sans Pareil* 2/7, *Standard* 1/3, *Teazer* -/1, *Thalia* -/4, *Thunderer* -/2, *Valiant* -/5.
Fire Ships: *Incendiary* and *Megaera*. Cutters: *Argus* and *Dolly*.
Hospital ship: *Charon* -/2.
The roll quotes Andrew McKenzie, 97th Foot, private soldier (HMS *Barfleur*), as having received this bar, also Samuel Cole, Chaplain (HMS *London*). The last is the third medal to a chaplain that is known.
VANOR (5)

Dido 24 June 1795

	1	1

Lowestoffe 24 June 1795

	1	6

(24 June 1795)

HMS *Dido* (Capt G. H. Towry) and *Lowestoffe* (Captain R. G. Middleton) captured the French frigate *Minerve* and defeated the *Artemise* off Toulon.

Recipients: HMS *Dido*—Ord Charles Ledditt. HMS *Lowestoffe*—Mid Edward Libby, ABs Thos Kemp, John Smith, George Salvedore and Gilbert White; Boy 2nd Class Wm Gibson.

Spider 25 Aug 1795

	1	1

(25 August 1795)

The Lugger *Spider*, whilst cruising in the North Sea, encountered two small French brigs and captured the *Victorieuse*.

Recipient: AB John Lean.

Port Spergui 17 March 1796

	3	4

(17 March 1796)

The *Diamond* (Captain Sidney Smith), *Liberty* (Lieutenant Geo. M'Kinley RN), and the lugger *Aristocrat* (Lieutenant Abraham Gossett), went into the port of Erqui, on the Brittany coast, and captured and set on fire the French corvette *Etourdie* and also destroyed seven other small French warships.

Recipients: HMS *Diamond*—Surgeon D. McArthur, Mid. J. Boxer and Lieut W. F. Carroll. HMS *Liberty*—Lieut Geo McKinley, RN.
There were no claimants from HMS *Aristocrat*.

Indefatigable 20 April 1796

	1	6

(21 April 1796)

The *Indefatigable* (Captain Sir Edward Pellew) captured the French frigate *Virginie* in the English Channel, off Ushant, after a fifteen-hour chase.

	No of HM Ships Engaged	No of Bars Issued

Recipients: Master's Mte T. Groube, Mid N. L. Pateshall, Vols 1st Class The Hon George Cadogan and John Harry, Qtr Gnr J. McKerlie, AB John Jones. VANOR (2) Mid John Gaze, AB Joseph Simpson.

Unicorn 8 June 1796
| | 1 | 4 |

Santa Margaritta 8 June 1796
| | 1 | 3 |

(8 June 1796)

The *Unicorn* (Captain T. Williams) and *Santa Margaritta* (Captain T. Byam Martin), when cruising off the Scilly Islands, encountered the French frigates *Tamise* and *Tribune* together with the corvette *Legère*. The two French frigates were captured after the *Unicorn* had chased the *Tribune* for 220 miles. Captain Williams was knighted for this action.

Recipients: HMS *Unicorn*—Mid C. J. Austen; Ord W. Dexter; Pte John Green, RM; Surgeon's Mate J. Mather. HMS *Santa Margaritta*—Capt T. B. Martin RN,* QM's Mate T. Price, and Joseph Bullen (rank not given).

Southampton 9 June 1796
| | 1 | 4 |

(9 June 1796)

For the boarding and capture of the French frigate *Utile*, off Toulon, by the *Southampton* (Captain Macnamara).

Recipients: Yeoman of BS Room J. Strachan, LM Joseph Goodall and Pte's James Dallimore and S. Spill, RM. VANOR (4)

Dryad 13 June 1796
| | 1 | 5 |

(13 June 1796)

In this action the *Dryad* (Captain Lord A. Beauclerk) captured the French frigate *Prosperpine* off Cape Clear.

Recipients: Lieut E. D. King, RN; 2nd-Lieut Thomas Sharman, RM; Ord Seaman John Allen; LM John Pusey; and Edward Verling whose rank is not stated. VANOR (1) Mid Colin McDonald.

Terpsichore 13 Octr. 1796
| | 1 | 3 |

(13 October 1796)

For the action in which the *Terpsichore* (Captain R. Bowen) captured the Spanish frigate *Mahonesa* off Carthagena and then towed her to Lisbon.

Recipients: Pte T. Ashford, RM; Ord T. Beautyman; Vol 1st Class W. L. Paterson.

Lapwing 3 Decr. 1796
| | 1 | 2 |

(27 November 1796)

For the action between the *Lapwing* (Captain Robert Barton), and the French ships *Vaillante* and *Decius* off St Kitts, Antigua. The *Decius* was captured.

Recipients: ABs T. Morrod and LM Wm. Levey.

---

*Chairman of the NGS medal committee.

Minerve 19 Decr. 1796
| | 1 | 4 |

Blanche 19 Decr. 1796
| | 1 | 2 |

(19 December 1796)

Commodore Horatio Nelson in the *Minerve* (Captain Geo. Cockburn), accompanied by the *Blanche* (Captain Bruce), was on his way from Gibraltar to fetch stores left at Port Ferrajo, on the north coast of the island of Elba, when he fell in with the Spanish frigates *Sabina* and *Ceres*. The *Minerve* (which was previously the French-owned frigate *Minerve* captured by the *Dido* on 24th June, 1795) engaged the *Sabina*, which surrendered. Nelson placed a prize crew on board under Lieutenants John Culverhouse and Thomas Hardy (later to be his Captain on the *Victory* at Trafalgar) and proceeded to tow her. Whilst so engaged the Spanish frigate *Matilda* approached. The *Minerve* cast off her tow and engaged the new arrival, but during this second action three more Spanish ships appeared and so the *Minerve* had to flee and abandon the *Sabina*.
Much the same happened to the *Blanche*, which had forced the *Ceres* to surrender, and whilst accepting it the arrival of the *Matilda* and *Perla* forced her to relinquish her capture and seek safety in flight.

Recipients: HMS *Minerve*—Capt Geo. Cockburn RN, Lieut W. H. Gage; ABs S. Blackmore and P. Brown. HMS *Blanche*—Mid R. Pridham; Vol 1st Class J. Clark. VANOR (2) ABs Thomas Evans and H. Greely.

Indefatigable 13 Jany 1797
| | 1 | 8 |

Amazon 13 Jany 1797
| | 1 | 6 |

(13 January 1797)

For the action fought by the *Indefatigable* (Captain Sir Edward Pellew) and *Amazon* (Captain C. Reynolds), which started off the south of Ireland and ended with the *Amazon* and the enemy ship *Droits de l'Homme* going ashore on the French coast. The crew of the *Amazon* was captured on shore. The *Indefatigable* was almost a wreck, having several feet of water in her, but she managed to get home.
The French ship, when sighted off the mouth of the Shannon, had on board General Humbert and about 1,350 soldiers and crew, so that the loss in the *Droits de l'Homme* during the action, which lasted thirteen hours, and the further loss when she went ashore was appalling—over 900 being either killed or drowned.
General Humbert at the time was in command of a division of 6,000 men, which, together with troops from Spain and Holland, all under General Hoche, hoped to land in Ireland to assist the Irish rebels under Lord Edward Fitzgerald.
It is pleasant to record that the survivors of the *Amazon* and others rescued by the *Droits de l'Homme* were treated with every care. Those who had been in the French ship were nursed back to health and returned by special ship to England in

No of HM Ships Engaged	No of Bars Issued

March, the remainder of the crew of the *Amazon* were exchanged in September of the same year.

Recipients: HMS *Indefatigable*—Mids H. Hart, J. Gaze, and N. L. Pateshall Vols 1st Class Geo. Earl of Cadogan and J. Harry; Master's Mte Thomas Groube, Surgeon's Mte R. P. Williams. Schoolmaster John McKerlie. VANOR (2) ABs John Jones and Joseph Simpson. HMS *Amazon*—Mids B. Reynolds and Wm. Croft; Vol 1st Class Richard Devonshire; ABs John Brown and Alex Dixie; LM John Ellender.

St Vincent

24	348

(14 February 1797)

For the battle off Cape St Vincent fought by Admiral Jervis to prevent the uniting of the Dutch, Spanish and French fleets off the west coast of Spain.
In this action Commodore Nelson captured two of the four ships taken from the enemy—namely, the *San Josef* and *San Nicolas*.
It was when the *San Josef* surrendered that Nelson ordered the Spanish Captain to summon his (the Spanish) officers to the quarterdeck. Here Nelson relates that 'Extravagant as the story may seem, did I receive the swords of the vanquished Spaniards, which, as I received, I gave to William Fearney, one of my bargemen, who put them with the greatest sangfroid under his arm.' Some of the Welch Regiment (then the 69th, South Lincolnshire Regiment) were serving as Marines during this action on Nelson's ship, HMS *Captain*. They had previously served with him on HMS *Agamemnon*, from which fact they earned their soubriquet of 'Old Agamemnons' from him.
Ships present: Admiral Jervis's flagship *Victory* 5/18, and *Barfleur* 6/23, *Blenheim* 8/16, *Britannia* 5/16, *Captain* 2/17, *Colossus* 1/12, *Culloden* 4/23, *Diadem* 2/11, *Egmont* -/17, *Emerald* -/1, *Excellent* 3/18, *Goliath* 4/16, *Irresistible* 1/12, *Namur* 3/2, *Orion* 1/21, *Prince George* 3/32; frigates *Dido*, *Lively* 1/6, *Minerve* 2/2, *Niger* -/1, *Southampton* 1/8; sloops *Bon Citoyenne* -/5, *Raven* -/1; cutter *Fox*.

Recipients of the Large Gold Medal: Admiral Sir John Jervis *Victory*; Vice-Admiral Charles Thompson *Britannia*; Vice-Admiral Hon William Waldegrave *Barfleur*; Rear-Admiral William Parker *Prince George*; Commodore Horatio Nelson *Captain*; Captain of the Fleet Robert Calder *Victory*.

Recipients of the Small Gold Medal: Capt George Grey *Victory*; Capt Thomas Foley *Britannia*; Capt James Richard Dacres *Barfleur*; Capt John Irwin *Prince George*; Capt Thomas Lenox Frederick *Blenheim*; Capt James Hawkins Whitshed *Namur*; Capt Ralph Willett Miller *Captain*; Capt Sir Charles H. Knowles, Bart *Goliath*; Capt Cuthbert Collingwood *Excellent*; Capt Sir James Saumarez *Orion*; Capt George Murray *Colossus*; Capt John Sutton *Egmont*;

No of HM Ships Engaged	No of Bars Issued

Capt Thomas Troubridge *Culloden*; Capt George Martin *Irresistible*; Capt George Henry Towry *Diadem*.

Military Recipients of the NGS Medal with this Bar: 11th Foot—Ptes Samuel Huston, HMS *Diadem* and James Moorfield, HMS *Captain*. 49th Foot—Pte John Smith*, HMS *Blenheim* (who also got MGS bar for Corunna when serving with the 51st Foot). 50th Foot—Pte John Milgrove, HMS *Diadem*. 69th Foot†—Capt Caleb Chute, Pte Samuel Chadwick HMS *Britannia*. (Surgeon's 3rd Mate (Later Sir) Wm Burnett, HMS *Goliath* received the NGS medal with this bar and those for Nile, Egypt and Trafalgar.)

San Fiorenzo 8 Mar. 1797

1	8

Nymphe 8 March 1797

1	4

(9 March 1797)

The *San Fiorenzo* (Captain Sir Harry Neale) and *Nymphe* (Captain John Cooke) intercepted and captured the French frigates *Résistance* and *Constance* which were returning to France after carrying an expeditionary force who hoped to destroy the towns of Bristol and Liverpool. As a matter of fact 1,400 of them landed at Fishguard, on the Pembrokeshire coast, but surrendered to 600 civilians and the Pembrokeshire Yeomanry. The interest lies in the fact that this regiment received 'Fishguard' as a Battle Honour, the only one for home service.

Recipients: HMS *San Fiorenzo* Lieut T. Renwick RN; Mid R. Mitford; Ords J. Brookman and J. Emmerson; Boys Benjamin Shepherd, W. Dally, Wm. Lewis. HMS *Nymphe* Surgeon B. F. Outram; Mid J. H. Godby; Master's Mte J. D. Markland; Pte John Cook, RM.
VANOR (1) AB Robert Bastin.

Camperdown

25	298

(11 October, 1797)

For the defeat of the Dutch fleet off their coast by Admiral Duncan.
The ships present with the approx. number of recipients from each were: Admiral Duncan's flagship HMS *Venerable** 2/17, and *Active* 1/2, *Adamant* 4/4, *Agincourt* 4/9, *Ardent* 3/8, *Bedford* 2/25, *Belliqueux* -/11, *Brackel* -/2, *Director* 2/13, *Isis* -/6, *Lancaster* 1/13, *Martin* 1/-, *Monarch* 5/19, *Montagu* 2/20, *Monmouth* 2/13, *Powerful* -/20, *Russell* 7/14, *Triumph* 3/20, *Veteran* 2/19; frigates *Beaulieu* 3/8, *Circe* 3/4, *Martin* -/1; cutters

---

*It is probable that this man was serving with the 51st Foot on board HMS *Blenheim*, on which there were twenty-five other members of the Regiment, the 49th were in the West Indies at the time.
†In 1891 Queen Victoria granted this regiment the right to bear 'St Vincent' on its Colours.
*The Town of Sunderland presented a special silver medal to Jack Crawford for nailing the flag to the mast after it had been shot away. The obverse of this medal bears a shield with the arms of Sunderland supported by two sailors. Below, on a scroll, is the motto 'ORBIS EST DEI.' Under these is the inscription 'THE TOWN OF SUNDERLAND TO JOHN CRAWFORD FOR GALLANT SERVICES ON OCT. 11th 1797.' On the reverse is a scene of the action with, above, the legend 'DUNCAN AND GLORY' and below 'BRITISH VALOUR.'

No of HM Ships Engaged	No of Bars Issued

Active -/3, *Diligent, King George* 1/2, *Rose* -/1; lugger *Speculator.*

Recipients of the Large Naval Gold Medal: Admiral Alan Duncan *Venerable;* Vice-Admiral Richard Onslow *Monarch.*

Recipients of the Small Naval Gold Medal: Capt Edward O'Bryen *Monarch;* Capt John Knight *Montagu;* Capt Sir Thomas Byard *Bedford;* Capt William O'Bryen Drury *Powerful;* Capt William Essington *Triumph;* Capt John Inglis *Belliqueux;* Capt John Williamson *Agincourt;* Capt John Wells *Lancaster;* Capt Richard Rundell Burgess *Ardent;* Capt George Gregory *Veteran;* Capt William Bligh *Director;* Capt James Walker *Monmouth;* Capt William Mitchell *Isis;* Capt William Hotham *Adamant;* Capt Henry Trollope *Russell;* Capt Francis Fayerman *Beaulieu;* Capt Peter Halket *Circe;* Capt Hon Charles Paget *Martin;* Capt William George Fairfax *Venerable.*

Phoebe 21 Decr. 1797
1   5
(21 December 1797)

For the capture of the French frigate *Néréide* in the Bay of Biscay by the *Phoebe* (Capt Sir Robert Barlow).

Recipients: Mid S. J. B. Pechell and Charles Prowett; Yeoman of Sheets Robert Allen; Ord John Reedin and Boy 3rd Class Stephen Laurie.
(For further particulars of Boy Laurie see the introduction to the NGS Medal.)

Mars 21 April 1798
1   26
(21 April 1798)

The *Mars* (Captain Alex Hood, who was killed in the action), when cruising off Brest in consort with the *Ramillies* and *Jason,* sighted the French ship *L'Hercule.* The *Mars* chased her and, with the help of the *Jason* which came up towards the end of the action, forced her to surrender. The *L'Hercule* was towed to Plymouth and transferred to the Royal Navy under the name of HMS *Hercules.*

Isle St Marcou 6 May 1798
2   3
(7 May 1798)

As a sort of trial run for Napoleon's intended invasion of Britain an expedition consisting of flat-bottomed boats attacked the two small islands of St Marcou, off Le Havre, which were defended by the crews of the *Badger* and *Sandfly* together with some Marines, all under the command of Lieutenant C. P. Price, RN. It was not a naval action, though fought, on the British side, entirely by the crews of the two ships.

Recipients: HMS *Badger*—2nd Lieut T. L. Lawrence, RM, and Pte John Campbell, RM; HMS *Sandfly*—2nd Lieut J. Ensor, RM.

Lion 15 July 1798
1   23
(15 July 1798)

For the capture of the Spanish ship *Santa Dorotea* off Carthagena by the *Lion* (Captain Manly Dixon).

VANOR (1) Lieutenant W. H. B. Tremlett (however known to have been issued as confirmed by recipient's own letter).

Nile
16   326
(1 August 1798)

Admiral Bruey's fleet of 13 ships-of-the-line, 4 frigates and others lay at anchor in line in Aboukir Bay. With 14 ships-of-the-line Nelson attacked in the late afternoon, positioning several ships between the French and the coastal shallows with the remainder on the seaward side, bringing the French under fire from two sides. Throughout the evening and night the British fleet advanced along the immobile French line, pouring a concentration of fire upon successive ships. Only two French ships-of-the-line and two frigates escaped the catastrophic defeat.

For his victory, Sir Horatio was made a peer with the title of Baron Nelson of the Nile and Burnham Thorpe. The King of Naples conferred on him the title of Duke of Bronte.

Ships present: Rear-Admiral Nelson's flagship *Vanguard* 6/21, and *Alexander* 6/29, *Audacious* 1/13, *Bellerophon* 4/19, *Culloden* 5/26, *Defence* 2/26, *Goliath* 6/19, *Leander* -/9, *Majestic* 3/20, *Minotaur* 5/21, *Orion* 4/14, *Swiftsure* 5/21, *Theseus* 2/13, *Zealous* -/17; lugger *Speculator* o; sloop *Mutine* 1/5.

Recipient of the Large Naval Gold Medal: Rear-Admiral Sir Horatio Nelson, KB *(Vanguard).*

Recipients of the Small Naval Gold Medal: Capt Edward Berry *Vanguard;* Capt Thomas Troubridge *Culloden;* Capt Henry D'Esterre Darby *Bellerophon;* Capt Thomas Louis *Minotaur;* Capt John Peyton *Defence;* Capt Alexander John Ball *Alexander;* Capt Samuel Hood *Zealous;* Capt Davidge Gould *Audacious;* Capt Thomas Foley *Goliath;* Capt George Blagden Westcott *Majestic;* Capt Benjamin Hallowell *Swiftsure;* Capt Ralph Willett Miller *Theseus;* Capt Thomas Boulden Thompson *Leander;* Capt Sir James Saumarez *Orion.*
NB: Captain Ralph Willett Miller never received the Medal having been killed before it could be delivered. The Medal was returned to the Admiralty by Lord St Vincent.

Espoir 7 Augt. 1798
1   1
(6 August 1798)

For the capture of the *Liguria,* a large Genoese pirate ship, which closed with the *Espoir* (Commander L. O. Bland) and summoned her to surrender.

Recipient: Ord Seaman Henry Chambers.

12 Octr. 1798
9   74
(12 October 1798)

This bar was awarded for the defeat by Sir John Borlase Warren of the attempted invasion of Ireland, and was fought off Tory Island. The French ship *Hoche* and two frigates were captured.

No of HM Ships Engaged	No of Bars Issued		No of HM Ships Engaged	No of Bars Issued

Ships present: Sir John Borlase Warren's flagship *Canada* 2/16, and *Amelia* -/3, *Anson* -/8, *Arethusa*, *Doris*, *Ethalion* 1/7, *Foudroyant* 4/12, *Magnamine* 2/4, *Melampus* -/3, *Robust* 2/10.

There is a medal to Ordinary Seaman John Boon of HMS *Canada* with this bar and those for St Domingo, Java, and Algiers. Corporal Wm. Hodgson, RM, received a medal with this bar for service on HMS *Ethalion*. He received another medal with the bar for Egypt for service as a sergeant on HMS *Sensible*.

VANOR (4)

Fisgard 20 Octr. 1798
     1   9

(20 October 1798)

For the defeat of the French frigate *Immortalité*, off Brest, by the *Fisgard* (Captain Thos. Byam Martin). The *Fisgard* was formerly the French frigate *Résistance* captured by the *San Fiorenzo* on 8th March, 1797, for which a bar was awarded.

Recipients: Capt T. B. Martin, RN; Lieut J. S. Carden; Mid Daniel Little Couch; Yeoman of Sheets Thos. Price; Master's Mate John Fleming; LM Geo. Bright; Boys Chas. Brady, Richard Maxworth and John Tiver.

Sybille 28 Feby 1799
     1   12

(1 March 1799)

For the capture of the French frigate *Forte* by the *Sybille* (Captain Ed. Cooke) off the Hoogly in the Bay of Bengal.

Recipients: Lieut Nicholas Manger, RN; Mid Arthur Lysaght; Ord Seamen James Coombe, Thos. Hurley, and John Triggs; AB W. E. Wright, Samuel Butler and James Long; Vol 1st Class Joseph Wright; Boy 2nd Class Peter Cloosterman and Supernumeraries (Unrated) J. Piercy and R. Ratcliffe.

Telegraph 18 March 1799
     1   0

(18 March 1799)

The small brig *Telegraph* (Lieutenant J. A. Worth) captured the French privateer *Hirondelle* off the Isle de Bas, near Brest. There were no claimants for this award.

Acre 30 May 1799
     3   41

(20 May 1799)

Given for the defence of Acre, but the date is wrong as the siege was terminated on night of 20/21st May. It was the inability of Napoleon to capture Acre and thus open the way to the conquest of the East and India, that caused him to remark that his destiny was foiled by an English post-captain. He was, of course, referring to Commodore Sir Sidney Smith, who had worked out the plans for the defence of Acre.

Ships present: *Alliance* 1/2, *Theseus* 3/8, *Tigre* 5/22.

VANOR (10).

Schiermonnikoog 12 Aug 1799
     5   9

(11 and 13 August 1799)

Given for the attack on the island of Schiermonnikoog, off Holland, during which the Dutch schooner *Vengeance* was captured and the British gunboat *Crash* recaptured.

Ships present: *Courier*, *Espiegle*, *Juno*, *Latona* and *Pylades*.

Recipients: HMS *Courier* Lieut T. Searle RN; Gnr John Besbeech; AB Richard Keys. HMS *Espiegle* AB David Wilson; HMS *Juno*—Mid Eaton Travers. HMS *Pylades*—Purser's Steward John Feary; Landsmen, William Briscoe, George Kilner and John Stroud.

Arrow 13 Septr 1799
     1   2

Wolverine 13 Sepr 1799
     1   0

(13 September 1799)

For the Capture of the Dutch brig *Draak*, of Harlingen, by the *Arrow* (Commander Portlock). During the same action the *Wolverine* captured the Dutch brig *Gier*, but there appear to have been no claimants for the medal from her crew.

Recipients: HMS *Arrow*—Clerk J. M. Perkins and Boy 2nd Class George Ricketts.

Surprise with Hermione
     1   7

(25 October 1799)

Captain Edward Hamilton of the *Surprise* found the Spanish frigate *Hermione* moored in Puerto Cabello Harbour, Venezuela, and covered by the shore batteries. He decided to capture her by a cutting-out expedition. The boats of the *Surprise*, which were manned and led by Captain Hamilton, were rowed alongside the *Hermione*. After a desperate struggle the *Hermione* surrendered and then, partly by sail and partly by being towed by the row boats, she was taken out of the harbour and eventually reached Port Royal, Jamaica, on 1st November.

The previous history of the *Hermione* is probably unique. In 1797, the year in which the Naval Mutinies occurred, she was the 32-gun British frigate *Hermione*, commanded by Captain Hugh Pigot. His tyrannical manner so annoyed the crew that on 21st September, 1797, whilst the ship was cruising off Porto Rico in the West Indies, they mutinied. They murdered all the officers except two, and sailed the ship to La Guayra and handed her over to the Spaniards, who re-armed her and added her to their fleet.

It is fitting to conclude this short account with a few words about the gallant commander during the action between the *Surprise* and *Hermione*. Captain Hamilton was wounded no less than six times, so that in the following April he had to return to England for medical treatment. During the voyage he was captured by a French privateer and subsequently taken to Paris. Here his record was personally investigated by Napoleon, who agreed to exchange him for six midshipmen! His return was greeted with tremendous enthusiasm and he was made a Freeman of the City of London. The Jamaicans presented him with a superb gold and enamel sword and he received a Small Naval Gold Medal.

No of HM Ships Engaged	No of Bars Issued

Recipients of Small Naval Gold Medal: Capt Edward Hamilton, RN.

Recipients of NGS Medal: Capt Ed. Hamilton, RN; Ship's Cpl Ed Bartlett; Pte John Ingram, RM; Ords John Young and T. Turner; LM Dennis McGivern; Boy 3rd Class C. Robardo.

Speedy 6 Novr 1799

1	3

(6 November 1799)

The *Speedy* (Commander Jahleel Brenton) defended a convoy which was attacked by fifteen Spanish gunboats off Gibraltar.

Recipients: Master's Mate G. Pedlar; Clerk C. S. Ricketts; AB John Luscombe.

Courier 22 Novr 1799

1	3

(23 November 1799)

The cutter *Courier* (Lieutenant Thos. Searle), whilst cruising off Flushing, captured the French privateer *Guerrier*.

Recipients: Lieut Thos. Searle (see bar for Schiermonnikoog, 12th August, 1799), Gnr AB Henry Keys, J. Besbeech.

Viper 26 Decr 1799

1	1

(26 December 1799)

The cutter *Viper* (Lieutenant John Pengelly) captured the French privateer *Le Furet* in the English Channel.

Recipients: AB C. File. VANOR (1) Mid S. H. Paddon

Harpy 5 Feby 1800

1	3

Fairy 5 Feby 1800

1	3

(5 February 1800)

For the capture of the French frigate *Pallas*, off St Malo, by the *Harpy* (Commander Henry Bazeley) and the *Fairy* (Commander Sydney Horton), assisted later in the action by the *Loire*, *Danae* and *Rallieur*. The *Pallas* was added to the Navy under the name of *Pique*, which figures again on 26th March, 1804. It is extraordinary that the *Danae* and *Railleur* should have gone unrewarded, or alternatively that there were no claimants from them.

Recipients: HMS *Harpy*—Vol 1st Class R. B. Mathews; Boys 2nd Class, William Talbot and R. Rider. VANOR (1) AB R. P. Jones. HMS *Fairy*—Purser's Steward J. Benjamen; Clerk J. Hewitt; LM Thomas Beddrell; Vol 1st Class A. Clark.

Loire 5 Feby 1800

1	1

(5 February 1800)

Mid Sir W. Owen Pell, HMS *Loire*, lost his left leg in this action, and later became a Rear-Admiral may have received this clasp or the *Harpy* or *Fairy* clasp.

Peterel 21 March 1800

1	2

(21 March 1800)

The *Peterel* (Commander F. W. Austen) captured the French frigate *La Ligurienne* from almost under the guns of the forts at Marseilles.

Recipients: Comdr F. W. Austen; and Ord S Horn.

Penelope 30 March 1800

1	11

Vinciego 30 March 1800

1	2

(30 March 1800)

General Vaubois, who was blockaded in Valetta Harbour, Malta, dispatched the *Guillaume Tell* to obtain help from Napoleon, but she was intercepted by the *Penelope* (Captain Henry Blackwood) and *Vinciego* (Commander G. Long). Later HMS *Lion* and *Foudroyant* arrived and, after a terrific but one-sided contest, the Frenchman surrendered. The *Guillaume Tell* was the last survivor in the French Navy of the Battle of the Nile, and, as HMS *Malta*, became the second largest ship in the Royal Navy.

Recipients: HMS *Penelope*—Mids William Borough, John Carter and Henry Prescott; Vol. 1st Class James Bayley; Master's Mates Charles Elphick and Robert Yule; AB John Small; Ord Seaman Darby Collins; Carpenter's Mate James Brown;* Marine Charles Ogden; Boy William Manning. HMS *Vinciego*—Lieut E. A. Down and Master's Mate John Osborne. Claims from HMS *Foudroyant* and *Lion* were 'disallowed'.

Capture of the Désirée

18	21

(8 July 1800)

For the capture of the French frigate *Désirée*, which was lying in Dunkirk Roads. It is the only case in which the bar is named after the enemy's ship. Probably this was done for brevity, as the following ships took part: HMS *Dart*, *Rosario*; fireships *Comet*, *Falcon*, *Wasp*; gunbrigs *Biter* and *Boxer*; cutters *Ann*, *Camperdown*, *Kent*, *Nile*, *Selbu*, *Stag*, *Teazer*, *Vigilant*; and boats from HMS *Andromeda*, *Babet* and *Nemesis*. VANOR (3) Lieut James Carthew; Mid Francis Duval; 2nd Lieut Jasper Farmar, RM.

Seine 20 Augt 1800

1	7

(20 August 1800)

The *Seine* (Captain David Milne) captured the French frigate *Vengeance* off Porto Rico.

Recipients: Lieut Ed. Chetham, RN (also named Strode); Mids Wm. C. C. Dalyell and Robert Oliver, ABs Wm. Crotty and James Fitzgerald, Pte Jas. Jarrett and LM Thos. Cullern.

Phoebe 19 Feby 1801

1	6

(19 February 1801)

For the capture of the French frigate *Africaine*, off Gibraltar, by the *Phoebe* (Captain Sir Robert Barlow). The former was added to the Navy and renamed *Amelia*.

Recipients: Mid S. J. B. Pechell and C. Prowett; Sgt Wm. Ward, RM; AB J. Reedin; Vol 1st Class R. Meredith; Boy 2nd Class Stephen Laurie. (See Introduction to the NGS Medal for full particulars concerning Stephen Laurie).

*James Brown also received the bar for Basque Roads.

Egypt

	No of HM Ships Engaged	No of Bars Issued
	117	618

(8 March to
2 September 1801)

Though 117 ships served off Egypt between 28th March and 2nd September, 1801, medals were only awarded to claimants from the following 115. This bar, like that for Egypt to the Military General Service Medal, was not sanctioned until 12th February, 1850. Ships present to which medals were awarded (*approx.* numbers to each shown in brackets): Admiral Lord Keith's flagship *Foudroyant* (38), and *Agincourt* (9), *Ajax* (28), *Alexander* (1), *Alligator* (6), *Athenian* (3), *Astraea* (3), *Blonde* (2), *Bonne Citoyenne* (3), *Brackel* (3), *Cameleon* (5), *Ceres* (4), *Charon* (6), *Cyclops* (7), *Cynthia* (4), *Dangereuse* (3), *Delft* (6), *Determinée* (4), *Diadem* (8), *Dido* (2), *Diana* (5), *Dictator* (8), *Dolphin* (1), *Dover* (1), *Dragon* (8), *Druid* (2), *Eurus* (3), *El Carmen* (5), *Europa* (15), *Expedition* (4), *Experiment* (3), *Flora* (5), *Florentina* (5), *Forte* (2), *Fox* (1), *Gibraltar* (4), *Good Design* (1), *Greyhound* (8), *Haerlem* (6), *Hebe* (6), *Hector* (12), *Heroine* (2), *Inconstant* (3), *Inflexible* (6), *Iphigenia* (1), *Kangaroo* (1), *Kent* (27), *Leda* (8), *Madras* (15), *Minerve* (10), *Minorca* (1), *Minotaur* (17), *Modeste* (8), *Mondovi* (5), *Monmouth* (17), *Niger* (7), *Northumberland* (22), *Pallas* (5), *Pearl* (7), *Pegasus* (6), *Penelope* (1), *Peterel* (3), *Pigmy* (2), *Pique* (9), *Port Mahon* (3), *Regulus* (3), *Renomee* (8), *Renown* (12), *Resource* (3), *Roebuck* (9), *Romney* (7), *Romulus* (5), *Salamine* (1), *Santa Dorotea* (5), *Santa Theresa* (2), *Sensible* (2), *Sheerness* (2), *Spider* (1), *Stately* (10), *Swiftsure* (18), *Termagant* (4), *Thetis* (8), *Thisbe* (4), *Tigre* (33), *Trusty* (5), *Vestal* (10), *Victor* (1), *Virago* (1), *Wilhemina* (2), *Winchelsea* (3), *Ulysses* (2). Bomb boats: *Fury* (3), *Tartarus* (1). Sgt Wm. Hodgson, RM, received one medal with this bar for service on HMS *Sensible*, and another medal with the bar '12th Oct. 1798' for service as a Cpl on HMS *Ethalion*.

Copenhagen 1801

	No of HM Ships Engaged	No of Bars Issued
	36	555

(2 April 1801)

Vice-Admiral Nelson with a detachment of ships from the fleet of Admiral Sir Hyde Parker, engaged a powerful array of Danish ships, armed hulks and shore batteries at Copenhagen. After an arduous five hour battle, Danish resistance was overcome. With the battle at its height, Nelson disregarded Parker's signal to 'Leave off action' and is reputed to have put his glass to his blind eye, saying, 'I have a right to be blind sometimes . . . I really do not see the signal.'
Ships present: Lord Nelson's flagship *Elephant* 5/14, and *Agamemnon* 1/14, *Ardent* 4/23, *Bellona* 5/28, *Defence* 3/8, *Defiance* 5/29, *Edgar* 6/35, *Ganges* 6/8, *Glatton* 2/13, *Isis* 2/10, *London* 5/13, *Monarch* 7/32, *Polyphemus* 6/20, *Raisonnable* 1/7, *Ramillies* 1/20, *Russell* 4/25, *Saturn* -/12, *Veteran* 3/16.
Frigates: *Amazon* 4/10, *Alcmene* 3/9, *Blanche* 1/9, *Désirée* 5/4, *Jamaica* 3/5. Sloops *Arrow* -/3, *Cruizer* -/3, *Dart* -/2, *Harpy* 1/5.
Bomb vessels: *Discovery* -/4, *Explosion* -/3, *Hecla* -/1, *Sulphur* -/1, *Terror* 1/4, *Volcano* 1/2, *Zebra* 1/3.
Brigs: *Otter* 2/1, *Tigress* 1/-, *Zephyr* 1/4.
Also: *Asp* -/1, *Caesar* -/1, *Eling* -/4, *Hasty* 1/1, *Hyena* -/1, *Kite* 1/-, *Lecla* 1/-, *Lynx* -/1, *Powerful* -/1, *St George* 3/24, *Shannon* -/1, *Standard* 1/-, *Teazer* 1/-, *Victorious* -/1, *Warrior* 1/13.

Military Recipients: Royal Artillery—Gnr Andrew Smith, HMS *Zebra*. 49th Foot—Capt Chas. Plenderleath, Ensign John Armstrong, HMS *Ardent*; Lt Col Roger H. Sheaffe, Pte Robert Young, Dmr Anthony Walsh, HMS *Bellona*; Cpl J. Cronchy, Ptes Wm. Booth, Wm. Donnelly, Pte Peter Plunkett, HMS *Defiance*; Ptes Laurence Dooley, Dennis Slaynes, Andrew Jameson, HMS *Edgar*; Capt Hugh Arbuthnot, Vol George Brock, Pte Edward Liston, HMS *Ganges*; Asst Surgeon Robert Brown, Vol Harry S. Ormond, HMS *Glatton*; Lieut James Dennis, HMS *Monarch*; Capt William Bird Bleamire, HMS *Polyphemus*; Dmr Charles Hawkes, HMS *Ramillies*; Pte Richard Cornerford, HMS *Russell*; Pte John Long, HMS *Saturn*. 95th Foot—Rifleman Hugh Pasley, HMS *Isis*; and James Stiff, HMS *St George*.
Ensign John Armstrong of HMS *Ardent* also received the MGS Medal with bars for Busaco, Fuentes d'Onor, Cuidad Rodrigo, Badajoz and Salamanca when serving with the 88th Foot.

Speedy 6 May 1801

	No of HM Ships Engaged	No of Bars Issued
	1	7

(6 May 1801)

This is probably one of the most extraordinary actions for which this medal was awarded. Captain Lord Cochrane with the little *Speedy*, which carried only 14 4-pounder guns, and a crew of 6 officers and 54 men, chased and boarded the 32-gun Spanish frigate *Gamo*. Laying the *Speedy* alongside, he boarded the Spaniard with the whole of his crew except for the doctor and two seamen! The *Gamo*, which had a crew of over 300, surrendered and was sailed to Port Mahon, on the east coast of Minorca. One of the boarding party was Lord Cochrane's brother, Mid The Hon Archibald Cochrane, whose name, however, does not appear on the medal roll.

Recipients: Capt Lord Thos. Cochrane, RN; Mid C. Ricketts; Coxswain John Thomson; Actg Carpenter David Rust; ABs John Luscombe, David Gray and Wm. Hutchinson (alias John Campbell).

Gut of Gibraltar 12 July 1801

	No of HM Ships Engaged	No of Bars Issued
	11	142

(12 July 1801)

For the action with the Spanish fleet off Algeciras.
Ships present: Admiral Saumarez's flagship *Caesar* 3/20, and *Audacious* 2/10, *Calpe* 1/2, *Carlotta*, *Hannibal*, *Louisa*, *Pompée* 1/17, *Spencer* 4/19, *Superb* 4/24, *Thames* 4/9, *Venerable* 3/19.
(James Bull, 57th Foot, received the Naval General Service Medal with this bar as Boy 2nd Class and the Military General Service

	No of HM Ships Engaged	No of Bars Issued

Medal with bars for Busaco, Vittoria and Pyrenees.)
VANOR (2).

Sylph 28 Sepr 1801
    1   2
(28 September 1801)

It is presumed that the *Sylph* (Commander Charles Dashwood) engaged the French frigate *Artémise* when cruising off the Spanish coast. Whatever the name of the enemy ship she mounted 44 guns to the *Sylph's* 28, and after a two hour battle sought safety in flight. For this engagement Commander Dashwood was promoted Captain.

Recipients: Comdr Charles Dashwood, RN; and Lieut S. Burgess, RN, who received a medal with five bars, 1st June, 1794; Sylph, 28th Sept, 1801; Trafalgar; Boat Service, 27th July, 1809; and Algiers.

Pasley 28 Octr 1801
    1   4
(28 October 1801)

For the capture of the Spanish privateer *Virgen del Rosario* by the *Sir Thomas Pasley* (Lieutenant Wooldridge), who received promotion for this action off Cape de Gata, south-east Spain.

Recipients: Lieut P. H. Douglas, RN; Boatswain W. Bignell; ABs R. Glanvill and J. Hill.

Scorpion 31 March 1804
    1   4
Beaver 31 March 1804
    1   0
(31 March 1804)

This was really more of a boat action than a naval engagement. Boats from the *Scorpion* (Commander G. N. Hardinge) and *Beaver* (Commander Pelley) entered the Texel Roads and captured the Dutch brig *Atlante*, which they eventually sailed back to England. Both the Commanders received promotion for this action.

Recipients: HMS *Scorpion*—AB George Salvedore (who also had bars for 14th March, 1795; and Lowestoffe, 24th June, 1795); LM T. Hacker (or Hasker); ABs W. Thoms and R. Flaxman.

Centurion 18 Sept 1804
    1   9
(18 September 1804)

Note the similarity in the name of one of the enemy ships with that of one in the last action quoted. This bar was awarded for the action in which the *Centurion* (Captain J. Lind), whilst waiting in Vizagapatam Roads ready to escort merchant ships to Madras, was attacked by the French Admiral Linois, who appeared in the Roads with the three ships *Atalante*, *Marengo* and *Sémillante*. After a most half-hearted exhibition, and in spite of having seriously crippled the *Centurion*, he made off. (See bar for Amazon, 13th March, 1806.)

Recipients: Lieut J. R. Philips, RN (who also got the bar for Camperdown); Act Lieut Wm. Carroll (who also received the MGS Medal with bar for Maida, 4th July, 1806); Lieut Thos. Colby (who also got the

bars for Camperdown, 12th October, 1798, Trafalgar; and unlisted Boat Service, 19th April, 1814); Qtr Gnr John Ward; QM's Mate John Symes; Clerk N. Haydon; ABs Thos. Anderton, George Webb, Ord James Cole.
VANOR (3) Master's Mate George Bowen, Carpenter's Crew Jacob Mears and AB John Thompson.

Arrow 3 Feby 1805
    1   8
Acheron 3 Feby 1805
    1   2
(4 February 1805)

The sloops *Arrow* (Commander R. B. Vincent) and *Acheron* (Commander A. Farquhar) were protecting a large convoy which was attacked by the French frigates *Hortense* and *Incorruptible* when off the coast of Algeria. Both the *Arrow* and *Acheron* were forced to surrender after a twenty-four hour battle. The *Arrow* eventually sank and the *Acheron* was so badly damaged that the French set her on fire.

Recipients: HMS *Arrow*—Lieut C. F. Daly, RN; AB George Longridge; Ords Richard Dane, Robert Greatrex, John Hurley; Landsmen Benjamin Brown, Thos. Wheeler; Carpenter Archibald Gray, RM; HMS *Acheron*—Mid J. Simpson; Ord J. Wheelan.
C. F. Daly also received the bar for Comet, 11th August, 1808—a unique combination.

San Fiorenzo 14 Feby 1805
    1   12
(13 February 1805)

For the capture of the French frigate *Psyche* off Ganjam on the Malabar coast of India, by the *San Fiorenzo* (Captain Henry Lambert).

Recipients: Lieut Edward Collier; Mid Samuel Marsingall; Ord George Barney (who also got the bar for San Fiorenzo, 8th March, 1808) and George Love; Landsman John Acton; ABs Peter Hughes, Nathaniel Kenny, John Pacey and David Piggott; Ship's Cpl P. Trout, RM; Ptes William Beck and Daniel Hoskins, RM.
VANOR (1) LM Samuel Finn.

Phoenix 10 Augt 1805
    1   26
(10 August 1805)

For the capture of the French frigate *Didon* off Cape Finisterre by the *Phoenix* (Captain Thomas Baker). The *Didon* was towed into Plymouth, where she was repaired and recommissioned into the Royal Navy.
VANOR (3) AB H. Acland; QMs Mate J. Cummings; Yeoman of Sheets B. Kennedy.

Trafalgar
    33   1,710
(21 October 1805)

For the major fleet action off Cape Trafalgar between the British fleet of Vice-Admiral Lord Nelson with 27 ships-of-the-line and the Franco-Spanish fleet of Vice-Admiral Villeneuve with 33 ships-of-the-line. Nelson attacking in two single line divisions engaged the centre of Villeneuve's straggling fleet. After a five hour battle, 9

French and 9 Spanish ships-of-the-line were captured with no British loss. The mortally wounded Nelson had effectively destroyed the Franco-Spanish fleet and had gained one of the most decisive naval victories in history.
Ships present: Lord Nelson's flagship *Victory* 18/115, and *Achilles* 7/56, *Africa* 6/31, *Agamemnon* 7/39, *Ajax* 6/33, *Belleisle* 14/59, *Bellerophon* 6/50, *Britannia* 11/84, *Colossus* 10/41, *Conqueror* 6/50, *Defence* 8/52, *Defiance* 6/37, *Dreadnought* 10/53, *Leviathan* 5/53, *Mars* 6/49, *Minotaur* 6/28, *Neptune* 10/49, *Orion* 7/45, *Polyphemus* 7/15, *Prince* 16/53, *Revenge* 10/49, *Royal Sovereign* 6/92, *Spartiate* 13/46, *Swiftsure* 8/39, *Temeraire* 7/49, *Thunderer* 7/34, *Tonnant* 7/46.
Frigates: *Euryalus* 5/16, *Naiad* 5/24, *Phoebe* 8/19, *Sirius* 2/17.
Schooner: *Pickle* 3/1, which brought home the news of the victory.
Cutter: *Entreprenante*, none awarded.

Recipients of Large Naval Gold Medals: Vice-Admiral Cuthbert Collingwood (second-in-command HMS *Royal Sovereign*); Rear-Admiral William the Earl of Northesk (third-in-command HMS *Britannia).* (Vice-Admiral Viscount Nelson *Victory*—medal was sent to the family).

Recipients of Small Naval Gold Medals: Capt Thomas Hardy *Victory*; Capt Edward Rotherham *Royal Sovereign*; Capt Charles Bullen *Britannia*; Capt Eliab Harvey *Temeraire*; Capt Richard Grindall *Prince*; Capt Thomas Francis Fremantle *Neptune*; Capt John Conn *Dreadnought*; Capt Charles Tyler *Tonnant*; Capt William Hargood *Belleisle*; Capt Robert Moorson *Revenge*; Capt George Duff *Mars*; Capt James Nicol Morris *Colossus*; Capt Henry William Bayntun *Leviathan*; Capt Richard King *Achilles*; Capt John Cooke *Bellerophon*; Capt Charles John Moore Mansfield *Minotaur*; Capt Edward Codrington *Orion*; Capt William Gordon Rutherford *Swiftsure*; Capt Robert Redmill *Polyphemus*; Capt Henry Digby *Africa*; Capt Sir Edward Berry *Agamemnon*; Capt Israel Pellew *Conqueror*; Capt Sir Francis Laforey *Spartiate*; Capt Philip Charles Durham *Defiance*; Capt George Johnstone Hope *Defence*; Lieut John Pilford *Ajax*; Lieut John Stockham *Thunderer*.

The medals of Captain George Duff and John Cooke were sent to their widows.

4 Novr 1805

No of HM Ships Engaged	No of Bars Issued
8	296

(4 November 1805)

For the destruction of the remainder of the French Fleet after Trafalgar, off Finisterre, by Captain Sir Richard Strachan in HMS *Caesar* 4/61, accompanied by the *Aeolus* 2/14, *Courageux* 1/29, *Hero* 6/50, *Namur* 1/55, *Phoenix* 3/24, *Revolutionnaire* 1/29 (some books give *Revolution*), and *Santa Margarita* 1/12.

Recipients of the Small Naval Gold Medal: Capt Sir Richard John Strachan, Bart,

HMS *Caesar;* Capt The Hon Alan Hyde Gardner, HMS *Hero*; Capt William Laurence Halsted, HMS *Namur*; Capt Richard Lee, HMS *Courageux*.

Ord. Samuel Challis, HMS *Namur*, received two Naval General Service Medals, one with this bar and another with the bars for Basque Roads, 1809 and BS 27 Sept, 1810 as a Steward's Mate.

St Domingo

No of HM Ships Engaged	No of Bars Issued
11	396

(6 February 1806)

For the destruction of the French Fleet under Admiral Leissegues which had been carrying stores to the island of St. Domingo and was preparing to sail home again.
Ships present: Admiral Sir John Duckworth's flagship *Superb* 16/56, and *Acasta* 4/23, *Agamemnon* 8/32, *Atlas* 4/27, *Canopus* 11/58, *Donegal* 8/37, *Epervier* 1/4, *Kingfisher* 3/7, *Magicienne* 1/12, *Northumberland* 9/41 and *Spencer* 8/32.

Recipients of the Large Naval Gold Medal: Vice-Admiral Sir John Duckworth *Superb;* Rear-Admiral The Hon Alexander Forester Cochrane *Northumberland;* Rear-Admiral Thomas Louis *Canopus*.

Recipients of the Small Naval Gold Medal: Capt Richard Good Keats *Superb*; Capt John Morrison *Northumberland*; Capt The Hon Robert Stopford *Spencer*; Capt Pilteney Malcolm *Donegal*; Capt Samuel Pym *Atlas*; Capt Sir Edward Berry *Agamemnon*; Capt Francis William Austen *Canopus*.

Amazon 13 March 1806

No of HM Ships Engaged	No of Bars Issued
1	29

London 13 March 1806

No of HM Ships Engaged	No of Bars Issued
1	27

(13 March 1806)

The French Admiral Linois, when on his way home from the East Indies, with the *Marengo* and *Belle Poule* (the *Atalante* having been lost), encountered the *Foudroyant, Amazon* and *London* when nearly home. The *Amazon* (Captain Wm. Parker) chased the *Belle Poule* and the *London* (Captain Sir Harry Neale) chased the *Marengo*. Both the French ships were brought to action off Brest and surrendered. (See bar for Centurion, 18th September, 1804.)
VANOR (1) AB James Nipper, *Amazon*

Pique 26 March 1806

No of HM Ships Engaged	No of Bars Issued
1	8

(26 March 1806)

For the capture of the two French corvettes *Phaeton* and *Voltigeur* off Porto Rico by the *Pique* (Captain Charles Ross).

Recipients: Lieut Christopher Bell, RM; Lieut Wm. Ward, RN; Mid Richard Lloyd; Caulker Thos. Moulding; AB John Williams, LM John Trusse and Ord Wm. Hungate; Boy Benjamin Burke.

Sirius 17 April 1806

No of HM Ships Engaged	No of Bars Issued
1	10

(17 April 1806)

For the capture by HMS *Sirius* (Captain Wm. Prowse) of the French corvette *Bergère* off Civita Vecchia, on the west coast of

	No of HM Ships Engaged	No of Bars Issued

Italy. In this action the small *Sirius* of 16 guns attacked a French flotilla, which appears to have made off, leaving the small *Bergère* of only 19 guns to her fate.

Recipients: Surgeon Thos. Robertson; Mids Morgan G. Crofton and John Turner; 1st Lieut Wm. Magin, RM; Carpenters Robert Beatson, Wm. Thomas and Henry Curley; Sgt. John Ingram, RM; Pte Patrick Connolly, RM; Boy 3rd Class John Hennessey (who also got the bar for Trafalgar).
VANOR (10) Gnr Hugh Perry, ABs John Davis and Jonathan Pricely; Ord Edward Mealy; Landsmen John Brownrigg, John Cremer, William German, Edward Sheehy and Pte Isaac May, RM; LM Dennis Scully.

Blanche 19 July 1806
	1	22

(19 July 1806)

For the capture by HMS *Blanche* (Captain T. Lavie, who was knighted for this action) of the French frigate *Guerriere* off the Faroe Islands.

Arethusa 23 Augt 1806
	1	6

Anson 23 Augt 1806
	1	6

(23 August 1806)

For the capture of the Spanish frigate *Pomona* off Havana Harbour, Cuba, by HMS *Arethusa* (Captain Charles Brisbane) and HMS *Anson* (Captain C. Lydiard).

Recipients: HMS *Arethusa*—Lieut Henry Higman, RN; Mids J. W. Aldridge, John H. Bellairs and Curtis Reid; Purser John Elliott; Ord Edward Fielding; VANOR (11) HMS *Anson*—Lieut Thos. Ball Sullivan; Coxswain Wm. Jeffrey; Qtr. Gnr. Robert Henley; Ord. James Burke, LM. Christopher Coucher; Pte Stephen Coward, RM; VANOR (5) Yeoman powder room Richard Leverton; Ords James Duglass, George Simons; Boys 2nd Class Thomas Costello and 3rd Class Charles Salmon.

Curacao
	4	65

(1 January 1807)

For the capture of the island of Curaçao in the West Indies. Commodore Charles Brisbane, with the four frigates *Arethusa* (flying his pennant), *Anson*, *Fisgard* and *Latona* is said to have given the town exactly five minutes to surrender. Receiving no reply, he promptly boarded a Dutch frigate lying in the harbour whilst Captain Lydiard of the *Anson* boarded another. Having captured these two ships, the boarding and landing parties then went ashore and captured the forts of Amsterdam and Republique guarding the harbour. The mere sight of these parties seems to have terrified the Dutch garrison, which hastened to surrender the forts and the island. The island was restored to the Dutch in 1814. The numbers awarded to each ship were: *Arethusa* 4/15, *Anson* 1/13, *Fisgard* 6/5, *Latona* 4/14, *Morne Fortunee* 2/1.

Recipients of the Small Naval Gold Medal: Commodore Charles Brisbane *(Arethusa)* and Capts Lydiard *(Anson)*, Bolton *(Fisgard)* and J. A. Wood *(Latona)*.

Pickle 3 Jany 1807
	1	2

(3 January 1807)

For the capture of the French privateer *La Favorite* off the Lizard by HMS *Pickle* (Lieut D. Calloway).

Recipients: Act Sub-Lieut Charles Hawkins, and Bosun's Mate James Rowden.

Hydra 6 Augt 1807
	1	11

(7 August 1807)

For the capture of the French ships *Caroline*, *L'Eugene* and *Rosario* in Bagur Harbour, in Spain, as the result of a cutting-out expedition by the boats of H.M.S. *Hydra* (Captain George Mundy) under Lieutenant Drury, who was promoted for this action.

Recipients: Capt Geo Mundy, RN; 1st Lieut Robert Hayes, RM; Mid. John Finlaison; Capt of Fore Top James Huntley; Capt of Main Top David Smith; Landsmen George King and Thos. Dredge; Clerk R. H. Goddard; Boy 2nd Class B. E. Quadline; Cpl John Lee, RM; Pte John Bennett, RM.
VANOR (1) Mid P. G. Panton.

Comus 15 Augt 1807
	1	10

(15 August 1807)

For the capture of the Danish frigate *Frederikscoarn* off Helsingborg by the *Comus* (Captain Edmund Heywood).

Recipients: Lieut Geo. E. Watts, RN; Mid W. L. Wraxall and Chas. H. Seale; AB Wm. Finley; Coxswain John Miller; Purser W. C. Hillier; AB W. Scammel; Purser's Steward James Thain; LM Thos. Saunders. (Thos. Saunders also received the bar for Mars, 21st April 1798.) and Pte RM David Pinnegar.
Sir Wm. Lascelles Wraxall, Bart, whose medal is indented 'WRAXALL', received the Military General Service Medal with bars for Vittoria, Pyrenees, Nive, Orthes and Toulouse when serving as a Lieut in the 34th Foot.

Louisa 28 Octr 1807
	1	1

(29 October 1807)

For the defeat of a privateer off the Dalmatian coast by HMS *Louisa* (Lieutenant Joseph Hoy).

Recipient: Supernumary Lieut H. B. Powell, RN.

Carrier 4 Novr 1807
	1	1

(14 November 1807)

For the capture by HMS *Carrier* (under temporary command William Milne) of the French ship *L'Actif* off the Dalmatian coast. It is rather extraordinary that the sole recipient of the medal should be the commanding officer.

Recipient: Act Lieut in command Wm. Milne, RN.

Ann 24 Novr 1807
	1	0

(24 November 1807)

The *Ann* (Lieutenant Mackenzie) was attacked by ten Spanish gunboats off Tarifa, two of which surrendered. There were no claimants for this bar.

	No of HM Ships Engaged	No of Bars Issued

Sappho 2 March 1808

	1	4

(2 March 1808)

The *Sappho* (Commander Geo. Langford) captured the Dutch brig *Admiral Jawl* off Scarborough.

Recipients: Mid Daniel McN. Beatty; Carpenter's Mate Thos. Nicholls; Landsman Chas. Parry; Pte Wm. Howes, RM.

San Fiorenzo 8 March 1808

	1	16

(8 March 1808)

For the capture of the French frigate *Piedmontaise* off the coast of Ceylon after a two-day chase. Captain Geo. F. Hardinge of the *San Fiorenzo* was killed at the start of the action, Lieutenant Dawson then assumed command.

Recipients: Capt of Fo'cle Peter Trout; Gnr Robert Bird; Purser Nathaniel Haydon; ABs Wm. Cromer, Henry Gauk, Nathaniel Kenny, John Pacey, Matthew Clark, Wm. Dixon; Ords Geo. Barney, John Finch, David Wyse, Geo. Love; Landsmen John Acton, Samuel Finn; Pte Daniel Hoskins, RN. VANOR (2) Lieut Edward Collier, RN and AB Peter Hughes.

Emerald 13 March 1808

	1	10

(13 March 1808)

HMS *Emerald*, at the time commanded by Lieutenant Charles Bertram, destroyed the batteries at Vivero on the north-west coast of Spain, and captured the small French schooner *Apropos* lying in the harbour.

Recipients: Lieut Chas. Bertram, RN; Mids Edward Saurin, Richard Connor; Master's Mate Daniel Baird; Sailmaker Thos. Potts; Carpenter's Crew John Gillman; AB Wm. Thompson; Vol per Order John McKillop; Pte John Norman, RM; Boy 2nd Class Edward Wylde.

Childers 14 March 1808

	1	4

(14 March 1808)

The *Childers* (Commander W. H. Dillon, RN) engaged the Danish brig *Lugen* off the Norwegian coast. For this action Commander Dillon received promotion. There appears to be a considerable divergence of opinion as to how the name of the Danish brig should be spelt. Various histories mention the following: Lügn, Lougen, Lugn, Lügen and Lougon. Where there is such variation one is unable to say which is correct.

Recipients: Comdr Wm. Henry Dillon, RN; Lieut Thos. Edmonds, RN; Vol 1st Class Chas. Parker; Act Master Geo. Wilson. (Comdr Dillon, later Rear-Admiral Sir Wm. Hy. Dillon, also received bars for 1st June, 1794; and 23rd June, 1795. He served as a Mid in HMS *Defence* on 1st June, 1794, so that his promotion was very rapid. 'Dillons Narrative' in two volumes published by the Navy Records Society, 1953 and 1956, makes excellent reading).

Nassau 22 March 1808

	1	31

Stately 22 March 1808

	1	31

(22 March 1808)

The *Nassau* (Captain R. Campbell) and *Stately* (Captain Geo. Parker) destroyed the Danish battleship *Prince Christian Frederick* off Grenaa, which is in the Kattegat on the north-east coast of Denmark.

Off Rota 4 April 1808

	3	19

(4 April 1808)

The *Alceste* (Captain M. Maxwell), *Mercury* (Captain James Gordon) and the brig *Grasshopper* (Commander Thos. Searle) attacked a Spanish convoy off Cadiz and captured seven of the escorted tartans. (A tartan is a small sailing vessel with a triangular sail common to the Mediterranean and the Italian lakes).

Recipients: HMS *Alceste* (3)—Landsman Wm. Disney; Pte. James Simpson, Ord Smith Nash (awarded but had not yet joined ship), RM. HMS *Grasshopper* (4)—Comdr Thos. Searle, RN; Mid Stephen Hodge; Clerk John Gain; Purser Thos. Bastin (who also got the bar for Grasshopper 24th April, 1808). HMS *Mercury* (12)—Capt James A. Gordon; Lieut W. O. Pell; Mid Wm. Parker; 1st Lieut James Whylock, RM (and Syria Acre in Gold); Master's Mate Chas. du Cane; LM Jas. French; Carpenter's Crew Joseph Phillips; AB John Richardson; Ords Samuel Watson and John Ragan; Vol 1st Class Geo. Broom (later Mid, who also got the bar for Guadaloupe); Boy 3rd Class Joseph Crouch.

Grasshopper 24 April 1808

	1	7

(24 April 1808)

Rapid 24 April 1808

	1	1

(24 April 1808)

Three weeks after the last action described, the *Grasshopper* (Commander T. Searle) and the brig *Rapid* (Lieutenant H. Baugh) chased a small convoy escorted by four Spanish gunboats off Faro, south of Portugal. The Spaniards took refuge in the port, but the forts were silenced and two of the Spanish gunboats were captured.

Recipients: HMS *Grasshopper*—Comdr T. Searle, RN; Mid Stephen Hodge; Purser Thos. Bastin; Clerk John Gain (all of whom also got the bar for Off Rota, 4th April, 1808); Landsmen James Legge and Samuel J. Pottinger; Pte James Holdeway, RM. HMS *Rapid*—Lieut Henry Baugh, RN.

Redwing 7 May 1808

	1	7

(7 May 1808)

For the destruction of a Spanish gunboat off Cape Trafalgar by HMS *Redwing* (Commander Thos. Ussher—promoted Captain for this action).

Recipients: Comdr Thos. Ussher, RN; Lieut John McP. Ferguson, RN; Mid Thos. Hallahan; Act Master John Davis; Purser R. L. Horniman; Boatswain Wm. Martin; Vol 1st Class Wm. H. Brand.

	No of HM Ships Engaged	No of Bars Issued

Virginie 19 May 1808

        1   21

(19 May 1808)

For the capture of the Dutch frigate *Guelderland* off Northern Ireland by the *Virgine* (Commander E. Brace).

Redwing 31 May 1808

        1   5

(1 June 1808)

For the destruction of the batteries at Tarifa and capture of two vessels by the *Redwing* (Captain Thos. Ussher).

Recipients: Capt. Thos. Ussher, RN; Lieut John McP. Ferguson, RN; Mid Thos. Hallahan; Vol 1st Class Wm. H. Brand; Boatswain Wm. Martin (See Redwing, 7th May, 1808).
VANOR (2) Act Master John Davis and Purser R. L. Horniman.

Seahorse Wh Badere Zaffere

        1   32

(5 & 6 July 1808)

Captain John Stewart in the *Seahorse* encountered the Turkish frigate *Badere Zaffer* in company with the *Ali Fezan*. The latter frigate, having received a broadside from the *Seahorse*, decided that she had had enough and fled. The *Badere Zaffer*, however, continued fighting all day and all night, but due to her terrible plight was forced to surrender in the morning, having had her masts shot away and no less than 170 men killed and 200 wounded. As a result of this action the *Seahorse* had only five killed and ten wounded—a splendid example of fine gunnery, magnificent seamanship and tactics. This is a rare and much-prized bar in spite of the number issued.

Recipient of Small Naval Gold Medal: Capt John Stewart (*Seahorse*)

Comet 11 Augt 1808

        1   3

(11 August 1808)

For the capture of the French ship *Sylphe*, in the Bay of Biscay, by HMS *Comet* (Commander Cuthbert F. Daly).

Recipients: Comdr C. F. Daly, RN; Pte E. Vanston, RM and Vol 1st Class G. Dew. VANOR (1) Boy 2nd Class Daniel Caffrey (on Java Roll).

Centaur 26 Augt 1808

        1   41

Implacable 26 Augt 1808

        1   41

(26 August 1808)

These two bars show the variety of opponents which the Royal Navy had during the period covered by the NGS Medal. As a result of the Russians signing the Treaty of Tilsit on 7th July, 1807, they recognized the Confederation of the Rhine and the appointment of Napoleon's brothers Joseph, Louis and Jerome to the thrones of Naples, Holland and Westphalia. In other words, this meant that Russia was now ranged against us, so Admiral Sir James Saumarez was ordered to the Baltic, with his flag in Nelson's old flagship, *Victory*. During his voyage a Russian squadron of 17 ships was sighted. The *Centaur* (Captain Webley), flying the flag of Sir Samuel Hood, and the *Implacable** (Captain Byam Martin) were ordered to give chase. The *Implacable* overtook and captured the *Sevolod*, but as the Russian fleet returned the *Implacable* had to retire. On the arrival of the *Centaur* the *Sevolod* was again attacked, captured and eventually ran ashore and was set on fire.
HMS *Centaur* VANOR (1), HMS *Implacable* VANOR (3).

Cruizer 1 Novr 1808

        1   4

(1 November 1808)

The *Cruizer* (Lieutenant T. Wells) was attacked by about twenty Danish cutters off Gothenburg. She captured one and drove off the others.

Recipients: Lieut J. Allen, RN; Mid F. W. Ellis, Ord. W. J. Walker; Vol 1st Class James R. Forrest.

Amethyst Wh Thetis

        1   31

(10 November 1808)

Captain Michael Seymour in the *Amethyst* whilst off Lorient encountered the French frigate *Thetis*, which was on its way to Martinique. The *Thetis* was captured after a terrific fight, having suffered no less than 134 killed and 102 wounded. After the surrender of the *Thetis*, HMS *Triumph* and *Shannon* arrived and took her in tow, but, having taken no part in the actual fight, received no awards. The *Thetis* was added to the Royal Navy under the name of *Brune*.

Recipient of Small Naval Gold Medal: Capt Michael Seymour.

Off the Pearl Rock 13 Dec 1808

        6   14

(12 and 13 December 1808)

The *Circe* (Captain F. Collier), *Amaranthe* (Captain E. Brenton), *Stork* (Captain Geo. Le Geyt), *Express* (Lieutenant Dowers), *Morne Fortunée* (Lieutenant Brown), and *Epervier* (Captain T. Tucker) destroyed the French frigate *Cygne* off the Pearl Rock, Martinique. No awards were made to HMS *Express*.

Recipients: HMS *Circe* (4)—Comdr Francis R. Collier, RN; AB Yeoman of Sheets Alexander Roberts; AB John Jago; Ord George Underwood. HMS *Amaranthe* (4)—Mid James Rigmaiden; Vol 1st Class Joseph Willans; AB Wm. Weatherhead; Ord James Garrick. HMS *Stork* (3)—Comdr Geo. Le Geyt; Pte RM Richard Fry; AB George Harding (who also received bar for Martinique). HMS *Morne Fortunée* (2)—ABs

*The *Implacable* was originally the French line-of-battle ship *Duguay Trouin*, launched at Rochefort in 1797. She was present at Trafalgar and later captured by Sir Richard Strachan in the action off Finisterre, for which the bar '4th Novr. 1805' was awarded. She lay in Portsmouth harbour for many years as a hulk, until finally condemned as unseaworthy and not worth the cost of repair. On 3rd December, 1949, she was towed out to sea and blown up off the Isle of Wight with the White Ensign and the Tricolour flying side by side at her stern. On her way out of harbour she passed the aircraft carrier HMS *Implacable*, then flagship of the Home Fleet. The final signal for the detonation of the charges was given from the destroyer HMS *Finisterre*. It is a strange reflection on the life of modern warships to think that the aircraft carrier *Implacable*, 26,000 tons was launched in 1944 and scrapped in 1955 as out-dated.

	No of HM Ships Engaged	No of Bars Issued

Alex Clark and Peter Russel. HMS *Epervier* (1)—Lieut. Joseph Harrison, RN.
VANOR (2) Act Lieut C. H. Crooke, *Circe* and Lieut Comdg J. J. Rorie, *Morne Fortunée*.

Onyx 1 Jany 1809

1   5

(1 January 1809)

The brig *Onyx* (Commander Chas. Gill) recaptured the brig *Manly* from the Dutch in the North Sea. For this action Commander Gill and Lieutenant E. Garrett received promotion.

Recipients: Lieut E. W. Garrett, RN; Master's Mate W. White; Qtr Gnr H. Edwards; Clerk Hewson Dutchman; Ord J. Barnes.

Confiance 14 Jany 1809

1   8

(14 January 1809)

Captain Sir L. Yeo in the *Confiance*, with the assistance of 500 Portuguese troops captured Cayenne, the present capital of French Guiana (see Cayenne Medal, page 30).

Recipients: Mid Wm. Moore; Yeoman of Sheets J. Blackman; Boatswain George Byerlee, LM Christopher Hosan; Ord T. Hinnick, Vol 1st Class H. J. O'Callaghan; Cpl T. Ward, RM; Mid Edward Bryant.

Martinique

44   486

(24 February 1809)

For the capture of the island of Martinique in conjunction with the Army. There were no military recipients of the Naval Medal, though there were six naval and marine recipients of the military one, whose names are given when dealing with the bar for Martinique on the Military General Service Medal (see page 83).
Ships present: Rear-Admiral Cochrane's flagship *Neptune* 17/60, and *Acasta* 5/16, *Aeolus* 5/7, *Amaranthe* 3/9, *Belleisle* 6/30, *Captain* 3/25, *Cherub* 2/3, *Circe* 2/8, *Cleopatra* 3/10, *Eclair* 1/-, *Ethalion* 6/18, *Eurydice* 2/6, *Express* 1/1, *Fawn* 3/6, *Forester* 3/8, *Floric* 2/-, *Gloire* 3/3, *Gorée* 1/4, *Haughty* 1/4, *Hazard* 2/4, *Intrepid* 7/14, *Pelorus* 2/2, *Penelope* 4/17, *Pompée* 11/41, *Recruit* 1/4, *Star* 1/7, *Stork* 1/7, *Swinger*, *Ulysses* 3/8, *Wolverine* 4/4, *York* 7/22.
Schooners: *Bacchus*, *Bellette* 1/2, *Cuttle* 1/-, *Demerara* -/3, *Dominica* 1/-, *Elizabeth* -/1, *Liberty* -/1, *Mozambique* 1/-, *Port d'Espagne* 4/-, *Poltustle* -/2, *Ringdove* -/5, *Snap* 2/1, *Subtle*, *Supérieure* 2/1, *Surinam* 3/8.

Horatio 10 Feby 1809

1   13

Supérieure 10 Feby 1809

1   1

(10 February 1809)

The *Horatio* (Captain George Scott) and the *Supérieure* (Commander W. Ferrie) captured the French frigate *Junon* off Saintes in the Virgin Islands.

Recipients: HMS *Horatio*—Dmr Thos. Young, RN; Purser John Warden; 1st Lieut Richard Blakeney, RM; AB Richard Plumb; Mid Nicholas Webb; Ord Joseph Allen; Pte Joseph Crawford, RM; Lieut Manly Hall

	No of HM Ships Engaged	No of Bars Issued

Dixon, RN; LM Morris Hurley; Boy 3rd Class Samuel Beswick; Sgt Geo. Vincent, RM; Boy 2nd Class G. R. T. Disney; Capt of Foretop John Lane; also HMS *Supérieure* Act Master B. G. S. Day.

Amethyst 5 April 1809

1   26

(5 April 1809)

With Captain Michael Seymour in command, the *Amethyst* engaged the French frigate *Niemen* in the Bay of Biscay. When the *Niemen* was on the point of capitulating the *Arethusa* came on the scene and, strange to say, the *Niemen* surrendered to her and not to the *Amethyst*. No awards were given to the *Arethusa*. Captain Seymour was given a baronetcy for this action.
VANOR (1) Boy 2nd Class J. Pearce.

Basque Roads 1809

35   529

(11 and 12 April 1809)

For the complete destruction of the French fleet in the Basque Roads, off St Nazaire, which was due to the enterprize and skill of Lord Cochrane, who organized and led the fleet of warships and fireships into the Roads. Lord Cochrane was given the Order of the Bath and Lord Gambier, who was the senior officer present, received a court martial. The Court not only exonerated him for his pusillanimity but seems to have gone out of its way to express extreme approbation of his conduct! In O'Meara's *Napoleon in Exile*, Napoleon is quoted as having remarked when referring to the French ships in the harbour: 'Lord Cochrane could not only have destroyed them, but he might and would have taken them out had your Admiral supported him as he ought to have done.'
Ships present: Admiral Lord Gambier's flagship *Caledonia* 8/24, and *Aetna* 5/11, *Aigle* 5/11, *Armide* -/1, *Arrow* -/1, *Beagle* 2/9, *Bellona* 4/7, *Caesar* 17/26, *Christian VII* -/4, *Conflict* 1/-, *Contest*, *Defiance* -/1, *Doterel* 3/5, *Donegal* 7/13, *Dreadnought* -/1, *Emerald* 3/9, *Encounter* -/2, *Fervant*-/1, *Foxhound* 1/1, *Gibraltar* 10/24, *Goldfinch* 1/-, *Growler*, *Hero* 3/4, *Illustrious* 3/22, *Impérieuse* 6/18, *Indefatigable* 5/28, *Insolent* 1/4, *Lyra* 2/5, *Martial* 2/2, *Mediator* -/2, *Pallas* 3/8, *Redpole* 2/4, *Resolution* 4/35, *Revenge* 7/26, *Theseus* 6/30, *Thunder* 2/6, *Unicorn* 3/17, *Valiant* 9/22, Schooner *Whiting* -/2, *Zephr* -/1.
Cutters *King George* and *Nimrod* 1/-.

Recipient of the Small Naval Gold Medal: Capt James Wooldridge *Mediator*.
NB: The special award of the Small Gold Medal and Gold Chain was granted to Capt Wooldridge for this action. (See medal No 49).

Recruit 17 June 1809

1   5

Pompee 17 June 1809

1   21

Castor 17 June 1809

1   5

(17 April 1809)

The date on this bar is substantially incorrect. It is difficult to understand how such an error could pass unnoticed. The conclusion must be that there was considerable lack of verification or checking of the findings of the Board of Flag Officers which recommended the actions for which awards were to be given. The French seventy-four *D'Hautpoul*, which had escaped from Lorient, was in company with two others of her size and three frigates when they were sighted by the *Pompée* (Captain W. Fahie) and the brigs *Recruit* (Commander Charles Napier) and *Hazard*, all of which gave chase together with other British ships present. The two brigs were eventually outstripped, whereupon the *Latona* and *Castor* (Captain W. Roberts) took up the action. The latter engaged, giving time for the *Pompée* to arrive. The Frenchman surrendered and was added to the Royal Navy under the name of HMS *Abercromby*. Commander Charles Napier, as a reward for the gallant way in which the *Recruit* had behaved during the action, was given command. The action took place off Isle de Saintes, a small island off the south coast of Guadaloupe. A company of the 63rd Foot was on board HMS *Pompée* during the action. There was only one medal with this single bar issued to the army and that was awarded to Lieut W. Cosby of the 63rd Foot, and he also received the MGS Medal with bars for Martinique and Guadaloupe. VANOR (26).

Recipients HMS *Recruit*: Comdr Charles Napier, RN; Qtr Mstr J. Pearson; Carpenter R. Mustard; LM Robert Pattinson; Boy 3rd Class J. Davis. VANOR (2) Capt of Forecastle Joseph Mott; Carpenter's Crew James Stewart.

Recipients HMS *Castor*: Lieutenant W. R. B. Sellon, RN; Surgeon J. McCarogher; Mid J. T. T. Dixon; Pte J. Ross, RM; Boy 2nd Class W. Andrews. VANOR (8) Cook Anthony Pevering, RM; Pte Joseph Huson, RM; AB James McLaughlan; AB Samuel Mills; AB Alexander Nesbitt; AB George Packe; Lieut Michael Raven; Surgeon John Forbes*.

Cyane 25 and 27 June 1809

No of HM Ships Engaged	No of Bars Issued
1	5

L'Espoir 25 and 27 June 1809

No of HM Ships Engaged	No of Bars Issued
1	5

(26 and 27 June 1809)

Capt T. Staines in the corvette *Cyane* in company with the brig *L'Espoir* (Commander T. Mitford) was attacked off Naples by the French frigate *Ceres* and corvette *Fama*. The action was too one-sided and in the end the *Cyane* and *L'Espoir* had to withdraw after being very badly damaged. Captain T. Staines was knighted for this action.

Recipients HMS *Cyane*—1st Lieut W. Stuart, RM; Mids J. Allnutt and John Taylor; Purser J. Tapson; Boy 3rd Class J. Crogan. HMS *L'Espoir*—Comdr R. Mitford, RN; Lieut W. H. Higgs, RN; Act Lieut R. Oliver, RN; Ord E. Boyce and LM John Taylor.

Bonne Citoyenne Wh Furieuse

No of HM Ships Engaged	No of Bars Issued
1	12

(6 July 1809)

The French frigate *Furieuse* had escaped from the blockade of Guadaloupe and was

*Entered on Pompee roll in error.

on her way back to France when, in mid-Atlantic, she encountered the sloop *Bonne Citoyenne* (Captain W. Mounsey). After a battle lasting seven hours, the Frenchman had expended all his powder and so was forced to surrender.

Recipient of Small Naval Gold Medal: Capt Mounsey.

Recipients: Lieut Wm. Sandom, RN; Lieut Joseph Symes, RN; Mid Nathaniel Routh; Capts of Foretop Richard Roberts and Eliazer Taysand; Carpenter Thos. Atwaters; Ords Wm. White and Ed. Buttonshaw; Boy 2nd Class John Crosdale; Ptes Joseph Smith, James Jolley and Richard Chapman, RM.

Diana 11 Septr 1809

No of HM Ships Engaged	No of Bars Issued
1	5

(11 September 1809)

For the capture of the Dutch brig *Zephr* (or *Zefir*), which was anchored off Amurang, in the north-east of the island of Celebes in the East Indies, by the *Diana* (Lieutenant W. Kempthorne).

Recipients: AB George Wilson; Ord R. Rowell; Ptes A. Brown and N. Brittal, RM; Boy 2nd Class James Burke. VANOR (3) with BS clasp 24 December 1810; Mid John B. Knocker; Ship's Cpl George White; Ord J. J. F. Newell.

Anse la Barque 18 Decr 1809

No of HM Ships Engaged	No of Bars Issued
9	40

(18 December 1809)

A British squadron consisting of the *Sceptre* (Captain S. Ballard), *Blonde* (Captain V. V. Ballard), *Freija* (Captain J. Hayes), *Thetis* (Captain G. Miller), *Castor* (Captain Roberts), *Hazard* (Captain Cameron), *Ringdove* (Captain Dowers), *Cygnet* (Captain Dix) and *Elizabeth* (Lieutenant C. Finch) encountered the French frigates *Loire* and *Seine*, which were escorting troops and stores to Guadaloupe. The latter ships sought protection under the batteries of Anse la Barque, but both they and the batteries were captured. This is a scarce bar on the market in spite of the number issued.
VANOR (12)

Cherokee 10 Jany 1810

No of HM Ships Engaged	No of Bars Issued
1	4

(11 January 1810)

For the capture of the French privateer *L'Aimable Nelly* in Dieppe Harbour by the *Cherokee* (Captain Richard Arthur).

Recipients: Lieut J. R. R. Webb, RN; Supn Pilots H. Barber and H. Pilcher; Ord G. Arguile.

Scorpion 12 Jany 1810

No of HM Ships Engaged	No of Bars Issued
1	5

(12 January 1810)

The *Scorpion* (Captain P. Stanfell) captured the French brig *L'Oreste* off the island of Guadaloupe. The *L'Oreste* was repaired and added to the Royal Navy as HMS *Wellington*.

Recipients: Lieuts George C. Blake, RN and (?) John Scott; Mid J. R. Benson (2 medals issued, one as a single bar, the other with bar Guadaloupe); AB Adam Peters; Sailmaker William Toms. VANOR (3) Lieut Samuel Strong, Bosun's Mate Robert Flaxman, LM Thos Hacker.

Guadaloupe

	No of HM Ships Engaged	No of Bars Issued
	45	483

(5 February 1810)

For assisting in the capture of the island of Guadaloupe. From its discovery by Christopher Columbus in 1493 its career, as regards ownership, is difficult to follow, and as its name appears so frequently when dealing with the NGS Medal perhaps collectors will be interested in this very short history.

As a result of its discovery by Columbus, the island was claimed for Spain by Ferdinand and Isabella, who financed his voyage, which incidentally included the discovery of Cuba, the Bahamas, and other West Indian islands. The French took possession in 1635 and spent a considerable sum in colonizing it in time for us to capture it in 1759. In 1763 it was handed back to France, but recaptured again in 1779, 1794 and 1810. After all this trouble it was given to Sweden as an incentive to join the alliance against France. On the ratification of the Treaty of Paris (14th May, 1814) the island was again returned to France, only to be again taken by the British on 10th August, 1815, and yet again restored to France in the following July. Since then it has remained a French possession. It came into the limelight again during 1940 when part of the French fleet took refuge there and had to be demilitarized.

Ships present: Vice-Admiral Sir A. Cochrane's flagship *Pompée* 12/45, and *Abercrombe* 6/18, *Alfred* 6/29, *Alcmène* 5/13, *Asp* 3/7, *Aurora* 1/8, *Amaranthe* 1/5, *Achates* 2/2, *Attentive* -/3, *Bacchus* 1/1, *Ballahou*, *Bellette* -/1, *Blonde* 4/14, *Caster* 2/9, *Cherub* 3/1, *Cygnet* 1/2, *Eclair* 2/-, *Elizabeth, Fawn* 2/4, *Forester* 1/3, *Freija* 3/15, *Frolic* 1/3, *Gloire* 2/7, *Grenada* 1/-, *Guadeloupe* 1/2, *Hazard* 2/5, *Laura* 1/1, *Loire* 5/19, *Melamphus* 4/10, *Morne Fortunee* -/2, *Netley* -/2, *Observateur* 2/4, *Orpheus* 1/15, *Pelorus* 2/5, *Perlen* 4/19, *Plumper* -/1, *Pultusk* 3/2, *Ringdove* 1/3, *Rosamund* 2/7, *St Christopher* 1/-, *St Pierre* 1/-, *Savage* 1/-, *Sceptre* 6/34, *Scorpion* 3/5, *Snap* 3/3, *Star* 2/6, *Statira* 5/12, *Subtle, Superieure* 2/1, *Surinam* 2/4, *Thetis* 5/6, *Tompée* -/1, *Vimiera* 1/6, *Wanderer* 1/3.

Thistle 10 Feby 1810

	No of HM Ships Engaged	No of Bars Issued
	1	0

(10 February 1810)

For the capture of the Dutch corvette *Havik* off Bermuda by the *Thistle* (Lieutenant Peter Proctor). There were no recipients of this bar.

Surly 24 April 1810

	No of HM Ships Engaged	No of Bars Issued
	1	1

Firm 24 April 1810

	No of HM Ships Engaged	No of Bars Issued
	1	1

(20 April 1810)

The *Surly* (Captain R. Welch)* and *Firm* (Captain J. Little)* captured the French

*The ranks of these officers are various quoted as Lieutenant, Commander and Captain. The name Welch is also found spelt Welsh. The commanding officer's report of this action quoted the date as the 20th April, 1810.

privateer *Alcide* in Granville Bay, on the east coast of the island of Grenada in the West Indies. HMS *Sharpshooter* was also engaged, but does not appear to have been rewarded, or at any rate there were no claimants for this medal from her.

Recipients: HMS *Surly*—Clerk, Abraham Norster. HMS *Firm*—Pte Henry Wigley, RM.

Sylvia 26 April 1810

	No of HM Ships Engaged	No of Bars Issued
	1	1

(26 April 1810)

For the capture of the Dutch ship *Echo* and two transports in the Sunda Sea between Java and Celebes by the *Sylvia* (Lieutenant A. Vere Drury).

Recipient: Act 2nd Master J. C. Chesnaye.

Spartan 3 May 1810

	No of HM Ships Engaged	No of Bars Issued
	1	30

(3 May 1810)

Captain Jahleel Brenton in the *Spartan* was the subject of a special expedition by Murat (one of Napoleon's marshals who had usurped the throne of Naples). Captain Brenton had been cruising off Naples, causing the Neapolitans a good deal of trouble. Murat sent the frigate *Ceres*, the corvette *Fama*, and several small brigs and gunboats to destroy the *Spartan*. Events did not materialize as intended by Murat, for the *Ceres*, which had embarked special troops to act as a boarding party, was terribly mauled, the *Fama* sheered off, and one of the brigs, the *Sparvière*, surrendered.

Royalist May and June 1810

	No of HM Ships Engaged	No of Bars Issued
	1	3

(23 February 1810)

The correct dates for this clasp should have been Nov. 1809-Feb. 1810. The *Royalist* (Captain G. S. Maxwell) patrolled the Channel on the watch for French privateers. The actions fought by her were with the following five privateers in 1809: *La Princesse* and *Le Grand Napoleon*, 17th November; *L'Heureuse Etoile*, 6th December; *Le Beau Marseille*, 10th December; *Le Francois*, 31st December; and the *Prince Eugène* on the 24th February, 1810. She captured her opponent in each of these actions, but was not engaged during either May or June, 1810.

Recipients: Mid H. A. D. Thornton, Supn Pilot Anthony Bowles, and Boy 3rd Class George Selby.

Amanthea 25 July 1810

	No of HM Ships Engaged	No of Bars Issued
	3	23

(25 July 1810)

The *Thames* (Captain Honorable G. Waldegrave), *Pilot* (Captain T. Nicolas) and *Weazel* (Henry Prescott) fought an action with a number of gunboats and destroyed some transports off Amanthea, Calabria, on the 'toe' of Italy.

Banda Neira

	No of HM Ships Engaged	No of Bars Issued
	4	68

(9 August 1810)

Captain C. Cole in the *Caroline*, together with the *Piedmontaise* (Captain Chas. Foote) and the brig *Barracouta* (Commander R. Kenah), together with a landing party of

100 of the Madras European Regiment, arrived off the island on the night of 8th-9th August. Early on the 9th the landing parties attacked the batteries and the castle guarding the town, which then surrendered. It seems strange that the forts, mounting a total of nearly 130 guns and over 1,500 defenders, should give in so easily against three ships mounting a total of only 92 guns and a landing party of only 180 seamen, marines and soldiers. Eventually the remaining islands of the Banda group in the Banda Sea, about 700 miles due north of the Northern Territory in Australia, surrendered, only to be handed back to the Dutch in 1816.

Recipient of the Small Naval Gold Medal: Capt Christopher Cole, *Caroline*. The numbers of bars awarded to the three ships were as follows: *Caroline* 1/34, *Piedmontaise* 5/15, and *Barracouta* 2/11.

	No of HM Ships Engaged	No of Bars Issued
Staunch 18 Sepr 1810	1	2
Otter 18 Sepr 1810	1	8
Boadicea 18 Sepr 1810	1	15
(18 September 1810)		

The *Ceylon* (Captain Chas. Gordon) sailed from Madras with detachments of the 69th and 89th Foot and Major General Abercromby on board. When off Réunion she encountered the French frigate *Venus* and corvette *Victor*. The *Ceylon* was forced to surrender. Shortly after, Commodore Rowley in the *Boadicea*, accompanied by the *Otter* (Captain J. Tomkinson) and *Staunch* (Lieutenant B. Street), sighted the *Victor* towing the *Ceylon*, and the *Venus*. The *Victor* released the *Ceylon* and made off, leaving the *Venus* to fight the three ships. Almost as soon as the *Boadicea* engaged her the *Venus* surrendered. She was taken to St Paul's Bay and renamed *Néréide*.

Recipients: HMS *Staunch*—Act Sub-Lieut R. T. Sainthill, RN; Ord J. Edwards (also at Malaga 29 April 1812), HMS *Otter*—Act Purser F. Taylor; Master's Mate J. McGladery; Ord J. Sutherland and AB John Jeffery; Qtr Gnr T. Manning; Pte J. Grassum, RM; Boy 2nd Class Owen Hearn and Pte Benjamin Pratt, 69th Foot. HMS *Boadicea*—Lieuts Thos. L. P. Laugharne and Edward Lloyd, Act Lieut H. J. Clifford; Mid Samuel Ramsey, and John Chamberlayne; Ord Wm. Carey; AB Wm. Page; LM Philip Lamb; Boys 3rd Class Stewart Stocker and James Wilson; Ord Wm. Taylor; Cpl Thos. Roberts, RM; Ptes Richard Griffiths, John Borrows and James Swigg, RM.

	No of HM Ships Engaged	No of Bars Issued
Briseis 14 Octr 1810	1	2
(14 October 1810)		

For the capture of the French privateer *Sans Souci* in the North Sea by HMS *Briseis* (Acting Commander G. Bentham).

Recipients: Act Comdr George Bentham, RN; and Lieut George Welsh, RN.

	No of HM Ships Engaged	No of Bars Issued
Lissa	4	124
(13 March 1811)		

The combined French and Venetian fleet, when cruising off Lissa in the Adriatic, was engaged by Captain W. Hoste in the *Amphion* with the *Active* (Captain J. A. Gordon), *Cerberus* (Captain H. Whitby) and *Volage* (Captain P. Hornby). After a severe fight the three French frigates *Favorite*, *Danae* and *Flora* and the Venetian ships *Corona*, *Bellona*, *Carolina*, and *Mercure* and four small vessels were severely beaten so much so that only the *Danae* and *Carolina* managed to escape capture or destruction. The *Flora* surrendered and then escaped, which in those days was not considered very laudable. The numbers of medals awarded to each ship were *Active* 10/35, *Amphion* 7/27, *Cerberus* 5/21, *Volage* 7/12.

Recipients of the Small Naval Gold Medal: Capts Sir Wm. Hoste, *Amphion*; James Alexander Gordon, *Active*; H. Whitby, *Cerberus* and Phipps Hornby, *Volage*

	No of HM Ships Engaged	No of Bars Issued
Anholt 27 March 1811	4	40
(27 March 1811)		

Captain J. W. Maurice, whilst commanding the garrison of 350 Marines and 31 Marine artillerymen on the small island of Anholt in the Kattegat, was attacked by a large flotilla of gunboats and 1,500 Danish troops. No less than 520 Danes surrendered and many were killed. After the attack the *Tartar* (Captain J. Baker) and *Sheldrake* (Commander J. Stewart) chased the fleeing expedition and captured three gunboats and a lugger and a further sixty men. This is a rare bar. (Island commissioned as HM Ship. See Master List ADM 37/3513).

	No of HM Ships Engaged	No of Bars Issued
Arrow 6 April 1811	1	0
(6 April 1811)		

For the action fought with French *chasse marées* off the coast of France by the *Arrow* (Lieutenant Samuel Knight, RN). No awards were claimed.

	No of HM Ships Engaged	No of Bars Issued
Off Tamatave 20 May 1811	4	79
(20 May 1811)		

The *Astraea* 9/16 (Captain C. Schomberg), *Phoebe* 5/19 (Captain J. Hillier)*, *Galatea* 7/12 (Captain J. Losack), *Racehorse* 2/9 (Captain J. de Rippe) captured the French frigates *Néréide* and *Renommée*, which were carrying munitions to Mauritius. It is nice to know that the *Renommée* was renamed, this time *Java*, and the *Néréide* was re-christened *Madagascar*.
VANOR (8).

	No of HM Ships Engaged	No of Bars Issued
Hawke 18 Augt 1811	1	6
(18 August 1811)		

The *Hawke* (Commander Henry Bouchier) captured the French brig *Heron* near Barfleur. This action, according to the commanding officer's report, took place on the 19th August.

Recipients: Comdr Henry Bouchier, RN; Lieut David Price, RN; Mid John Langworthy; Ords John Keady and Wm. Perkis; Carpenter's Crew John Monteith.

---

*This officer is quoted as given above and also as Captain T. Hillyar, whilst Captain Losack's initial is found as W. as well as J.

	No of HM Ships Engaged	No of Bars Issued

Java

	33	665

(July-18 September 1811) For the assistance given by the Navy in the capture of the island of Java. This island, like so many others over which we had spent so much blood and money, was handed back to the Dutch in 1814. The attack on Java provides the only case known of when two ships of the same name were on the same side. In this case there was HMS *Psyche* and the HEI Company's cruiser of the same name.†

For the troops engaged see the Military General Service Medal from page 80). Ships present: Rear-Admiral Hon R. Stopford's flagship *Scipion* 20/65, and *Akbar* 3/16, *Barracouta* 2/9, *Bucephalus* 2/11, *Caroline* 4/30, *Cornelia* 2/23, *Dasher* 1/2, *Doris* 5/8, *Harpy* 3/11, *Hecate* 2/6, *Hesper* 5/8, *Hussar* 7/35, *Illustrious* 14/54, *Leda* 3/19, *Lion* 7/38, *Minden* 6/37, *Modeste* 3/22, *Nisus* 8/31, *Phaeton* 4/31, *Phoebe* 6/24 *Presidente* 8/41, *Procris* 3/11, *Psyche, Samarange* -/8, *Sir Francis Drake* 3/21.

HEI Company's Cruisers: *Ariel* 1/-, *Aurora* 1/-, *Malabar* 1/-, *Mornington* 1/-, *Nautilus* 1/-, *Psyche, Thetis* 1/-, and *Vestal* 1/-.

Skylark 11 Novr 1811

	1	4

Locust 11 Novr 1811

	1	2

(10 November 1811) For the capture of a French brig off Boulogne, after an action with the Boulogne Flotilla, by the *Skylark* (Commander J. Boxer) and *Locust* (Lieutenant J. Gedge).

Recipients: HMS *Syklark*—Comdr James Boxer, RN; Lieut W. Walford, RN; Boy 2nd Class Wm. Bird, unknown alias aboard or rate Richard Dyer. HMS *Locust*—Lieut John Gedge, RN, and AB Samuel Bachell.

Pelagosa 29 Novr 1811

	3	64

(29 November 1811) For the action off Pelagosa in which the *Active* (Captain James A. Gordon), *Alceste* (Captain Murray Maxwell), and *Unité* (Captain E. Chamberlayne) encountered the French frigates *Pauline* and *Pomone*, which were escorting the store-ship *Persanne*. The *Pomone* surrendered; the *Pauline* escaped to Ancona. The *Persanne* was also trying to escape thither, but was overhauled by the *Unité* and surrendered. In spite of the numerous awards, this is a scarce bar. The distribution of bars is as follows: *Active* 12/22, *Unité* 7/12 and *Alceste* 3/8. VANOR (10) *Active*.

Victorious with Rivoli

	1	67

Weazel 22 Feby, 1812

	1	6

(22 February 1812) These two bars were given for what was really the same battle, though in a sense each of the two ships fought a separate action. When cruising off Venice, Captain J. Talbot in the *Victorious*, in consort with the *Weazel* (Commander J. W. Andrew), encountered the French 74-gun *Rivoli* and the brig *Mercure*. Whilst the *Victorious* fought the *Rivoli*, the *Weazel* engaged the *Mercure*, which after about an hour, blew up. Having finished off her own adversary so satisfactorily, the *Weazel* then engaged the *Rivoli*, which by then was quite ready to surrender and did so.

Recipients of the Small Naval Gold Medal: Captain Talbot, *Victorious;* Comdr J. W. Andrew, HMS *Weazel.*

Recipients: HMS *Weazel*—Comdr J. W. Andrew; Asst Surgeon F. Kiernan; Ords J. Milly and J. Saxton; Ptes J. Feather and Wm. Young, RM.

Rosario 27 March 1812

	1	7

Griffon 27 March 1812

	1	3

(27 April 1812) The *Rosario* (Captain B. Harvey) and *Griffon* (Commander G. B. Trollope) captured two French brigs off Boulogne.

Recipients: HMS *Rosario*—Surgeon Wm. Watson; Mid Jas. Rothery; Pilot Jas. Gillman; Purser George Starr; Gnr John Webber; Act Master John Brown; Pte George Norris, RM; HMS *Griffon*—Comdr G. B. Trollope; Lieut B. Shepherd, RN; Master's Mate C. Price.

Malaga 29 April 1812

	4	17

(22 April 1812) The boats from the *Hyacinth* (Captain T. Ussher), *Goshawk* (Captain J. Lilburn), *Resolute* (Captain J. Keenan) and gunboat No. 16 (Lieutenant T. Cull), captured the French corsairs *Brave* and *Napoleon* off Malaga, on the south coast of Spain.

Recipients: HMS *Hyacinth* (9)—Capt Thos. Ussher, RN; Clerk J. M. Hoffmeister; Armourer Thos. Wiltshire; Ord John Andrews; Pte John Barber, RM; Capt of Foretop Geo. Weeks; Act Bosun Joseph Bell; Lieut Thos. Hastings, RN; Clerk Chas. Blatchley. HMS *Goshawk* (5)— Carpenter Wm. Leaper; Yeoman of Powder Room Chas. File; Master George L. Parrott; AB Chas. Shackle; Lieut Allen Otty, RN. HMS *Resolute* (3)—Ptes Richard Bird and John Vassey; and Pte Marshal Heaviside, RM.
VANOR (2) Lieut Thos. Cull and Carpenters Crew John Edwards.

Northumberland 22 May 1812

	1	63

Growler 22 May 1812

	1	1

(22 May 1812) The *Northumberland* (Captain Hon Henry Hotham) and *Growler* (Lieutenant J. Weeks) were detailed to watch for the French frigates *Ariane* and *Andromaque (Andromache?)* and the brig *Mameluk* which had been causing considerable depredation to British merchantmen. They were sighted on their return to port off the Isle de Groix off Lorient. It is rather extraordinary that

† Captain G. Sayer, of HMS *Leda*, landed in command of a large party of seamen and marines from the *Hesper, Illustrious, Leda, Procris,* and *Scipion,* for which service he received an Army Gold Medal, the only one awarded to a Naval officer. Captain Richard Bunce, RM, received a similar medal.

	No of HM Ships Engaged	No of Bars Issued

as a result of the action that followed, all three French ships blew up! In spite of the number issued, the bar to HMS *Northumberland* is rare.

Recipient: HMS *Growler*—Mid Hy. Edwards (Mid Wm. L. Stephens; AB Robert Rowe and LM Robert Dillon on *Growler* Roll but all were aboard *Northumberland*).

Off Mardoe 6 July 1812

4   47

(6 July 1812)

For the destruction of the Danish frigate *Nayaden* and three brigs off Mardoe, on the Norwegian coast, by the *Dictator* (34) (Captain J. P. Stewart), *Calypso* (7) (Commander H. Weir), *Podargus* (5) (Commander W. Robilliard) and *Flamer* (1) (Lieutenant T. England).

Sealark 21 July 1812

1   4

(21 July 1812)

For the capture of the French privateer *Ville de Caen* off Start Point, Devon by the *Sealark* (Lieutenant T. Warrand).

Recipients: Licut T. Warrand, RN; Gnr's Mate J. Cummings; AB Thomas Durnford; Cpl J. Wakeham, RM.

Royalist 29 Decr 1812

1   3

(29 December 1812)

For the capture by the *Royalist* (Commander G. Downie) of the French privateer *La Ruse* which was then off Hythe, Kent.

Recipients: Mid L. Rees; Coxswain A. Brown. AB Henry Hackman. VANOR (1) Surgeon W. F. Carter.

Weazel 22 April 1813

1   5

(22 April 1813)

For the destruction of six French gunboats in the Adriatic by the *Weazel* (Commander J. Black).

Recipients: Lieut M. Quinn, RN; Asst Surgeon F. Kiernan; Ords John Bryan, J. Saxton, and W. Watson. VANOR (3) with bar for Weazel 22 Feb. 1812, AB John Milly; Ptes RM James Feather and Wm. Young.

Shannon Wh Chesapeake

1   42

(1 June 1813)

Captain Philip Bowes Vere Broke reconnoitered Booton Harbour, where he found the *Constitution* and *Chesapeake* refitting. He lay off the harbour and sent Captain Lawrence of the *Chesapeake* a challenge to come out. At noon on 1st June, the *Chesapeake* came out, accompanied by several pleasure boats. The action lasted exactly fifteen minutes. Captain Broke was severely wounded on board the *Chesapeake* when leading a boarding party. The *Chesapeake* suffered 48 killed and 96 wounded. The *Shannon* was taken out of action by Lieutenant Provo Wallis (later Admiral, who died at the age of 101), and Lieutenant Falkiner assumed command of the *Chesapeake* and took her to

Halifax, where she arrived on 6th June. She was added to the Navy under the same name. This medal is much sought after and commands a high price.

Recipient of the Small Naval Gold Medal: Captain Philip Bowes Vere Broke, *Shannon*.

Pelican 14 Augt 1813

1   4

(14 August 1813)

For the capture of the American brig *Argus*, which had taken the American minister to France and on her way back had caused depredations in the Bristol Channel. The *Pelican* (Commander J. F. Maples) sailed from Cork and encountered the *Argus* which had recently captured a Spanish wine ship. It would be unwise to jump to conclusions, but the fact remains that the *Pelican* seemed to have had little trouble in capturing her, during which process she suffered only one killed and five wounded.

Recipients: Mid Henry Cox (also Gold and Silver Life Saving Medals); Cook F. Fox; AB William Baker; Pte Wm. Maides, RM.

St Sebastian

18   293

(8 September 1813)

For assisting in the capture of St. Sebastian. For the troops engaged, see the Military General Service Medal. Some ships' boats were employed in the inner blockade. In many cases the name of their parent ship is not quoted among those of the blockading squadron.

Ships present: Capt Sir G. Collier's ship *Surveillance* 4/34, and *Ajax* 13/38, *Andromache* 6/20, *Arrow* 1/1, *Beagle* 1/13, *Challenger* 2/4, *Constant* 2/5, *Dispatch* 2/10, *Epervier* -/1, *Freija* 4/6, *Holly*, *Juniper* -/5, *Leda* -/1, *Lyra* 4/3, *Magicienne* 8/14, *Magnificent* -/1, *Nimble*, *President* 8/21, *Revolutionnaire* 7/24, *Rover* 1/-, *Royalist*, *Sparrow* 7/5, *Stork* 2/1 and Gunboats Nos. 14 -/2, 16 1/1, 19 1/3, 20 -/1 and 22 -/1; *Racer* 1/-.

The following from HMS *Reindeer* which is not given among the list of ships present, received this bar: Lieut Robert Loney, RN (who also received bars for Basque Roads, 1809, and Java). Act Master Richard Johns; Capt of Forecastle, Joshua Carson; Ord James Wallace. Capt P. Faddy, RA, who was on board HMS *Freija*, received the NGS Medal with this bar.

Thunder 9 Octr 1813

1   7

(9 October 1813)

For the capture of the French privateer *Le Neptune* off the Owers in the English Channel by the *Thunder* (Commander W. Owen Pell).

Recipients: Comdr W. Owen Pell, RN (had lost his left leg Feb. 1800); Lieut T. H. McKenzie, RN; Mid Wm. S. Whittmee; Qr Mr David Finn; Qr Master's Mate Thomas Thompson; Purser C. E. Cotterel; Gnr's Mate James Webb. VANOR (2) AB John Ham, and Ord John Elmore.

	No of HM Ships Engaged	No of Bars Issued

Gluckstadt 5 Jany 1814

	6	42

(5 January 1814)

For the capture of the Fortress of Gluckstadt, near the mouth of the Elbe, by Captain A. Farquhar, in the *Desirée* 8/15 together with the *Shamrock* 1/2 (Captain J. Marshall), *Hearty* -/3 (Captain J Rose), *Blazer* 1/1 (Captain F. Banks), *Piercer* 1/1 (Commander J. Kneeshaw), *Redbreast* -/2 (Commander Sir G. M. Keith), and eight gunboats numbered 1, 2, 3, 4, 5, 8, 10, 12 in Flotilla 5/2
VANOR (2)

Venerable 16 Jany 1814

	1	42

Cyane 16 Jany 1814

	1	7

(16 and 20 January 1814)

The *Venerable* (Captain A. J. Worth) and the *Cyane* (Captain T. Forrest) captured the French frigates *Alcmene* and *Iphigenie* off the Canary Islands.

Recipients: HMS *Cyane* (7)—Surgeon Wm. Aiton; Act Lieut Edward Grant, RN; Master's Mate James Thompson; Mid Daniel Young; Capt Mast John Truss (who also got the bars for Copenhagen, 1801; Pique, 28th March, 1806; Anse la Barque, 18th Dec., 1809; and Guadaloupe), and Supn Boys 2nd Class J. Hurwood, Wm. Scull.

Eurotas 25 Feby 1814

	1	32

(25 February 1814)

Captain J. Phillimore in the *Eurotas* captured the French frigate *Clorinde*, off Brest. The *Clorinde* was added to the Navy as HMS *Aurora*. The *Clorinde* actually surrendered to the *Achates*, which, in company with the *Dryad*, arrived on the scene whilst the original contestants had broken apart to repair damage.

Hebrus with L'Etoile

	1	40

(27 March 1814)

On 27th March, 1814, the French frigate *L'Etoile* was returning from the Cape Verde Islands, where she had fought a desperate action with HMS *Creole* and *Astraea*, when she was sighted by the *Hebrus* (Captain E. Palmer) off the island of Alderney. After suffering over one hundred casualties she surrendered and was added to the Navy as HMS *Topaze*.

Recipient of the Small Naval Gold Medal: Capt Edmund Palmer.

Phoebe 28 March 1814

	1	31

Cherub 28 March 1814

	1	7

(28 March 1814)

The *Phoebe* (Captain James Hillyar) and *Cherub* (Captain T. Tucker) had been cruising up and down the South American coast in search of the American frigate *Essex*, which had destroyed several merchantmen and whaling ships. Early in February, 1814, she was found sheltering in the harbour of Valparaiso with her prizes and a sloop called the *Essex Junior*. Captain Porter of the *Essex*, having failed in one or two attempts to escape, lay in harbour until

28th March, when a heavy off-shore wind drove him out to sea. The *Essex* surrendered after a short fight. The *Essex Junior* did not take any part in the action, but was captured, together with all the prizes.

Recipients: HMS *Cherub*—Comdr Thomas T. Tucker, RN; Surgeon Peter Ramsay; Supn LM Wm. Crombie; Ord Wm. Salter; AB Thos. Skiddy; Vol 1st Class John Randall and Boy 2nd Class Jonathan Griffin.
VANOR (5) *Phoebe.*

The Potomac 17 Aug 1814

	8	108

(29 August 1814)

For the destruction of American ships nearly fifty miles up the Potomac river. This is a scarce bar in spite of the number issued.
Ships present: *Aetna* 6, *Devastation* 9, *Euryalus* 30, *Meteor* 4, *Seahorse* 40. Rocket Vessels: *Erebus* 13 and *Fairy* 4. *Regulus* 2 (not present).

Endymion Wh President

	1	58

(15 January 1815)

The *President* had been blockaded in New York, but, having escaped, was chased by the *Endymion* (Captain Henry Hope) and brought to action off Sandy Hook. Owing to the *Endymion* having suffered considerable damage to her sails, the *President* managed to get away, but was again brought to action by HMS *Pomone* and *Tenedos,* to whom she eventually surrendered. Whilst taking the prize to Bermuda a terrible gale was encountered and when they eventually arrived the *Endymion* and *President* were practically empty, as everything movable had been jettisoned. The *Endymion* had lost two of her masts and the *President* all three! This is a scarce bar.
The *Pomone* and *Tenedos* were not awarded any bars.

Recipient of the Small Naval Gold Medal: Capt Henry Hope. This was the last action for which a Naval Gold Medal was issued.

Gaieta 24 July 1815

	2	88

(8 August 1815)

For the attack on Gaieta, near Naples, by the *Berwick* (Captain Edward Brace) (49) and *Malta* (Captain W. Fahie) (39). This, in spite of the numbers issued, is a somewhat scarce medal.
The names of Private Ed. Hooper, RM, and Private Wm. Spooner of HMS *Woodlark* and AB Edward Richmond of HMS *Princess Augusta* appear on the roll but these ships were not present.
VANOR (1) *Berwick.*

Algiers

	20	1,328

(27 August 1816)

For the action at Algiers in which the combined English and Dutch fleets attacked the town. The combined fleets were under the command of Admiral Lord Exmouth, of whom we heard before when he was Captain Edward Pellew of HMS *Nymphe,*

No of HM Ships Engaged	No of Bars Issued

which gained the first bar to the NGS Medal for the action fought on 18th June, 1793, and again as Sir Edward in command of HMS *Indefatigable*, 20th April, 1796, and 13th January, 1797. He commanded HMS *Phaeton* at Java, August and September, 1811. He died on 23rd January, 1833, so consequently did not receive a medal. There were 19 Military recipients of the NGS Medal with this bar, as follows:

Military recipients: Rocket Trp, RHA— Lieut John Thomas Fuller, Sgt Edward Howe, Ord Clerk John Miller (HMS *Minden*); Conductor of Stores Edward Sargent; Artificer John Dickenson; Gnr Daniel McLeod (HMS *Queen Charlotte*); Gnr Joseph Allen (HMS *Granicus*); Sappers and Miners—Lieut Frederick William Whinyates; Sprs Thomas Jewry and Richard Parry; Dmr Alexander Smith (all HMS *Impregnable*). Capt William Reid; Lieut George Hotham; Sgt Nemen Melville; Sprs James Bond, Thomas Farmer, Alexander McKenzie, Francis Rogers, William Stuart (all HMS *Queen Charlotte*, which had on board 84 men of the 7th Company, 1st Bn Royal Sappers and Miners).

Ships awarded medals: Lord Exmouth's flagship *Queen Charlotte* 39/190, and *Albion* 18/90, *Beelzebub* 6/12, *Britomart* 4/12, *Cordelia* 4/11, *Falmouth* 1/3, *Fury* 6/8, *Granicus* 10/54, *Glasgow* 22/70, *Hebrus* 8/44, *Hecla* 13/13, *Heron* 5/19, *Impregnable* 21/150, *Infernal* 2/9, *Leander* 19/85, *Minden* 22/105, *Mutine* 5/19, *Prometheus* 5/16, *Severn* 17/47, *Superb* 26/120.

Navarino
12   1,142
(20 October 1827)

For the Battle of Navarino, in which the combined fleets of Britain, France, and Russia took part under Vice-Admiral Sir Edward Codrington. Only three or four of the Turkish and Egyptian ships, numbering over eighty at the start of the battle, were left afloat.
Ships present: Flagship *Asia* 26/212 and *Albion* 21/167, *Cambrian* 11/89, *Dartmouth* 11/96, *Genoa* 24/179, *Glasgow* 15/91, *Talbot* 14/66. Brigs *Brisk* 3/14, *Mosquito* 7/21, *Philomel* 6/23. Corvette *Rose* 5/26. Cutter *Hind* 1/1. One would particularly value a medal to HMS *Hind* (Lieutenant J. Robb), which with ten 6-pdr. guns and a crew of only thirty took on two frigates, a corvette and a brig, and then rammed another frigate for good measure and ended the day with only fifteen of her crew not killed or wounded.
James Hawkins received a medal with this bar and a second medal with a bar for Syria.
The only military recipient of this bar was Lieutenant Colonel John Hobart Cradock for service on board HMS *Asia*.

Syria
34   6978
(4 November 1840)

In 1840, Mehemit Ali, Viceroy of Egypt broke his agreement to leave Syria alone and invaded it. As Britain, Austria, Russia and Prussia had guaranteed to act in the event of any further trouble, a combined fleet, under Admiral Stopford, was sent to evict him. Acre was bombarded and captured on 3rd November.
Ships present: Admiral Sir Robert Stopford's flagship *Princess Charlotte*, and *Asia, Bellerophon, Benbow, Cambridge, Carysfort, Castor, Daphne, Dido, Edinburgh, Fury, Ganges, Hastings, Hazard, Hecate, Implacable, Lady Franklin, Magicienne, Medea, Pique, Powerful, Revenge, Rodney, Talbot, Thunderer, Vanguard, Wasp, Zebra* and the following steamers, as they were then called: *Cyclops, Gorgon, Hydra, Phoenix, Stromboli,* and *Vesuvius*.
Seventy officers and men of the army received the medal with this bar RA 5/42, RE/S & M 6/12, 7th Foot 1/1, Staff Corps 2/-.

Boat Service Bars

We now come to the bars issued with the Naval General Service Medal for what are termed Boat Actions. The bars are inscribed: '28th AUG. BOAT SERVICE 1809; 28th JUNE BOAT SERVICE 1810'; etc. The words 'BOAT SERVICE' separate the month and year. The bars were only sanctioned for occasions on which an officer received promotion, usually being the leader of the expedition or action concerned.

As will be seen, more than one boat action took place on some of the dates. In the case of some of the bars no corroborative evidence can be found that any action took place on the dates mentioned.

In the column headed 'No. of HM Ships engaged' the number of warships is given from which the small boats were supplied.

15 Mar Boat Service 1793
1   1
(15 March 1793)
Boats from HMS *Syren* captured some of the French guns erected to bombard the fortress of Willemstadt, Holland.

Recipient: Mid The Hon F. W. Aylmer.

17 Mar Boat Service 1794
28   29
(17 March 1794)
The boats from Admiral Jervis's flagship *Boyne* and the other ships captured the French frigate *Bienvenue* in Fort Royal Bay, Martinique.
HM Ships engaged: Flagship *Boyne*, and *Alarm, Asia, Assurance, Audacious, Aurora, Avenger, Beaulieu, Blonde, Dromedary, Experiment, Irresistible, Nautilus, Quebec, Rattlesnake, Roebuck, Rose, Santa Margarita, Seaflower, Spiteful, Tormentor, Ulysses, Vengeance, Venom, Vesuvius, Veteran Winchelsea, Woolwich, Zebra*.
The bars awarded were: *Veteran* -/6, *Boyne* -/4, *Irresistible* 1/3, *Quebec* -/3, *Vengeance* -/2, *Assurance* -/2, and one each to *Alarm, Blonde, Dromedary, Experiment, Nautilus, Rose, Ulysses* and *Vesuvius*.

29 May Boat Service 1797
2   3
(29 May 1797)
The boats of the *Minerve* and *Lively* captured the small French brig *Mutine* at anchor in Santa Cruz Bay.

Recipients: HMS *Minerve*—Lieut W. H. Gage, RN; Act Lieut T. J. Maling, RN; AB A. B. Blackmore. *Lively* (nil).

	No of HM Ships Engaged	No of Bars Issued

9 June Boat Service 1799

	1	4

(9 June 1799)

For the action in which boats from the *Success* captured a Spanish polacca, a small three-masted vessel common to the Mediterranean, in La Selva Harbour, NE Spain.

Recipients: Lieut G. Stupart, RN; Master's Mate J. Gregory; Ord Geo. Harding; Pte Edward Smith, RM.

20 Dec Boat Service 1799

	2	3

(21 December 1799)

The boats of the *Queen Charlotte* and *Emerald* recaptured the British ship *Lady Nelson* off Cabitra. The *Lady Nelson* had been previously captured by 3 French privateers.

Recipients: From *Queen Charlotte*, 2nd Lieuts W. Ferguson and T. Peebles, RM; AB Joseph Perkins.

29 July Boat Service 1800

	2	4

(29 July 1800)

The boats from the *Viper*, *Impetueux* and *Amethyst* captured the French brig *Cerbere* in Port St Louis.

Recipients: *Impetueux* (3) Master's Mate Nicholas L. Pateshall, Mid Henry Hart and LM Hugh Dunn. *Viper* (1) Mid Silas H. Paddon.

29 Aug Boat Service 1800

	9	25

(30 August 1800)

Twenty boats from the *Amelia*, *Amethyst*, *Brilliant*, *Courageux*, *Cynthia*, *Impetueux*, *London*, *Renown* and *Stag* attacked and captured the French privateer *Guepe* off Vigo.

27 Oct Boat Service 1800

	1	5

(28 October 1800)

Three boats from HMS *Phaeton* captured the Spanish polacca *San Josef* in Fuengirola Harbour, near Malaga.

Recipients: Lieut Francis Beaufort, RN (of windscale repute); 2nd Lieut D. Campbell, RM; Gnr E. Deagon; Master's Mate A. B. P. P. Hamilton; AB John Sherrard.

21 July Boat Service 1801

	5	7

(22 July 1801)

The boats from the *Beaulieu*, *Doris*, *Robust*, *Uranie*, and *Ville de Paris*, captured the French corvette *Chevrette* in Camaret Bay. Of the fifteen boats which left the warships with 280 men, only nine, under Lieutenant Maxwell, actually took part in the attack.

Recipients: HMS *Beaulieu* (1)—Pte Wm. Beck, RM; HMS *Doris* (3)—Capt Edward Boxer, RN; Master's Mate J. Clephan; Sgt John Inch, RM. HMS *Uranie* (3)—Yeoman of Sheets J. Morice; ABs J. Barry and R. Biggins.

27 June Boat Service 1803

	1	5

(28 June 1803)

Two boats from HMS *Loire* captured the French brig *Venteux* off the Isle de Bas.

Recipients: Lieut F. Temple, RN; Mid G. Ferguson; ABs James Cameron and R. Whitaker; Clerk Thomas Bastin.

4 Nov Boat Service 1803

	1	1

(4 November 1803)

A boat from the *Blanche* captured the French schooner *Voltigeuse*, off St Domingo.

Recipient: Mid Maurice F. F. Berkeley.

4 Feb Boat Service 1804

	1	10

(4 February 1804)

Four boats from the *Centaur* captured the French brig *Curieux* in Fort Royal Bay, Martinique.

Recipients: Carpenter's Crew John Messervey; ABs Joseph Edwards and Henry Manning; Ords Jeremia Dobson, John James and George Warner; Boy Benjamin Windsor; Ptes Joseph Backhouse, Richard Church and Robert Cockburn, RM.

4 June Boat Service 1805

	1	10

(4 June 1805)

The boats from the *Loire* landed and demolished some forts at Muros, near Cape Finisterre, where the garrison commander and about one hundred men surrendered.

Recipients: Lieut Charles Bertram, RN; Lieut Joseph Douglas, RM; Mid Richard Connor; Vol 1st Class John McKillop, Edward Saurin; AB James Cameron, Richard Collins and Richard Whitaker; Ord John Southern; Clerk Thos. Bastin (see bar for Boat Services, 27th June, 1803).

16 July Boat Service 1806

	9	51

(16 July 1806)

Twelve boats from HMS *Achille, Centaur, Conqueror, Indefatigable, Iris, Monarch, Polyphemus, Prince of Wales* and *Revenge* cut out two French corvettes in the River Gironde. The only casualties were suffered by the crew of the *Revenge*.
The number of awards to each ship was as follows: HMS *Achille* -/3, *Centaur* 1/10, *Conqueror* 1/4, *Indefatigable* 1/3, *Iris* -/3, *Monarch* 1/11, *Polyphemus* 1/5, *Prince of Wales* -/4, *Revenge* 1/2.
VANOR (1) LM J. Conway *Revenge*.

2 Jan Boat Service 1807

	1	3

(2 January 1807)

The boats of HMS *Cerberus* captured two French privateers in St Pierre Harbour, Martinique.

Recipients: Lieut W. Coote, RN; Mid G. Sayer and Dmr T. Gilmore, RM.

21 Jan Boat Service 1807

	1	8

(21 January 1807)

The boats from the *Galatea* fought the French corvette *Lynx* off Caracas, Venezuela.

No of HM Ships Engaged	No of Bars Issued	

Recipients: AB Wm. Mills,** Jas. McCarthy,** and John Norris**; LM Benjamin Rouse, Wm. Howard and Caulker Thomas Burnett; Ptes James Williams and M. L. Browning, RM.

**Had joined from HMS *Diamond Rock*—see Note to Zebra 17 March 1794. It is still the custom to pipe *'Diamond Rock'* when passing as she was never officially decommissioned.

19 April Boat Service 1807

1	Nil
(20 April 1807)	

The boats of the *Richmond* captured the small Spanish privateer *Galliard* in Paderneira Harbour, Portugal.

13 Feb Boat Service 1808

1	2
(14 February 1808)	

Two boats from the *Confiance* captured the French gunboat *Canonnier* in the mouth of the River Tagus.

Recipients: Surgeon David Lewis; Yeo of Sheets John Blackman.

10 July Boat Service 1808

1	8
(10 July 1808)	

The boats of the *Porcupine* captured an armed merchant vessel off Port d'Anzio. This is the same Anzio which became famous for its beach-head in the Second World War. It is about thirty miles south along the coast from the mouth of the Tiber, on which Rome stands. The merchantman was lying under the protection of the batteries of Mount Circio and guarded by two gunboats.

Recipients: Master H. Smartley; Master's Mate H. Parry; Clerk G. Anderson; Vol 1st Class C. J. Adams; AB John Campbell; LM G. D. Lane; Pte Thos. Townsend, RM; Boy Francis Johns.

11 Aug Boat Service 1808

3	15
(9 August 1808)	

The boats of HMS *Brunswick*, *Edgar* and *Superb* under Captain J. Macnamara of the *Edgar* entered Nyborg Harbour in the Baltic and captured the small Danish brig *Fama*.
The number of bars awarded were: *Brunswick* 1/1, *Edgar* 1/7, *Superb* 2/3.
VANOR (2) Mids G. Raymond and H. E. Temple *Edgar*.

28 Nov Boat Service 1808

1	2
(29 November 1808)	

Three boats from HMS *Heureux* captured two French vessels in Mahault Harbour, Guadaloupe.

Recipients: Lieut D. Lawrence, RN, and Carpenter J. Milne.

7 July Boat Service 1809

4	34
(7 July 1809)	

Seventeen boats containing 270 men from HMS *Bellerophon*, *Implacable*, *Melpomene* and *Prometheus* attacked eight Russian gunboats off Percola Point in the Baro Sound, off Finland. The number of bars awarded to each ship were: *Bellerophon* 4/8, *Implacable* 2/14, *Melpomene* -/5, *Prometheus* -/1.
VANOR (1) Act 1st Lieut J. T. Cracknell, *Implacable*.

14 July Boat Service 1809

1	7
(16 July 1809)	

The boats of the *Scout* stormed and captured the batteries commanding the mouth of the River Rhone.

Recipients: Lieut John Farrant, RN; Mid John Adams; Capt of Foretop Thos. Howard; Carpenter Robert Blackmore; AB's Thomas Atkins, Philip Brown; Pte James Houlder, RM.

25 July Boat Service 1809

1	Nil
(26 July 1809)	

Two separate actions were commemorated by a clasp of this date. No applicants claimed for this affair which involved the cutting out and capture of a French cutter and a schooner in St Marie Bay, Guadaloupe, by boats from HMS *Fawn*.

25 July Boat Service 1809

4	36
(25 July 1809)	

Seventeen boats from HMS *Cerberus*, *Minotaur*, *Princess Caroline* and *Prometheus* attacked four Russian gunboats at Frederikshavn in the Gulf of Finland. The numbers of bars awarded to each ship were: *Cerberus* 2/1, *Minotaur* 3/9, *Princess Caroline* 3/14 and *Prometheus* 1/3.

27 July Boat Service 1809

5	10
(27 July 1809)	

This bar was awarded for the attack on French troops and destruction of the forts at Gessendorf, near Cuxhaven, by the boats from HMS *L'Aimable*, *Briseis*, *Ephira*, *Mosquito* and *Pincher*.

Recipients: HMS *L'Aimable* (2)—Lieuts John Reeve, RN; A. M. Hawkins, RN. HMS *Briseis* (2)—Lieut Geo. Welsh, RN; Surgeon Wm. Hy. Banks. HMS *Ephira* (1)—Comdr Geo. Ed. Watts. HMS *Mosquito* (2)—AB Edward Frost and Pte Wm. Bird, RM; HMS *Pincher* (2)—Lt Comdr Samuel Burgess and Mid R. E. Cotgrave.

29 July Boat Service 1809

3	11
(29 July 1809)	

The boats from the *Acorn*, *Bustard* and *Excellent* entered Duino Harbour, near Trieste, and attacked the batteries covering the harbour. They also captured several fully laden merchant ships which had just arrived in convoy.

Recipients: HMS *Bustard* (7)—Comdr J. D. Markland, RN; Lieut John Hilton, RN; Purser James Wise; Master Mate Samuel Laston; Ord Wm. Richards; Pte Thos. Sainsbury, RM; and Wm. Wolfe. HMS *Excellent* (4)—Lieut John Harper, RN; Mids James John Foord and Wm. Prowse; Pte Thos. How, RM.

	No of HM Ships Engaged	No of Bars Issued

28 Aug Boat Service 1809

1   15

(27 August 1809)

The awards were given to the crew of the boats of HMS *Amphion* who stormed a battery at the mouth of the Piave, in the Adriatic, and demolished the guns and also captured six Italian gunboats at Cortelazzo.

Recipients: Lieuts C. G. R. Phillpott, Wm. Slaughter; Surgeon John Angas; Mids Charles Bruce, Chas. H. Kempthorn, Chas. Henry Ross and Joseph Gape. Lieut Thomas Moore, RM; Master's Mates John W. Dallings and Thomas Boardman. Capt of Foc'sle Francis Blyth; Yeo of Sheets David Buchanan; Ord John Bailey; LM Wm. Whisker; Pte George Weston, RM.

1 Nov Boat Service 1809

8   110

(1 November 1809)

Boats from the *Apollo, Cumberland, Philomel, Scout, Tigre, Topaze, Tuscan* and *Volontaire* attacked a convoy in Rosas Bay, off the extreme north-east coast of Spain. The convoy consisted of five warships and seven merchant vessels all of which were destroyed (Lieutenant J. Tailour, RN). This is a rare bar in spite of the number issued.
The number of bars awarded to each ship was: *Apollo* 3/10, *Cumberland* 3/15, *Philomel* 3/2, *Scout* 2/3, *Tigre* 11/19, *Topaze* 4/17, *Tuscan* 1/3, *Volontaire* 3/9. In addition to these, Vol John McDougall and Lieut Wm. Waldegrave of HMS *Ville de Paris* were awarded this bar.

13 Dec Boat Service 1809

5   8

(12 December 1809)

Boats from the *Achates, Attentive, Bacchus, Pultusk* and *Thetis* captured the French corvette *Nisus* in Hayes Harbour, Guadaloupe.

Recipients: HMS *Achates* (1)—Comdr Thomas Pinto, RN; HMS *Attentive* (2)—AB John Ross; Ord Alexander Underhill. HMS *Bacchus* (1)—Mid William Hole. HMS *Pultusk* (1)—Lieut John Davis Mercer, RN. HMS *Thetis* (3)—2nd Lieut Jervis Cooke, RM; Purser Beniamin Soden; Boatswain Daniel Murrey.
VANOR (1) 2nd Lieut Geo. Ruel, RM, HMS *Thetis*.

13 Feb Boat Service 1810

3   20

(13 February 1810)

Three boats from HMS *Christian VII*, three from HMS *Armide* and two from HMS *Seine* destroyed three French ships aground off La Rochelle in the Basque Roads.

Recipients: HMS *Christian VII* 4/8, *Armide* 4/4, *Seine* Nil.

1 May Boat Service 1810

1   15

(1 May 1810)

A landing party 105 strong from HMS *Néréide* went ashore at Jacotel, in the Bay of Biscay, and destroyed a battery. They then captured a French merchant ship and sailed it out of the harbour.

	No of HM Ships Engaged	No of Bars Issued

28 June Boat Service 1810

3   25

(29 June 1810)

Boats from the *Active, Amphion,* and *Cerberus* destroyed stores and captured twenty vessels in Grado Harbour, north-east of Venice.

Recipients: *Active* 5/5, *Amphion* 5/6, *Cerberus* 1/3.
VANOR (2) LM Geo Christie; Capt after Guard, Evan Davies.

27 Sep Boat Service 1810

3   33

(28 September 1810)

Boats from the *Armide, Caledonia* and *Valiant* captured two French brigs off Pointe du Ché, in the Basque Roads.

Recipients: HMS *Armide* 2/3, HMS *Caledonia* 9/9 and HMS *Valiant* 3/7.
VANOR (3) Lieut W. Kelly *Caledonia*, Lieut J. Phepoe *Armide*, Mid E. Pope *Valiant*.

4 Nov Boat Service 1810

1   1

(4 November 1810)

Boats from HMS *Blossom* captured the small Spanish privateer *Caesar* off Cape Sicie, S. W. Toulon.

Recipient: Ord Jamus Barrington

23 Nov Boat Service 1810

24★   40

(23 November 1810)

The boats of Rear-Admiral Sir R. Keat's squadron, under command of Captain R. Hall, attacked the French fleet lying off Point St Mary during the siege of Cadiz by the French.
The siege lasted from 1810 to 1812. It was not until after Wellington's defeat of Marshall Marmont at Salamanca on 22nd July, 1812, and his subsequent entry into Madrid, that Napoleon, already heavily engaged in eastern Europe, decided to withdraw from southern Spain.
Historians are inclined to lay emphasis on the parts played by the boats of HMS *Devastation, Aetna* and *Milford*, though it has been impossible to trace any award of medals to the first named. Captain George Landmann, RE, received the NGS Medal with this bar for his service on HMS *Milford*. HMS *Achille* 1/-, *Aetna* -/3, *Alfred* -/2, *Atlas* -/3, *Colossus* 2/-, Gunboat *Flotilla* 4/-, *Hardy* 1/1, *Hound* -/2, *Milford* 4/5, *Norge* 4/3, *Revenge* 1/1, *Thunder* 1/1, and *Mors Aut Gloria* 1/-.

24 Dec Boat Service 1810

1   6

(24 December 1810)

Boats from HMS *Diana* completed the destruction of the French frigate *Elisa* which was ashore in the La Hogue Roads.

Recipients: Mid Julius J. F. Newell; Master's Mate John B. Knocker; Vol 1st Class Wm. Maxwell; Ship's Cpl George White; Ptes Noah Brittal and Ambrose Brown, RM.

---

*Excluding gunboats.

	No of HM Ships Engaged	No of Bars Issued

4 May Boat Service 1811

	2	10

(5 May 1811)

Seamen and marines from the *Alceste* and *Belle Poule* destroyed a French brig in Parenzo Harbour, off Istria in the north-east Adriatic. It is interesting to note that although over 300 men took part only 10 bars were claimed.

Recipients: HMS *Alceste* (3)—Mid John King and Chas. Croker; LM P. Stanbury. HMS *Belle Poule* (7)—Lieut Robert B. Boardman, RN; Mid Chas. M. Chapman, ABs Arthur Gros, Geo. Belly; Ord Geo. Rowcliffe; Ptes Robert Woodward and James Bowden, RM.

30 July Boat Service 1811

	1	4

(30 July 1811)

Capture of Fort Marrack, Java by two boats of *Minden*.

Recipients: Lieut Edmund Lyons, RN*; Qr Gnr Wm. Ellmore; ABs Stephen Roberts and Wm. Scott.

2 Aug Boat Service 1811

	6	9

(3 August 1811)

Ten boats containing 117 men from HMS *Alert, Exertion, Princess Augusta, Quebec, Raven* and *Redbreast* entered the River Jade, in north Germany, and captured four French gunboats at Nordeney.

Recipients: HMS *Alert* (1)—Pte John Smith, RM; HMS *Exertion* (1)—Sub Lieut Thomas Hare, RN; HMS *Princess Augusta* (2)—ABs Edward Wright (or Richmond?), Wm. Russel. HMS *Quebec* (4)—Lieut Chas. Wolrige, RN; Master's Mate Robert Cock; LM Benjamin Hawkins; Pte John Tate, RM; HMS *Raven* (1)—Carpenter's Crew Wm. Clark.

20 Sep Boat Service 1811

	1	6

(2 September 1811)

Boats from HMS *Victory* entered Wingo Sound, in the Baltic, where they captured and brought out two Danish privateers.

Recipients: Lieut David L. St Clair; Mid Edward Purcell; Qtr Gnr Gabriel Land; AB Joseph Roston; Ptes John Bason, Charles Mountford, RM.

4 Dec Boat Service 1811

	1	19

(4 December 1811)

For the capture of the French brig *Languedoc* off Bastia, on the north-east coast of Corsica, by boats from HMS *Sultan*.

4 April Boat Service 1812

	1	4

(4 April 1812)

For the capture of the French xebec *Martinet* off Cape de Gatt, south-east Spain, by the boats of HMS *Maidstone*.

Recipients: Master's Mate Wm. Caswell, RN; Lieut A. C. Rea, RM; Ord George Lightbody, Pte Wm. Smith, RM.

*Later Naval C-in-C. Crimea

1 & 18 Sep Boat Service 1812

	1	21

(1 September 1812)

A party of sixty-five men from HMS *Bacchante* cut out and captured two French gun-boats, the xebec *Tisiphone* and seven vessels of a convoy.

17 Sep Boat Service 1812

	1	11

(17 September 1812)

Boats from HMS *Eagle* attacked coastal trading vessels in the mouth of the River Po in northern Italy, capturing twenty-one of them.

Recipients: Lieut B. M. Festing, RN; 2nd Lieut S. Lloyd, RM; Mate Chas. Moore; Qr Mr Jas. Nicholson; Caulker's Mate Charles Clarke; LM Robert Bines; Ord Chas. Hussey; ABs Joseph Cemmett, and Samuel Seymour; Ptes John Good and Richard Heine.

29 Sep Boat Service 1812

	2	25

(29 September 1812)

A small party from HMS *Aboukir, Ranger* and gun-boats attacked the booms and batteries guarding Mittau in the Gulf of Riga, Estonia.

Recipients: HMS *Aboukir* 7/18, Gun-boats -/-.

6 Jan Boat Service 1813

	2	26

(6 January 1813)

Boats from the *Bacchante* and *Weazle* attacked French gunboats in Otranto Harbour.

Recipients: *Bacchante* 5/19, *Weazle* -/2.

21 March Boat Service 1813

	2	3

(21 March 1813)

Boats from the *Blazer* and *Brevdageren* went up the Elbe and captured two Danish gunboats.

Recipients: HMS *Blazer*—Pte Charles Whiteman, RM; HMS *Brevdageren*—Mid Frederick Devon; Asst Surgeon Thos. Davies.

29 April Boat Service 1813

	1	2

(29 April 1813)

Boats from the *Orpheus* under Lieutenant Dance burnt the American ship *Wampoe** off the North American coast.

Recipients: Lieut W. F. Dance, RN; Mid G. G. MacDonald.

---

*The *Wampoe* was a 'Letter of Marque' and is quoted in some books as Danish, which is probably wrong.

As this is the only occasion on which this term has been listed in actions dealing with the award of medals, perhaps the following account may be interesting.

A 'Letter of Marque' is a letter of authority from the owner's government permitting the captain of a private ship to act as a commerce raider against the declared enemy of the government concerned. The crew did not wear uniform and neither was the ship compelled to fly its colours during the engagement, so that it really amounted to a form of licensed piracy. This form of privateering was very prevalent during the early seventeenth century, the Spaniards making particular use of it in their war with Holland.

These 'letters' were purchased from the government by the owner for £3,000

	No of HM Ships Engaged	No of Bars Issued

29 April Boat Service 1813
Ap & May Boat Service 1813

| | 9 | 57 |

(29 April and 3 May 1813) This bar was given for two separate actions fought on 29th April and 3rd May, both up the Elk river in Chesapeake Bay. The same landing parties under the personal command of Rear-Admiral Sir George Cockburn were engaged in each action. 29th April, 1813: The boats from HMS *Dolphin* 1/-, *Dragon* 4/10, *Fantome* 3/2, *Highflyer* -/2, *Maidstone* 1/3, *Marlborough* 6/16, *Mohawk* 2/-, *Racer* -/1, and *Statira* 2/5 went up the river to destroy five American ships and stores. This took until the early hours of the morning of 3rd May.
3rd May, 1813: On the way back to their ships they were fired on by a battery on the banks of the river, so they landed and destroyed it.
Two differently dated bars were issued, early applicants receiving one dated '29 April' whilst later ones were engraved 'AP and MAY'. The change took place probably to avoid confusion with the previous Boat Service bar.

2 May Boat Service 1813

| | 4 | 48 |

(2 May 1813) One hundred marines under Captain M. Ennis, RM, from HMS *Redwing, Repulse, Volontaire* and *Undaunted* landed in the small harbour of Morgiou, near Toulon, and destroyed a battery. In the meantime, another party captured some laden merchant-ships which they sailed out of the harbour (Lieutenant Isaac Shaw).

Recipients: HMS *Redwing* 3/1, *Repulse* 2/14, *Volontaire* 4/9, *Undaunted* 6/9.

8 April Boat Service 1814

| | 4 | 24 |

(8 April 1814) This bar was given for the destruction of twenty-seven vessels and a considerable quantity of stores up the Connecticut River by men from HMS *Boxer, Endymion, Hogue* and *Maidstone*.

Recipients: HMS *Boxer* 1/1, *Hogue* 3/12, *Maidstone* 2/3, *Endymion* 2/-.

24 May Boat Service 1814

| | 1 | 12 |

(25 May 1814) The boats from HMS *Elizabeth* under Lieutenant M. Roberts captured the French ship *L'Aigle* off Vide, in Corfu. Some histories quote this action as having been fought on 29th April, 1814.

Recipients: Lieut Mitchell Roberts, RN; Mid Edwin Lipscomb; Master's Mate

Richard Keays; Carpenter's Crew Daniel McAdam; Ords John Evans, Henry Taylor; LMs Wm. Aaron, John Savory, John Stoddard (who also got the bars for Trafalgar and St. Domingo); Henry Towning; AB Thos. Robinson; and Pte John Collier, RM.

3 & 6 Sep Boat Service 1814

| | 1 | 1 |

(3 and 6 September 1814) The only bar issued was awarded to Lieutenant Andrew Bulger of the Royal Newfoundland Fencible Infantry, which was being blockaded on Lake Huron. The boats from HMS *Nancy* assisted the Regiment to destroy the American schooners *Tigress* and *Scorpion*, and were under the command of Lieutenant Miller Worsley. (Lieutenant Bulger also received the MGS Medal with bars for Fort Detroit and Chrystler's Farm.)

14 Dec Boat Service 1814

| | 22 | 205 |

(14 Dec 1814) This action, which took place off New Orleans, was the largest-scale boat action for which awards were given. Prior to capturing the town of New Orleans, the guard-ships had to be destroyed. A fleet of ships' boats, all under the command of Captain Nicholas Lockyer, carrying about a thousand men were dispatched by Admiral Cochrane to do the job. By capturing one of the enemy's guard ships and using it against the others they eventually destroyed them all.
The boats came from Admiral Cochrane's flagship *Tonnant* 10/26, and the *Alceste* -/8, *Armide* 2/4, *Asia* 1/4, *Bedford* 3/16, *Belle Poule* -/1, *Carron* -/1, *Cydnus* 3/6, *Diomede* -/5, *Gorgon* -/1, *Hydra* -/1, *Meteor* 2/2, *Norge* 2/16, *Ramillies* 7/17, *Regulus* -/2, *Royal Oak* 4/19, *Seahorse* 3/18, *Sophie* -/11, *Traave* -/6, *Weser* -/2 and unknown ships -/2.
Lieutenant de Lacy Evans of the 3rd (King's Own) Light Dragoons received the NGS Medal with this bar for service on HMS *Meteor*—he was later to command The British Legion in the Carlist War (1835-40).

---

when his ship had a crew of over 150 men. Those with smaller crews paid half this sum. The owner reimbursed himself by capturing and bringing into port as many prizes as he could, because he received a percentage of the subsequent sale of his prize and her cargo.

The European powers decided to abolish privateering in 1856, but the Americans refused to agree unless the right of blockade was also abolished. The system was in use during the American Civil War under the authority of the President of the Southern Confederacy, Jefferson Davies. Abraham Lincoln, however, declared it to be piracy and curiously, on the 19th April, 1861, ordered

the blockade of the southern ports.

One has been unable to trace the earliest use of these letters, but probably some similar system was used as far back as the thirteenth century. There was a very thin line between what we would now call the armed merchantman and the licensed pirate. As long as somebody was having a crack at the actual, or supposed enemy his authority for doing so does not appear to have been very closely investigated!

Privateering and the use of 'Letters of Marque' were universally abolished in 1898.

This concludes the summary of all the bars awarded with the NGS Medal, and it gives ample proof, though none is needed, of the extraordinary versatility of the Navy. A study of the brief descriptions will show that the destruction of any dreams of world conquest or a shore battery were all in a day's work.

When reading the full account of all the actions mentioned, one is amazed at the hardships which the sailors of those days had to endure. One reads not once, but scores of times, of men with the most terrible wounds undergoing amputations without any anæsthetic, of being on deck when their ship has received broadsides at pistol or even half pistol range. They cleared away broken masts and rigging within a few yards of the enemy. No finer example of the range at which these fights took place can be given than the reminder that the greatest Admiral in British history, in the most important naval action in which the nation has ever been involved, received his mortal wound from a musket-ball fired from the mizen-top of one of the enemy's ships.

Reading these accounts one realizes that even today we are using, or have used, many ideas which are only elaborations of what these men were using. They had their hand grenades, incendiary shells, landing barges, convoys, rockets and many other ideas which we are inclined to think originated in the 1914-1918 or 1939-1945 wars.

55 The 'Endymion' Crook, or Midshipmen's Badge 1815

General   A silver crook with a ring for suspension, not hallmarked.
Obverse   The letters 'ENDYMION' in raised characters.
Reverse   Plain
Naming   Plain or engraved. Example known engraved to 'A Boyter' (afterwards Lieut Alex Boyter) ex Payne collection.

Awarded as a badge of distinction to the midshipmen of HMS *'Endymion'* after the capture of the American frigate *'President'* on 15th January 1815 by Captain Henry Hope. (See page 56).

56 St. Jean D'Acre Medal 1840

Obverse   The Turkish flag flying over the Fortress of Acre, six stars and an Arabic inscription 'The country of Syria and the fortress of Acre, 1256, AH'.
Reverse   The Sultan's cypher within a laurel wreath.
Size   29.5mm. diameter
Metal   Gold, silver and bronze
Ribbon   28mm wide, pink with white edges.
Naming   The medals were issued unnamed.

For the capture of Acre and services along the Syrian Coast in 1840. The Sultan of Turkey awarded a medal which was given in gold to Naval Captains and Field Officers and above, in silver to all other officers and warrant officers, and bronze to seamen, marines and soldiers. It was awarded to all who received the NGS bar for Syria except for those who served on board the *Dido, Fury* and *Lady Franklin*—a distinction for which one is unable to account. (See page 57).

<h2>57 Gold Collar and Cross</h2>

The special gold collar and cross awarded to the Duke of Wellington and Marshal Viscount Beresford.

a) Duke of Wellington's Collar

Composed of alternate gold lions and oval medallions, each approximately 5cm wide, connected together by a double gold chain. The medallions have the Union Badge in enamels, surrounded by a gold oak wreath. Across the centre of the Badge is the name of a battle or siege in which the Duke had been engaged, these being: Ciudad Rodrigo, Badajoz, Salamanca, Vittoria, Toulouse, Pyrenees, Nivelle, Orthes, Nive and Waterloo. Below the Waterloo medallion hangs a royal crown which is suspended by two gold chains. Suspended from the crown is the gold cross.

Cross

Gold pattée cross with ornamental borders approximately 6.5cm across, generally similar in design to the Army Gold Cross (page 65). In the centre, on one side a winged figure of Victory with outstretched arms with a laurel wreath in each hand, and on the other side a lion. On the four limbs of the Cross on the side bearing the figure of Victory, are the names of the following actions: Roleia and Vimiera, Talavera, Busaco and Fuentes d'Onor.

Designer	Possibly Sir George Nayler.
Manufacturer	Rundell and Bridge of London.
Naming	On the edges of the 'east, south and west' limbs of the Cross is the inscription, 'Field Marshal Arthur Duke of Wellington.'

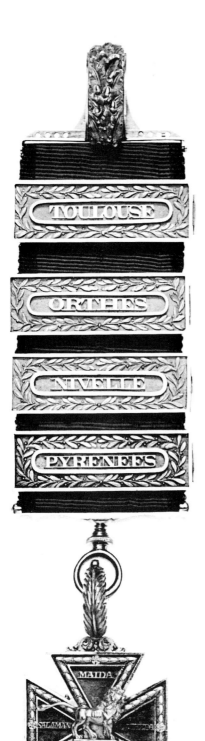

b) Viscount Beresford's Collar and Cross

Believed to be similar to that of the Duke's except for the following points:

a) The enamelled medallions of the collar are surrounded by a gold laurel wreath.

b) As Viscount Beresford was not present at Waterloo, in place of the 'Waterloo' medallion is a royal crown from which the gold cross was suspended.

The gold Collar and Cross were bestowed by King George IV in about the year 1827. That of the Duke of Wellington's is to be found with his other insignia at Apsley House, London. The present whereabouts of Viscount Beresford's Collar and Cross in unknown and the points of difference noted above are based on the portrait by Sir William Beechey RA of Beresford wearing the insignia.

58 *Army Gold Cross*

Obverse	A Pattée cross having bright gold raised double borders between which is a border of laurel. In the centre in bold relief a lion is standing facing to the right. On each of the four arms is the name of a battle or siege, the first action being on the top division.
Reverse	As above
Size	38.5mm square
Ribbon	44mm. wide, crimson with dark blue edges
Suspension	A gold ring adorned with oak leaves and acorns through which the ribbon passes, this is joined to a plain gold ring which swivels from a straight suspender. Worn by General Officers around the neck.
Designer	T. Wyon, Junior
Naming	The name and rank of the recipient are engraved on the edges of three of the arms in capital letters.
Bars issued	Awarded when the recipient was present at more than four actions. Rectangular, having bright gold raised double borders between which is a border of laurel. The centre contains the name of the battle in bright gold raised letters. Placed on the neck ribbon without being connected by rivets.

The total number of Crosses issued was 163. The greatest number of bars issued with any one Cross was nine, this being awarded to the Duke of Wellington.

Cross only	61
Cross and one bar	46
Cross and two bars	18
Cross and three bars	17
Cross and four bars	8
Cross and five bars	7
Cross and six bars	3
Cross and seven bars	2
Cross and nine bars	1

The following extracts from the *London Gazette* dated 7th October, 1813, make the reason for, and descriptions as to their recipients, so clear that no further amplification is necessary.

HORSE GUARDS, *7th Oct, 1813.*

'Whereas considerable inconvenience having been found to attend the increased number of medals that have been issued in commemoration of the brilliant and distinguished events . . . the Prince Regent has been pleased to command, in the name and on the behalf of His Majesty, that the following regulations shall be adopted in the grant and circulation of such marks of distinction, namely:

1 That one medal only shall be borne by each officer recommended for such distinction.

2 That for the second and third events, which may be subsequently commemorated in like manner, each individual recommended to bear the distinction, shall carry a gold clasp attached to the ribbon to which the medal is suspended, and inscribed with the name of the battle, or siege, to which it relates.

3 That upon a claim being admitted to a fourth mark of distinction, a cross shall be borne by each officer, with the names of the four battles, or sieges, respectively inscribed thereupon; and to be worn in substitution of the distinctions previously granted to such individuals.

4 Upon each occasion of a similar nature, that may occur subsequently to the grant of a cross, the clasp shall again be issued to those who have a claim to the additional distinction, to be borne on the ribbon to which the cross is suspended, in the same manner as described in No. 2 of these regulations.'

The regulations concerning the distribution of those medals were as follows:

'1 That no general, or other officer, shall be considered entitled to receive them, unless he has been personally and particularly engaged upon those occasions of great importance and peculiar brilliancy, in commemoration of which the Prince Regent, in the name and on behalf of His Majesty, may be graciously pleased to bestow such marks of distinction.

2 That no officer shall be considered a candidate for the medal, or badge except under the special selection and report of the Commander of the Forces on the spot, as having merited the distinction by conspicuous services.

3 That the Commander of the Forces shall transmit to the Commander-in-Chief returns signed by himself, specifying the names and ranks of those officers whom he shall have selected as particularly deserving.

4 The Commander of the Forces in making the selection, shall restrict his choice to the undermentioned ranks, namely: General Officers; Commanding Officers of Brigades; Commanding Officers of Artillery, or Engineers; Adjutant General; and Quartermaster General; Deputies of Adjutant General; and Quartermaster General having the rank of Field Officers; Assistants Adjutant and Quartermaster General, having the rank of Field Officers, and being at the head of the Staff with a detached corps, or distinct division of the army; Military Secretary, having the rank of Field Officer; Commanding Officers of Battalions, or corps equivalent thereto; and officers who may have succeeded to the actual command during the engagement in consequence of, the death or removal of the original commanding officer.'

'The Prince Regent is therefore graciously pleased to command, in the name and on behalf of His Majesty, that in commemoration of the brilliant victories attained by His Majesty's arms in the battle of Roleia and Vimiera, Corunna, Talavera de le Reyna, Busaco, Barossa, Fuentes d'Onor, Albuhera, and Salamanca, and in the assaults and captures of Ciudad Rodrigo and Badajoz, the officers of the army, present on those occasions, shall enjoy the privilege of bearing badges of distinction and His Royal Highness having approved of the crosses, medals and clasps, which have been prepared, is pleased to command that they shall be worn by the general officers, suspended by a ribbon of the same colour as their sash, with a blue edge, round the neck; and by the commanding officers of battalions, or corps equivalent thereto, and officers who may have succeeded to the actual command during the engagement, the chiefs of military departments and their deputies and assistants, (having the rank of field officers), and such other officers as may be specially recommended, attached by a ribbon of the same description to the buttonhole of their uniform.'

'The Prince Regent is also pleased to command, in the name and on behalf of His Majesty, that those badges which would have been conferred upon the officers who have fallen at, or died since the above-named battles and sieges, shall, as a token of respect for their memories, be transmitted to their respective families.'

The point to note is that the crosses were only issued to those who would normally have become entitled to a gold medal and three bars. This means that the maximum number of bars to the gold medal was two. It is also interesting to note that this is the first occasion on which clasps are mentioned. They were worn so that the first battle commemorated was farthest from the cross/medal.

After the termination of the Peninsular War the conditions governing the awarding of the Order of the Bath were revised. The awarding of Gold Crosses and Medals was discontinued and those who would have received either a Gold Medal or Cross received one of the three classes into which that Order was subdivided in 1815. Those awarded a Cross, Large or Small Medal were not entitled to the appropriate bars on the Military General Service Medal.

59 *Army Large Gold Medal*

Obverse	A seated and helmeted figure of Britannia, who holds a laurel wreath in her right hand and a palm branch in her left, which is resting on a shield bearing the Union Crosses.
Reverse	The name of the battle for which it was awarded is engraved in the centre surrounded by a laurel wreath. The medal for Barrosa has the name of the battle embossed instead of engraved. The reason for this exception having been made cannot be traced.
Size	54mm diameter for issue to General Officers.
Ribbon	44mm. wide, crimson with dark blue edges
Suspension	A plain gold ring attached to the medal by a gold loop. Worn from the neck.
Designer	T. Wyon, Junior
Naming	The name and rank of the recipient are engraved around the edge in capital letters.
Bars issued	As described for the Gold Cross (page 65).

The medal is set in a gold frame, being glazed on both sides. The total number of medals issued was 85.

60 *Army Small Gold Medal*

Obverse	A seated and helmeted figure of Britannia, who holds a laurel wreath in her right hand and a palm branch in her left, which is resting on a shield bearing the Union Crosses.
Reverse	The name of the battle for which it was awarded is engraved in the centre surrounded by a laurel wreath. The medal for Barrosa has the name of the battle embossed instead of engraved. The reason for this exception having been made cannot be traced.
Size	33mm diameter. For issue to Field Officers.
Ribbon	44mm. wide, crimson with dark blue edges
Suspension	A triangular shaped gold swivel bar. Worn at the buttonhole.
Designer	T. Wyon, Junior
Naming	The name and rank of the recipient are engraved around the edge in capital letters.
Bars issued	As described for the Gold Cross (page 65).

The medal is set in a gold frame being glazed on both sides. The number of medals issued was 596.

The undermentioned gold awards were authorized:

Action	Small Medal	Bars	Large Medal	Bars	Cross	Bars
Albuhera	29	3	6	2	23	—
Badajoz	28	13	1	3	48	3
Barrosa	15	—	1	—	9	—
Benevente	1	—	—	—	—	—
Busaco	22	6	2	3	32	2
Chateauguay	2	—	—	—	—	—
Chrystler's Farm	6	1	—	—	—	—
Ciudad Rodrigo	11	5	1	2	22	1
Corunna	20	4	10	1	22	—
Fort Detroit	10	—	1	—	—	—
Fuentes d'Onor	21	8	1	4	32	1
Guadaloupe	8	7	6	4	3	—
Java	27	1	5	—	—	—
Maida	11	—	2	—	4	—
Martinique	18	1	9	—	5	2
Nive	34	28	2	5	53	39
Nivelle	30	13	—	1	69	30
Orthes	32	36	—	1	38	47
Pyrenees	18	24	1	3	61	18
Roleia	2	—	—	—	—	—
Roleia & Vimiera	18	—	5	—	9	—
Sahagun & Benevente	4	—	1	—	2	—
Salamanca	73	18	11	2	81	11
St. Sebastian	17	10	1	3	19	11
Talavera	36	5	13	1	23	1
Toulouse	21	30	—	—	22	50
Vimiera	9	—	2	1	1	—
Vittoria	73	24	7	7	99	21

The small gold medals awarded for North American actions 1812/14 were issued to:

Fort Detroit
Maj Gen Sir I. Brock (large gold medal). [Killed in 1812]; Maj P. L. Chambers CB, 41st Ft (Died in 1828); Maj M. C. Dixon RE; Col M. Elliott, Canadian Militia; Maj J. B. Glegg, Asst Adj Gen (Retired in 1836); Maj P. Latouche, 41st Ft; Capt A. Muir, 41st Ft (Retired in 1818); Lt Col R. Nichol, Qmtr Gen, Canadian Militia; Lt Col T. B. St George CB, KCH, Inspecting Field Officer (Died in 1836); Capt J. Tallon, 41st Ft (Retired in 1821); Lieut F. Troughton RA (Died in 1815).

Chateauguay
Lt Col G. MacDonell CB, Inspecting Field Officer, Canadian Militia, late 79th Ft; Lt Col C. Saluberry CB, 60th Ft.

Chrystler's Farm
Col M. Clifford CB, KH, 89th Ft (Died in 1837); Lt Col J. Harvey KCB, KCH, Dep Adj Gen (Died in 1852); Maj Gen F. G. Heriot KG, CB, Canadian Voltrs, late 49th Ft (Died in 1844); Lt Col H. G. Jackson RA (Died in 1849); Col J. W. Morrison CB, 44th Ft (Died in 1826); Lt Gen Sir T. Pearson CB, KCH, 85th Ft (Died in 1847), received gold medal for Albuhera with bar for Chrystler's Farm; Lt Col C. Plenderleath CB, 49th Ft.

61 *Military General Service Medal* 1793-1814

Obverse   The diademed head of Queen Victoria and legend 'VICTORIA REGINA' with the date '1848'.

Reverse   Queen Victoria standing on a dais about to place a laurel wreath on the Duke of Wellington, who is kneeling on his left knee. Beside the dais is a diminutive representation of the British Lion dormant. Around the top half of the circumference is the inscription 'TO THE BRITISH ARMY'. In the exergue are the dates '1793-1814' although the first action commemorated by a bar is Egypt 1801, it can only be presumed that the authorities had in mind earlier actions, hence the date 1793 in the exergue.

Size   36mm diameter

Ribbon   32mm wide crimson with 6mm wide dark blue borders

Suspension   By a plain straight swivelling suspender

Designer   W. Wyon, RA

Naming   In indented large roman capitals

Bars issued   Twenty-nine

This silver medal was authorized by a General Order dated 1st June, 1847, and issued in 1848—thirty-four years after the last battle it commemorates. For some inexplicable reason the medal is often referred to as the Peninsular Medal, even though the medal commemorates such places as Egypt, the East and West Indies, USA, etc. Personal application had to be made for the medals, and Carter, in his book *Medals of the British Army,* gives an amusing account of an old officer who had to refer to the records to see whether he was present at a particular action or not, 'having been in so many at such a distant date'.

Medals were awarded to the next-of-kin of those who applied for them but who died before the medals were issued.

There were about 25,650 applications for the medal, for which twenty-nine bars were awarded, fifteen being the most to any recipient. The bars are fixed in multiples of three where applicable.

There were two recipients of the medal with fifteen bars and eleven with fourteen, though in the latter case the medal roll only gives nine.

15 Bars	James Talbot, 45th Foot. Daniel Loochstadt, who appears on the roll of the 60th and King's German Legion.
14 Bars	John Hughes, RA George Legg, RA, who is credited with only thirteen bars on the medal roll. Sgt John Hardy, 7th Foot, who received bars for Martinique, Talavera, Busaco, Albuhera, Ciudad Rodrigo, Badajoz, Salamanca, Vittoria, Pyrenees, St Sebastian, Nivelle, Nive, Orthes, Toulouse. (His brothers, Corporal Peter Hardy and Private James Hardy, received the medal with thirteen bars. They were not present at the Battle of Talavera). Drum-Major John Green, 45th Foot Edwin Kean, 45th Foot James Nixon, 45th Foot Major James Campbell, 50th Foot Patrick Haggerty, 52nd Foot James Morris, 52nd Foot Lieutenant Sir J. A. Schoede, 60th Foot Sergeant Joseph Hindle, 95th Foot

The following table shows the approximate order of scarcity of the bars when awarded singly and in conjuction with others. The value of the medals is not, however, in the same order.

Single Bars	With two or more Bars
Benevente	Benevente
Roleia	Sahagun
Sahagun	Chrystler's Farm
Ciudad Rodrigo	Chateauguay
Nivelle	Sahagun and Benevente
Pyrenees	Fort Detroit
Sahagun and Benevente	Java
Orthes	Guadaloupe
St Sebastian	Maida
Busaco	Martinique
Vimiera	Barrosa
Albuhera	Roleia
Fuentes d'Onor	Egypt
Badajoz	Vimiera
Nive	Albuhera
Guadaloupe	St Sebastian
Chrystler's Farm	Fuentes d'Onor
Chateauguay	Ciudad Rodrigo
Martinique	Talavera
Fort Detroit	Badajoz
Barrosa	Busaco
Talavera	Corunna
Salamanca	Nive
Maida	Nivelle
Java	Orthes
Vittoria	Salamanca
Toulouse	Pyrenees
Egypt	Toulouse
Corunna	Vittoria

Officers and men received bars for actions when attached to other than their parent units, so that it is difficult to say to which the medal should be credited. The unit given on the medal is not consistently given as the first or last with which a man served although it is known for officer's medals to contain up to three different units and more than one rank on a medal.

Several officers were attached to the Portuguese Forces and received medals with a greater number of bars than normally awarded to members of their regiments.

The Peninsular War

Though twenty-nine bars were issued with the Military General Service Medal, only twenty-one of them were awarded for service in the above mentioned War. The historical reasons for the award of the other eight are given separately.

The cause of the War is to be found in the discontent in Portugal and Spain in the year 1808 and the rising of the Spaniards caused by the dislike of Napoleon, especially by the transference of his brother Joseph from Naples to Madrid. This was done, of course, to give Napoleon control of the Iberian Peninsula. Portugal was to all intents and purposes under his control by virtue of the fact that a French army, under Marshal Junot, occupied the country in considerable strength.

Space will not permit a discussion as to why British forces were sent out, so we must confine ourselves to a very brief statement of what happened after they arrived.

Two forces were dispatched under the supreme command of Sir Arthur Wellesley with a view to affording the Spanish and Portuguese nations every possible aid in 'throwing off the yoke of France', to quote the instructions received by Sir Arthur from the Duke of York.

The troops sailed from Cork on 10th July, 1808, arrived off Mondego Bay, about ninety miles to the north-west of Lisbon, on the 26th and started disembarkation on 1st August. Further reinforcements were sent which arrived on 20th August.

As soon as possible the advance inland commenced. The first encounter with the French occurred on 15th August at Lourinha, where General Laborde, commanding the French, had sited his outpost line to guard Lisbon. On 17th August Wellesley fought his first battle against the French at Rolica, as a result of which they were driven back towards Lisbon.

As further reinforcements were due to arrive at Maceira, about thirty miles north-west of Lisbon, Wellesley decided to wait until they had joined him before continuing his advance.

Marshal Junot, who had taken over command from Laborde, attacked Wellesley in his position around Vimiera on 21st August, but was heavily defeated. During the action Lieutenant General Sir Harry Burrard arrived, but did not take over command. The next day Sir Hew Dalrymple assumed command.

On 22nd August a treaty was signed with the French which was ratified on the 30th under the title of Convention of Cintra, by the terms of which Junot and the French army were to be evacuated from Portugal in British ships.

It is hardly to be wondered at that the authorities at home were somewhat puzzled to say the least, as to the reasons for such a pact so soon after two crushing defeats of the French, and Wellesley, Burrard and Dalrymple were ordered home to attend a court of inquiry. Sir John Moore was then given supreme command.

The French were evacuated from Portugal and landed in Brittany, whence they promptly crossed the Pyrenees and re-entered Spain from the north, having been rested and re-equipped and being resolved to do better next time!

Moore was left the almost impossible task of clearing the French out of Spain while having his hands tied by having to consider his forces 'an Auxiliary to the Spanish Forces to support the attempts of Napoleon to subjugate them, and should the Spanish Government appoint a Commander-in-Chief, he was to consider himself as under his command'. The Spaniards never did make an appointment and Napoleon was able to give instructions for the destruction of the isolated forces piecemeal.

The Spaniards, flushed by a victory under Castanos, at Baylen on 22nd July, 1808, not only resented but were almost hostile to the presence of British troops.

General Baird was ordered to land at Corunna in the extreme north-west of Spain, with instructions to march towards Madrid to make a junction with Sir John, who was receiving the most encouraging reports concerning the results of actions between the Spanish and French. The truth was that the Spanish had been heavily defeated, and instead of an unharassed meeting between himself and Baird he found that his total force of about 25,000 men was opposed to some 300,000 Frenchmen, the rigours of winter, the embarrassing presence of Spanish troops, and the complete apathy of the local population and government.

Sir John, realizing that far from being able to clear the French out of Spain, he would be lucky if his armies escaped annihilation, ordered a retreat towards Corunna, from which place the army could be re-embarked.

We cannot go into the interesting details of Napoleon's attempt to entice Moore to Madrid, so must concentrate on the retreat to Corunna and the attempts of Napoleon to prevent it.

On 21st December, 1808, the army halted at Sahagun, where a cavalry charge was made. A few days later another was made at Benevente. Luckily for Moore, Marshal Soult, to whom Napoleon had delegated the task of driving the British into the sea, made no determined attack on the retreating army and allowed it to concentrate at Lugo, outside Corunna, between 6th and 16th January, 1809.

On the 14th the fleet had arrived at Corunna to embark the army, but on the 17th the French attacked (during which Lieutenant-General Sir John Moore was killed), so that it was not until the 18th that the embarkation was completed. This ended the first phase of the Peninsular War.

The court of inquiry exonerated Wellesley and he was now appointed to command another army. This disembarked at Lisbon on 22nd April, 1809, and crossed the River Douro on 12th May. Soult was driven out of Oporto and up the valley of the Tagus to Talavera, where the French grouped their forces under Marshal Victor.

On the evening of 27th July the French attacked, but were defeated on the 28th after severe fighting during which the touch of humanity, that even the heat of battle cannot obliterate, showed itself. Between the contending armies was a small stream to which both sides went to draw water for their wounded and themselves; yes, and to exchange remarks and souvenirs in much the same way as happened in the 1914-18 War for no other reason than physical exhaustion and the mutual realization of the horrors and futility of human slaughter.

After the battle of Talavera, Wellesley was created a peer with the style of Lord Wellington of Wellington, in Somerset, and Talavera. Marshal Victor was given the title of Duke of Talavera by the French. It is a strange if not unique occurrence for commanders to take their titles from the place where they were opposed to each other.

The exhaustion and losses were such that Wellington could not take immediate advantage of his victory; in fact, he had to withdraw into Portugal.

In May 1810, Napoleon ordered Messéna to drive Wellington out of Portugal, but he remained completely inactive for some months before besieging the frontier fortress of Almeida. He started his advance on 15th August and by a lucky chance exploded the defenders' ammunition store. Wellington, who had moved up to help the garrison, realized that nothing could be done, so retired to the valley of the Mondego. Messéna remained inactive till the 15th September, when he advanced down the right bank of the river to where Wellington had taken up a strong position along the high ridge of the Sierra de Busaco.

Though the action that followed was an allied victory, it was fought as a delaying action to give the Portuguese inhabitants of the area time to get behind the prepared defences of Torres Vedras.

Once again Messéna was slow to follow up, thus giving the allies time to make an unhurried withdrawal to behind these thirty miles of prepared positions, where they spent the period from September, 1810, to March, 1811, during which the weather and conditions in the area made all but a few sporadic engagements impossible.

The scene now shifts to the South of Spain to Barrosa, which is a few miles south of Cadiz. Here General Graham, who had disembarked at Algeciras, on the other side of the bay from Gibraltar, joined forces with a Spanish army under General Lapena with a view to operating in the rear of the French. There appears to have been a certain amount of confusion between the two generals, and of this Marshal Victor was quick to take advantage. The Spaniards were no sooner attacked than defeated, leaving the British, not for the last time in war, alone. After two hours of heavy fighting the French retired, thus leaving open the way to Cadiz.

We must now return to the north, where Masséna had crossed the River Agueda at Ciudad Rodrigo on 2nd May, 1811, remembering that the battle to which this place gives its name was not fought until January of the next year. Masséna's movement was a continuation of the withdrawal forced on him by the approach of the Portuguese in his rear and the poor condition of his troops due to sickness and lack of supplies, not to mention the fact that he was also being closely pressed by Wellington. His reputation had suffered a severe blow as a result of this retreat, so he decided to draw Wellington away from Lisbon and then sidestep and get in behind him. His intentions were anticipated and the two forces met at Fuentes d'Onor, where Masséna's defeat was so decisive that he was relieved of his command and returned to France.

To the west and slightly north of Fuentes d'Onor is the town of Almeida, in which a French garrison under General Brennier was surrounded. Whether it was partly due to mistakes on our part or not, one cannot but admire the skill with which this garrison escaped and joined Marmont, who, having taken over command from Masséna, now withdrew towards Salamanca.

During the early part of May the British were also besieging Badajoz. Marshal Soult left Seville with strong forces to relieve it, but was intercepted at Albuhera on 16th May by Marshal Sir William Beresford.

Here it is well to remind the reader that our forces in the Peninsula were small compared with those opposing them. To operate with small forces of tired troops on long lines of communication which would only get longer as the French were driven back would have been the very acme of folly. We find, therefore, that after those two battles there was a lull in the operations as regards major battles. We had in 1809, as already explained, to withdraw from the Peninsula. The Spanish army and people were unreliable, so that defeat or another withdrawal might have had unpredictable consequences.

After the two major battles of Fuentes d'Onor and Albuhera the position was serious, and it was as well that Soult did not realize it or at any rate take advantage of it. Be that as it may, Wellington was given time to reorganize, so that by the beginning of January, 1812, he was ready to take the offensive again.

His first move was to capture Ciudad Rodrigo, the siege of which lasted from 8th to 10th January. For this action he was granted an earldom, and the Spanish Government conferred on him the title of Duke of Ciudad Rodrigo.

Before a general advance could begin, a further garrison fortress had to be captured for the third time during the campaign. This was Badajoz, which after a heroic defence by General Phillipon and terrible slaughter on both sides fell on 5th April, 1812.

There was another French garrison in Salamanca, after which the next

battle is named. The town was surrounded by small forts, and these, though strong after the three weeks' work that had been spent on them, did not hold out so long as Marmont expected. His tactics here are extremely difficult to understand, because, though he had spent considerable time and labour in putting it in a strong state of defence, he withdrew all the garrison, except 800 men, as soon as Wellington approached on 16th June. The town was captured on the 17th.

Once again Marmont's tactics are hard to understand: though in the neighbourhood with large forces he appears to have made no effort to come to the assistance of the garrison.

As soon as he knew that Salamanca had fallen he withdrew behind the River Duero in two columns, both of which had to cross at least two rivers before they could get into their new positions. As it turned out it was a case of *reculer pour mieux sauter*, Wellington, for reasons which are not clear, was very slow in following up, thus giving Marmont the initiative. On 17th July he recrossed the Duero and from then onwards to the end of the battle a study of thrusts, parries and counter-thrusts of these two masters of war make fine reading.

In the end, all else being equal, victory goes to the general who makes the fewest mistakes. By the night of 22nd July the French were in full retreat. The British casualties had been in the region of 8,000, with those of the French about double.*

For this action Wellington was created a Marquis and granted a bounty of £100,000.

The way to Madrid was now open, and the capital was entered by Wellington on 12th August, 1812. Here he halted and became involved in a certain amount of politics with the Spanish and Portuguese Governments. He was, however, appointed Commander-in-Chief of the Spanish forces, so that at last there was that essential to success where allies are concerned—a unified command.

On 14th September, 1812, Napoleon entered Moscow. In the following month began the world-famous retreat of the Grande Armée.

From August, 1812, to May, 1813, Wellington reorganized the Spanish and Portuguese armies, the latter of which was commanded by British officers. By May the strengths of the opposing forces were about equal; perhaps Wellington's forces were slightly the stronger.

On 4th June, 1813, the advance towards the Pyrenees began. It was undertaken in three columns, the left under Graham and the right under Hill, with Wellington in the centre. On the 20th the French were encountered holding a position at Vittoria, on the River Zadora. Once again Wellington's brilliant tactics were too good for the French under Marshal Jourdan, who were forced to withdraw. Marshal Jourdan's baton was captured, together with the personal baggage of King Joseph Bonaparte, in addition to the greater part of the French artillery, ammunition and wagons.

For this outstanding victory Wellington was made a Field Marshal. Napoleon now appointed Marshal Soult to command the French armies in Spain.

After the battle of Vittoria the French withdrew to the extreme north of Spain, leaving behind garrisons at Pampeluna and St Sebastian. Wellington, however, pushed on. He left the Spaniards to deal with Pampeluna and Graham to attack St Sebastian. When he reached the Pyrenees he was met and attacked by Soult. The battle which takes its name from the mountains was fought where they run down to the Bay of Biscay near Irun. It lasted for four days, but in the end the French were forced back on to their own soil.

St Sebastian did not fall as soon as expected, so Wellington, considering it inadvisable to continue his advance into France, decided that the place had to be taken.

Weapons used in mobile warfare are not suitable for siege work, so there was some delay. Though the town was surrounded, one must remember that Soult was in considerable strength not far away and was obviously intent on relieving it. This he tried to do by crossing the Badossa in force on 30th August.

Though the investment started on 17th July, the town did not fall until 31st August. The battle to which the town gives its name, continued until 8th September.

Having found no evidence to the contrary, one presumes that the bar for St. Sebastian was awarded to those who had taken part in the siege and/or the subsequent battle which took place in the neighbourhood.†

---

*The bar to the Military General Service Medal was awarded for the Battle of Salamanca and not for the capture of the town.
†The *London Gazette* of 1st June, 1847, quotes just 'August and September, 1813'. The days of the month are not stated.

Pampeluna, for the capture of which no bars were awarded, did not fall until 31st October.

The losses on both sides in and around St Sebastian were considerable and once again a halt was made until reinforcements arrived. Meanwhile, Soult withdrew and took up a defensive position along the River Nivelle.

Whilst the events with which we have just been dealing were taking place even greater ones were happening, or were about to happen, elsewhere which, though outside the scope of this short account, had a very great bearing on those that follow. Between 16th and 19th October, 1813, there was fought the battle of Leipzig or 'The Battle of the Nations' as it has been called, in which Napoleon with 160,000 men was decisively defeated by the combined armies of Austria, Russia and Prussia, numbering about 400,000. The French losses were tremendous in men, artillery and, above all, in morale. It was obvious that after this shattering blow the French forces opposing Wellington could not expect much in the way of reinforcements to make good subsequent losses and that if they were given one or two more hard knocks the war would be over. The fact that the fighting continued until the following April was due, so some say, to the personal vanity of Soult. The Marshal should be given credit for his skill and to the bravery of his army which, though continually defeated and forced to withdraw for hundreds of miles, fought with a gallantry undiminished by events which they could see for themselves and those which they must have heard about through the most demoralizing of all methods, rumour.

Further reinforcements having arrived from England, Wellington attacked and captured the mountain of La Rhune which overlooked the French position along the Nivelle. After this the French left wing, resting on Amotz, was attacked and turned on 10th November, 1813. Hill, who was now on the allied left, forded the river at its mouth just above St. Jean de Luz. These two movements 'rolled up' the French army, which now withdrew to the River Nive, running almost parallel to the Nivelle at a distance varying from twelve to eight miles.

The weather at the end of November and in early December made further military operations impossible, so that once again there was a hiatus, this time for a month.

On 9th December, 1813, the advance continued and the battle along the Nive commenced.

There were three crossings over the river, one at Cambo on the British right, one at Ustaritz in the centre, and another at Bayonne on the left. The battle raged from the 9th to the 13th December, when the French had their left flank turned and were compelled to withdraw, leaving a garrison in Bayonne which did not surrender until after the war was over.

After the fighting along the Nive the behaviour of the Spanish troops so annoyed the Basque peasants that they rose in revolt and formed, under the leadership of Harispe, what in the 1939-45 War would have been termed a Maquis. They caused considerable trouble and hindered the subsequent operations. Among the other things which they did was to gain time for Soult to take up another position on the high ground between St Boes and Orthez from which, after the battle of the latter name, he was forced to withdraw on 27th February, 1814. In this action Wellington was wounded, though not seriously, in the thigh.

After several further engagements which are not commemorated on the medals, Soult withdrew to his home town of Toulouse, on the River Garonne. Apart from the fact that he was fighting on his home ground, the site was well chosen, as it was a focal point of the roads leading into the heart of France. It is also located in an area traversed by many rivers. He could, if occasion arose, retire to the Lyons area.

Through good marching and local knowledge he withdrew his forces so expeditiously that he gained three days—three valuable days—in which to reorganize and prepare for the attack by the British forces which arrived in the neighbourhood on 8th April, 1814.

On the 10th the attack on Toulouse started. The town was surrounded by battlements and intersected by the Garonne. From the west to the south-east, about half a mile outside these battlements, was the Languedoc Canal. Beyond were a range of hills and a few isolated crests, all of which were strongly fortified. By some unaccountable failure Beresford was allowed to get into position to attack the outer ridge of high ground without being molested, with the result that after terrific fighting round the whole perimeter Soult was forced to evacuate the town on 12th and retire on Villefranque.

Napoleon abdicated on 31st March 1814 and the Peninsular War ended.

———————

This brief account of the campaign should show that the battles commemorated on the Military General Service Medal were not fought in a sequence as a result of one long advance. There were two distinct phases to the campaign, the first of which ended with the British evacuation from Corunna.

During the campaign units known as 'Battalions of Detachments' were formed from details of various strengths from many regiments. It is on account of this that medals are found to regiments which were not present as a whole, and it is also the reason why some men received many more bars than those normally gained by their regiment. Officers were attached to the Portuguese forces, so that they received bars not normally awarded to their parent units.

There is no finality in the compilation of statistics concerning the Military General Service Medal. Rolls obtained from different sources disagree as to the spelling of the names and, what is far more important, as to the title of the bars to which they quote the man as being eligible.

The following three examples will illustrate the difficulty of obtaining complete accuracy:
1. Private R. Atkinson, 3 Foot Guards, received a medal with bars for Talavera, Ciudad Rodrigo, Salamanca and Vittoria, whereas the roll shows him as being entitled to bars for Busaco, Fuentes d'Onor, Nivelle and Nive in addition. 2. Charles Shepperd, 29 Foot, received a medal with the single bar for Vimiera, though the roll shows him as being entitled to those for Vittoria, Talavera and Albuhera in addition. 3. Wm. Chadwick, 12th Light Dragoons, received a medal with bars for Salamanca and Nivelle, though some rolls show him as entitled to those for Salamanca and Vittoria.

The following historical detail mainly taken from the catalogue of the Captain A. E. Whitaker Collection.

Egypt 2nd March-2nd September 1801

Napoleon, as everyone knows, had visions of world conquest, but before this could be achieved he, like Hitler after him, realized that Egypt was the steppingstone to the East.

At the beginning of the year 1801 Egypt was occupied by Napoleon's 'Army of the East' under General Menou.

An expedition to conquer the country was dispatched from England under General Sir Ralph Abercromby, and additional forces were sent from India and the Cape of Good Hope. These were commanded by Major General Baird.

The troops from home assembled at Marmorice, in Asiatic Turkey. Sailing from thence on 2nd March, 1801, they arrived in Aboukir Bay during a heavy storm. A landing was made on the 8th, and the French were forced back towards Alexandria. They took up a position at Mandora (borne on the Colours of the 90th and 92nd Foot) which was attacked on the 13th. They were then driven back into Alexandria itself, which lies on a thin neck of land with the sea on the north and Lake Mareotis on the south.

The two armies faced each other on this strip from 13th to 21st March, on which latter day the French attacked the British position and, led by the Invincible Legion, broke through. Wheeling left, it encircled the 28th Foot, which, attacked both in front and rear, earned its right to wear two badges on the head-dress, one in front and one behind. After severe fighting, the Invincible Legion surrendered to Major Stirling of the 42nd Foot, and handed over their Standard.

General Abercromby was wounded in this battle and Lieutenant-General Hutchinson assumed command; he contained the French garrison in Alexandria and attacked Cairo, which surrendered on 27th June.

General Menou, now besieged in Alexandria, refused to surrender, so a landing was made by General Coote to the west of the town. The fort of Marabout, which stood on an island in the harbour, was attacked and captured by the 54th Foot, which is the only regiment to have this honour on its colours.

Severe fighting ensued both to the west and east of the town, which capitulated on 2nd September.

Maida 4th July 1806

The battle of Maida was fought on 4th July, 1806. The French had assembled a body of troops in Calabria, for the invasion of Sicily. Major- General Stuart, who commanded the British troops in Sicily, formed the design of penetrating Calabria and attacking the French Division, under General Reynier. Disembarking at St Euphemia from the ships under the command of Admiral Sydney Smith, Major General Stuart advanced to the attack, and finally routed the enemy with great slaughter. The French loss was estimated at over 2,000 men, and the British had only 1 officer and 44 men killed, with 11 officers and 271 men wounded. Heaviest casualties fell on the 78th and 81st Foot. Major- General Stuart received the thanks of Parliament, with £1,000 a year for life, was created a Knight of the Bath, and also Count of Maida by the King of Naples. The City of London voted him its Freedom and a sword.

Roleia 17th August 1808

This is the spelling used on the bar, though the correct one is Rolica as used on the regimental colours.

Roleia was the first victory gained in the Peninsula. The battle was fought on the 17th August, 1808, the British Army being under the command of Lieutenant-General Sir Arthur Wellesley, and that of the French under General Laborde. On nearing the French position, General Laborde fell back from the plain in front of the village to the heights of Zambugiera. The approaches were only by a few difficult tracts through deep ravines, or water courses, diverging from the foot of the heights to their crests. The enemy was forced from the heights, and retired during the night, leaving three guns behind. Sir Arthur Wellesley, in his despatch, observed: 'The troops actually engaged in the heat of the action were, from unavoidable circumstances, only the 5th, 9th, 29th, the riflemen of the 60th and 95th, and the flank companies of Major General Hill's brigade, being a number by no means equal to that of the enemy; their conduct, therefore, deserves the highest commendation.'

Although no medals are known to have been issued, the casualties of the 82nd (25 killed and wounded) indicate that they took some part in the assault. Wellesley's loss amounted to 4 officers and 66 men killed, 20 officers and 315 men wounded, 4 officers and 78 men missing; in all 487 casualties, of which 190 fell upon the 29th Foot. The French losses were 1,000 killed, wounded and taken prisoner.

There were only 11 recipients of the medal with this as a single bar. They were:

Staff	Samuel Brown (who was carrying despatches)
5th Ft	Adam Lloyd, Joseph Stevenson, Wm Tollerday
9th Ft	Capt Samuel Sanky, Lieut Samuel Nicholls, Thos Fuller (on Muster Roll only)
29th Ft	Joseph Beer
91st Ft	James Bennett
95th Ft	Sergt John Wheeler
Medical Department	John Winter, Purveyor's Clerk

Vimiera 21st August 1808

Two days after the victory at Roleia, 21st August, 1808, the battle of Vimiera took place. The French Army, under Marshal Junot, in the hope of taking Sir Arthur Wellesley by surprise, commenced this action, and after a succession of furious attacks, which were successfully resisted, the enemy was driven back and retreated in great disorder. Thirteen guns, several hundred prisoners, and a great quantity of ammunition were captured. The French casualties amounted to nearly 2,000 killed, wounded and taken prisoner. The British casualties amounted to 4 officers, and 131 men killed, 37 officers and 497 men wounded, 2 officers and 49 men missing, making 720 altogether. The regiments that suffered most severely were the 50th with 89 casualties, the 43rd with 118; and the 71st with 112.

Sahagun 21st December 1808

A cavalry action, which took place in Spain, on the 20th December, 1808. About 800 French Dragoons, under the Brigadier-General Debelle, were in cantonment. Lieutenant-General Lord Paget, with the 15th Hussars and 12 soldiers of the 7th Hussars, determined to surprise them. The Hussars arrived in the vicinity of Sahagun before daylight, but the French patrol galloped off and gave the alarm. On nearing Sahagun, the French Dragoons were discovered formed up. In numbers the French were about two to one, but Lord Paget at once charged, and completely overthrew them. Thirteen officers, including two lieutenant colonels, and 132 men were taken prisoners.

British casualties, to the 15th Hussars were 2 men killed, 2 officers and 18 men wounded.

Only twenty *single* bars were issued, all to 15th Hussars. The recipients were: Major F. Forrester; Captain J. Broadhurst; Captain A. Gordon; Paymaster E. P. Henstowe; Tp. Qr. Mr T. Ledger; T. Bannister; J. Barnett; J. Bartholomew; J. Clarke; G. Edmonds; Sergeant-Major R. Harvey; Sergeant B. Loach, F. May; J. Pluckett; W. Pontin; W. Skinner; S. Skuse; L. Taylor; Wm. Thackeray and J. Westcot.

Benevente 29th December 1808

A cavalry action, on the 29th December, 1808. At the moment of the evacuation of Benevente by the rear-guard of the British Army, General Lefebre Desnouettes, with 600 chasseurs à cheval of the Imperial Guard, forded the River Esla and drove back the videttes. The British pickets advanced and repeatedly charged the enemy. Lord Paget bringing up the 10th Hussars in support, the pickets, with a loud cheer, dashed at their numerous opponents, but before they could close the French wheeled round, fled to the ford, and plunged into the river, leaving behind them about 30 men killed, 25 wounded, and 70 prisoners, among whom was the French Commander, General Desnouettes.

British casualties were 12 killed and over 70 wounded, the heaviest sufferers being the 3rd Hussars KGL, having 3 killed and 43 wounded.

Four single bars were awarded to 10th Hussars; Sergeant W. Ace; Jas. Foster; W. Humbert; Jas. Scrambler. Four bars were awarded to 7th Hussars: A. Barry; W. Lyne; J. Norse; Jonathon Brown and M. McCartney, 18th Light Dragoons.

One medal with this single bar was awarded to the Royal Artillery: Captain Henry Eveleigh, RHA—a total of ten bars only to the unit.

Sahagun and Benevente

This bar was awarded to those present at both battles.

Corunna 16th January 1809

After the disastrous and ever memorable retreat from Sahagun, under Lieutenant-General Sir John Moore, the British Army reached Corunna on the 11th January, 1809. No transports were there to receive them, and the Army occupied the adjacent villages and suburbs. The next day the French Army, under Marshal Soult, appeared in front of the town, and on the 14th the British fleet of transports hove in sight. As the enemy made no demonstration to attack, orders were given, on the 16th, to prepare for embarkation during the night; but at two o'clock in the afternoon the enemy advanced, and desperately attempted to pierce the British positions. The French were foiled at every point, their centre broken, their left turned, and, night coming on, they fell back. Sir John Moore fell by a cannon shot in the midst of the battle, and his remains, wrapped in a military cloak, were consigned to their resting place in the citadel of Corunna. The main body of the Army embarked during the night, and the rear-guard on the 17th January. The British loss was 800 killed and wounded, with the 1st Foot Guards, the 42nd Foot and the 81st Foot suffering heaviest casualties. The French loss was in the region of 900.

Martinique 30th January-24th February 1809

The Island of Martinique was in the possession of the French. A British force under Lieutenant-General Beckwith, proceeded to its capture, and arrived and landed, without opposition, on the 30th January, 1809. On the 1st February some skirmishing took place, but on the 2nd the enemy made a determined stand, and a sharp action followed, the French being driven from their position with considerable loss. The enemy retired into Fort Bourbon. A vigorous siege commenced, and the garrison surrendered to the English on the 24th February. Three eagles and several brass drums were captured. The British force numbered about 10,000, and its loss was 3 officers and 81 men killed, and 9 officers and 325 men wounded. The French force outnumbered that of the British, and was under Vice-Admiral Villaret Joyeuse.

Talavera 27th-28th July 1809

The British, having determined to make another effort to liberate the Peninsula from the aggression of Bonaparte, appointed Sir Arthur Wellesley to the command of the British Army in Spain. After the passage of the Douro, a very brilliant exploit, although no clasp was given for it, Sir Arthur pursued the flying enemy for some days. Marshal Victor, having taken up a position at Talavera, to which place he had retreated on hearing of Soult's expulsion from Oporto, and Sir Arthur having formed a junction with the Spanish General, the combined forces proceeded along the valley of the Tagus and arrived at Talavera. On the afternoon of the 27th July, the French, by a *ruse de guerre*, turned on the left of Donkin's brigade and gained the hill in its rear; but the brigade discovered its error, and, being supported by Hill's brigade, the whole force poured in a destructive fire, charged with the bayonet, and drove the assailants down the hill with great slaughter. At midnight the attack was renewed, but was again gallantly repulsed, both armies then bivouacked for the night. Soon after daybreak on the 28th, a cannon shot was the signal for the advance of the French columns; they again and again pressed forward to within a few paces of the summit of the hill but were repulsed in all their attempts, leaving the ground covered with slain. A pause ensued till mid-day, when under cover of 80 pieces of artillery and crowds of voltiguers, four heavy columns advanced to the attack of the right and centre of the English line. After being received with well-directed volleys, numerous charges with the bayonet, and gallant charges by the cavalry, the enemy was repulsed at all points, and retreated under cover of the smoke of its guns and numerous cavalry. Seventeen guns, two tumbrils with ammunition, 17,000 stands of arms and several silk standards were captured. The loss to the British was 2 generals, 31 officers and 761 men killed; 3 generals, 193 officers and 3,718 men wounded; 9 officers and 643 men missing. The Spanish returned their loss at 1,200. The French loss, according to their returns, was 944 killed, 6,294 wounded, and 156 prisoners, but Sir Arthur's estimate was one quarter of their army, and the statement made by the French War Office was 8,794 men. The English Army numbered nearly 19,000 and the French 56,174, but only 16,000 of the English and 38,000 of the French were engaged in the battle, the remainder being kept in reserve. Sir Arthur Wellesley was created Viscount Wellington of Talavera and Baron Douro.

Guadaloupe 30th January-4th February, 1810

Guadaloupe was the only island remaining to the French in the West Indies, and in January, 1810, an expedition, under Lieutenant General Sir George Beckwith, was despatched to capture it. A landing was effected without opposition. The French, under General Ernout, appeared in force, but their flanks were turned and they were compelled to retire. Shortly afterwards, the conquest of the Island was completed. The British loss was 4 officers and 48 men killed, and 16 officers and 234 men wounded. The loss of the French was between 500 and 600.

Busaco 27th September 1810

The Battle of Busaco was fought on the 27th September, 1810. The French were under Marshal Massena, and the combined British and Portuguese Armies were under Lieutenant General Viscount Wellington. The English General had taken up his position on the heights of Busaco. At the first light of dawn the French commenced the attack, and two Divisions, under Regnier, advanced in front of Picton's Division and gained the summit of the ridge; they were furiously charged and driven down the declivity in confused masses with fearful slaughter. Meanwhile Ney attacked, with three corps, the left Division, under Brigadier Craufurd, and also gained the heights. A charge with bayonets overthrew the foe, and three terrible volleys at only a few yards distance, drove the shattered and wavering masses down the hill. The enemy withdrew from the contest, and by 2 o'clock the battle had

ceased. Of the allies, 197 were killed, 1,014 wounded and 68 missing, among whom were 74 officers. Of the enemy, 2,000 were killed, about 3,000 wounded and nearly 300 were taken prisoner, among whom was one general killed, three wounded and one taken prisoner. The army, under Lord Wellington, numbered 25,000 British and a like number of Portuguese, and he computed the enemy at 70,000 men. The British regiments which suffered most severely were the 45th Foot (150 casualties) and the 88th Foot (134 casualties).

Barrosa 5th March 1811

On the 5th March, 1811, the Allied Armies were on the heights of Barrosa. The Spanish General, Lapena, being in chief command, directed Lieutenant General Thomas Graham (afterwards Lord Lynedoch) to march with the British Army through a pine forest and take possession of the Burmeja ridge; this was a movement Graham did not approve of, but he obeyed the order. No sooner had the English General entered the pine forest than the Spanish General quitted the heights, leaving a small force to protect his baggage. Marshal Victor, the French General in command, as soon as he observed Lapena's false movements, and that the English were involved in the wood, rushed forward to seize the heights; the Spanish fled, and Lieutenant Colonel Brown, with a battalion of light companies of the several regiments, alone remained on the heights. Unable to resist the torrent, he formed his battalion into a square and sent to Graham for orders. One Division of the French Army was advancing along the edge of the forest within cannon shot, and another was rapidly ascending the left side of the Barrosa Hill. Lieutenant General Graham, relying on the bravery of his troops, determined to encounter with his little band the host of the enemy and recover the key of the battlefield. Unable in the thick forest to countermarch his column, he faced it about, and as they issued from the wood formed line and pushed forward to the attack. The left wing assailed the Division on the edge of the forest, whilst the right attacked the Division which was ascending the hill. A furious cannonade commenced with fearful execution; the British left wing advanced firing, and fixing bayonets charged the first line of the enemy, drove it back on the second, and both were broken by the shock. The enemy's other Division, confident of victory, descended the hill half-way to meet the right wing; a desperate conflict ensued, but the struggle was not of long duration; the enemy was forced back and driven down the other side of the heights in confusion, leaving two pieces of cannon in possession of the victors. The enemy attempted to rally, but the English artillery rendered this impossible, and they fled precipitately to their lines. Six guns and one eagle were captured. The loss of the enemy was about 3,000 men in killed, wounded and taken prisoner, and among the latter were the General of Division Rufin, the General of Brigade, Rousseau (mortally wounded), the chief of Staff, General Bellegarde, an aide-de-camp of Marshal Victor, the Colonel of the 8th Regiment, and several other officers; 440 prisoners remained in the hands of the victors, who did not lose a single prisoner. The loss to the English exceeded one-fourth of the army—7 officers and 195 men were killed, and 55 officers and 985 men were wounded. The thanks of both Houses of Parliament were unanimously voted to Lieutenant General Graham and the officers and men under his command for this victory.

Fuentes D'Onor 5th May, 1811

The Battle of Fuentes D'Onor took place on the 5th May, 1811. The British forces were commanded by Lord Wellington, and those of the French by Marshal Massena. The English General had blockaded Almeida, and his object was to prevent the enemy having communications with the garrison. On the 2nd, the French Army passed the Azava, and, continuing its march the next morning, the light division of the British Army, with its cavalry, fell back on Fuentes D'Onor (Fountain of Honour), and in the evening a fierce attack was made on the village, which was successfully resisted. A reinforcement of three British regiments arrived, a vigorous charge was made, and the enemy was driven from the lower part of the village, of which he had obtained a temporary position; night coming on, he withdrew across the Duas Casa. The whole of the 4th May was occupied by the French General in reconnoitring the British position. At daylight of the 5th, two columns of the French and all the cavalry advanced against the village of Poco Velho, and Houston's advanced guard was driven back, the right of his Division turned, and the village was carried by the enemy. Houston's advanced brigade retiring in good order. The light division, the cavalry, and a troop of horse artillery were sent to Houston's assistance, but the British cavalry were furiously charged by the whole of the enemy's horse, and, though the weak squadrons sustained the shock of the overpowering numbers of the enemy, they were obliged to retire behind the light division which formed into squares. The 7th Division, at the same time, took advantage of some ground intersected by stone walls and rocks, and the united force poured in so destructive a fire that the enemy at once fell back in disorder. The principal effort of the enemy throughout the day was directed against the villages of Fuentes D'Onor, but the French were never able to gain more than a temporary possession. Every house in the lower town was taken and retaken in the course of the day, and one by one abandoned as the entrances were choked up with the dead. In this desperate affair, bayonets were repeatedly crossed. The contest lasted until night, and the British still held their post. At daylight of the 6th, the whole of the French Army was in motion and on the 10th retired across the Azava in full retreat for Ciudad Rodrigo. The loss of the British was over 1500 killed, wounded and missing, while that of the French is said to have exceeded 3,000. The British Regiments which suffered most severely were the 71st Foot (127 casualties), and 79th Foot (256 casualties).

Albuhera 16th May 1811

The first seige of Badajoz was undertaken by the British early in the month of May, 1811, but on the 12th intelligence was received that Marshal Soult was marching from Seville to relieve that fortress, and the siege was broken up. The whole of the allied army, under the command of Marshal Beresford, except the 4th Division, which remained to maintain the blockade, moved forward to meet the enemy, and on the 15th reached the village of Albuhera, sometimes written, 'Albuera.'

The battle has been described as 'one of the fiercest on human record.' A little before 8 o'clock on the morning of the 16th May, the battle began by the enemy driving the Spanish troops from the heights on which they had been posted by Marshal Beresford. To dislodge the enemy from this commanding position, Major General Stewart was ordered to bring up Colonel Colburn's brigade, which, while deploying into line, were attacked by a large body of Polish Lancers and French Hussars, who, concealed by a mist and heavy rain, galloped round on their rear; they were mistaken for Spanish Cavalry, occasioned by their calling out as they advanced 'Vivan los Ingleses,' 'Vivan los amigos de Espana,' and were allowed to approach without a shot being fired; the whole brigade, except the 31st Regiment, was either slain or driven forward into the enemy's lines. The 3rd Brigade of General Stewart's Division, under the General Houghton, was now brought up to restore the battle, and a most bloody contest ensued. On gaining the summit of the disputed heights, a murderous fire of artillery and musketry was opened on the English, but they pushed on until prevented by a steep gully from reaching the enemy with bayonet; the brigade halted and opened fire, but both sides maintained their position with desperate courage. A perfect hurricane of grape and canister was poured in, very often at a distance of but twenty paces, which was only interrupted by partial charges with the bayonet by the British. Of the 57th, which numbered 24 officers and 570 privates, only one officer remained standing, and above 400 privates had fallen. From this stubborn resistance the 57th gained the sobriquet of the 'Die-Hards.'

The 4th Division, which had come up from Badajoz after the action had commenced, was now ordered to advance, and on crowning the heights was received with a tremendous fire; but it pushed on to the aid of Houghton's brigade. Withering volleys were exchanged, but the foe was discomfited, and its shattered battalions were driven down the hill in confusion. The French corps threw away their arms to expedite their flight, and the reserve was overwhelmed in the confusion. The French Artillery came to the rescue and arrested the advance of the victors, or the whole French Army would have been annihilated. The enemy retreated under cover of the guns, and the battle ceased a little before 3 o'clock.

The allies lost, in killed, wounded and missing, over 6,000, including 2,500 Spaniards, Germans, and Portuguese. The precise loss of the English was 984 killed, 2,993 wounded and 570 missing (the 48th suffered 621 casualties), but of the prisoners, nearly 300 rejoined, having escaped from the French bivouac during the night. The French loss is estimated to have been in excess of 8,000.

Java 14th-26th August 1811

The Government of Calcutta, being determined on the capture of Java, the only colonial settlement in the East Indies remaining in possession of the Batavian Republic, despatched an expedition from Madras, consisting of a number of ships-of-war and nearly 12,000 troops, one half of whom were Europeans, the Governor General of India, Lord Minto, organized the expedition. The naval forces were commanded by Rear Admiral the Honourable Robert Stopford. Though Lord Minto accompanied the force, the command of the troops was given to Lieutenant General Sir Samuel Auchmuty.

A landing was affected on the 4th August, 1811, at Chillinching, about ten miles from the city of Batavia. The French and Dutch Troops at once abandoned that place, and took refuge in the intrenched camp at Meester Cornelis, about one mile from the city. The command of the Island of Java was under the French General Jansens. On the 10th August, he was attacked at Weltervreeden, and driven back on his entrenched position on the heights of Cornelis, at a loss of not less than 500 men; his army consisted of about 20,000, and the place was strongly fortified. On the morning of the 26th, the assault was made, and after the capture of a number of redoubts, which were carried at the point of the bayonet, the enemy was completely defeated and fled from the field. 750 pieces of brass and iron cannon and mortars, with an enormous quantity of shot, shell and ammunition, were taken. The enemy's loss was severe, and 1,700 prisoners were taken. The loss of the British in the two actions was 154 killed and 786 wounded.

Ciudad Rodrigo 8th-19th January 1812

Viscount Wellington commenced the investment of this fortress on the 8th January, 1812, and on the night of the following day the first parallel was established; on the 13th, the convent of Santa Cruz was carried by escalade, and at noon on the 14th, during the interchange of the tour of duty by the Divisions, a sortie was made by the enemy for the purpose of destroying the parallels and spiking the guns in the battery; the attack was, however, defeated and the enemy retreated into the town. On the night of the 14th, the fortified convent of San Francisco was taken.

On the 19th, two breaches were established, the width of one being 100 feet and that of the other 30 feet, and intelligence having been received of the advance of Marmont for the relief of the place, Lord Wellington ordered the assault to be made at 7 o'clock on the evening of that day. The duty of carrying the main breach was assigned to the 3rd Division, under Picton, and that of the lesser breach to the Light Division, under Crauford. At the appointed hour, both Divisions moved to the points of attack, each preceded by its forlorn-hope and stormers. As soon as the sappers had thrown some bags into the ditch, so as to reduce its depth from 14 to 8 feet, the forlorn-hope and stormers of the 3rd Division jumped down and rushed forward to the breach; at the same moment every gun on the ramparts that could bear on the spot opened a tremendous fire. Williams, in his 'Life and Campaigns of the Duke' writes:—'A battalion of the 5th, under Major Ridge, and a wing of the 94th, under Colonel Campbell, which had been directed to move forward for the purpose of clearing away any obstacle that might interrupt the advance of the main storming party, descending the counterscarp by ropes and gaining the main breach unobserved, rushed up, and cutting down the artillerymen, impetuously carried everything before them, notwithstanding the difficulties sustained by the explosion of the bombs and grenades rolled down upon them from the summit of the breach, and of the bags of powder deposited among the slopes of its ruins and the destructive force of the grape from the two guns planted on the summit. So rapid had been their movements that, when they appeared on the top of the breach, they were fired at by their countrymen outside the walls, from the supposition that they were the enemy defending the breach.' The enemy was driven from the opening and retired under cover. Here, and from the neighbouring houses, the foe kept up a fire of musketry with great rapidity and destruction, but the 3rd Division maintained the terrible struggle with desperate resolution. The stormers of the Light Division carried the lesser breach, which was not intrenched, at the point of the bayonet, and the fortress was eventually won. Captain Dubourdieu of the 5th Fusiliers, was the first who placed a scaling ladder and entered the enemy's works, and the first of the foe who fell that night at the escalade was by his hand. The garrison, consisting of 80 officers and 1,700 men, were taken prisoners. It may be seen from the great loss sustained by the British how desperate was the resistance and how fearless the attack with over 550 allied casualties suffered during the siege and at least a further 500 allied casualties suffered during the assault.

Badajoz 17th-18th March 1812

The siege and capture of the fortress of Badajoz present to us one of the most desperate and sanguinary conflicts fought during the Peninsula War. Having strengthened the defence of Ciudad Rodrigo, Lord Wellington marched with the Allied Army from that town, on the 5th March, 1812, leaving in it a garrison of Spaniards; on the 16th, a pontoon and two flying bridges were thrown across the Guadiana, and the 3rd, 4th, and Light Division crossed and invested Badajoz. On the night of the 17th, in the midst of rain and storm, ground was broken at 160 yards from the Picurina Fort. On the 19th, sorties from the town and fort entered the trenches but were vigorously charged and repulsed with the loss of 300 men. At 10 o'clock, on the night of the 24th, an assault was made on the Picurina Fort by 500 men of the 3rd Division; the fort was escaladed and captured and its garrison either slain or taken prisoner.

The general attack was made on the night of the 6th of April from three points, the castle by escalade and the bastions of Trinidad and Santa Maria by storming the breaches. The troops for the storm of the castle consisted of the 3rd Division, and those for the storm of breaches of the 4th and Light Divisions. After two hours efforts, in the midst of terrible slaughter, they were unable to carry the breaches. A staff officer was sent to Lord Wellington to apprise him that 2,000 men had fallen in the breaches, and that the troops were without leaders. At the same moment, another staff officer arrived with the tidings that the 3rd Division was in possession of the castle, and orders were sent to General Picton to retain it at all costs, and the Divisions at the breaches were withdrawn.

Williams, in his 'Life and Campaigns of the Duke,' describes the part taken by the 3rd Division thus:—'The 3rd Division, having been obliged, from the circumstances of a lighted carcass having fallen close to it, and discovering its array, to begin the attack half-an-hour before the appointed time, rushing up the rugged steep to the foot of the castle walls, raised, under a destructive fire, their ladders against the walls; but they were no sooner planted than they were grappled by the garrison with hooked pikes of enormous length, and thrown down with the men who had mounted on them; at the same moment, stones, crushing logs of wood, bars of iron, loaded shells, and other destructive missiles, with which the tops of the walls were garnished, were hurled down on the heads of the assailants. Some of the ladders, also broke with the weight of the troops that in their eager haste to meet the foe, swarmed upon them, and precipitated the men who had mounted them upon the bayonets of their comrades below. The heroic troops, however, persevered, but all who first ascended fell by musketry or the bayonet. But undaunted by the terrific reception they met, fresh assailants swarmed round the feet of the ladders eager to ascend, but all in vain; the assault seemed hopeless. Many men of the 45th and Packenham's brigade, though they reached the top of the rampart, were thrown down wounded. Receding a few paces, the assailants reformed, and Picton, who had been wounded in the early part of the assault, redirecting ladders to be placed in an embrasure where the wall was lower, Lieutenant Colonel Ridge, of the 5th Fusiliers and a German officer, of the name of Girsewald caught up the ladders, and, planting them against the walls, mounted, followed by their men. Having gained a footing, a fierce contest ensued between the combatants, and the ground was, foot by foot, won and lost, until, after a fierce contest of an hour, the intrepidity of the assailants surmounted every obstacle and drove the enemy from his post, when in a moment the castle was won, its garrison escaping through the sally-port. Had not the castle gate been bricked up the victors would have marched down on the rear of the defenders of the breaches.' The governor, General Philippon, finding the town in possession of the assailants, retired with the garrison into Fort San Christoval, but at daylight of the following morning surrendered to the victors.

The original garrison consisted of 5,000 men, of whom 1,200 were killed or wounded during the operations, besides those lost in the assault, and about 3,500 prisoners were captured. The loss of the Allied Army was great 77 officers and 963 men being killed, and 306 officers and 3,481 men wounded. When Wellington heard of the great sacrifice that had been made in gaining this fortress, his usual firmness gave

way, and he burst into a flood of tears at the loss of so many of his gallant soldiers.

Salamanca 22nd July 1812

The battle of Salamanca was fought on 22nd July, 1812, the French Army being under the command of Marshal Marmont, and the Allied Army under Lord Wellington in person. After much manoeuvring between the two commanders, the action commenced at 4 o'clock in the afternoon, by the extension of the French columns to its left, near which was posted the Third Division and D'Urban's Cavalry, but concealed by the nature of the ground. Lord Wellington, perceiving the error of the enemy, made immediate disposition for the attack. The British suddenly rushed down the slope of the hill on which they were posted, and in the hollow beneath effected their formation amidst a storm of grape and bullets. The Third Division then advanced, supported by General D'Urban's Cavalry, two squadrons of the 14th, the Light Dragoons and two brigades of artillery. Ascending the opposite slope, the advanced lines of the enemy were driven upon their supports. On gaining the ridge, the main body of the enemy was found drawn up in squares. Firing a volley, the Third Division rushed on the foe with fixed bayonets, broke the squares, and scattered them in confusion; the Cavalry now advanced and completed discomfiture of the enemy. After this the French were unable to rally, and an author gives the following description of this attack: 'He fell upon them like a thunderbolt, and the issue of the attack was as decided a rout upon the part of the French as was, perhaps, ever experienced by an army. Their broken and discomfited masses, swept away before our victorious troops, were precipitated upon the Tormes, in crossing which many were drowned. Had it not been for the protection afforded them by the night immediately coming on, few of them could have escaped.'

The loss of the enemy was 7,000 killed and wounded, including Marshal Marmont, who lost an arm, and 5 general officers; eleven cannon, two eagles and 7,000 prisoners, including 1 general and 6 field officers, were taken. The estimated loss of the Allied Army was: British, 1 general officer, 27 officers and 472 men killed; 5 general officers, 173 officers, 2,922 men wounded; 101 men missing.

Portuguese, 13 officers and 338 men killed; 74 officers, 1,574 men wounded; 207 missing.

Spanish, 2 men killed and 4 wounded.

Regiments suffering the most heavy casualties were the 11th Foot "Bloody Eleventh": 16 officers, 325 men; 2nd/53rd Foot: 11 officers and 131 men; 1/61st Foot: 24 officers and 342 men.

Fort Detroit 16th August 1812†

Having declared war on Britain on 18th June, 1812, the United States intended to invade Upper Canada.

Fort Detroit was situated at the extreme north-western end of Lake Erie on the south bank of the Detroit river, on the opposite bank of which were the British garrisons of Sandwich and Amherstburg.

An American force, under Brigadier General William Hull, reached Fort Detroit on 8th August and then crossed the river and occupied Sandwich without opposition. Instead of immediately continuing his advance to Amherstburg, some twenty miles away, he decided to wait for heavy artillery. Whilst waiting he became overawed by the apparent magnitude of his task and withdrew his force to the American bank.

The Commander-in-Chief in Upper Canada was Brigadier General Isaac Brock, who noticing the half-heartedness of the Americans, decided to cross the river and attack Fort Detroit. This he did on 16th August under cover of the fire of his artillery and the supporting fire from the *Queen Charlotte*. No sooner had his attackers got in position to start the assault when the garrison surrendered.

The units taking part in the capture of the fort were 30 men of the Royal Artillery, 250 men of the 41st Foot (Welch Regiment), 50 men of the Royal Newfoundland Regiment, and about 650 Indians.

---

†Fort Detroit was the original name of the present city of Detroit. The site was first visited by the French in 1610 and then again by them under Antoine de la Mothe Cadillac in 1701, when he founded Fort Detroit. It was ceded to the British in 1763. In the same year it was unsuccessfully besieged by Chief Pontiac with his Ottawa Indians. In 1783 it was given back to the United States, but was not occupied by them until 1796. It was captured again, as related, by the British on 16th August, 1812; and recovered by the United States in 1813.

The Welch Regiment also have the honour 'Miami' (state of Ohio) for the action fought on 23rd April, 1813. It is rather extraordinary that this action and those of Queenstown (26th October, 1813), Niagara (19th December, 1813), and Blandensburg (24th August, 1814) should have been considered as worthy of being given the status of battle honours, but not warrant a bar to the Military General Service Medal.

The medal to J. B. Lapierre, Canadian Militia, is the only one awarded with the bars for Fort Detroit, Chateauguay and Chrystler's Farm.

Vittoria 21st June 1813

On the 21st June, 1813, near the City of Vittoria, in the province of Alava, the French Army, commanded by Joseph Bonaparte assisted by Marshal Jourdan was posted on the neighbouring heights arrayed in order of battle occupying a line nearly eight miles in extent. Lord Wellington on the previous day had surveyed this position and determined to attack it on the following morning. Both armies were of about equal strength.

At daybreak the Allied Army was under arms. The enemy's left rested on the heights at Puebla de Arganzan. Lieutenant General Sir Rowland Hill directed a Spanish brigade to drive the enemy from this position, but the Spaniards making but little impression, the 71st Light Infantry and the 2nd Division under Colonel Cadogan, were sent to their support. After a severe contest the post was won. but Colonel Cadogan fell mortally wounded. The enemy now, finding his right threatened by the 1st and 5th Divisions, and fearing to lose his communication with Bayonne, fell back in successive masses. At this time a Spanish peasant came up and informed Lord Wellington that the bridge of Tres Puentes was negligently guarded. Major General Kempt's brigade of the light Division and the 15th Hussars dashed over the bridge and occupied a deep ravine. A few round shots were thrown to dislodge them, one of which carried off the head of the peasant. Meanwhile, the 3rd and 7th Divisions approached the Bridge of Mendoza, under a heavy fire of the French artillery, and Colville's brigade of Picton's Division, consisting of the 5th Fusiliers, the 83rd, 87th and 94th Regiments, passed over, the other brigades of the 3rd Division forded the river, followed by the 7th and light Divisions. The British centre now advanced to the attack, and the French retreated on their reserves, posted on a second range of heights. 'Colville's brigade of the *fighting third* led up to the attack, and gallantly, not only repulsed the force opposed to it, but encountered its two supporting lines at the bayonet's point and captured their guns.' The village of Arinez was carried by the bayonet, and Margarita and Hermandad were stormed. A running fight was maintained for nearly six hours, and, between the villages of Ali and Armentia, the columns of the French were re-formed, and a desperate resistance was made under cover of 80 guns. Under a murderous cannonade and musketry fire, the 3rd Division, which was most in advance, could scarcely retain its ground; the 4th, 7th and light Divisions, however, charging them in flank, the enemy was driven from the position and fled in confusion, leaving in his trail broken-down wagons, cars and coaches, some laden with eatables, cooked and uncooked, sacks of flour, casks of brandy, boxes of dollars and doubloons, wearing apparel, jewellery, paintings and sculpture, besides books and correspondence from the chests of the military and civil offices. The carriage of King Joseph and the baton of Marshal Jourdon fell into the victor's hands; 151 pieces of artillery, 450 caissons, the colours of the 106th Regiment, and the military chest, containing five and a half millions of dollars were taken. Lord Wellington, in his despatch states:— 'All their ammunition and baggage, and everything they had, were taken close to Vittoria. I have reason to believe that the enemy carried off with them one gun and one howitzer only.'

The French, according to their own account, lost, in killed and wounded, 8,000. The loss of the allies was: British, 501 killed, 2,807 wounded; Portuguese, 150 killed, 899 wounded; Spanish, 89 killed and 406 wounded; making a total of 4,910, which included 33 officers killed and 230 wounded. Regiments suffering particularly heavy casualties were the 5th, 28th, 39th, 59th, 71st, 87th and 88th Foot.

A vote of thanks, by both House of Parliament, was accorded to the troops, and Lord Wellington was appointed Field Marshal in the British Army.

Pyrenees 25th July-2nd August 1813

The battles of the Pyrenees took place between the 25th July and the 2nd August, 1813. The British forces occupied the whole of the frontier passes under the Marquis of Wellington, and the French consisted of three Army Corps, of about 78,000 men, under Marshal Soult.

The scattered remnants of the French Army defeated at Vittoria, having been reinforced and reorganized, it was the intention of Marshal Soult to force the passes and re-enter Spain. On the 25th July, the French made an attack on the pass of Maya. A British picket was posted at the entrance at a long distance from its supports. By a circuitous path, the enemy gained the summit of the mountain and opened a destructive fire on the 20th Regiment, which was forming to meet the attack. 'A' company was ordered to charge the enemy and drive them back. Captain Tovey (afterwards of the 5th Fusiliers) dashed forward against the front of the 6th French Light Infantry with the bayonet. The French, seeing so few opponents, called out to them to lay down their arms; Tovey's answer was to his men, 'Bayonet away! Bayonet away!' This gallant exploit kept the enemy in check until the reserves were able to reform, and the overwhelming forces of the enemy were eventually driven back. While this attack was proceeding, Soult advanced to the pass of Roncesvalles and attacked Byng's brigade of 1,500 men which was posted on the summit of a rugged rock. This position was resolutely maintained, whilst volleys of musketry, as the enemy swarmed up the heights, kept them at bay. In the evening in consequence of Byng learning that a Spanish Division had been driven back on Cole, he retired on that Division also. Cole also fell back during the night. Picton hearing of Cole's retreat, advanced the following morning with the 3rd Division to his support and as senior officer took command and made a new disposition of the troops. Lord Wellington shortly afterwards arrived at the scene of the action, and some skirmishes took place. On the morning of the 28th, the 6th Division joined and occupied the left of the valley of the Lauz. While taking up their position they were attacked by a large enemy force; this was soon driven back, with immense loss, from fire on their front, both flanks and rear. The enemy, in order to extricate their troops from their difficulty, attacked the heights on the left of the 4th Division, and the 7th Cacadores were driven from their position, but, being reinforced by the 27th and 40th Regiments, the enemy was charged by the whole and driven down the hill with great loss. The battle now became general along the whole front of the heights occupied by the 4th Division. With shouts of 'Vive l'Empereur, ' the enemy came on to within a few paces of their opponents, who, firing a volley, charged them down the heights with terrible loss. Every regiment of the 4th Division charged with the bayonet, and the 7th, 20th, 23rd and 40th four different times.

Soult now determined to turn the left of the Allied front, and made his dispositions on the night of the 29th; he was, however, out-manoeuvred by Lord Wellington, who in his turn, with the 7th Division, under Dalhousie, turned the enemy's right, and Picton, with the 3rd Division, crossing the heights of Zubaldica, turned the left of their position. The enemy, now attacked in the front, gave way and retired vigorously followed by the Allies, until darkness closed the pursuit. The enemy continued the retreat during the night of the 30th, and, early on the morning of the 31st, his rear-guard was attacked with great loss. The pursuit was followed up with much slaughter, and Soult was in a critical situation; he attempted to rally his disorderly masses: 'Cowards,' said he, 'where are you fleeing to? You are Frenchmen, and you are running away! In the name of honour, halt, and face the enemy!' But the fugitives made the best of their way through the passes. The light Division, from the summit of a precipice, assailed one division of the enemy while in the gorge of a pass, great slaughter and confusion followed, and the bridges, road and ravine were covered with the dead and dying. On the 1st of August, the pursuit was continued; on the 2nd, the enemy was driven from his last position within the Spanish territory, and the British were again established on nearly the same positions which were occupied at the commencement of these bloody conflicts.

The loss of the French, during these operations was about 15,000 men killed and wounded and 6,000 prisoners. A few cannon, large quantities of baggage and a convoy of provisions were captured. The loss of the Allies was 41 officers and 847 men killed; 328 officers, 5,172 men wounded; and 705 missing.

St Sebastian 17th July-8th September 1813

The first attempt to capture the fortress of St Sebastian, in July, 1813, was unsuccessful on account of the disadvantages under which the attacking force laboured, and the desperate and valiant resistance made by the defenders. The besiegers, however, were successful in an attack on the convent and redoubt of San Bartolomeo. These positions were held with advantage during the subsequent operations.

The siege was resumed by Sir Thomas Graham, on the 26th August. On the 31st, breaches having been made which were deemed practicable, a second and successful assault was made. Crossing the river Urumea, which was fordable at low tide, the British rushed up to the main breach, but were met by such a storm of shot and shell that each man, as he mounted, was swept down. Again and again fresh bodies of the dauntless assailants mounted the breach, and again and again they were swept down by the resistless hurricane of fire that poured upon them. Thus the slaughter continued for two hours; the attack seemed hopeless, and it appeared that the British would have to retire a second time, repulsed from the walls of St Sebastian. Sir Thomas Graham, seeing the state of affairs, after consulting with Colonel Dickson, commanding the artillery, resolved upon the desperate expedient of firing over, and within a few feet of, the heads of the attacking party on the breach. A fortunate shell fell amongst some powder barrels, grenades and other combustibles stored up behind the breach, the explosion of which fired a mine prepared for the destruction of the assailants. The French were, for a time, paralysed by this disaster, which blew up 300 of their grenadiers. Under cover of the smoke and confusion which ensued, the British mounted the breach and entered the town. With desperate impetuosity they drove the enemy before them, who retired into the castle. Preparations, were now made for the taking of the castle, and on the 8th September, after two hours bombardment, the governor, General Rey, surrendered with 1,800 men. The loss of the Allies during these operations was 951 officers and men killed and 2,490 wounded.

Chateauguay 26th October 1813

In September, 1813, the United States decided to capture Montreal, which lies on the St Lawrence below where it is joined by the Chateauguay.

A force under Major General Wade Hampton advanced down the left bank of the Chateauguay, whilst another, under Colonel Purdy, kept touch on the other.

The British, with a force of 800 regulars and militia, and 170 Indians, under Lieutenant Colonel Charles de Saluberry, had taken up a defensive position near the mouth of the Chateauguay.

On 26th October, the advance elements of Colonel Purdy's force were surprised by fire from a well concealed position which caused them to withdraw and then start a spirited action with the remainder of their comrades. When General Hampton heard of the confusion on the opposite bank, he withdrew his own troops after only a few minutes' contact with the British on his side of the river.

The British loss was 5 men killed, 2 officers and 10 men wounded, and 4 men missing.

Three British artillerymen received this bar: James Dougherty, John Gibson and John Purdie. The remainder were awarded to Canadians and Indians. Lieutenant Colonel Charles de Saluberry of the 1st Battalion the 60th Foot was awarded a gold medal for this action.

Nivelle 10th November 1813

After the fall of St Sebastian, it was necessary to reorganize the Army, and more than a month elapsed before hostile operations could be resumed. The advanced position of the French was on the right of the Bidassoa, a few miles in rear of which was a strongly fortified line of works along the Nivelle. On the 7th October, 1813, the passage of the Bidassoa was made with considerable loss on both sides; the enemy was driven from the heights, 500 prisoners and three guns were captured, and the invasion of France was now commenced.

Before daybreak on the 10th November, 1813, the Allied Army had taken up its position to attack the fortified works along the Nivelle. Lord Wellington, with his staff, awaited the dawn under cover of a small wood, within 600 yards of the redoubt which was to be the first object of assault. On a signal of three guns, a general attack was made along the whole line, and an impression having been made by the

artillery, the light Division stormed the entrenchments on the mountains. The 4th and 7th Divisions carried two redoubts and advance against Sarré. This village, being also threatened on its left by the 3rd Division, was abandoned by the enemy. The enemy's main position was then attacked; the 3rd and 7th Divisions carried the redoubts on the left, and the enemy retired. In the meantime the enemy's right position was attacked by the 6th Division, and all the entrenchments and redoubts were carried. A large force of the enemy was now concentrated on the heights above St Pé and Ascain. The 3rd and 7th Divisions crossed the river, and, attacking, gained the heights, and the enemy retreated in disorder to their third line of defence, about 8 miles in rear of their first line. Darkness now set in, and during the night Soult withdrew, and the British were left masters of the whole line. The loss to the French was about 3,000 killed and wounded, 1,400 prisoners, 51 guns and a large quantity of magazine stores and provisions. The loss to the British was 26 officers, 297 men killed, 2 general officers, 155 officers and 2,123 men wounded. Regiments suffering particularly heavy casualties were the 5th, 52nd, 87th and 91st Foot.

Wellington mentions in his dispatch concerning this action that the bomb ketch *Vesuvius*, together with the *Challenger*, *Sparrow* and *Racer*, were sent up the River Nivelle to co-operate with the army although no medals were awarded to the Navy for this service.

Chrystler's Farm 11th November 1813

After the American defeat at Chateauguay a further attempt was made by them to capture Montreal.

The British force engaged in this action numbered about 830 men, including 30 Indians, under the command of Colonel Morrison of the 81st Regiment. It formed a corps of observation, organized by Lieutenant General Sir George Prevost, to prevent the advance of the enemy down the River St Lawrence to Montreal. It was the intention of the American General, James Wilkinson, to co-operate with General Hampton, who was advancing down the Chateauguay River.

On the 11th November, 1813, a Division of the American force, consisting of upwards of 3,000 men under Major General Boyd, and the British corps of observation met at Chrystler's Farm. Colonel Morrison drew up his men in a favourable position, with the river on his right and a wood on the left. On account of the heavy rainfall of the previous night, the Americans were compelled to advance to the attack over ploughed ground, knee-deep in mud. The American General endeavoured to turn the flanks of the British force, but in every attempt he was gallantly repulsed. After two hours hard fighting the British advanced, and the Americans gave way at all points and retired. Want of cavalry and the inferiority of numbers prevented Colonel Morrison from immediately pursuing the enemy. The British loss was 1 officer and 21 men killed, 10 officers and 137 men wounded, and 13 men missing. Of the American force, about 100 prisoners and one gun were taken, and its loss in killed and wounded was 339.

Soon after this defeat General Wilkinson learned that General Hampton was taking no part in the advance. Being now on the Canadian bank and sandwiched between two advancing forces, he decided to return to the American side. Thus ended the American invasion of Lower Canada, though the war did not end until the signing of the Peace of Ghent on 24th December, 1814.

The medals with this bar are to be found with additional unofficial bars for Stoney Creek, Fort George and Queenstown affixed to the ribbon.

Six artillerymen received this bar; they were John Boyle, Thomas Gosling, Dennis Martin, Samuel Nuttall, Joseph Sterland (entitled to Fort Detroit) and Joseph Wells.

Nive 9th-13th December 1813

Marshal Soult, after his defeat on the Nivelle, retired, on the night of the 11th November, into his entrenched camp in front of Bayonne. In consequence of the inclemency of the weather and the impracticable state of the roads, the English and Portuguese Armies were placed in cantonments, between the Nive and the sea, about 2 miles from Bayonne, and headquarters were established at St Jean de Luz. The Spanish troops, in consequence of disregarding the orders forbidding maurauding, were, with the exception of one corps, sent back to Spain. During the inactivity which ensued, a friendly intercourse was established between the contending troops. The English soldiers purchased brandy and tobacco from the French, and other acts of civility took place between the contending Armies from the banks of the Nive.

At length the weather cleared up, and Lord Wellington, to relieve himself from his confined position, and also to cut off the supplies which the enemy received from Bordeaux by the River Adour, determined to force the passage of the Nive. The battle commenced at 8 o'clock in the morning of the 9th December, 1813. The 6th Division forced the passage of a pontoon bridge. Hill's right wing forded the river above Cambo, and his left at Halson, and by 1 o'clock the enemy's advanced posts were driven from the right bank of the river. The 5th Division swept the whole space of the heights to the banks of the Adour, and the enemy, under cover of the darkness, retired into his camp before Bayonne.

On the morning of the 10th, the enemy, with the main body of his army, consisting of 35,000 men, attacked the Allied Army; the action was continued throughout the day, with various results and with great slaughter. At night both sides rested upon their arms on the field of battle, and the Allied forces occupied nearly the same ground they held in the morning. The morning of the 11th was wet and stormy. Some skirmishing ensued; but at about noon the firing ceased on both sides. At 3 o'clock the enemy made a sudden attack, and the allied pickets were driven in; the battle lasted till nightfall, when the combatants occupied the same ground on which they rested the previous night. At about 2 o'clock on the afternoon of the 12th, the attack was renewed by Soult, and skirmishing continued during the greater part of the day. The enemy, being foiled at all points, retired during the night into the entrenched camp.

At daylight of the 13th, Soult moved out of his entrenchments with the main body of his Army, and a severe engagement followed. Bloody conflicts ensued throughout the action, and at length Lord Wellington assumed the offensive. Major General Byng was ordered to dislodge a great force of the enemy on some rising ground; placing himself at the head of his brigade, with the colours of the 31st Regiment in his hand, he advanced unchecked by a storm of grape and musketry, and planted them in the enemy's lines. The enemy was driven from his position, and the French Marshal then withdrew into his entrenched camp. General Byng was permitted to bear, as an honourable augmentation to his arms, the colours of the 31st Regiment, as an especial mark in appreciation of the heroic valour displayed by him. The loss of the Allies during these operations was 32 officers, 618 men killed; 5 general officers, 228 officers, 3,674 men wounded; and 504 taken prisoners. The loss of the French has been estimated at 6,000, and two guns and some prisoners were taken.

Orthes 27th February 1814

After the passage of the Nive and the battles in front of Bayonne, the weather became very wet and wintery, the rivers and streams became swollen and impassable, and active operations against the enemy were suspended. Soult, considering his position before Bayonne to be impregnable crossed to the right bank of the Adour, leaving his right wing in the entrenched camp. On the 14th February, 1814, the weather became more favourable, active operations were resumed, and some actions occurred in which the enemy were driven from their positions and retired, destroying all the bridges behind them. The Allies followed in pursuit as soon as the bridges could be restored, and on the 17th the French retired across the Gave d'Oleron. Soult, concentrating his forces, took up a strong position on the ridge of Sauveterre, covering the road that leads to Orthes and destroying all the bridges behind him. On the 23rd, pontoons arrived and Hill crossed the Gave d'Oleron at Villeneave on the following day, and the 3rd and light Divisions crossed at the same place. Soult's position was turned and he hastily retreated to Orthes.

The Allied Army arrived in front of the strong position which the French Marshal had taken up on the 26th. On the 27th, the 4th Division assaulted the village of St Boës, and then, supported by the 6th Division, advanced to attack the heights occupied by the French left and centre, but from its difficult position were obliged to retire. The village of St. Boës was now repeatedly gained and lost: 'Five times breaking through the scattered houses did Ross carry his battle into the wider space beyond; yet ever as the troops issued forth the French guns from the open hills smote them in front, and the reserve battery on the Dax

road swept through them with grape from flank to flank; at the same moment the enemy's supporting masses rushed forward with a wasting fire, and lapping the flanks with skirmishers, which poured along the ravines on either hand, forced the shattered columns back into the village.'

The crisis now became urgent and Picton was directed to advance with the 3rd and 6th Divisions, also Bernard's brigade of the light Division and the 7th Division. Wading through a deep morass, sinking in mud and water above the knees, and in some places nearly up to the waist, the gallant troops pressed forward, and, gaining the top of the heights, dislodged the enemy. The French now retired contesting each point. Meanwhile Hill had crossed the river above Orthes, and advanced parallel to the line of Soult's retreat, whose object was to gain the bridge of Sault de Navailles. The retreat had been slow and leisurely, but when Soult perceived Hill's parallel movement he hurried the march of his columns. Afraid of being intercepted, the French now threw away their arms and knapsacks and passed the bridge like a scared flock of fleeing sheep. The English cavalry, nearing the bridge, sabred about 300 and took many prisoners. Night coming on, the pursuit ceased. The loss of the enemy was about 4,000 men, and that of the Allies 18 officers, 255 men killed, 132 officers, 1,759 men wounded; and 73 missing. Regiments suffering particularly heavy casualties were the 6th, 20th, 45th, 87th and 88th Foot. Six pieces of cannon and a great many prisoners were taken.

Toulouse 10th April 1814

The Battle of Toulouse, which was fought on the 10th April, 1814, was the last of the general actions in the Peninsular War. Soult continued his retreat after the Battle of Orthes, pursued by Wellington. The town of Toulouse was surrounded on three sides by the canal of Lanquedoc and the Garonne, and the left of that river was fortified with strong field works in front of the ancient walls. Beyond the canal was a range of heights which was strongly fortified with five redoubts connected by lines of entrenchments.

The battle commenced at 7 o'clock in the morning. The advanced posts of the enemy were driven in by the Light and 3rd Divisions within the fortified positions. Marshal Beresford, with the 4th and 6th Divisions, crossed the Ers, carried the village of Montblanc, and, proceeding up the river, formed up opposite the enemy's extreme right. The Spaniards, under Lieutenant General Freyre, boldly advanced to attack the left of the position under a heavy fire, but were repulsed and driven down the hill with great slaughter. Picton was directed to make a feint attack on the Jumeau Canal Bridge, which he converted into a real attack, hoping thereby to check the progress of the French in pursuit of the fleeing Spaniards. Arriving at the counterscarp of the redoubt which defended the bridge, he found it protected by a ditch 6 feet deep and as many broad. Being without scaling ladders, his brave Division jumped into the ditch, and, by climbing on one another's shoulders, tried to reach the top of the wall; the attempt was impracticable, and Picton withdrew with the loss of 400 men and officers. Meanwhile, Marshal Beresford, with the 4th and 6th Divisions, gained the heights on the enemy's right and the redoubt which, protected that flank. The movement was continued along the ridge, and the two principal redoubts and fortified houses in the enemy's centre were carried by the 6th Division. The enemy were afterwards driven, at the point of the bayonet, from the two remaining redoubts and entrenchments on the left, and the whole range of heights was in possession of the British. The enemy retired during the night, leaving Generals Harispe, Baurot, St Hilaire, and 1,600 prisoners in the hands of the victors. According to the French account their loss was a little more than 3,000, but this account is not reliable. One gun was taken in the field and eight in the town, together with a large quantity of stores. The loss of the allies was 31 officers. 564 men killed; 248 officers, 3,798 men wounded; 3 officers and 15 men missing. Regiments suffering particularly heavy casualties were the 11th, 36th, 42nd, 61st, 79th and 88th Foot.

It is interesting to note that of the thirteen recipients of the Military General Service Medal with fourteen or more bars, whose names appear on page 69, eleven of them received this bar, though it commemorates the last action fought in the Peninsular War. Ten of these men received the bars for Nive and Orthes; eight those for Nivelle, Nive and Orthes; whilst Haggerty and Nixon were not present at any of these four actions.

Military General Service Medals

Regiment	Egypt	Maida	Vimiera	Roleia	Sahagun and Benevente	Benevente	Sahagun	Corunna	Martinique	Talavera	Guadaloupe	Busaco	Barrosa	Fuentes d'Onor	Albuhera	Ciudad Rodrigo	Java	Badajos	Salamanca	Fort Detroit	Chateauguay	Chrystler's Farm	Vittoria	Pyrenees	St Sebastian	Nivelle	Nive	Orthes	Toulouse	Number of Medals	Max bars: Officers	Max bars: Other ranks
1st Life Gds																							72						84	*106*	2	2
2nd Life Gds																						1	62						76	*94*	2	2
Rl Horse Gds																							121						116	*158*	2	2
3rd Dgn Gds								1		97				2	83								92	1					112	*150*	4	4
5th Dgn Gds								1							79				101				109						140	*156*	3	3
1st Rl Dgns								1							79				89				113	3					105	*151*	4	3
3rd Lt Dgns																			89				112						122	*137*	3	3
4th Dgns										98				55	81				92				95						99	*131*	7	6
6th Dgns																									1					*1*	2	2
7th Lt Dgns					1	4		85	2																		18	145	116	*206*	4	4
8th Lt Dgns	7																													*7*		1
9th Lt Dgns																					1	1								*2*		1
10th Lt Dgns						4		93	1														142					105	163	*215*	4	4
11th Lt Dgns	10																1		87				1							*98*	2	2
12th Lt Dgns	48																1		86				104			1	28	30		*128*	5	4
13th Lt Dgns	1														90								92	3		16	22	53	85	*124*	7	6
14th Lt Dgns	1									102		53	1	79				72	109				133	91		42	47	95	125	*184*	11	11
15th Lt Dgns							99							1									132					95	142	*184*	4	4
16th Lt Dgns										86		48		62					71				80				30	2	3	*126*	6	6
18th Lt Dgns						1		79				1											90			28	5	69	124	*165*	7	5
20th Lt Dgns		4	17	33																										*36*	3	2
22nd Lt Dgns	46																54													*93*	1	2
23rd Lt Dgns	34							1		60												1								*123*	2	2
Rl Art	48	39	55	81	1	1	9	433	48	168	21	216	147	181	133	10	308	382	582	6	3	4	1023	537	621	194	195	403	740	*2134*	12	14
Rl Engrs	3	3	3	2					6	5	3	3	2	5		3		8	13	1			8	2	12	11	12	5	6	*46*	8	—
Rl Sprs & Mnrs	8								3	1	1	1			15		3	9	29	1			28	13	56	56	46	33	33	*118*	—	7
1st Ft (Gren) Gds								348					108												63	241	259			*606*	3	4
2nd (Cold) Ft Gds	70									141			104	36	108	116			161				175		27	72	80			*337*	6	10
3rd Ft (Scots) Gds	63									164			119	73	139	169		1	109				239		42	105	155	1	1	*425*	6	9

LINE REGIMENTS

Regiment	Egypt	Maida	Vimiera	Roleia	Sahagun and Benevente	Benevente	Sahagun	Corunna	Martinique	Talavera	Guadaloupe	Busaco	Barrosa	Fuentes d'Onor	Albuhera	Ciudad Rodrigo	Java	Badajos	Salamanca	Fort Detroit	Chateauguay	Chrystler's Farm	Vittoria	Pyrenees	St Sebastian	Nivelle	Nive	Orthes	Toulouse	Number of Medals	Max bars: Officers	Max bars: Other ranks
1st Ft	29							74	2		7	114		38		110		147	174				145		35		59			*327*	6	9
2nd Ft	28			74				67			18			1	2	1		1	76				90	66	13	30	9	11	68	*163*	6	10
3rd Ft								5		130				64	165				2				164		88	87	62		125	*281*	7	8
4th Ft				2				88			6				21	1		106	217				154		171	38	62			*321*	6	7
5th Ft			54	69				105			16	64		39		65		73	195				145		96	87	44	127	154	*322*	12	11
6th Ft			60	92				100				17		1									255	195		107		217		*337*	7	8
7th Ft									111	100					179	2	256		124		159	156	213	193	41	57	46	179	205	*438*	13	13
8th Ft	42										113																			*142*	1	2
9th Ft	1		76	203				85				90	42	32				1	150				186		196	51	97			*359*	7	10
10th Ft	60																													*60*	1	1
11th Ft														71		1		2	1	62			2	148	5	105	78	89	160	*277*	6	7
12th Ft																																
13th Ft	24									70		60																		*88*	2	2
14th Ft								79														74								*149*	2	2
15th Ft									26		44																			*47*	2	2
16th Ft																																
17th Ft														1		2				2	1	2				1	1		1	*2*	8	—
18th Ft	12																													*12*		
19th Ft																																
20th Ft	103	72	1	63				85				14											164	124	18	28	29	110	90	*269*	10	11
21st Ft																																
22nd Ft																																
23rd Ft	31		1	1					68	77					121	84		120	118				117	107	30	53	37	130	140	*295*	10	12
24th Ft	21									115		63		78		81		3	99				89	82		24		75	1	*184*	9	9
25th Ft	34										42		104								1	1								*125*	6	3

The final two columns, **Officers** and **Other ranks**, fall under the heading **Maximum number of bars awarded**.

Regiment	Egypt	Maida	Roleia	Vimiera	Sahagun	Benevente	Sahagun and Benevente	Corunna	Martinique	Talavera	Guadaloupe	Busaco	Barrosa	Fuentes d'Onor	Albuhera	Ciudad Rodrigo	Java	Badajos	Salamanca	Fort Detroit	Chateauguay	Chrystler's Farm	Vittoria	Pyrenees	St Sebastian	Nivelle	Nive	Orthes	Toulouse	Number of Medals	Officers	Other ranks
26th Ft	12	122						162											1					1			1	1	1	173	1	5
27th Ft	90	122						1		1		113	1		2	55		2	165	132			146	126	28	81	47	113	144	445	9	13
28th Ft	27							124		18		74	132		127	1		3	3				220	160	1	90	103	101	146	376	8	8
29th Ft			90	88						103		65			114									1						150	8	5
30th Ft	20														42			11	102	77										136	4	7
31st Ft	1									121		68			116			2					122	97		52	53	55	83	184	9	9
32nd Ft			77	109				126		4				1	1			197					1	146		101	79	114	76	283	8	9
33rd Ft																												1		1	1	
34th Ft												78			145								162	134		49	70	70	112	198	8	
35th Ft	1	46																												46	1	2
36th Ft			33	87				72		6		1			2				113				2	112	10	68	55	69	121	212	9	10
37th Ft																							1							1		1
38th Ft			39	65				85		12		62			8			67	165				119		134	23	38		12	243	7	9
39th Ft			1									66			128								207	162		82	95	102	209	344	8	8
40th Ft	25		51	114				1		135		101			1	35		126	116	137			210	146	8	83	27	125	176	373	10	13
41st Ft																						62								62	1	1
42nd Ft	65	1						141		9				103		206			90					248		224	166	162	228	252	448	7	10
43rd Ft				126				101		23		48		140		268		269	252				307	191	21	162	138	3	291	485	12	12
44th Ft	53														42			93	80											153	3	4
45th Ft	1		73	121				3		144		115			65			140	143	142			170	129		76	43	145	155	278	11	15
46th Ft											21	18																		23	2	2
47th Ft														51									90		90	29	41			108	4	5
48th Ft										200		101			190			83	137	98			140	132	17	80	20	110	138	310	11	12
49th Ft								1							1?	2			1	1	5	61								74	9	1
50th Ft	22		36	112				103				11		15	47			2					180	149		39	53	60	107	271	9	10
51st Ft			1	83				85				62		73					114				135	120	23	79	5	77		202	6	8
52nd Ft								62		26		175	1	121		302		260	251				269	215	52	135	115	214	239	452	10	14
53rd Ft	47									79		54						1	1	75			61	50	11	18	12		80	129	6	9
54th Ft	47																													47	1	1
55th Ft																																
56th Ft															122								172	131		86	80	51	125	237	7	8
57th Ft													69						52				35	29		13		23		173	5	5
58th Ft	24	102						1																								
59th Ft								78				6					104		1				120		115	17	37			275	5	4
60th Ft	9		13	15				6	8	15	15	14			10	2		16	14	18			24	19	1	7	8	10	16	77	14	15
61st Ft	36	24						1		136		74		1				2	154				3	113	1	66	62	96	131	277	9	8
62nd Ft																										64	83			89	2	2
63rd Ft											46	39																		59	2	2
64th Ft																																
65th Ft																																
66th Ft										97		56			99				1				110	104		37	43	52	92	172	8	9
67th Ft													67																	67	1	1
68th Ft																			96				136	94	18	45		93		151	5	6
69th Ft	2																105													105	2	1
70th Ft									1			8																		9	1	1
71st Ft			104	147				131		3				123									237	182		90	131	141	182	388	8	10
72nd Ft																																
73rd Ft																																
74th Ft														118	96	111		90	113				142	124		69	35	129	141	223	11	11
75th Ft																																
76th Ft								124																		73	99		1	169	3	3
77th Ft		97														64		76					1	1			1	1	1	89	2	7
78th Ft		97						1									107						1		1		1			185	2	2
79th Ft	58							146		12		149		182					175					175		142	142		212	360	10	9
80th Ft	7							1																						7		
81st Ft		119						98						2	2															213	7	2
82nd Ft			44	79				63		24			43		2			2					114	99	20	67		87	1	218	6	8

| | | | | | | | | | | | | | | | | | | | | | | | | | | | | | | | Maximum number of bars awarded | |
Regiment	Egypt	Maida	Vimiera	Roleia	Sahagun and Benevente	Sahagun	Benevente	Corunna	Martinique	Talavera	Guadaloupe	Busaco	Fuentes d'Onor	Barrosa	Albuhera	Ciudad Rodrigo	Java	Badajos	Salamanca	Fort Detroit	Chateauguay	Chrystler's Farm	Vittoria	Pyrenees	St Sebastian	Nivelle	Nive	Orthes	Toulouse	Number of Medals	Officers	Other ranks
83rd Ft												117	72		79	1		89	99			81	110	60		62	18	94	98	203	11	12
84th Ft																												88	151	155	2	2
85th Ft														1		54										86	89	96		146	3	4
86th Ft	8																													8	1	1
87th Ft												86			110								102	57	5	59	22	72	70	173	7	8
88th Ft	20											124	163			206		200	195				162	229	173	153	121	201	220	408	10	13
89th Ft	32																41		1			80								150	1	2
90th Ft	44							98			120								1											176	2	3
91st Ft			95	141				105				14												195		141	132	161	177	283	8	8
92nd Ft	79							140				11			130				2				193	168		64	103	116	131	310	7	9
93rd Ft																																
94th Ft													1		120			109	134			130	163	121		112	78	140	164	221	10	10
95th Ft			40	105				192		1		11	1			163	110	153				186	300	308	403	314	59	162	167	299 421	691	12 14
96th Ft												19																		19	1	1
97th Ft	7			2	69							70		63		36														88	4	6
98th Ft																						1								1	1	
Rl York Rgrs									34		33																			47	2	2
Rl Staff Corps			3	5				17				6	1	10	3	3		16	25	21			22	11	1	14	12	5	34	60	8	8
Rl Wgn Train			3	7			2	36				15	13	2	3	16		26	43	45			70	31	24	8	7	21	59	130	6	11
Staff Officers	10	2	15	13	2			5	28	8		22	30	5	10	23	7	29	32	29	1	2	38	31	16	33	23	21	24	127	12	12
Chaplains												2										1	1		1			2	2	3		4
Comm Dept Offrs		1	5	5				2	11	12		2	17	3	9	6		8	4	27			46	19	3	29	26	27	32	85	11	11
Medical Staff	3	2	6	6				7	3	2		4	4	3	3	1	1	4	6	10		1	13	12	6	12	10	11	13	53	11	11
Payr Gen Dept	1	1	1	1						2		1		2					1				5	3	1	1	1	3	8	14	7	
Cav Staff Corps					1														2				5	12		10	8	10	15	19	7	
Civil Artificers																				2			1		2					3	3	
Newfndlnd Fencbls																						3								3		3
Canadian Militia (Upp & Low)																				224	250	67								533	1	1
1st W Ind Regt									25		6																			25	2	2
3rd W Ind Regt									42		42	5																		43	2	2
6th W Ind Regt											5																			5		
8th W Ind Regt									15		17																			17		
Rl W Ind Rgrs									3		9																			9		
HEI Co Service	5																41													46		
Chasseurs Brit															2							3		2	2	1	1	1		5	5	
Corsican Rgrs	?	3																												?		
4th Rl Veterans Bn														1																1	?	
Ind Warrs (Can)																						?								?	?	
York Lt Inf												1		1																?		?
Ind Chfs & Warrs																				15	75	10								102		

KING'S GERMAN LEGION

												Busaco	Fuentes d'Onor	Barrosa	Albuhera	Ciudad Rodrigo	Java	Badajos	Salamanca	Fort Detroit	Chateauguay	Chrystler's Farm	Vittoria	Pyrenees	St Sebastian	Nivelle	Nive	Orthes	Toulouse	Number of Medals	Officers	Other ranks
Staff Officers												1		1		1		1		2			1	1	1	2	2			3	8	
Art Officers												3		3		3		2	3	3			4	3	3	2	2	3	3	9	8	
Art Other Ranks												58		51		4	53	23	9	48			52	32	32	11		45	50	82		12
1st Lt Dgns												3		1		1		1	77				67			1		2	72	84	7	4
2nd Lt Dgns														1					92				70					2	80	100		
1st Hsrs												81		72	1	71	1	66	74				69	73	3	83	5	74	74	112	10	11
2nd Hsrs															43			1	2				2	1	1	1	1			43	1	5
3rd Hsrs							96																				1	1		96	1	3
1st Lt Bn												4		5		5	111		3	108			124	1	115	114	116	1	1	137	7	9
2nd Lt Bn												6		7		9	97	4	2	114			115	1	118	107	109	1	7	144	9	8
1st Line Bn							1					66		62	1	73	1	69	3	72			64		61	58	58		1	95	9	9
2nd Line Bn												80		71		72	1	70	78				76		74	72	74			101	9	9
5th Line Bn												78		71		60	73	76					73		68	70	69			98	9	9

	Egypt	Maida	Roleia	Vimiera	Sahagun	Benevente	Sahagun and Benevente	Corunna	Martinique	Talavera	Guadaloupe	Busaco	Fuentes d'Onor	Barrosa	Albuhera	Java	Ciudad Rodrigo	Badajos	Salamanca	Fort Detroit	Chateauguay	Chrystler's Farm	Vittoria	Pyrenees	St Sebastian	Nivelle	Nive	Orthes	Toulouse	Number of Medals		
7th Line Bn										28		19			17															34	3	5
Duke of Bruns Hsrs																						2								2		2
Bruns Oels Lt Inf			1	1											15	1		10	11	24			27	8	5	10	11	5	1	39	9	6
Offrs Corps of Guides											3		3		2				2	1			1				1	2	1	4	7	
OTHER RECIPIENTS																																
Rl Navy		1							6		2					8									2							
Rl Marines									3		4					10																
de Watteville's Regt		?																														
Dillion's Regt	?																															
de Rolle's Regt	?																															
Stuart's Regt	?																															
Ancient Irish Fencbls																																
Maltese Pnrs	?																															
Foreign Corps	?																															
2nd Bombay NI	?																															
13th Bombay NI	?																															

Military General Service Medals to Naval Recipients

Bars	Ranks and Name	Ship
Maida (1)	* Lieut Wm F. Carroll, RN, Flag Lt to Sir S. Smith	
Martinique (6)	Lieut Wm B. Bigland	*Pompée*
	* Lieut Thos Burdwood	*Belleisle*
	Mid Chas S. Jackson	*Captain*
	Master's Mate Edwin Richards	*Pompée*
	* Master's Mate James Scott	*Pompée*
	AB William Wells	*Amarouth*
Guadaloupe (2)	Surgeon John Neill	*Sceptre*
	* Lieut E. W. Pitt	*Sceptre*
Java (8)	Master's Mate John E. Cabburn	*Cornelia*
	Master's Mate Lawrence Dennehy	*Illustrious*
	Act Capt Robert Festing	*Illustrious*
	* Lieut Edward Lloyd Vol. on Staff of Gen. Auchmuty	
	Mid Wm C. Simmons	*Illustrious*
	LK Thomas Birtles	*Scipion*
	Coxswain John Norris	*Leda*
	Seaman James Reynolds	

Henry Barrister, Ord, *Illustrious,* whose name does not appear in this list also received the medal for Java. Possibly there are some others omitted.

Bars		
St Sebastian (2)	Ord Colewell	
	Ord Colville Thos	*Surveillante*

Military General Service Medals to Royal Marine Recipients

Bars	Rank and Name	Ship
Martinique (3)	2nd Lieut William Balhetchet	*Neptune* (also Guadaloupe)
	2nd Lieut George Hookey	*Acasta*
	Capt John Robyns	*Neptune*
Guadaloupe (4)	*Capt Christopher Abbott	*Pompée*
	2nd Lieut William Balhetchet	*Pompée*
	* Lieut James Clarke	*Pompée*
	2nd Lieut Samuel R. Wesley	*Abercombie*
Java (10)	* 2nd Lieut William Calamy	*Nisno*
	Lieut Samuel Garriston	*Bucephalus*
	Lieut George Gill	*Scipion*
	* Lieut Richard W. Pascoe	*Phoebe*
	2nd Lieut Matthew F. Steele	*Illustrious*
	Sgt John Cressly	*President*
	Pte Francis Field	*President*
	Pte Dennis Fox	*Scipion*
	* Pte William Morgan	*Phoebe*
	Pte James Platt	*Scipion*

*These also received the corresponding Naval Medal with bars for naval services.

62 *Portuguese Commander's Cross and Medal*

A **Commander's Medal for one or two actions**

Type 1

General	Circular, skeletal medal, in the centre a green enamel laurel leaf inscribed with the name of an action on the obverse and reverse, held by a circlet of gold, bearing a laurel wreath upon blue enamel. Two inscribed laurel leaves for two actions.
Size	30mm diameter
Other details	As for Type 2.

Type 2

General	Solid circular medal
Obverse	Plain gold with a green enamel laurel leaf inscribed with the name of an action superimposed across its centre. Two inscribed laurel leaves for two actions.
Reverse	Plain; may be engraved with recipient's name, etc
Size	32mm diameter
Metal	Gold
Ribbon	Watered, dark blue with red edges.
Suspension	Straight bar suspension.

B **Commander's Cross for Three or More Actions**

General	Star with three or more white enamel double pointed arms, each point tipped with a gold ball, arms linked by a green enamel laurel wreath. Along the length of each arm a green enamel laurel leaf inscribed with the name of an action. Star surmounted by a crown.
Obverse	In the centre a gold bust of King John VI upon a blue enamel background.
Reverse	In the centre the initials of the recipient upon white enamel.
Metal	Gold
Ribbon	Watered dark blue with red centre and edges.
Suspension	Ring passing through crown apex and attached to a scalloped bar. Worn as a breast badge.

Instituted by King John VI of Portugal on the 28th June, 1816. Granted to officers of the Portuguese Army holding command during a designated action. Those commanding a division, brigade, regiment or battalion during an action were eligible, as were junior officers who took command upon the death or disablement of their superiors. Officers above the rank of major attached to an eligible general were also awarded the distinction.

In the original decree, sixteen actions were designated:
Vimiera, Corunna, Talavera, Busaco, Fuentes d'Onor, Albuhera, Siege of Ciudad Rodrigo, Siege of Badajoz, Salamanca, Vittoria, Pyrenees, Siege of St Sebastian, Nivelle, Nive, Orthes and Toulouse. In addition, several undesignated actions are found on certain crosses and medals and include:
Almaraz, Arapiles, Arroyo de Molinos, Gariz and Maya.

Portuguese sources state 161 awards were authorized, of which 83 were to British officers. Sub-divided as follows:

26 for 1 action	4 for Busaco
15 for 2 actions	2 for Fuentes d'Onor
15 for 3 actions	1 for Albuhera
13 for 4 actions	1 for Badajoz
4 for 5 actions	4 for Salamanca
4 for 6 actions	2 for Vittoria
2 for 8 actions	5 for Pyrenees
2 for 9 actions	2 for Nive
2 for 10 actions	2 for Orthes
	3 for Toulouse
	26

As with the Campaign Cross (No 63), these figures were undoubtedly exceeded. Notably, two prominent omissions from the Portuguese list were the awards to Sir Denis Pack, with a cross for eleven actions, and that to Viscount Beresford with the following twelve:
Corunna, Buzaco, Ciudad Rodrigo, Albuhera, Badajoz, Salamanca, Vittoria, Pyrenees, Nivelle, Nive, Orthes, Toulouse.

---

63 *Portuguese Campaign Cross* 1816

A Portuguese Pattern

General	Pattée Cross with broad ornamental borders and a green enamel wreath between two arms.
Obverse	In the centre, the arms of Portugal enclosed by a blue enamel band inscribed 'GUERRA PENINSULAR'.
Reverse	In the centre, a numeral '1-6' enclosed by a laurel wreath. A variation has the numeral enclosed by a blue enamel band inscribed, 'CAMPANHAS'.
Size	38mm diagonal diameter
Other details	As for English pattern.

B English Pattern

General	Pattée Cross, arms with a broad border ornamented with laurel.
Obverse	In the centre within a laurel wreath the legend in three lines, 'GUERRA/PENINSU/LAR'.
Reverse	In the centre within a laurel wreath a Roman numeral 'I-VI'.
Size	38mm diameter
Metal	Gold or silver
Ribbon	Watered dark blue with red edges.
Suspension	Straight bar suspension.
Naming	May be engraved on the limbs of the cross

Instituted by King John VI of Portugal on 28th June 1816. Awarded to officers for the campaigns of 1809-1814. The number on the cross corresponding to the years of campaign service. Issued in silver for 1-3 years, and gold for 4-6 years. A smaller silver cross was authorized to designated Portuguese 'Other Ranks'.

British officers serving with the Portuguese Army were eligible for the Officer's Cross. Portuguese sources state that 1,745 crosses were authorised of which 210 were to British Officers. Of the 210, 75 were for two campaigns, 61 for '3', 42 for '4', 26 for '5', and 6 for '6'. However, these official figures were undoubtedly exceeded. Differences also occur between the campaign number authorised for a particular officer, and that of the cross eventually procured.
   Obtaining their own crosses, British Officers may be found with a cross of English, Portuguese or private pattern.
   Variations abound for this particular award.

64 *Waterloo Medal* 18th June 1815

Obverse	The laureated head of the Prince Regent with the legend 'GEORGE P. REGENT.'
Reverse	The winged figure of Victory seated on a pedestal and holding a palm branch in her right hand and an olive branch in her left; below the pedestal is the word 'WATERLOO' within a rectangle. The date 'JUNE 18 1815' is in two lines underneath. The word 'WELLINGTON' is above the seated figure.
Size	35mm diameter
Ribbon	39mm wide, crimson with 6.5mm wide dark blue edges.
Suspension	The medals were originally issued with a steel clip on the piece through which passed a steel ring 28mm diameter, through which the ribbon was threaded. Many recipients removed the method of suspension as issued and replaced it with designs of their own.
Designer	T. Wyon
Naming	In large impressed roman capitals.

Though styled the Waterloo Medal, it was awarded to anyone who had taken part in one or more of the following battles: Ligny, 16th June; Quatre Bras, 16th June; Waterloo, 18th June. Every soldier present at either of these battles was credited with two extra years service, to count for all purposes.

By a General Order dated 29th July 1815, the 1st Regiment of Foot Guards were granted the title of 'Grenadiers' for their service during the battle of Waterloo.

This is the first general medal issued by the British Government to *all* soldiers present. This statement must not be confused and read as if this were the first battle for which a general issue was made. The Dunbar Medal of 1650 was issued to both officers and men, but there is no verification of its having been given to *all* officers and men. The Military General Service Medal commemorates earlier battles, but was not issued until 1848.

It is also the first *campaign* medal awarded to the next-of-kin of men killed in action.

This medal has another distinction in that it was the first on which the recipient's name was impressed around the edge by machine.

The Waterloo Campaign

Napoleon's return from exile on Elba (1st March, 1815), his triumphant entry into Paris and resumption of full powers, brought resolute action from his main opponents: Great Britain, Prussia, Russia and Austria. Declaring him an outlaw, they determined upon his downfall and planned a concerted and overwhelming invasion of France. Opposing them, Napoleon hoped to defeat individual allied member states before their combined strength could be brought to bear. Calculating the Russian and Austrian threat would not materialize until mid-July, Napoleon proposed to deliver a knock-out blow to the Anglo-Dutch and Prussian armies mustered in the Netherlands posing the most immediate threat.

With dazzling energy and efficiency, Napoleon raised and organised his country's forces, reserving for himself a field force of 124,000—the 'Army of the North' for the Netherlands campaign. Ranged against him in the Netherlands; an Anglo-German-Dutch army of 103,000 under the Duke of Wellington and the Prussian 'Army of the Lower Rhine' numbering 124,000 under Prince Blucher von Wahlstadt.

Secretly concentrating his forces in the north, Napoleon launched his army into the Netherlands (15th June) with the objective of driving a wedge between his enemies and defeating each in detail. By the end of the first day, some measure of success had been achieved; screening units of both armies had been encountered and forced back by divergent routes; the Prussians retreating north-east towards Sombreffe, Nassau units north upon Quatre Bras.

For 16th June, Napoleon planned to strike with his centre and right wing (65,000 men) against the Prussians who were in the process of concentrating three of their four army corps (85,000 men) at Sombreffe. The left wing commanded by Marshal Ney (42,000 men) was ordered to seize Quatre Bras and then fall upon the flank and rear of the Prussians to complete their destruction.

At Quatre Bras on 16th June, Ney with 22,000 men available, delayed his advance against the 8,000 strong Dutch/Nassau contingent under the Prince of Orange until the afternoon. Then, with the attack under way at 2pm, he was on the point of overwhelming this force when Wellington and the first of a series of allied reinforcements arrived to frustrate it. (Brigades of Kempt, Pack and Best, Brunswick cavalry and infantry, Van Merlen's Dutch cavalry.) A more substantial attack followed and succeeded in driving back the Dutch and Brunswick held right and centre; during the course of which the Duke of Brunswick was mortally wounded. On the left, the allied line was tenaciously held by the brigades of Kempt and Pack.

Meanwhile, Ney, who increasingly counted upon the arrival of D'Erlon's corps (20,000 men) to clinch the battle, was informed of their diversion by Imperial Order to the battlefield at Ligny. Furious, Ney dispatched orders that they resume their march to Quatre Bras, with the result that the corps, vital to both fields of battle, participated in neither.

Further reinforcements then bolstered the allied line (C. Halkett's and Kielmansegge's Brigades) and Ney, still fuming, ordered a series of savage cavalry attacks upon the allied left and centre. Halkett's Brigade was severely tested, with cavalry crushing the 69th Foot and driving the 33rd and 73rd into cover. But the attacks were held and with successive allied reinforcements, weight of numbers were beginning to tell against the French. At 6pm with the arrival of the British Guards Brigade, Wellington counter-attacked and drove the French back. By 9pm, the battle had ended inconclusively with both armies holding their initial positions.

French casualties numbered 4,200, those of the allies, 4,800.

That same day, at Ligny, Napoleon gained a hard won victory over the Prussians forcing them to retreat north upon Wavre. Prussian casualties numbered 16,000 and included Blucher, injured whilst leading a cavalry charge. A further 8-10,000 disaffected Germans abandoned their colours soon after the battle. French casualties numbered 10,000.

On 17th June, believing the Prussians to be decisively beaten and of no further threat, Napoleon turned his attention to Wellington and casually dispatched Marshal Grouchy with 33,000 men after the retreating Prussians.

With his position at Quatre Bras made untenable, Wellington withdrew north to maintain contact with Blucher. Ney, again slow in moving, permitted the allied army to retreat unhindered. Not until Napoleon arrived in person did the pursuit begin in earnest, only to be thwarted by a torrential rainstorm.

By the end of the day, Wellington's army had taken position about Mont St Jean and with the promise of Prussian support was resolved to fight the next day.

Battle of Waterloo

Wellington's army approximately 69,000 strong opposed the French with 72,000. A further 17,000 men of Coleville and Prince Fredericks' command were stationed ten miles to the west at Hal and Turbize against possible flanking moves, but took no active part in the battle.

To achieve the decisive victory he sought, Napoleon planned to break the allied centre by a mass attack supported by concentrated artillery fire. Because the sodden nature of the ground made manoeuvre difficult, the attack timed for 9am was postponed until 1pm.

With his polyglot force, Wellington's plan was one of containment until such time as the French attack became exhausted or until the Prussians made their promised appearance.

Unknown to Napoleon, Grouchy had lost effective contact with the Prussians and Blucher had restored his defeated army to such an extent that by 2pm, three of his four army corps were on the move west to aid Wellington.

At 11.30 the battle began with an attack on Hougoumont by Jerome's division. The original garrison of the Chateau and grounds consisted of four light companies of the Foot Guards with Hanoverian and Nassauer contingents under the command of Colonel Macdonell and Lord Saltoun. In an epic day long action, all attempts by the French were repulsed as what was initially intended as a diversionary attack proved increasingly to be a drain on French resources.

At 1pm, with preparations for the grand attack nearing completion, forward units of Bulow's IV Prussian Corps were observed in the distance. To counter the threat, Napoleon ordered Lobau's Corps with Domon and Subervie's Cavalry Divisions east to cover his right flank.

At 1pm, French batteries opened fire in preparation for the main attack and at 1.30pm D'Erlon's four divisions with cavalry support advanced upon the allied centre-left. Durutte's Division successfully took Papelotte from the Nassauers. Quiot's failed to dislodge the 2nd Light Battalion KGL under Major Baring from La Haye Sainte. but drove the 95th from their supporting position nearby. In the centre, Bijlandt's Dutch Brigade, demoralised by the intense bombardment, fled leaving Kempt and Packs' Brigades to stem the attack. Picton was killed as both brigades counter-attacked and halted the unwieldly mass. Nevertheless, French numbers began to take effect and Pack's Brigade wavered under pressure. However, Uxbridge had noted the crisis in the British line and had readied his heavy cavalry for a counter-stroke. Unleashed, Somerset's Household Brigade scattered cavalry and infantry on D'Erlon's left and simultaneously Ponsonby's Union Brigade tore into the divisions of Donzelot and Marcognet with fearful effect. The French broke and fled in chaos leaving countless dead and 3,000 prisoners. Flushed with their success, the two cavalry brigades continued their charge forward and attacked the French batteries before them, oblivious of orders to halt. On tired mounts and in a disorganised state, they then fell prey themselves to a counter-attack by fresh French cavalry. Ponsonby was killed as the British cavalry was driven back with heavy loss; Vandeleur's cavalry covering the retreating remnants.

When at 3.30pm sufficient numbers of D'Erlon's Corps had been re-assembled, Napoleon ordered Ney to take La Haye Sainte as a prelude to a larger attack. An attack was mounted on La Haye Sainte but failed. However, Ney noted what he took to be a general movement to the rear amongst the allied ranks beyond La Haye Sainte. Misconstruing this movement of wounded, prisoners etc as the beginnings of a general retreat, Ney ordered cavalry forward to exploit the situation.

At 4pm upon Ney's order, Milhaud's cavalry moved forward, followed, on his own initiative, by that of Lefebvre-Desnoette's, a total of 5,000 advancing on the unbroken allied centre-right between Hougoumont and La Haye Sainte. Despite heavy losses, the cavalry gained the position of the allied artillery and infantry, but unable to break any square, and making no attempt to disable or remove captured artillery, they were driven off by Uxbridge's allied cavalry. Reforming, the French repeated the attack, but only to the same effect.

Although considering these attacks premature, Napoleon nevertheless dispatched Kellerman and Guyots' cavalry to Ney's support and at 5.30pm, a total of 9,000 cavalry assaulted the beleaguered squares.

French reserve cavalry was wrecked as successive attacks failed, lacking as they did close artillery and infantry support. Only at 6pm were units of Foy and Bachelu's Divisions sent forward, but with the cavalry support greatly weakened, they were driven back with heavy loss.

Successive charges had also depleted the best of Uxbridge's cavalry and weaker elements had begun to falter: sections of Trip's cavalry refusing to advance and the Cumberland Hussars fleeing the field rather than fight.

Meanwhile, on the French right the first of Blucher's army corps had arrived. At 4.30pm, the head of Bulow's IV Corps debouched from Paris Wood and by 6pm had driven Lobau's Corps from Plancenoit. A counter-attack by the Young Guard soon restored it to French control, yet Prussian pressure in this quarter increasingly placed a demand on Napoleon's attention and his reserves, deflecting both from Wellington.

In the centre, following the failure of the cavalry charges, Napoleon ordered a further attempt upon La Haye Sainte. Soon after 6pm, with Baring's men largely out of ammunition, Ney succeeded in its capture. Taking immediate advantage, Ney brought forward artillery and infantry and from advanced positions poured a destructive fire upon the allied centre. Alten's Division and the Brigades of Pack, Kempt and Lambert were devastated—Ompteda was killed and his line battalions slaughtered in attempting to counter-attack, while the 27th Foot were nearly destroyed in holding their exposed position.

With the allied centre in tatters, Ney appealed for fresh troops to force the decisive breakthrough. Fourteen battalions of the Old and Middle Guard were available but with the Prussians pressing hard upon the flank, Napoleon refused to commit his only reserve—and the vital moment was lost.

By 7pm two battalions of Old Guard had again evicted Bulow's men from Plancenoit and with his right flank stabilized, Napoleon brought forward the Guard for a final attempt upon Wellington's line. With Ney at their head, five battalions of the Middle Guard advanced upon the allied centre-right, supported on their right by D'Erlon's divisions and on the left by Reille making yet another attempt upon Hougoumont. Under intense fire, the Guard gained the crest of the allied ridge. In the centre, the leading battalion was broken and pursued by Maitland's Guard Brigade. To the right, two battalions clashed with Sir Colin Halkett's Brigade and the Brunswick Corps and were only repulsed with difficulty. To the rear and left, the appearance of two more battalions turned back Maitland's advance. Moving forward with other rallied Guard elements, they came under fire from Colborne's 52nd Regiment positioned along their left flank. Further assailed to their front by the re-organised Maitland Brigade, and rear by W. Halkett's Hanoverians, the Guard, demoralised and overwhelmed, broke when charged by Colborne.

With the Guard in retreat, the heart went out of the French army and everywhere their line crumbled. Soon after 8pm, sensing the French had come to the end of their resources, Wellington ordered a general advance to finish the battle.

Spearheaded by Vivian's and Vandeleur's cavalry and the brigades of Adam and W. Halkett, the long suffering allied army swept forward. Simultaneously, on Wellington's left, Zeiten's I Corp went into action, thrusting deep into the collapsing French right. In conjunction with this, Blucher, with both Bulow's IV and Pirch's II Corps again attacked Plancenoit and only tenacious resistance by the Guard prevented its early capture. Elsewhere, the bulk of the French army disintegrated before the onslaught, although stubborn Guard battalions made heroic resistance and attempted an orderly withdrawal. From the protection of these battalions, Napoleon made his way south to safety. The joint allied advance continued until after 9pm when Wellington and Blucher met near La Belle Alliance when it fell to the Prussians to continue the pursuit.

Casualties: Wellington's Army 15,000, Prussians 7,000, French over 30,000.

Meanwhile, 10 miles east at Wavre, Theilmann's III Corps had held Grouchy thereby allowing the bulk of Blucher's army to march unhindered to Wellington's aid. On the 19th, Grouchy renewed his attack and defeated Theilmann, but to no avail; the vital battle, and with it the Empire, had been lost at Waterloo on 18th June, 1815.

Napoleon abdicated for a second time on 22nd June 1815 and died in exile on St Helena on 5th May, 1821.

*Extract from the official 1815 reports.

List of Regiments* under the command of Field Marshal Duke of Wellington on Sunday 18 June 1815

and the total British, Brunswick and Hanoverian loss from 16 to 26 June 1815 to which is added the computed losses of the Dutch and Prussians During the Campaign in the Netherlands

**Based on strength of the unit and the percentage of casualties.

	Officers			Rank and File				Strength of unit	** Desir- ability
	Killed	Wounded	Missing	Killed	Wounded	Missing	Total		
General Staff	12	46	3				61	—	—
1st Life Gds	2	4		24	49	4	83	228	36%
2nd Life Gds	1		1	16	40	97	155	231	67%
Rl Horse Guards	1	4	1	19	61	20	106	237	45%
1st Dragoon Gds	3	4	4	40	100	124	275	530	52%
1st, or Rl Dgns	4	9	1	86	88	9	197	394	50%
2nd, or Rl NB Dgns	6	9		96	89		199	391	51%
6th Dragoons	1	5	1	72	111	27	217	396	55%
7th Hussars		7	3	62	109	15	196	380	52%
10th Hussars	2	6		20	40	26	94	390	24%
11th Lt Dragoons	2	5		10	34	25	76	390	19%
12th Lt Dragoons	2	3		45	61		111	388	29%
13th Lt Dragoons	1	9		11	69	19	109	390	28%
15th Hussars	2	3		21	48	5	79	392	20%
16th Lt Dragoons	2	4		8	18		32	393	8%
18th Hussars		2		13	72	17	104	396	26%
23rd Lt Dragoons		5	1	14	26	33	79	387	20%
1st Lt Dgns KGL	3	11		30	99	10	153	462	33%
2nd Lt Dgns KGL	2	4		19	54	3	82	437	19%
1st Hussars KGL		1		1	5	3	10	493	2%
3rd Hussars KGL	4	8		40		78	130	622	21%
Royal Artillery	5	26		62	228	10	331	5030	7%
KGL Artillery	1	6		19	51	4	81	526	—
Rl Engineers		2					2	—	—
Rl Staff Corps		2					2	—	—
Rl Sprs and Mnrs		1			2		3	—	—
1st Ft Gds, 2nd Bn	3	9		73	353		438	976	45%
1st Ft Gds, 3rd Bn	4	12		101	487		604	1021	59%
Cold Gds, 2nd Bn	1	7		54	242	4	308	1003	31%
3rd Ft Gds, 2nd Bn	3	9		39	195		246	1061	23%
1st Ft Rl Scots, 3rd Bn	8	26		33	295		362	604	60%
4th Ft, 1st Bn		9		12	113		134	669	20%
14th Ft, 3rd Bn		3		7	26		36	571	6%
23rd Ft, 1st Bn	5	6		13	80		104	647	16%
27th Ft, 1st Bn	2	13		103	360		478	698	68%
28th Ft, 1st Bn	1	19		29	203		252	557	45%
30th Ft, 2nd Bn	6	14		51	181	27	279	615	45%
32nd Ft, 1st Bn	1	30		49	290		370	662	56%
33rd Ft	5	17		49	162	58	291	561	52%
35th Ft, 2nd Bn				5			5	570	1%

**Based on the strength of the unit and the percentage of casualties in approximate terms.

	Officers			Rank and File			Total	Strength of unit	** Desir-ability
	Killed	Wounded	Missing	Killed	Wounded	Missing			
40th Ft, 1st Bn	2	10		30	159	18	219	761	29%
42nd Ft, 1st Bn	3	21		47	266		337	526	64%
44th Ft, 2nd Bn	2	18		14	151	17	202	455	44%
51st Ft, 1st Bn		2		11	29		42	549	8%
52nd Ft, 1st Bn	1	8		16	174		199	1038	19%
54th Ft, 1st Bn				2	2		4	541	1%
59th Ft, 2nd Bn					2		2	461	2%
69th Ft, 2nd Bn	4	7		51	162	15	240	516	46%
71st Ft, 1st Bn	1	14		24	160	3	202	810	25%
73rd Ft, 2nd Bn	6	16		54	219	41	336	563	60%
79th Ft, 1st Bn	3	27	1	57	390	1	479	703	68%
91st Ft, 1st Bn	4	2		1	6		13	824	2%
92nd Ft, 1st Bn	2	27		49	322		402	588	68%
95th Ft, 1st Bn		15		28	175		220	604	36%
95th Ft, 2nd Bn		14		34	178	20	246	585	42%
95th Ft, 3rd Bn		4		3	36	7	50	188	27%
1st Lt Inf Bn KGL	4	9		37	82	13	145	423	34%
2nd Lt Inf Bn KGL	3	9	1	40	120	29	202	433	47%
1st Line Bn KGL	1	6		22	69	17	115	437	26%
2nd Line Bn KGL	1	2		18	79	7	107	437	24%
3rd Line Bn KGL	1	5		17	93	31	147	494	30%
4th Line Bn KGL	1	7		13	77	15	113	416	27%
5th Line Bn KGL	2	3		36	47	74	162	379	43%
8th Line Bn KGL	3	4		44	80	16	147	388	38%
Hanover									
Prince Regents' Hsrs							0	596	
Bremen & Verden Hsrs							0	589	
Cumberland Hsrs	1			17	33	10	61	497	
Fld Bn Bremen	1	8		11	113	106	239	512	
Fld Bn Verden		7		63	94	138	302	533	
Fld Bn York	2	2		22	68	127	221	607	
Fld Bn Luneburg	3	5	1	106	189	179	483	595	
Fld Bn Grubenhagen	1	6		15	72	122	216	621	
Fld Bn Jager Corps		3		12	38	19	72	321	
Landwehr Batt									
Bremervorde	2	4	7	16	17	29	75	632	
Osnabruck	3	6		17	62	41	129	612	
Quakenbruck	1			1	10	25	37	588	
Salzgitter		2		20	60	27	109	622	
Hamelm		4		9	60	24	97	669	
Gifhorn	2	3		13	69	19	106	617	
Hildesheim		1		3	20	12	36	617	
Peine		2		8	40	20	70	611	
Verden	2	4	3	10	97	49	165	621	
Luneburg		5		10	37	6	58	624	
Osterobe	2	5		12	93	18	130	677	
Munden		6		12	97	21	136	660	
Artillery				8	27		35	465	
Staff		2					2		
Brunswick									
Hussars	3	7		42	72		124	690	
Uhlans		2		4	23		29	232	
Advance Guard Bn		5		16	63		84	672	
Guard Bn		6		29	142		177	672	
1st Lt Inf Bn		3		4	44		51	672	
2nd Lt Inf Bn	2	5		55	122	Total Brunswick 'Missing' 260	184	672	
3rd Lt Inf Bn	1	5		35	75		116	672	
1st Line Bn	1	2		25	132		160	672	
2nd Line Bn	3	5		25	168		201	672	
3rd Line Bn		3		14	70		87	672	
Horse Artillery	1			2	6		9	510	
Foot Artillery					18		18		
Staff	2	4					6		
THE DUTCH ARMY	27	115		2058	1936		4136		
THE NASSAU CONT							1255	7025	
THE PRUSSIAN ARMY							33120		

Effective strength and composition of the Anglo-Allied Army under the command of the Duke of Wellington at Waterloo

taken from the official 1815 returns

		Men
First Corps HRH The Prince of Orange		
1st Division Maj Gen G. Cooke		
1st British Brigade	2nd Bn 1st Guards	976
Maj Gen P. Maitland	3rd Bn 1st Guards	1,021
2nd British Brigade	2nd Bn Coldstream Guards	1,003
Maj Gen Sir John Byng	2nd Bn 3rd Guards	1,061
Artillery	Capt Sandham's British Foot Bty	
Lt Col S. G. Adye	Maj Kuhlmann's KGL Horse Bty	
3rd Division Lt Gen Sir Charles Alten		
5th British Brigade	2nd Bn 30th Regt	615
Maj Gen Sir Colin Halkett	33rd Regt	561
	2nd Bn 69th Regt	516
	2nd Bn 73rd Regt	562
2nd Brigade KGL	1st Lt Bn KGL	423
Col Baron von Ompteda	2nd Lt Bn KGL	337
	5th Line Bn KGL	379
	8th Line Bn KGL	388
1st Hanoverian Brigade	Fld Bn Bremen	512
Maj Gen Count Kielmansegge	Fld Bn Verden	533
	Fld Bn York	607
	Fld Bn Luneburg	595
	Fld Bn Grubenhagen	621
	Fld Bn Jager Corps	321
Artillery	Maj Lloyd's British Foot Bty	
Lt Col J. S. Williamson	Capt Cleeve's KGL Foot Bty	
2nd Dutch Division Lt Gen Baron de Perponcher		7,700
1st Brigade	27th Dutch Jager Bn	
Maj Gen Graf van Bijlandt	7th Belgian Line Bn	
	5th Dutch Militia Bn	
	7th Dutch Militia Bn	
	8th Dutch Militia Bn	
2nd Brigade	1st Bn 2nd Nassau Regt	
Maj Gen HSH Prince Bernard	2nd Bn 2nd Nassau Regt	
of Saxe-Weimar	3rd Bn 2nd Nassau Regt	
	1st Bn Orange Nassau Regt	
	2nd Bn Orange Nassau Regt	
	Nassau Vol Jager Co	
Artillery	Capt Bijleveld's Dutch Horse Bty	
	Capt Stievenart's Belgian Foot Bty	
3rd Dutch Division Lt Gen Baron de Chasse		6,669
1st Brigade	35th Belgian Jager Bn	
Col H. Detmers	2nd Dutch Line Bn	
	4th Dutch Militia Bn	
	6th Dutch Militia Bn	
	17th Dutch Militia Bn	
	19th Dutch Militia Bn	
2nd Brigade	36th Belgian Jager Bn	
Maj Gen A. K. J. G. d'Aubreme	3rd Belgian Line Bn	
	12th Dutch Line Bn	
	13th Dutch Line Bn	
	3rd Dutch Militia Bn	
	10th Dutch Militia Bn	
Artillery	Capt de Bichin's Belgian Horse Bty	
	Capt Lux's Belgian Foot Bty	

		Men
Second Corps Lt Gen Lord Hill		
2nd Division Lt Gen Sir Henry Clinton		
3rd British Brigade	1st Bn 52nd Regt	1,038
Maj Gen F. Adam	1st Bn 71st Regt	810
	2nd Bn 95th Regt	585
	3rd Bn 95th Regt	188
1st Brigade KGL	1st Line Bn KGL	411
Col G. C. A. du Plat	2nd Line Bn KGL	437
	3rd Line Bn KGL	494
	4th Line Bn KGL	416
3rd Hanoverian Brigade	Landwehr Bn Bremervorde	632
Col W. Halkett	Landwehr Bn Osnabruck	612
	Landwehr Bn Quackenbruck	588
	Landwehr Bn Salzgitter	622
Artillery	Capt Bolton's British Foot Bty	
Lt Col C. Gold	Maj Sympher's KGL Horse Bty	
4th Division Lt Gen Sir Charles Colville		
4th British Brigade	3rd Bn 14th Regt	571
Col Mitchell	1st Bn 23rd Regt	647
	1st Bn 51st Regt	549
6th British Brigade	2nd Bn 35th Regt	570
Maj Gen Johnstone	1st Bn 54th Regt	541
	2nd Bn 59th Regt	561
	1st Bn 91st Regt	824
6th Hanoverian Brigade	Fld Bn Lauenburg	553
Maj Gen Sir James Lyon	Fld Bn Calenberg	634
	Landwehr Bn Nienburg	625
	Landwehr Bn Hoya	629
	Landwehr Bn Bentheim	608
Artillery	Maj Brome's British Foot Bty	
Lt Col J. Hawker	Capt von Rettberg's Hanoverian Foot Bty	
Dutch Corps Prince Frederick of the Netherlands		
1st Dutch Division Lt Gen J. A. Stedman		6,437
1st Brigade	16th Dutch Jager Bn	
Maj Gen F. d'Hauw	4th Belgian Line Bn	
	6th Dutch Line Bn	
	9th Dutch Militia Bn	
	14th Dutch Militia Bn	
	15th Dutch Militia Bn	
2nd Brigade	18th Dutch Jager Bn	
Maj Gen D. J. de Eerens	1st Belgian Line Bn	
	1st Dutch Militia Bn	
	2nd Dutch Militia Bn	
	18th Dutch Militia Bn	
Artillery	Capt Wijnand's Dutch Foot Bty	
Indian Brigade	1st Bn 5th East Indian Regt	3,499
Lt Gen C. H. W. Anthing	2nd Bn 5th East Indian Regt	
	Bn of Flankers (19th-21st East Indian Regts)	
	10th West Indian Jager Bn	
	11th West Indian Jager Bn	
Artillery	Capt Riesz's Dutch Foot Bty	

		Men
Reserve		
5th Division Lt Gen Sir Thomas Picton		Men
8th British Brigade	1st Bn 28th Regt	557
Maj Gen Sir James Kempt	1st Bn 32nd Regt	662
	1st Bn 79th Regt	703
	1st Bn 95th Regt	549
9th British Brigade	3rd Bn 1st Regt	604
Maj Gen Sir Denis Pack	1st Bn 42nd Regt	526
	2nd Bn 44th Regt	455
	1st Bn 92nd Regt	588
5th Hanoverian Brigade	Landwehr Bn Hamelm	669
Col von Vincke	Landwehr Bn Gifhorn	617
	Landwehr Bn Hildesheim	617
	Landwehr Bn Peine	611
Artillery	Maj Roger's British Foot Bty	
Maj A. Heisse	Capt Braun's Hanoverian Foot Bty	

		Men
6th Division Lt Gen Hon Sir Lowry Cole		
10th British Brigade	1st Bn 4th Regt	669
Maj Gen Sir John Lambert	1st Bn 27th Regt	698
	1st Bn 40th Regt	761
4th Hanoverian Brigade	Landwehr Bn Verden	621
Col Best	Landwehr Bn Luneburg	624
	Landwehr Bn Osterobe	677
	Landwehr Bn Munden	660
Artillery	Capt Sinclair's British Foot Bty	
Lt Col Bruckmann	Maj Unett's British Foot Bty	
British Reserve Artillery	Lt Col Sir Hew Ross's British Horse Bty	
	Maj Beane's British Horse Bty	
	det of Capt Hutchesson's British Foot Bty	
	det of Capt Ilbert's British Foot Bty	

		Men
Brunswick Corps Duke Frederick William of Brunswick		5,376
	Advance Guard Bn	672
Light Brigade	Guard Bn	672
Maj Gen Olfermans	1st Lt Inf Bn	672
	2nd Lt Inf Bn	672
	3rd Lt Inf Bn	672
Line Brigade	1st Line Bn	672
Lt Col von Buttler	2nd Line Bn	672
	3rd Line Bn	672
Artillery	Capt von Heinemann's Brunswick Horse Bty	
Maj von Lubeck	Maj von Moll's Brunswick Foot Bty	

Nassau Cont Maj Gen A. H. E. von Kruse		2,880
1st Bn 1st Nassau Regt		
2nd Bn 1st Nassau Regt		
1st Nassau Landwehr Regt		

		Men
Cavalry Lt Gen The Earl of Uxbridge		
British and King's German Legion Cavalry		Men
1st Brigade (Household Bde)	1st Life Gds	228
Maj Gen Lord E. Somerset	2nd Life Gds	231
	Royal Horse Gds	237
	1st Dragoon Gds	530
2nd Brigade (Union Bde)	2nd Dgns (Scots Greys)	391
Maj Gen Hon Sir William Ponsonby	1st or Rl Dragoons	394
	6th or Inniskilling Dgns	396

		Men
3rd Brigade	1st Lt Dgns KGL	462
Maj Gen Sir William Dornberg	2nd Lt Dgns KGL	419
	23rd Lt Dragoons	387
4th Brigade	11th Lt Dragoons	390
Maj Gen Sir John Vandeleur	12th Lt Dragoons	388
	16th Lt Dragoons	393
5th Brigade	7th Hussars	380
Maj Gen Sir Colquhoun Grant	15th Hussars	392
6th Brigade	1st Hussars KGL	493
Maj Gen Sir Hussey Vivian	10th Hussars	390
	18th Hussars	396
7th Brigade	3rd Hussars KGL	622
Col Sir F. Arentschildt	13th Lt Dragoons	390
British Horse Btys attached to the Cavalry:	a) Major Bull's Howitzers	
	b) Lt Col Webber Smith's	
	c) Lt Col Sir Robert Gardiner's	
	d) Capt Whinyate's (with rockets)	
	e) Capt Mercer's	
	f) Capt Ramsay's	

		Men
Hanoverian Cavalry		
1st Brigade	*Prince Regent's Hsrs	596
Col Baron von Estorff	*Bremen and Verden Hsrs	589
	Cumberland Hussars	497
Brunswick Cavalry	Regt of Hussars	690
	Sqdrn of Uhlans	232

Dutch Cavalry Lt Gen Baron J. A. de Collaert		3,405
Heavy Cavalry Brigade	1st Dutch Carabiniers	
Maj Gen A. D. Trip	2nd Belgian Carabiniers	
	3rd Dutch Carabiniers	
1st Lt Cavalry Brigade	4th Dutch Lt Dgns	
Maj Gen Baron de Ghigny	8th Belgian Hussars	
2nd Lt Cavalry Brigade	5th Belgian Lt Dgns	
Maj Gen J. B. van Merlen	6th Dutch Hussars	
Artillery	Capt Petter's Dutch Horse (half) Bty	
	Capt van Pittius's Dutch Horse (half) Bty	

Other detachments present

	Men
2nd Hussars KGL	12
6th Line Bn KGL	6
7th Line Bn KGL	26

		Guns	Men
Artillery			
British	7 Foot Btys of 6 guns each	42	3,630
	3 Foot Btys of 4 guns each	12	
	8 Horse Btys of 6 guns each	48	
KGL	1 Foot Bty of 6 guns	6	526
	2 Horse Btys of 6 guns each	12	
Hanoverian	2 Foot Btys of 6 guns each	12	465
Brunswick	1 Foot Bty of 8 guns	8	
	1 Horse Bty of 8 guns	8	
Dutch	4 Foot Btys of 8 guns each	32	
	2 Horse Btys of 8 guns each	16	
	1 Foot half Bty of 4 guns	4	
	1 Horse half Bty of 4 guns	4	

*Probably not present

The following were present in Belgium/Netherlands but took no part in the fighting. British units were not awarded the Waterloo Medal.

At Brussels

Det of 10th British Brigade	2nd Bn 81st Regt

At Ostend, Antwerp, Nieuport

7th Division Maj Gen McKenzie		Men 3,233
7th British Brigade	2nd Bn 25th Regt	
	2nd Bn 37th Regt	
	2nd Bn 78th Regt	
	13th Veteran Bn	
	1st Foreign Bn	
	2nd Garrison Bn	
Artillery	Maj Morisson's British Foot Bty	
	Capt Hutchesson's British Foot Bty (less det)	
	Capt Ilbert's British Foot Bty (less det)	

At Antwerp

Hanoverian Res Corps Lt Gen Baron von de Decken

1st Hanoverian Res Brigade Lt Col von Bennigsen	Landwehr Bn Bremerlehe
	Landwehr Bn Molln
	Landwehr Bn Bothmer
2nd Hanoverian Res Brigade Col von Beaulieu	Landwehr Bn Nordheim
	Landwehr Bn Ahlefeldt
	Landwehr Bn Springe
3rd Hanoverian Res Brigade Lt Col von Bodecken	Landwehr Bn Otterndorf
	Landwehr Bn Zelle
	Landwehr Bn Ratzeburg
	Landwehr Bn Luchew
4th Hanoverian Res Brigade Lt Col von Wissel	Landwehr Bn Hanover
	Landwehr Bn Uelzen
	Landwehr Bn Neustadt
	Landwehr Bn Diepholz

At Courtrai

Det of 5th Cavalry Brigade	2nd Hussars KGL (less det)	564

The Waterloo Medal was awarded to General Colville's Division which was out on the right flank and took no part in the actual fighting. The medals to members of his Division are not so highly prized by collectors. His division, less Mitchell's 4th British Brigade (present at Waterloo), consisted of the 6th British Brigade: 2/35, 1/54, 2/59, 1/91, 6th Hanoverian Brigade, and Major Brome's British Foot Battery. Stationed with Colville was Prince Frederick's Dutch Corps.

Regiments present: Two sqdns each of 1, 2 Life Gds; two sqdns Rl Horse Gds; 1 Dragoon Gds; 1 Rl Dragoons; 2nd Rl North British Dragoons (Scots Greys); 6 Inniskilling Dragoons; 7, 10, 15, 18 Hussars; 11, 12, 13, 16, 23 Lt Dragoons; RA; Corps of Artillery Drivers; RE; Sappers and Miners; Waggon Train; Staff Corps; Medical Staff; Ordnance Dept; Commissariat Dept; 2, 3 Grenadier Gds; 2 Cold Gds; 2 Scots Gds; 3/1, 1/4, 3/14, 1/23, 27, 28, 2/30, 1/32, 1/33, 2/35, 1/40, 1/42, 2/44, 1/51, 1/52, 1/54, 2/59, 2/69, 1/71, 2/73, 1/79, 1/91, 1/92, 1/95, 2/95, 3/95 (two Cos) Ft.

65 *Brunswick Waterloo Medal* 18th June 1815

Obverse	Head of Duke Frederick William of Brunswick (who was killed at Quatre Bras, 17th June 1815), facing left and wearing cap; with the legend, 'FRIEDRICH WILHELM HERZOG'.
Reverse	In the centre the year '1815' enclosed by a wreath of laurel and oak. Legend around upper circumference, 'BRAUNSCHWEIG SEINEN KRIEGERN'. Lower circumference, 'QUATREBRAS UND WATERLOO'.
Size	35mm in diameter
Metal	Bronze
Ribbon	Yellow with a pale blue stripe near the edge.
Suspension	Steel claw and ring
Designer	C. Häseler
Naming	Large impressed roman capitals

Instituted 11.6.1818 by the Prince Regent of Great Britain as Guardian of the young Duke. Made of bronze from captured French guns.

In 1824 another medal was issued by the Duke of Brunswick to those who had fought in the Peninsular War. The medal which was given in silver gilt to officers and bronze to men, bears the word 'PENINSULAR' on the obverse, surrounded by a wreath, the left half of which is composed of oak leaves, and the right laurel leaves. The reverse shows a collection of military trophies on a stand, consisting of three flags, a drum and a cannon with three cannon balls. In the centre, askew, is a shield. The medal was suspended from a crimson ribbon similar in colour to that of the Victoria Cross. It was not, of course, as the name thereon shows, given for service at Waterloo.

66 *Dutch Silver Cross* 1813-1815

Obverse	In the centre, the date '1813'.
Reverse	In the centre, the date '1815'.
Size	35mm in diameter
Metal	Silver star with five indented arms.
Ribbon	Yellow with a white stripe towards each edge.
Naming	Issued unnamed

Instituted by the Royal Decree of 10.5.1865 to be awarded to surviving veterans of the campaigns of 1813-15. Approximately 6,000 issued.

67 *Hanoverian Waterloo Medal* 18th June 1815

Obverse	Laureated head of the Prince Regent facing right with the date '1815' below, with the legend, 'GEORG.PRINZ.REGENT.'
Reverse	In the centre 'WATERLOO/JUN XVIII', a trophy above, a partial wreath of laurel below. Legend around circumference, 'HANNOVERSCHER TAPFERKEIT'.
Size	35mm in diameter
Metal	Silver
Ribbon	Bright crimson with light blue edges
Suspension	Steel claw and ring
Designer	W. Wyon
Naming	Large impressed roman capitals

Instituted in December 1817 by the Prince Regent for all his Hanoverian troops present at Waterloo.

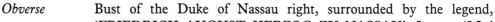

68 *Nassau Waterloo Medal* 18th June 1815

Obverse	Bust of the Duke of Nassau right, surrounded by the legend, 'FRIEDRICH AUGUST HERZOG ZU NASSAU'. Letters 'J.L.' beneath the bust.
Reverse	Winged 'Victory' crowning a classical warrior with the victor's laurel. Legend around the circumference, 'DEN NASSAUISCHEN STREITERN BEY WATERLOO'. In the exergue, 'DEN 18 JUNI/1815'.
Size	29mm in diameter
Metal	Silver or gold
Ribbon	Dark blue ribbon with orange edges
Naming	Issued unnamed

Instituted by the Duke of Nassau on 23.12.1815 and issued in silver to all troops who had been present.

69 *Prussian Campaign Medal* 1815

Obverse	Pattée cross with rays between the arms; year '1815' at its centre surrounded by a wreath of laurel and oak leaves.
Reverse	Crowned monogram 'FW' above the legend in two lines 'PREUßENS TAPFERN/KRIEGERN'. Legend around circumference, 'GOTT WAR MIT UNS, FHM FEY DIE EHRE!'.
Edge	Impressed in upright capitals, 'AUS EROBERTEM GESCHUTZ'.
Size	29mm in diameter
Metal	Bronze
Ribbon	Orange central band with equal stripes of black and white (outermost) and a thin edge of black.
Naming	Issued unnamed

70 *Saxe-Gotha-Altenburg Campaign Medal* 1814-15

Obverse	The crown of Saxe Gotha surrounded by the legend 'IM KAMPFE FUER DAS RECHT'.
Reverse	Five-petalled rose surrounded by an ornate design.
Edge	Impressed in upright capitals, 'HERZOGTH.GOTHA.UND. ALTENBVRG.MDCCCXIV.MDCCCXV'.
Size	41mm in diameter
Metal	Bronze
Ribbon	Bright green with black edges, the black having horizontal gold stripes.
Suspension	Ball and ring (17mm) suspension
Naming	Issued unnamed

Instituted on 28.10.1816 to officers, NCOs and men.

Medal for officers in bronze-gilt, for NCOs in bronze with gilt inscription, ornamentation and centres. Issued to other ranks in bronze with gilt inscription.

Saxe-Gotha-Altenburg contingents served in the North German Corps and the Army of the Upper Rhine.

71 *Pistrucci Waterloo Medal*

This medal, which was to have been about 140mm diameter, was intended by the Prince Regent to be issued to the heads of Allied countries who participated in the downfall of Napoleon. After various squabbles over who should design it, the whole idea of giving a medal was abandoned in 1849, by which time the alliances of 1815 were somewhat moth-eaten, so that the presentation of this or any other medal would not have had the desired effect. However, electrotypes are seen from time to time.

It might interest collectors of the Long Service and Good Conduct and Distinguished Conduct Medals to know that the early issues of these were designed by Benedetto Pistrucci, an Italian, who was chief medallist at the Royal Mint at the time of their inception (Royal Warrants dated 30th July 1830 and 4th December 1854).

72 *Army of India Medal* 1799-1826

Obverse	The diademed head of Queen Victoria with the legend 'VICTORIA REGINA'.
Reverse	A seated figure of Victory holding a laurel branch in her right hand and a wreath in her left. In the left background is a palm tree. Around the top is the wording 'TO THE ARMY OF INDIA'. In the exergue are the dates '1799-1826'.

Medals are to be found on which the length of the hyphen between the dates varies. Those with the long hyphen are thought to have been sent out to India unnamed and were then named in Calcutta and issued to those serving or living in India when the claims were made. Those with a short hyphen with the designer's initials 'WW' were mostly issued to the Queen's Ships and Regiments.

Size	35mm in diameter
Metal	Silver
Ribbon	32mm wide, light blue
Suspension	By an ornate swivelling suspender.
Designer	W. Wyon RA
Naming	Generally in indented capitals, similar to the Military General Service Medal, to British and European troops. In various types of indented capitals or script to natives.
Bars issued	Twenty-one

An Order dated 21st March 1851 authorized the East India Company to issue a medal to all survivors (and this point must be remembered) who served in India between 1799 and 1826. It should be noted that the first action commemorated was that of Allighur, fought on the 4th September 1803. A similarity occurs here with the MGS and NGS medals in that Queen Victoria was not born when many of the actions were fought and the date of the first action does not agree with the first date in the exergue.

The order of the bars is different from most medals in that the last award is placed nearest the medal, ie, the correct order reads downwards. The medal was always issued with a bar.

As is only natural when twenty-one bars were issued, there are a great many varieties of combinations in existence, and medals with three or more bars are extremely rare. The Army of India medal roll, compiled by Major G. H. Edwards MBE, gives a full list of European recipients, as well as an extensive summary of combinations etc. However, this has been partly superseded by a further roll compiled by Mr R. W. Gould and Captain K. J. Douglas-Morris DL, RN.

The Duke of Wellington received bars for Assye, Argaum and Gawilghur, of which combination only thirteen were issued. Glazed silver-gilt specimens of this combination appear on the market.

The records of medals awarded to native troops are very sketchy indeed and therefore all figures quoted should be treated as guides rather than facts.

It is curious to note that whilst the bars for Ava and Bhurtpoor are the commonest, only the following thirteen medals were awarded with this dual combination:

Lieut David Williams	Sub-Asst Commissariat Gen
Asst Surgn William Mitchelson	Field Hospital
Lieut E. C. Archbold	8th Cav
Lieut R. G. MacGregor	Bengal Art
Brev Capt G. T. Finnicane	14th Ft
Lieut Francis Hawkins	44th Ft
Lieut A. R. J. Swinton	22nd and 3rd NI
Capt R. Seymour	26th NI
Capt George Chapman	36th NI
Capt James Steel	41st NI
Lieut W. C. Ormsby	63rd NI
Lieut E. M. Orr	58th NI
Ensign Hugh Boyd	62nd NI

Lieutenant J. C. C. Gray, 1st Grenadiers and 21st NI, was awarded the medal with three bars; Nepaul, Ava and Bhurtpoor.

Much fighting had taken place between the times of the battles commemorated by the medal and the date of its issue, to survivors only, so that the number of recipients is very small compared with those involved.

The medals to the 76th Foot are particularly interesting as they were the only European regiment present under General Lake in the Second Mahratta War 1803-4. Five men of this regiment received medals with five bars; Allighur, Battle of Delhi, Laswarree, Battle of Deig, Capture of Deig, and four received four bars; Allighur, Battle of Delhi, Laswarree, Battle of Deig. Surgeon C. Corfield of the regiment received the bars for Allighur, Battle of Delhi and Laswarree.

The greatest number of bars on any one medal was on that awarded to Drummer William Colston who received the following seven— Allighur, Battle of Delhi, Laswarree, Battle of Deig, Capture of Deig, Nepaul and Bhurtpoor. He served with the 2/15th Native Infantry in the first six actions, and at Bhurtpoor with the 31st Native Infantry. Two medals are known named to this man. The first, with the short hyphen reverse, is officially engraved to the 31st NI, whilst the second, with the long hyphen reverse, is impressed Calcutta style to the 15th

NI. The fact that Colston appears on the medal rolls of both Regiments possibly explains the existence of the two medals.

Two medals were issued with six bars to Major J. Greenstreet, 15th Native Infantry, and to Captain H. W. Carmichael-Smyth, Engineers. Both medals have bars for Allighur, Battle of Delhi, Laswarree, Battle of Deig, Capture of Deig and Nepaul. The former medal is in a private collection and the latter is in the Honeyman Collection, LA County Museum of National History.

Ten medals were issued with five bars, twenty-three with four bars, and one hundred and forty-nine with three bars.

Allighur 4th September 1803

Regiments present: 27 (15), 29 (11) Lt Dgns; 1, 2, 3, 4 Bengal Cav; 76 (17) Ft; 4 (1), 1/15 (3), 17 Bengal NI; Bengal Art (2).

The assault on this fortress was carried out by four companies of the 76th Foot, 1/4, 2/4, 2/12, 1/15, 2/15, four companies 17 Bengal NI and two guns of the Bengal Artillery. The 27th Light Dragoons also received casualties. A grand total of 60 bars awarded to Europeans (none as singles).

General Mossom Boyd received a medal with bars for Allighur, Battle of Delhi and Laswarree.

The medal awarded to Sepoy Sunkhar Bhowan, 23 NI, is the only one with this single bar that is known.

Battle of Delhi 11th September 1803

Regiments present: 27 Lt Dgns (20); 2, 3 Bengal Lt Cav; Bengal Art; 76 Ft (20); Pioneers; 1/2, 2/2, 1/4, 2/4, 2/8, 2/9, 1/12, 2/12, 1/14, 1/15, 2/15, 2/16 Bengal NI. Four companies of the 2/17 Bengal NI were acting as baggage guard and took no part in the fighting. A grand total of 57 bars awarded to Europeans.

There is an impressed medal to Newal Singh Jagarnath, Pioneer, with this bar and another medal with this bar and Capture of Deig to Sepoy Kedar Nath to the 30th NI, which was then numbered 1/15. NI.

Two medals were awarded to Europeans as a single bar. They were awarded to J. Cook, 27 Light Dragoons, and H. S. Montagu, 15 NI. 58 bars in all awarded to Europeans.

Lieutenant Curzon, 6 Light Cavalry, was awarded bars for Battle of Delhi, Capture of Deig, Nagpore and Bhurtpoor, but he must have been serving with some other regiment at the time.

Assye 23rd September 1803

This battle was the first of Major-General Arthur Wellesley's great victories. With about 4,000 troops he routed the Rajah of Berar's forces of over 50,000.

Regiments present: 19 Lt Dgns (14); 4, 5, 7 Madras Cav; 3rd, 5th Cos Bombay Art; Madras Art and Madras Pioneers; 74 (20), 78 (35) Ft. The following are the only native infantry that actually took part in the attack 1/2, 1/4, 1/10, 2/12 Madras NI.

This bar was awarded singly to ten Europeans. Eighty-five in all were awarded to Europeans. The sole occasion on which it was awarded in conjunction with other bars to this medal, one of which was not that for Argaum, was in the case of the medal to John McGough, 78 Foot, who received bars for Assye and Gawilghur. This is a unique medal and, incidentally, he also received the Military General Service Medal with the bar for Java.

Asseerghur 21st October 1803

It is difficult to understand why this rare bar, of which only fifty-two were awarded to Europeans, was sanctioned, as the fort surrendered without being attacked, after an hour's bombardment.

Regiments present: 3, 6 Madras Cav and detachments of Madras Art; 94 Scotch Bde (39) [which later became the 2nd Bn The Connaught Rangers]; 2/2, 5, 1/6, 2/7, 2/9, 1/11, 2/11, 19 Madras NI; 2 Madras Pioneers.

Major J. L. Basden, 89th Foot, received a medal with this bar and those for Argaum, Gawilghur and Ava; he was serving with the Scotch Brigade as a Lieutenant at the time.

Laswarree 1st November 1803

Regiments present: 8 (27)*, 27 (18), 29 (14) Lt Dgns; 1, 2, 3, 4, 6 Bengal Lt Cav; Bengal Art*; 76 Ft (17)*; 1/2, 2/2, 1/4, 2/4, 2/8, 2/9, 1/12, 2/12*, 2/15, 2/16*, 2/17 Bengal NI.

One hundred and four bars were awarded to Europeans.

There is a medal to Lieutenant-Colonel Parlett Starling, 32nd NI, then numbered 2/16th Bengal NI, with this bar and that for Bhurtpore.

*These were the only units to sustain any casualties.

Argaum 29th November 1803

This is a rare bar, of which only 122 were awarded to Europeans. The Bombay and Madras Artillery, 74th, 78th Foot and 2nd NI received bars for Assye, Argaum and Gawilghur on one medal.

Regiments present: 19th Lt Dgns (10); 3, 4, 5, 6, 7 Madras Cav; 3rd, 5th Cos Bombay Art; detachments of Madras Art; two Cos Bombay Pioneers; 74 (15), 78 (34), 94 (40), Ft; 1/2, 2/2, 1/3, 2/3, 1/6, 2/7, 1/8, 1/11, 2/11, 2/12, 2/18 Madras NI.

Gawilghur 15th December 1803

This is a rare bar of which only two single ones and one hundred and thirteen in all were issued to Europeans.

Regiments present: 19th Lt Dgns (7); Bombay and Madras Art; 74 (14), 78 (22), 94 (38) Foot; 1/2, 2/2, 1/3, 2/3, 1/6, 2/7, 1/8, 1/11, 2/11, 2/12, 2/18 Madras NI.

Defence of Delhi 8th-14th October 1804

Only six bars, all with unique combinations, were issued:
  Lt Gen Sir John Rose, KCB, 2/14th NI.
  [Allighur, Battle of Delhi, Defence of Delhi]
  Gen Edmund Frederick Waters, commanding Dingapore Bn.
  [Allighur, Battle of Delhi, Defence of Delhi, Nepaul, Ava]
  Lt Gen Sir Arthur Galloway, 2/14th NI.
  [Defence of Delhi, Capture of Deig]
  Lieut Alex Duncan, Bde Maj.
  [Laswarree, Defence of Delhi]
  Sgt J. Brown, Bengal Art.
  [Allighur, Laswarree, Defence of Delhi, Battle of Deig, Capture of Deig]
  Riding Master C. J. Davis, 4th Lt Cav.
  [Allighur, Defence of Delhi, Battle of Deig, Bhurtpoor]

No British regiments took part in the defence. The regiments present were the following: 2/4, 2/14, 2/17, 1/21 Bengal NI; 3rd and 4th Bengal Light Cavalry.

A medal was also awarded to Virzhall Tulsidass, Sappers and Miners.

Battle of Deig 13th November 1804

Medals with this bar are extremely rare. Only forty-nine were awarded, eight as single bars (to Europeans).

Regiments present: 2, 3 Bengal Lt Cav; Bengal Art (4); 76 Ft (22) and 1 Bengal European Regt (10) [later to become the 1st Bn Royal Munster Fus]; 1/2, 1/4, 7, 1/8, 1/12, 2/15, 2/22 Bengal NI.

Capture of Deig 11th-23rd December 1804

Regiments present: 8 (33), 27 (6), 29 (8) Lt Dgns; 2, 3, 6 Bengal Lt Cav; Bengal Horse and Field Art; two Cos each of 22 (8) and 76 (16) Ft; 1 Bengal European Regt (1); 1/2, 1/4, 1/8, 1/12, 2/12, 1/15, 2/15, 2/22 Bengal NI. One hundred and three bars were awarded to Europeans.

Nepaul October 1814 to March 1816

Natives who had received the HEI Co Medal (see No 73) did not receive this bar, which was only issued to those who had taken part in actual fighting and not to those who were merely in Nepaul during the campaign.

Regiments present: Bengal Horse Art; 8 Lt Dgns (14); Skinner's Horse; Gardner's Horse; 2 Rohilla Cav (13/12); 2, 6, 7, 8 Bengal Cav; 14 (16), 17 (52), 24 (95), 53 (17), 66 (90), part of 67 (7), 87 (54) Ft; 1/1, 1/2, 2/2, 2/3, 2/4, 1/5, 2/5, 1/6, 2/6, 1/7, 2/7, 1/8, 2/8, 1/9, 2/9, 1/10, 2/10, 1/11, 1/12, 2/12, 1/13, 1/14, 2/14, 1/15, 2/15, 2/16, 1/17, 2/17, 1/18, 2/18, 2/19, 1/21, 2/21, 1/22, 2/22, 2/24, 1/25, 2/25, 1/26, 1/27, 1/30 Bengal NI.

A total of four hundred and ninety-one were issued to Europeans.

Kirkee 5th November 1817

This is an extremely rare bar, only five to Europeans (all single bars) and two to natives known:
Pte Joseph Morgan, 65 Ft
Pte William McKenzie, 103rd Bombay European Regt
Pte Joseph Thompson, 103rd Bombay European Regt
Cornet F. Hunter, 1st Lt Cav
Cornet James Morrison, 2nd Lt Cav
Sepoy Gopal Bhave, 7th Bombay NI
Sepoy Nadir Rai, 12th Bombay NI

Regiments present: Detachment of 6th Co Bombay Artillery; small detachments of Madras Artillery and Pioneers; detachment of 65 Ft (1); Bombay European Regt (2), 2/1, 2/6, 1/7 Bombay NI; Dapuri Battalion.

Poona 11th-16th November 1817

Only 42 bars issued to the 65th Foot and 27 to other Europeans
Regiments present: 65 (42) Ft; Bombay European Regt (6); 2/1, 1/2, 1/3, 1/4, 2/6, 1/7, 2/9 Bombay NI; Bombay and Madras Pioneers; Bombay and Madras Art (3 officers and 9 men).

Private T. Carrotts and Private J. Dickinson, 14th Foot, were serving with the 65th Foot at Poona. Private T. Curtis and Private J. Strong, 38th Foot, were serving with the 65 Foot at Poona and received a medal with bars for Poona and Ava.

Kirkee and Poona 5th-16th November 1817

Seventeen of these bars were awarded to the 65th Foot and sixty-seven to other Europeans.
Regiments present: 65 Ft (17); Bombay European Regt (46); 2/1, 2/6, 1/7 Bombay NI; HEI Co Art (2/6).

Seetabuldee 26th-27th November 1817

This bar is extremely rare and only two were awarded to Europeans (Gunner William Pegge, Madras Artillery and Lieutenant Colonel V. Pedler, Nizam's Cavalry).
Regiments present: Madras Bodyguard; 6 Bengal Cav; Det of Madras Art; 1/20, 1/24 Madras NI; 61 Native Pioneers.

Nagpore 16th December 1817

Only one hundred and forty-seven were awarded to Europeans.
Regiments present: 6 Madras Native Cav; 6 Bengal Native Cav; Madras Horse and Foot Art (17); 2/1 Ft (95); 1/2, 1/11, 1/12, 2/13, 2/14, 1/20, 1/22, 1/24 Madras NI; 6, 1/22 Bengal NI; 61, 81 Native Pioneers.

Seetabuldee and Nagpore 26th-27th November and 16th December 1817

A total of nineteen bars were awarded to Europeans serving in the 3rd, 6th Bengal Cavalry; 20, 24 and 28 Madras NI; Artillery (3) and Staff.

The 1/24 Madras NI were later redesignated 1/1 and medals to them are so numbered.
Sir Richard Jenkins, Resident at Nagpore
Lieut A. Gordon, Assistant to Resident at Nagpore
Sir William Lloyd, Resident's Escort
Brig Hopton S. Scott, Commanding 24th NI
Capt William Stone, Staff
Capt John B. Hearsey, 6th Lt Cav (+ Bhurtpoor)
Capt Lucius H. Smith, 6th Lt Cav (+ Bhurtpoor)
Lieut Charles Fitzgerald, 6th Lt Cav
Lieut Charles O. Fothergill, 20th NI
Lieut L. W. Watson, 24th NI
Lieut A. Inglis, 28th NI
Asst Surgn William Mansell, 3rd Lt Cav (+ Laswarree, Battle of Deig, Capture of Deig)
Dresser John Anthony
Bugler John Pairah, 12th NI
Dmr Heath, 20th NI
Gnr John Baldock, Madras Art
Gnr James Perkins, Madras Art
Gnr Daniel Smith, Madras Art
Gnr Thomas White, Madras Art

Maheidpoor 21st December 1817

A total of one hundred and sixty-seven bars were awarded to Europeans.
Regiments present: 22 Lt Dgns (28); 3, 4, 8 Madras Cav; Mysore Horse; Madras Horse Art and Rocket Train (39); 1 Ft (38); Madras European Regt; 1/3, 2/6, 1/14, 2/14, 1/16 Madras NI; Det of 22 Bengal NI; 27 NI; Madras Pioneers; Madras Sappers.

Corygaum 1st January 1818

Issued to Europeans once only as a single bar and three times in conjunction with other bars. The total strength of the garrison, when attacked by three divisions, was only about 900.
Regiments present: Madras Art (1); Poona Auxiliary Horse; 2/1 Bombay NI (1); 2nd Native Infantry.
The four Europeans who received this bar were:
Pte George Bainbridge, 65th Ft (Poona, Corygaum)
Lieut Charles Swanston, 102nd Madras European Regt (Kirkee and Poona, Corygaum)
Asst Surgn John Wylie, Madras Art (Poona, Corygaum)
Bugler John Nicholas, Bombay Rifle Corps (Corygaum).

Ava 1824-1826

No native troops received this bar as they were given the HEI Company's Medal for Burma, 1824-26 (see No 75). European officers of native regiments did, however, receive it: 2,294 bars were awarded.
Regiments present: 1 (118), 13 (112), 14 (265), 38 (119), 41 (149), 44 (96), 45 (120), 47 (175), 54 (79), 87 (195), 89 (205) Ft; 1 Madras European Regt (113); HEI Co Art (164).
Three hundred and six medals were issued to the RN as follows:
Alligator (10/20); *Arachne* (8/17); *Boadicea* (17/43); *Champion* (11/8); *Larne* (12/19); *Liffey* (13/36); *Slaney* (7/25); *Sophie* (8/18); *Tamar* (8/13); *Tees* (3/10).
In addition, 34 were issued to officers and 19 to ratings of the Bombay Marine.

Bhurtpoor Siege of, 17th-18th January 1826

Regiments present: 8th Lt Dgns (2); 11 Lt Dgns (198); 16 Lancers (178); 3, 4, 6, 8, 9, 10 Bengal Cav; Bengal Horse and Foot Art (140); Bengal Sappers and Miners (9); 14 (246), 59 (184) Ft; 1 Bengal European Regt (79); 6, 11, 15, 18, 21, 23, 31, 32, 33, 35, 36, 37, 41, 44 (1), 58, 60, 63 Bengal NI; one hundred men from each of the Nusseeree and Sirmoor Bns of Gurkhas. 1,528 medals were awarded to Europeans.

First Mahratta War 1778-84

For which the Deccan Medal was awarded (see No 31)

Second Mahratta War 1803-05

The native rajahs of this time had their own well trained armies, among the most powerful of which were those of Holkar of Indore, The Peshwar of Poona, Scindhia of Gwalior and Bhoonsla of Berar. Holkar had defeated several of the others including the Peshwar who had fled to British protection and with whom he signed a treaty of alliance. Fearful of expanding British influence threatening their own sovereignty, Scindhia and Bhoonsla prepared for war. The British countered by invading the hostile territories.

General G. Lake with 10,500 men opposed Scindhia's 35,000 strong army in the Hindustan. Major General Sir Arthur Wellesley and Colonel James Stevenson with 25,000 men faced armies of Scindhia and Bhoonsla numbering 50,000 in the Deccan.

Deccan Campaign

20th March 1803. Unopposed recapture of Poona.
9th-11th August 1803. Capture of the town and fort of Ahmednuggar.
23rd September 1803. Battle of Assaye. Wellesley with some 6,000 men attacked and defeated the joint army of Bhoonsla and Scindhia, 50,000 strong.
21st October 1803. Capture of the fort of Asseerghur by Stevenson after nominal opposition.
29th November 1803. Battle of Argaum. The disheartened Mahratta army decisively defeated by Wellesley.
15th December 1803. Fortress of Gawilghur stormed. With this and the action of Lake (below) Scindhia and Bhoonsla sued for peace.

Hindustan Campaign

4th September 1803. Capture of Allighur.
11th September 1803. Battle of Delhi. Scindhia's army under Frenchman M. Louis Bourquien heavily defeated by Lake.
17th October 1803. Capture of Agra.
1st November 1803. Battle of Laswari. Scindhia decisively defeated by Lake.

Holkar of Indore who had remained aloof from his erstwhile allies, then began operations against British and allied territory.
8th July-31st August 1804. Disastrous retreat by Colonel Monson in the face of Holkar's forces.
7th-15th September 1804. Holkar's unsuccessful siege of Delhi.
13th November 1804. Battle of Deig. Holkar's army aided by the Rajah of Bhurtpoor's troops from the fortress of Deig, defeated by Major General J. H. Fraser and Colonel Monson.
17th November 1804. Battle of Farruckabad. Holkar's cavalry force decisively beaten by Lake.
11th-25th December 1804. Siege and capture of the fortress of Deig.

2nd January-23rd February 1805. Lake's unsuccessful siege of Bhurtpoor.
17th April 1805. Peace arranged with the Rajah of Bhurtpoor.
24th December 1805. Peace concluded with Holkar.

Nepaul War 1814-16
For details see No 73.

Pindari and Third Mahratta War 1817-19

Organised raids on British territory by hordes of Pindaris (outlaws and marauders) prompted the Governor-General Lord Hastings to mount a concerted offensive against them. Mahratta chieftains who supported the Pindaris broke into open revolt.

5th November 1817. Battle of Kirkee. Colonel C. B. Burr with 3,000 men defeated some 26,000 troops of the Peshwar of Poona.
11th-16th November 1817. Capture of Poona by the combined forces of Colonel Burr and Brigadier General Lionel Smith.
26th-27th November 1817. Battle of Seetabuldee. Colonel H. S. Scott and a small force of native troops withstood heavy attacks by Bhoonsla of Berar.
16th December 1817. Capture of Nagpore. Brigadier General J. Doveton reinforced Scott and advanced on nearby Nagpore. Bhoonsla pretended to surrender but had to be driven out.
21st December 1817. Battle of Maheidpoor. Holkar of Indore with 35,000 men was decisively defeated by some 9,000 under Lieutenant General Sir Thomas Hislop.
1st January 1818. Defence of Corygaum. Captain F. F. Staunton with 900 men encountered the Peshwar's army 28,000 strong. Seizing the village of Corygaum, Staunton held it against all attacks.
16th May-18th June 1818. Siege and capture of Malleygaum.
3rd June 1818. Surrender of the Peshwar.
17th February-6th April 1819. Siege and capture of Asseerghur. (With casualities over 300 it is remarkable that the 1819 siege went unrewarded whilst participants of the 'trivial' 1803 siege received a bar).

War in Ava 1824-6
For details see No 75.

Siege of Bhurtpoor 10th December 1825 to 18th January 1826

Doojan Sal, the nephew of the late and friendly Rajah Baldeo Singh, usurped the throne which the British had agreed should go to Baldeo Singh's son. Repeated remonstrances having produced no result, the city was attacked by Lord Combermere and after heavy fighting, it surrendered.

A notable feature of the siege was the desertion to the enemy of three British artillerymen. All were captured upon the fall of the fortress; Gunner Herbert who had served at Waterloo was hanged, the two others, of Irish extraction, were transported.

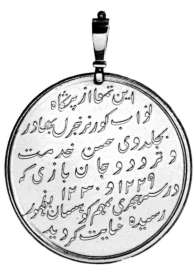

73 *Nepaul War Medal* 1814-1816

Obverse	A scene of hills and stockades; on the left is a field gun.
Reverse	A Persian inscription. (Translation: 'This medal was conferred by the Nawab Governor-General Bahadur, in testimony of the energy, good service, skill and intrepidity which was displayed during the campaigns in the hills, in the years of Hegira, 1229 and 1230'.)
Size	51mm diameter
Metal	Silver
Ribbon	The medal was suspended from either a ribbon or cord of no specified colour in a similar manner to the medal for Seringapatam.
Suspension	A loop is riveted to the top of the piece through which the ribbon or cord is threaded.
Engraver	The dies were engraved and the medals struck at the Calcutta Mint.
Naming	It was issued unnamed

The issue of this silver medal (300 thought to have been awarded) was sanctioned by a General Order, signed at Fort William on the 20th March, 1816, for award to native troops who had shown zeal and gallantry. The British troops who took part received the Army of India Medal with the bar Nepaul, as did the native troops who were not awarded the Nepaul War Medal. For the regiments present see the bar for Nepaul awarded with the Army of India Medal 1799-1826.

> Nepaul was first conquered by the Gurkhas in 1768 and treaties of friendship were signed between them and the British in 1791 and 1801. In spite of these, however, they made continuous raids over the border until it was decided to invade their country.
>
> War started on the 1st November, 1814, and ended on the 27th April, 1815. A new treaty was signed on the 2nd December, 1815, but in January, 1816, trouble broke out again and a further expedition under Major-General Sir David Ochterlony, KCB, was sent into the country.
>
> After battles at Mukwampore and Sierapore the Rajah of Nepaul sued for peace and a further treaty was concluded on the 4th March, 1816. After this treaty Prince Jung Bahadoor came to London and opened an embassy.
>
> The Nepaulese remained loyal during the Mutiny and since then the bravery and devotion of the Gurkhas has never failed to earn the admiration of all.

74 *Ceylon Medal* 1818

Obverse	The inscription 'CEYLON 1818' within a wreath.
Reverse	'REWARD OF' above, 'MERIT' below, with name of recipient engraved in the centre.
Size	38.5mm in diameter
Metal	Gold (2), silver (45)
Ribbon	38.5mm wide blue ribbon
Designer	Unknown. Issued by the Ceylon Government.
Naming	Engraved

Regiments present 19th, 73rd, 83rd Foot, 1st, 2nd Ceylon Regiment and 7th, 15th and 18th Madras NI. Awarded for gallant conduct during the Kandian Rebellion in 1818, details of which are shown in General Orders of 7 July, 1818 and 2 June, 1819, reproduced below.

'In concluding these orders it is with feeling no less gratifying that the Commander of the Forces places on record a display of heroism most honourable to the individuals who achieved it, in the instance of Lance Corpl. McLaughlin, of the 73rd, and a detachment of four rank and file of the 2nd Ceylon, when on their march on the 16th ult. from Passera to Badulla.

This small party was beset about mid-way by a horde of rebels in a thick jungle, who fired on the detachment from their concealment, killing two soldiers of the Light Infantry, 73rd. (Jas. Southerland and Wm. Chanleer), on the spot, and immediately showing themselves in numbers around this little band of brave soldiers, whom they no doubt considered a certain prey, but regardless of their menaces and faithful to their fallen comrades, ten of these gallant men encompassed the dead bodies of their brother soldiers, while Corpl. McLaughlin, with the remaining five, fought their way to Badulla at two miles distance through some hundred Kandyans, to report the situation of the detachment they left, surrounded by so immense and disproportionate a

force, in conflict with which they continued for two hours, when being relieved by a party detached by Major MacDonald under the command of Lt. Burns of the 83rd Regiment from Badulla, they had the triumph of seeing the insurgents fly before them, and of bringing in the dead bodies of their comrades to be honorably interred.

The Commander of the Forces has not language sufficient to extol the noble trait of generous feeling, to save from barbarous insult and mutilation the bodies of their dead comrades, which he ventures to believe is without parallel, and to mark his admiration of such an act, the Lt. Genl. is pleased to promote Lance Corpl. McLaughlin, to be a supernumerary serjeant in the 73rd to bear date on the 16th ult., and to succeed to the 1st effective vacancy that occurs in the regiment, and with respect to the detachment that he commanded. The Commander of the Forces desires that Major MacDonald will report their names, that the Lt. Genl. may consider how it may be in his power adequately to distinguish them.'

75 *Burma Medal* April 1824-February 1826

Obverse	The elephant of Ava crouching before the British Lion. Behind the lion is the Union Flag and behind the elephant the Burmese standard submissively lowered. Palm trees in the background. In the exergue is a Persian inscription. (Translation: 'The Elephant of Ava is obedient to the Lion of England, Year 1826').
Reverse	A scene of the storming of the Pagoda at Rangoon, to the left is the Irrawaddy flotilla, General Campbell directs the attack from under a palm tree. In the exergue is a Persian inscription. (Translation: 'A medal for the victorious British soldiers on Ava').
Size	38mm diameter
Metal	Gold and silver. Silver-gilt specimens are also found.
Ribbon	38mm wide, crimson with blue edges. (This was the first ribbon issued by the Honourable East India Company).
Suspension	Either by means of a ring attached to a steel clip which passes through the piece, or by a straight bar attached to a steel claw.
Naming	The medal was issued un-named.
Bars issued	Nil

This medal was sanctioned at Fort William on the 22nd April, 1826. It was issued in gold and silver; about 750 of the former were awarded to native officers and officials and about 24,000 silver ones to native troops from Bengal and Madras. Some silver medals were probably also issued to the members of the Royal Indian Marine present.

For a complete list of the British troops and units of the Royal Navy and Royal Indian Marine see the bar of Ava awarded with the Army of India Medal (see page 98).

Native Regts present: 1 Madras Cav; 4, 5, Bengal Art; 2 Madras Art; 1st Co Bombay Foot Art; 1, 3, 7, 8, 9, 10, 16, 2/17, 18, 22, 26, 28, 32 Madras NI; 2, 7, 14, 26, 39, 44, 45, 49, 52 Bengal NI; 61 Native Pioneers; Native Levies.

The war in Ava, as it is generally called, was caused by the continual depredations of the Burmese into Sylhat and Cachar.

A force was organized under Brigadier-General Sir Archibald Campbell to capture Rangoon and blockade the Irrawaddy river, whilst at another one under Brigadier-General Morrison advanced through the Aracan.

The length of the war was mainly caused by the difficult nature of the country, rain, fog, inundations and the difficulty of maintaining supplies, not to mention the stout resistance of the Burmese.

Most of the fighting took place in the neighbourhood of Rangoon. The following nine battles were fought:

1824: Kemmendine, 10th June.
1825: Syriam, 12th January; Bassein, 24th February; Aracan, 1st April; Donabew, 2nd April; Prome, 1st December.
1826: Melloon, 13th January; Moulmein, 28th January; Pagham Mew, 9th February.

76 *Spanish St Sebastian Medal* 1836

Obverse	In the centre a lion, standing facing left, surrounded by the collar of the Golden Fleece. Above, 'ESPANA', below 'AGRADECIDA'.
Reverse	Pattée cross with rayed interiors, crown between arms, centre enclosed by laurel wreath, having '1836', 'SAN SEBASTIAN 5 DE MAYO' at its centre.
Size	Circular medal, pewter 36.5mm, silver 37mm in diameter
Metal	Issued in silver to officers, grey metal to other ranks. Silver medals were possibly all struck in Britain by Messrs Loewenstark & Son of London.
Ribbon	Watered blue with a yellow stripe towards each edge for British Legion. Yellow with red stripe towards each edge for Spanish troops.
Suspension	Variable. Medal may be pierced at top for ring suspension; suspension for silver medals generally less crude.
Namimg	Issued unnamed

The medal authorized on 23rd April 1842 was awarded to those British volunteers who saw action on the heights of San Sebastian on 5th May 1836.

> The volunteers, part of the 'Spanish Legion' under General Sir George de Lacy Evans KCB, fought on the side of Christinists against the Carlists in the Carlist War of 1834-39.
> Also aiding the Christinists, was a British naval squadron under Lord John Hay, a battalion of marines commanded by Colonel Owen, and a Royal Artillery contingent under Major Colquhoun.

77 *Cross for the Liberators of Bilbao* 1836

General	Gold Maltese Cross in light blue enamel with white enamel borders, cross points tipped with gold balls, gold grenades protruding from the 'V' of each arm, crossed cannon in the angles. Cross suspended from a wreath with ring suspension.
Obverse	In the centre a gold castle upon a red enamel ground, enclosed by a white enamel band upon which is inscribed 'SALVO A BILBAO'.
Reverse	Enamelled centre depicting a ruined wall, enclosed by a white enamel band bearing the inscription 'EN SU TERCER SITIO 1836'.
Size	36mm x 24mm
Metal	Gold and enamel for officers, silver for other ranks
Ribbon	Watered ribbon with three equal stripes of green/yellow/green. Also seen and described as having a yellow ribbon with a blue stripe towards the edge.

'Other Ranks' Version
Similar design as that for officers except Maltese Cross is in silver only, with a plain reverse and obverse inscription 'BILBAO 1836'.

Authorized by Queen Isabella II of Spain on 3rd January, 1837. Conferred upon British Officers and men involved in raising the siege of Bilbao in December 1836. Awarded to Royal Naval, Royal Marine and Royal Artillery personnel who assisted General Espartero in the actions of 24th and 25th December 1836.

The final and successful attempt to raise the siege commenced on Christmas Eve, 1836, when in the midst of a heavy snowstorm General Espartero embarked eight picked companies in boats and on rafts which were towed up the River Nervion by the crews of HM ships 'Saracen', 'Ringdove' and 'Comet' under the command of Commander William Frederick Lapidge and Lieutenant Thomas P. Le Hardy.

This flotilla proceeded up the river and made a landing which permitted the main body of the Christinist army to cross the river and on the following morning a severe engagement took place in which the Carlists were defeated and forced to abandon the siege.

On the 22nd and 23rd December, in preparation for the final assault, artillery manned by the seamen from HMS Saracen and Ringdove together with men of the Royal Marines and Royal Artillery under Major Colquhoun played a significant part in silencing Carlist batteries.

Members of the Royal Artillery present: Brev Maj J. N. Colquhoun, Lieut R. Basset, Sgt H. Ormrod, Bdr G. Gurnett, Gnrs and Dvrs G. Hunter, R. Carmichael, T. Colman, J. Lee, G. Runnet, E. Curson, F. Holt, P. McLaughlin, J. Haggions, P. Young, W. Cassin, C. Taylor, G. Lander, A. McMaster, J. Hill and J. Spring.

Others known to be present include Lieut Hamnet Parke RMA, Lieut Langley RMA, Lieut Vickers RE.

Some Royal Navy personnel present are listed in NAVAL MEDALS 1793-1856 by Capt K. J. Douglas Morris DL, RN.

The Cross for the Liberators of Bilbao was awarded to Surgn Charles Benson Brearey MD on service with the Spanish army, who also received the St Sebastian Cross, 1836 (named) and the Irun Medal, 1837 (named).

78 *Coorg Medal* April-May 1837

Obverse	A Coorg warrior holding a knife in his raised right hand and a musket in his left, and a Canarese inscription around the perimeter, 'A MARK OF FAVOUR GIVEN FOR LOYALTY TO THE COMPANY'S GOVERNMENT IN SUPPRESSING REBELLION IN THE MONTHS OF APRIL AND MAY, 1837.'
Reverse	Some war trophies and the inscription 'FOR DISTINGUISHED CONDUCT AND LOYALTY TO THE BRITISH GOVERNMENT.' Exergue, 'COORG APRIL 1837.'
Size	50mm diameter and of various thicknesses
Metal	Gold and silver
Suspension	Medals awarded to officers were suspended from chains which passed through a loop in the piece. Medals awarded to other ranks were suspended from a cord of no specified colour.
Designer	The dies were engraved and the medals struck at the Calcutta Mint.
Naming	They were issued unnamed.

Only forty-four gold and three hundred silver medals were issued to the Coorg soldiers who remained loyal during the Canara rising. Some of these medals are to be found with a decided flaw in them as if made from a cracked die.

Copper specimens occasionally appear which, in some cases, give the appearance of having been worn. None were officially awarded and the only inference can be that they are copies.

The order authorizing this medal was dated the 28th August, 1837.

The First Afghan War 1839-42

Historical detail forming the background of the Ghuznee Medal (No 79); the Candahar, Ghuznee and Cabul Medals (No 80); the Jellalabad Medals (No 81); and the Defence of Kelat-i-Ghilzie Medal (No 82).

The historical reasons for their award are so correlated that a brief account of the war will show why so many medals were given. It must be remembered that at this time the principle of awarding bars had not been instituted, though at a later date medals were issued to commemorate actions fought prior to those to which we shall now refer.

Afghanistan was considered a buffer state between India and Persia, so that it was necessary for the tranquility of the former that whosoever ruled in Afghanistan should be strong and above all friendly.

The ruler at the time was Shah Soojah-ool-Moolk, who was weak and thoroughly unpopular. He was driven out by the Persians under Prince Mahomed Khan, who then proceeded to divide Afghanistan into several states and to nominate their chiefs.

To drive the Persians out and reinstate Shah Soojah-ool-Moolk, an

army 27,000 strong, subsequently known as 'The Army of the Indus,' was formed. The command of it was given to Lieutenant-General Sir John Keane. This army was divided into the Bengal and Bombay Columns under Major-Generals W. Cotton and T. Willshire respectively.

The Bombay Column advanced up the Indus and occupied Hyderabad. It then crossed the Bolan Pass and occupied Dadur and then Quetta, where it halted. When the advance was continued, Candahar, the capital of Western Afghanistan, was reached on the 27th April, 1839, after several skirmishes with recalcitrant tribes on the way.

On the 27th June the column moved off again on its way to Ghuznee, which had been heavily fortified by Hyder Khan. When the fort was reached, on the 21st July, it was considered to be too strong to attack until a gate could be blown by explosive. This task was performed under a covering party of the 13th Foot and the fort occupied on the 23rd, and Mahomed Khan fled for safety towards Cabul, the capital of Eastern Afghanistan.

Whilst the fighting for Ghuznee was taking place large numbers of

Afghans had remained in the neighbourhood waiting to see which horse to back. Having learned of the defeat of Mahomed Khan they dispersed, so that Cabul was entered unopposed.

Shah Soojah-ool-Moolk was then restored to the throne and a British envoy appointed in Cabul.

It was to show his appreciation at his reinstatement that Shah Soojah intended to present the medal for Ghuznee to all who had taken part in the siege, and the Order of the Dooranee Empire to field officers and above.

This weakling became so unpopular that in October, 1841, the Afghans rose in revolt and murdered the British envoy in Cabul, compelling the garrison, under Major General W. G. K. Elphinstone to retreat. (4500 men and substantial followers; 44th Ft, 1/1 Bengal Horse Art, 5th Bengal Lt Cav, 5th, 37th, 54th Bengal NI, Bengal Sappers and Miners, Shah's men and Irregulars). On their way towards Jellalabad this force was attacked and annihilated, 80 officers and men were captured; Dr Bryden was the only British officer to escape and arrive at Jellalabad.

Prior to the attack on Cabul the 13th Foot had formed part of the garrison, but they had been sent out to quell local disturbances. They were on their way back to Cabul when the trouble broke out. Rather than let them fight their way to Cabul it was decided that they should withdraw to Jellalabad and hold it until the garrison in Cabul could get out. As already stated, this garrison was annihilated during its withdrawal.

On arrival at Jellalabad, Major-General Sir Robert Sale placed it in a state of defence and then withstood a siege from the 12th November, 1841, to the 7th April, 1842, when, as a result of an attack in force by the garrison and a threatening one from the relieving column under Major-General Sir George Pollock, Mahomed Khan (who had again come on the scene) fled with his Afghan followers.

General Pollock had really been little more than a threat as he met with stiff opposition in the Khyber Pass on the 5th April and did not reach Jellalabad until the 16th, when he found that the garrison had, by their own efforts, dispersed the enemy.

After his arrival at Jellalabad, General Pollock tried to impress on the Governor-General the necessity for the re-occupation of Cabul, but for several reasons he was not allowed to move out until the 20th August. During this period the troops suffered severely from the heat and the results of constant raiding of the convoys by the local tribes, in particular the Shinwarees. A brigade, under Brigadier-General Monteath, was sent out to deal with them. They were defeated at Mazenia, which appears on some of the unauthorized bars to be found.

The route to be followed by General Pollock from Jellalabad to Cabul exactly suited the tactics of the Afghans, who took up a strong position in the Tazeane Pass from which they had been driven out. This action is also commemorated by some unofficial bars. In this action Mahomed Khan was so completely defeated that there was no further opposition to the advance and Cabul was entered on the 15th September, 1842.

At Candahar, Major-General Sir William Nott had refused to surrender and was being besieged by Prince Sufter Jung, the son of Shah Soojah. The defence was far from a static one, for many foraging and punitive sorties were made by the garrison into the surrounding country. One of these sorties, under the immediate command of Colonel Wymer, relieved the garrison of Khelat-i-Ghilzie, the defenders of which received a special medal.

General Nott's relief was similar to that of General Sale in Jellalabad in that he bided his time until the weather was favourable and the disposition of the Afghans gave him an opportunity to defeat them *en masse*. The similarity is heightened by the fact that Major-General Sir Richard England was on his way to relieve him in the same way that General Pollock was on his way to relieve General Sale.

The situation in Ghuznee was worse than that in Candahar and Cabul and the garrison (27th Bengal NI) through starvation was compelled to surrender on the 6th March 1842.

On the 10th August General Nott set out from Candahar to relieve Cabul. On the 30th August he encountered and defeated a strong force of Afghans at Gonine. On the 5th September he reached the outskirts of Ghuznee, which was strongly held by the enemy. Dispositions were made for the attack, but on the morning of the 6th it was found that the enemy had evacuated their positions before Ghuznee, which was immediately entered. The force remained here until the 10th, when the advance to Cabul continued. Cabul was reached on the 17th, two days after its relief by General Pollock.

Collectors will now understand why medals were awarded bearing the single name of Candahar or that of Cabul, also the two names Ghuznee and Cabul and the three names Candahar, Ghuznee and Cabul.

79 *Ghuznee Medal* 21st-23rd July 1839

Obverse	The Fortress of Ghuznee with the word 'GHUZNEE' below.
Reverse	Within two laurel branches tied at the base, a mural crown. Above, '23RD JULY'; below, '1839'.
Size	37mm in diameter
Metal	Silver
Ribbon	38.5mm wide. Originally intended to be half yellow and half green. However, this was changed to half crimson and half green.
Suspension	A non-swivel plain straight suspender.
Designer	Designed by a committee
Naming	Issued unnamed, however, engraved in the field in either running script or neat capitals. Also found engraved or impressed around the rim in bold capitals.
Bars issued	No official bars issued. However, unofficial bars are found engraved Ghuznee, Kelat (Kellatt), Ponulla (Punulla), Monsantonsh (Mansantosh) and Mnaher (Monohur).

Two sets of dies are known for the medal, one having the fortress as being narrower and taller, whilst the detail on the reverse is much sharper. Medals from these dies were issued to the 17th Foot, as possible tailors' copies. (For historical detail see above.)

Issued by General Order, dated Camp, Buddee, November 23rd, 1842; 'The Governor-General being informed that the Medals once intended to be given in the name of Shah Shooja, to the Officers and Soldiers engaged in the capture of Ghuznee in 1839, have been manufactured in the Govt. Mint at Calcutta, and considering that it is not just that, in consequence of the death of Shah Shooja, the glorious achievement of the capture by assault of the Ghuznee should remain without due commemoration by the conferring of a personal decoration upon those engaged therein, is pleased to direct that the Medals shall be given, in the name of the Govt. of India, to the officers and men entitled thereto for such service; and the several Officers commanding the Regiments and Corps employed at Ghuznee on 23rd July, 1839, will transmit to the Govr.-Genl. nominal lists of the Officers and men then present, and now surviving.'

Her Majesty had given her sanction to wear this Medal in March, 1841.

NUMBERS ISSUED

European Commissioned Officers	239
Native Officers	153
European Warrant Officers	6
Sgts and Havildars	456
Rank and file	7,467
Misc	50
Total	8,371

REGIMENTS PRESENT

4 Lt Dgns; 16 Lancers; 1 Bombay Lt Cav; 2, 3 Bengal Lt Cav; Skinner's Horse; Poona Irreg Horse; 2/2 Bde Bengal Horse Art; 2/6 Bengal Foot Art; 3, 4 Tps Bombay Horse Art; 2/2 Bn Bombay Foot Art; 1/Shah Sooja's Horse Art; 1 Co Golundaz Native Art; 2, 3 Cos Bengal Sappers and Miners; 2, 13, 17 Ft; 1 Bengal European Regt (later 1 Rl Munster Fus and often named to European Lt Infy); 16, 35, 48 Bengal NI; 19 Bombay NI

In addition to the above, certain units of Shah Soojah's Force also received the medal.

There is an unpublished issue of this medal in tin. These are fitted with a ring at the top of the piece and thence by a swivel on to a triangular suspender. The edges are inscribed with the Sepoy's name and regiment.

a) *Ghuznee Medal* 1839 Rt Hon The Earl of Auckland's Medal

Obverse	The fortress of Ghuznee covering the whole of the field; the British Army entering at the principal gate.
Reverse	Within two laurel branches tied together at the base, inscribed in raised characters, in three lines, 'AFGHANISTAN—GHUZNEE—23RD JULY 1839.'
Size	41mm in diameter
Metal	Silver
Suspension	None
Naming	Unnamed

A special medal for Ghuznee was presented to the Earl of Auckland, as Governor-General of India.

80 *Candahar, Ghuznee and Cabul Medals* October 1841-October 1842

There are four different strikings of this silver medal, authorized by a General Order, issued in Simla, on the 4th October, 1842, not counting the two which appear to have been mistakes. The first of the latter kind have the legend 'VICTORIA REGINA' on the obverse instead of 'VICTORIA VINDEX'; the second, which refers to the medal for Cabul only, has this place spelt 'CABVL'. Fifteen of these medals were issued.

As all the types are the same except for the reverses, one general description will suffice and the reverses will be dealt with separately. The order of rarity is as follows: (1) Ghuznee, Cabul; (2) Candahar; (3) Candahar, Ghuznee, Cabul; (4) Cabul. (For historical detail see pages 103-4.)

Obverse	The diademed head of Queen Victoria with the legend 'VICTORIA VINDEX'.
Reverse	See individual headings below.
Size	36mm diameter
Metal	Silver
Ribbon	41mm wide. Rainbow pattern watered red, white, yellow, white and blue.
Suspension	By means of a straight steel suspender fastened by a pin to a steel clip affixed to the piece, however, medals are often seen with a variety of replacement suspensions.
Designer	W. Wyon, RA
Naming	Some in script, some in indented capitals, whilst a few were issued unnamed. The medals of the 40th foot and the Artillery are generally found engraved in script, whilst those to the 41st Foot are named in engraved roman capitals.
Bars issued	Nil

a) **Candahar** May 1842

Reverse   'CANDAHAR' with the date '1842' underneath and surmounted by a crown: the whole surrounded by a laurel wreath.

Europeans received approximately 130 medals and natives approximately 2,485.

Regiments present. Staff and details (5); HM 40th Ft (64); HM 41st Ft (26); 3/1st Bn Bombay Art (2); 3/2nd Bn Bengal Art (1); 4/2nd Bn Bengal Art (28); 1st Trp, Shah's Horse Art (127); 2nd Trp, Shah's Horse Art (1); 1st Bengal Irreg Cav (17); 1st Shah's Cav (198); Poona Irreg Horse; 25th Bombay NI; Bombay Lt Inf Bn; 2nd Bengal NI (65); 16th Bengal NI (31); 38th Bengal NI (107); 42nd Bengal NI (79); 43rd Bengal NI (37); 1st Shah's Inf (640); 2nd Shah's Inf (592); 5th Shah's Inf (595).

b) **Cabul** 15th September 1842

Reverse   'CABUL' with the date '1842' underneath and surmounted by a crown—the whole surrounded by a laurel wreath. Also the very rare variety with 'CABVL'.

The bars for 'Marzenia 1842' and 'Tazeane 1842' are found attached to this medal, but they are quite unofficial.

The battle of Mazenia, or Mazeena, was fought on the 26th July, 1842, by the 31st Foot and the 32nd and 53rd Native Infantry.

The battle of Tazeane, or Tazeen, was fought in, and for, the Tazeen Pass on the 13th September, 1842. The complete defeat of Akbar Khan in this action annihilated his forces and opened the way to Cabul, which was reached on the 15th September, 1842.

No regiment is allowed to add bars to medals unless they have been authorized by a General Order and therefore medals fitted with such bars are merely interesting curios.

Europeans received approximately 3,500 medals and natives 9,241.

Regiments present: Staff, etc (38); 3/1st Bde Bengal Horse Art (129); 3/2nd Bde Bengal Horse Art (139); 2/2nd Bn Bengal Art (97); 2/6th Bn Bengal Art (123); 4/6th Bn Bengal Art (109); Mountain Train (56); E Co Syce Drivers (153); HM 3rd Lt Dgns (489); 1st Bengal Lt Cav (453); 5th Bengal Lt Cav (142); 10th Bengal Lt Cav (498); 3rd Tait's Irreg Cav (739); HM 9th Ft (831); HM 13th Ft (745); HM 31st Ft (826); 6th Bengal NI (3rd Co only) (112); 26th Bengal NI (1,004); 30th Bengal NI (920); 33rd Bengal NI (947); 35th Bengal NI (837); 53rd Bengal NI (915); 60th Bengal NI (1,012); 64th Bengal NI (927); 5th Co Bengal Sappers & Miners (125); Shah's Sappers (Broadfoot's) (375).

Ptes M. Doyle of the 50th Foot received this medal, as did Wm Hewett of the 22nd Foot and I. Simpson. Pte Ed Branagan, 40th Foot, received one of the 'Victoria Regina' medals.

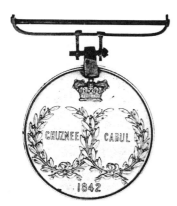

c) Ghuznee and Cabul

Reverse Two laurel wreaths forming the letter W. The word 'GHUZNEE' is written in the first loop and 'CABUL' in the second. The whole is surmounted by a crown, and the date '1842' appears at the bottom under the wreaths.

Europeans received approximately 360 medals and natives 1,163.

Regiments present: Staff and details (3); HM 40th Ft (3); HM 41st Ft (105); 1st Trp, Bombay Horse Art (138); 3/1st Bn Bombay Art (25); 3/2nd Bn Bengal Art (87); 4/2nd Bn Bengal Art (38); 2nd Soojah's Horse Art; Bengal Sappers and Miners (details 2nd and 3rd Cos) (24); Madras Sappers and Miners, C Co (28); 3rd Bombay Lt Cav (354); 1st Bengal Irreg Cav (17); 1st Shah's Cav (1); 2nd Bengal NI (4); 16th Bengal NI (4); 38th Bengal NI (5); 42nd Bengal NI (1); 43rd Bengal NI (169); 3rd Shah's Inf (521).

d) Candahar, Ghuznee, Cabul

Reverse The names of these three places with the date '1842' underneath—on four lines. The whole is surmounted by a crown and surrounded by a laurel wreath.

Europeans received approximately 400 medals and natives 4,811.

Regiments present: Staff and details (23); HM 40th Ft (669); HM 41st Ft (494); 3/1st Bn Bombay Art (91); 3/2nd Bn Bengal Art (17); 4/2nd Bn Bengal Art (10); 2nd Troop, Shah's Horse Art (121); Bengal Sappers and Miners (details 2nd and 3rd Cos) (3); Madras Sappers and Miners, C Co (1); 1st Bengal Irreg Cav (282); 1st Shah's Cav (469); 2nd Bengal NI (893); 16th Bengal NI (795); 38th Bengal NI (854); 42nd Bengal NI (852); 43rd Bengal NI (637).

81 *Jellalabad Medals* 12th November 1841-7th April 1842

This medal was issued in two distinct types, generally referred to as a) Mural Crown and b) Flying Victory. The first type was considered inartistic, and in any case, not enough of the first type were struck to issue to the next of kin, so it was decided to strike a further issue in London—the first issue having been minted in Calcutta. Though a free exchange was offered to those who received the first type it is recorded that only five men of the 13th Foot made the change. (For historical detail see pages 103-4.)

a) **First Type**

Obverse	A mural crown superscribed 'JELLALABAD'.
Reverse	The date 'VII APRIL, 1842' occupying three lines.
Size	39mm diameter
Metal	Silver
Ribbon	Rainbow pattern watered red, white, yellow, white and blue 44mm wide
Suspension	By means of a straight steel suspender fastened by a pin to a steel clip affixed to the piece, however, many are seen with replacement suspensions particularly by means of a ring.
Naming	This seems to vary considerably, so that the medal cannot have been named when issued. Some are found with names on the edge and others with the name of the recipient on the obverse under the crown. The medals issued to the 13th Foot were named round the edge at the Commanding Officer's expense, though some are seen to this regiment with the name above the crown and the regiment underneath, also with the name impressed on the rim as well as on the reverse.
Bars issued	Nil

b) **Second Type**

Obverse	The diademed head of Queen Victoria with legend 'VICTORIA VINDEX', but a few medals were later struck with 'VICTORIA REGINA'.
Reverse	The winged figure of Victory with wreaths in her right hand and holding the staff of a Union Jack in her left hand whilst flying over the fortress of Jellalabad. Around the top is the inscription 'JELLALABAD VII APRIL'. In the exergue is the date 'MDCCCXLII'.
Size	36mm diameter
Metal	Silver
Ribbon	As above
Suspension	A straight suspender fastened by means of a pin to a steel clip affixed to the piece, however, also seen with replacement suspensions, particularly scroll and 'China 1842' suspensions.
Designer	W. Wyon, RA
Naming	The recipient's name and regiment are indented on the edge in block capitals.
Bars issued	Nil

A 'Mural Crown' medal is known to the 50th Foot.

Mural Crown Medals were awarded by the Governor General, Lord Ellenborough, at Ferozepore to Major General Sale's force in November 1842 and were the first awarded for the war. As the awarding of medals went, and goes now, this is pretty prompt service. Compare this lapse of seven months with the fifty-six years in the case of the first bar to the Naval General Service Medal 1793-1840.

Recipients:

1 Sqdrn 5th Bengal Lt Cav (Capt Oldfield)	122
1 Sqdrn Shah Soojah's Horse (Lieut Mayne)	100
Political Agent (Capt MacGregor) and party of Duran's Horse .	25
Abbott's Bty Bengal Art (2 Co 6 Bn)	244
Backhouse's Mountain Train, Shah's Art	61
Broadfoot's Sappers (3 Cos—Broadfoot)	342
13th Lt Inf (Col Dennie)	774
35th Bengal NI (Col Monteath)	846
Followers including camel drivers	125
Brigade HQ	14
Dr Brydon, 44th Ft—Sole survivor from Kabul	1
	2654

82 *Defence of Kelat-i-Ghilzie Medal* February–May 1842

Obverse	A shield with 'KELAT-I-GHILZIE' thereon occupying three lines. The shield is surrounded by a laurel wreath and surmounted by a mural crown.
Reverse	A collection of military trophies surmounting a rectangular plaque with 'INVICTA MDCCCXLII' thereon.
Size	36mm diameter.
Ribbon	Rainbow pattern of watered red, white, yellow, white and blue, 41mm wide
Suspension	The ribbon passes through a straight steel suspender which is affixed to the piece by a somewhat crude metal clip.
Designer	W. Wyon, RA
Naming	The recipient's name and regiment are engraved in script on the edge.
Bars issued	Nil

This silver medal, whose issue was sanctioned by a General Order from Simla dated 4th October, 1842, was awarded to the garrison under Capt John Halkett Craigie, which consisted of 55 Europeans and 877 natives as follows: Staff (7); 4th Co 2nd Bn Bengal Art (86); details from the 2nd and 3rd Bengal Sappers and Miners (23); three Cos of the 43rd Bengal NI under Capt Webster (247); and 569 men of the 3rd Shah Soojah's* Inf.

Lieut G. Piercy, 2nd Ft, received this medal in addition to that for Ghuznee. It was also awarded to Surgn Gen C. Mackinnon, who also received the CB, Ghuznee 1839 Medal, Ghuznee-Cabul 1842 Medal, Punjab Medal and the Mutiny Medal.

Kelat-i-Ghilzie was a fort between Cabul and Candahar, about eighty miles north-east of the latter, which withstood siege for four months until relieved by Maj-General Nott on the 26th May, 1842. (For historical detail see pages 103-4.)

For its gallant conduct during the siege the Shah's Regt was subsequently added to the establishment of the Bengal Army as the 12th (Kelat-i-Ghilzie Regt) Bengal NI. They later became the 2nd Bn (Kelat-i-Ghilzie) Bombay Pioneers. They were disbanded on the 10th February, 1933.

*This name is variously spelt Shoojah, Soojah, Soujah and Sujah.

83 *China War Medal* 5th July 1840 to 29th August 1842

Obverse	The diademed head of Queen Victoria with the legend, 'VICTORIA REGINA'.
Reverse	A collection of war trophies with an oval shield with the Royal Arms in the centre, all positioned under a palm tree. Above is the inscription 'ARMIS EXPOSCERE PACEM'. In the exergue is the word 'CHINA' and the date '1842' underneath.
Size	36mm diameter
Metal	Silver
Ribbon	35mm wide with a crimson band 23mm wide down the centre and yellow edges.
Suspension	A straight nickel silver suspender with a 5.5mm neck in the centre, which is soldered directly on to the piece.
Designer	Wm Wyon RA
Naming	Impressed in bold well-spaced roman capitals. The space between the above mentioned neck either before and/or after the naming is filled in with stars.
Bars issued	Nil

a) *China War Medal* Original Design

Reverse   British Lion, crowned, trampling the fallen Chinese Dragon, whose body and tail are curved over the back of the Lion. Above is the inscription 'ARMIS EXPOSCERE PACIM'. In the exergue, 'NANKING' with the date '1842' underneath.

Designer   William Wyon RA

Naming   Unnamed

(see above for other details)

The original design was considered to be offensive to the Chinese and was therefore replaced. Though never issued with the original reverse, specimens do exist.

The award of this medal was originally suggested by the Governor-General of India in October 1842 for presentation to all ranks of the Honourable East India Company's Forces. It was, however, subsequently awarded by the Home Government in 1843 to those who had taken part in certain specified actions. (see below)

'DOWNING STREET,
5th January, 1843

'MY LORD DUKE,

I am commanded by the Queen to acquaint your Grace that Her Majesty has been pleased to give directions that a Medal should be prepared for the purpose of commemorating the signal success of Her Majesty's Naval and Military Forces upon the Coast and in the interior of the Empire of China.

'Although Her Majesty is of opinion that the award of a distinction of this nature should be reserved, as it has hitherto been, for very peculiar and special occasions, and the great evil would arise from the frequent and indiscriminate grant of Medals for the commemoration of Naval or Military exploits of an ordinary character, yet it appears to Her Majesty that in the instance of the recent events in China an exception can properly and safely be made from a rule which ought to be generally observed.

'On a consideration of all these circumstances, although in other exploits of Her Majesty's Arms there may have been more equality in the contending forces, more obstinate resistance may have been shewn, and more formidable obstacles surmounted, yet Her Majesty deems it fitting that the conclusion of a War, leading to such important results, should be commemorated by the issue of a Medal, to be granted to those, to whose skill and gallantry such results are mainly attributable. The Queen is well aware that in the course of that War, while all engaged have had an equal desire, all have not had equal opportunities, of distinguishing themselves; but Her Majesty, anxious that no invidious distinctions should appear to be drawn between Men, who, as occasions have offered, have performed their duties with equal zeal, has been pleased to order that the Medal which Her Majesty has directed to be struck in commemoration of the recent great successes, should be bestowed upon each Admiral, General and other Officers of the Navy and Army, including the Officers, European and Native, of the service of the East India Company, Petty Officers, Seamen and Marines of the Navy of Her Majesty and of the East India Company, and the Non-Commissioned Officers and Soldiers of Her Majesty's Army, and of the East India Company, including the Native Non-Commissioned Officers and Soldiers, belonging to such Regiments, Corps, Ships and other Vessels as have served with distinction at any of the following operations of 1841:

'In the Canton River, in the operations:

At Chusan in 1841 and 1842

At Amoy, at Ningpo, at Chinpae, at Tsekee, Chapoo, in the River Woosung, in the Yangtse Kiang, and at the Assault of Ching-Kiang Foo.

Her Majesty is pleased to direct that the above list should comprise the Officers serving on the Staff of the several Armies, including those of the Ordnance, the Medical and Commissariat Staff, and Her Majesty's Superintendent and the Officers employed under his direction.

'In order to enable me to give effect to Her Majesty's gracious intentions as above explained, I have to request that your Grace will call upon Lieut.-General Sir Hugh Gough to furnish a nominal list of the Officers, Non-Commissioned Officers and Privates of Her Majesty's Army, who may be entitled to receive Medals under the foregoing Instructions. Copies of this letter, accompanied by similar requests, will be transmitted to the Lords Commissioners of the Admiralty, to the Commissioners for the Affairs of India, and to her Majesty's Superintendent; and on the receipt of the returns thus called for, immediate orders will be issued to the Master of Her Majesty's Mint for the preparation and distribution of the Medals.

'I have, etc.,

STANLEY.

Field Marshal,
HIS GRACE THE DUKE OF WELLINGTON, K.G., etc.'

REGIMENTS PRESENT

1 Coy 8 Bn RA, C Trp Madras HA, B and C Coys 2 Bn and D Co 3 Bn Madras FA; A, B and F and a few from C, D and E Co Madras Sprs and Mnrs; 18, 26, 49, 55, 98 Ft; 2, 6, 14, 36, 37, 39, 41 Madras NI; 1, 2 Bengal Volunteers.

HM SHIPS

Algerine (80), *Alligator* (139), *Blenheim* (550), *Blonde* (365), *Calliope* (235), *Cambrian*, *Childers* (124), *Clio* (118), *Columbine* (140), *Conway* (169), *Cornwallis* (735), *Cruizer* (113), *Dido* (151), *Druid* (287), *Endymion* (337), *Harlequin* (96), *Hazard* (132), *Herald* (149), *Hyacinth* (126), *Larne* (107), *Melville* (455), *Modeste* (168), *Nimrod* (117), *North Star* (173), *Pelican*, *Plover* (65), *Plyades* (130), *Royalist*, *Samarang* (145), *Starling* (55), *Sulphur* (102), *Vixen* (138), *Volage*, *Wanderer* (106), *Wellesley* (605), *Young Hebe* (12).

INDIAN AND BENGAL MARINE SHIPS

Ariadne (41), *Atalanta* (80), *Auckland* (103), *Enterprize* (93), *Hooghly* (72), *Madagascar* (69), *Medusa* (51), *Nemesis* (92), *Phlegethon* (73), *Pluto* (32), *Proserpine* (55), *Queen* (133), *Sesostris* (105), *Tenasserim* (89).

TROOPSHIPS

Apollo (107), *Belleisle* (265), *Jupiter* (103), *Rattlesnake* (49), *Sapphire* (68).

HOSPITAL SHIP

Minden

The ships present varied considerably in size, consequently, the numbers issued affect the value.

The troubles which led to the war centred upon the British monopoly of the importation of opium into China; a highly profitable trade the Chinese Government wished to prohibit.

In January 1839, the Chinese seized and destroyed vast quantities of opium stored by British merchants in Canton. The British Commissioner, Captain Elliot, RN, and residents were forced to evacuate Canton on the 24th May 1839 and hostility towards the British was shown in many acts of incendiarism and pillage all over China.

At Cheunpi on the 3rd November 1839, HMS *Volage* and *Hyacinth* were unsuccessfully attacked by a large fleet of junks. On 6th December 1839, an edict was published prohibiting all trade with Britain.

Sir Gordon Bremer commenced the blockade of Canton on the 28th June 1840, and a small force under Brigadier-General George Burrel was dispatched from Madras. This consisted of the 18th, 26th and 49th Foot, together with Bengal Artillery and Sappers, also a composite unit of Bengal Volunteers. It arrived off Ting-lai on the island of Chusan, in Hanchow Bay, on the 2nd July. The island surrendered on the 5th.

A blockade of the whole coast of China was started and a series of treaties and agreements arranged with bewildering frequency.

On the 7th January 1841 the fort of Chuenpi south of Canton was captured and on the 26th February 1841 the British occupied Hong Kong. On the 1st March 1841 the Navy moved up the river to Canton and General Sir Hugh Gough, who had arrived with considerable reinforcements, took over the military command.

Canton was taken on the 26th May 1841 only to be ransomed and evacuated a few days later. Moving up the Chinese coast Amoy was bombarded and captured on the 26th-27th August and Chusan, earlier returned to the Chinese, was recaptured 1st October 1841. The capture of Chinhai was effected on the 10th October and Ningpo surrendered on the 13th. In early March 1842, the Chinese attacked the garrisons at Ningpo and Chinhai, but were repulsed with heavy loss.

The Chinese were defeated at Tzeki 15th March 1842. At Chapu 18th May 1842 Gough was again victorious, British casualties totalling 65, Chinese over 1,200. On the 13th June a naval squadron under Admiral Sir William Parker proceeded up the Woosung River and anchored off Shanghai on the 16th, entering the city on the 19th.

On the 21st July 1842 Gough captured Chinkiang and in the hardest engagement of the War, British casualties numbered 144. Then with Nanking threatened with attack, the Chinese Government sued for peace and on the 17th August hostilities were suspended. On the 29th a treaty was signed on board HMS *Collingwood* by Sir Henry Pottinger and the Chinese representative, Keying Elepoo. Under the terms of the treaty, China agreed to cede Hong Kong to Britain and pay an indemnity of 21 million dollars.

---

84 *Scinde Campaign Medals* 6th January-24th March 1843

There are three different strikings of this silver medal, which differ only as regards their reverses, which will be dealt with separately:

Obverse	Diademed head of Queen Victoria and legend 'VICTORIA REGINA'.
Reverse	See individual headings.
Size	36mm diameter
Ribbon	45mm wide. Rainbow pattern watered red, white, yellow, white and blue.
Suspension	Either by a straight suspender, or a large ring, passing through a steel clip attached to the piece.
	Lieutenant Colonel J. L. Pennefather, 22nd Foot (wounded at Meeanee) at his own expense had the steel suspenders replaced by silver ones on medals awarded to the 22nd Foot.
Designer	W. Wyon RA
Naming	In block lettering, either engraved or impressed.
Bars issued	Nil

a)   **Meeanee** 17th February 1843

Reverse   'MEEANEE' above the date '1843' and surmounted by a crown and surrounded by a wreath.

Regiments present: 9 Bengal Cav; Scinde Horse (90); Poona Horse (14); 2/2 Bn Bombay Art (63); 3 Golundaz Bombay FA; C Co Madras Sprs and Mnrs (14); 22 Ft (65); 1 Bombay Grenadiers (148); 12 (153); 25 (206) Bombay NI.

Indus flotilla ships *Planet* (45), *Satellite* (44), Flat No 1 (20). (38 medals to Europeans, 71 to natives).

The naval recipients were not present at the Battle of Meeanee, but received the Meeanee Medal for their part in the 'Residency' action of the 15th February.

b)   **Hyderabad** 24th March 1843

Reverse   'HYDERABAD' within a wreath and surmounted by a crown above the date '1843'.

Regiments present: 3 Bombay Cav; 9 Bengal Cav; Scinde and Poona Horse; 1 Trp Bombay Horse Art; 2/1, 2/2, 3 Co's Bombay Art; C Co Madras Sprs and Mnrs; 22 Ft; 1 Bombay Grenadiers; 6, 8, 12, 21, 24, 25 Bombay NI.

Indus flotilla ships *Comet* (33), *Meteor* (35) *Nimrod* (46). (53 medals to Europeans, 61 to natives.)

Two of these medals were awarded to Lieutenant Frederick Foster Taylor, 3rd Bombay Cavalry. He also received the medal for Ghuznee and Cabul.

c)   **Meeanee and Hyderabad** 1843

Reverse   'MEEANEE HYDERBAD' on two lines surrounded by a wreath and surmounted by a crown.

Regiments present: 9 Bengal Cav; Scinde and Poona Horse; 2/2 Bombay FA; 3 Co Golundaz Bombay FA; Madras Sprs and Mnrs; 22 Ft; 1 Bombay Grenadiers; 12, 25 Bombay NI.

Two men of the 40th Foot received this medal, one of whom was William Arbott. He also received the medal for Candahar.

Thomas Nugent, 32nd Foot, and Ensign W. Pirie, 1st Grenadier NI, received this medal, but one cannot trace the presence of either regiment.

One was also awarded to an Assistant Pilot of the Indian Marine.

The medal was authorized on the 22nd September 1843 to be awarded to those who accompanied Sir Charles Napier in his campaign against the Amirs of Scinde: Rustam, Nasir Khan and Shere Mahomed; their hostility during the First Afghan War prompting the British to seek redress.

The first operation of the campaign was the destruction of the unoccupied fortress of Emaum Gur on 15th January. Situated deep in the desert, it served as an example to the Amirs that no stronghold, however remote or strong, was immune from attack.

The Resident of Hyderabad, Major James Outram, in attempting to arrange a peaceful solution with the Amirs, was besieged in his Residency on 15th February. A company of the 22nd Foot held off 8,000 Baluchis for four hours before successfully withdrawing to the ships *Planet* and *Satellite* and joining Napier. On 17th February, Napier, with 3,000 men, attacked and defeated a force of 30,000 at Meeanee. The action lasted four hours and in that time some 2,000 Baluchis had fallen. Napier's loss amounted to 62 killed and 194 wounded [22nd Foot: 24 killed, 58 wounded.]

Following the battle most of the Amirs surrendered, the exception being Shere Mahomed who remained at large with a considerable force. Napier entered Hyderabad on 20th March and there awaited reinforcements. These having arrived, he marched out on 24th March, with 5,000 men to confront Mahomed with over 25,000 at Dubba on the outskirts of Hyderabad. In the ensuing battle, Mahomed was heavily defeated and suffered over 4,000 casualties. Napier's losses numbered 39 killed and 231 wounded [22nd Foot: 23 killed, 129 wounded].

With the victory, the power of the Amirs was broken and the conquest of the Scinde soon accomplished.

85 *Gwalior Campaign Stars* 29th December 1843

Obverse	The centre of the main six pointed bronze star carries a small (29mm diameter) silver one of the same pattern, in the centre of which is the date '29TH DEC^r.' in two lines. Around the date is the name of the action for which it was awarded, either, 'MAHARAJPOOR 1843' or 'PUNNIAR 1843'.
Reverse	Plain except for the naming
Size	50mm diameter
Metal	Bronze with silver
Ribbon	The ribbon adopted was the then current type for Indian military medals: 45mm wide, watered red, white, yellow, white and blue.
Suspension	It would appear that the stars were originally intended to be worn directly on the jacket, for which purpose brass hooks were fitted on the reverse. However, most were altered by the recipients and fitted with various means of suspension so as to be worn from a ribbon.
Designer	Both stars were produced and probably designed by the Calcutta Mint.
Naming	In script, on the reverse

By a General Order dated 4th January, 1844, sanction was given for the award of bronze stars, made from captured guns, to all troops under Sir Hugh Gough or Major-General Grey. There are two of these stars, generally referred to as the Punniar and Maharajpoor Stars, named after the actions for which they were awarded. As these actions were fought on the same day, some twenty miles apart, it was naturally impossible for one recipient to receive both.

It is recorded that owing to the expense that would have been involved, the original design of the star was altered and the proposed small silver elephant centrepiece was replaced by a silver inner star. However, a star of the proposed type was awarded to and worn by Sir Hugh Gough.

The campaign was made necessary by the disturbances in the state of Gwalior following the death of the Maharajah in February 1843. As a result, Lord Ellenborough ordered the formation of an 'Army of Exercise' under Sir Hugh Gough to operate along the border. However, in late December it became necessary to cross into Gwalior and on 29th December battles were fought at Maharajpoor and Punniar.

In the Battle of Maharajpoor, Gough defeated the Mahrattas who were strongly entrenched around the villages of Maharajpoor, Skirkapoor and Chonda. The Gwalior army was destroyed as a fighting force in the encounter for the approximate loss to Gough of 800 men. [Casualties: 39th (214), 40th Foot (162), 16th Bengal NI (179)].

On the same day, Grey defeated the Mahrattas who were entrenched in the hills about Punniar. Grey's casualties were approximately 215 [3rd (72), 40th Foot (42), 39th Bengal NI (62)].

On 31st December, a peace treaty was signed and the Gwalior army reduced in number.

Maharajpoor Star 29th December 1843

Regiments present: 16 Lancers; Governor-General's Bodyguard; 1, 4, 5, 8, 10 Bengal Light Cavalry; 4 Irregular Cavalry (NB—the 5th and 8th Bengal Light Cavalry only had detachments present); 2/2, 3/2, 2/3 Bengal HA: 1/1, 1/4, 2/4, 3/4, 4/4 Bengal Foot Artillery; 3, 4, 7 Company Bengal Sappers and Miners; 39, 40, 50 (1)* Foot; 2, 4, 14, 16, 31, 39 (a detachment), 43, 56, 62, 70 Bengal NI (the 62nd and 70th were not engaged in the fighting).

Punniar Star 29th December 1843

Regiments present: Two Sqdrns of 9 Lancers; 5, 8, 11 Bengal Light Cavalry; 8 Irregular Cavalry; 1/3, 3/3 Bengal HA; 6/6 Bengal FA; 1 Company Bengal Sappers and Miners; 3, 50 Foot; 39, 50, 51, 58 Bengal NI.

a) *Lady's Star for Maharajpoor* 1843

General	A six pointed gold star
Obverse	In the centre, a blue enamel circle bearing the head of Queen Victoria facing left.
Reverse	Red enamel circle, having at its centre '1843' with 'MAHARAJPOOR 29 DECEM^R' about it's circumference.
Suspension	The star is suspended from it's uppermost point by a gold ring and straight bar suspension to which is attached a gold and enamel imitation riband, with buckle.

The Governor-General, Lord Ellenborough, presented a special star to each of the four ladies, who, because of the speed of events, found themselves present at the Battle of Maharajpoor. The ladies present were:

Lady Gough, Lady Smith (wife of Sir Harry Smith), Mrs Curtis (wife of Captain Curtis, deputy-assistant commissary-general) and Miss Gough (later Lady Grant).

*This star was awarded to Major Thomas Ryan, Knight of Hanover, of the 50th Foot, who was attached to the 39th Foot.

86 *Sutlej Campaign Medal* 18th December 1845-22nd February 1846

Obverse	The diademed head of Queen Victoria with the legend 'VICTORIA REGINA'.
Reverse	The standing figure of Victory, facing left. In her outstretched right hand she holds a wreath and in her left an olive branch. At her feet is a collection of trophies. The legend 'ARMY OF THE SUTLEJ' is written around the circumference. There are four different exergues which contain one of the following: (1) 'MOODKEE 1845'; (2) 'FEROZESHUHUR 1845'; (3) 'ALIWAL 1846'; or (4) 'SOBRAON 1846'.
Size	36mm diameter
Metal	Silver
Ribbon	32mm wide. Dark blue with crimson edges.
Suspension	An ornamental swivelling suspender
Designer	Wm. Wyon RA
Naming	Indented in capital letters or light roman skeleton lettering.
Bars issued	Three: Ferozeshuhur, Aliwal, Sobraon.
Variant	Glazed, silver-gilt specimens of this medal with three bars.

Sanction was given by a General Order dated the 17th April 1846 for the award of a medal to the Army of the Sutlej.

The medal awarded for this campaign was the first with bars to be given to both officers and men. The Army Gold Medals and Crosses were only awarded to officers. The previously issued China 1842 Medal had no bars. The Army of India Medal, though awarded to commemorate much earlier battles, was not issued until 1851.

The first action in which the recipient took part was given in the exergue on the reverse, so that four distinct types had to be issued. This is the only time this has been done in the case of a battle, though we find the date, or dates, of the campaign either in the exergue or on the reverse as is the case with the medals for Afghanistan 1878-80, Egypt 1882, and the British South Africa Company's medals for Matabeleland, 1893 etc.

Collectors should note that the only regiments present as a whole at all four actions were the 31st and 50th Foot, the 24th and 47th Bengal NI and the 5th Bengal Light Cavalry. Consequently, the rivets joining the bars should be carefully examined for forgeries as three-bar medals are rare. The only Ferozeshuhur Medal that is known of with two bars was awarded to Henry Allward, 62nd Foot. The Moodkee Medals with the Ferozeshuhur—Aliwal combination are rare.

1st Sikh War

With the death of Ranjit Singh (1839) a state of anarchy ensued within the Punjab. With the army becoming increasingly dominant in the State's internal affairs and being substantially anti-British, war was the natural outcome.

The Sikh army was reckoned to number upwards of 60,000 European-trained men with over 200 guns, and to be supported by numerous irregular forces. Opposing them, an Anglo-Indian army of approximately 35,000 with 100 guns, based primarily at Ferozepur, Ludhiana, Ambala and Meerut.

The Sikh army crossed the Sutlej into British territory (December 11 1845) and the British, commanded by General Sir Hugh Gough, not entirely surprised by this action, marched to meet them.

At Mudki (December 18) Gough and 12,000 men were confronted late in the day by a detached force of 15,000 to 25,000 Sikhs. Whilst the Anglo-Indian infantry deployed for action, the battle commenced with

an artillery duel. Meanwhile successful British cavalry charges on both flanks had foiled possible Sikh moves at envelopment with their numerically superior cavalry. Infantry attacks were then pressed, and with difficulty the British succeeded in driving the Sikhs from the field; the brunt of the fighting falling to the British Regiments. Swirling dust and approaching night caused untold confusion and many casualties were suffered by native infantry units firing at each other! Sikh casualties were also heavy and 17 of their estimated 40 guns were captured. Anglo-Indian casualties (killed or wounded) numbered 870. [3 Lt Dgns (86), 9 (52), 31 (157), 50 (109), 80 (24), Foot, 5 Bengal Lt Cav (49), 2 Bengal NI (71), 42 Bengal NI (89)].

Pressing on towards the main Sikh concentration, Gough and a reinforced army encountered a fortified encampment of 50,000 Sikhs led by Lal Singh at Ferozeshah (December 21). For the forthcoming action Gough's superior, Governor-General Sir Henry Hardinge agreed to serve as his second-in-command. However, such an arrangement soon came to grief. A disagreement between the two prevented the attack being made until late afternoon when reinforcements under Sir John Littler arrived from Ferozepur; these having evaded another Sikh army under Tej Singh. Upon his arrival the Anglo-Indian force numbered 18,000. The battle commenced with Littler on the far left making a premature and unsupported attack on the entrenched Sikh positions; to be driven back with heavy loss, especially to the 62nd Regiment. Coordinated attacks by other units managed to penetrate the encampment but could not drive the Sikhs from it. Confused fighting continued all night. The following day (December 22), Gough finally cleared the camp, only to be opposed by 35,000 fresh troops under Tej Singh who had been menacing Ferozepur. In a serious situation, having suffered many casualties, and the remaining men exhausted and short of ammunition, Gough made a brave show against the new arrivals. Fortunately, Tej Singh, perturbed by the capture of the camp, made only half-hearted attacks and was then content to withdraw.

Sikh losses at Ferozeshah numbered 10,000 with 74 guns captured. Anglo-Indian casualties (killed or wounded) were over 2,800, again falling most heavily on the British. [3 Lt Dgns (152), 9(280), 29(184), 31(142), 50(124), 62(260), 80 Foot (81), Bengal European Regiment (204)].

Another Sikh force under Ranjur Singh, making for Ludhiana and threatening Gough's line of communications, was countered by a force under Major-General Sir Harry Smith. A skirmish near Ludhiana (January 21) cost Smith 200 casualties, but caused Ranjur to fall back to the Sutlej at Aliwal. Here Smith, with 10,000 men, fought Ranjur with 20,000 (January 28). Smith's right wing, spearheaded by the 16th Lancers, broke the Sikh left and attacked their rear. Despite gallant efforts to repair the damage, Ranjur's force was relentlessly demolished. Sikh losses numbered at least 3,000, many of whom were drowned or cut down attempting to cross the river to safety. 67 guns were captured or destroyed. Anglo-Indian casualties (killed or wounded) numbered 589. [16th Lancers (144), 50 Foot (73)].

The final battle of the war was fought at Sobraon (February 10), 45 miles south east of Lahore. The Sikhs held a strongly fortified position on the east side of the Sutlej, supported by additional artillery on the west bank. Gough, reinforced to approximately 20,000 faced opposition numbering 35,000. Action began in the early morning with an artillery bombardment of the Sikh positions; curtailed after two hours through lack of ammunition. Infantry attacks then followed. Initially repulsed with heavy loss, a penetration of the Sikh fortifications was finally effected and their army inexorably pushed back, then driven across the river in chaos. The Sikhs suffered 10,000 casualties, many perishing in an attempt to cross the Sutlej. 67 guns were captured. Gough had 2,385 casualties. [9(44), 10(132), 29(187), 31(154), 50 Foot (239), Bengal European Regiment (197), Nasiri Battalion (88)].

With the power of the Sikh army broken at Sobraon, Gough crossed the Sutlej (February 10) and entered Lahore (February 20). Under the Treaty of Lahore (March 8) formally ending the war, the Punjab paid an indemnity, reduced its army, ceded land and became a British Protectorate.

Moodkee 18th December 1845

Regiments present: 3 Lt Dgns (57 killed, 519 medals claimed 73, for Moodkee only.) 4, 5, Bengal Lt Cav; 4, 9 Irreg Horse; Bodyguard Cav; 1/1, 2/1, 3/1, 1/3, 2/3, 4/3 Bengal HA; 3/4, 2/6 Bengal FA; Bengal Sprs and Mnrs; 9(899), 31(877), 50(703), 80(824) Ft; 2, 16, 24, 26, 42, 45, 47, 48, 73 Bengal NI.

Ferozeshuhur 21st-22nd December 1845

Regiments present: 3 Lt Dgns (55 killed, 8 medals claimed with Ferozeshuhur in exergue, total issue of 446) 4, 5, 8 Bengal Lt Cav; 3, 9 Irreg Horse; Bodyguard Cav; 1/1, 2/1, 3/1, 5/1 [including 6 medals with Sobraon bar], 1/3, 2/3, 3/3, 4/3 Bengal HA; 2/4, 3/4, 4/4, 2/6, 4/6, 2/7 Bengal FA; No 6 Co Bengal Sprs and Mnrs; 9(866), 29(784), 31(721),

50(509), 62 [120 killed, 870 claims], 80(817) Ft; 1 Bengal European Regt [later 1st Bn Rl Munster Fus] (696) [131 as Ferozeshuhur only and 565 with Sobraon bar], 2, 12, 14, 16, 24, 26, 33, 42, 44, 45, 47, 48, 54, 73 Bengal NI.

Also receiving the award for Ferozeshuhur:
a) units left at Mudki to guard the wounded: 11, 41 Bengal NI
b) garrison left by Littler at Ferozepur:
27, 63 Bengal NI; 2/2 Bengal FA; Det 2/7 Bengal FA; Bengal Sprs and Mnrs.

Aliwal 28th January 1846

Regiments present: 3 Lt Dgns (51, 50 having Aliwal in the exergue); 16 Lancers (551); 1, 3, 5 Bengal Lt Cav; 4 Irreg Cav; Bodyguard Cav; 1/1 [13 with no bar], 1/2, 3/2, 2/3 Bengal HA; 2/7 Bengal FA; Det of No 6 Co Bengal Sprs and Mnrs; 31(524), 50(629), 53(708), 62 [4 as Aliwal only and 47 with Sobraon], 80 [6 as Aliwal only and 18 with Sobraon] Ft; 13, 24, 30, 36, 47, 48 Bengal NI; Shekhawattee Inf and Cav; Nasiri Bn [1 Gurkhas], Sirmoor Bn [2 Gurkhas].
Also receiving the award for Aliwal:
the garrisons at Ludhiana and Buddhowel Forts:
Detachments of 24 Bengal NI
2/4, 4/4, 4/6 Bengal FA.

Sobraon 10th February 1846

Regiments present: 3 Lt Dgns (384, 20 with Sobraon in exergue); 9(637), 16(436) Lancers; 3, 4, 5 Bengal Lt Cav; 2, 4, 8, 9 Irreg Cav; Bodyguard Cav; 1/1, 2/1 [3 with no bar], 3/1 [3 with no bar], 5/1, 1/2, 2/2, 3/2, 1/3, 2/3, 3/3, 4/3 Bengal HA; 2/2, 3/3, 4/3, 1/4, 2/4, 3/4, 4/4, 1/6, 2/6, 3/6, 4/6, 2/7 Bengal FA; 2, 3, 4, 5, 6, 7 Cos Bengal Sprs and Mnrs; 9(637), 10(778), 29(612), 31(503), 50(571), 53(760), 62(662), 80(694) Ft; 1 Bengal European Regt (565); 4, 5, 9, 12, 16, 24, 26, 33, 38, 41, 42, 43, 47, 59, 63, 68 Bengal NI; Nasiri Bn [1 Gurkhas], Sirmoor Bn [2 Gurkhas].

Also receiving the award for Sobraon:
(a) troops at Rhodawalla: 73 Bengal NI
(b) those guarding the C-in-C' camp
(c) those guarding the C-in-C's camp

The 11th Irregular Horse was ordered to be raised in January 1846. A nucleus of Anglo-Indian personnel designated for the 11th but serving with other units at the time, received medals to the 11th Irregular Horse.

87 *Punjab Campaign Medal* 7th September 1848-14th March 1849

Obverse	The diademed head of Queen Victoria with the legend 'VICTORIA REGINA'.
Reverse	Major-General Sir Walter Gilbert, on horseback receiving the surrender of the Sikhs. In the background is a hill with a large palm tree on it. Around the top is the inscription 'TO THE ARMY OF THE PUNJAB'. In the exergue is the date 'MDCCCXLIX'.
Size	36mm diameter
Metal	Silver
Ribbon	32mm wide. Dark blue with a yellow stripe near each edge
Suspension	An ornamental swivelling suspender
Designer	Wm. Wyon, RA
Naming	In impressed roman capitals. The name of the recipient's ship, in the case of medals awarded to the Indus flotilla, is not given
Bars issued	Three—Mooltan, Chilianwala, and Goojerat
Variant	Glazed, silver-gilt specimens of the medal with three bars exist

A General Order dated the 2nd April 1849 granted the award of a medal to all employed in the Punjab between the 7th September 1848 and the 14th March 1849.

The bars to this medal should read downwards—ie, the more recent bar nearest the medal. As the bars were issued to be affixed locally a great number of genuine medals are found with the correct bars in the wrong order. It should be noted that medals to the 1/60th with the single bar for Mooltan are rare. As a general rule medals to units which were present at Mooltan and Goojerat are more valuable with the single bar than the double. For this reason medals with the single bar for Mooltan should be carefully examined to see whether there are any signs of a second bar having been taken off.

Many medals are found with no bars. The units which received the medal and yet saw no fighting are the following: 2nd Bengal European Regiment (35), 7th Bengal Cavalry, Bengal Horse and Foot Artillery, 53rd (367) Foot, 98th Foot (503), Bengal Pioneers, two regiments of the Sikh Infantry and the 1, 3, 4, 18, 22, 29, 37, 50, 53 (367), 71, 73 Bengal NI. Fifty-four medals were awarded without bars to members of the Indus flotilla.

At the Battle of Chilianwala the 24th Foot suffered twenty-one officer and 503 other-rank casualties.

There were no medals issued with three bars, and no unit received a medal with the bars for Mooltan and Chilianwala.

Second Sikh War

The defeats of the earlier war left an uneasy peace in the Punjab. Many of the Sikh leadership, unhappy with the result, sought the means to renew the conflict and restore their sovereignty. The means occurred at Multan in the south west Punjab (April 20 1848), when two British Residents were murdered by the soldiery of the Governor, Mulraj Singh. The incipient revolt was confined within Multan after defeats were inflicted upon Mulraj by Lieutenant H. E. Edwards and a force of irregulars (June 18 and July 1). General W. S. Whish was then dispatched from Lahore (July 24) with an Anglo-Indian force to invest the city. Arriving in early September, assaults were made on outlying Sikh positions (September 10 and 12) causing them to fall back to the city walls. However, the revolt worsened when a Sikh army under Shere Singh, ostensibly sent to assist Whish, instead declared for the rebels. Whish, his position at Multan untenable, abandoned the siege and withdrew (September 15).

Meanwhile, the rebellion had spead to the north west Punjab, principally under the direction of Shere's father, Chattar Singh. By the end of October, several Sikh garrisons within the region, notably Bannu and Peshawar, had rebelled.

Departing from Multan (October 9), Shere marched north to effect a junction with the other rebels; eventually concentrating his forces at Ramnagar on the River Cheneb, 55 miles north west of Lahore.

The British C-in-C, Lord Gough, his preparations complete, marched from Ferozepur via Lahore to confront Shere Singh at Ramnagar. Arriving (November 22), he found the Sikhs concentrated mainly on the north side. A series of cavalry actions followed around the ford between the two armies. In the course of which, the 14th Lt Dragoons and 5th Bengal Light Cavalry, advancing recklessly, were entrapped and were only extricated with difficulty. [Casualties: 14 Light Dgns (49); 5 Bengal Lt Cav (23)]. More devastating still was the loss of Brigadier Cureton, the divisional cavalry commander, whilst attempting to halt the advance.

Unwilling to press on with an opposed crossing, Gough sent a detachment to cross further upstream and outflank Shere's position. This was accomplished and after a skirmish at Sadullapur (December 14) Shere withdrew. Gough was then able to cross the Cheneb with his main force.

At Multan, with the departure of Shere Singh, Whish had re-established the siege. Receiving reinforcements (December 21) he was at length able to storm and take the city, bar the citadel (January 3). The citadel, the last refuge of Malraj eventually surrendered (January 22) so terminating hostilities in the area.

Meanwhile Gough, after a delay advanced (January 12) to confront the army of Shere Singh now established on the east side of the River Jhelum at Rasul. Reaching the village of Chilianwala (January 13) Gough prepared to camp, deferring action against the nearby Sikh army for another day. However, an artillery bombardment on British positions caused a change of plans and Gough prepared for action that same day. The Sikhs commanded by Shere and Lal Singh numbered 30,000 with 62 guns and held a strong position west of Chilianwala between Rasul and Lakhniwala. Gough commanded 12,000 Anglo-Indian troops with 66 guns. Overlapped on both flanks, Gough decided upon a general frontal assault. This was made difficult by the terrain through which the Anglo-Indian forces would have to pass. This consisted of scrub and jungle that impeded both vision and movement, disrupting co-ordination between units. The Anglo-Indian army formed up for battle. On the right, a division commanded by Major General Gilbert with brigades under Godby and Mountain. On the left, the division of Brigadier C. Campbell with brigades under Pennycuick, Hoggan and (in reserve) Penny. On the left flank Brigadier White and on the right Brigadier Pope commanded brigades of cavalry. All units were supported by horse or field artillery with a concentration of heavy batteries in the centre between the divisions.

Because of the difficult terrain Campbell felt unable to control his two forward brigades adequately and so left Pennycuick in independent command of his brigade with the added injunction that they should attack with bayonet, not bullet. The Anglo-Indian left advanced but Pennycuick's brigade (24th Foot, 25th and 45th Bengal NI) pressing ahead soon lost contact with that of Hoggan's. Furthermore, Pennycuick in his haste with the 24th Foot soon left behind his native regiments and lost touch with his artillery support. It was thus that the 24th finally found themselves in an unsupported and disordered state emerging from the jungle under heavy fire before the Sikh positions. The 24th charged with the bayonet and took the Sikh positions to their front after a fierce fight. However, in a weakened and even more disordered state, they were unable to withstand the Sikh counter-attack and were driven back with heavy loss, carrying with them in their flight the 25th and 45th Bengal Native Infantry.

Campbell, with Hoggan's brigade, met with more success. Destroying the Sikhs to his front, he then wheeled right and advancing along the Sikh line rolled it up. The left wing cavalry was likewise successful in dealing with its opposition. The right wing cavalry found itself ineptly led by Pope. Thoroughly demoralised through his handling, the brigade, on his apparent order, suddenly turned about and made for the rear. Order soon dissolved and the majority galloped off as in rout, disorganising their supporting horse artillery and all in their path until rallied by members of Gough's staff.

The right division under Gilbert, finding itself bereft of cavalry support, nevertheless pressed on with its attack, defeating Sikhs to their front whilst repelling attacks to flank and rear in a series of hard fights until meeting with Campbell's advancing troops.

The success of Campbell and Gilberts' advance gave Gough a hard won victory, but left both sides exhausted. The Sikhs retreated to defensible Rasul, Gough gathering his wounded retired to Chilianwala; unfortunately, allowing many of the captured Sikh guns to be reclaimed. Sikh casualties numbered over 8,000 with 12 guns captured. Anglo-Indian casualties (killed or wounded) numbered 2,357 with 4 guns lost. [24th (524), 29th (241), 30th Bengal NI (285), 56th Bengal NI (316)].

This costly victory was received badly in England and orders were given to replace Gough by Sir C. Napier. However, the war reached its climax before this could be implemented.

Shere Singh reinforced with the army of Chattar Singh, moved from Rasul and after failing to draw Gough into further battle, set up a position to the east at Gujrat (February 14), west of the River Cheneb. As a precaution against possible Sikh moves to cross the river, Gough dispatched units to the east bank at Waziribad. Gough too was reinforced, receiving units under General Whish who, following his victory, had moved up from Multan.

Thus reinforced, Gough prepared again for battle and confronted the Sikhs at Gujrat (February 21). Shere Singh's army numbered 60,000 men with 59 guns, Gough's army numbered 24,000 with 96 guns.

A destructive 2½ hour long British artillery bombardment silenced the Sikh artillery and severely shook their infantry. The Anglo-Indian infantry advance proved to be irresistible and only in the Sikh centre around two villages south of Gujrat did the Sikhs fight with any determination. Sikh cavalry on both wings attempting flanking attacks also failed, being skilfully countered by cavalry and horse artillery. With Gough's men in pursuit, the Sikhs fled in great disorder with all hopes wrecked, leaving numberless dead and 56 guns captured. Anglo-Indian casualties numbered 801 [2nd Bengal European (150)].

A force under Gilbert continued the pursuit of the remaining Sikh strength. At Rawalpindi (March 14) he received the surrender of Shere and Lal Singh with 20,000 men and 41 guns. Continuing further west, he pursued the Sikh's retreating Afghan allies under Dost Mohammed to their homeland and recovered Attock (March 17) and Peshwar (March 21) so bringing the war to an end.

The whole Punjab was then annexed to the other British dominions in India.

Mooltan Seige of, 7th September–22nd January 1849

Two thousand nine hundred of these bars were issued to Europeans and 16,067 to natives.

Regiments present: Guides Cav; 1, 2 Scinde Horse; 1 Bombay Lt Cav; 11 Bengal Lt Cav; 7, 11 and 1 Sqdrn 14 Irreg Cav; 4/1, 4/3 Bengal HA; 2/2, 3/3, 4/3, 6/7 Bengal FA; 3 Bombay HA; 2/1, 4/2, 1/4, 2/4 Bombay FA; 1, 2, 3 Co Bengal and 1, 2, Co Bombay Sprs and Mnrs; 2, 3 and part of 5 Bengal Pioneers; 10 (843), 24 (2), 32 (1105), 1/60 (998, 100 of which were single bars), 103 (102 as single bars and 789 with Goojerat) Ft; 8, 49, 51, 52, 72 Bengal NI; 3, 4, 9, 14, 19 Bombay NI; Scinde Camel Corps; a hundred men from the Indus flotilla with bar and fifty-four without bar.

Chilianwala 13th January 1849

Four thousand three hundred bars were awarded to Europeans and 16,153 to natives.

Regiments present: 3 Lt Dgns (586), 9 Lancers (651 but only 1 as a single bar), 14 Lt Dgns (564), 1, 5, 6, 8 Bengal Lt Cav; 3, 9 Irreg Cav; 1/2, 2/2, 3/2, 4/2, 1/3, 2/3 Bengal HA; 1/1, 3/1, 1/4, 2/4, 4/4, 3/7 Bengal FA; 4, 5, 6, 7 Co Bengal Pioneers; 24 (524 killed and wounded, 1,060 medals), 29 (948), 61 (835) Ft; 2 Bengal European Regt (36 single bars and 700 with Goojerat); 20, 25, 30, 31, 36, 45, 46, 56, 69, 70 Bengal NI.

Goojerat 21st February 1849

Six thousand two hundred bars were issued to Europeans and 26,760 to natives.

Regiments present: 3 Lt Dgns (565); 9 Lancers (666 but 14 only as a single bar); 14 Lt Dgns (549), 1, 8 Bengal Lt Cav; Guides Cav; Scinde Irreg Horse; 3, 9, 11, 14 Irreg Cav; 4/1, 1/2, 2/2, 3/2, 4/2, 1/3, 2/3, 4/3 Bengal HA; 1/1, 3/1, 2/2, 3/3, 4/3, 1/4, 2/4, 4/4, 3/7, 6/7 Bengal FA; 3 Bombay HA; 2/1 Bombay FA; 2, 3 Co Bengal Sprs; 1 Co Bombay Sprs and Mnrs; 2, 3, 4, 5, 6, 7 Bengal Pioneers; 10 (790), 24 (694), 29 (824), 32 (975), 53 (611), 1/60 (912), 1/61 (888) Ft; 2 Bengal European Regt (13 single bars and 700 with Chilianwala); 1 Bombay European Regt; 8, 15, 20, 25, 30, 31, 36, 46, 51, 52, 56, 70, 72 Bengal NI; 3, 19 Bombay NI, Scinde Camel Corps.

The following troops were in reserve: 5, 6 Bengal Lt Cav; 2/1 Bn Bombay Art; 45, 69 Bengal NI.

Waziribad contingent receiving the bar: 12 Irreg Cav, Det of 6/7 Bengal FA; 53 Ft, 13 Bengal NI.

88 *South Africa Medal* 1834-1853

Obverse	The diademed head of Queen Victoria with the legend, 'VICTORIA REGINA'.
Reverse	A lion representing Africa depicted crouching in a token of submission in front of a Protea bush. Above are the words 'SOUTH AFRICA' and in the exergue the date '1853'.
Size	36mm diameter
Metal	Silver
Ribbon	32mm wide. Pale orange, watered with two wide and two narrow dark blue stripes
Suspension	Ornamental scroll swivelling suspension
Designers	Obverse: Wm Wyon RA
	Reverse: L. C. Wyon
Naming	Indented in roman capitals as found on the Military General Service Medal
Bars issued	Nil

This medal is commonly called the 'Kaffir' Wars medal, a term of Arabic origin meaning 'unbeliever' once used to encompass different native tribes. It was earned by those who had been engaged in, and survived, one or more of the frontier wars of 1834-5, 1846-7 and 1850-3, and was the first medal specially struck for military service in the Continent of Africa that was available to all ranks.

The intention of awarding a medal for the campaign of 1850-3 was established in March 1854; proposed rules had been drawn up by July and design suggested. Word of this reached Sir James Alexander in Canada, who in 1840 had tried to obtain a medal for survivors of the Peninsula wars, and he wrote to the Duke of Newcastle, Secretary of State for War and the Colonies, asking that those who had served in the wars of 1834-5 and 1846-7 and against the Boers in Natal (1842) and at Boomplats (1848) should 'not be overlooked'.

Alexander had a particular interest for he had served as an Aide to Major General Sir Benjamin D'Urban at the Cape in 1834-5. Possibly he envisaged an Africa General Service medal on the lines of the MGS, NGS and Army of India medals for British troops had fought against the Boers in 1795 and 1806 and had to deal with native rebellions in 1798, 1811 and 1819. If so, it is a pity he did not press the matter on that basis, but perhaps he felt more limited objectives stood a better chance of being achieved. In the event he was largely successful; his suggestions were referred to Lord Hardinge, C-in-C at the Horse Guards who decided 'it would scarcely be possible to resist the claims of those engaged in two former wars against the same enemy'. Hardinge ignored the actions against the Boers but in fact almost all of the British troops who took part in those engagements qualified though one or other of the three wars.

When General Order No 634 was issued from the Horse Guards on 22nd November 1854 it laid down that the medal was to be conferred on 'Surviving Officers, non-commissioned Officers and Soldiers of the regular forces . . . who actually served in the field against the enemy in

South Africa'. This soon came to the eye of Lieutenant General Sir Harry Smith, former Governor of the Cape who raised the question of the eligibility of Seamen and Marines. Shore detachments of the latter had frequently been engaged with the enemy but the Horse Guards did not take to the notion of the Navy sharing the award. Ships of the Royal Navy had made a considerable contribution to the campaigns, but it was only with some deft manoeuvring by the Admiralty that all War Office resistance was overcome. Even so, diehards tried to salvage something from the defeat nearly a year later when attempts were made to limit the number of medals to the Naval force on the grounds that they had not 'served in the field'. But again the Admiralty prevailed and the entire crews of the ships concerned during the 1850-3 campaign were admitted to the award. Just the same it is surprising no one pressed for recognition of ships' crews employed during the two earlier rebellions and the only claims respecting them came from a handful of Marines serving in HMS *President* during 1846-7.

The original suggested design of the medal incorporated the date '1853'. The decision to extend qualification to embrace the wars of 1834-5 and 1846-7 naturally threw that aspect into question. This posed the War Office a problem for many soldiers had served in more than one campaign and regimental returns already received often did not accurately record such detail. A cost conscious Government Department had no wish to spend time and money upon revising the returns, nor in meeting additional costs which would have ensued from producing strikings of varying date combinations or bars, as was later done with the New Zealand (1845-1866) or South Africa (1877-8-9) medals. They were also in the middle of a war with Russia and consequently took the easiest course by letting well alone and, to the puzzlement of later generations, sticking by the meaningless '1853'.

A common misconception of the design concerns the posture of the lion symbolizing Africa. The beast is usually incorrectly described as 'stooping to drink', when in fact its 'couchant' pose was intended to convey submission. An Under-Secretary expressed worry at the time that the 'Lion doing penance will be taken for a British Lion'!

The ribbon first issued with the medal in October 1855 was without doubt of a pale orange with dark blue stripes, but it has been asserted that the deeper orange of the SA 1877-8-9 ribbon indicates fading of the 'Kaffir' ribbon. This is nonsense and stands logic on its head; there is overwhelming evidence that the orange of both ribbons was very different. Almost certainly it was intended that the so-called 'Zulu' ribbon should imitate the colour and design but it is very difficult to perfectly reproduce exact colours in different batches of pigment, and if the manufacturers tried—which is doubtful—they failed dismally.

Kaffir Wars

The uprising of 1834-5 is known to medal collectors as the First Kaffir War, but is numbered in South Africa's history as the Sixth Frontier War.

It sprang from a minor incident in December 1834 when a patrol of the Cape Mounted Rifles was attacked during an attempt to recover stolen horses. The trouble spread and marauding Kaffir bands fell upon settlements in the Albany district to steal and slaughter livestock. This escalated into widespread pillage and murder. Settlers fled to Grahamstown or the protection of the nearest military forts. In January 1835 Colonel Harry Smith made a famous 600 miles' ride in 6 days from Cape Town to Grahamstown where he brought order from confusion. Small columns were pushed out to take the fight to the enemy and very soon reinforcements were reaching the frontier.

Operations to drive the foe from the bush along the Kat and Great Fish rivers and then the fastnesses around Fort Willshire up to the Keiskamma occupied February and March. Four divisions then swept the Amatola mountains and in ensuing months the dissidents were relentlessly pursued wherever they could be found, but not until September 1835 was a peace treaty ratified.

The Second (or Seventh) Frontier War, known as the War of the Axe, was sparked off when the escort for a Kaffir prisoner accused of the theft of an axe were massacred in March 1846. Failure to surrender the murderers resulted in a punitive force being sent to strike at Chief Sandili's Kraal in the Amatolas, but the troops found themselves facing swarms of the enemy and lost half of their wagon train near Burns Hill before retiring. Elated by this success the natives poured into the eastern district and destroyed a wagon train on the Fish River. In June, warriors massing for an attack on Trompetters Post were caught in open country and suffered heavily in the battle of Guanga.

During the next three months extensive sweeps as far as the Kei river seemed to break the back of the rebellion but the following May trouble flared again and it was not until the end of 1847 that all resistance was crushed.

The Third (or Eighth) and greatest Kaffir War began in December 1850 when a British column was ambushed in Boomah Pass. Lieutenant General Sir Harry Smith was trapped in Fort Cox and made a celebrated dash through the beseigers with an escort of Cape Mounted Riflemen. Again the settlers, many of them discharged soldiers, took the brunt of savage fury and over 40 were murdered. This time, many Hottentots jointed with the dissidents and seriously spread the troubles throughout British Kaffraria.

No sooner had columns driven through the fortresses of the Amatolas and the Waterkloof than the elusive enemy returned to their familiar hideouts, and it took nearly two years of harrassment before all resistance ceased, peace being proclaimed in March 1853. During November and December 1852, before all the Kaffir chiefs had finally submitted, an expedition was despatched across the Orange River to deal with a threat from the Basutos. It was found that the Basutos were of a different quality and at the battle of Berea the cavalry were near to suffering a disaster. Chief Mosesh promised no further trouble and General Sir Geo Cathcart, now Governor in place of Smith, thankfully withdrew.

The Third Kaffir War was marked by an incident famous in British history—the sinking of the *Birkenhead*.

The *Birkenhead* struck an uncharted rock off Danger Point at 1.50am on 26th February 1852. In less than 25 minutes the *Birkenhead* had broken up and sunk. Of the 638 persons on board, 445 lost their lives, the survivors amounting to only 193. The following table provides a summary of the survivors:

	On Board	Died	Survived
Children	13	nil	13
Women	7	nil	7
Ship's Officers	17	11	6**
Ship's Crew	121	68	53
Army Officers	14	9	5***
Other Ranks	465	356	109
Civil Servant	1	1*	nil
Total	638	445	193

Included in the ship's crew survivors was a small detachment of Royal Marines under Colour Sergeant John Drake RM.

Valiant work by the ship's officers and crew who manned the two undamaged cutters and a small gig resulted in the saving of 85 lives. Of the remaining 108 survivors, 40 clung to the rigging attached to the top of the main mast which protruded from the water and were rescued the following afternoon by the Schooner *Lioness* which had already picked up the survivors from the two cutters. The gig with 9 people on board including Surgeon Culhane landed at Point D'Urban. The remaining 68 survivors clung to floating wreckage in shark infested waters and made their own way to land. Captain Wright of the 91st Regiment the senior surviving military officer took charge of the party which had reached land until the arrival on the 29th of HMS *Rhadamanthus*, which was the first war ship to reach the scene.

The epic bravery of the troops on board so impressed King William of Prussia that he had the full story read out on parade in every barrack in Germany. Medals to survivors who later took part in the campaign are particularly sought after.

Throughout the 1850-53 campaign her Majesty's ships *Castor*, *Dee*, *Hermes*, *Rhadamanthus* and *Styx* were engaged in the movement of troops and stores between the various ports of Cape Colony. The landing of troops, horses and stores on selected beaches from open anchorages was hazardous work as the ships' boats were compelled to negotiate the heavy surf. The ships' logs for the period frequently carry entries relating to ships' boats being swamped and capsizing and stores

---

* Andrew White
** Asst Surgn W. Culhane, Asst Engr 1st Cl C. R. Renwick, Asst Engr 2nd Cl B. Barber, Masters Asst R. B. Richards, Clk G. W. S. Hire, Gnr 3rd Cl J. Archbold.
*** Capt W. W. C. Wright, 91st Regt; Lt J. F. Giradot 43rd Ft; Engn G. A. Lucas 73rd Regt; Cor S. Bond 12th Lncrs; Staff Surgn R. Bowen.

being lost. A substantial number of both sailors and troops are recorded as having died from drowning.

The award of medals to the various ships engaged was as follows: *Castor* (494); *Dee* (88); *Hermes* (143); *Rhadamanthus* (84); *Styx* (183).

A total of 866 Officers and Men of the Royal Navy and 126 Officers and Men of the Royal Marines.

A small number of recipients later served during the Kaffir and Zulu wars of 1877-8-9. It was intended they should be awarded a bar only but the widths of the suspenders to the 1853 and 1877-8-9 medals differ and the former needed adjustment to receive a bar. In fact, several men received a SA 1853 medal with bar attached (see OMRS Journal 1981 page 236).

Diagrammatic Chart of Medals Awarded

	ARMY OFFICERS								OTHER RANKS						
	1834-5	1846-7	1850-3	1834-5 and 1846-7	1846-7 and 1850-3	1834-5 1846-7 and 1850-3	1834-5 and 1850-3	Total	1834-5	1846-7	1850-3	1834-5 and 1846-7	1846-7 and 1850-3	1834-5 1846-7 and 1850-3	Total
Staff	3	8	8	—	3	3	1	26	—	—	—	—	—	—	—
Staff MS	—	5	9	—	8	—	—	22	—	—	—	—	—	—	—
7th Dgn Gds	—	20†	—	—	—	—	—	20	—	149	—	—	1	—	150†
12th Lncrs	—	—	27	—	—	—	—	27	—	—	339	—	1	—	340
Rl Art	1	5	6	—	2	—	—	14	—	—	K	—	—	—	212*
Rl Engrs	1	7	12	—	1	—	—	21	—	—	—	—	—	—	244*
2nd Regt	—	—	24	—	—	—	—	24	—	—	577	—	—	—	577
6th Regt	—	10	16	—	12	—	—	38	—	47	175	—	378	—	601
12th Regt	—	—	25	—	—	—	—	25	—	—	510	—	—	—	511
27th Regt	9	8	—	4	—	—	—	21	26	70	—	84	—	—	180†
43rd Regt	—	—	24	—	1	—	—	25	—	—	585	—	—	—	585
45th Regt	—	17	13	—	10	—	—	40	—	—	—	—	—	—	711*
60th Regt	—	—	23	—	1	—	—	24	—	—	553	—	—	—	553
72nd Regt	10	—	—	—	—	—	—	10	128	—	—	1	—	—	129
73rd Regt	—	11	17	—	6	—	—	34	—	27	180	—	327	—	534
74th Regt	—	—	25	—	1	—	—	26	—	—	558	—		—	558
75th Regt	12	—	—	—	—	—	—	12	116	—	—	—	—	—	116
90th Regt	—	14	—	—	—	—	—	14	—	243	—	—	1	—	244
91st Regt	—	21	15	—	9	—	—	45	—	179	222	2	355	1	759
1st Rif Bde	—	9	14	—	11	—	—	34	—	161	420	—	150	—	731
CMR	7	7	20	2	16	6	1	59	—	22	471	5	271	36	805
								561							8,540

*Estimated
†Including one of uncertain date
K Medal known

Royal Navy	831 Officers and men
Royal Marines	93
Royal Marine Artillery	40
Commissariat	118
Colonial/Levy Forces	30 Approximately

The Mint records show that 10,558 medals were struck between April 24th 1855 and March 31st 1862. This number includes two patterns which were presented to Queen Victoria; those issued to deserters and later cancelled, replacements, duplicates and others of which we have no record also effect the figure.

Extracted from 'The South Africa 1853 Medal' by G. R. Everson, Sampson Books.

89 *India General Service Medal* 1854-1895

Obverse	The diademed head of Queen Victoria and the legend 'VICTORIA REGINA'.
Reverse	The winged and standing figure of Victory, who is crowning a seated warrior. In the exergue is a lotus flower and four leaves denoting the connection with the East.
Size	36mm diameter
Metal	Silver and bronze
Ribbon	32mm wide. Red with two dark blue stripes.
Suspension	By means of a floreated swivelling suspender.
Designers	Obverse—W. Wyon, RA; Reverse—L. C. Wyon.
Naming	Although this varies considerably, as a general guide medals will be found engraved in running script. Exceptions to this style will be noted under the relevant bar.
Bars issued	Twenty-four: Pegu, Persia, North West Frontier, Umbeyla, Bhootan, Looshai, Perak, Jowaki 1877-8, Naga 1879-80, Burma 1885-7, Sikkim 1888, Hazara 1888, Burma 1887-89, Burma 1887-9, Chin Lushai 1889-90, Samana 1891, Hazara 1891, NE Frontier 1891, Hunza 1891, Burma 1889-92, Lushai 1889-92, Chin Hills 1892-93, Kachin Hills 1892-93, Waziristan 1894-95

General Order of the Governor-General dated 22nd December 1853, announced the institution of the medal with bar 'Pegu'.

The Governor-General had earlier recommended that to avoid unnecessary multiplication of medals a single service medal with bar would be awarded and additional service would be represented by further bars. This recommendation was approved on 1st March 1854.

This medal could never be awarded without a bar. The maximum number of bars to any known medal is seven, this being to General Sir A. W. Lockhart. However the 'Official History of the Services of the Bengal Army' states that 'some officers and native soldiers possessed as many as nine or ten' although this cannot be confirmed.

As these bars were issued individually over a number of years, they are often found in an incorrect order. The bars may be found fitted together by a variety of means.

Pegu 28th March 1852-30th June 1953

The bar was authorized on 22nd December 1853.

Naming: Impressed in block capitals, the letters on the Naval medals are smaller than those found on the Army medals.

Regiments present: Detachment of Irregular Horse; 2 Co. 5 Bn. Madras and Bengal Artillery; Madras and Bengal Sappers and Miners; Ordnance Department; Quartermaster General's Department; 18 (1,028), 51 (900), 80 (460) Foot; 1 European Bengal Fusiliers (1 Royal Munster Fusiliers); 1 Madras Fusiliers (1 Royal Dublin Fusiliers); 5, 9, 19, 26, 30, 35, 46, 49, 79 Madras NI; 10, 37, 40, 67, 68 Bengal NI; 4, 15 Sikhs.

HM Ships: *Bittern* (136), *Cleopatra* (235), *Contest* (107), *Fox* (426), *Hastings* (530), *Hermes* (159), *Rattler* (163), *Salamander* (138), *Serpent* (130), *Spartan* (180), *Sphinx* (236), *Styx* (157), *Winchester* (479).

Bengal Marine ships: *Bhagurette* (25), *Damoodah* (100), *Enterprise* (94), *Fire Queen* (214), *Indus* (67), *Krishna* (100), *Lord William Bentinck* (121), *Luckia* (23), *Mahanuddy* (125), *Nemesis* (84), *Nerbuddah* (98), *Phlegethon* (127), *Pluto* (174), *Proserpine* (134), *Soane* (25), *Spy* (58), *Sutledge* (30), *Tenasserim* (284).

Indian Marine Ships: *Berenice* (255), *Feroze* (275), *Hugh Lindsay and Medusa* (84), *Moozuffer* (351), *Sesostris* (178), *Zenobia* (351).

This, the second, campaign in Burma was caused by the refusal of the King of Ava to abide by the Treaty of Yendaboo signed on 24th February, 1826, at the conclusion of the first Burma war, which allowed trading facilities in the port of Rangoon. In addition to the molestation

of shipping, the British Resident was insulted and British warships fired upon. After attempts at obtaining satisfaction proved useless, war was declared on 2nd April, 1852. A squadron under Commodore G. Lambert and an expeditionary force under Major-General Godwin were dispatched on 28th March, 1852. Martaban was captured on 5th April; Rangoon on 14th April; Bassein on 19th May; Pegu, which had been captured on 4th April, was recaptured on 21st November; Prome on 10th October. On 20th December the Province of Pegu was annexed. After this a revolution broke out which resulted in considerable banditry, of which Myat-Toon was the chief instigator with his stronghold near Donubyu. It was at the capture of this that Ensign Garnet Wolseley, 80th Foot, distinguished himself. The war ended on 30th June, 1853.

Persia 5th December 1856-8th February 1857

The bar was authorized on 12th April 1858.

Naming: Impressed in block capitals, the letters on the naval medals are smaller than those found on the army medals.

Regiments present: 14 Light Dragoons (366); 3 Bombay Cavalry; Scinde Horse; Poona Horse; Aden Irregular Horse; 3, 5 Light Field Batteries, RA; 3rd, 4th Troop Bombay Horse Artillery, 1, 2, 3, 4, 5 Bn Bombay Foot Artillery; 4th Company 4th Bn (Native) Artillery; 2, 4 Companies Bombay Sappers and Miners; Ordnance Department; 64 (1,025), 78 Foot; 1, 2 Bombay Fusiliers (1,040) (2 DLI); 2, 3, 4, 5, 6, 8, 9, 11, 15, 19, 20, 21, 22, 23, 25, 26, 28, 29 Bombay NI.

Indian Marine ships: *Ajdaha* (301); *Assaye* (339); *Assyria* (39); *Berenice* (112); *Clive* (153); *Comet* (61); *Constance* (32); *Euphrates* (89); *Falkland* (114); *Lady Falkland* (42); *Feroz* (275); *Hugh Lindsey* (83); *Napier* (61); *Nitocris* (17); *Planet* (54); *Punjaub* (244); *Semiramis* (258); *Victoria* (133).

The war was caused by the reoccupation of the city of Herat by the Persians. This city, said to be the key to Afghanistan, was formally annexed by them on 25th October, 1856. War was declared on 1st November, and on the 10th an Indian naval squadron commanded by Commodore Young bombarded Bushire, which surrendered. On the arrival of Major-General Sir James Outram with an expeditionary force an advance was made inland from Bushire to Boorzgoon (or Brazjun), where many stores were captured. During the withdrawal the force was attacked at Kooshab on 7th February, 1857. The Persians were heavily defeated. After his return to Bushire, Outram left Major-General Stalker to hold the town, whilst he (Outram) crossed the Persian Gulf to the delta of the Euphrates, up which he advanced to Mohamrah, some sixty miles inland. On 26th March the Navy bombarded the strong Persian positions and forts. After a short while they were either silenced or completely destroyed, so that troops were landed under Brigadier-General Havelock, who promptly entered the city and captured a further large supply of stores. He very generously gave full credit for the ease with which he accomplished his mission to the Navy, who in turn owed its immunity from heavy casualties to the foresight of Commander Rennie, who gave orders for the bombarding ships to be surrounded with trusses of hay!

The Persians withdrew to Akwaz, about a hundred miles up the Karoon river, where they were again attacked by Commander Rennie and a small force composed of about 300 men of the 64th and 78th Foot under Captain Hunt. The town was captured on 1st April, after which the force returned to Mohamrah, where it learnt that peace had been signed in Paris on 4th March under the terms of which Herat was to be evacuated by the Persians.

The North Staffordshire Regiment and the Durham Light Infantry both carry Bushire and Koosh-ab on their colours.

Three Victoria Crosses were awarded during this expedition—Colonel J. A. Wood 20th Bombay Native Infantry, Major General A. T. Moore, 3rd Bombay Light Cavalry and Captain J. G. Malcolm, 3rd Bombay Light Cavalry.

North West Frontier 3rd December 1849-22nd October 1868

This bar was authorized on 1st July 1869 for 15 expeditions (below). The same bar was authorized on 14th June 1884 for Colonel Macdonell's action at Shabkadar. (See 15 below).

Naming: Engraved in running script and to some British officers in block capitals.

1. 3rd-11th December 1849: Two expeditions under Lieutenant-Colonel J. Bradshaw, CB to Yusafzai to collect revenue from the village of Sanghao.

Regiments present: 13 Irregular Cavalry; 2 Troop 2 Brigade Bengal HA; 1 Bombay Sappers and Miners; 60 (77), 61 (74) Foot; 3 Bombay NI; Guides Cavalry and Infantry; 1 Punjab Infantry (116).

2. 9th-15th February 1850: An expedition under Brigadier-General Sir Colin Campbell, KCB, to the Kohat Pass to punish troublesome Afridis.

Regiments present: 15th Irregular Cavalry; 1 Punjab Cavalry; 2 Troop 2nd Brigade Bengal HA (52 Battery RFA). (This battery used elephant transport to carry its two 5½in. mortars.) Two companies each of 60, 61, 98 Foot; 23, 31 Bengal NI; 1 Punjab Infantry, Guides.

3. 11th March-22nd May 1852: An expedition under Brigadier-General Sir Colin Campbell, KCB, against the Ranizais, in Turangai between 11th and 22nd March, 1852, and another in Shakot and Dargai from 15th to 24th May, 1852.

Ranizai Expedition: Regiments present: 15 Irregular Cavalry; 1 Troop 1 Brigade, Bengal HA; 32 (600) Foot. A wing of the 29 Bengal NI and 66 Gurkhas (later the 1 King George's own Gurkha Rifles).

Medals are known to the 53rd Foot (120) although not entitled. They were issued due to an administrative error.

Shakot and Dargai Expedition: Regiments present: Guides Cavalry; 2nd Irregular Cavalry; two squadrons of 1 Punjab Cavalry; 1 Troop 1 Brigade Bengal HA; detachments 2, 3 Company 4 Battalion Bengal Artillery; detachment of 19 Light Field Battery; 2 Company Sappers and Miners; 32 (350) Foot, Guides Infantry; 1, 28 Bengal NI; 66 Gurkhas, 1 Punjab Infantry.

4. 15 April-14th May 1852: Two expeditions, under Brigadier-General Sir Colin Campbell, KCB, against the Mohmans at Panjpao on 15th April 1852, and another against the Utman Khel villages of Nawadan and Prangarh between 28th April and 14th May, 1852.

Panjpao Expedition: Regiments present: 7 Light Cavalry (87); 15 Irregular Horse (179); 2 Troop 1 Brigade Bengal HA.

Nawadan and Prangarh Expeditions: Regiments present: one squadron 2 Irregular Cavalry; one squadron Guides Cavalry; 1 Troop 1 Brigade Bengal HA; detachments of 2 and 3 Companies 4 Bn Bengal Artillery; 2 Company Bengal Sappers and Miners; 32 Foot, Guides Infantry; 1 (300), 28 (300) Punjab NI; 66 Gurkhas.

5. 19th December 1852-2nd January 1853: An expedition under Lieutenant-General F. Mackeson, CB, against the Hassanzais.

Regiments present: 16 Irregular Cavalry; 5 Troop 1 Brigade Bengal Artillery; Hazara Mountain Battery; 7 Company Bengal Sappers and Miners; Guides, Cavalry, Infantry; 1 Sikh Infantry; two regiments of

Dogras; 3 Bengal NI; Rawal Pindi Police (176).

6. 30th March-12th April 1853: Two expeditions under Brigadier-General J. S. Hodgson against the Shiranis from 30th March to 2nd April, 1853, and another against the Kasranis from the 11th to 12th April, 1853.

Shirani Expedition: Regiments present: 4, 5 Punjab Cavalry; Scinde Camel Corps; 2 Punjab Light Field Battery and detachment of 4 Company Bengal Garrison Artillery; detachments from each of 1 and 3 Punjab NI and the 2 and 6 Native Police Battalion.

Kasrani Expedition: Regiments present: 1, 4 Punjab Cavalry; 6 Police Battalion, 1 Punjab Infantry.

7. 29th November 1853: A punitive expedition under Colonel S. B. Boileau against the Bori Afridis.

Regiments present: 1 squadron 7 Irregular Cavalry; 2 Company 2 Battalion Bengal Artillery; 2 Bengal Sappers and Miners; 22 Foot (438); 20 Bengal NI (169); 66 Gurkhas (467), Guides.

8. 31st August 1854: An expedition under Colonel S. J. Cotton to the villages of Dabb, Sadin and Shah Mansur Khel.

Regiments present: 10 Light Cavalry, 1 Irregular Cavalry (one squadron each); 1 Troop 3 Brigade Bengal HA; 2 Company 2 Battalion Bengal Artillery; Mountain Train Battery; 2 Company Bengal Sappers and Miners; 22 Foot (199); 1 Sikh NI; 1, 9 Bengal NI; Rawal Pindi Police.

9. 27th March 1855: An expedition under Lieutenant-Colonel J. H. Craigie, CB, against the Aka Khels and Bussi Khels.

Regiments present: Two troops of 16 Irregular Cavalry; Peshawar Mountain Battery; detachments of 4, 9, 20 Bengal NI.

10. 4th April, 1855: An expedition under Brigadier-General N. B. Chamberlain to the Miranzai Valley.

Regiments present: 4 Punjab Cavalry; Nos 1 and 3 Punjab Light Field Batteries; 2 Bengal Sappers and Miners; 66 Gurkhas; 1, 3 Punjab NI and the Scinde Rifle Corps [in 1856 this was renamed 6 Punjab Infantry and later became 59 Royal Scinde Rifles (Frontier Force)].

11. 6th-21st March 1857: An expedition under Brigadier-General N. B. Chamberlain against the Bozdars.

Regiments present: 2, 3 Punjab Cavalry; Nos 1, 2 and 3 Punjab Light Field Batteries; 1 Bengal Sappers and Miners; 1, 3 Sikh NI; 1, 2, 4 Punjab NI; Levies.

12. 22nd April-5th May 1858: For the operations of the Sittana Field Force under Major-General Sir Sydney J. Cotton, KCB, in Panjtar and Lower Sittana.

Regiments present: Guides Cavalry, Infantry, 7, 8 Irregular Horse; Peshawur Light Horse; Peshawur Light Field Battery and Mountain Train (23rd Peshawur Mountain Battery); Hazara Mountain Train Battery; Bengal Sappers and Miners; 81, 98 Foot; Guides Infantry; 8, 9, 12, 18, 21 Bengal NI; Kelat-i-Ghilzie Regiment, 2nd Sikh Infantry.

13. 15th December 1859: An expedition under Brigadier-General N. B. Chamberlain, CB, against the Kabul Khel Waziris.

Regiments present: Guides Cavalry, Nos. 1 and 2 Punjab Light Field Batteries; Peshawur and Hazara Mountain Train Batteries; 4, 5 Bengal Sappers and Miners; Guides Infantry; 4 Sikh Infantry; 1, 3, 4, 6, 24 Bengal NI.

14. 16th April 1860: An expedition under Brigadier-General N. B. Chamberlain, CB, against the Mahsud Waziris.

Regiments present: Guides Cavalry; 3 Punjab Cavalry; Multani Cavalry; Nos 2 and 3 Punjab Light Field Batteries; Peshawur and Hazara Mountain Trains; 5 Bengal Sappers and Miners; Guides Infantry; 4 Sikh Infantry; 1, 2, 3, 4, 6, 14, 24 Punjab NI; Hazara Gurkhas; 6 Native Police Battalion.

15. 5th December-2nd January 1864: Between these dates Sultan Muhammed Khan attacked the fort of Shabkadar with a body of Mohmands and Bajouris and was defeated by a force under Brevet-Colonel A. F. Macdonell, CB.

Regiments present: Three troops of 7 Hussars (155); 2, 6 Bengal Cavalry; D Battery 5 Brigade RHA (54); 79 Foot (131); 3 Battalion Rifle Brigade (716); 4 Sikh Infantry; 2 Gurkhas.

16. 3rd-22nd October 1868: An expedition under Major-General A. T. Wilde, CB, CSI, against the Bazotee Black Mountain Tribes.

Regiments present: Guides Cavalry; 9, 16 Bengal Cavalry; D. F. Battery, B Brigade RHA; E Battery 19 Brigade RA, 2 Battery 24 Brigade RA; Peshawur and Hazara Mountain Trains; 2, 7 Companies Bengal Sappers and Miners; 1/6 (648), 1/19 (720), 38, 77 Foot; 3 Sikhs; 2, 19, 20, 24, 30, 31 Bengal NI; 23 (Pioneers) Bengal NI; 1, 2, 4, 5 Gurkhas.

Given below is a combined list of those entitled to the North West Frontier bar
Regiments present:
CAVALRY
7 (155) Hussars; 1, 2, 7, 8, 13, 15, 16, 18 Irregular Cavalry; 1, 2, 3, 4, 5 Punjab Cavalry; 2, 6, 9, 16 Bengal Cavalry; Guides Cavalry; 7, 10 Light Cavalry; Peshawur Light Horse; Multani Cavalry; Scinde Camel Corps.

ARTILLERY
D, F Battery B Brigade, D Battery 5 Brigade RHA; E Battery, 19 Brigade RA; 2 Battery, 24 Brigade RA; 1, 2, 3 Brigade Bengal HA; 2, 4, 19, 2/24 Garrison Batteries RA; Sappers and Miners 1, 2, 3; 19 Punjab Light Field Batteries, 1, 2, 4 Bengal Artillery; Peshawur and Hazara Mountain Train Batteries, detachment of 19 Light Field Battery; 2, 4, 5, 7 Bengal and Bombay (160) Sappers and Miners.

BRITISH INFANTRY
1/6 (650), 1/19 (720), 1/22 (438), 32 (600), 38, 53, 60 (105), 61 (74), 77, 79 (130), 81 (205), 1/87 (37), 2/98 (335) and 3 Rifle Brigade (980).

NATIVE INFANTRY
Guides Infantry; 1, 2, 3, 4 Punjab Infantry; 1, 3, 4 Sikhs; 1, 2, 3, 4, 6, 8, 9, 12, 14, 18, 19, 20, 21, 23, 24, 28, 29, 30, 31 Bengal Infantry; 3 Bombay Infantry; 1, 2, 4, 5, 7, 66 Gurkhas; Dogras; Scinde Rifle Corps; 2, 6 Native Police Battalion; Rawal Pindi Police; Levies; Kelat-i-Ghilzie Regt.

Umbeyla 20th October-23rd December 1863
This bar was authorized on 1st July 1869 to troops who had been engaged under Brigadier-General Sir N. B. Chamberlain, KCB, and subsequently under Major-General Sir J. Garvock, KCB.
Naming: The medals are named in block capitals.

Regiments present: 1st Brigade: Half 'C' Battery 19th Brigade RA; Peshawar Mountain Train; 71 Foot; 1, 3, 5, 20, 32 (Pioneers) Punjab NI; 5 Gurkhas.
2nd Brigade Peshawar and Hazara Mountain Trains; 101 Bengal Fusiliers; 6, 14 (Pioneers) Punjab NI; 3 Sikhs; Guides Cavalry and Infantry; Bengal Sappers and Miners; 4 Gurkhas; 11 Bengal (Probyn's Horse) Cavalry.
The following units joined the Expeditionary Force in the latter part of November: 1/7 (470), 93 Foot, 3 Sikhs, 23 Punjab NI; 3 Punjab Light Field Battery.

This bar was awarded for an expedition against the Muslim fanatics in Sittana and their village of Malka. The Yusafzai Field Force of approximately 5,600 men under General Sir Neville Chamberlain advanced up the Umbeyla Pass and encountered strong opposition. Heavy casualties were sustained during attempts to hold the 'Eagle's Nest' and the 'Crag Piquet'.
Eventually the Commander-in-Chief, Sir Hugh Rose, decided to send further reinforcements and appointed Major-General Garvock to succeed General Chamberlain. The troops were organized into two brigades which drove the rebels out of the valley, and then a small party under Colonel Reynell Taylor with an escort of Guides went forward and burnt Malka. This expedition suffered over 900 casualties.
Two Victoria Crosses were awarded during this campaign: Lieutenant George V. Fosbery, 4th Bengal European Regiment and Lieutenant Henry W. Pitcher, Bengal Staff Corps.

Bhootan December 1864-February 1866
This bar was authorized on 22nd March, 1870 and was awarded for service in the Bhootan compaign of 1864-66.
Naming: These medals are named in square capitals to Europeans and in script to natives.
Regiments present: 5, 14 Bengal Cavalry; 7/22, 5/25, 6/25, 3/25 Batteries RA, and the Eurasian (Christian) Battery; 2, 4, 5, 6, 7, 8 Companies Bengal Sappers and Miners; 55, 80 Foot; 11, 12, 17, 18, 43, 44 Bengal NI; 19, 29, 30, 31 Punjab NI; 2 and 3 Gurkhas; Frontier Police.

As a result of insults to the Hon. Ashley Eden, who headed a mission into Bhootan and for the continued raids into British territory, the Indian Government decided on punitive action.
Four columns advanced into Bhootan under the command of Brigadier-General W. E. Mulcaster. Slight resistance was met with and overcome at Dhalimcote, Bhumsong and Charmoorchee. With the campaign apparently at an end the Bhootanese then attacked the various Anglo-Indian positions, with serious results. A further expedition was then despatched under Brigadier-General Sir H. Tombs, VC, KCB, who captured Dewangiri on 2nd April, 1865. A further expedition was mounted in 1866 after which the Bhootanese accepted defeat.
Two Victoria Crosses were awarded during this campaign: Lieutenant James Dundas and Major William S. Trevor, Royal Bengal Engineers.

Looshai 9th December 1871-20th February 1872
The bar was authorized on 1st December 1872.
Naming: The medals are named in thin running script.
Regiments present: 3 (Peshawur) Mountain Battery; Sappers and Miners; Commissariat Transport Corps (800); 22, 27 Punjab NI; 42 (500), 44 (500) Assam NI, 2, 4 Gurkhas; Native Police (100).
No British units were engaged. (Medals to No 113 Pte H. Thompson, 55th Foot and one to the 80th Foot with this bar are known.)

An expedition was mounted against the Looshais following the massacre at the Winchester Plantation and the abduction of the tea-planter's daughter, Mary Winchester. This incident was the climax to a series of raids mounted by the Looshais.
In response two columns known as the Cachar Column, under Brigadier-General G. Bourchier, CB, RA, and the Chittagong Column under Brigadier-General C. W. Brownlow, CB, were formed.
After many skirmishes and capture of villages the Looshais eventually agreed to the terms of peace dictated to them by General Bourchier and subsequently released Mary Winchester.
One Victoria Cross was awarded for this campaign, to Major Donald MacIntyre, Bengal Staff Corps.

Perak 2nd November 1875-20th March 1876
A bar for 'Perak 1875-76' was authorized by the Queen in General Order N° 111, dated 1st September, 1879. However, for an unknown reason the bar was issued with the dates omitted.
Naming The naming is in large sloping capitals.
Regiments present: 3rd Battery 5th Brigade and 9 Battery, 2nd Brigade, RA (120); 'C' Company Madras Sappers and Miners (80); 1/3 (600), 10 (460), 19, 80 (300) Foot; 66 Gurkhas; Army Hospital Corps, Control Department.

Naval Brigade: Admiralty Order of 23rd February, 1880, authorized the award of medals to all who were serving off the coast of Perak and adjacent rivers during the period August 1873 to March 1874. The medal was refused to the officers and men of the *Midge* which was engaged in adjacent waters. Admiralty Order of 6th June, 1881, extended the grant of the medal to officers and men of *Charybdis* and *Hart* for services up the Lingie and Lukhut rivers between 27th November and 10th December, 1874. A total of 1,117 medals and bars were awarded to the officers and men of the eight ships engaged: *Charybdis* (257); *Egeria* (139); *Fly* (103); *Hart* (74); *Modeste* (258); *Philomel* (77 + 14 Seedies); *Ringdove* (106); *Thistle* (75).

Perak, situated on the west side of the Malay Peninsula, suffered from constant strife between the Chinese and Malays which, in turn, disturbed the peace of the adjoining British territory. This culminated in the murder of the British Resident, Mr W. J. Birch, by the Ismail. They then encouraged the Rajahs to join them, causing much trouble. General Colbourn commanded an expedition to Perak with Brigadier General Ross, they distinguished themselves at Kinta and Kotah Lama. The success of these operations were greatly due to the aid given by the Naval Brigades, as rocket and gun Parties.
One Victoria Cross was awarded for the campaign to Brevet-Major George Nicholas Channer, Bengal Staff Corps.

Naga 1879-80: 1875 and December 1879-January 1880

The bar for the expedition of 1879-80 was authorized on 24th June 1881. It was later extended to cover the earlier 1875 expedition.
Naming: In thin running script.

1875 Expedition: In January 1875 a surveying party of natives under Lieutenant Holcombe were attacked by the Nagas. A force under Colonel Nuthall was despatched to punish the tribe.
1879-80 Expedition: The Nagas of Konoma murdered Mr Damant, the Local Commissioner on 14th October, 1879, they then besieged the garrison at Kohima. A force under Lieutenant Colonel Johnstone was despatched to relieve Kohima. An expedition under Brigadier General J. L. Nation then marched on Konoma, the Naga stronghold. After much fighting of a desperate nature the Nagas retreated from Konoma and took position in the Chaka Forts. They agreed to terms of surrender in March 1880.
No European troops were engaged in either of these expeditions, but the medal and bar were given to the Native regiments employed, and their British officers.
Regiments present: 34 Bombay Infantry; 18 Bengal NI; 42, 43 Assam Light Infantry; 44 Sylhet Light Infantry; Frontier Police; Bengal Sappers and Miners.
The artillery consisted of two 7-pdrs. and a hundred 9-pdr. rockets. They were manned by Lieutenant A. Mansel and three bombardiers from the 16/9 Battery, RA.
One Victoria Cross were awarded for this campaign to Colonel Richard Kirby Ridgeway, Bengal Staff Corps.

Jowaki 1877-8 9th November 1877-19th January 1878

The bar was authorized on 1st March, 1879.
Naming: The medals are named in impressed block capitals.

The Jowaki Afrideis occupied the territory between Peshawar and the Kohat Pass. After continuous attacks by the ferocious Jowakis upon neighbouring tribes, two forces under command of Brigadiers C. P. Keyes and C. C. G. Ross were sent to suppress them. Brigadier Keyes with the main body attacked and captured Jummoo, the principal stronghold of the tribe on the 1st December, 1877.'
Regiments present: Brigadier-General Keyes' Force (Kohat Column); 13/9 RA; 2 Punjab Cavalry; Nos. 1 and 2 Mountain Batteries; 4, 5, 6, 29 Punjab NI; 1, 3 Sikh Infantry; 5 Gurkhas.
Brigadier-General Ross's Force (Peshawur Column): Regiments present: 13/9th RA (38); 17 Bengal Cavalry; half of I/C Battery RHA (137); No 4 Hazara Mountain Battery; 2, 3 and detachment of 4 Bengal Sappers and Miners; 9 (15 Officers and 559 other ranks), 51 Foot (536) and 4 Rifle Brigade; 14, 20, 22, 27 Bengal NI.

Burma 1885-7 14th November 1885-30th April 1887

The bar was authorized on 1st August 1887. Bronze medals were also authorized for the first time to be awarded to all authorized Government followers who accompanied the troops.
Naming Naval medals impressed, others in light script.

The origins of the expedition to Burma stemmed from the irrational behaviour of King Thebaw of Burma, whose reign of misgovernment and massacre ended with his interfering with the Bombay and Burma Trading Company's timber trade. Arbitration having failed, the Viceroy of India, Lord Dufferin, sent an ultimatum which demanded protection for British subjects and interests. This was rejected, so that war was declared on 8th November, 1885. An expedition under Major-General H. N. D. Prendergast, VC, composed of three brigades, was dispatched.
The frontier was crossed and the forts of Minhla and Gurgyong captured on 17th November, 1885. On the 26th Thebaw agreed to unconditional surrender; the Ava forts were occupied on the 27th, and General Prendergast entered Mandalay on the 28th.
After Thebaw's surrender his brother issued a proclamation against the British whereupon banditry became rife. Engagements between the troops and the dacoits (bandits) took place at Nyadan on 2nd December, 1885; at Bhamo on the 28th; Moutshobo on the 29th; Kadol on 16th January, 1886; Kunnah on the 16th; Yindawango on 18th March; Zemethen on the 26th; Salem on 12th June and Tummoo on the 19th.

The amount of banditry increased so much in July that more troops were sent from India, and General Macpherson assumed supreme command on 17th September, 1886. He died on 20th October, and was succeeded by General Sir Frederick Roberts, who arrived in Mandalay on 18th November.
Further actions against the bandits continued and are covered in the later sections dealing with 'Burma' bars.
Regiments present: 7th Dragoon Guards (1); 12th Lancers (5); 1, 2 Madras Cavalry; 1 Bombay Lancers; 7 Bengal Cavalry; 7, 9 Battery 1 Brigade Northern Division R.A.; Q/1 Battery RFA; 4/1 Battery North Irish Division RGA; 3/1 Battery South Irish Division RGA; 2/1, 9/1 Batteries Cinque Ports Division RGA; 3/1, 5/1, 6/1 Batteries Scottish Division RGA; 7/1, 9/1 Batteries Northern Division RGA; 4/1, 8/1 Battery London Division RGA; 5/1, 6/1 Batteries Southern Division RGA; Military Staff Corps; 1, 2, 4, 7 Native Mountain Batteries; 2, 4, 5 Companies Bengal Sappers and Miners; 2 Company Bombay Sappers and Miners; 2 Queen's, 2 King's, 2 Somersets, Cheshire's (4), 2 Hants, 1 Royal Welch Fusiliers, 1 KOYLI; 2 South Wales Borderers, 2 Munster Fusiliers, 2 Royal Scots Fusiliers, 1 and 4 Battalions Rifle Brigade; 1, 2/2, 5, 11, 12, 13, 15, 16, 18, 26, 27, 33, 44 Bengal NI; 3, 12, 13, 15, 16, 17, 21, 23, 25, 27 Madras Infantry; 1, 5, 7, 23, 25, 27 Bombay Infantry; 4 Punjabis; 2, 3 Infantry (Hyderabad Contingent); 2, 3 Gurkhas; Madras Transport and Commissariat Department; Levy Militia; Military Police Battalion; Rangoon Volunteer Artillery; IMS.
HM Ships: *Bacchante* (253), *Mariner* (80), *Ranger* (59), *Sphinx* (32), *Turquoise* (139), *Woodlark* (62), Indian Marine Ships: Steamers: *Kathleen, Irrawaddy.* Gunboats: *Bulldog, Spitfire.* The name of the ship is not always shown on the medal. Frequently the abbreviation 'HMIMS' (Her Majesty's Indian Marine Ship) follows the name and rank of the recipient.
Irrawaddy Flotilla Company's vessels: The name of the individual vessel is rarely found on the medal, the recipient's name and rank is frequently followed by 'Irrawaddy Flotilla'.
Aloungpyah, Ananda, Ashley Eden, Ataran, Burma, Colonel Fytche, Doowoon, Kah-Byoo, Mindoon, Ngawoon, Palow, Panlang, Panthay, Okpho, Rangoon, Schwaymyo, Talifoo, Thambyadine, Thooreah, Waikemo, White Swan, Yunan, Yunkeetown.
The Irrawaddy Pilot Launches *Alerto, Apollo, Buffalo, Dromio, Jingo* and *June* were used as Picket Boats.
Medals with this bar are also known to the following ships 'Investigator', 'Jaboona', 'Mac Wor', 'Sladen', 'Tigris'.

Sikkim 1888 15th March-27th September 1888

The bar was authorized on 1st June 1889. Silver and bronze medals were issued.
Naming: Thin running script.

Sikkim is a small Himalayan state adjoining Tibet. It had been allied to the Indian Government since 1814, and trade and free passage through the state had been agreed upon.
In early 1888 the Tibetans persuaded the Rajah to erect a fort, in strict contravention of the treaty, at Lingtu to obstruct the route through the state. In spite of remonstrances from the Viceroy the work continued so that in March a force under Colonel T. Graham, RA, was dispatched to capture the fort and drive the Tibetans out of Sikkim.
The fort was captured on 20th March and destroyed the next day, after which the force withdrew to Darjeeling; but it had to return in July owing to further incursions.
On 24th September the Tibetans were found to be fortifying a position in the Jelapla Pass, from which they were driven on the 25th. After this defeat, in which they suffered about four hundred casualties, the Tibetans retired from Sikkim.
Regiments present: 4 guns 9/1 Northern Division, RA; detachment of 5 Company Bengal Sappers and Miners; two companies 2 Derbys (481); 13 Bengal Infantry (400); 32 Bengal Pioneers; 2/1 Gurkhas (514).
Medals are also known to the 8 Hussars, 49, 52 Foot.

Hazara 1888 3rd October-9th November 1888

The bar was authorized on 1st June 1889. Silver and bronze medals were issued.
Naming: Thin running script.
This bar was awarded to the Hazara Field Force, commanded by Major-

General J. W. McQueen, CB, ADC. This is generally referred to as the 'Black Mountain Expedition', as it was undertaken against the Black Mountain tribes of Hassanzais, Akazais, Chagarzais, etc.

The cause of the trouble was the murder of Major L. Battye and Captain H. B. Urmiston, together with five sepoys, who were surveying in the territory occupied by the Akazais.

The expedition sent to deal with them advanced in four columns and defeated the Chagarzais at Kotgai and Maidan. Many villages were destroyed before the tribes surrendered.

Regiments present: 15 Bengal Cavalry; 3/1 South Irish Division, RGA; 2/1 Scottish Division, RGA; No. 2 (Derajat) and No. 4 (Hazara) Mountain Batteries; 3 Company Bengal Sappers and Miners and Telegraph Section; 2 Royal Northumberland Fusiliers; 1 Suffolks; 2 Royal Irish Regiment; 2 Seaforth; 2 Royal Sussex; 3, 14, 25, 45 Sikhs; 4, 24, 29 Punjab Infantry; 40 Bengal Infantry; 34 Sikh Pioneers; Kaiber (Khyber) Rifles; 5 Gurkhas; Field Hospital.

Burma 1887-89 1st May 1887-31st March 1889

This bar was authorized in 1st December 1889. Silver and bronze medals were issued.
Naming: Thin running script.
For the numerous operations that continued against bandits, etc. throughout Burma, the bar 'Burma 1887-89' was awarded succeeding 'Burma 1885-7'.
A Victoria Cross was awarded for this campaign to Surgeon John Crimmin, Bombay Medical Service.

Regiments: As well as the units entitled to the earlier Burma bar the following units were entitled to the bar 'Burma 1887-89'. No 2 and 6 Mountain Batteries; 7 Dragoon Guards (2); 1 Norfolks (6 Officers and 200 other ranks); 2 Leicesters; 1 and 2 Cheshires; 1 Hants; 2 Munster Fusiliers (238 single bars); 4 Gurkhas; Mimbu and Burma Police (many individuals received both bars).

Indian Marine: The officers and men of the Indian Marine ships *Irrawaddy*, *Sir William Peel* and *Sladen* received this bar, as did a number of officers attached to the field force as Marine Transport Officers.

Burma 1887-9

This very rare bar was issued by the Royal Mint, and has the same criteria as the above.

Chin Lushai 1889-90 13th November 1889-30th April 1890

The bar was authorized on 1st February 1891. Silver and bronze medals were issued.
Naming: Bold running script.
This bar was awarded to (a) The Burma Column under Brigadier General W. P. Symons against the Chin tribe. (b) The Chittagong Column under General Tregear against the Lushai tribe.

Those in the Burma Column employed on the lines from Gangaw to Yezagyo, and the garrisons of Fort White and intermediate posts to Kalemyo from the date of concentration at Gangaw were also entitled to the bar.

Regiments present: Burma Column: No 1 (Bengal) Mountain Battery; 5, 6 Companies Madras Sappers and Miners; 7th Dragoon Guards. (Private J. Foster—with Lushai 1889-92 and Captain J. W. Peters— with Hazara 1891 and Burma 1889-92); KOSB (approx 520) and detachments of 1 Norfolks (29), 1 Cheshire, Border Regt (30) and Wiltshire Regt (4); 2 Madras Infantry; 10, 38 Bengal Infantry, Chittagong Column—2 Company Bengal Sappers and Miners; 3, 9 Bengal Infantry; 28 Bombay Pioneers; 2/4 (part), 42 Gurkhas; Surma Valley and Chittagong Police.

Indian Marine: The officers and men of the Indian Marine Ships *Bhamo* and *Irrawaddy* received this bar for services in support of the land operations. A small number of bars were awarded to officers of the Indian Marine who were on detached duty and saw service with the field force as Marine Transport Officers.

Samana 1891 5th April-25th May 1891

The bar was authorized on 1st December, 1891. Silver and bronze medals were issued.
Naming: Thin running script.
This bar was awarded to members of the Miranzai Expeditionary Force commanded by Brigadier-General Sir W. S. A. Lockhart, KCB, CSI which operated in the Miranzai Valley and against the Samana Heights where the fanatical priest Syed Mir Basha was proclaiming a 'jihad'.

Miniature medals with the bar 'Miranazai 1891' are known.

Regiments present: No 1 Column—No 3 Mountain Battery, RA (88); 1 KRRC (650); HLI (7); DLI (2); Wiltshire Regiment (13); 1 Punjab Infantry; 27 Bengal Infantry; 1/5 Gurkhas. No 2 Column—No 3 (Peshawur) Mountain Battery; 3 Sikh Infantry; 2 Punjab Infantry; 15 Bengal Infantry. No 3 Column—No 2 (Derajat) Mountain Battery; 6 Punjab Infantry (47). 19, 29 Bengal Infantry. Divisional Troops—Punjab Garrison Artillery; two squadrons 5 Punjab Cavalry (300); 19 Bengal Lancers; 5 Company Bengal Sappers and Miners; two companies 2 Manchester Regiment (311); 1/4 Gurkhas, Military Police.

Hazara 1891 12th March-16th May 1891

The bar was authorized on 1st February, 1892. Silver and bronze medals were issued.
Naming: Running script
This bar was awarded for the operations of the Hazara Field Force under Major-General W. K. Elles, CB, against the Hussanzais and Akazais in the Black Mountain.

The operation was carried out by two columns, commanded by Colonels Williamson and Hammond which advanced from Derband. There was little fighting; what there was consisted mostly in repelling raids on the columns when on the march or road-making. During the operations a party of rebels was chased up, and eventually captured on, the Machai Peak, 9,800 feet high.

Regiments present: King's Dragon Guards (5); 2 (6), 3 (10), 7 Dragoon Guards (5); 11 Bengal Lancers, 1, 9 Mountain Battery, RA; 2 (Derajat) Mountain Battery; 4 Company Bengal Sappers and Miners; Queen's Regiment (2); Northumberland Fusiliers (3); Royal Fusiliers; Royal Irish Regiment (9); Wiltshire Regiment (5); 1 Royal Welch Fusiliers; 1 KRRC; 2 Seaforth; 2 Manchester Regiment (8); HLI (8); DLI (3); 4 Sikhs; Guides Infantry; Kaiber (Khyber) Rifles; 11, 19, 27, 28, 32, 37 Bengal Infantry; 1/5, 2/5 Gurkhas; 32 Punjab Pioneers.

Hunza 1891 1st-22nd December 1891

The bar was authorized on 1st September 1892. Silver and bronze medals were issued.
Naming: Running script.
This bar was awarded for an expedition under Lieutenant-Colonel A. G. A. Durand to Gilgit, Hunza and Nagar, where the tribesmen continually attacked the road-making parties. Colonel Durand was wounded during the capture of the fort at Nilt, the only serious action of the campaign.

Three Victoria Crosses were awarded for this campaign, these being to Captain F. J. Aylmer, RE; Lieutenant G. H. Boisragon, 5th Gurkhas and Lieutenant J. M. Smith ISC.

Regiments present: No British units were engaged, though medals to British officers of Indian units were awarded.

Silver medals: No 4 (Hazara) Mountian Battery (76); No 4 Company Bengal Sappers and Miners (12); 1 (1030), 2 (404) Kashmir Infantry; 20 Punjab Infantry (32); 5 Gurkhas (200); Peshawur and Unorganised Transport (159); Native Signallers (12)

Bronze medals: Staff (28); 1/5 Gurkha Rifles (23); 4 Mountain Battery (29); Kashmir Troops (81).

N. E. Frontier 1891 28th March-7th May 1891

The bar was authorized on 1st June 1892. Silver and bronze medals were issued.
Naming: Running script

About 3,000 of these bars were awarded for the Manipur Expedition, which was divided into three columns, commanded by Colonel R. H. F.

Rennick, Major-General H. Collett, CB, and Brigadier-General T. Graham, CB.

The small state of Manipur adjoins Assam and Burma. It possessed a small army, but relied on the British for protection against attacks from the Burmese. In 1886 the Rajah, Chandra Kirti Singh, died, leaving eight sons, each of whom headed a rival party for the throne. One brother, Takendrajit Singh, occupied the post of senaputti or commander-in-chief. He deposed the ruler and appointed his brother Kula Chandra Dhuya Singh to the throne.

On 21st February, 1891, Mr. J. W. Quinton, Chief Commissioner for Assam, was instructed to remove the Senaputti. He was well received, but failed to get the Senaputti to resign. On 24th February Colonel Skene with 250 men surrounded the Senaputti's residence, but when it was entered he had escaped. The Manipuris attacked Colonel Skene's force, but after a while a parley was agreed upon, whereupon the Colonel, accompanied by Mr. Quinton and others went forward to meet the Manipuris. None of the party were ever seen alive again. As the fighting had broken out again, it was decided to withdraw towards Lakhipur, which was reached on 20th March.

In the meanwhile the three columns had started their advance and converged on Manipur on 26th April. The palace had been burnt, and the Regent, Senaputti and other princes had fled. The heads of the party that went to the parley were found in the palace grounds.

Chandra Dhuya Singh, his brother Prince Angao Sana and the Senaputti were captured in May. The Senaputti was tried and executed, and the other two were exiled to the Andaman Islands in the Bay of Bengal.

One Victoria Cross was awarded for this campaign to Lieutenant C. J. W. Grant, Indian Staff Corps.

Regiments present: Surma Valley Light Horse; Royal East Kent (10), Royal East Surrey (6), Devons (4).

Cachar Column: Two guns of No 2 Mountain Battery RA (62); 1/2 (708), 42 (99), 43 (275), 44 (112) Gurkhas, 18 Bengal NI (364), Calcutta Volunteer Pioneers (48).

Kohima Column: Three guns of No 8 Bengal Battery; 42 (200), 43 (300) Gurkhas; 13 Bengal NI; Assam Police (200).

Tamu Column: Four guns of No 8 Bengal Battery; 4 KRRC (443); 12, 32 Madras NI; 2/4 Gurkhas.

Lines of Communication troops: 5 Madras NI.

In addition medals are known to the Military Police.

Burma 1889-92 16th April 1889-18th April 1892

The bar was authorized on 1st September 1893. Silver and bronze medals were issued.
Naming: Thin running script.

For the eleven operations against bandits, etc. throughout Burma, the bar 'Burma 1889-92' succeeded the bars 'Burma 1885-7' and 'Burma 1887-89'.

Poukhan Expedition Brigadier General G. B. Wolseley, CB, Commanding. 16th April to 16th May, 1889.
Tonhon Expedition—Major J. E. Blundell, 1st Battalion, Hampshire Regiment, Commanding. 17th December, 1889 to 8th April, 1890.
Thetta Column—Captain P. M. Carnegy, 2nd Battalion, 4th Gurkha Rifles, Commanding. 1st to 4th January, 1891.
Chinbok Column—Captain E. S. Hastings DSO, Madras Infantry, Commanding. 8th January to 14th February, 1891.
Momeik Column—Major R. E. Kelsall, afterwards Major J. H. Yule, 2nd Battalion, Devonshire Regiment. 27th January to 28th March, 1891.
Wuntho Field Force—Brigadier-General G. B. Wolseley, CB, Commanding. 18th February to 7th May, 1891.
Tlang-tlang Column—Lieutenant D. E. Mocatta, 39th Bengal Infantry, Commanding. 29th March to 3rd April, 1891.
Baungshe Column—Major R. H. Gunning, 4th Battalion, King's Royal Rifle Corps, Commanding. 25th December, 1891 to 29th February, 1892.
Irrawaddy Column—Major J. H. Yule, 2nd Battalion, Devonshire Regiment, Commanding. 15th December, 1891 to 18th April, 1892.
North-Eastern Column—Captain T. A. H. Davies, 2 Battalion Devonshire Regiment, Commanding. 15th December, 1891 to 7th April, 1892.
Chinbok Column—Lieutenant Rainey, Commanding. 1st to 20th January, 1890.

A Victoria Cross was awarded during this campaign to Surgeon F. S. Le Quesne, RAMS.

In addition to the units already listed as being present in the previous two 'Burma' campaigns the following units were present for the Burma 1889-92 expeditions.

Regiments present: British troops—Devons; Cheshires; 1 DCLI; 1 Hants; 2 Oxford and Bucks Light Infantry; 4 KRRC; 4 Rifle Brigade. Indian troops—22 Madras Infantry; 24 Bengal Infantry; 2nd Sappers and Miners.

Lushai 1889-92 11th January 1889-8th June 1892

The bar was authorized on 1st September, 1893. Silver and bronze medals were issued.
Naming: British troops: Large bold block letters. Medals to the KRRC were named in engraved script. Native troops: Engraved script.

This bar was awarded for five small expeditions into the Lushai Hills:
1 Lushai Expeditionary Force was under the command of Colonel V. W. Tregear, 9th Bengal Infantry. 11th January to 5th May, 1889.
2 An attack made by Lushais on Forts Aijal and Changsil. (Relieving force under command of Lieutenants Swinton, Cole and Watson). 9th September to 9th December, 1890.
3 Expedition under command of Captain F. P. Hutchinson against the village of Jacopa to avenge the attack on Mr. Murray. 20th February to 3rd March, 1891.
4 Expedition under command of Captain G. H. Loch in consequence of a general rising of the Eastern Lushais, commencing with the attack on a force under Mr. M'Cabe at Lalbura. 1st March to 8th June, 1892.
5 Operations undertaken to quell a general rising of the Eastern Lushai clans. Advance of a force under Captain Shakespear in South Lushai Hills. 16th March to 13th May, 1892.

Regiments present: Bengal Sappers and Miners; 4 KRRC (1 Co); 2, 3, 9 Bengal Infantry; 2 Gurkhas; 28 Bombay Pioneers; 4 Madras Pioneers and Military Police; Detachment of Civilian Telegraphists.

Chin Hills 1892-93 19th October 1892-10th March 1893

The bar was authorized on 9th January 1903. Silver and bronze medals were awarded.
Naming: Small running script. Those to the Norfolks are often seen as having been issued officially renamed.

This bar was awarded for small punitive expeditions, under Brigadier-General Palmer, against the Chin tribes.

Regiments present: RA (15); 7 Mountain Battery; Queen's Own Madras Sappers and Miners; 19th Horse (5); 200 men of 1 Norfolks; 10, 21 Madras Infantry; 31, 33 Burma Light Infantry; 39 Bengal Infantry; Garhwal Rifles; 21 Madras Pioneers; two battalions of Burma Police; Mimbu Native Police; 21 Military Train; Telegraph (Postal) Department; Indian Medical Service.

Indian Marine: The officers and men of the Indian Marine ship *Pagan* received this bar for services in support of the various land expeditions against the Chins. A small number of officers who served on shore with the field force as Marine Transport Officers also qualified for this bar.

Kachin Hills 1892-93 3rd December 1892-3rd March 1893

The bar was authorized on 9th January, 1903.
Naming: In bold running script.

This bar was awarded for punitive expeditions into the Kachin Hills. Silver and bronze medals were awarded.

A Victoria Cross was awarded for this campaign to Surgeon Major O. E. P. Lloyd, AMS.

Regiments present: 6 Mountain Battery; 2 Yorkshire Regiment (112); DCLI (6); 1 Sikhs; 2, 4, 6 Punjab Infantry; 20, 33, 38 Bengal Infantry; 1/1, 4, 5 Gurkhas; 21 Madras Pioneers; 10, 32 Madras Infantry; Magwe Battalion; Magaung and Chin Levies; Indian Medical Department; The Ava, Sagaing and Chin Hills Military Police.

Indian Marine: The officers and men of the Indian Marine ship *Pagan* became entitled to this bar for services in support of the various field forces operating in the area. Officers on detached service as Marine Transport Officers were also entitled.

In the RN Museum, Portsmouth, Medal Collection there is a four-bar medal to Engine Driver (an official rate in the Indian Marine) Essack of the tender *Pagan* with bars for 'Burma 1885-87', 'Burma 1887-89', 'Chin Hills 1892-93' and 'Kachin Hills 1892-93'.

Waziristan 1894-5 22nd October 1894-13th March 1895

The bar was authorized on 1st September 1895. Silver and bronze medals were awarded.
Naming: Running script.

The operations were necessary owing to the continual attacks by the Waziris on the Afghan Frontier Delimitation Party, which was commanded by Colonel A. H. Turner. Though the tribesmen suffered heavy casualties from the party's escort, it was not possible to deal with them effectively until the arrival of more troops.

The Waziristan Field Force, commanded by Lieutenant-General Sir

Wm. Lockhart, KCB, CSI, was formed on 2nd December, 1894, and disbanded on 30th March, 1895. This bar was however, also awarded to the Waziristan Delimitation Escort, composed entirely of some of the troops given below, which operated between 22nd October, 1894, and 13th March, 1895.

Regiments present: 1st Brigade—1 Punjab Cavalry; No 3 Mountain Battery; No 2 Company Bengal Sappers and Miners; 2 Border Regiment; 3 Sikhs; 20 (Punjab) Bengal Infantry; 1/1 Gurkhas. 2nd Brigade—1 and 2 Punjab Cavalry; No 8 (Bengal) Mountain Battery; No. 5 Company Bengal Sappers and Miners; one Machine-Gun Section of Devons (10); 4, 33 Punjab Infantry; 38 Dogras; 1/5 Gurkhas. 3rd Brigade—3 Punjab Cavalry; No 1 (Kohat) Mountain Battery; one Machine-Gun Section 2 South Wales Borderers; 3rd Foot (8); Devon Regiment (8); Derby Regiment (4); Argyll and Sutherland Highlanders (4); Gordon Highlanders (11); Seaforth Highlanders (3 known); 1 Sikhs; 2, 6, 19 Punjab Infantry.

90 *Baltic Medal* March 1854-August 1855

Obverse	The diademed head of Queen Victoria and the legend 'VICTORIA REGINA'
Reverse	The seated figure of Britannia holding a trident in her right hand and looking over her left shoulder. Behind her are depicted the fortresses of Bomarsund and Sveaborg, with the word 'BALTIC' above. In the exergue are the dates '1854-1855'
Size	36mm. diameter
Metal	Silver
Ribbon	33mm. wide. Yellow with blue edges
Suspension	An ornamental swivelling suspender
Designers	Obverse—W. Wyon, RA; Reverse—L. C. Wyon
Naming	The medals were issued unnamed except for those awarded to the Royal Sappers and Miners (one hundred and six in all). These being impressed in block capitals. Many other recipients had their medals privately engraved
Bars issued	Nil

These medals are to be found in two thicknesses, and there are two different types of claws, one plain, the other more ornate at the top.

Lieutenants C. B. P. Nugent, RE, and J. C. Cowell, RE, one sergeant and nineteen Royal Sappers and Miners were on board HMS *Duke of Wellington*. Captain F. W. King, RE, commanding No. 2 Company, eighty strong sailed on board the transport *Julia*. The medals to these three officers and their men are named in impressed roman capitals. Those to the men give their rank, name and corps. Collectors should be on their guard against *inscribed* specimens which are not official issues. They are nothing more than the Baltic Medal engraved with a probably fictitious number, rank and name.

The following ships were present:
Sir Charles Napier's flagship *Duke of Wellington*, *Aeolus*, *Ajax*, *Alban*, *Algiers*, *Amphion*, *Archer*, *Arrogant*, *Basilisk*, *Belleisle*, *Blenheim*, *Boscawen*, *Bulldog*, *Caesar*, *Calcutta*, *Centaur*, *Conflict*, *Cornwallis*, *Colossus*, *Cossack*, *Cressy*, *Cruizer*, *Cuckoo*, *Cumberland*, *Dauntless*, *Desperate*, *Dragon*, *Driver*, *Edinburgh*, *Esk*, *Euryalus*, *Exmouth*, *Falcon*, *Firefly*, *Geyser*, *Gladiator*, *Gorgon*, *Hannibal*, *Harrier*, *Hastings*, *Hawke*, *Hecla*, *Hogue*, *Imperieuse*, *James Watt*, *Janus*, *Leopard*, *Lightning*, *Locust*, *Magicienne*, *Majestic*, *Merlin*, *Miranda*, *Monarch*, *Neptune*, *Nile*, *Odin*, *Orion*, *Otter*, *Pembroke*, *Penelope*, *Pigmy*, *Porcupine*, *Prince Regent*, *Princess Royal*, *Plyades*, *Resistance*, *Retribution*, *Rhadamanthus*, *Rosamund*, *Royal George*, *Royal William*, *Russell*, *St George*, *St Jean D'Acre*, *St Vincent*, *Sheerness Water Tank*, *Sphinx*, *Stromboli*, *Tartar*, *Termagant*, *Tribune*, *Tyne*, *Valorous*, *Volage*, *Volcano*, *Vulture*, *Wrangler*, *Zephyr*.

In 1855 the following Steam screw Gun Boats (SGB) and Mortar Vessels (MV) were also present attached to parent ships (above).
SGB *Badger*, MV *Beacon*, SGB *Biter*, MV *Blazer*, MV *Carron*, MV *Cracker*, SGB *Dapper*, MV *Drake*, SGB *Gleaner*, MV *Grappler*, MV *Growler*, MV *Havock*, SGB *Hind*, SGB *Jackdaw*, SGB *Lark*, SGB *Magpie*, MV *Manly*, MV *Mastiff*, SGB *Pelter*, MV *Pickle*, SGB *Pincher*, MV *Porpoise*, IPP *Princess Alice*, MV *Prompt*, MV *Redbreast*, SGB *Redwing*, MV *Rocket*, SGB *Ruby*, MV *Sinbad*, SGB *Skylark*, SGB *Snap*, SGB *Snapper*, SGB *Starling*, SGB *Stork*, MV *Surly*, SGB *Swinger*, SGB *Thistle*, SGB *Weasel*. (The crews of these vessels are on the medal roll under their parent Ship's name).

This medal was sanctioned on the 23rd April, 1856, as an award for services in the Baltic under Admiral Sir Charles Napier and Rear-Admiral the Hon. R. Dundas.

Admiral Napier entered the Baltic in March 1854. The forts at Hango Head were attacked and later, when a French Fleet under Admiral Dechasnes arrived, an attack was made on Cronstadt. Russian merchant ships were destroyed in the Gulfs of Bothnia and Riga.

Bomarsund was attacked on the 16th August, 1855, and the Sappers and Miners were landed to place demolition charges against the forts, which surrendered on the 16th.

In the summer of 1854 Captain Lyons (son of Admiral Lyons, who was later Naval Commander-in-Chief, Crimea), with the *Miranda* and *Brisk*, entered the White Sea and attacked Kola, at the same time the port of Petropaulovski, on the Kamtschatka Peninsula in the north-east of Russia in Asia, was attacked by Captain Sir Frederick Nicholson, who had with him the *President, Pique, Virago, Forte* and *Eurydice* (these vessels were not eligible for the Baltic Medals). The attack was in charge of a French admiral, who was present with three French ships. Seven hundred seamen and marines were landed under Captain Burridge of the *President*, but the affair was not a success.

Another fleet, this time under Rear-Admiral Dundas, was sent to the Baltic, Sveaborg was attacked from the 9th to 11th August, and Helsingfors (now called Helsinki), farther up the Sound, was practically burnt out. It is interesting to note that specially constructed mortar and rocket boats were used in these attacks in March 1855. Nothing further was done after the destruction of Helsingfors and the fleet withdrew from the Baltic in December 1855.

Royal Engineers and Royal Sappers and Miners entitled to the Baltic Medal

Brig Gen Harry D. Jones[1]
Capt Frederick W. King[2] (M)
Capt Harry St George Ord[3] (P)
Lieut John C. Cowell[4]
Lieut Charles Nugent* (P)
Lieut The Hon. George Wrottesley[5]

Royal Sappers and Miners

Col Sgt Harry Brown[6]	Carpenter
Sgt Thomas Barrow[7]	Carpenter
Sgt Cornelius Godfrey[8]	Carpenter
Sgt John Jones*[9] (P)	Mason
Sgt Richard P. Jones[10]	Miner
Cpl John J. Harris[8] (P)	Tailor
Cpl Peter Leitch[11] (M)	Carpenter
Cpl George Luke*[12]	Miner
Cpl James Pitts[13] (P)	Collar Maker
Cpl William Shadbolt[14]	Carpenter
2nd Cpl John Ferguson (P)	Smith
2nd Cpl Francis Irwin[15]	Carpenter
2nd Cpl William James[16]	Bricklayer
2nd Cpl Leonard Roberts[17]	Painter
2nd Cpl William Wood*[18] (P)	Carpenter
Bugler Richard Bullock[8] (M)	
Bugler Henry Kenyon[21] (M)	
Pte William Adams[19]	Carpenter
Pte Richard Allen[8]	Painter
Pte Robert Allison*[20]	Mason
Pte John Ancell*[21]	Smith
Pte Alfred Andrews*[22]	Collar Maker
Pte John Bassett	Shoemaker
Pte Thomas Bates[23]	Carpenter
Pte Hiram J. Boyt[24] (M)	Wheeler
Pte Samuel Bracher[8]	Mason
Pte William Bradley[8]	Mason
Pte Richard Bridgman[25]	Bricklayer
Pte John Bromfield[26] (P)	Painter
Pte John Carson[8] (P)	Mason
Pte Henry Cawte*[8]	Smith
Pte James Chesterman[8]	Mason
Pte Stephen Chittenden[27]	Bricklayer
Pte Samuel Cole[28] (P)	Smith
Pte Francis Collings[8]	Carpenter
Pte William Collings[29]	Miner
Pte David Cuthbert[30]	Mason
Pte Richard Davis*[8]	Tailor
Pte Francis Downey[8]	Miner
Pte George Drake*[31]	Mason
Pte Joseph Dunham[32]	Painter
Pte John Eddy[8] (P)	Miner
Pte John Edwards[33]	Carpenter
Pte Francis Enright*[34] (M)	Carpenter
Pte John Evans	Smith
Pte William Ferguson[8]	Smith
Pte Jeremiah Fish[21]	Carpenter
Pte Charles Foot[8]	Smith
Pte George Fox*[8]	Miner
Pte Samuel Garrett[8]	Painter
Pte George Gasson[35] (P)	Brickmaker
Pte Philip Gould[36]	Smith
Pte Andrew Greig[8]	Carpenter
Pte Charles R. Harris*[21]	Mason
Pte George Harris[37]	Smith
Pte William Harris[38]	Mason
Pte Alexander Hattrick[8] (P)	Carpenter
Pte Jesse Head[8]	Miner
Pte William Heathcote*[39]	Carpenter
Pte George Heather*[8]	Miner
Pte John Hillman[8]	Miner
Pte Robert Hopkins[40]	Carpenter
Pte Alexander Hosie[41]	Mason
Pte Alexander Ingram[8]	Mason
Pte John Lethbridge[42]	Mason
Pte James Lush*[43]	Bricklayer
Pte William Martin	Smith
Pte Donald McArthur[44]	Mason
Pte Thomas McLaren[45]	Tailor
Pte James McLeish[8]	Plasterer
Pte David Miller[46]	Mason
Pte James Moncur[47]	Smith
Pte John Morrison[48]	Carpenter
Pte Thomas Muir[49]	Bricklayer
Pte William Pauley[21]	Mason
Pte William Pedler[8]	Mason
Pte George Peters[50]	Mason
Pte Thomas Prentice[51]	Carpenter
Pte James Ramsay*[52]	Collar Maker
Pte William Relf[53]	Carpenter
Pte Joseph Riordan[21]	Painter
Pte James Roberts[8]	Painter
Pte William Robertson[21]	Plumber
Pte John Ross[54] (M)	Mason
Pte Thomas Ross[55] (M)	Carpenter
Pte John S. Rowley[56]	Smith
Pte William Smale*[57]	Mason
Pte Stephen Stammer[8]	Bricklayer
Pte George Sussex*[58]	Miner
Pte Rodrick Stewart[8]	Mason
Pte William Tout[21]	Smith
Pte Francis Trevett[59]	Carpenter
Pte John Vietch*[60] (M)	Carpenter
Pte Alexander Wallace[45]	Mason
Pte John Williams (1)*[61]	Mason
Pte John Williams (2)[62]	Smith
Pte Samuel Williams[61]	Mason
Pte John Williamson[63]	Cooper
Pte George Wilson[8]	Smith
Pte John Wright[64]	Mason

Notes

1. Commanded the Bn of Marines and Sappers accompanying the Baltic fleet
2. Killed in the Crimea April 1855
3. Brigade Major to Gen Jones
4. ADC to Gen Jones. Accidentally wounded by his own pistol. Also served in the Crimea
5. Posted to the 2nd Company 14.7.54 and mortally wounded on Bomarsund on 15.8.54, dying the same day
6. Also served in the Crimea. Papers in WO/97 series at PRO Quartermaster Sgt at discharge
7. Also served in the Kaffir War and the Crimea. Quartermaster Sgt at discharge. Papers in the WO/97 series
8. Also served in the Crimea
9. Sgt of the detachment who built the first battery on Bomarsund. Narrowly escaped when attempting to draw a plan of Fort Tzee which was on fire and eventually blew up. Served in the Crimea and said to be the inventor of iron bound gabions. Rose to Sgt Major
10. An accomplished diver who was engaged in the destruction of the wreck of the *Royal George* at Spithead
11. In charge of the carpenters responsible for laying the platform of the first battery to be constructed at Bomarsund. Wounded during the storming of the Redan in the Crimea and awarded the VC
and Legion D'Honor. Sgt Major at discharge. Papers in WO/97 series
12. Overseer of the road built on Bomarsund to hau the guns to the breaching battery and commended for his demolition work. Killed in the trenches before Sebastopol 17.7.55
13. Also served in the Crimea and China 1860. Papers in the WO/97 series
14. Died of sickness in the Crimea 1.5.55
15. Col Sgt at discharge. Papers in the WO/97 seri¢
16. Killed in the trenches in the Crimea 17.6.55
17. Died from cholera at Bomarsund 23.8.54
18. Also served in the Crimea. Sgt at discharge. Papers in the WO/97 series
19. Also served in the Crimea and the Indian Mutiny. Col Sgt at discharge. Papers in the WO/97 series
20. Died from cholera before Sebastopol, 8.1.55
21. Transferred to the 5th Co. 1.11.54
22. Died from cholera off Cronstadt in June 1854
23. Died of sickness in the Crimea 1.5.55
24. Died of sickness at Balaclava 27.2.55
25. Also served in the Crimea. Sgt at discharge. Papers in the WO/97 series
26. Also served in the Crimea. Papers in the WO/9 series
27. Also served in the Crimea and Indian Mutiny. Col Sgt at discharge. Papers in the WO/97 seri¢
28. Won the DCM and Legion D'Honor in the Crimea. Rose to Captain
29. Probably the same William Collings—described as a Mason—who was killed in the trenches 17.8.55. Not to be confused with William Collins (carpenter) who died of wounds 24.7.55
30. Also served in the Crimea and wounded in an arm. Papers in the WO/97 series
31. Served with the 1st Co in the Crimea and the 23rd Co during the Indian Mutiny. Drowned at sea on his way to the China War of 1860. (Falsely named medal known to exist)
32. Died of sickness at Balaclava hospital 29.1.55
33. Died at Bomarsund of cholera 24.8.54
34. Commended for his 'boldness, resolution and zeal' at Bomarsund
35. Died of sickness in the camp before Sebastopol, 26.11.55
36. Also served in the Kaffir War and Crimea. Papers in the WO/97 series
37. Died of camp fever before Sebastopol, 19.5.55
38. Died at Scutari 20.2.55
39. Received the NGS for Syria and also served in the Crimea. Papers in the WO/97 series
40. Died of fever before Sebastopol, 20.7.55
41. Wounded in the throat by shell splinter in the Crimea. Papers in the WO/97 series
42. Killed in the trenches in the Crimea, 15.4.55
43. Died of cholera at Basso Sound, 24.6.54
44. Died 24.4.55 before Sebastopol of wounds and fever

91 *Crimea War Medal* 28th March 1854-30th March 1856

Obverse	Diademed head of Queen Victoria with the date '1854' underneath, and the legend 'VICTORIA REGINA'
Reverse	A Roman warrior holding a sword in his right hand and a circular shield in front of him with his left whilst being crowned by a small winged figure of Victory. The word 'CRIMEA' is written vertically on the left
Size	36mm. diameter
Ribbon	27mm. wide, light blue with yellow edges
Suspension	By means of a foliated suspender peculiar to this medal
Designers	Obverse—W. Wyon, RA; Reverse—B. Wyon
Naming	The medals were originally issued unnamed, but could be returned for naming free of charge. Those which were officially named were done in indented square or engraved capitals.

In the Public Record Office there is a memo from Lord Panmure to a Mr Elliott 'Officers and men who have received medals without names in the Crimea, if they require their names to be engraved on them, and send them in for the purpose, Lord Panmure has no objection to its being done' 5th Dec 1855. This note *may* indicate that all the medals sent out to the Crimea were unnamed whilst those issued in the UK were named.

Those awarded to members of four selected ships were officially impressed, namely:— HM ships *London* (743), *Niger* (187), *Rodney* (851), *Wasp* (180).

Bars issued	Five—Alma, Balaklava, Inkermann, Sebastopol and Azoff. The maximum number of bars awarded to any one recipient was four

This medal, of which 275,000 were awarded, is often found with the bars arranged in the wrong order, the correct order from the bottom upwards being: Alma, Balaklava, Inkermann, Sebastopol.

It is interesting to note that the medal and bars were not authorized at the same time.

The deeds of the Army so stirred the Queen that orders were issued on 15th December, 1854, for a medal with bars for Alma and Inkermann to be awarded to all present. The bar for Balaklava was sanctioned on 23rd February, 1855, and that for Sebastopol on 13th October, 1855. Many medals were issued before the last bar was distributed, consequently one finds a variety of fittings and many recipients did not bother to fit it on at all or sewed it on to the ribbon. It must also have happened that many men died from wounds, etc., before the award of the bar for Sebastopol, though they had been present at some time during the siege.

The fact that the medal was originally awarded to commemorate the battles of Alma and Balaklava only accounts for it bearing the single date '1854' and not the dual ones as does that for the operations in the Baltic. The colours of the two ribbons were intended to be the same though arranged in the reverse positions.

There were of course many awarded without bars to those who were present in the Crimea but had not taken part in any of the actions for which bars, with the unique leaf and acorn pattern, were awarded.

The British Medal was also awarded to some of the French military and naval personnel, some of which do not bear the date '1854' on the obverse. These medals are sometimes found with the bars Traktir, Tchernaia, Mer d'Azoff and/or Malakof. The French medals were all issued un-named.

[45] Also served in the Crimea. Papers in the WO/97 series

[46] Wounded in the back while on the *Julia* 22.8.54 when the mate of the ship accidentally discharged a captured Russian rifle. Papers in the WO/97 series

[47] Received the DCM while in the Crimea. Also served in the Kaffir Wars of 1846/7 and 1850/3

[48] Killed in the trenches before Sebastopol 2.9.55

[49] Died of sickness before Sebastopol 15.5.55

[50] Accompanied Sgt Jones into burning Fort Tzee. Also served in the Crimea. Sgt at discharge. Name sometimes shown on musters as Peter. Papers in the WO/97 series

[51] Died of sickness before Sebastopol 6.3.55

[52] Died of cholera on board the *Duke of Wellington* off Cronstadt, 17.6.54

[53] Wounded in the knee in the Crimea. Papers in the WO/97 series

[54] Won the VC in the Crimea. Sgt when discharged. Papers in the WO/97 series

[55] Died of sickness in camp before Sebastopol 5.1.55

[56] Accompanied Sgt Jones into burning Fort Tzee. Also served in the Crimea. Papers in the WO/97 series

[57] Killed in the trenches before Sebastopol 17.6.55

[58] Also served in the Crimea. Papers in the WO/97 series

[59] Died at Scutari 14.2.55

[60] Commended for his 'boldness, resolution and zeal' at Bomarsund. Died of cholera in the Crimea 28.12.54

[61] Also served in the Crimea, transferred to No 3 Co 1.1.55

[62] Died of fever in the Crimea, 9.4.55

[63] Papers in the WO/97 series

[64] Killed in the trenches in the Crimea 1.6.55

The symbol * indicates those officers and men of the first detachment who went aboard the *Duke of Wellington* on March 9th 1854

PRO references:—
    AD/38/32/3/4
    WO/11/135/139/143
and Soldiers' Records WO/97 series

(P) Indicates medal known to be in private collection
(M) Medal in Royal Engineers' Museum
For this information we are indebted to Mr Graham Hornby and Gordon R. Everson.

Crimea War

Thinking that Turkey was in the throes of disintegration, Russia invaded the provinces of Moldavia and Wallachia in July 1853. After fruitless negotiations, Turkey declared war in late October, and on 4th November an army under Omar Pasha defeated the Russians at Oltenitza in Wallachia. However, on 30th November, a Russian fleet destroyed a Turkish squadron at Sinope and then bombarded the town. As a result, and fearing further Russian expansion might lead to the seizure of the Bosporus and with it an outlet to the Mediterranean, both Britain and France sent naval forces to the Black Sea to protect Turkish shipping. On 23rd March 1854, the Russians crossed the Danube and advanced further into the Turkish provinces; in response, both Britain and France declared war with Russia.

An Anglo-French force was dispatched to Varna to assist the Turks in repelling further advances; however, threatened with Austrian intervention and suffering defeats in battle with the Turks, the Russians withdrew from their recent conquests.

With the Russian withdrawal, the primary objective of the Anglo-French expedition was achieved. However, in order to substantially reduce Russian strength in the area it was decided to mount an expedition to the Crimea Peninsular and neutralize Sebastopol, the major Russian naval base on the Black Sea.

The British, under Major General Fitzroy James Henry Somerset, Lord Raglan, and the French under Marshal Armand J L de Sainte-Arnaud, sailed from Varna on 7th September 1854 and made an unopposed landing at Eupatoria on the 13th, and the Old Fort, Kalamita Bay on 14th to 18th September, the latter being 30 miles north of Sebastopol. On the 19th, the expeditionary force, approximately 62,000 strong (27,000 British, 28,000 French, 7,000 Turkish) advanced towards Sebastopol.

On 20th September, the allies encountered the Russian army under Prince Alexander Sergeievich Menshikov occupying a position commanding the Alma River. Under heavy fire, the river was crossed and the heights stormed, forcing Menshikov to withdraw. Approximate British casualties 360 killed and 1,600 wounded; French casualties were under 500; Russian casualties 1,800 killed, over 3,000 wounded, with numerous prisoners. Lord Raglan favoured an immediate advance on Sebastopol, but the French disagreed, with the result that the brilliant Russian engineer Count Franz Todleben was given time to prepare the defences of the base.

The combined allied forces were insufficient to surround the town, so a base was established at Balaklava about ten miles south-east of it and from there siege operations began.

Arriving before Sebastopol with little opposition, the town was bombarded on the 17th, 18th and 19th of October. On the 25th, Menshikov attempted to break through between the besieging lines at Balaklava. Russian cavalry advancing to exploit the situation charged the 93rd commanded by Sir Colin Campbell. In line (the 'Thin Red Line') instead of the usual square, the highlanders repelled the attackers. A larger mass of cavalry faced British heavy cavalry under Brigadier General James York Scarlett. The Scots Greys and the 6th Inniskilling Dragoons charged uphill and broke through the first line of cavalry, then charged at the second in company with the 1st Dragoons and the 4th and 5th Dragoon Guards routing the Russians. Approximate British casualties 80; Russian 200, out of a total of 800 and 3,000 respectively. Then through an error in the transmission of orders, the light cavalry brigade under Lord Cardigan charged massed Russian artillery in that most famous of all cavalry charges. With artillery to their front and on flanks, the cavalry gallantly attacked the guns before them and engaged the gunners and their cavalry support before being forced to retire. Out of a total force of 675, 247 were casualties.

On 26th October, the British repulsed the Russians in the first battle of Inkermann. On 5th November the main battle of that name was fought when Menshikov again attempted to break through between the besieging troops and their base. In a savage day long 'soldiers' battle, the Russian attacks were beaten back. Russian casualties were high, estimated at over 15,000 killed and wounded; British casualties were over 2,500.

After the Battle of Inkermann, the siege proper of Sebastopol began. It was then that the gross inefficiency of supply and transport became apparent. There were no proper hospitals and the death rate among those admitted to the hastily converted buildings exceeded 88%. Four men died from disease to every one killed by enemy action.

In January 1855 the first of a 15,000 strong Sardinian contingent arrived to bolster the allied cause.

On 17th February, the Russians, under Prince Michael Gorchakov, attacked Turkish positions at Eupatoria but were repulsed. On 24th May, Kertch at the entrance to the Sea of Azov was seized, blocking supplies coming to the Russians from that quarter and allowing squadrons entry to the Sea.

Attacks were made on the Russian outer defences of Sebastopol on 7th June 1855, the British taking the Quarries, the French the Mamelon position. Approximate British casualties 700; French 5,000; Russian 8,500.

On 17th to 18th June the allied assault on Sebastopol was renewed with the French attacking the Malakoff and the British the Redan positions. Both attacks were beaten off with heavy loss to all parties. Approximate British casualties 1,500; French 3,550, Russians 5,400.

On 28th June Lord Raglan died and was succeeded by General Sir James Simpson.

On 16th August at the Battle of Traktir, 60,000 Russian troops, under Prince Gorchakov, failed to break through a force of 12,000 French and 10,000 Sardinians. The French casualties numbered 1,500, the Sardinians 250; the Russians in the region of 9,000.

On 8th September the key positions to the defence of Sebastopol—the Malakoff and the Redan—were stormed, the French capturing the former, the British repulsed from the latter. However, the French bombarding the Redan from the Malakoff drove the defenders from their position.

Losses were enormous, the allies suffering some 10,000 casualties, the Russians over 11,000. That night the city and remaining fortifications were evacuated and set on fire by the Russians.

With the fall of the fortress the war neared it's end. In February 1856 hostilities ceased and on 30th March a treaty of peace was signed. The last of the British troops departing the Crimea on 12th July 1856.

When the Crimea War broke out there was no organized Medical Service as we know it today. The Director-General at the time (Sir Andrew Smith) had urged the necessity of enlisting able-bodied men for the sole duty of looking after the sick and wounded, but his advice was disregarded. Instead, a force of some 300 old-age pensioners were sent to the Crimea for that purpose and they were to be known as the 'Hospital Conveyance Corps', also sometimes called the 'Ambulance Corps'. They proved a complete failure, half of them died of Cholera and the remainder 'hit the bottle'. It was left to the Regimental Surgeons and their orderlies, taken from the ranks, and the bandsmen to collect the wounded. Such was the inglorious beginning of the RAMC as we know it today.

There was one incident that took place in the campaign which is of interest and very far from generally known. It concerns the inventiveness, experiences and pluck of Boatswain John Shepheard, RN, for which he was awarded the Victoria Cross.

In the 1914-18 War the Italians sank the Austrian battleship *Viribus Unitis* when in Pola harbour by means of an explosive charge placed against her hull. This charge had been carried in a small two-man torpedo through the boom defences. In the 1939-45 War a similar feat was performed by the Italians on 18th December, 1941, against HMS *Queen Elizabeth* and *Valiant* whilst they were in Alexandria Harbour.

Boatswain Shepheard, of HMS *Jean d'Acre*, constructed a sort of punt with a freeboard of only three inches in which he proposed to carry an explosive charge. He was then going to paddle it into the harbour of Sebastopol and attach the charge to the Russian flagship *The Twelve Apostles* and explode it by means of a time fuse.

His scheme met with a certain amount of opposition and ridicule until he showed the feasibility of his idea by attaching a large dummy bomb to his own admiral's flagship.

It is a sidelight on how war was carried out in those days to read that both Admiral Lyons and Lord Raglan considered the whole idea very unsporting, and so would not sanction its use against the enemy. The French, however, had no such qualms and borrowed Shepheard and his boat.

On the 15th July, 1855, Shepheard entered Careening Bay but, although he got past the guard ships undetected, he could not get through the large number of small boats that were ferrying troops across the bay. He managed to hide his craft and himself all the next day, whilst keeping careful watch of the enemy's movements. He returned to his starting-point the next night with much useful information. He repeated his performance on the 16th August, but once again was unable to dodge the traffic running across the bay.

Though he sank no enemy ships, there can be little doubt that the germ of the idea of limpet bombs and one-man torpedoes originated, or at any rate grew in Shepheard's mind.

A total of one hundred and eleven Victoria Crosses were awarded for the campaign, including those for Azoff (see page 131).

Alma 20th September, 1854

Regiments present: 4, 8, 11, 13 Hussars; 17 Lancers; C and I Troops HA; 1/3, 8/3, 2/8, 1/11, 3/11, 4/11, 5/11, 4/12 RA; Sappers; Medical and Transport Corps; Ambulance Corps; 3/1, 1/2, 1/3 Foot Guards; 2/1, 4, 7, 19, 20, 21, 23, 28, 30, 33, 38, 41, 42, 44, 46 (6 officers and 225 men), 47, 49, 50, 55, 63, 68, 77, 79, 88, 93, 2/95 Foot; 1st and 2nd Bns Rifle Brigade.

(Surgeon J. B. Greene received a medal with this single bar and another medal with bars for Alma, Inkermann and Sebastopol. A naval officer, who was ADC to Lord Raglan, received a medal with bar Alma.)

Balaklava 25th October, 1854

Regiments present: **The Light Brigade** composed of 4th Light Dragoons, 8th and 11th Hussars, 13th Light Dragoons, and the 17th Lancers. The 13th Light Dragoons and the 17th Lancers formed the Light Brigade Front line, the 11th Hussars the 2nd line and the 4th Light Dragoons, and 8th Hussars the 3rd line. On the anniversary of Balaklava, 25th October, 1913, there were fifteen known Light Brigade survivors still alive, namely:

John Boxall, Pte 4th Lt Dgns age 83 living at Tunbridge Wells
John Whitehead, Pte/Sgt 4th Lt Dgns age 89 living at Camberley
Henry Wilsden, Pte 4th Lt Dgns age 92 living at Oxford
Edward Phillips, Lieut/Maj 8th Hsrs age — living at Reading
Wm Fulton, Pte 8th Hsrs age 81 living at Edinburgh
Geo Gibson, Pte 13th Lt Dgns age 82 living at Linlithgow
Jas Mustard, Pte/Sgt 17th Lncrs age 87 living at Twickenham
Thos Watt, Pte 11th Hsrs age 86 living at Dorchester
John Parkinson, Pte/Sgt 11th Hsrs age 84 living at Birmingham
Percy Smith, Lieut/Capt 13th Lt Dgns age 88 living at Southampton
Jas Olley, Pte 4th Lt Dgns age 88 living at Elsing, Norfolk
John Kilvert, Cpl/TS Maj 11th Hsrs age 87 living at Wednesbury
Wm Pennington, Pte/Cpl 11th Hsrs age 80 living at Stoke Newington,
died 1923
Edwin Hughes, Pte SS Maj 13th Lt Dgns age 96 living at Blackpool
Sir Fitzroy Maclean (Born 1835 died 1936)—the last survivor of 'The Gallant Six Hundred'.

The Heavy Brigade was composed of: 4, 5 Dragoon Guards; 1, 2 and 6 Dragoons.

Other ranks killed, missing and wounded from the Heavy Brigade at Balaklava.

2nd Dragoons

Killed
Cpl A. P. Clifford
Pte H. Campbell

Wounded
TSM Mathew Brown
TSM James Dearden
TSM James Davidson
Sgt Thomas Kneath
Sgt John Wilson
Sgt David Gibson
Cpl Francis Campbell
Pte Owen Ward
Pte Richard Foster
Pte William Jackson
Pte A. D. Gardiner
Pte William Johnston
Pte Henry Lochrie
Pte Thomas Ghofley

Pte James Hunter
Pte Robert Kerr
Pte William Henwood
Pte Alex Weir
Pte John McNee
Pte Charles Glany
Pte Robert Barnet
Pte Thomas Langdon
Pte James Taylor
Pte Peter Burley
Pte William Leggie
Pte William Hammond
Pte Robert Thompson
Pte George Alexander
Pte William Davis
Pte William Caulfield
Pte James Aitken
Pte George Burns
Pte William Donaldson
Pte James McPherson
Pte James Hackett

Pte James Bothwicke
Pte John Borland
Pte Donald Davidson
Pte Walter Fawke
Pte A. S. Lang
Pte Thomas Traill
Pte William Marshall
Pte James Watson
Pte William McPherson
Pte William J. Allis
Pte James Allen
Pte Richard Livingstone
Pte William Conmell
Pte Charles Currie
Pte James Calter
Pte John Knowles
Pte William Morrison
Pte McAdam Galbraith

1st Dragoons

Killed
Pte Charles Middleton
Pte Thomas Shore

Wounded
Sgt M. Noake
Trmpt G. Stacey
Pte J. R. Astlett
Pte James Blake
Pte George Taylor
Pte B. Kennedy
Pte Samuel Woodward

4th Dragoon Guards

Killed
Pte Thomas Ryan

Wounded
TSM John Evans
Sgt William Percy

Pte James Anchinclass
Pte Henry Preece
Pte William Scanlon

5th Dragoon Guards

Killed
Cpl James Taylor
Pte Bernard Callery

Wounded
Cpl Charles M'Keegan
Pte Edward Malone
Pte Henry Herbert
Pte John McCabe
Pte William Wilson
Pte Charles Babbington
Pte Joseph Jenkins
Pte G. H. Dickson
Pte William Morris

6th Dragoons

Killed
Pte Robert Elliot
Pte Alex Latimer

Wounded
TSM Alex Shields
Sgt Richard Jeffreys
Sgt Frederick Bolton
Cpl John Kidney
Pte Michael Rourke
Pte Robert Turner
Pte Charles Clarke
Pte John McCanna
Pte Robert Keane
Pte James Backler
Pte William Breadin
Pte John Davis
Pte William Lyons

The famous **Thin Red Line** was composed of the 93 Foot (2nd Bn. The Argyll and Sutherland Highlanders), which is the only *line* regiment to receive Balaklava as a Battle Honour.

In addition to the 93rd Foot and cavalry regiments which received Balaklava as a Battle Honour, medals with this bar are found awarded to almost every unit present in the Crimea, though they, as a whole, took no part in the fighting.

What was known as a 'Battalion of Detachments' was formed. These detachments consisted of about one officer, one sergeant and thirty men from several regiments. Medals were issued to the following regiments, but this list must not be considered as in any way complete. 20, 23, 42, 46, 55, 63, 68, 79, 88 (35) Foot; Rifle Brigade, C and I Troops HA; 1/3, 2/8, 1/11, 3/11, 5/11, 4/12 RA and the Royal Marine Brigade drawn from a number of ships; Ambulance Corps.

Inkermann 5th November, 1854

Regiments present: 5 Dragoon Guards; 6 Dragoons; 4, 8, 11, 13 Hussars; 17 Lancers; CJ Troop HA; 1/3, 8/3, 2/8, 3/11, 4/11, 5/11, 6/11, 7/11, 8/11, 1/12, 2/12, 3/12, 4/12, 6/12, 7/12 RA; Sappers; Ambulance Corps; 3/1, 1/2, 1/3 Foot Guards; 1, 4, 7, 19, 20, 21, 23, 28, 30, 33, 38, 41, 44, 46 (6 officers and 201 men), 47, 49, 50, 55, 57, 63, 68, 77, 79, 2/95 Foot; 1st and 2nd Rifle Brigade; Naval Brigade and Royal Marine Brigades drawn from a large number of ships.

Sebastopol 11th September, 1854—9th September, 1855*

Regiments present: 1, 4, 5, 6 Dragoon Guards; 1 Royal Dragoons; 2, 6 Dragoons; 4, 8, 10, 11, 13 Hussars; 12, 17, Lancers; RHA; RA;

*The dates for the Royal Navy were 1st October, 1854-9th September, 1855.

Sappers; Medical and Transport Corps; Ambulance Corps; 3/1, 1/2, 1/3 Foot Guards; 1/1, 2/1, 1/3, 1/4, 7, 9, 13, 14, 17, 18, 19, 20, 21, 23, 28, 30, 31, 33, 34, 38, 39, 41, 42, 44, 46, 47, 48, 49, 50, 55, 56, 57, 62, 63, 68, 71, 72, 77, 79, 82, 88, 89, 90, 93, 95, 97 Foot; 1st and 2nd Rifle Brigade and Royal Marine Brigades drawn from a large number of ships.

HM ships: *Agamemnon, Albion, Arethusa, Bellerophon, Britannia, Cyclops, Diamond, Firebrand, Furious, Highflyer, London, Lynx, Niger, Queen, Resistance, Retribution, Rodney, Samson, Sanspareil, Sphinx, Spitfire, Terrible, Trafalgar, Tribune, Triton, Vesuvius.*

It is interesting to note that in the early days of the siege our men were paid for each Russian shot that they salvaged so that they could be fired back again!

Azoff 25th May-22nd September, 1855†

This bar was only awarded to Naval personnel and Marines who entered the Sea of Azoff.

HM ships: *Agamemnon* (86), *Algiers* (144), *Ardent* (83), *Arrow* (77), *Beagle* (79), *Boxer* (32), *Clinker* (34), *Cracker* (26), *Curlew* (130), *Danube* (37), *Fancy* (32), *Grinder* (32), *Hannibal* (62), *Industry* (48), *Jasper, Lynx* (71), *Medina* (105), *Miranda* (236), *Moslem* (25), *Princess Royal* (59), *Recruit* (65), *Royal Albert* (63), *Snake* (80), *Sphinx, Stromboli* (151), *St Jean d'Acre* (62), *Sulina* (33), *Swallow* (130), *Vesuvius* (159), *Viper* (79), *Weser* (72), *Wrangler* (77).

Victoria Crosses awarded to the navy for 'commando-type' raids on the northern shores of the Sea of Azoff, listed in chronological order, were:
Cecil W. Buckley Lieut, RN (first of his two exploits) *Miranda* 29 May 1855 Genitchi
Hugh T. Burgoyne, Lieut, RN *Swallow* 29 May 1855 Genitchi
John Robarts, Gnr, RN *Ardent* 26 May 1855 Genitchi
Henry Cooper, Boatswain, RN *Miranda* 3 June 1855 Taganrog
Cecil W. Buckley, Lieut, RN *Miranda* 3 June 1855 Taganrog
Joseph Trewavas, Ordy Seaman (loaned from *Agamemnon*) *Beagle* 3 July 1855 Genitchi
Joseph Kellaway, Boatswain, RN *Wrangler* 31 Augt 1855 Marionpol
George F. Day, Lieut, RN *Recruit* 16 Sept 1855 Spit of Arabat
John E. Commerell, Comdr *Weser* 11 Oct 1855 Spit of Arabat
William T. Rickard, Quarter Master *Weser* 11 Oct 1855 Spit of Arabat

List of the Recipients of the French Military Medal for the Crimea

4th Dragoon Guards
RSM William Joyce; Sgt Maj Joseph Drake; Sgt Richard Cooke; Pte Patrick Hogan
5th Dragoon Guards
RSM J. Russell; TSMs S. Griffith, William Stewart; Sgt M. Davidson
6th Dragoon Guards
RSM William Lyons; Pte Thomas Edwards
1st Dragoons
TSMs John Norris, Matthew Bailey; Pte John Savage
2nd Dragoons
RSM John Geene; TSM George Tilsley; L/Sgt James Borthwick; Pte Andrew Wilson
4th Light Dragoons
RSM James Kelly; Sgt John Andrews; Ptes Thomas Guthre, George McGregor
6th Dragoons
TSMs T. Wakefield, Andrew Morton; Trumpeter Thomas Monkes; Pte Humphrey Polkinghorn
8th Hussars
TSM John Pickworth; Sgt Charles Macauley; Cpl James Donaghur; Pte John Martin
10th Hussars
TSM William Finch
11th Hussars
RSM G. L. Smith; TSM Rourke Trevan; Sgt Seth Bond; L/Cpl Thos. Harrison; Pte Cornelius Teehan

†The *London Gazette* of 2nd May, 1856, gives the final date as 22nd November for officers and men who were employed in operations in the Sea of Azoff, but a later *Gazette*, dated 5th August, 1856, quotes the inclusive dates as given above.

12th Lancers
Cpl J. Cannings; Trumpeter John Earson
13th Light Dragoons
RSM T. G. Johnson; Sgt Richard Davis; Ptes George Dearlove, John Fenton
17th Lancers
RSM Chas. Wooden; Sgts J. Shearingham, J. Nunnely; Pte Chas. Watson
Royal Artillery
Sgt Conductors J. Buchanan, J. Boggie, Job Smith; Sgt Maj W. Flockhart; Sgts William Kempton, William Scott, F. Iles, Rd. Perkins, Chst. Fitzsimons, John Adams, John Acland, John Fairfax, J. McGarrity, Joseph Smith, J. McPherson, H. Bacchus, T. Walsh, S. Ewing, J. McKown; Cpls Thomas Betts, Patrick Conway, James Browne, M. Fenton, James Hamilton, Joseph Milligan; Bombardiers Willm Hewitt, John Bower, A. Sutherland, J. Trotter, W. Ramsey; Acting Bombardiers John Hagan, C. Henderson, D. Jenkins, G. Gibson, W. Burrows; Gnrs and Drivers H. Wood, R. Botfield, J. Douglas, J. Cannell, J. M'Ardle, J. Hay, G. Davis, J. Powell, M. O'Donohue, M. Malowney, J. Magee, G. Bines, J. McGrath, J. Norton, J. Vance, P. Knight, R. Woodbridge, T. Margree, E. O'Brien, H. Davis, W. Hovenden, T. Reynolds; Driver Rbt Smeaton; Trumpeter J. McLaren
Royal Engineers
Col Sgt K. Knight; Cpls W. Lendrim, J. McMurphy, J. Ross, R. Hanson; Second Cpl W. Conning
Grenadier Guards
Pay Sgt R. Powley; Col Sgt C. Sargent; Ptes J. Archer, T. Elger, A. Hale, J. King, W. Myers, W. Williams, W. Nurton
Coldstream Guards
Sgt Maj S. Carter; Drill Sgt J. Burnett, Sgts W. Reed, G. Walden; Cpl F. Vile; Ptes J. Winter, P. Balls, C. Tutt, J. Bott
Scots Guards
Pay and Col Sgts W. M. M'Gregor, J. Badenoch, G. Attrill; Drill Sgts J. Lennox, G. Sharp; Sgt D. Manson; Cpl J. Judd; Act Cpl J. Coulter; Pte J. Drummond
1st Regiment
Sgt Maj S. Hunter; Col Sgt A. Stewart; Sgts W. Sparks, J. Mulvany; Cpls J. Horsfall, W. Sullivan; Ptes D. Moran, J. Colver, A. Campbell, C. Pulfer, F. Lock; Drummer H. Clarke
3rd Regiment
Sgt W. Heyes; Ptes W. Brown, J. Connor, J. Eagan, J. Hall, J. Walsh
4th Regiment
Col Sgts W. O'Grady, A. Flemming, R. Marshall; Sgt J. Newth; Cpl J. Clarkson; L/Cpl J. Fitzgerald; Ptes T. Murray, J. Murphy, J. Fitzpatrick
7th Regiment
Sgt Majs J. Bell, W. Bacon; Col Sgt J. Watts; Sgts J. Laws, T. Poulton, W. White; Cpls P. Hanlon, W. Marshall; Pte M. Edwards
9th Regiment
Sgts G. Ripton, E. Firmin, A. Rielly; Cpl M. Monaghan; Ptes D. M'Mahaon, C. Farrell, J. Redmond
13th Regiment
Sgts J. Godwin, T. Coopen; Cpl E. Tallman; Ptes V. Corry, F. Stokes
14th Regiment
Sgts T. Cooper, J. MacDonald, T. Brown; Ptes R. Harrison, T. Caby, P. Canty
17th Regiment
Sgt C. Collins; Cpl P. Smith; Ptes J. Davis, R. Hogan, T. Lawless, B. Vaughan
18th Regiment
Col Sgt E. Dunne; Sgts J. Harvey, J. Gleeson; Cpl N. O'Donnell; Ptes J. Cox, E. Langton, J. Byrne
19th Regiment
Col Sgt W. Britts; Sgts W. Murphy, W. Smith, H. Strick, T. Murphy, G. Rolins; Ptes H. Higgins, J. Duffy, S. Evans
20th Regiment
Sgts J. Moss, G. Boxall, J. Brown; Ptes J. Brown, G. Kirkham, W. Hennessy, H. Gray, P. Callaghan, J. Lowe
21st Regiment
Col Sgts J. Higdon, R. Ellis; Sgts J. Sim, P. Kelly, J. Russell, E. Marshman; Ptes T. Driscoll, M. M'Phely, P. Crowley
23rd Regiment
Sgt Maj W. Handley; Col Sgts J. O'Neill, C. Coviton, J. Boyse; Sgts J. Collins, C. Godden, W. Andrews, W. Parkinson; Ptes T. Gerraghty, J. Brown

28th Regiment
Sgts W. Cook, G. Dunnery; Ptes J. Carson, M. Connell, W. Dunn, J. Blake, J. Tobin, J. Hill, P. Tulley

30th Regiment
Col Sgts H. McAllister, T. M'Donogh, J. Richardson; Sgt O. Curran; L/Cpl M. Byrne; Ptes J. Smith, W. Nicholl, C. Quigley, T. McDonald

31st Regiment
Col Sgt J. Foley; Ptes R. Stapleton, J. Ruth, L. Ryan, J. Spelman

33rd Regiment
Sgt Maj W. Barwell; Col Sgts W. Meanaing, P. Read, J. Bacon; Sgts P. Whelan, W. Crane; Ptes F. Crotty, W. Douglas, P. M'Guire

34th Regiment
Col Sgt W. Smith; Sgts W. Quirk, J. Haydon, W. Carney; Cpl W. Coffer; Ptes C. Brophy, W. Gill, T. Loft

38th Regiment
Sgt Maj P. M'Fadden; Sgt A. Clarke; Cpl T. Brennan; Ptes J. Walsh, R. Longheed, M. Murphy, B. Newhall, W. Moore, J. Blackmore

39th Regiment
Col Sgt J. Garrett; Sgt G. Pegram; Cpl T. Omealy; Ptes M. Boyle, L. Lond, M. Ryan

41st Regiment
Col Sgts J. Smith, A. Madden, W. Davis, J. Kelly; Cpl C. Nelson; Ptes P. Garvey, J. Kennelly, T. M'Quade, M. Rogerson

42nd Regiment
Col Sgt T. Ridley; Sgts W. Strathern, G. Fox; L/Cpls R. M'Nair, W. Bennett; Ptes D. M'Kenzie, N. Carmichael A. Cromtie

44th Regiment
Quartermaster Sgt D. Reddin; Col Sgt J. Donelan; Sgt T. Brown; Cpls R. Murray, J. Drenon, D. Canty; Ptes J. Edlow, J. Burnside, T. McCarthy

46th Regiment
Col Sgt S. Harbour; Sgts G. Blagdon, W. Brommell, L. Gooding; Cpl W. Watt; Ptes J. Hunt, J. Condon

47th Regiment
Col Sgts G. M'Donald, Gill; Sgts W. Bowler, R. Court; Cpl C. O'Loghlin; Ptes J. McDermond, J. Dinneen, J. Dillon, D. Flanagan

48th Regiment
Sgt Maj S. Francis; Cpls T. Kelly, T. Goorly; Pte J. Downey

49th Regiment
Col Sgts G. Vayng, J. M'Coy, J. Thompson, C. Barnes; Sgt M. Rooney; Cpl W. Reilly; L/Cpl A. Pendridge; Pte R. McKenna

50th Regiment
Sgt Maj R. Foley; Col Sgt W. Turner; Sgt R. Newcombe; Ptes M. Hannan, J. Brennan, W. Cooney, L. Ward

55th Regiment
Col Sgts H. Hendrick, P. Pope; Sgts W. Spencer, W. Campion; L/Cpl W. M'Lachlin; Ptes J. Dunn, J. Wilson, J. Whelan, T. Johnstone

56th Regiment
Col Sgts W. Dibbs, J. Whittaker, J. Lord, L. Hogan; Pte J. Butler

57th Regiment
Col Sgts J. McCardle, J. Coughlin, J. Jones; Sgt J. Andrews; Cpl T. Connell; L/Cpls W. Kinnarney, T. Anderson; Pte J. Murray

62nd Regiment
Sgts W. Reilly, J. Warren; Ptes M. Brophy, J. McKie, T. Carney, J. McCarthy, J. McSharry; Drummer T. Finnigan

63rd Regiment
Sgt Maj R. Hughes; Col Sgts J. Ward, W. Morris, J. Brophy; Sgts A. Roberts, W. Ahern; Ptes J. McGowan, D. Sullivan

68th Regiment
Sgt Maj J. Gibbons; Sgts P. Delany, T. Watson; Cpls Donohue, P. Finns; Ptes J. Sims, W. Ferris, C. Ross, J. Mitchell

71st Regiment
Col Sgt J. Hughes; Ptes W. Don, R. Martin, A. Rattray, J. Cousins, J. Laughlin

72nd Regiment
Cpl A. Duncan; Ptes T. Alison, J. Harper, S. McNeish

77th Regiment
Col Sgt J. Toohey; L/Cpl W. Wilson; Ptes A. Wright, M. Charleston, W. M'Guire, J. Quinlan, Drummer T. McGill

79th Regiment
Col Sgt J. Spence, A. Goodbrand; Sergeants C. Campbell, W. Davie, W. Gunn, Ptes R. Bruce, J. Wilkie, J. Sloan

88th Regiment
Sgt Maj S. Conyngham; Col Sgts H. Kelly, M. Canty; Sgt J. Myers;

Cpl H. McKeon; Ptes H. Spellacy, T. Handley, B. M'Namara, M. Ryan; Drummer R. Grannon

89th Regiment
Sgt J. Grant; Cpl J. Tremwith, Ptes P. Kineally, D. Lenaghan, W. Heffernan

90th Regiment
Col Sgt C. Sanderson; Cpl H. Hill; Ptes J. Alexander, J. Lawless, T. Bayley, J. Goldsmith, M. Whelan; Bugler E. Flaxman

93rd Regiment
Col Sgt A. Knox; Sgts J. Kiddie, A. Crabtree; L/Cpl W. M'Kenzie; Ptes J. Cobb, J. Forbes, J. Leslie, J. Davidson, P. M'Kay

95th Regiment
Sgt N. Ormond; Cpls S. Webb, J. Linn; Ptes W. Harris, J. English, P. Gallagher, J. Jacques, P. Dooley, J. Cody

97th Regiment
Col Sgt F. Wedgeworth; Sgts P. Donellan, W. Newmann, Cpl A. Curran; Ptes H. Jackson, J. Cotterill, P. M'Miltry, W. Fitzgerald

Rifle Brigade
Sgt Majs J. Waller, R. Cornelius; Col Sgts C. Munro, D. Fisher, J. Hicks; Sgts T. Burge, J. Harrywood; Cpl J. Bradshaw; Ptes C. Dencer, M. Benn, M. M'Cormick, C. Frough, W. Eagle, J. King, P. M'Cann, H. Bailey, T. Davis, J. Green, B. M'Mahon

---

List of the Recipients of the Sardinian War Medal for the Crimea—all engraved by E. Nash, a Royal Mint sub-contractor, the medals having been struck in Turin

General Officers
Gen Sir G. Brown, Lt Gen Sir R. England; Maj Gens Sir H. Bentinck, Lord Rokeby, Sir J. Scarlett, Sir H. Jones, Sir W. Eyre, J. Dupuis

Staff
Lt Cols Hon Adrian Hope, E. B. Hamley; Brev Lt Cols G. W. Mayow, Hon L. Curzon, K. D. Mackenzie, Hugh Smith, J. E. Thackwell, R. L. Ross, L. Shadwell, A. M. Cathcart, J. V. Kirkland; Brev Majs V. Wing, E. Fellowes, J. Hackett, A. P. S. Wortley, Hon G. Elliott, W. Faussett, A. C. Snodgrass, Hon W. Colville, A. Garrett, F. A. Thesiger, R. Luard, R. L. Pearson, F. Hammersley, C. W. St Clair; Maj A. Pitcairn; Capts A. Ponsonby, H. C. Jervoise, Hon C. J. Keith, R. Swire, C. E. Mansfield, R. G. Ellison, W. Earle, H. H. Day, G. M. Stopford

4th Dragoon Guards
Lt Col T. W. M'Mahon; Brev Lt Col W. C. Forrest; Brev Maj F. R. Forster; Assistant Surgn W. Cattell; TSM J. Evans; L/Sgt J. Gamble

1st Dragoons
Col J. Yorke; Capt G. Campbell; Sgt J. Hill

2nd Dragoons
Col H. D. Griffith, Capt G. Buchanan; Sgt Maj J. Wilson

4th Light Dragoons
Col Lord George Paget; Brev Lt Col A. Lowe; Brev Maj R. Portal; TSM W. Waterson

6th Dragoons
Capt E. D. Hunt, Trumpeter J. Hardy

8th Hussars
Lt Col R. De Salis; Brev Maj E. Tomkinson; Trumpeter W. Wilson

10th Hussars
Col W. Parlby

11th Hussars
Lieut and Adjutant J. Yates; Sgt R. Davis

12th Lancers
Maj T. G. A. Oakes

13th Light Dragoons
Capt P. S. Smith; Cpl W. Gardiner

17th Lancers
Col J. Lawrenson; Cornet J. Duncan; Sgt A. Ranson

Royal Artillery
Brev Lt Cols J. C. Fortescue, C. H. Morris, S. E. Gordon, Hon E. T. Gage, C. S. Henry, H. J. Thomas; Maj F. B. Ward; Brev Majs P. G. Pipon, G. L. Tupper, C. H. Ingilby, H. P. Yates, J. F. Pennycuick, A. C. Hawkins, G. Shaw, E. Mowbray, W. Barry, J. Mitchell, G. Henry, J. Sinclair, L. Penn, E. Taddy, P. L'Estrange, R. Champion, W. Andrews, W. Le Mesurier; Lieuts B. Humphrey, Sir J. Campbell E. Ward, F. Anley, C. Browne, H. Maule, C. Roberts; Staff Surgn W. Perry; Assistant Surgn R. Bowen; TSM J. Beardsley; CSM J. Hamilton; Sgts J. Hamilton, S. Ewing, D. Dowling, G. Symonds, M. Hunter; Bombardier D. Cambridge, W. Ramsey, H. Collier; Gnrs and Drivers E. O'Brien, J. M'Garry, T. Arthur, J. Barrett, J. Death

Royal Engineers
Cols J. W. Gordon, F. E. Chapman; Lt Cols E. Stanton, J. Manners Browne; Majs H. W. Montague, F. C. Hassard, C. B. Ewart, F. H. De Vere; Lieuts W. O. Lennon, A. Leary, F. E. Pratt; Cpl W. Baker; Ptes A. M'Caughey, W. Tumble

Grenadier Guards
Col C. W. Ridley; Lt Col Lord Arthur Hay; Capts C. N. Sturt, H. W. Verschoyle, R. W. Hamilton; Col Sgt R. Minor; Pte T. Sharpe

Coldstream Guards
Lt Cols C. W. Strong, Lord A. FitzRoy; Brev Majs P. Crawley, Sir James Dunlop, J. A. Connolly; Sgt G. Haynes; L/Sgt F. File

Scots Fusilier Guards
Col E. Forestier Walker; Brev Majs Hon W. Coke, Hon A. E. Frazer; Capts S. J. Blane, J. Scott; Sgts J. McBain, J. Stewart

1st Regiment
Lt Col A. Montgomery; Brev Lt Cols Hon C. D. Plunkett, F. G. Urquhart; Maj W. J. Gillum; Capts W. F. Rudd, W. Cookworthy; Lieut F. H. Hope; Sgt Maj R. Henshall; Col Sgt W. M'Dowell; Pte G. Woodhouse

3rd Regiment
Col C. Van Straubenzee; Brev Maj G. Ambrose; Pte J. Fahey

4th Regiment
Lt Col J. J. Hort; Capt A. J. Sykes; Lieut J. Howley; Sgt J. M'Ardell; Pte T. Scannells

7th Regiment
Lt Col R. Y. Shipley; Brev Lt Col J. R. Heyland; Brev Maj H. R. Hibbert; Lieut W. Hope; Ptes W. Barrack, J. M'Guire

9th Regiment
Lt Col F. D. Lister; Capt W. Nugent; Sgt P. Donohue

14th Regiment
Col M. Barlow; Brev Lt Col Sir J. E. Alexander; Brev Maj W. C. Trevor; Capt J. G. Maycock; Sgt W. Hopkins

18th Regiment
Lt Col J. C. Kennedy; Brev Lieut Col F. S. Call; Lieut T. D. Baker; Pte J. Weir

19th Regiment
Lt Col R. Warden; Capts H. T. Uniacke, G. A. Warburton; Lieut and Adjutant T. Thompson; Sgt J. Sherlock; Pte J. Halloran

20th Regiment
Col F. Horn; Maj W. P. Radcliffe; Capt C. E. Parkinson; Lieut H. B. Vaughan; Col Sgt J. Whybrow; Pte P. Rowe

21st Regiment
Col. C. R. Sackville; Brev Maj G. Boldero; Capts H. King, R. Stephens, S. H. Clerke; Sgt Maj W. Fowler; Col Sgt R. Ellis

23rd Regiment
Col D. Lysons; Maj F. E. Drewe; Capt S. C. Millett; Lieut L. O'Conner; Cpls E. Luby, T. Symonds

28th Regiment
Col F. Adams; Lt Col R. Baumgartner; Brev Lt Col E. Hallewell; Maj T. Maunsell; Capts S. A. Messiter, T. L. Bell; Cpl J. M'Loughlin; Pte W. Gleeson

30th Regiment
Lt Col J. Mauleverer; Brev Lt Col T. Pakenham; Maj R. Dillon; Lieut and Adjutant G. Sanders; Sgt T. Shaw; Pte J. Andrews

31st Regiment
Col G. Staunton

33rd Regiment
Lt Col G. V. Mundy; Brev Lt Col J. E. Collings; Capt A. B. Wallis; Lieut R. H. De Montmorencey; Assistant Surgn T. Clarke; Ptes P. Leary, J. Bond

34th Regiment
Brev Lt Col J. Simpson; Brev Maj J. Jordan; Lieuts A. W. Boyce, F. Peel; Col Sgt J. Pratt; Cpl D.Coughlin

38th Regiment
Lt Col J. P. Sparkes; Brev Lt Col W. J. Loftus; Lieuts C. W. Gaynor, A. J. Ewen; Ptes P. McGuire, T. Reynolds

39th Regiment
Maj T. W. Hudson; Lieut and Adjutant T. W. Bennett; Pte J. M'Cluskey

41st Regiment
Lt Col R. Pratt; Majs G. Skipworth, H. S. Bush; Capt G. Peddie; Cpl W. Crawford; Pte P. Collins

42nd Regiment
Col D. A. Cameron; Lt Col A. Cameron; Capts H. Montgomery, Sir Peter Halkett; Col Sgt D. Dalgleish; Pte E. M'Millan

44th Regiment
Col Hon A. A. Spencer, Lt Col C. W. Staveley; Brev Lt Col W. M'Mahon; Brev Maj W. Fletcher; Capt R. Baille; Lieut W. A. Wood; Ptes W. Doole, W. Woodgate

46th Regiment
Col Sir Robert Garrett; Brev Lt Col C. F. Campbell; Capts N. Dunscombe, G. H. Knapp; Col Sgt P. Cullen; Pte P. Flinn

47th Regiment
Lt Col R. T. Farren; Brev Lt Col J. Villiers, J. H. Lowndes; Capts Hon B. M. Ward, H. J. Buchanan; Sgt W. Grant; Pte E. M'Mahon

48th Regiment
Cpt W. H. Cairnes; Sgt R. Batlin

49th Regiment
Lt Cols J. T. Grant, J. H. King; Capts G. K. Chatfield, W. Young; Surgn J. Davis; Sgt Maj R. Holden; Pte J. Gibbons

50th Regiment
Col R. Waddy; Lt Col J. L. Wilson; Brev Lt Col H. E. Weare; Maj E. G. Hibbert; Lieuts M. G. Clarke, J. Lamb; Ptes A. O'Leary, T. Reghan

55th Regiment
Col C. Warren; Lt Col A. Capel Cure; Lieuts W. B. Johnson, J. Scott; Sgt J. Meara; L/Sgt J. O'Donnell

57th Regiment
Lt Col J. A. Street; Brev Maj G. J. Forsyth; Lieut A. F. Slade, Drummer M. Norton; Pte J. Healy

62nd Regiment
Col C. Trollope; Lt Col W. L. Ingall; Brev Maj C. Cooch; Captain G. H. Wilkinson; Sgt J. Warren; Private J. Farrell

63rd Regiment
Lt Cols Hon R. A. Dalzell, C. E. Fairclough; Capt F. T. Paterson; Pte P Ceaton

68rd Regiment
Col H. Smith; Lt Col G. Macbeath; Lieut S. Grace; Lieut F. Saunderson; Ptes S. Burrows, J. Magner

71st Regiment
Capts F. J. Halkett, J. O. Wemyss; Ptes H. Gourley, J. Cathcart

72nd Regiment
Lt Col Parke

77th Regiment
Brev Lt Col G. H. Willis; Capt R. Willington; Assistant-Surgns R. Burton, A. Humfrey; Sgt R. Bushell; L/Cpl G. Brown

79th Regiment
Lt Cols J. Douglas, R. C. Taylor; Brev Lt Col R. Clephane; Capt H. H. Stevenson; Quarter-Master R. Jameson; Sgt J. Anderson; Pte W. Campbell

88th Regiment
Col H. Shirley; Lt Cols G. V. Maxwell, E. Vesey Brown; Brev Majs T. Gore, E. Maynard; Capt J. E. Riley; Lieut G. Priestly; Ptes J. Sullivan, W. Durwoode

89th Regiment
Lt Col C. Egerton; Majs R. B. Hawley, L. Skynner; Cpl P. Scott

90th Regiment
Brev Lt Col T. Smith; Brev Maj J. Perrin; Capt J. H. Wade; Sgt Maj A. Kirkland; Pte W. Smith

93rd Regiment
Lt Col W. B. Ainslie; Brev Lt Col J. A. Ewart; Capt J. Dalzell; Lieut R. A. Cooper; Col Sgt G. Allan; L/Cpl J. Robertson

95th Regiment
Lt Col A. T. Hayland; Brev Majs J. A. Raines, A. J. Macdonald; Capt B. C. Boothby; Col Sgt F. Cluney; Pte J. Keenan

97th Regiment
Maj F. Burton; Capt G. H. Ware; Lieut C. H. Brown; Sgts W. Kemmy, W. Moore

Rifle Brigade
Col W. S. Norcott; Lt Cols A. H. Horsford, A. Macdonell; Brev Lt Cols C. J. Woodford, Lord Alexander Russell, Brev Maj Hon James Stuart; Lieuts G. R. Saunders, F. W. Freemantle, J. C. Moore; Sgt J. Cherry; Cpls J. Rudling, T. Tarrant; Pte E. Tarvish

Royal Navy
Rear Admirals Sir J. Lushington, Hon Henry Keppel; Capts W. Peel, vc, T. S. Brock, W. Moorsom, J. J. Kennedy; Comdrs R. B. Oldfield, H. J. Raby, F. W. Gough, E. Hardinge, HSH Prince Victor of Hohenlohe; Lieuts W. N. Hewett, vc, J. C. Evered, A. J. Kennedy, J. E. Hunter, G. C. Sinclair; Midshipman C. A. Hayward; Surgns D. J.

Duigan, G. Mason; Engineer G. Murdoch; Assistant Payr M. G. Autey; Gnrs R. Rowe, G. G. Dunlop; Boatswains W. Guys, J. Sheppard, VC, J. Sullivan, VC; Carpenter J. Casey; Petty Officers J. Murdock, T. Dunning; Chief Gnr's Mate J. Cleverly

Royal Marines

Col T. Hurdle; Brev Col T. Holloway; Lt Col W. F. Hopkins; Brev Lt Col G. Alexander; Brev Majs W. H. March, G. B. Payne; Capts H. Timpson, C. J. Ellis; 1st Lieuts A. Douglas, RMA, H. J. Jull, RMA; A. Wolrige, C. J. Napier Sgt Maj G. White; Col Sgts E. Richards, T. Hatch, RMA; Sgt J. Prettyjohn, VC; Gnr J. Bull, RMA; Ptes J. Perry, J. Tozer, J. Hucknall

92 *Turkish Crimea Medals* 1855

Obverse	Map of the Crimea spread over the wheel of a cannon that is resting on the Russian flag. To the left are three cannon balls and a ramrod, to the right, an anchor and mortar. Issuing from behind the cannon are the four flags of the allies. The British medal: the Union Jack flies second from the right; in the exergue, 'CRIMEA 1855'. The French medal: the Tricolour flies second from the right; in the exergue, 'LA CRIMEE 1855'. The Sardinian medal: the Sardinian flag flies second from the right; in the exergue, 'LA CRIMEA 1855'.
Reverse	Enclosed within a wreath of laurel, the Sultan's cypher, below in Turkish script 'CRIMEA' and the year 1271 A.H. (1855 AD).
Size	36mm in diameter
Metal	Silver
Ribbon	Watered crimson with green edges. The original ribbon was 18mm wide, but medals were often altered so that the more normal 31mm width ribbon could be worn.
Suspension	Many and varied. The medals were originally issued with a small ring through which the ribbon was passed. These rings were generally removed and either a similar suspender to that of the Crimea Medal or one of the Indian medals fitted.
Naming	The medals were issued unnamed, but as many of the recipients had their British medals named privately, they must have had these done at the same time, as some are to be found named in similar ways.
Bars issued	Nil

The Sultan of Turkey issued medals to the British, French and Sardinian troops who had taken part in the war. The medals were of three different types and issued according to nationality. However, the ship carrying medals to Britain was wrecked and many British troops received a French or Sardinian issue instead.

Sardinian medals are seen which, one assumes, were made privately of purer silver content than any of the general issues, with excellent relief work, and the initials 'C.B.' With no date to go by, it is probable that these medals, which are of a slightly different size from the usual ones, were made at the instigation of certain officers who were disappointed with the workmanship of their originals. As the sizes were not the same, it would be safe to classify them as 'unofficial'. One cannot say who 'C.B.' was, how many medals were struck, or why the Sardinian issue was copied. This may have been because the instigator of the idea of having the original copied and improved upon had himself been awarded the more common Sardinian type, so could hardly wear a copy of a medal of which he had not been awarded the original.

Sardinian type medals of a superior quality are believed to have been produced by the firm of Hunt & Roskell; these medals are frequently found with a buckle on the ribbon stamped 'Hunt & Roskell'. It is interesting to note that this firm also produced insignia of the Order of the Bath and Turkish Orders of the period.

93 *Turkish General Service Medal*

Obverse   Sultan's cypher within a beaded circle; star and crescent above; on either side a flag, pennon and laurel branch.

Reverse   Twelve pointed star with a six pointed star at its centre; below a scroll inscribed 'Medal for Glory' in Turkish characters. Small six pointed star at 3 and 9 o'clock, another at 6 o'clock beneath the scroll with a laurel branch at either side.

Size   Circular medal 31mm in diameter

Metal   Gold and silver medals issued

Ribbon   Watered red with green edges

Suspension   Scroll bar suspension, or various types of ring fitting.

Awarded to British officers and men for services in conjunction with Turkish forces against the Russians. Most notably at Silistria (May/June 1854) and Giurgevo (July/August 1854).

> Medal awarded in gold to Colonel J. L. A. Simmons RE. Awarded in silver to Captain G. Bent RE and sixteen men of the 10th Company RE for their part in bridging the Danube at Giurgevo.
> Also awarded to Lieutenant H. C. Glyn, Midshipman Prince Ernest of Leiningen and up to thirty seamen for participating in bridge construction and in manning Turkish gunboats in the vicinity.
> British officers present at and surviving the Battle of Giurgevo (7th July 1854) are likely to have received this medal. They include General Cannon, Lieutenant Colonel Ogilvy, and Lieutenants J. Hinde, 26th Bengal NI and J. A. Ballard, Bombay Engineers.

94 *Turkish Medal for Silistria* 1854

Obverse   Within a beaded border, the Sultan's cypher surrounded by a wreath of laurel and oak.

Reverse   Within a beaded border, the Fortress of Silistria amongst hills, flags flying, Danube in the foreground. In the exergue on a scroll 'Silistria' and the year '1271 A.H.' (1854 A.D.) in Turkish script.

Size   Circular medal 36mm in diameter

Metal   Gold and silver medals issued

Ribbon   Watered red with green edges

Suspension   Variable

Naming   Issued unnamed

Granted by the Sultan for the Defence of the Fortress of Silistria 19th May-22nd June 1854. The Turkish garrison in Silistria under Mussa Pasha was surrounded by 30,000 Russians under Prince Paskievitch.

> Seven British officers were present in the garrison:
> Colonel (Later Field Marshal Sir) J. L. A. Simmons RE (gold medal);
> General Cannon HEI Company Service;
> Lieutenant Colonel Ogilvy;
> Lieutenants J. A. Ballard, Bombay Engineers, J Hinde 26th Bengal NI,
> Major C. Nasmyth;
> Captain Butler.

95 *Turkish Kars Medal* 1855

Obverse	Within a beaded border, the Sultan's cypher surrounded by a wreath of laurel and oak.
Reverse	Within a beaded border the town of Kars with citadel and flag flying on hill above. In the exergue the word 'Kars' and the year '1272 A.H.' (1855 A.D.) in Turkish script.
Size	Circular Medal 36mm in diameter
Metal	Gold and silver medals issued.
Ribbon	Watered red with green edges
Suspension	Variable
Naming	Issued unnamed

Silver medals were awarded, to Brigadier General W. F. Williams, Colonel H. A. Lake RE, Lieutenant C. C. Teesdale RA, Captain H. Langhorne Thompson, Humphrey Sandwith MD, C. T. Kean and other British officers for their services during the defence of Kars.

It was here that General Williams organized the Turkish garrison, 15,000 strong, to withstand a siege by 50,000 Russians, under General Mouravieff. After repeated assaults, all of which were repulsed, the garrison was compelled to surrender owing to an outbreak of cholera and famine. On accepting General Williams's surrender, Mouravieff made one of the nicest compliments ever paid to a vanquished foe. He said: 'General Williams, you have made a name in history; and posterit will stand amazed at the endurance, the courage, and the discipline which the siege has called forth in the remains of an army. Let us arrange a capitulation that will satisfy the demands of war without disgracing humanity.'

General Williams was subsequently created a baronet with the title of Sir William Fenwick Williams of Kars. His ADC, Lieutenant C. C. Teesdale RA, was awarded the Victoria Cross for conspicuous gallantry in rallying the Turks at a critical moment. He was also personally thanked by General Mouravieff for preventing the Turks from butchering wounded Russians.

96 *Indian Mutiny Medal* 1857-1858

Obverse	Diademed head of Queen Victoria with the legend 'VICTORIA REGINA'.
Reverse	A standing helmeted figure of Britannia holding a wreath in her outstretched right hand and over her left arm is the Union Shield. Behind her is the British Lion and above the word 'INDIA'. In the exergue are the two dates '1857-1858'.
Size	36mm diameter
Metal	Silver
Ribbon	32mm wide. White with two 6mm scarlet stripes.
Suspension	A cusped swivel suspension bar.
Designers	Obverse—W. Wyon, RA; Reverse—L. C. Wyon.
Naming	The recipient's name and regiment, or ship, is indented in roman capitals.
Bars issued	Five—Delhi, Defence of Lucknow, Relief of Lucknow, Lucknow and Central India. These bars are fish-tailed and separated from the suspender and each other by rosettes. Bars should read downwards.

This medal was sanctioned by General Order No. 363 dated 18th August, 1858, and No. 733 of 1859, to the troops engaged against the mutineers. General Order No. 771 of 1868 (note the lapse of time) extended the award to all persons who had borne arms or had been under fire.

The latter order may account for the large number of these medals, the last of the Honourable East India Company's to be found without bars from the total of 290,000 awarded.

On January 21st, 1859, the Government of India sanctioned the reissue of medals gratis to all officers and men who had lost their awards during the Mutiny. This is an important point to bear in mind when considering war medals issued prior to the Mutiny, as re-issues are not generally considered as valuable as originals.

Indian Mutiny

The issuing of greased cartridges to the native soldiers was no more the only cause of the Indian Mutiny than the assassination of the Austrian Archduke Ferdinand, at Sarajevo in July, 1914, was the sole reason for the First World War, 1914-18. Both these events were enlarged upon and then used in such a way that only the most gullible person would believe that they, and they only, were the sole causes of the catastrophes that followed.

Trouble in India had been brewing for some time. Serious unrest started after the annexation of the provinces of Oudh and the Punjab in 1856, because the native princes feared that they would lose their territories and their thrones.

In July, 1855, there was a mutiny of the Sonthals, a tribe of Northern India, which was not suppressed until May, 1856.

On the 7th February, 1856, the Province of Oudh (or Oude) was annexed. The King and Queen of Oudh went to London to appeal against this annexation, but to no avail. It is certain that when he returned to India, embittered by what had happened, the King fomented trouble and kindled a hatred against the British presence in the country and the British rule in particular.

In March, 1857, seven companies of Bengal Native Infantry mutinied at Barrackpore. A rumour spread amongst the sepoys that they were all going to be Christianized and another that a new type of ammunition was going to be introduced which required greasing with cow or pig fat. The seeds for the coming general outbreak were now well sown.

On the 10th of May 1857, the sepoys mutinied at Meerut; the first soldier killed being Colonel Finnis, the commanding officer of the 11th Bengal Native Infantry. Lack of effective British action in suppressing the outbreak allowed the mutineers to escape to Delhi where they were joined by other native regiments. A general slaughter of Europeans ensued and the rebels proclaimed the Great Mogul, Bahadur Shah, their ruler. As word of the rebellion spread, the native Bengal army broke into open revolt.

The Commander-in-Chief, General George Anson, collected available troops and began to march on Delhi, but he died of cholera on 27th May. He was succeeded by Major-General Sir Henry Barnard. After several actions culminating in the Battle of Badli-ke-Serai (8th June), the British army arrived before Delhi. On 5th July, Barnard died of cholera and was briefly succeeded by General Reed and, on the 17th of July, by Brigadier General Archdale Wilson. On 14th September, an assault was made on the city. Brigadier General John Nicholson, commanding the attack, was killed as stubborn resistance was encountered. Not until the 20th of September was the capture complete. The unfortunate Bahadur Shah was captured, and his sons shot.

At Cawnpore the British garrison under Major-General Sir Hugh Wheeler surrendered to the mutineers under Nana Sahib on the 26th of June after a gruelling three week siege. The garrison and their families were promised safe conduct to Allahabad, but on the 27th as the troops began to embark on board boats for the journey down the Ganges, they were treacherously attacked and slain and the women and children imprisoned.

At Lucknow, Sir Henry Lawrence had most ably prepared for the defence of the Residency against an ever increasing rebel presence. However, on the 30th of June, he was rashly persuaded to advance against a large force of rebels at Chinhut and was badly defeated. The rebels closed in and the siege began in earnest. On 2nd July, Lawrence was mortally wounded and Brigadier John Inglis took command of the garrison.

A small British force under Brigadier General Sir Henry Havelock moved up from Allahabad on the 7th of July to attempt to relieve Lucknow. With a meagre 1,500 men, he defeated the forces of Nana Sahib at Fatehpur (12th July) Aong and Panda Nandi (15th July) and Cawnpore (16th July). Havelock entered Cawnpore the next day only to find that the captured British women and children had been butchered.

His small force weakened by losses through enemy action and disease, Havelock was compelled to await reinforcements before continuing his advance on Lucknow. These arrived under Major-General Sir James Outram and increased his command to 3,000 men. Although his

superior, Outram put aside his military rank and agreed to serve as a volunteer under Havelock so as to give him the honour of the relief. The advance on Lucknow was resumed and on 25th September, Havelock's column broke through to the garrison. The loss was heavy with 535 men killed or wounded. Too weak to withdraw, Outram then took command of the augmented but still besieged garrison.

A second relief being necessary, another column under the Commander-in-Chief Sir Colin Campbell advanced on Lucknow. Combining with the forces of General Hope Grant and Captain Peel RN at the Alum Bagh, Campbell advanced into the city on 14th November. On the 16th, the strongly defended Secundra Bagh was stormed. The following day attacks by both Campbell and Havelock dislodged the remaining rebels, separating the two British forces. By the 23rd, the Residency was successfully evacuated; an achievement marred only by the death of Havelock on the 24th.

Leaving Outram with a force to hold the Alum Bagh, Campbell withdrew from Lucknow and proceeded to Cawnpore. There, on the 6th of December, he defeated the rebels under Tantia Topi. On 2nd March 1858, an augmented force under Campbell returned to the Alum Bagh and from there proceeded to systematically reduce rebel-held Lucknow. By the 21st of March, the city had been taken.

A force under Major-General Sir Hugh Rose operated against the rebels in Central India. The fort of Rathghur was captured (27th January, 1858) and the rebels defeated at Barodia (31st January) prior to the relief of Saugor on the 3rd of February. The rebel stronghold of Jhansi was then captured (5th April) after a short siege. Whilst in progress, Rose, with 1,500 men, defeated Tantia Topi with 22,000 at Betwa on the 1st of April.

Major-General Whitlock, with a column from the Madras Presidency defeated the rebels at Banda (19th April).

Advancing towards the rebel-held Kalpi, Rose defeated Tantia at Kunch (7th May) and a further victory at Gowlowlee (22nd May) was followed by the capture of Kalpi on the 23rd.

Tantia Topi, the Rhani of Jhansi and other leaders then descended upon Gwalior. The Maharajah fought them at Morar but was defeated and Gwalior and it's treasures fell to the rebels. Rose advanced on Gwalior and defeated the rebels at Kotah-ke-Serai (17 June) during which the Rhani was killed. Gwalior was recaptured on the 20th of June.

With the fall of Gwalior, the Great Mutiny was virtually over although small scale actions continued into 1859 against Tantia Topi and others. Tantia was finally captured on the 7th of April and hanged on the 18th of April 1859.

A List of Indian Regiments involved in the Mutiny

Bengal Native Infantry

1st Regiment
Mutinied at Cawnpore on the 5th of June, 1857, less three companies, stationed at Banda, who mutinied on the 14th of June, 1857.
2nd Regiment
Disarmed at Barrackpore on the 14th of June, 1857.
3rd Regiment
Mutinied at Phillour on the 8th of June, 1857.
4th Regiment
Disarmed at Kangra; Disbanded 1861.
5th Regiment
Disarmed at Umballah.
6th Regiment
Mutinied at Allahabad on the 6th of June, 1857.
7th Regiment
Mutinied at Dinapore on the 25th of July, 1857.
8th Regiment
Mutinied at Dinapore on the 25th of July, 1857.
9th Regiment
Mutinied 21st-23rd of May, 1857. Headquarters at Allygurh with detachments at Mynpoorie, Etahwah and Boolundshuhur.
10th Regiment
Mutinied at Futtehgurh on the 18th of June, 1857.
11th Regiment
Mutinied at Meerut on the 10th of May, 1857.
12th Regiment
The Left Wing mutinied at Jhansi on the 5th and 6th of June, 1857.

The Right Wing mutinied at Mowgong on the 9th of June 1857.

13th Regiment
Part of the Regt. mutinied at Lucknow on the 30th of May, 1857, the bulk remained loyal and helped defend the Residency until the final relief.

14th Regiment
Mutinied at Jhelum on the 7th of July, 1857.

15th Regiment
Mutinied at Nasiribad on the 28th of May, 1857.

16th Regiment
Disarmed at Mean-Meer and disbanded for disaffection May, 1857.

17th Regiment
Mutinied at Azimgarh on the 3rd of June, 1857.

18th Regiment
Mutinied at Bareilly on the 31st of May, 1857.

19th Regiment
Disbanded for disaffection on the 31st of March, 1857. Barrackpore.

20th Regiment
Mutinied at Meerut on the 10th of May, 1857.

21st Regiment
Disarmed at Peshawar, Remained loyal.

22nd Regiment
Mutinied at Faizabad on the 7th of June, 1857.

23rd Regiment
Mutinied at Mhow on the 1st of July, 1857.

24th Regiment
Disarmed and disbanded at Fort Mackeson, Peshawar May, 1857.

25th Regiment
Disbanded for disaffection.

26th Regiment
Disarmed for disaffection at Mean-Meer on the 13th of May, 1857.

27th Regiment
Disarmed and disbanded for disaffection at Peshawar on the 29th of May, 1857.

28th Regiment
Mutinied at Shahjehanpore on the 31st of May, 1857.

29th Regiment
Mutinied at Moradabad on the 3rd of June, 1857.

30th Regiment
Mutinied at Nasiribad on the 28th of May, 1857.

31st Regiment
Remained loyal throughout and saw action against the mutineers of other Regt's.

32nd Regiment
Two companies mutinied at Deogarh on the 9th of October, 1857. The remainder stayed loyal.

33rd Regiment
Disarmed at Phillour on the 25th of June, 1857. The bulk of the Regt. having remained loyal they were re-armed at Jullundur on the 17th of January, 1859.

34th Regiment
Seven companies of the Regt. were disbanded at Barrackpore on the 6th of May, 1857. The three remaining companies mutinied at Chittagong on the 18th of November, 1859.

35th Regiment
Disarmed and disbanded for disaffection, Phillour, 25th of June, 1857.

36th Regiment
Mutinied at Jullundur on the 7th of June, 1857.

37th Regiment
Mutinied at Benares on the 4th of June, 1857.

38th Regiment
Mutinied at Delhi on the 11th of May, 1857.

39th Regiment
Disbanded for disaffection, Jhelum 1857.

40th Regiment
Mutinied at Dinapore on the 25th of July, 1857.

41st Regiment
Mutinied at Seetapore on the 3rd of June, 1857. Some officers (11) and some bandsmen made their way to Lucknow and helped defend the Residency until relieved by Sir C. Campbell. 9 officers and 10 bandsmen survived the siege.

42nd Regiment
Part mutinied at Saugor on the 1st of July, 1857. Part remained loyal and the Regt. was not disbanded.

43rd Regiment
Disarmed at Barrackpore on the 14th of June, 1857. They remained faithful and the Regt. was not disarmed.

44th Regiment
Mutinied at Agra on the 31st of May, 1857.

45th Regiment
Mutinied at Ferozepore on the 14th of May, 1857.

46th Regiment
Mutinied at Sealkote on the 9th of July, 1857.

47th Regiment
Remained faithful and volunteered for service in China, where they arrived in May, 1858.

48th Regiment
Mutinied at Lucknow on the 30th of May, 1857. Some 50 other ranks remained faithful and with the officers helped defend the Residency until relieved by Sir C. Campbell

49th Regiment
Disarmed at Mean-Meer on the 13th of May, 1857, and disbanded.

50th Regiment
Mutinied at Nagode on the 27th of August, 1857.

51st Regiment
Mutinied at Peshawar on the 22nd of May, 1857.

52nd Regiment
Mutinied at Jubbulpore on the 18th of September, 1857.

53rd Regiment
Mutinied at Cawnpore on the 5th of June, 1857.

54th Regiment
Mutinied at Delhi on the 11th of May, 1857.

55th Regiment
Mutinied at Hoti-Mardan on the 25th of May, 1857.

56th Regiment
Mutinied at Cawnpore on the 5th of June, 1857.

57th Regiment
Mutinied at Ferozepore on the 14th of May, 1857.

58th Regiment
Disarmed at Rawalpindi, July, 1857. Disbanded 1861.

59th Regiment
Disarmed at Amritsar on the 9th of July, 1857. Stayed loyal.

60th Regiment
Mutinied at Rhotak on the 8th of June, 1857.

61st Regiment
Mutinied at Jullundur on the 7th of June, 1857.

62nd Regiment
Mutinied at Mooltan on the 10th of June, 1857.

63rd Regiment
Disarmed at Berhampore on the 1st of August. Stayed loyal and were not disbanded.

64th Regiment
Mutinied at Peshawar, June, 1857

65th Regiment
Disarmed at Ghazeepore. Remained faithful and volunteered for service in China, where they arrived in May, 1858.

66th Regiment
Remained faithful. Saw action against mutineers and other Regiment's.

67th Regiment
Mutinied at Agra on the 31st of May, 1857.

68th Regiment
Mutinied at Bareilly on the 31st of May, 1857.

69th Regiment
Mutinied at Mooltan on the 10th of June, 1857.

70th Regiment
Disarmed at Barrackpore on the 14th of June, 1857. Remained faithful and volunteered to serve in China, where they arrived in February, 1858.

71st Regiment
Mutinied at Lucknow on the 30th of May, 1857. Some 50 Natives remained loyal and helped defend the Residency until relieved by Sir C. Campbell.

72nd Regiment
Mutinied at Neemuch on the 3rd of June, 1857.

73rd Regiment
Part mutinied at Pacca on the 22nd of November, 1857. The Regt. was not disbanded until 1861.

74th Regt.
Mutinied at Delhi on the 11th of May, 1857.

Bengal Light Cavalry

1st Regiment
The Left Wing mutinied at Neemuch on the 3rd of June, 1857. The Right Wing mutinied at Mhow on the 1st of July, 1857.
2nd Regiment
Mutinied at Cawnpore on the 5th of June, 1857.
3rd Regiment
Mutinied at Meerut on the 10th of May, 1857.
4th Regiment
Disbanded in 1858 for disaffection.
5th Regiment
Disarmed at Peshawar on the 22nd of May, 1857, disbanded for disaffection, 1858.
6th Regiment
Mutinied at Jullundur on the 7th of June, 1857.
7th Regiment
Mutinied at Lucknow on the 30th of May, 1857. About 20 Natives remained loyal and helped defend the Residency until relieved by Sir C. Campbell.
8th Regiment
Disarmed at Mean-Meer on the 13th of May, 1857, disbanded for disaffection, 1858.
9th Regiment
One Wing of the Regt. mutinied at Sealkote on the 9th of July, 1857, the remainder of the Regt. was part of Nicholson's Moveable Column, and was disarmed when Nicholson heard of the Sealkote mutiny. (9th of July)
10th Regiment
Mutinied at Ferozepore, 1857.

On the 2nd August, 1858, the authority of the Honourable East India Company was transferred to the Crown, but it was not until the 1st January, 1877, that Queen Victoria was proclaimed Kaisar-i-Hind, Empress of India, by simultaneous proclamations in Delhi, Calcutta, Madras and Bombay.

A total of one hundred and eighty-two Victoria Crosses were awarded for the campaign.

ROYAL NAVAL BRIGADE PARTICIPATION

In May, 1857, the news reached Calcutta of the disasters at Delhi and Meerut, whereupon the Governor-General, Lord Canning, immediately asked for help.

At this time Lord Elgin was on his way to China with reinforcements for the campaign which had started out there. Whist waiting at Hong-Kong he heard of Lord Canning's predicament and, in agreement with Admiral Sir Michael Seymour, it was decided that the three ships HMS *Sanspareil* (Captain Key), HMS *Shannon* (Captain Peel) and HMS *Pearl* (Captain Sotheby) should be dispatched to Calcutta at once.

On arrival at Calcutta, Captain Key landed his Marines at Fort William, whilst Captain William Peel, son of Sir William Peel, founder of the Police Force, formed a naval brigade of 408 seamen and marines from his crew. He also prepared for use ashore the following artillery pieces which were to prove so useful later on: six 68-pdrs., two 8in. howitzers, eight 24-pdrs., two small guns and eight rocket tubes.

On the 13th August, 1857, the brigade started on its march to Allahabad, where it was joined on the 20th October by a contingent of 124 volunteers, under Lieutenant Vaughan, from the merchant shipping lying at Calcutta. It remained in Allahabad until the 28th October, when it left for Cawnpore, being joined on the way by Colonel Powell and part of the 53rd Regiment. The brigade reached Futtehpore on the 31st. Here it was joined by a detachment of the 93rd Highlanders.

On the 1st November, the force attacked the mutineers at Kudjna, where Colonel Powell was killed and Captain Peel assumed command. The mutineers were defeated and the advance to Lucknow was continued. It is worth noting that this must be one of the very rare occasions in which a naval officer has commanded a mixed force in action in the field.

Reaching the Alum Bagh on the 15th November, the brigade came under the command of Sir Colin Campbell, who ordered it to start bombarding the defences, part of which consisted of the Shah Nujeef, a mosque surrounded by a garden and a high wall, which had been heavily reinforced and defended. This mosque was to be the particular task of the Naval Brigade, which earned four Victoria Crosses in the

process of its capture. The recipients were Lieutenant Thomas Jones, Lieutenant Nowell Salmon, John Harrison and Captain of Foretop William Hall, who was a negro from Nova Scotia.

Lieutenant Salmon earned his V.C. for sniping from a tree which he had climbed to get a view over the wall, Whilst so employed he was kept supplied with loaded rifles by a private of the 93rd.

In these days when the mention of the words Combined Operations conjures up visions of fleets of landing craft, bombarding squadrons, air cover and all the paraphernalia of modern war, one likes to think of this sailor, up a tree, 500 miles from the nearest sea, with his ghillie below, giving a very good example of a Combined Operation on the 16th November, 1857!

After the relief of Lucknow the brigade took part in the relief of Cawnpore.

The *Pearl* Brigade under Captain Sotheby, RN, 253 strong, operated under Brigadier Rowcroft. It fought in no fewer than ten battles during its existence of fifteen months.

Members of the Naval Brigade from HMS *Shannon* could get two bars—namely, Lucknow and Relief of Lucknow. The Brigade from HMS *Pearl* as a complete brigade received no bars, though perhaps some members of it received the one for Lucknow.

The awards to the *Shannon* and *Pearl* Brigades were as follows:

Ships	Bars	Officers	Other Ranks
Shannon	Relief of Lucknow and Lucknow	15	140
Shannon	Relief of Lucknow	2	26
Shannon	Lucknow	13	271
Shannon	Nil	3	63
Pearl	Nil	23	230
		56	730

Both Brigades suffered heavy casualties. Out of a total force of 533 officers and men landed from *Shannon,* 4 officers and 100 men were killed or died from wounds or disease. 1 officer and 17 men were later invalided, and a further 7 officers and 51 men were wounded in action. The *Pearl's* Brigade which consisted of 253 officers and men, lost 1 officer and 17 men killed or died, with a further 16 men wounded in action.

The maximum number of bars carried on one medal was four. Less than 200 of these four-bar medals were awarded to the 3rd Company Bengal Artillery, including 85 to natives serving in the unit.

The 9th Lancers were the only British Regiment to have been awarded as many as three bars.

The following units were in India during the period of the Mutiny, 10th May, 1857-30th December, 1858, and many of their members received a medal without a bar:

CAVALRY: 1, 2 (69), 3, 6 (495), 7 Dragoon Guards; 6 Dragoons; 7 (103), 8, 14 (689) Hussars; 9 (95), 12 (90), 17 Lancers; 4 European Light Cavalry.

ARTILLERY: 3, 4 and 5 Bns.; Field Bty; 6, 8 and 14 Bn. R.H.A.: D and E Troops. Bengal Artillery: 1 and 2 Cos. 1st Bn., 1 and 3 Cos. 2nd Bn., 1, 2, 3 and 4 Cos. 3rd Bn., 2, 3 and 4 Cos. 4th Bn., 1, 2 and 4 Cos. 5th Bn., 1, 2 and 4 Cos. 6th Bn. Bengal Horse Artillery: 1 and 2 Troops, 1st Bde., 1 and 3 Troops, 3rd Bde. Madras Horse Artillery: B Troop. Nagpore Irregular Force Artillery; Hyderabad Contingent—2nd Co. Artillery; Engineers; Medical Services; Commissariat Dept.; Ordnance Dept., 2nd Btn. Military Train; Civil Service; Chaplains.

INFANTRY: 1/4 (20?), 1/5 (159), 1/6, 8 (310), 1/10 (236), 1/13 (980), 1/20, 1/23, 1/24 (281), 27 (925), 28, 29 (326), 32 (267 with no bar), 33, 34 (196), 35 (471), 37, 38 (501), 42 (54), 43 (755), 51, 52 (44), 53 (337), 54, 56 (22), 1/60 (332), 2/60 (363), 3/60, 61 (79), 64 (600), 66, 67, 69, 70 (634), 71 (716), 72, 73, 74 (444), 75 (101), 78 (121), 79 (135), 80 (811), 81 (960), 82, 83, 84 (167), 86, 87 (1,073), 88 (134), 89 (80), 90 (74), 92 (428), 93, 94, 95, 97 (90), 98, 99 Foot; 2nd and 3rd Bns. Rifle Brigade; 1 Bengal Fusiliers (100); 1 Madras European Regt.; 1 Bombay Fusiliers; 2 Bengal Fusiliers; 2 Madras European Light Infantry; 2 Bombay European Regt. (271); 3 Bengal European Infantry (1,005); 3 Madras European Regt. (150); 3 Bombay European Regt.

NATIVE AND LOCAL UNITS: Bengal Light Cavalry; 3rd Madras

Cavalry: 3, 5 and 7th. Bombay Light Cavalry: 2 and 3rd. Bengal Native Infantry: 3, 6, 12, 18, 21, 32, 36, 37, 38, 44, 47, 58, 59, 61, 62, 63, 66, 67, 73 and 74th. Madras Native Infantry: 17, 24, 26, 28, 33 and 35th. Bombay Native Infantry: 4, 24, 26 and 28th. Hyderabad Contingent: 4, 5 and 6 Infantry. Punjab Units: 4th Punjab Rifles, 16 and 23rd Punjab Infantry, 2nd Sikh Cavalry, 1st Sikh Infantry. Darjeeling Sappers and Miners; Belooch Btn.; Golconda Local Corps; 1st Khandeesh Bheel Corps; 2nd Khandeesh Bheel Corps; Kumaon Levy; Kuppoorthulla Contingent; Musseeree Gurkha Btn; Sawunt and Warree Local Corps; Sylhet Lt. Infantry; Behar and Shahabad Police; Dumoh Military Police; Jubbulpore Police Btn.; 11th Regt. Oudh Police; Alexanders Horse; Benares Horse; Bengal Yeomanry Cavalry; 2nd Troop Bengal Yeomanry Cavalry; Jat Horse Yeomanry; Maynes Horse; Mooltanee Regt. of Cavalry; Mysore Horse; Nagpore Irregular Cavalry; 1st Nagpore Irregular Cavalry; Pathan Horse; Poona Irregular Horse; Rohilcund Horse; Sind Irregular Horse; 1st Regt. South Mahratta Horse; Volunteer Cavalry.

NAVAL BRIGADES: HMS *Shannon* (Captain Peel); HMS *Pearl* (Captain Sotheby).

INDIAN NAVAL BRIGADE, including many small river vessels: *Berhampooter, Calcutta, Coromandel, Dallah, Damoodah, Diana, Enterprise, Fire Queen, Ganges, Hoorungotta, Jumna, Koladyne, Lord Wm. Bentinck, Loorma, Mahanuddy, Megna, Myoo, Nemesis, Nerbuddah, Phlegathon, Pluto, Prosperine, Punjab, Sanspareil, Sesostris, Soornia, Tenasserim, Thames* and *Zenobia*.

Delhi 30th May-14th September, 1857

This bar was awarded to the troops employed in the recapture of the city. The relieving forces, owing to illness and death, had no fewer than four commanders between 14th May and 14th September, 1857. They were General Sir George Anson, Major-General Sir Henry Barnard, General Reed, and finally Brigadier-General Archdale Wilson.

Regiments present: 6 Dragoon Guards (223), 7(1), 8 Hussars (13); 9 Lancers (533); 1, 2, 5 Punjab Cavalry; 4 Irregular Horse; Guides Cavalry; Multan Horse; 1/1, 2/1, 5/1, 2/3, 3/3 Bengal H.A.; 3/1, 3/3, 2/4, 3/4, 4/4, 4/6, Bengal F.A.; Peshawar Mountain Train; Bengal Engineers; Bengal Sappers and Miners (129); 8 (636), 52 (716), 1/60 (680), 61 (871), 75 (798) Foot; 1 (763), 2 (748) Bengal Fusiliers; 1, 2, 4, 24 Punjab N.I.; 4 Sikh Infantry; 20 and 60 Bengal NI; 6th Bengal Light Cavalry; Guides Infantry; a battalion of each of the Sirmoor, Kumaon and 1 Balooch NI; Towana Horse; Jummoo Contingent.

Defence of Lucknow 29th June-22nd November, 1857

The medals to the original defenders, under Sir Henry Lawrence, and after his death under Major-General Sir John Inglis, are the most prized. The first relief force under Sir Henry Havelock also received this bar. A few civilians received medals with this bar.

Original Defenders: These numbered 1,538 soldiers and 160 civilians who were co-opted to serve. 4/1 Bengal FA; 32 Foot (19 officers and 517 other ranks); 84 Foot (50); 7 Bengal Lt. Cav.; Oudh Irregular units: 1, 2 and 3 Cavalry, 1, 4, 5, 7, 9 and 10 Infantry, 3rd Horse Bt. Arty.; and in excess of 1,000 natives of the 13, 15, 41, 48, 71 NI.

1st Relief Force under Sir Henry Havelock: 13 Irregular Cavalry (95); Volunteer Cavalry composed of civilians (20); 3/8 RA; 2/3 Bengal FA; 1/5 (370), 64 (137), 78 (640), 84 (190), 90 (440) Foot; 1 Madras Fusiliers (1 Royal Dublin Fusiliers) (376); 14 Ferozepore Sikhs (448); Military Train; Barrow's Vol. Cavalry.

Relief of Lucknow November, 1857

This bar was awarded to the troops under Sir Colin Campbell engaged in the relief of the city, who were composed as follows:

Cavalry: 8th Hussars (19); 9 Lancers (330); 1, 2, 5 Native Cavalry; Hodson's Horse.

Artillery: 4/5, 5/13, 6/13 RA; 1/1, 2/3, Bengal HA, 3/1, 1/5, 3/5 Bengal FA; E. Tp. Madras HA Peshawar Mountain Train.

Engineers: One Company RE and two companies of Bengal and Punjab Sappers and Miners.

Infantry: 5 (208, 16 as single bars); 8 (331); 23 (wing); 32nd L.I. (23); 53 (wing 73); 64 (183); 75, 78 (358); 82 (two companies), 84 (5 Officers and 23 Other Ranks); 90 (419, 47 as singles); 93 (963 including 113 as singles) Foot; 1 Madras Fusiliers (1 Royal Dublin Fusiliers), 1 Bengal Europeans (1 Royal Munster Fusiliers 414); 2, 4 Punjab NI; Regt. of Ferozepore; 57 Bengal NI.

Naval Brigade from HMS *Shannon* and HEIC ship *Calcutta*.

Seventeen medals with the bar were awarded to the Royal Marine Artillery.

Lucknow November, 1857-March, 1858

This bar was awarded to the troops under Sir Colin Campbell who took part in the final operations which resulted in the capture of the city.

Cavalry: 2 Dragoon Guards (464); 7 Hussars (435); 8 Hussars (6); 9 Lancers (462, 73 as single bars); 1, 2, 5 Punjab Cavalry; 1, 2 Hodson's Horse; Benares Horse; Barrow's Vol. Cavalry; 1, 3 Sikh Cavalry.

Artillery: E and F Tps.; 8/2, 3/8, 6/11, 5/12, 5/13, 6/13, 3/14 RA; 1/1, 2/1, 2/3, 3/3 Bengal HA; 4/1, 2/3, 1/5, 3/5, 4/5 Bengal FA; A/4 Madras FA.

Engineers: Royal Engineers; Bengal and Madras Sappers and Miners.

Infantry: 5 (449), 1/8, 10 (719), 20 (714), 23, 32, 34 (586), 38 (993), 42 (893), 53 (386), 75 (12), 78 (550), 79 (846), 82, 84, 90 (683), 93 (850), 97 (657) Foot; 2 and 3 Bns. The Rifle Brigade; 1 Bengal Fusiliers (103) (1 Royal Munster Fusiliers); 1 Madras Fusiliers (1 Royal Dublin Fusiliers); 2, 4, 24 Punjab NI; 32 Bengal NI; six battalions of Gurkhas; 27 Madras NI.

Military Train.

Naval Brigade from HMS *Shannon*.

Central India January-June, 1858

This bar was awarded to those who served under Major-General Sir Hugh Rose against Jhansi, Calpee and Gwalior, and those who served with Major-General Roberts in the Rajpatana Field Force, and Major-General Whitlock of the Madras Column, between January and June, 1858.

Cavalry: 8 (511), 14 Hussars; 12 (387), 17 Lancers; 3 Sikh Cavalry: 4, 6, Madras Light Cavalry; 1, 2, 3, 4 Hyderabad Contingent Cavalry; 1, 2, 3 Bombay Light Cavalry; Meades Horse.

Artillery: 5/14, 6/14, 7/14 RA; 3/1, 1/4, 2/6 Bengal FA; 1, 2, 3 Bombay HA; 1/2, 4/2, 2 and 4 Reserve Cos., 3/3 Bombay FA; A and E Trps. Madras HA; A/4, B/4 Madras FA; Peshawar Mountain Train.

Engineers: Royal Engineers; Bombay and Madras Sappers and Miners.

Military Train.

Infantry: 67, 70 (a detachment only), 71 (119), 72 (637), 80 (153), 83, 84, 86, 88 (874), 95 (752) Foot; 2 and 3 Rifle Brigade (detachments); 3 Madras European Regiment (806) (2 Royal Inniskilling Fusiliers); 3 Bombay European Regiment (689) (2 The Prince of Wales's Leinster Regiment); 13, 15 Bengal NI; 10, 12, 13, 19, 24, 25 Bombay NI; Sikh Police, Camel Corps; Rajpootana Field Force; 1, 10, 19, 25, 27 and 50 Madras NI; 3rd Hyderabad Infantry; 22 Punjab Infantry.

97 *Second China War Medal* 1856-1863

Obverse	The diademed head of Queen Victoria and the legend 'VICTORIA REGINA'.
Reverse	A collection of war trophies with an oval shield, with the Royal Arms in the centre, all positioned under a palm tree. Above is the legend 'ARMIS EXPOSCERE PACEM'. In the exergue is the word 'CHINA'.
Size	36mm diameter
Metal	Silver
Ribbon	32mm wide. A variant had five equally spaced stripes, reading from the left: blue, yellow, red, white and green representing colours of the Chinese flag. The adopted ribbon was crimson with yellow edges.
Suspension	Exactly the same as that for the Mutiny Medal, namely a cusped swivel suspension bar.
Designer	Wm. Wyon RA
Naming	The medals issued to the Royal Navy were unnamed; a few of those to the Marines and Indian Marine are, however, to be found named as those to the Army, in neat indented roman capitals.
Bars issued	Six—China 1842, Fatshan 1857, Canton 1857, Taku Forts 1858, Taku Forts 1860, Pekin 1860.

There is one five-bar medal and that was awarded to Thomas Cole, RMA, HMS *Cruiser* (although the roll only supports four bars), who received all the bars except that for China, 1842. There are a number of made up five-bar medals on the market which are usually referred to as either unnamed medals to the Royal Navy or Royal Mint specimens.

The medal is often found without bars, so we give a complete list of all Naval and Military forces present during the period covered for the award—ie, 25th May, 1857, to 13th October, 1860—as approved by Royal Warrant on 6th March, 1861.

Regiments present: two squadrons 1st Dragoon Guards (3 issued without bars); 11, 19 Bengal Cavalry; 4/2, 1/4, 2/4, 6/12 (9), 3/13, 4/13, 7/14, 8/14 Batteries RA; A/5 Madras Artillery; 1/5 Supplemental Artillery and a Mountain Train; RE; 'A' and 'K' Companies QO Madras Sappers and Miners; 2/1 (15 without bar), 1/2 (22 without bar), 1/3, 2/31 (10 without bar), 44 (36), 59, 2/60, 67 (7 without bar), 99 Foot; 15, 23 Sikhs; 19, 20, 22, 27 (37) Punjab NI; 7, 10, 11 Bengal NI; two officers and forty men of the 38 Madras NI; 3, 5 Bombay NI; Military Train; Medical Staff Corps. Fifteen members of the British Embassy Staff were awarded the medal without bar.

HM ships: *Acorn, Acteon, Adventure, Algerine, Amethyst, Assistance, Bante, Barracouta, Beagle, Belleisle, Bittern, Bouncer, Bustard, Calcutta, Cambrian, Camillia, Centaur, Chesapeake, Clown, Cockchafer, Comus, Cormorant, Cruiser, Drake, Elk, Encounter, Esk, Firm, Flamer, Forester, Furious, Fury, Grasshopper, Hardy, Haughty, Havoc, Hesper, Highflyer, Hong Kong, Hornet, Imperieuse, Inflexible, Insolent, Janus, Kestrel, Lee, Leven, Magicienne, Nankin, Niger, Nimrod, Odin, Opossum, Pearl, Pioneer, Pique, Plover, Prince Arthur, Racehorse, Raleigh, Retribution, Reynard, Ringdove, Roebuck, Sampson, Sanspareil, Scout, Simoon, Sir Charles Forbes, Slaney, Snake, Snap, Sparrowhawk, Spartan, Sphinx, Starling, Staunch, Surprise, Sybille, Tribune, Urgent, Valiant, Volcano, Vulcan, Watchful, Weazel, Winchester, Woodcock.*

Indian Marine ships: *Auckland, Berenice, Coromandel, Ferooz, Prince Arthur, Zenobia.* (Issued with impressed medals with full details.)

There were a few other ships present, such as tugs and gunboats, to which no medals were awarded.

China 1842

The details of the issue of this bar have always been veiled in obscurity, however a letter from the Secretary of State for India to the Governor General dated 28th February, 1861 states that a clasp for China 1842 had been especially granted *in addition* to the clasps already approved

for the 1857 Medal. The 1842 bar was to be awarded to those of Her Majesty's forces who had *already* received the China 1842 Medal *and* had served in the operations from 1856-63. The Admiralty stated that 93 'China 1842' bars were issued.

Instructions were given that in the preparation of the rolls for the 1857 Medal that those already in possession of the 1842 Medal should receive the bar only for services 1856-63. In other words it was expected that those who had received the 1842 Medal should not be issued with a second medal but would be awarded bars to be added to their first medal. However it appears to have been overlooked that the suspender of the 1842 Medal was not at all suitable to carry bars and this aspect seems to have been discovered after the issue of the loose bars had commenced. Consequently it would appear that the 1842 recipients were then sent medals from the 1856-63 die so that the medal could be married up with the loose bar already sent. In the meantime however it is more than likely that some had already fixed their bars to the 1842 Medal by altering the original suspender at their own expense. Unfortunately as the second medal was issued unnamed (unlike the 1842 Medal), it makes it impossible to check these with the rolls.

It is known that General Sir James Hope Grant was issued a medal for the Second China War, this having a China 1842 bar as well as two others for the 1856-63 period, the medal was fully impressed as 'Commander of the Forces'. However a group to an Admiral in the Douglas-Morris collection has the 1842 medal with a suspender from the 1857 medal with a bar affixed for 1842.

Fatshan 1857 25th May-1st June, 1857

This bar was only awarded to Naval and Marine personnel from HM ships *Bustard, Calcutta, Coromandel, Cruiser, Elk, Forester, Fury, Haughty, Highflyer, Hong Kong, Hornet, Nankin, Niger, Plover, Raleigh, Starling, Staunch, Sybille, Tribune.*

Canton 1857 28th December, 1857-5th January, 1858

Regiments present: 4/2, 4/12, 6/12 (105) RA (3 Batteries); RE; RMLI; Medical Staff Corps; 59 Foot; 38 Madras NI (2 officers and 40 men).

Naval Brigade from HM ships: *Acorn, Actaeon, Calcutta, Cruiser, Esk, Furious, Fury, Highflyer, Hornet, Inflexible, Nankin, Niger, Racehorse, Samson, Sanspareil, Sybille.*

Taku Forts 1858 20th May, 1858

This bar was only awarded to Naval and Marine personnel from HM ships: *Bustard, Calcutta, Cormorant, Furious, Fury, Magicienne, Nankin, Nimrod, Opossum, Slaney, Staunch.*

Taku Forts 1860 21st August, 1860

Regiments present: 1 Dragoon Guards (two Squadrons, approx. 317, 15 as single bars); 11 Probyn's and 19 Fane's Horse (11 and 19 Bengal Cavalry); 4/2, 1/4, 2/4, 6/12 (133), 3/13 (231), 4/13, 7/14, 8/14 RA; 1 Madras FA; RE; Military Train; RMLI; 2/1 (51 as singles), 1/2 (613), 1/3, 2/31 (890), 44 (960), 57 (1),* 2/60 (760), 67 (851), 99 (8) Foot; 20, 22, Punjab NI (then numbered 8 and 15), 23 Punjab NI.

HMS *Chesapeake, Clown, Drake, Furious, Janus* and *Woodcock;* Indian Marine ships *Coromandel, Ferooz* and *Prince Arthur.*

Pekin 1860

Regiments present: Two Squadrons of 1 Dragoon Guards (approx. 318 as 2 bar medals, 1 only as a single bar); 11, 19 Bengal Cavalry; 1/4, 2/4, 6/12, (127), 3/13 (25), 4/13, 7/14, 8/14 RA; RE; 2/1 (17 as single bars); 1/2 (532), 2/31 (51), 44 (28), 2/60, 67 (751), 99 (531) Foot; 20, 22, 23 Punjab NI. Medals were awarded to members of both the Royal Navy and Royal Indian Marine (*Zenobia*).

The causes that led up to this war were very similar to those that caused the First China War in 1842—namely, maltreatment of Europeans.

On the 8th October, 1856, the Chinese in Canton boarded the *Arrow*† and took off twelve of her crew of fourteen. The flag was also hauled down. Admiral Sir Michael Seymour demanded redress, but none was forthcoming. On the 23rd October, 1856, he seized the Barrier Forts and entered the city. The forces at his command were not strong enough for the work in hand, so he appealed to the Governor-General of India for troops and the Home Government for naval reinforcements. They all arrived during March, 1857. In May, 1857, Commodore Elliot destroyed the Chinese fleet in Escape Creek and Admiral Seymour, with Commodore Keppel, those in Fatshan Creek.

The Indian Mutiny had drained British military resources so that, although a few troops had arrived, it was not until December, 1857, that the commanders on the spot felt justified in commencing combined operations on a large scale.

Major-General Sir Charles Van Straubenzee was given command of the British troops. The French also supplied a Naval Brigade.

Canton was captured on the 5th January, 1858; Yeh was taken prisoner and sent to Calcutta, where he died on the 9th April, 1859.

Lord Elgin had insisted that the Treaty of Peace should be signed in Pekin, but when the envoys arrived off the mouth of the Peiho river they met with a most hostile reception and a blank refusal to be allowed to pass up to Tientsin. It was obvious to Admiral Seymour that the Taku Forts which guarded the mouth of the river would have to be attacked. After a heavy bombardment by a combined British and French fleet a landing party went ashore. The forts surrendered on the 20th May. On the same day, Tientsin was reached and a treaty signed by Lord Elgin, Baron Gros (for the French) and Keying Elepoo, who had signed the treaty after the first war.

It was soon made very obvious that the Chinese had not the slightest intention of honouring any treaty and simply looked upon them as a means of lulling suspicion and getting their forts rearmed and collecting fresh supples of warlike materials.

By the peace signed in May, 1858, it was agreed that Britain and France should be represented by ambassadors at Pekin. Sir Frederick Bruce, whilst on his way to Pekin to take up his appointment, was stopped in the Peiho River by fire from the Taku Forts. Admiral Sir James Hope, who had succeeded Admiral Seymour, was forced to stage a full-scale attack on the 18th and 19th June, 1859. This attack was unsuccessful, so the Mission and the fleet had to withdraw. No bar was awarded for this action, presumably because it was a failure.

Matters could not be left like this, so the British and French Governments decided that a combined expeditionary force should be sent to China. This was composed of about 13,000 European and Indian troops with a French contingent 6,700 strong. In addition there was, of course, a combined fleet. The British troops were commanded by Lieutenant-General Sir Hope Grant, the French by General Mountauban.

Operations started in August, 1860, and the Taku Forts at the mouth of the Peiho river were captured on the 21st. On arrival at Tientsin, which is about forty miles up the Peiho river, the Chinese again tried to bargain for time, but both the allied commanders agreed that it was essential to get to Pekin. The capital was entered on the 13th October after two severe actions at Chang-kia-wan on the 18th September and Pa-li-chian on the 21st.

A further treaty was signed on the 24th October. Kowloon was exchanged for the island of Chusan and a large indemnity had to be paid. Pekin was evacuated on the 5th November.

Affairs in China after this were far from peaceful as an extraordinarily complicated inter-state struggle then started between the Chinese, Tartars and Taepings on the mainland, whilst at sea, piracy, smuggling and banditry of all forms continued on a large scale for many years.

A total of eight Victoria Crosses were awarded for the campaign.

---

*This medal was awarded to Lieutenant Edward Brutton, who was serving on the staff. He also obtained the New Zealand medal dated 1861-66.

†The *Arrow* was a lorcha sailing under British colours. A lorcha is a type of vessel peculiar to the Chinese coast. Their hulls look of European build, whilst their sails are of distinctly Chinese origin and design like those of a junk.

98 *New Zealand Medal* 1845-1847 and 1860-1866

Obverse	Diademed head of Queen Victoria with a veil covering the back of her head. Around the head is the legend 'VICTORIA D:G:BRITT:REG:F:D'
Reverse	In the centre, surrounded by a wreath of laurel, is the date or dates of service. Above are the words 'NEW ZEALAND' and below 'VIRTUTIS HONOR'.
Size	36mm diameter
Metal	Silver
Ribbon	32mm wide, dark blue and a red stripe 10mm wide down the centre.
Suspension	By means of a straight ornamental swivelling suspender, of a type only used for this medal.
Designers	J. S. Wyon and A. B. Wyon
Naming	Indented in very neat well-spaced capitals. Some of the medals which bear no date on the reverse are to be found with a date, or dates, engraved on the edge. The rolls indicate many late claims, some after 1900, which probably explains the later style naming. The New Zealand Ministry of Defence released a number of unclaimed medals to registered NZ collectors about 1969. The original names were partly obliterated by an engraved line and 'specimen'.
Bars issued	Nil

New Zealand was first discovered by Tasman in 1642. It was circumnavigated by Captain Cook, in the *Endeavour,* during the voyage in which he went round the world (30th July, 1768-12th June, 1771).

Captain Hobson, the first Governor, landed on the 29th January, 1840, and signed the Treaty of Waitangi, on the 6th February, as a result of which the native chiefs agreed to the ceding of large tracts of land.

There can be little doubt that the outbreak of war in 1845 was caused by the natives resenting the gradual infiltration of the white man, who began taking a lot more than the Treaty permitted. Whatever the real cause, the natives rose in rebellion, headed by their chiefs Hone-Heke and Kawiti.

The only regiments in the country at the time were the 58th and 99th Foot, under Colonel Despard. After considerable bush fighting the troubles ended on the North Island in 1846, and on the South Island in 1847.

During this period about thirty-five officers and 360 men of the Royal Navy and Marines were employed. The discrepancy between these figures and the number of naval medals awarded is probably due to their not having been sanctioned until 1869, and then only to survivors who had landed *and* engaged the enemy.

It was during this campaign that British troops first encountered the native fortifications known as 'pahs'. These were high wooden stockades, generally of two walls with earth in between and surrounded by a deep ditch. They were proof against the small firearms of those days.

In March, 1860, the Maoris, under Chief Wiremu Kingi, again rose in revolt due to their belief, not without considerable foundation, that they were being made to part with their lands at prices all too favourable to the Government.

The natives of Tauranga, south of Auckland on the Bay of Plenty, who had remained quiet during the fighting of 1845-47, were incited by the natives of Waikato to revolt. The incitation was acted upon with such enthusiasm that it became necessary to dispatch troops from Burma, India and Britain to Tauranga and Taranaki, on the West Coast.

General Pratt, who arrived first with troops from Australia, took command. The natives were defeated at Mahoetahi on the 6th November. Peace was again established in March, 1861.

On 4th May, 1863, fighting broke out again and spread rapidly. More troops were sent, some of whom encamped at the end of a narrow peninsula called Te-pap. The natives were allowed to build an enormous pah between the camp and the mainland which effectively isolated the troops from the region they had come thousands of miles to enter! This pah being the gate to the mainland, became known as the Gate Pah.

On the 28th April, 1864, the attack on the Gate Pah started. Owing to confusion among the sailors and soldiers involved the attack was repulsed and heavy casualties suffered.

The war continued until the 3rd July, 1866, though it cannot be said that all native disturbances ceased much before 1881. The last British troops were withdrawn from New Zealand in January, 1870.

It is worth noting that although there was no 'official' fighting between 6th November, 1861, and 4th May, 1863, medals were issued bearing these dates and many with dates which include them.

The medal was sanctioned on 1st March, 1869, for issue to survivors only of those who had taken part in suppressing the Maori risings on the North Island between 1845 and 1846, South Island during 1847 and/or service in New Zealand between 1860 and 1866.

As medals for the two campaigns are the same, except for the date or dates on the reverse, they have been taken together.

There were thirty-one different medals issued. Thirty of these carry a year date(s) on the reverse and one was undated.

Medals with engraved dates could quite possibly be late issues where the relief dates have been officially removed.

Army Medals

Medals with no dates. These are to be found to the following units: Staff Corps; Artillery; Engineers; Army Hospital Corps; Commissariat Corps (64); 12 (146), 14, 18, 40, 43, 50 (276), 57, 58, 65, 68 (67), 70, 96 (for 1844-6) (25) and 99 Foot (101), Military Train, 1, 2, 3, 4 Waikato Militia; Auckland Militia.

The following local forces received medals which were all *undated* and which were engraved by the jeweller in the district to which the medals were sent. Members of local forces and civilians who were employed by the Imperial Commissariat Corps were issued with an impressed medal dated 1861-66 although a few medals of the undated variety were impressed to members of the Waikato Militia.

Numbers issued		Numbers issued	
Alexandra Cavalry Volunteers	1	Napier Cavalry Volunteers	3
Arawa Contingent	2	Napier Military Settlers	18
Armed Constabulary	478	Napier Militia	119
Armed Police	3	Napier Rifle Volunteers	40
Auckland Cavalry Volunteers	3	Native Contingent	94
Auckland Coastguard	1	New Zealand Militia	30
Auckland Defence Force	14	Onehunga Naval Volunteers	2
Auckland Engineer Volunteers	17	Opotiki Rangers	5
Auckland Militia	356	Otahuhu Cavalry Volunteers	6
Auckland Naval Volunteers	12	Patea Rangers	18
Auckland Rifle Volunteers	28	Patea Rifle Volunteers	16
Auckland Volunteers	57	Patea Yeomanry Cavalry	7
Bay of Islands Militia	1	Petone Cavalry	5
Bay of Islands Volunteers	2	Poverty Bay Cavalry	10
Bay of Plenty Volunteer		Poverty Bay Volunteers	9
Cavalry	6	Pukekohe Rifle Volunteers	6
Carlyle Volunteers	1	Taita Militia	2
Chatham Islands Guard	1	Taranaki Bush Rangers	22
Civilians in Imperial		Taranaki Cavalry Volunteers	20
Commissariat Corps	239	Taranaki Military Settlers	203
Clive Militia	1	Taranaki Militia	142
Colonial Defence Force	90	Taranaki Mounted Volunteers	13
Commissariat Transport Corps	9	Taranaki Rifle Volunteers	228
Corps of Guides	3	Taranaki Volunteers	159
East Coast Expeditionary Force	2	Tauranga Cavalry Volunteers	6
European Contingent	4	Wairea Rifle Volunteers	41
Forest Rangers	86	Waiuku Volunteers	6
Friendly Natives	108	Wanganui Rangers	31
Hawke's Bay Cavalry	3	Wanganui Cavalry	91
Hawke's Bay Military Settlers	29	Wanganui Militia	50
Hawke's Bay Militia	12	Wellington Defence Force	15
Hawke's Bay Volunteers	12	Wellington Militia	12
Howick Royal Cavalry		Wellington Rangers	22
Volunteers	2	Wellington Rifles	33
Hutt Militia	8	1st Waikato Regiment	595
Interpreters to the Forces	7	2nd Waikato Regiment	483
Kai-iwi Volunteer Cavalry	37	3rd Waikato Regiment	663
Mauku Rangers	4	4th Waikato Regiment	17
Mauku Rifle Volunteers	25		

1845 to 1846
Bombay European Artillery (15) on board HEIC ship *Elphinstone*.
Medals to G. Williams, 99th Foot and Capt W. M. Biddlecomb, RE are also known.

1845 to 1847
Issued primarily to the Navy.
Gnr. J. Simpson, Bombay Artillery was awarded the medal for service aboard HEIC ship *Elphinstone*. The Northamptonshire Regt Museum report that they have a medal dated 1845 to 1847 to Lieut G. H. Page, 58th Foot.

1846
Issued to the Navy only.

1846 to 1847
Issued to the Navy only.

1846 to 1865
One awarded to Col R. H. McGregor, Commanding Officer of the 65th Regiment and now in the Napier Museum.

1846 to 1866
Unnamed specimens of this medal are known to exist.

1847
One awarded to Captain T. B. Collinson, RE.

1848
One awarded to Lieutenant-Colonel Andrew Clarke, RE.

1860
Lieutenant-Colonel V. T. Mairis, RE and six other ranks of the Sappers.
Australian volunteers were present during this year.

1860 to 1861
Royal Engineers (33); 12th (3), 40th Foot (13). Lieutenant E. C. MacNaughton, RA received a medal with these dates.

1860 to 1863
Only three medals known: No 6108 Sapper Thomas Ellis, RE, Corporal Henry Barnes RE, No 2124 James Phillips, 4th Battalion Military Train.

1860 to 1864
No 3 Battery, 12 Brigade RA (31); I Battery 4th Brigade RA (12); Royal Engineers; 12 (4), 40, 65 Foot.

1860 to 1865
2 Battery Coast Brigade; J. Battery, 4th Brigade RA (3); 12 (9), 40, 65, 70 Foot.

1860 to 1866
Only thirteen medals with this date known. 1/12, 40 Foot; RE, 12th Brigade RA.

1861
Only known to Lieutenant Arthur Stewart Hunter, RA, No 349 Driver William Matthews, C Battery, 4th Brigade, RA and Gunner B. Donegan RMA of HMS *Falcon*.

1861 to 1863
Medals to 2377 Sergeant Chas Moore, 57th Foot and D. Gleed, 57th Foot are known but have not been verified.

1861 to 1864
12 (5), 40, 57 Foot; RA; RE (1).

1861 to 1865
65 Foot. Only one medal known.

1861 to 1866
C Battery, 4th Brigade RA (27); RE; 1/12 (85), 2/14, 57 (349), 68, 70 Foot; 1, 2, 3 Waikato Regiments, Auckland Militia.

1862 to 1866
Two known to Captain Edward Mills, 57th Foot and Ensign, C. Picot, 57th Foot.

1863
RE; 1/12, 2/14, 2/18 (1), 40 (14), 50 (29), 57, 65, 70 (3) Foot; Military Train and Naval Brigade.

1863 to 1864
RE (19); 12 (20), 40, 43 (30), 50 (15), 65, 68, 70 Foot (66).

1863 to 1865
12 (27), 14, 2/18 (2), 40, 43 (71), 50 (3), 65 (8), 68, 70 Foot.

1863 to 1866
C (58) and I (8) Batteries 4th Brigade, 17 Brigade RA; RE (7); Military Train; 1/12 (243), 2/14, 2/18 (463), 43 (377), 50 (342), 57 (10), 65, 68, 70 Foot.

1864
I Battery RA (97); 11th RA; RE (2); 40 (33), 43 (5), 50 (1), 68, 70 Foot; 4th Battalion Military Train; Commissariat Transport Corps.

1864 to 1865
I Battery, 4th Brigade (3), 17 Brigade RA; 2/18 (1), 50 (1), 65 (25), 68, 70 Foot (65); RE.

1864 to 1866
9th Battery, 2nd Brigade (25), 10th Battery RA; 1st Battery 11 Brigade RA; 2nd Battery RA; 5, 7, 19 Batteries Coastal Brigade RA; C (40) and J (36) Batteries 4 Brigade RA; RE (3); Gunner Riding Establishment; 1/12 (158) 2/18 (68), 40, 43 (109), 50 (102), 57 (61), 65, 69 Foot; Commissariat Staff Corps (13).

1865
RE; 2/18, 43, 50, 65 (38), 68 Foot.

1865 to 1866
RA; RE (14); 2/18 (30), 43 (possibly 3, including Assistant Surgeon O. Owen), 57 (40), 68, 70 Foot; 4th Battalion Military Train (76).

1866
1/12, 14, 18 (2), 50 (8), 68 Foot; 4th Battalion Military Train.

The following British regiments were engaged in New Zealand between 1845-47 and 1860-66, but not necessarily for the whole of both periods: RA; RE; Military Train; 1/12, 2/14, 2/18, 40, 43, 50, 57, 58, 65, 68, 70, 96, 99 Foot.

Naval Medals

Undated Medals
Some undated medals were issued to satisfy late claims whilst others were issued with engraved dates, these engraved dates appear to have been issued between 1875 and 1880. These factors have made it difficult to be absolutely certain regarding numbers issued, especially the undated varieties.

Ships present: *Calliope* (?), *Esk* (3), *Harrier* (1)—T. Rodda A. B., issued 9.5.1911, *Iris* (?), *Miranda* (?), *Niger* (?).
1845 to 1846
Ships present: *Calliope* (?), *Castor* (69), with the dates '1845 to 1846' or '1845 to 1847', *Driver* (1)—Master-at-Arms A. Alpe, *Hazard* (35), *North Star* (41), *Osprey* (11), *Racehorse* (1)—Commander's Cook Joseph Crew, HEIC Ship *Elphinstone* (5).
1845 to 1847
Ships present: *Castor* (69), with the dates '1845 to 1846' or '1845 to 1847', *Racehorse* (36).
1846
Ships present: *Calliope* (1)—Lieutenant W. Thorpe (in lieu of '1846 to 1847'), *Driver* (10).
1846 to 1847
Ships present: *Calliope* (63).
1847
Ships present: *Inflexible* (20).
1860
Ships present: *Cordelia* (1)—Commander C. E. H. Vernon, *Iris* (3)—Commander W. Loring, Danl. Catmore, AB and Chas. M. Cooke, AB, *Niger* (3)—Lieutenant (later Captain) W. H. Blake, Acting Mate Wm. W. Smythe and Lieutenant Wm. Watson-Smyth. (All in lieu of 1860 to 1861).
1860 to 1861
Ships present: *Cordelia* (29), *Iris* (72), *Niger* (63), *Pelorus* (117), Colonial Ship *Victoria* (40), it is believed that only 10 medals were distributed.

Some of the naval medals were issued with an undated reverse and dated 1860-61 on the edge.
1863
Ships present: *Himalaya* (1)—Captain E. Lacy.
1863 to 1864
Ships present: *Curacoa* (187), *Eclipse* (1)—W. Clay, Captain of the Foretop, *Esk* (120), *Harrier* (79), *Miranda* (91).
1863 to 1865
Ships present: *Eclipse* (75).
1863 to 1866
Ships present: *Hazard* (1)—Lieutenant Klintberg, Swedish Navy.
1864
Ships present: *Falcon* (12).
1865
Ships present: *Brisk* (13), *Eclipse* (6?), Private T. Archer, RM, Private H. Rowe, RM, Private T. Bath, RM and Boy 1st Class M. Swain, Boy 1st Class Henry Balcon, Assistance Paymaster, A. Le. B. Corrie.

Other naval units present: Auckland Naval Volunteers (9), dates unknown.

It should be noted that medals were only issued to the survivors who actually landed and engaged the enemy.

A total of fifteen Victoria Crosses were awarded of which two were for the 1860-1861 campaign (Leading Seaman William Odgers RN and Sergeant-Major John Lucas, 40th Regiment). The remainder were for the 1863-1866 campaign.

99 *Abyssinian War Medal* 4th October 1867-19th April 1868

Obverse	A small veiled and coroneted bust of Queen Victoria surrounded by an ornate nine-pointed star, between each point of which is one of the letters of the word 'ABYSSINIA'.
Reverse	Within a beaded circle, surrounded by a wreath of laurel, tied at the base, the recipient's name and regiment or ship stamped in relief. The Indian troops had their names and regiments engraved. Medals are also found having an additional circular back plate affixed by a centrally placed rivet on which the recipient's details are struck in relief around its border. These are believed to be officially corrected medals.
Size	32.5mm diameter
Metal	Silver
Ribbon	38mm wide. White with a broad red band down the centre.
Suspension	Above the circular disc is the imperial crown at the top of which is a ring through which the ribbon is threaded.
Designer	Designed by Owen Jones and engraved by Joseph S. Wyon and Alfred B. Wyon.
Naming	See *reverse* above
Bars issued	Nil

About 14,000 (12,000 to the Army and 1,981 to the Navy) of these medals were issued for the expedition under Lieutenant-General Sir Robert Napier, who afterwards became Lord Napier of Magdala.

This campaign was one of the most bloodless in which the British Army has ever been involved, the total casualties amounting to two killed and twenty-seven wounded. It may have been this fact which tempted the Italians to embark on a similar expedition which resulted in almost total annihilation of their forces at Adowa on 1st March, 1896.

The disembarking and final embarking were in the hands of one who was later to become famous, Major Frederick Roberts, VC, who became Field-Marshal Earl Roberts of Kandahar.

The medal, which was sanctioned on 1st March, 1869, is said to be the most expensive of all the British general-issues, on account of the fact that the recipients' details were embossed, thus necessitating a separate die for each medal.

The following troops took part in the campaign:
3 Dragoon Guards (219); 11 Hussars (9); 3 Scinde Horse; 3 Bombay Light Cavalry; 10 (643), 12 (483) Bengal Cavalry; G/14 (148), 3/21, 5/21 (116), 5/25 (124) Batteries RA; No 1 (Bombay) Mountain Battery;

Munition Battery; 1, 2, 3, 4 Companies Bombay Sappers and Miners; G, H, K Companies Madras Sappers and Miners (368); 10 Company RE; Bombay Medical Department; Army Hospital Corps; Army Works Corps; Commissariat; Land Transport Corps; Ordnance Corps; 1/4, 26 (800 approx.) 33, 45 (644), 46 (1), 92 (2), 96 (21), 108 (10), 109 (15) Foot; 1,* 2, 3, 4, 5, 8, 10, 18, 21 (785), 25, 27 Bombay NI; 23 Punjab Pioneers (755), James Pollard, 102 Foot, received this medal.

A Naval Brigade (83) under Captain Fellowes, RN, was drawn from some of the following ships and manned twelve 12 pounder rocket tubes: HMS *Argus* (177), *Daphne* (170), *Dryad* (151), *Nymphe* (167), *Octavia* (611), *Satellite* (285), *Spiteful* (180), *Star* (101), *Vigilant* (97), hospital ships *Golden Fleece, Queen of the South* and *Mauritius*. The transport service received 42 medals of which 12 also appear on the roll of HMS *Octavia*.
Naval awards were made to all the crews of the ships on duty in the Red Sea and to those whose service was in any way connected with the war. They were not confined to those who landed or formed part of the Naval Brigade.

This war was caused by the penchant of King Theodore for imprisoning foreigners, among whom were Captain Cameron, the British Consul, as well as missionaries and other British subjects. Most of them were put in chains and sent to Magdala, the capital, in November, 1864. In 1865 the British Political Resident in Aden, Mr Hormuzd Rassam, together with Lieutenant Prideaux and Doctor Blane, negotiated for nearly a year with the Emperor, with the result that the prisoners were released in March, 1866, only to be re-arrested the next month, together with the negotiators. At about this time, with amazing aplomb on the part of the Emperor and extraordinary imbecility on the part of the British, workmen were requested and sent from England, as a result of a visit by Mr Flad the Emperor's representative. On his return, Mr Flad was thanked and, like the workmen who arrived later, cast in prison.

A period occupied in dispatching ultimatums and formal letters then followed. The first, which apparently never arrived, was sent in September, 1867; then came a proclamation by Sir Robert Napier, commanding the Bombay army; then the Queen proclaimed war in a speech on 19th November. This was followed by another ultimatum from Sir Robert, who landed at Annesley Bay, below Massowah, in January, 1868. As soon as sufficient troops had arrived and the necessary arrangements had been made, Napier started on the 300 or more miles to Magdala. The battle of Arrogie was fought on 10th April, and Magdala entered on the 13th. It was found that Theodore had committed suicide, so with the prisoners rescued, Magdala was razed to the ground on the 17th, and the return journey was started.

Two Victoria Crosses were awarded during this campaign, these being to Drummer M. Magner and Private J. Bergrin, both of the 33rd Regiment.

100 *Canada General Service Medal* 1866-1870

Obverse	A veiled bust of Queen Victoria with the legend 'VICTORIA REGINA ET IMPERATRIX'.
Reverse	The Canadian flag surrounded by a maple wreath with the word 'CANADA' above.
Size	36mm diameter
Metal	Silver
Ribbon	32mm. Three equal stripes of red, white and red.
Suspension	A plain straight swivel suspender.
Designers	Obverse, T. Brock; Reverse, G. W. de Saulles.
Naming	These medals are to be found with several different types of naming as follows:

(a) In large indented block capitals.
(b) In indented lower case letters.
(c) Engraved in large or small capitals. The Naval medals are generally found with the latter.
(d) The medals to the English regiments were impressed in capitals or engraved.

Bars issued Three—Fenian Raid 1866; Fenian Raid 1870; Red River 1870. The medal was always issued with a bar. 4 different dies were used to strike the 1866 bar, 5 for 1870 and 3 for Red River.

By Army Order No 7 January, 1899 (Army Order No 256 of 1906 extended the period for applying for the medal to 1st July 1907, which was later extended to the end of 1928) approval was given for the Canadian Government to issue a medal to members of the Imperial and Canadian Forces which had taken part in the suppression of the Fenian Raids and Riel's First Rebellion. Approximately 16,121 were issued including 15,300 to Canadians.

The variety of styles of naming is partly due to the fact the medal was issued over a very long period. As the medal was not issued until 1899 many who were entitled did not live to receive it.

*This regiment did not land in time to take part in any of the fighting.

Fenian Raid 1866

British Regiments present: 7 R Fus (158), 15 York R (20); 16 Bedford R (121); 17 Leicester R (145); 22 Cheshire R (1); 25 KOSB (99); 30 E Lancs R (94); 47 Loyal R (119); 53 Shropshire R (2); 1/60 KRRC (6); 4/60 KRRC (109); 1/Rifle Bde (92); 4/Rifle Bde (175); 4, 10, 15 Bde RA (280); RE (40); AHC (1); ASC (16); Staff (10).

The medal awarded to No 1173 Private R. Birmingham, 30th Foot, with this bar and that for 'Fenian Raid 1870' is the only two-bar one that is known to this regiment.

The Dunville Naval Volunteers (29).

HM ships: *Aurora* (131), *Baracouta* (1); *Britomart* (15), *Cherub* (6), *Constance* (2), *Demon* (6), *Duncan* (17), *Fawn* (7), *Heron* (11), *Lily* (1), *Niger* (41), *Pylades* (60), *Rescue* (1), *Rosario* (16), *Royal* (3), *Simoom* (1), *Wolverine* (10).

The following ships were also present: *Cadmus, Canada, Cordelia, Hercules, Michigan, Minstrel, Philomel, Phoebe, Prince Albert, Royal Alfred* and *Tamar*. As these vessels were mainly manned from HM Ships *Aurora, Niger* and *Pylades*, it is most probable that medals issued to these men were named to their parent ship.

Fenian Raid 1870

British Regiments present: 7 R Fus (3); 17 Leicester R (32); 25 KOSB (4); 30 E. Lancs R (1); 1/60 KRRC (16); 4/60 KRRC (7); 69 S Lincs R (160); 1/Rifle Bde (74); 4/Rifle Bde (69); 3, 4 Bde RA (29); RE (8); ASC (6); Staff (3).

Red River 1870

British Regiments present: 7 R Fus (1); 16 Bedford R (1); 1/60 KRRC (123); 4/60 KRRC (6); 69 S Lins R (1); 4/Rifle Bde (1); H Bty 14 Bde RA (6); RE (8); ASC (7); Staff (5).

Canadian Units

The following units served and were entitled to medal with bars:

Staff; District Staff; Gov Gen's Body Gd; 1-24, 26-31, 33-35, 37, 38, 41-56, 58-61, 64, 65, 69, 70, Battalions; 1 Admin Bn; 1, 2 Provisional Bn.

Albion I Co	Clinton I Co	Georgetown I Co	1st King's Regt
Algoma R Co	Coburg Cav	Goderich GA	Kingston Cav & I Co
Almonte I Co	Coburg GA	Goderich GB	Kingston FB
Alton I Co	Coburg I Co	Goderich I Co	Komoka R Co
Amherstberg I Co	Coburg R Co	Goderich R Co	Lakefield I Co
Annapolis Co Bde	Collingwood I Co	Gordon Rifles	Leamington I Co
Arthabaskaville I Co	Columbus R Co	Grahamsville I Co	Leith R Co
Ashburnham I Co	Como R Co	Granby I Co	Lennoxville I Co
Athelstan I Co	Cookshire Cav	Grand Trunk Ry Bde	Lisgar Rifles
Aurora I Co	Cookstown R Co	Greenwood I Co	Lloydtown I Co
Aylmer I Co	Cornwall I Co	Grimsby Cav	London Cav
Barrie I Co	Cornwall Mtd Patrol	Guelph R Co	London FB
Barrie R Co	Cornwall R Co	Gunboat 'Royal'	London LI
Becacour I Co	Dalhousie I Co	Haldimand R Co	Lotbiniere I Co
Beauce Prov Bn	Danville R Co	Halifax Art & Art Mil	Loughborough Cav
Beauharnois I Co	Darlington R Co	Halifax FA	Lucan I Co
Bells Corners I Co	Dartmouth Engrs	Halifax FB	Marbleton I Co
Belleville R Co	Delaware R Co	Halifax GA	Markham Cav
Berthier I Co	Derry West I Co	Halifax EVB	Meaford R Co
Bishop's Coll I Co	Derry West Vols	Halifax Bn	Megantic R Co
Blenheim I Co	Despatch Office	1st Halifax Bn	Melbourne I Co
Bothwell I Co	Digby Co Mil	Halifax Prov Bn	Merrickville R Co
Bowmansville I Co	Dorchester Prov Bn	Halifax Vol Bn	Mil School Cadets
Bradford I Co	5th Dragoons	Hamilton FB	Millbrook I Co
Brampton I Co	Drumbo LI	Hamilton Naval Bde	Missisquoi Home Guards
Brampton R Co	Dundas I Co	Hants Mil	Montreal Cav
Brantford R Co	Dufferin R Co	Harrietsville I Co	Montreal Engrs
Brantford Highland R	Dunnville Naval Co	Hastings R Co	Montreal FA
Brockville & Ottawa GA	Dunville R Co	Havelock R Co	Montreal FB
Brockville I Co	Durham I I & I Cos	Hemmingford I Co	Montreal GA
Brockville R Co	Elora R Co	Hemmingford Rangers	Montreal HSC Corps
Brockville Vol Bn	Embro R Co	Hespeler V Bn	Montreal LI
Brooklin R Co	Exeter I Co	Hinchingbrooke I Co	Montreal Rangers
Bruce Mines Vols	Fenwick R Co	Huntingdon I Co	Moore I Co
Buckingham I Co	Fergus I Co	Huntingdon Scouts	Mooretown I Co
Burham (?Durham) I Co	Fitzroy I Co	Huntley I Co	Mooretown Mtd I
Burritts Rapids I Co	Franklin I Co	Huron R Co	Morrisburg GA
Bury I Co	Fraserville I Co	Ingersoll I Co	Mount Forrest I Co
Caledonia R Co	Fredericton R Co	Ingersoll R Co	Mount Pleasant R Co
Campbellford I Co	Frelightsburg I Co	Iroquois GA	Napanee Cav
Carleton Pl I Co	Frontenac Cav	Joliette I Co	Napanee GA
Charlotte Co Mil	Galt I Co	Kamouraska Pr Bn	New Brunswick GA
Chatham I Co	Gananoque GA	Kincardine GA	New Brunswick Engrs
Chicago Vols	Gananoque R Co	Kincardine I Co	New Hamburg I Co
Civil Service R Co	Garden Island Nav Co	King I Co & Mil Rifles	Nicolet I Co

North Ridge R Co	Prince Alfred R Co	St John's VB	Thorold I Co
Norval I Co	PWDG	St Martine I Co	Three Rivers I Co
Nova Scotia Mil	Princeton R Co	St Melanie I Co	Tilsonburg I Co
Oakridge Cav	Quebec PG	St Norbert I Co	Toronto FB
Oakville I Co	Quebec Cav	St Paul's Bay I Co	Toronto GA
Oakville R Co	Quebec FB	St Pie I Co	Toronto Mil School
Ontario Rifles	Quebec GA	St Placide I Co	Toronto Naval Bde
Orangeville I Co	Quebec PB	St Remi I Co	Toronto Pr Bn
Ormstown I Co	Quebec Rifles	St Simon I Co	University R Co
Oshawa I Co	Queenstown Mtd Inf	St Stephen R Co	Upper Canada CC Co
Oshawa R Co	Rawdon I Co	St Sylvestre I Co	Upper Canada CR Co
Ottawa FB	Richmond I Co	St Therese R Co	Uxbridge I Co
Ottawa GA	Rimouski Pro Bn	St Thomas Cav	Varennes I Co
Ottawa Rifles	Riviere du Loup I Co	St Thomas R Co	Victoria Rifles
Ottawa & Prescott GA	Rockburn I Co	Sandwich I Co	Victoria R o BC
Owen Sound I Co	Roxham I Co	Sarnia GA	Victoriaville I Co
Oxford R Co	Royal Guides	Sarnia GB	Vienna I Co
Paisley I Co	St Andrew's Art	Sarnia I Co	Villa Nova R Co
Pakenham R Co	St Andrew's Cav	Sarnia Pro Bn	Walsingham Centre R Co
Paris R Co	St Benoit I Co	Sault Ste Marie I Co	Wardsville I Co
Perth I Co	St Catherine's Cav	Scarboro' R Co	Warwick I Co
Perth R Co	St Catherine's GA	Seaforth I Co	Waterloo I Co
Peterboro I Co	St Catherine's GB	Sherbrooke Cav	Welland Canal FB
Peterboro R Co	St Ed de Gentilly I Co	Sherbrooke GA	Whitby I Co
Philipsburg I Co	St Elizabeth I Co	Sherbrooke R Co	Whitby R Co
Port Arthur I Co	St Eustache I Co	Simcoe Foresters	Widder I Co
Port Hope E Co	St Gabriel I Co	Smith's Falls I Co	Windsor FB
Port Hope I Co	St George's Vol Mil	Southampton R Co	Windsor GA
Port Hope LI	St Gertrude I Co	Stewarttown I Co	Windsor I Co
Port Hope R Co	St Hyacinthe PB	Stormont R Co	Windsor R Co NS
Port Neuf Pro Bn	St Hyacinthe I Co	Storrington R Co	Windsor Vols
Port Rowan R Co	St Jacques I Co	Stratford I Co	Wolfestown I Co
Portsmouth I Co	St Jean Baptiste I Co	Stratford R Co	Woodstock V Bn
Port Stanley Marines	St John's Cav	Strathroy I Co	Wotten I Co
Prescott GA	St John's GA	Streetsville I Co	York Cav
Prescott Rifles	St John's VA	Temiscouta P Bn	York I Co
Press	St John's B	Terrebonne I Co	York Rangers
Prince Alfred I Co	St John's Co Mil	Thamesford I Co	York Rifles

Total number of medals issued, including Fenian Raid 1866, Fenian Raid 1870, and Red River 1870 are 16,121. Approximately 15,300 were issued to Canadian units.

One Bar Fenian Raid, 1866	7,000
One Bar Fenian Raid, 1870	7,135
One Bar Red River, 1870	365
Two Bar Fenian Raid 1866 and 1870	1,421
Two Bar Fenian Raid 1866 and Red River	150
Two Bar Fenian Raid 1870 and Red River	30
Three Bar Fenian Raid 1866, 1870 and Red River	20

In November 1837, French-Canadian leader Louis J. Papineau led a brief rebellion, as did republican leader William MacKenzie in December of that year, both intending to sever Canada's connection with Britain.

In the 1860's it was the Fenians who presented a challenge to the British Crown.

Fenians is the name of the old Irish National Militia which took the title of 'Brotherhood' in the United States and vowed its intention to 'liberate Ireland and establish a Republic'. The Fenian oath is as follows: 'I promise by the divine law of God to do all in my power to obey the laws of the society F.B. and to free and regenerate Ireland from the yoke of England. So help me God.'

Having a large following in the United States and with Civil war veterans available, sights were set on the invasion of Canada. On 31st May 1866 'Colonel' John O'Neill with a small force of 800 men crossed the Niagara River and on 1st June defeated Canadian troops at the Battle of Ridgeway. However when news that a strong force of Canadian Volunteers was approaching many Fenians deserted and the remainder were compelled to retreat to the United States. On the 3rd June the remainder surrendered to the American warship *Michigan*. President Johnston proclaimed against the Fenians on 7th June, 1866 and they remained quiescent until 1870.

On the 26th May 1870 O'Neill crossed the border near Franklin, Vermont, but this incursion was soon dispersed by Canadian Volunteers and O'Neill was captured by the United States authorities on his return. Upon his release he instigated another invasion, this time in Manitoba. O'Neill himself was unable to participate as he was again arrested on the US side of the border.

The reason, for the Red River Expedition stems from the area's history.

Hudson Bay was first discovered by Cabot in 1512 and then again by Henry Hudson in 1610 when searching for the 'Northwest Passage'. The Hudson Bay Company was then founded and obtained a Royal Charter from Charles II in 1670. On 9th April, 1869, the Charter having expired, the whole of what was known as the Hudson Bay Territory was transferred to the Dominion for £300,000 and incorporated into the State of Manitoba. This transference was resented by many people, and Louis Riel, styling himself a General, seized the Company's treasury in January, 1870, seized Fort Garry, imprisoned many British residents, and started a rebellion. One of his prisoners, Thomas Scott, escaped and was recaptured by Riel, and after a sham court-martial was ordered to be shot. The firing party only wounded him twice; he was then shot in the face at point blank range, but still not killed. He was then placed in a rough wooden box, in which he remained alive for a further ten hours.

Riels' rebellion encouraged the Fenians to consider a further invasion. However in the previous four years the Canadian Militia had become organised and were able to prevent further border activity.

The fact that British subjects were imprisoned, murdered and maltreated was the concern of the Government, which promptly ordered Colonel Garnet Wolseley to lead an expedition to Fort Garry. Colonel Wolseley's expedition left Toronto on 14th May and reached Fort Garry on 24th August, 1870, having covered 1,118 miles. Remains of the old Fort Garry may still be seen in Winnipeg, the capital of Manitoba. The fort is commemorated by a Canadian regiment, The Forty Garry Horse.

The 6th Battalion Canadian Infantry have a part of the old fort incorporated in their badge.)

Riel escaped before Wolseley's arrival. He was later able to lead the 'Second Riel Rebellion' in 1885 for which the North West Canada Medal was given.

One Victoria Cross was granted under unique circumstances as it was not won in the face of the enemy but for extinguishing a fire in an ammunition wagon. This was awarded to Private Timothy O'Hea, 1/Rifle Brigade for 19th June 1866.

The following is a list of the Canadians killed and wounded in the action at **Ridgeway**:

Queen's Own Rifles
Killed
Ensign Malcolm McEachren; L/Cpl Mark Defries; Pte William Smith; Pte Christopher Alderson; Pte Malcolm McKenzie; Pte Wm. F. Tempest; Pte J. H. Mewburn; Sgt Hugh Matheson; Cpl F. Lackey.

Wounded
Ensign Wm. Fahey; Pte Oulster; Pte Wm. Thompson; Capt. J. B. Boustead; Lieut J. H. Beaven; Pte Charles Winter; Pte Chas. Lugsdin; Pte Chas. Bell; Pte Copp; Lieut W. C. Campbell; Cpl Paul Robbins; Pte Rutherford; Sgt; W. Foster; Pte E. T. Paul; Pte R. E. Kingsford; Pte E. G. Paterson; Pte W. H. Vandersmissen; Col Sgt F. McHardy; Pte White; Pte Alex Muir; Sgt Forbes.

Thirteenth Battalion
Died
Pte Morrison.

Wounded
Lieut Routh; Pte McKenzie; Pte George Mackenzie; Pte Edwin Hillier; Pte Stuart; Pte Powell; Sgt J. M. Young; Pte H. W. Simons; Pte B. W. Sutherland; Pte Alex. Henderson; Pte John Crossman; Pte James Cahill; Pte W. Irving; Private W. T. Urquhart; Pte W. B. Nicholls.

York Rifles
Wounded
Sgt. Jack; Pte B. J. Cranston; Pte Oneida.

101 *Ashantee Medal* 9th June 1873-4th February 1874

Obverse	The diademed and veiled head of Queen Victoria with the legend 'VICTORIA REGINA'.
Reverse	A scene of bush fighting around a tree between British soldiers and natives.
Size	36mm diameter
Metal	Silver and bronze
Ribbon	33mm wide. Yellow with black borders and two thin black stripes down the centre.
Suspension	By a straight bar, swivelling suspender.
Designers	Obverse: L. C. Wyon, Reverse: Sir Edward Poynter, RA
Naming	In engraved roman capitals. Rim dated 1873-4.
Bars issued	One: 'Coomassie'. However those who later qualified for the East and West Africa Medal, 1887 were awarded the bar(s) only, for attachment to the Ashantee Medal, 1873.*

This medal, sanctioned on 1st June 1874, was awarded for Major-General Sir Garnet Wolseley's campaign against the Ashantis under King Kofi Karikara.

The chief cause of the war was the transfer of the port of Elmina from the Dutch to the British (2nd April, 1872). The King had received an annual payment from the Dutch for its use but when the British took over this was stopped. In January 1873 an Ashanti army moved south across the Pra river and attacked friendly tribes of the British Gold Coast Protectorate.

Wolseley was sent to rectify the situation. He and his staff arrived on 2nd October 1873, the British regiments, the mainstay of his army, arrived in December.

Prior to the arrival of Sir Garnet Wolseley, the only European forces in the country were a hundred marines under Colonel Festing who landed on 9th June 1873.

On the 5th July Commodore Edmund J. Commerell VC assumed command. With boats from the *Angus* and *Rattlesnake,* he attempted to reconnoitre the Pra river. The boats were fired upon and he, Commander Luxmore of the *Argus* and others were wounded. In response the towns of Chamah and Takoradi were shelled.

Shortly after his arrival, Sir Garnet with two hundred seamen and marines under Captain Freemantle together with a battalion of the West India Regiment disembarked at Elmina and on the 14th October defeated a force of Ashantis at Essaman. Colonel Festing also defeated them at Escaber on the 17th October.

A force of fifty seamen and marines under Lieutenant Wells RN, together with local troops were attacked at Abrakrampa on the 5th November, but were able to hold out until relieved.

The main advance on the Ashanti capital of Coomassie (variously spelt: Kumasi, Kumassi) began on the 5th January 1874.

On the 19th January, three hundred men of the Naval Brigade, 23rd Fusiliers and local volunteers fought a small action at Borborassie.

On the 31st January in the first major action of the war, Wolseley defeated the Ashantis, under difficult conditions at Amoaful. The next day the town of Bekwai was captured.

On the 4th February, in another battle made difficult by the terrain, Wolseley defeated the Ashantis at Ardahsa (variously spelt: Odasu,

*Those awarded the Witu 1890 bar for wear with this medal were: Rear Admiral Freemantle, Lieut A. H. D. Ravenhill, Lieut W. Ainger, Staff Paymr. F. R. C. Whidden, Cmdr. A. M. Gardner and P.O. 2nd., W. H. Still.

Ordahsu, Ordashsa). The Black Watch under Colonel John McLeod distinguished themselves by spearheading the attack that lead the way into Coomassie.

Although Coomassie was taken, King Kofi refused to come to terms and the bulk of the Ashanti army was still at large. Troubled by the increasing number of sick and wounded and lack of supplies Wolseley decided to withdraw and on the 6th February Coomassie was set on fire and the army began to retire.

However, the appearance of Captain J. Glover RN with a force of seven hundred Hausas and Yorubas approaching Coomassie from the east induced King Kofi to come to terms and on 13th February a peace treaty was signed whereby the King renounced claims to various outlying areas and agreed to pay an indemnity.

In the campaign four Victoria Crosses were awarded, these being to Lieut. E. D. Gifford (Lord), 24th Foot; Major R. W. Sartorius, 6 Bengal Cav.; L/Sgt. S. McGaw, 42nd Foot and Lieut. M. S. Bell, RE.

The following troops and naval ships were employed during the campaign. Where known the first figure indicates medals issued without a bar, the second figure medals with the bar Coomassie.

1/17 Bde. RA (20); Rait's Artillery; 28th Co. RE (93/60); 2/23 (617/302), 1/42 (688/651), 2 Rifle Brigade (700/621); 1, 2 West India Regiments; Glover's Force; Fantee Force; Army Hospital Corps (133/22); Army Hospital Services (76/31); Army Service Corps (61/10); Wood's and Russel's Native Regiments; Hausas (210); Kassoos (100); Elminas (50); Armed Police (10); Control Department

HM Ships: *Active* 568 (117 with bar); *Amethyst* 235 (39 with bar);

Argus 176 (33 with bar); *Barracuta* 301 (3 with bar); *Beacon* 90 (no bars); *Bittern* 106 (no bars); *Coquette* 68 (no bars); *Decoy* 69 (1 with bar); *Dromedary* 81 (no bars); *Druid* 212 (47 with bar); *Encounter* 229 (1 with bar); *Himalaya* 278 (1 with bar); *Merlin* 62 (no bars); *Rattlesnake* 295 (no bars); *Seagull* 90 (no bars); *Simoom* 200 (7 with bar); *Tamar* 223 (1 with bar); *Victor Emmanuel* 275 (no bars).

Medal without bar to Lieut. C. S. Shuckbury, RN, Transport *Manitoban*.

In addition to the above, several other British regiments contributed between one and three men and received medals. Medals with and without bars were also issued to native Kroomen etc. The crews of HM Ships frequently gave these locally recruited 'sailors' imaginative nicknames such as John Bull, Prince of Wales, Sea Breeze, Ben Liverpool, Johny Walker, Tom Poor Fellow, Moses Snowball, Jack Dandy, etc. Many of these Kroomen were subsequently to receive further bars for service during the East and West Africa campaigns.

Coomassie

The bar 'Cooomassie' was granted to all present at the battle of Amoaful (21 January 1874) and the actions between that place and Coomassie, including the capture of the capital on 4 February 1874, and to those who, during the five days of those actions, were engaged to the north of the Pra in maintaining and protecting the communications of the main army. With respect to those serving at Prahsu, the bar was restricted to those who were actually serving at the Tete-du-pont on the north side of the river, or beyond.

102 *South Africa Medal* 25th September 1877-2nd December 1879

Obverse	The diademed head of Queen Victoria and the legend, 'VICTORIA REGINA'.
Reverse	A lion representing Africa depicted crouching in a token of submission in front of a Protea bush. Above are the words 'SOUTH AFRICA'. in the exergue, a Zulu shield and four crossed assegais.
Size	36mm in diameter
Ribbon	32mm wide, watered, orange-yellow with two wide and two narrow dark blue stripes.
Suspension	Ornamental scroll swivelling suspension slightly wider than that of the South Africa Medal 1853.
Designers	Obverse: W. Wyon RA; Reverse: L. C. Wyon.
Naming	Engraved in capital letters.
Bars issued	Seven: 1877; 1877-8; 1877-8-9; 1877-9; 1878; 1878-9; 1879.

Often referred to as the Zulu War Medal it was awarded for operations against various tribes between September 1877 and December 1879. More accurately called the South Africa General Service Medal it was doubtless thought of as such by authorities at the time who ordered that the design and ribbon should be 'similar to those awarded in 1853'. And so they were, except that the date of 1853 in the exergue was replaced by a shield and four assegais while the ribbon emerged as a deeper orange with slightly lighter blue stripes.

When the first Royal Warrant was applied for in January 1880 the War Office envisaged the issue of two bars—'Caffraria 1877-9' and 'Zululand 1879'—to recognize the fighting against the Gcalekas, Gaikas, Griquas and Zulus. By April 1880 a third bar was decided upon for operations against the Basuto Chief Sekukuni in 1879, but when it was proposed to provide a fourth for service against another Basuto, Moirosi, the prospect of a multiple-bar medal brought pause for thought. The whole position was re-examined; a no-bar medal for the Moirosi troubles and a different medal altogether for the Zulu war were just two suggestions

put forward. It did not help that no-one in the War Office seems to have had a clear understanding of the different tribes, chiefs or territories, but eventually it was decided to issue only one bar per medal, the bar denoting the year or years during which the recipient was employed against an enemy. So, after three Royal Warrants had been issued, General Order 103 was published in August 1880. The actual wording reflects War Office uncertainties and it was soon pointed out that operations against Sekukuni had taken place in 1878 as well as 1879. This was covered by amending General Order 134 in October

1880. For easier understanding the operations provided for can be taken as follows:

1) Against the Gcalekas and Gaikas, under Chiefs Kreli, Sandile, Macomo, etc., the Tambookies and other Kaffir tribes, 26 September 1877-28 June 1878.
2) Against Chief Pokwane, 21st-28th January 1878.
3) Against the Griquas, 24th April-13th November 1878.
4) Against the Zulus under Chief Cetewayo 11th January-1st September 1879.
5) Against the Basutos under Chief Sekukuni 11 November-2nd December 1879.
6) Against Chief Moirosi 25th March-20 November 1879.

General Order 103 assumed that bars for '1877-8', '1878', '1878-9', '1879' and '1877-8-9' would provide for all eventualities but late in 1881 it was learned that a small number of Colonials had served in 1877 only and fewer still had turned out in 1877 and 1879 but not during 1878. As a result two more dies were made bringing the total number of bars to seven and meeting every possible combination. No amending General Order was issued as only Colonials were involved. Many writers have erroneously stated that the '1877' and '1877-9' bars were unofficial. In fact, the dies lie in the Royal Mint Collection.

All this did little for the clerks in the War Officer charged with allotting the bars. They never quite made sense of it and collectors should not assume that the double or treble dated bars always accurately reflect the years of active service as they should. To offer just one example, the 2nd Batt. 24th Regt. arrived in the Cape in March 1878, yet were presented with the three date bar as was the properly qualified 1st Battalion.

In 1978 D. R. Forsyth published 'South African War Medal 1877-8-9. The Medal Roll' which incorporated interesting official correspondence and facsimiles of forms, but to determine the particular campaigns under which recipients qualified it is necessary to consult the official Rolls in the PRO (WO/100/46-50).

Some 36,600 medals were struck; 5,600 were issued without a bar and went to officers and men who were part of the operations against the Zulus between January 11th and September 1st 1879 but did not cross into Zululand from Natal.

The approximate apportionment of the bars was as follows:

1879	18,330
1877-8	5,820
1877-8-9	3,520
1878	2,000
1878-9	1,180
1877	150
1877-9	8

These figures rely upon those given by Major Charles E. C. Townsend TD in his invaluable article in the OMRS Journal (Spring 1979). They are at variance with the larger numbers listed by Forsyth, but this can be accounted for by duplicated and even triplicated submissions when Colonials changed units.

Applicants who were in possession of a SA 1853 medal were supposed to declare the fact, whereupon they should have received an appropriately dated bar for attachment to the earlier medal. Only 20 men are known to have served before 1853. One, an officer, entitled to an 1877-8-9 medal without a bar received it and thus obtained both medals. But so did a few others despite confessing that they held the 1853 award (see OMRS Journal Winter 1981).

Operations against Gcalekas and Gaikas 1877-78

The Fingoes were long oppressed by the Gcalekas but the yoke was removed when they allied themselves to Government forces during the earlier frontier wars and came under British protection. They were encouraged to settle in Gcalekaland between the Kei and Bashee rivers and the hatred between the two tribes burst into flame in 1877 following an incident at a wedding feast.

At first the trouble was regarded as a minor tribal squabble and a small force of Frontier Armed and Mounted Police was sent to deal with it. In trying to assist some Fingoes against a Gcaleka force at Gwadana a patrol found itself heavily outnumbered and beat a hasty retreat to its camp at Ibeka. Digging themselves in around a brick house 180 police and 2,000 Fingoes were attacked on September 29th 1877 by thousands of warriors. Fortunately the defenders had a gun and

Congreve rockets and inflicted such casualties that the Gcalekas broke and fled.

It was now decided to deal with them once and for all and to annex their territory. In October a force of 500 police, 1,000 Colonials and 6,000 Native levies swept into Gcalekaland, scattering the inhabitants but doing little real harm. Believing that the disturbances were now over most of the Militia went home but on December 2nd a mounted patrol was attacked in dense bush. Riding for their lives they fell back to a trading store called Holland's shop where 225 police and volunteers joined some artillerymen with two guns and successfully held off all attacks until the dispirited Gcalekas slipped away.

General Sir Arthur Cunynghame, CIC of Imperial troops in South Africa was now instructed to take control. He had few Imperial troops at his immediate disposal—1st/24th and the 88th Regiments—but he was intent upon settling matters quickly and soon had a mixed force moving through Gcalekaland. But now the Gaikas chose to join the rebellion and attacked posts between the Kei and King William's Town. The Tambookies too revolted but were soon suppressed by the Frontier Armed and Mounted Police and Fingo Levies.

Running short of food and ammunition the dissident tribes combined to try to capture a supply depot at Centane Mountain. It was defended by the 1st/24th, a body of Fingoes and two guns, and came under attack on February 6th 1878. Every assault was crushed and the Gcalekas suffered such heavy losses they never fought again.

The Gaikas now crossed the Kei and sought refuge in the Amatola Mountains. Government forces had been reinforced by the 90th Regiment and two batteries of the RA and in March the 2nd/24th landed in the Cape. Early the same month Lt Gen The Hon Frederick Thesinger took over command from Cunynghame and was soon organising limited operations in the bush. They met with indifferent success until at the end of April 4,000 Imperial and Colonial troops went into the Ntaba ke Ndoda region. A company of the 90th ran up against the heaviest resistance and lost 15 men before the enemy was flushed from the valleys and dispersed in small groups.

During May Thesinger was relentless in clearing the Pirie bush, the Fish River Valley and the Waterkloof, capturing cattle and destroying Gaika food supplies. Chiefs Sandile and Seyolo were killed and fugitive bands ruthlessly hunted down until protests in the Cape Town House of Assembly led the way to an amnesty on July 2nd. Casualties during this 9th Kaffir War have been estimated at 60 Europeans and 133 Native levies killed.

Operations Against the Griquas 1878

The Griquas, a race of mixed origin, were settled in two distinct areas; Griqualand East, a district in the Eastern Cape Province, and Griqualand West, 250 miles distant and a region north of the Orange River. Here in the area of the Diamond Fields the Griquas and Boers were uneasy neighbours.

Disturbances arose early in 1878 and rebellious Griquas established themselves in a mountain stronghold. On June 11th a force of Frontier Armed and Mounted Police and Colonial volunteers attacked the fortress and drove them out after six hours of fighting. The survivors scattered over a wide area and some took refuge in the Magnet Hills where they successfully defended inaccessible caves. Small scale skirmishes continued for a couple of months before the troubles were ended and led to an amnesty. Only Colonial units were engaged.

Operations Against Sekukuni 1878 and 1879

Sekukuni's people were Bapedi, a Basuto tribe at the centre of unrest in the Transvaal. From his natural rocky mountain fortress their chief ravaged the surrounding country. He defied the Boers and was contemptuous of the Colonial government until a raid on a chief under British protection forced the Commissioner to move against him. In October 1878 a small mixed force of the 13th Regiment and some Frontier Light Horse sent to bring him to heel found themselves inadequately prepared for the task and withdrew without accomplishing anything. With trouble brewing in Zululand it was decided to suspend operations for the time being and a year passed before attention was again focused on Sekukuni.

In November 1879 a force of 1,400 Imperial troops from the 21st, 80th and 94th Regiments, some 800 Colonials and several thousand Native levies moved against the reputedly impregnable stronghold. On the 28th they launched a three-pronged attack and quickly over-ran the position. A race to the summit developed though the defenders were driven from their trenches and caves with difficulty. The Basutos fought well but the native levies gave no quarter and few escaped. One who did was Sekukuni. He surrendered a few days later. Government casualties amounted to 10 European officers and men killed with 49 wounded.

Operations Against Moirosi 1879

The outbreaks in Kaffraria gave rise to anxieties that a confederation of native tribes might form to oppose the Government and it was decided to enforce disarmament on all tribes in the Cape Colony. The Basutos could not imagine life without their firearms and Moirosi, a Baphuti witch doctor of high repute, became so troublesome that in March 1879 a force of some 450 men of the Cape Mounted Rifles and Cape Mounted Yeomanry with Fingo Levies and a few friendly Basutos moved into his country around the junction of the Orange and Quthing rivers. With 1,500 followers Moirosi took refuge in a fortified stronghold known as Moirosi's Mountain. Three sides were virtually perpendicular and the fourth was protected by a series of loopholed walls and traverses.

An assault was made on April 8th preceded by a bombardment with seven pounders. It failed with the loss of 23 killed and wounded. The beseigers were reinforced but the Baphuti grew so confident that during May they twice attacked the piquets. On June 5th another attack failed ignominiously and the investment dragged on with occasional clashes well into November. The irresolute Yeomanry were sent home and the CMR took full responsibility with a few volunteers and levies. On the night of the 20th the eastern face of the mountain was successfully scaled and simultaneous assaults on the northern and southern faces crushed the surprised defenders. Moirosi died with his warriors. The campaign saw three Victoria Crosses awarded to the CMR

The Zulu War 1879

Using minor border incidents to issue Chief Cetewayo an ultimatum so worded as to be inevitably rejected, the High Commissioner Sir Bartle Frere brought about his sought for confrontation with the formidable Zulu army.

On January 11th 1879 British forces moved into Zululand. Three columns were intended to effect a junction at the royal Kraal at Ulundi while two other bodies were positioned to prevent Zulu incursions into Natal and the Transvaal. Under Thesinger, now Lord Chelmsford, the main force crossed the Buffalo from the camp at Rorke's Drift. A short sharp action cleared the way to Isandhlwana where camp was established.

In the belief that the main Zulu army had been located a few hours march away, Chelmsford moved out of camp before dawn on the 22nd January with a force principally composed of the 2/24th Regiment and with four guns of the Royal Artillery. Contact was made with the enemy and some casualties inflicted but the Zulus melted away. Messages then came that the camp at Isandhlwana was under attack and orders were given to return immediately. It was already too late.

Chelmsford had left at the camp two guns of the RA, some 600 of the 1st/24th, 110 mounted men of the Mounted Infantry and Colonial Units and 420 of the Natal Native Contingent. While at breakfast vedettes reported Zulus in the vicinity and the men fell in under arms. At the same time they were reinforced by men of the Natal Native Horse, the Natal Native Contg. and a rocket battery, but the Zulu army now bearing down on the unentrenched camp was overwhelming. The Natal Native Contg. withdrew in disorder and it was impossible to form an unbroken defensive perimeter. Short of ammunition, outflanked and surrounded, the defenders fought hand to hand and died hard. As the camp was over-run some managed to escape the slaughter on horseback, but 858 whites and 471 of the Natal Native Contg. were killed.

Three Victoria Crosses were awarded for gallantry displayed at Isandhlwana.

The troops under Chelmsford regained the camp after dark and slept by the bodies of their comrades. The next day they retired to Rorke's Drift, where 'B' Company, 2nd/24th and a few others, 139 men in all, had gallantly and successfully defended the post against several thousand Zulus. Eleven VC's were awarded for gallantry displayed at Rorke's Drift.

The Isandhlwana disaster forced the other two columns to abandon their plans and one was besieged at Eshowe. Colonial units were

mustered and reinforcements hurried from England. A base camp at Kambula beat off a determined Zulu attack on March 29th and Eshowe was relieved on April 2nd.

A second invasion of Zululand was organised with Ulundi again being the objective. One division was to strike at Cetewayo's kraal after crossing the Buffalo river near Dundee, while another carried out diversionary movements in south east Zululand. Fifteen Imperial infantry and cavalry regiments took part as well as the RA, RE, Mounted Colonial units and the Natal Native Contg. Both divisions took time to assemble and movement was slow through April and May. During June there was a series of minor skirmishes and earthwork forts were established to protect communications. On July 3rd the Mounted Infantry and Colonial horsemen under Lt Col Buller were in action on the Mahlabatini plain within sight of Ulundi. The following day Chelmsford's troops advanced in hollow square.

A screen of mounted men retired to the square when opposed and the Zulu warriors bravely came on until cut down in swathes. As they faltered the 17th Lancers were sent out to pursue the survivors. Catewayo's kraal was burned but the chief was not captured until August 28th.

From December, 1877, to December, 1879, the Navy played a part which is worthy of a longer account than space permits. In December, 1877, a brigade of three hundred seamen and Marines from HMS *Active* was landed at East London under Captain Wright, RN. They fought under Colonel Glynn, against Pokwane in the Battle of Quintana early in 1878. In 1878, men of this brigade also fought against the Gaikas in the Peri Bush and then rejoined their ship. On 19th November, 1878, a further brigade under Captain Campbell, RN, and Lieutenants Craigie and Hamilton, landed at Durban. It was 172 strong with three guns and two rocket tubes. It formed, together with forty reinforcements from HMS *Tenedos,* part of the garrison at Eshowe for some time. A Naval Brigade, under Captain Brackenbury RN, was present at Ginghilovo. When Lord Chelmsford crossed the Tugela river into Zululand he took with him a Naval Brigade consisting of forty-one officers and 812 seamen and Marines.

The following figures summarise the Naval awards of this medal inclusive of those awarded to locally employed 'Kroomen'.

No bar (1829), 1877-8 (75), 1878 (nil), 1878-9 (nil), 1877-8-9 (123), 1879 (847).

A total of twenty-nine Victoria Crosses were awarded during these campaigns, those for the major actions being:

Isandhlwana 22nd January 1879, VC recipients
Lieut. T. Melville, 24th Regiment; Lieut. N. J. A. Coghill, 24th Regiment; Pte S. Wassall, 80th Regiment.

Killed at Isandhlwana: 22nd January 1879

Europeans	Officers	NCO's & Men
Staff	2	9
N/5 RA	1	61
Rocket Battery, RA	1	6
RE	1	4
1/24th	16	400
2/24th	5	178
ASC		3
AHC	1	10
Army Medical Corps	1	1
Mounted Infantry		13
Natal Mounted Police		26
Natal Carbineers	2	20
Newcastle Mtd. Rifles	2	5
Buffalo Border Guard		3
Sikali's Horse	1	
1st Bn 1st Regt Natal Native Contg.	2	10
1 Bn 3rd Regt Natal Native Contg.	8	29
2nd Bn 3rd Regt Natal Native Contg.	9	28
Total Europeans	52	806
Natives killed—Reported total		471
Total Reported Killed		1329

Rorkes Drift 23rd January 1879, VC recipients
Lieut John Chard, RE; Lieut G. S. Bromhead, 24th Regiment; Pte John Williams, 2nd/24th Regiment; Pte Henry Hook, 2nd/24th Regiment; Pte William Jones, 2nd/24th Regiment; Pte Robert Jones, 2nd/24th Regiment; Cpl William Allen, 2nd/24th Regiment; Pte Frederick Hitch, 2nd/24th Regiment; Surgeon-Major J. H. Reynolds, AMD; Actg Asst James Langley Dalton, Commissariat and Transport Dept; Cpl F. C. Schiess, Natal Native Contingent

Killed at Rorke's Drift, 23rd January 1879

	NCO's and Men
1/24th	4
2/24th	9
Commissariat and Transport Corps	1
Natal Mounted Police	1
Estimated Zulu Casualties	600

Ulundi 3rd July 1879, VC recipients
Sgt Edmund O'Toole, Frontier Light Horse; Captain Cecil D'Arcy, Frontier Light Horse;

———

The Colonial units changed their titles with such bewildering frequency that they may have been mentioned twice against the same bar or given the wrong title at the time. The medals were, of course, issued after the campaigns, and one suspects that those entitled to a medal gave the present title of their unit if still serving or the title at the time of the campaign if they had been demobilized. This would account for two titles to the same unit and, with the constant changes already referred to, probably a good many more. In many cases although the rolls indicate that reasonable numbers were issued, a large proportion were returned to Woolwich; where the number returned is known these are shown thus: (60.W20).

———

No bar. Numerous Imperial and Colonial units received the medal without a bar.
HM Ships *Active* (201), *Boadicea* (249), *Euphrates* (261), *Himalaya* (228), *Orontes* (226), *Shah* (307), *Tamar* (215), *Tenedos* (142).

1877

The advance against the Gcalekas did not start until 26th September, 1877, so that this bar is particularly rare.
List of '1877' Bars on South African 1877-79 Medal
to Colonial Units, after deducting numbers returned to Woolwich:

Aliwal North Mounted Vols	16
Bowkers Rovers	34
Prince Alfred's Volunteer Guard	24
Fort White Mounted Vols.	11
Sidbury Mounted Rangers	5
East London & Chalumna Cavalry	6
Miscellaneous	11
Add medals known but not found on rolls	3
Total:	110

The following medals are known:
Pte A. Freeman, PAVG; Tpr J. Pentland, Bowker's Horse; No. 422 Pte J. Hennetz, 88th Foot; Trooper J. Kemp, Bowker's Rovers; Pte T. Murray, PAG Rifle Volunteers; No. 1806 Pte. J. Wales; Lieut Vononheim, Cape Mounted Rifles; Pte H. F. McLachlan, PAG Rifle Vols; Tpr Searle, Bowker's Rovers; Tpr. J. C. McCall, Aliwal N. Mtd. Vols; Pte C. Hickey, Fort White Mtd. Vols; Pte S. Roberts, PAG Rifle Vols and Civil Practitioner E. S. Stevenson.

1877-8

Imperial Troops present: N/5 (2), 8/7 (23), 11/7 (3) RA; RE (33); 1/13, 1/24, 2/24 (44), 80, 88 (195), 90 (70) Foot. AHC, ASC, Army Dept. Commissariat and Transport.
Colonial Troops present: Adelaide Vol. Cav. (74.W*28); Albany Fingoe Levy (53.W49); Albany Mounted Rangers (or Rifles) (43); Albert Burghers (262.W148); Albert Vols. (37.W23); Alexandra Mounted Rifles (42.W15); Aliwal North Mounted Volunteers; Barber's Horse (75.W58); Beaufort Rangers Cavalry Volunteers (59); Berlin Volunteer Cavalry (122); Berlin Volunteer Mounted Infantry (3); Bolotwa Tembus (136.W32); Bolotwa Volunteers; Bowker's Horse (101.W60); Bowker's Rovers (74W36); Buckley's Native Levy (51.W45); Buffalo Mounted Vol. Rifles (18.W7); Buffalo Vol. Rifles and Levy (104.W53); Cape Field Arty. (10); Cape Mounted Rifles (392.W159); Cape Mounted Rifles Frontier Armed Mounted Police (14.W3); 1 Chalumna Volunteers (Cavalry); Clan-William Vol. Corps (40); Colesburg Light Horse (53); Cradock Vol. Rifles (11); Diamond Fields Horse; District Native Police (8); Duke of Edinburgh's Own Vol. Rifles (55.W16); East London Burghers (20.W10); East London Engineers; East London Volunteer Guard (28); First City Volunteers (53.W20); Fort Beaufort Mounted Volunteers (84); Fort White Mounted Volunteers (12); Frankfort Burghers (41.W27); Frontier Armed Mounted Police (74.W22); Frontier Armed and Mounted Police (146.W30); Frontier Light Horse (98.W1); Frontier Mounted Rifles (210); German Burghers Horse Arty. (73.W16); German Grahamstown Horse Artillery; Grahamstown Rifle Volunteers (11); Hottentot Militia (or Levy) (149); Kaffrarian Volunteer Artillery (12.W3); Kaffrarian Mounted Rifles (36); Kaffrarian Rangers (110); Kaffrarian Volunteers (117); Khama's Levies (113.W40); Keiskama Hoek Burghers (40); Keiskama Hoek Vol. Rifles (20); Keiskama Volunteer Infantry (20); Keiskama Hoek Mounted Volunteers (59); Kimberley Horse (29); Kingwilliamstown Veterans (29); Komgha Fingoe Levy (103); Leach's Fingoes (94.W69); Lonsdale's Horse; Murraysburg Volunteer Cavalry (31); Murrays Orange Rovers; Natal Native Contingent (21); Nelson Burghers (18.W5); Northern Border Horse (9); Northern Border Police (56.W26); Officer's Fingoe Levies (10); Port Elizabeth Militia (42.W28); Port Elizabeth Vol. Horse (56); Prince Albert's Guard Rifle Volunteers (130.W28); Prince Albert's Arty. Vol. (27.W2); Prince Alfred's Own Cape Vol. Arty. (44.W6); Pulleine's Rangers (37); Pullen's Fingoe Levy (51.W45); Queenstown Burghers Force (115.W84); Queenstown Burghers Force Levies (26.W24); Queenstown Burghers (115.W86); Queenstown Rifle Volunteers (323); Queenstown Volunteer Rifles (21); Queenstown Native Levy (26.W24); Sansom's Horse; Sidbury Rangers (14); Stutterheim Foot Police (32.W27); Stutterheim Mounted Vols. (17.W8); Stutterheim Light Infantry Volunteers (38.W13); Snyman's Burghers (33); Somerset East Volunteers (124); Southeys Rangers (33); Stevenson's Horse (40); Stockenstroom Rangers (28); Streatfields Fingoes (13); Tambookieland Volunteers (5.W1); Transkei Rifles (82); Tshumie Volunteers (153.W141); Upington's Foot (30); Wodehouse Volunteers (6); Yeomanry Regt. (15).
Naval contingents from HM ships *Active* (75).

1877-8-9

Imperial troops present: 1st Royal Dragoons (1); N/5 (178), 8/7 (11), 11/7 (38) RA; 1/13, 1/24 (551), 2/24, 80, 88 (349), 90 (550) Foot.
Colonial troops present: Alexandria Mounted Rangers (8); Baker's Horse (8); Bettington's Horse (7); Cape Field Artillery (41); Cape Mounted Rifles (340.W57); Colesbury Light Horse (4); Fort Beaufort Volunteers (1); Frontier Armed Mounted Police (76.W7); Frontier Mounted Riflemen (200); Grahamstown Volunteer Horse Artillery (6). Keiskama Hoek Volunteers; Kimberley Horse; Lonsdale's Horse (4), Natal Horse; Natal Native Contingent (49.W8); Natal Native Infantry (10); Northern Border Horse, Port Elizabeth Volunteers (7); Prince Albert's Guard Volunteer Rifles (5); Queenstown Volunteer Rifles (31); Stevenson's Horse (30); Stockenstroom Rangers (10); Wodehouse Volunteers (9).
124 members of the crews of the ships present in 1877 and 1878 received this bar including HMS *Active* (119), *Boadicea* (4).

1877-9

Colonial Troops present: 2 Cape Mounted Yeomanry (8.W3).

———

*'W' indicates the number of medals which were not claimed and eventually returned to Woolwich.

1878

Imperial Troops present: 1/13 (25), 1/24, 80 (170), 88, 90 Foot.

Colonial troops present: Baker's Horse (14); Barkly Rangers (63.W38); Bowker's Rovers; Buffalo Volunteer Horse; Cape Town Volunteer Artillery; Colesburg Light Horse (33); Corps of Guides (13.W8); Diamond Fields Horse (2); East London Volunteer Guard (12); Ferreira's Horse (17.W9); First City Volunteers; Fort White Mounted Volunteers (59); Frontier Light Horse; George Town Volunteers (28); Grahamstown Volunteer Horse; Griqualand West Constabulary or Light Infantry (117.W16); Griquatown Burg. Force; Griqualand West Native Contingent (9.W1); Griqualand West Volunteer Arty. (26.W15); Hottentot Militia (or Levy); Humansdorp Volunteer Horse; Jamestown Mounted Volunteer Rifles (40); Komgha Fingoes; Murray's Orange Rovers (68); Northern Border Horse; Northern Border Police; One Star Diamond Contingent (266.W84); Panmure Volunteer Horse; Princes Horse Pulleines Rangers (5); Raaf's Horse; Riversdale Burghers (52); Ronald Maclean's Fingoes; Sidbury Mounted Rifles (10); Siwani's Kaffirs (9.W6); Somerset East Volunteers (78.W51); Tamacha Fingoes; Tarka South Rangers (20); Transvaal Artillery (13.W4); Vincent's Volunteer Horse; Winterberg Grey's Volunteers (29); Wodehouse True Blues (75).

1878-9

Imperial troops present: 11/7 RA (6); 3, 1/13, 1/24 (35), 80, 88 Foot.

Colonial Troops present: Baker's Horse; Border Horse (12); Cape Mounted Rifles (37.W12); Cape Town Volunteer Artillery (34); Clarke's Police; Diamond Fields Horse; Ferreira's Horse; Frontier Light Horse; Grahamstown Horse Volunteer Artillery; Kimberley Horse (29); Kimberley Rangers; Natal Native Contingent (21); Southey's Rangers; Stockenstroom Volunteers Rifles (19); Transvaal Artillery (4).

HMS *Shah*.

1879

Imperial troops present: M/6 (160), N/6 (180), 0/6 (180), 8/7 (57), 10/7, 11/7 (97) RA; Gatling Train (81), 2, 5, 7, 30 Company RE, C Troop RE, ASC Army Hospital; Army Hospital Corps; 1st Life Guards (2); 2nd Dragoon Guards (3); 3rd Dragoon Guards (3); 4th Dragoon Guards (2); 1 King's Dragoon Guards (600); 16 (6), 17 Lancers; Frontier Light Horse;* 2/3, 2/4 (1,000), 1/13 (950), 2/21, 1/24, 2/24 (119), 57, 58, 3/60, 80 (820), 88 (336), 90 (380), 91, 94, 99 Foot. Also four to The Scots Greys.

Colonial troops present: Alexandra Mounted Rifles (30); Amangwi Scouts; Amatonga Scouts; Baker's Horse (21); Bolotwa Volunteers (18); Border (or Weatherley's) Horse (230); Buffalo Border Guard (196.W91); Cape Field Artillery; Cape Mounted Rifles; Cape Mounted Rifles Artillery; Cape Mounted Yeomanry (250); Duke of Edinburgh's Own Volunteer Artillery; Diamond Fields Horse; Dunn's Scouts; Durban Mounted Rifles (72), Eckersley's Native Contingent; Ferreira's Horse (130); Fort Beaufort Volunteers (33.W26); Frontier Light Horse (5); Grahamstown Horse Artillery Volunteers (7); Griqualand West Border Police; Herschel Mounted Volunteers (59.W3); Herschel Native Contingent (1037.W320); Isipingo Mounted Rifles (101.W46); Mafunzi's Mounted Natives; Murray's Orange Rovers; Natal Carbineers (76); Natal (or Bettington's) Horse; Natal Hussars (40); Natal Mounted Police (167); Natal Mounted Volunteers; Natal Native Cavalry (or Horse) (19); Natal Native Contingent (104); Natal Native Pioneers (8); Nettleton Ltd. Horse; Newcastle Mounted Rifles (37); Northern Border Horse; Nourse's Horse; Pietermaritzburg Carbineers; Pietermaritzburg City Guard; Pietermaritzburg Rifles; Piet Uys Horse (or Burgher Force); Pretoria Carbineers (or D'Arcy's Horse); Pretoria Rifles; Pulleine's Rangers; Queenstown Volunteer Rifles (35); Rustenburg Contingent; Shepstone's Native Horse (79.W17); Stanger's Rifles (55); Stockenstroom Rifle Volunteers (18); Stockenstroom Rangers (6); Swazie Contingent; Transvaal Artillery (21); Transvaal Mounted Rifles; Transvaal Rangers (or Raaf's Horse); Transvaal Mounted Volunteer Force (13); Umvoti Mounted Rifles; Victoria Mounted Rifles (49); Weenan Yeomanry (19); Wood's Irregulars; Zoutpansberg Native Contingent.

HM Ships: *Active* (56), *Boadicea* (223), *Forester* (111), *Shah* (398), *Tenedos* (59).

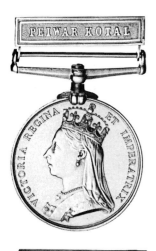

103 *Afghanistan Medal* 1878-1880

Obverse	The crowned and draped head of Queen Victoria and legend 'VICTORIA REGINA ET IMPERATRIX'.
Reverse	A scene of troops on the march with an elephant carrying a gun in the centre. Around the top is the word 'AFGHANISTAN' and in the exergue the dates '1878-79-80'.
Size	31mm diameter.
Metal	Silver and bronze.
Ribbon	32mm wide. Green with crimson stripe on each edge.
Suspension	By means of a plain, swivelling suspender.
Designers	Obverse—J. E. H. Boehm; Reverse—R. Caldecott. The engraving was carried out by L. C. Wyon.
Naming	The medals to the British troops were engraved in upright or sloping capitals and those awarded to natives are found named in capitals or script.
Bars issued	Six: Ali Musjid, Peiwar Kotal, Charasia, Ahmed Khel, Kabul and Kandahar. The bars are somewhat large, being 8mm x 35mm. They have no rosettes, as is common with Indian medals to cover the junctions.

The medal was sanctioned on 19th March 1881 for the Afghanistan campaigns of 22nd November 1878 to 26th May 1879 and 3rd September 1879 to 20th September 1880.

The following British regiments served during the war and many received the medal with no bar. In addition to the Artillery, Sappers and Miners and ancillary services: 6 Dragoon Guards; 8, 10, 15 Hussars; 9 Lancers (46); 1/5, 2/5, 2/7, 1/8, 2/8, 2/9, 2/11, 12, 2/14, 2/15, 1/17, 18, 1/25, 31, 34 (31), 51 (454), 59 (13), 2/60, 63*, 65†, 66, 67, 70, 72, 78, 81, 85, 92, Foot and Rifle Brigade (83).

The following Artillery units took part in the war and were issued with medals without bars, numbers shown in brackets: A Brigade: D (236), F (177) and I (133) Batteries; B Brigade: A (65), D (136) and E (52) Batteries; C Brigade: H (154) and I (87) Batteries; 1st Brigade: I (144) and H (184) Batteries; 2nd Brigade: C (18), D (188) and F (168) Batteries; 3rd Brigade: C (230), E (38) and G (83) Batteries; 4th Brigade: A (136), C (208), E (175) and G (43) Batteries; 5th Brigade: L (142) Battery; 8th Brigade: C (29), No 1 (134), No 5 (99), No 13 (102) and No 16 (10) Batteries; 9th Brigade: 13th (23), 14th (93) and 15th (43) Batteries; 11th Brigade: 5th (29), 6th (19), 8th (11), 9th (4), 10th (90) and 11th (29) Batteries; Siege Train: Kandahar Field Force (26); 12/9, Battery RGA; 13/8, 16/8, 8/11 Siege Trains RA; 1, 2, 3, 4 Mountain Batteries; 5 Garrison Battery.

---

*A few men of the 1st Bn. The Manchester Regiment received four bars, though the battalion as a whole did not participate in the fighting.

†6 officers and 22 other ranks were employed on lines of communications signals.

Ali Musjid 21st November 1878

Regiments present: 10 Hussars; two Squadrons 11 Bengal Lancers; two Squadrons Guides Cavalry; I/C Bty RHA; E/3 Bty RFA (158); 11/9 Mountain Bty (104); 13/9 Garrison Bty (72); No 4 (Hazara) Mountain Bty; Bengal Sappers and Miners; 1/17, 51, 81 Foot and 4 Rifle Brigade; Corps of Guides; 1, 14, 45 Sikhs; 6, 20, 45 Bengal NI; 20 and 27 Punjab NI; 4 Gurkhas.

It is most unusual to find this bar and that for Ahmed Khel on the same medal.

Peiwar Kotal 2nd December 1878

Regiments present: One Squadron 10 Hussars (38); 12 Bengal Cavalry; 5 Punjab Cavalry; F/A Bty RHA (26); G/3 Bty RFA (74); No 1 (Kohat) and No 2 (Derajat) Indian Mountain Batteries; Bengal Sappers and Miners; 2/8, 72 Foot; 2, 5, 29 Punjab NI; 23 Pioneers; 5 Gurkhas.

Charasia 6th October 1879

Regiments present: A Squadron of 9 Lancers (87); 5 Punjab Cavalry; 14 Bengal Lancers; 12 Bengal Cavalry; G/3 Bty RA (143); F/A Bde RHA (58); and No 2 (Derajat) Mountain Battery; Bengal Sappers and Miners; 67, 72, 92 Foot; 5 and 28 Punjab NI; 3 Sikhs; 23 Pioneers; 5 Gurkhas.

Pte. T. Munro, 8th Hussars, received this bar and that for Kabul.

Kabul 10th-23rd December 1879

Awarded to those who were engaged in operations at or near Kabul between 10th and 23rd December, including the column under Brigadier-General C. J. S. Gough vc, which joined Sir Frederick Roberts vc, on 24th December.

Regiments present: 9 Lancers (253); 10, 14 Bengal Lancers; 5 Punjab Cavalry; Guides Cavalry; F/A Bde RHA (135); G/3 Bty RA (143); No 1 (Kohat), No 2 (Derajat) and No 4 (Hazara) Mountain Batteries; Bengal

Sappers and Miners; 2/9, 67, 72, 92 Foot; Corps of Guides; 28 Bengal NI; 23 Pioneers; 5 Punjab Inf.; 3 Sikhs; 2, 4, 5, Gurkhas.

Ahmed Khel 19th April 1880

Regiments present: 19 Bengal Lancers; 1, 2 Punjab Cavalry; A/B Bde RHA (168); G/4 Bty RA (123); 6/11 Heavy Bty RA (96); 11/11 Mountain Bty RA; ten men of PWO Sappers and Miners; 59, 2/60 Foot; 19, 25 Punjab Infantry; 570 men of 2 and 15 Sikhs; 3 Gurkhas. Also known to the 53 Foot.

It is most unusual to find this bar and that for Ali Musjid on the same medal.

Kandahar 1st September 1880

Awarded to those under Sir Frederick Roberts VC engaged in the action on 1st September 1880 and also granted to those who took part in the reconnaissance of the city on 31st August 1880 but who did not participate in the attack the next day.

Regiments present: 9 Lancers (244); 3 Bengal Cavalry; 3 Punjab Cavalry; 3 Bombay Cavalry; Central India Horse; Poona Horse; 3 Scinde Horse; E/B RHA; C/2, 6/8, 11/9, 5/11 RA; 2 Mtn Bty; 2 Bombay Sappers and Miners; 23 Pioneers; 2/7, 22 (6), 50 (13), 2/60, 66 (309), 72, 92 Foot; 2, 3, 15 Sikhs; 24, 25 Punjab NI; 1, 3, 4, 9 28, 29, 30 Bombay NI; 2, 4, 5 Gurkhas. Also known to the 56 Foot.

In 1873 the boundaries between Afghanistan and India were agreed upon by the British and Shere Ali, the Amir, for the peaceful recognition of which he was to be paid a substantial subsidy. In 1877, Shere Ali refused to have a British Resident at Kabul, raised an army and did all he could to promote bad feeling between the border tribes and the British. He refused to receive a Mission sent by the Viceroy and threatened the advance party of another led by Sir Neville Chamberlain which left Peshawur on 21st September 1877. In August 1878, he signed a treaty with Russia giving her the guardianship of himself and the right to protect Afghanistan.

The increasingly pro-Russian stance by Afghanistan upset the delicate balance of power in the area and was seen as a threat to British India. Britain responded by sending an ultimatum to Shere Ali on 28th October 1878 to which a reply was demanded by 20th November. Meanwhile troops were concentrated at Peshawur, Kohat and Quetta in readiness for action.

As no answer was received by 20th November, the Army, which had been organised into three columns, began to cross the frontier on 21st November, 1878. The three columns were as follows: the first, the Peshawur Valley Field Force under Lieutenant-General Sir Samuel Browne, VC, KCSI, CB, the second, the Kurram Valley Field Force under Major-General Frederick Roberts, VC, CB; the third, the Kandahar Field Force under Lieutenant-General Donald Stewart.

The Peshawur Force crossed the border at Jamrud on 21st November and captured the hill fortress of Ali Musjid on the same day.

The Kurram Force crossed the border and defeated the Afghans in the Peiwar Kotal,* at the entrance to the Kurram Valley route to Kabul, on 2nd December.

After these two actions Shere Ali fled from Kabul and his son Yakub Khan assumed command. General Roberts annexed the Kurrum Valley

and after a little more desultory fighting Yakub Khan, on 30th May 1879, concluded peace. By this peace he agreed to a British Resident being in Kabul. The Khyber Pass, the Kurrum and Pisheen Valleys were to be occupied by the British. The Amir was to be paid an annual subsidy of £60,000 to be on his good behaviour.

Sir Louis Cavagnari, KCB, CSI, was appointed Resident at Kabul, where he arrived on 24th July 1879. On 3rd September, Sir Louis, and other British residents, together with the bodyguard of the Corps of Guides, were murdered.

General Roberts was ordered to march to Kabul with the Kabul Field Force. He started on 27th September and on the way defeated the Afghans at Charasia on 6th October. He entered Kabul on the 8th, where he was practically surrounded. He concentrated his troops in the cantonments at Sherpur, where they were severely attacked on 23rd December 1879. Reinforcements under General Gough arrived on the 24th and Kabul was reoccupied. It was for fighting in and around Kabul between the 10th and 23rd December that the bar 'Kabul' was awarded.

In April, 1880, General Stewart moved out of Kandahar with a view to clearing the lines of communication to Kabul. When nearing Ghuznee he encountered the Afghans at Ahmed Khel on 19th April and defeated them. He reached Kabul on 2nd May.

After Charasia, Yakub Khan abdicated, to be replaced as Amir on 22nd July 1880 by the pro-British Abdur Rahman, nephew of Shere Ali. However Ayub Khan the brother of Yakub Khan also claimed the throne. From Herat which he had earlier seized, he marched with 25,000 men and 30 guns towards Kandahar. General G. R. S. Burrows was despatched from Kandahar with an Anglo-Indian force of 2,500 men and 6 guns to support an Afghan force against Ayub Khan; however this Afghan force mutinied.

At Maiwand on 27th July 1880 Burrows was badly defeated when his artillery ammunition gave out and his small force overwhelmed. The remnants of his force retired to Kandahar closely followed by those of Ayub Khan who placed the city, and the forces under General Primrose, under siege.

Units at Maiwand: E Bde, B Bty. RHA; 2 Company Bombay Sappers and Miners; 66 Regiment; 3 Bombay Light Cavalry; 3 Scinde Horse; 1, 30 Bombay NI; Bombay Ordnance Department; Bombay Commissariat Department; 2 Field Hospital.

Over 1,100 of the Anglo Indian force were killed or wounded plus numerous followers, bearers etc. Casualties: RHA 34, 66 Regiment 319, 1 Bombay NI 426, 30 Bombay NI 245, 3 Bombay Light Cavalry 45, 3 Scinde Cavalry 18.

General Roberts with 10,000 men then advanced from Kabul to relieve Kandahar. On 1st September 1880 he attacked and defeated Ayub Khan at Kandahar. For his memorable march between Kabul to Kandahar a special Star (No 104) was awarded.

With this battle the war was brought to a close and with the Afghanistan government in the hands of Abdur Rahman, the British withdrew.

A total of sixteen Victoria Crosses were won in the Afghan campaign including two for Maiwand.

It is interesting to note that five Generals who were holders of the Victoria Cross took part in the campaign: Generals Browne, Gough, Macpherson, Tytler and Roberts.

---

*Kotal means pass.

104 *Kabul to Kandahar Star* 9th-31st August 1880

General	A five-pointed star with a ball between all the points except the two uppermost where is fixed a crown.
Obverse	In the centre is the monogram 'V.R.I' around which is a raised circular band. On this border in raised lettering around the top is, 'KABVL TO KANDAHAR', at the bottom is the date '1880'.
Reverse	Plain except for the recipient's name engraved around the hollow centre
Size	Height to top of crown, excluding the suspension ring 62mm. Maximum width 48mm.
Metal	Bronze
Ribbon	38mm wide, a rainbow pattern of red, white, yellow, white, blue (a thinner version than that for the First Afghan War Medals).
Suspension	By means of a ring attached to the back of the crown near the top.
Designer	Not known. Manufactured by Messrs H. Jenkins & Sons, Birmingham.
Naming	In indented capitals to British troops. Those issued to natives are found engraved in capitals and in script. A frequent error with specimens that have been named is the use of 'Foot' instead of 'Regt.' Examples are also found unnamed.
Bars issued	Nil

The star, usually issued in conjuction with the Afghanistan Medal with the bar Kandahar was made from guns captured from the army of Ayub Khan. Authorized by the Queen on 19th March 1881.

It was awarded to all who took part in General Roberts' famous march of about three hundred and ten miles from Kabul to Kandahar between 9th and 31st August 1880. In addition to the men from Kabul it was also awarded to the troops of the garrison of Kelat-i-Ghilzie who accompanied Roberts to Kandahar.

The force under General Roberts' command consisted of an Infantry Division and a Cavalry and Artillery Brigade as follows:

Cavalry: 9 Lancers (243); 3 Bengal Cavalry; 3 Punjab Cavalry; Central India Horse. Artillery: 6/8, 11/9 British and No 2 (Hazara) Indian Mountain Batteries. Infantry: 59 (9)*, 2/60, 65 (4), 66 (detachment), 72, 81 (1)†, 92 Foot; 23 Pioneers; 24, 25 Punjab NI; 2, 3, 15 Sikhs; 2, 4, 5 Gurkhas.

The garrison at Kelat-i-Ghilzie consisted amongst others of two companies of the 66th Foot under Captain McKinnon.

---

*965 R. Hogan; 1420 G Burbridge; 1081 G. Harrison; 1239 M. Kempson; 1199 J. Carver; 472 G. Tomkinson; Lieut H. A. L. Boulderson; Lieut C. Hodgkinson and 2/Lieut W. G. Small.
†L/Cpl. Moon.

105 *Cape of Good Hope General Service Medal* 1880-1897

Obverse	The bust of Queen Victoria wearing a veil and a small crown, with the legend, 'VICTORIA REGINA ET IMPERATRIX'.
Reverse	The arms of Cape Colony with the legend, 'CAPE OF GOOD HOPE'.
Size	36mm diameter.
Metal	Silver
Ribbon	33mm wide, darkish blue with a sandy-coloured yellow stripe down the centre.
Suspension	By means of a swivelling straight suspender
Designer	G. W. de Saulles
Naming	Engraved in the UK in thin, rather faint, block capitals. Some later issues were named in Cape Town, being impressed in fairly crude, squarish capitals.
Bars issued	Three—Transkei, Basutoland, Bechuanaland.

Authorized by the Cape of Good Hope Government with the approval of the Queen on 4th December 1900.

Just over 5,000 medals were awarded for services in suppressing small risings in the places mentioned on the bars. Medals were awarded to all survivors and claimants who during any of the campaigns saw active service in the field, served as guards at any point where an attack was expected or who were detailed for some specific or special military duty.

An analysis of the Issue Register at Defence Headquarters, Pretoria reveals the following issues:

One Bar 'Transkei'	562
One Bar 'Basutoland'	1589
One Bar 'Bechuanaland'	2483
Two Bars 'Transkei & Basutoland'	490
Two Bars 'Transkei & Bechuanaland'	18
Two Bars 'Basutoland & Bechuanaland'	77
Three Bars	23
No Bar	10
TOTAL	5252

The following were authorized to receive the medal without a bar: Pte S. R. Daniel, CMR; Cpl S. K. C. Daly, Papkuil Rifles; Col Sgt V. Ewers, Stutterheim LI Vol; Sgt W. Haig, DEOV Rifles; Pte H. H. Norton, CMR; Nurse G. A. Rogers; Sp Policeman A. A. Smith, Cape Police D 1; Pte E. G. Smith, DEOV Rifles; Sgt J. Wilson, CMR; Pte P. A. Williams, CMR.

With the exception of Nurse Rogers, Pte Williams and Sgt Wilson it is probable that the others were in fact issued a medal with a bar.

Medals issued with all three bars:
Dvr J. Bobbins, PAOCV Arty; Capt A. L. Chiapini, CM Yeo; Gnr E. C. A. Coombs, Cape F Arty; Pte J. Wirran, Nesbitts L Horse; Sgt E. H. Dye, Cape Police Dist No 1; Lieut F. W. H. Gillwald, Cape Police Dist No 1; Surgn Maj E. B. Hartley, vc, CM Rifles; Capt A. N. M. Hutcheons, Wodehouse B Rovers; Pte J. Lust, Nesbitts L Horse; Sapper R. McArthur, CTV Engrs; Sgt H McDonald, Nesbitts L Horse; Tpr E. McGuire, CM Yeo; Capt R. McLean, Buffalo Vol; Sgt Maj C. S. March, Landreys Horse; Pte C. Nielsen, Nesbitts L Horse; Sgt T. C. Peakman, CF Arty; Lieut R. Pillans, DEOV Rifles; Pte R. Quine, CT Rifles; L/Cpl T. Rodwell, DEOV Rifles; Pte S. Strutt, Nesbitts L Horse; Pte A. Turner, Ushers Contgt; Sgt A. J. White, CM Rifles; Pte W. D. Willemite, CT Rangers.

Transkei 13th September 1880-15th May 1881

This bar was awarded for operations in Tembuland and Griqualand East, in both of which the natives rose in revolt on account of having to hand in their firearms. They showed marked hostility towards the settlers in the districts of Tsolo, Maclear, Matatiele and Qumbu, in all of which it became necessary to employ troops to restore order.

It is difficult to separate the fighting for which this and the next bar were awarded.

Basutoland 13th September 1880-27th April 1881

After the termination of the fighting in 1879 (see No 102) the natives were ordered to hand in their firearms. Certain chiefs, such as Jonathon and Letsi, complied with the order, but no sooner had they done so than they were attacked by Chiefs Lerothodi, Masupha and Moletsane, together with others. In September 1880, they attacked the white officials. The situation soon became so serious that troops and volunteers were mobilized.

The first encounter took place near Mafeteng on 17th September, when a detachment of Cape Mounted Riflemen, under Colonel F. Carrington, was attacked by Chief Lerothodi. When they reached Mafeteng they were again attacked and the place besieged by rebel Basutos. On 10th and 28th October the Basutos attacked Maseru, but were repulsed on both occasions. On 19th October Brigadier-General M. Clarke, now in command of all the forces, was attacked at Kalabani. Lerothodi's village was stormed and captured by Colonel F. Carrington on 22nd October, and on the 31st that of Moletsane by Brigadier-General Clarke.

From November 1880, to February 1881, there were several encounters. In the latter month an armistice was arranged, but sporadic skirmishes continued until peace was concluded in May 1881, though

Chief Masupha did not submit until September. The troubles continued in 1882, 1883 and 1884, in which latter year there were battles between the Chiefs Khetisa and Masupha on one side and Lerothodi on the other.

In response to representations by the Basutos the Home Government agreed that Basutoland should become a Crown Colony. The change-over took place in March, 1884.

Bechuanaland 24th December 1896-30th July 1897

In April 1896, a severe cattle disease broke out in Bechuanaland which necessitated the slaughtering of cattle belonging to the natives. They resented this and rose in revolt. The first engagement took place at Pokwani, where the natives under Chief Galishwe attacked a detachment of the Cape Mounted Police on 24th December. In January, 1897, the Batlaros rose in revolt, to be followed shortly by practically all the other native tribes. It became obvious that a considerable force would be necessary, so that units were raised, equipped and placed under the command of Lieutenant-Colonel Dalgety, of the Cape Mounted Rifles. The main actions were the attacks on Gamasep Kloof and Riet Kloof, but in neither of these actions were the rebels completely defeated, so that there had to be a pause in the operations whilst more reinforcements were raised for the Bechuanaland Field Force. In July, when all was ready, a 'drive' started which ended with the action at Langberg on 30th July-1st August 1897, as a result of which the ringleaders were either killed or surrendered.

No British units were present for these campaigns, although fifteen were awarded to the following regiments:

IMPERIAL RECIPIENTS

	Basutoland	Transkei	Bechuanaland
3rd KRRC	3	8	1
3rd R Irish Fus	—	—	1
7th Hussars	—	—	2

LOCAL UNITS

BASUTOLAND
Abalondolozi Regt. (14)
Adelaide Mounted Infantry (9)
Albany Rangers (25)
Albert Burghers (4)
Aliwal North Contgt (1)
Aliwal North Vols (3)
Amatembu Regt (1)
Baca Contgt (2)
Bakers Horse (31)
Barkley's Native Contgt (1)
Basutoland Mounted
   Police (5)
Busuto Native Contgt (10)
Beaufort Rangers (4)
Beaufort West Burghers (1)
Beaufort West Vol Rifles (2)
Bedford Burghers (1)
Bredasdorp Burghers (1)
Buffalo Mounted Vols (28)
Buffalo Rangers (4)
Bullers Mounted (1)
Burghersdrop Burgher F (2)
Caledon Burghers (1)
Cape Field Artillery (32)
Cape Infantry (1)
Cape Medical Staff
   Corps (1)
Cape Mounted Riflemen   (355)
Cape Mounted Yeomanry (314)
Cape Police Dist No 1 (9)
Cape Town Rangers (40)
Cape Town Rifles (50)
Cape Town Vol Engineers (3)
Cathcart Burghers (6)
Chalumna Mounted Vols (5)
Colesburg Burghers (9)

Colonial Forces (5)
Commissariat Dept (18)
Cradock Burghers (21)
Despatch Rider (1)
Diamond Fields Arty (1)
Diamond Fields Horse (6)
Dicks Kaffrarian Levies (7)
D of Edinburgh Own Vol
   Rifles (187)
Dymes Rifles (38)
East Griqualand Forces (1)
East London Arty (1)
East London Vol Infantry (3)
Ferreiras Horse (4)
Field Force (2)
Fingo Levies (1)
First City Vols (71)
Fort Beaufort Vols (1)
Fort White Vols (1)
Frontier Armed and
   Mounted Police (2)
Frontier Carabineers (1)
General Clarke's Staff (3)
George Burghers (2)
Gonubie Horse (1)
Graff Reinet Burghers (5)
Graff Reinet Rovers (4)
Grahamstown Vol Horse
   Arty (13)
Griqualand West Brigade (1)
Griqualand West Native
   Contgt (4)
Hampshire Arty (1)
Harveys Horse (2)
Herschell Native Contgt (14)
Hopetown Burghers (7)
Hunts Vols (1)

Irregular Horse (Nettleton) (1)
Kaffrarian Levies (3)
Kaffrarian Rifles (1)
Kaffrarian Vol Arty (16)
Kamatone Fingos (2)
Keiskama Hoek Vols (9)
Kimberley Light Horse (63)
Kimberley Rifles (1)
Knysna Vols (1)
Kokstad Mounted Rifles (10)
Landreys Light Horse (70)
Leaches Rifles (3)
Leribe Native Levy (3)
Lonsdale Rifles (3)
Maclear Constab (1)
Mafeteng Contgt (6)
Malmesbury Burghers (2)
Malmesbury Levies (1)
Maseru Native Levies (1)
Maseru Vols (1)
Middleburg Burghers (3)
Mohali Hoek Contgt (1)
Muters Rangers (10)
Natal Mounted Police (28)
Natal Mounted Rifles (1)
Native Contgt (3)
Native Levies (1)
Nesbitts Light Horse (105)
Ordnance Department (2)
Oudtshoorn Burghers (2)
Paarl Burghers (18)
Paarl Western Levies (1)
Port Elizabeth Rifles (2)
Prince Alfred's Own Cape
   Vol Arty (1)
Prince Alfred's Vol Guard (135)
Pullens Rangers (1)
Queenstown Burghers (17)
Queenstown Rifle Vols (1)
Qutheng and Masitisi Native
   Contgt (1)
Richmond Burghers (9)
Ross and Hicksons Horse (1)
Ross Light Horse (1)
Salem Rangers (1)
Somerset East Burghers (18)
Special Border Police (2)
Stanfords Police (1)
Stantons Light Horse (9)
Stellenbosch Burghers (4)
Sterkstroom Rifles (1)
Stockenstroom Burghers (3)
Stockenstroom Hott Contgt (1)
Stockenstroom Rangers (3)
Strachans Native Contgt (1)
Stutterheim LI Vols (7)
Swellendam Burghers (1)
Tambookie Ward Burghers (1)
Tarkastad Burghers (4)
Tembu Levies (1)
Transport Corps (3)
Transvaal Horse (43)
Uitenhage Burghers (4)
Umtata Volunteers (2)
Ushers Contgt (1)
Ushers Rangers (1)
Victoria Rangers (1)
Walkers Rifles (20)
Warrells Column (2)
Websters Rovers (1)
Western Levies (4)
Willoughby's Horse (39)
Willowmore Burghers (1)
Winterberg Greys (16)
Wodehouse Border Rangers (3)

LOCAL UNITS

TRANSKEI
Abalondolozi Regt (17)
Adelaide Mounted Infantry (10)
Albany Rangers (2)
Albert Burghers (1)
Alexandria Burghers (14)
Aliwal North Contgt (1)
Aliwal North Vols (1)
Ametembu Regt (5)
Baca Contgt (7)
Bakers Horse (53)
Barkley Vols (1)
Basuto Native Contgt (1)
Beaufort Rangers (4)
Beaufort West Burghers (4)
Beaufort West Vol Rifles (10)
Bedford Burghers (12)
Border Police (1)
Bredasdorp Burghers (3)
Buffalo Mounted Vols (21)
Buffalo Rangers (2)
Bullers Mounted (1)
Caledon Burghers (1)
Cape Field Artillery (12)
Cape Infantry (1)
Cape Mounted Riflemen (32)
Cape Mounted Yeomanry (29)
Cape Police Dist No 1 (4)
Cape Town Rangers (42)
Cape Town Rifles (3)
Cape Town Vol Arty (1)
Cape Town Vol Engineers (51)
Cathcart Burghers (4)
Ceres Burghers (6)
Colonial Forces (1)
Commissariat Dept (10)
Diamond Fields Horse (4)
Dicks Kaffrarian Levies (3)
D of Edinburgh Own Vol
   Rifles (10)
Dymes Rifles (2)
East London Vol Infantry (4)
Ferreiras Horse (1)
Fingo Scouts (1)
First City Vols (2)
Frontier Carabineers (10)
Frosts Column (2)
George Burghers (13)
Gonubie Horse (10)
Gordonia Vols (1)
Graff Reinet Burghers (26)
Graff Reinet Rovers (4)
Grahamstown Vol Horse
   Arty (3)
Grays Gonubie Vols (5)
Griqualand West Native
   Contgt (2)
Hampshire Arty (1)
Harvey's Horse (10)
Helvens Horse (1)
Herschell Native Contgt (4)
Humansdorp Burghers (2)
Idutwa Milita (2)
Intelligence (1)
Jamestown Vols (1)
Kaffrarian Rifles (4)
Kaffrarian Vol Arty (2)
Kamatone Fingos (2)
Kimberley Light Horse (2)
King Williams Town Vol
   Arty (11)
Kokstad Mounted Rifles (22)
Komgha Mounted Vols (2)

Lady Frere Native Levy (1)
Landreys Light Horse (34)
Leaches Rifles (2)
Learys Native Levies (1)
Maclear Constab (4)
Malmesbury Burghers (15)
McNicholas Horse (1)
Mount Ayliff Vol (2)
Murraysburgh Burghers (1)
Muters Rangers (10)
Natal Constabulary (1)
Natal Mounted Police (1)
Native Contgt (1)
Native Contgt Tembuland (1)
Native Levies (1)
Nesbitts Light Horse (102)
Ordnance Department (5)
Oudtshoorn Burghers (19)
Paarl Burghers (18)
Paarl Western Levies (1)
Prince Albert Burghers (2)
Prince Alfred's Own Cape
   Vol Arty (40)
Prince Alfred's Vol Guard (5)
Pullens Horse (1)
Queenstown Burghers (9)
Queenstown Division (1)
Queenstown Flying Col (1)
Queenstown Rifle Vols (2)
Qumbu Contgt (1)
Ross and Hicksons Horse (1)
Ross Light Horse (12)
Scouts (1)
Southeyville Levies (1)
Special Border Police (2)
Stanfords Police (2)
Stellenbosch Burghers (12)
Stockenstroom Hott Cont (3)
Stockenstoom Rangers (3)
Strachans Native Contgt (2)
Swellendam Burghers (13)
Tarka Vol Rifles (2)
Tarkastad Burghers (8)
Tembu Levies (4)
Thompson Relief Column (1)
Transkei Native Contgt (7)
Transport Corps (3)
Transvaal Horse (5)
True Blues (1)
Tsolo Native Militia (3)
Uitenhage Burghers (13)
Umtala Volunteers (17)
Ushers Contgt (1)
Ushers Rangers (2)
Victoria Rangers (17)
Vol Medical Staff Corps (1)
Walkers Rifles (20)
Warells Column (2)
Websters Rovers (9)
Western Levies (4)
Willoughby's Horse (31)
Willowmore Burghers (1)
Winterberg Greys (3)
Wodehouse Border Rangers
   (18)
Worcester Burghers (14)

BECHUANALAND
Albany Rangers (2)
Army Ordnance Corps (1)
Bakers Horse (2)
Beaufort West Vol Rifles (1)
Bechuanaland FF (11)
Buffalo Mounted Vols (2)

Cape Field Artillery (6)
Cape Medical Staff Corps (24)
Cape Mounted Riflemen (133)
Cape Mounted Yeomanry (13)
Cape Police Dist No 1 (574)
Cape Police Dist No 2 (192)
Cape Police (131)
Cape Town Highrs (110)
Cape Town Rangers (1)
Cape Town Rifles (1)
Cape Town Vol Engineers (1)
Colesburg Burghers (1)
Commissariat Dept (9)
Cradock Burghers (1)
Dennisons Horse (7)
Despatch Riders (6)
Diamond Fields Arty (23)
Diamond Fields Horse (127)
D of Edinburgh Own Vol
   Rifles (241)
Dymes Rifles (3)
Fingo Levies (1)
First City Vols (106)
Frontier Carabineers (1)
Geluk Mounted Vols (1)
Gordonia Vols (76)
Grahamstown Mtd Infy (1)
Griqualand West Brigade (11)
Hunts Vols (1)
Intelligence (3)
Kaffrarian Levies (1)
Kaffrarian Rifles (87)
Kimberley Light Horse (4)
Kimberley Rifles (176)
Landreys Light Horse (3)
Leaches Rifles (1)
Leribe Native Levy (1)
Mafeking Mounted Rifles (1)
Malmesbury Levies (1)
Mount Temple Horse (4)
Natal Mounted Rifles (1)
Native Basuto Levy (1)
Nesbitts Light Horse (7)
Ordnance Department (2)
Oudtshoorn Vol Rifles (42)
Papkuil Rifles (13)
Prince Alfred's Own Cape Vol
   Arty (40)
Prince Alfred's Vol Guard (138)
Queenstown Rifle Vols (66)
Ross Light Horse (2)
Schermans Burghers (1)
Stellaland Light Horse (18)
Tarkastad Burghers (1)
Taungs Gun Detachment (1)
Telegraphic and Intell Staff (1)
Thompson Relief Column (1)
Transkei Mounted Rifles (1)
Transkei Native Contgt (7)
Transport Corps (19)
Umtata Volunteers (1)
Upington Special Police (1)
Ushers Contgt (1)
Victoria Rangers (1)
Victoria Rifles (1)
Vol. Medical Staff Corps (11)
Vryburg Vols. (39)
Websters Rovers (1)
Western Rifles (1)
Willowvale Native Contgt. (3)
Wodehouse Border Rangers (4)

106 *Egypt Medal* 1882-1889

Obverse   The diademed and veiled head of Queen Victoria with the legend, 'VICTORIA REGINA ET IMPERATRIX'.

Reverse   The Sphinx on a pedestal with the word 'EGYPT' above. In the exergue is the date '1882' for those awarded in the first campaign; those awarded later have a plain exergue.

Size   36mm diameter

Metal   Silver

Ribbon   32mm wide. Three bright blue and two white stripes of equal width.

Suspension   By a straight swivelling suspender.

Designers   Obverse: L. C. Wyon; Reverse: J. Pinches.

Naming   Dated medals are engraved in sloping capitals. Undated medals are impressed in sloping capitals to British troops except those awarded to the Royal Marines which are named in large upright bold capitals. Medals awarded to Indian troops are named in neat small running script. Those awarded to Egyptian troops are named or numbered in Arabic.

Bars issued Thirteen: Alexandria 11th July, Tel-el-Kebir, Suakin 1884, El-Teb, Tamaai, El-Teb-Tamaai, The Nile 1884-85, Abu Klea, Kirbekan, Suakin 1885, Tofrek, Gemaizah 1888, Toski 1889.

The medal was instituted in October 1882 at the conclusion of the Egyptian War of 1882. At the time of its institution two bars were sanctioned, for 'Alexandria 11th July' and 'Tel-el-Kebir'.

When additional bars were awarded the recipient returned those already received for a completely new set. Therefore, the rivets of all genuine multiple bar medals should be the same.

Men who lost their medals and had them officially replaced received undated medals irrespective of the type of the original. With the result that on some of these medals it is possible to find bars that would normally be on a dated medal.

Egypt Medals are difficult to find in mint condition as they were generally worn next to the Khedive's Star which pitted them; this is especially so as regards medals awarded to mounted men.

A medal with seven bars was issued to Captain J. R. Beech, CMG, DSO. Six were issued with six bars to officers and their gallopers. Medals with five bars are rare and those with four are not common.

There are a great number of medals in existence to units which did not take part in the campaign as a whole.

The following medals without bars with either the dated or undated reverse were awarded: 1st Life Guards (51); 2nd Life Guards (60); Royal Horse Guards (52); 4th Dragoon Guards (208); 7th Dragoon Guards (115); 19th Hussars (202); 'N' Bty 'A' Bde (34); 'G' Bty 'B' Bde RHA (29); A/1 (25); D/1 (19), F/1 (14); H/1 (7), N/2 (19), I/2 (11), C/3 (14), J/3 (10), 1/1 S Div (139), RA; 4/1 (106), 5/1 (147) London Division RA; No 7 Battery (19); 5/1 Scottish Division (144); 6/1 Scottish Division RA (145); HQ RA (21); Loyal Malta Artillery (93); Royal Engineeers: Staff (26), A Troop (17), C Troop (66), Field Park (32), 8th (28), 17th (12), 18th (103), 21st (56), 24th (187), 26th (144); Grenadier Guards 2nd Bn (83); Coldstream Guards (49); Scots Guards (58); 8 (63), 35 (927), 38 (1,036), 42 (26), 45/95 (778), 46 (135), 49 (866), 50 (755), 53/85 (785), 63/96 (676), 68, 74 (63), 75 (75), 79 (28), 84 (84), 87 (84) Foot; RAMC, etc; Military Police (15); Army Chaplain's Dept (18); Interpreters (138); Malta Auxiliaries (214, but many not claimed).

Numerous Naval vessels were present in Egyptian waters including the under-mentioned, the crews or part of the complements received the medal without bar with either the dated or undated reverse: *Achilles* (43); *Agincourt* (783); *Albacore* (51); *Arab* (76); *Briton* (200); *Carysfort* (30); *Chester* (21); *Cockatrice* (67); *Condor* (20); *Coquette* (7); *Don* (50); *Dragon* (135); *Dryad* (99); *Eclipse* (224); *Euphrates* (257); *Euryalus* (460); *Falcon* (113); *Hecla* (65); *Helicon* (29); *Humber* (90); *Inconstant* (570); *Iris* (297); *Jumna* (180); *Malabar* (269); *Minotaur* (837); *Mosquito* (63); *Myrmidon* (81); *Northumberland* (820); *Orion* (340); *Orontes* (234);

Rambler (94); *Ranger* (81); *Ready* (81); *Ruby* (234); *Salamis* (88); *Seagull* (108); *Seahorse* (63); *Seraphis* (220); *Sphinx* (68); *Supply* (24); *Tamar* (214); *Thalia* (460); *Tourmaline* (223); *Turquoise* (190); *Tyne* (65); *Woodlark* (60); *Wye* (76). Indian Government Ship *Amberwitch*.

By Admiralty Circular, October 1882, a dated medal was sanctioned to officers and men of the naval forces present in Egypt between 11th July and 14th September, 1882.

By the General Order of 17th October, 1882, a dated medal was granted to all troops who landed and served in Egypt between 16th July and 14th September, 1882.

The following regiments received the 1882 Medal without bars: 35, 38, 49, 50 (one company received the bar for Tel-el-Kebir), 53, 95, 96 Foot, Royal Marines (840 sent out especially from the U.K.).

Dated medals found to the following HM ships seldom have any bars. HM ships: *Achilles*, *Agincourt*, *Amberwitch*, *Arab*, *Calabria*, *Chester*, *Cockatrice*, *Coquette*, *Dee*, *Don*, *Eclipse*, *Euphrates*, *Falcon*, *Humber*, *Inconstant*, *Iris*, *Jumna*, *Malabar*, *Mariner*, *Minotaur*, *Northumberland*, *Orion*, *Orontes*, *Rambler*, *Ranger*, *Ready*, *Ruby*, *Salamis*, *Sandfly*, *Seahorse*, *Seraphis*, *Supply*, *Tamar*, *Thalia*, *Tourmaline*, *Wye*.

Medals without bar were also awarded to 'Masters' of Transport Vessels (105).

Alexandria 11th July 1882

Sanctioned in October. Given to those actually present at the bombardment of Alexandria on 11th July by the ships under Admiral Seymour. Medals with the bar 'Alexandria 11th July' have the date '1882' in the exergue.

Flagship *Invincible* (560), *Alexandra* (821), *Beacon* (82), *Hecla* (236), *Inflexible* (481), *Monarch* (562), *Penelope* (352), *Rambler* (5), *Sultan* (658), *Superb* (623), *Temeraire* (594), *Turquoise* (190), Gunboats *Bittern* (95), *Condor* (104), *Cygnet* (61), *Deacon* (88), *Decoy* (66), *Euphrates*. Despatch Boat *Helicon* (85).

(Medals to HMS *Coquette* and HMS *Minotaur* are known, which ships, however, did not take part in the bombardment.)

Tel-el-Kebir 13th September 1882

Sanctioned on 17th October, 1882. Awarded to those troops who took part in the night march from Kassassin and the assault at Tel-el-Kebir. Medals with the bar 'Tel-el-Kebir' have the date '1882' in the exergue.

Regiments present: Three squadrons each of 1 (109) and 2 (103) Life Guards; Royal Horse Guards; 4 (335), 7 (450) Dragoon Guards; 1st R Dragoons (9); 3 (6), 4 (9), 11 (11), 19 (374) Hussars; 'N'/'A' (148), 'G'/'B' (143) RHA; A/1 (177), D/1 (183), F/1 (186), H/1 (147), N/2 (181), I/2 (187), C/3 (159), J/3 (164) RA; No 7 Battery (94), HQ RA (15); RMA; RE (570); 'A' and 'I' Companies Madras Sappers and Miners; 2/1 (660), 2/2 (705), 1/3 (715) Foot Guards; 2/18 (625), 1/42, 46 (645), 50 (One Company) (59), 3/60, 1/63, 1/72 (564), 2/74 (775), 1/75 (766), 78 (197), 1/79 (795), 84 (726), 87 (725), 88 (6), 96 (2) Foot; Mounted Infantry; 2, 6 Bengal Cavalry; 13 Bengal Lancers; 7 Bengal NI; 20, 29 Punjab NI; Malta Auxiliary Transport; C and T Corps; Interpreters (42); Army Veterinary Corps (30); Army Chaplains (10); Army Service Corps: Military Police (59).

A Naval Brigade formed of seamen and marines from the following ships served at the battle of Tel-el-Kebir: HMS *Alexandra* (35); *Carysfort* (28); *Euryalus* (1); *Hecla* (2); *Helicon* (1); *Inflexible*; *Monarch* (19); *Mosquito*; *Orion* (41); *Penelope* (22); *Seagull*; *Superb* (32); *Temeraire* (27).

Suakin 1884 19th February-26th March 1884

Authorized on 20th June 1884. A medal or bar was awarded to troops who landed at Suakin or Trinkitat between the above dates. Those eligible received an undated medal if they had not previously received a dated medal for the 1882 Egypt campaign. Those eligible who had received a dated medal were awarded the bar 'Suakin 1884'.

Regiments present: 19 Hussars; 6/1 Scottish Div RA; 24, 26, Co RE; 1/42, 60, 75 79 (5) Foot.

HM ships: *Albacore*, *Alexandra*, *Arab* (97), *Briton* (144), *Carysfort*

(224), *Coquette*, *Cygnet*, *Decoy* (66), *Euryalus* (304), *Falcon*, *Hecla* (195), *Helicon*, *Humber* (67), *Inconstant*, *Inflexible*, *Iris* (36), *Jumna* (37), *Malabar*, *Minotaur*, *Myrmidon*, *Northumberland*, *Orion*, *Orontes* (67), *Ranger* (9), *Ready*, *Seraphis* (19), *Skylark*, *Sphinx* (11), *Sultan*, *Temeraire*, *Thalia*, *Tyne*, *Woodlark*.

El-Teb 29th February 1884

Authorized on 20th June 1884. Awarded to all those present at the action at El-Teb. For this and subsequent actions the undated medal was awarded to all who had not already received a medal. Four thousand two hundred of these bars were issued. A medal with this single bar is unusual.

Regiments present: 10 Hussars; 19 Hussars (410); Mounted Infantry (125); 6/1 Scot Div RA (126); 26 Company RE (100); RMA; RMLI; Carrier and Transport Corps; 1/42, 3/60, 65, 75, 89 Foot; 150 sailors and 400 Marines from HM ships: *Briton* (6), *Carysfort* (38), *Decoy*, *Dryad* (2), *Euryalus* (20), *Hecla* (7), *Humber*, *Inconstant*, *Ranger*, *Sphinx* (2) and a few from HMS *Ready*.

Medals to the 84, 87 and 92 Foot are known. Captain Wilson RN of HMS *Hecla* gained the VC at this action.

Tamaai 13th March 1884

Authorized on 20th June 1884. Awarded to all those present at the action at Tamaai. A medal with this single bar is unusual.

Regiments present: One squadron each of 10 (approx 12) and 19 Hussars; M/1 Battery and 6/1 Scot Div RA; 26 Company RE; 42, 3/60, 65, 70, 75, 89 Foot; Native Camel Transport; fourteen officers and 464 seamen and Marines from HM ships: *Briton* (36), *Carysfort* (15), *Dryad* (5), *Euryalus* (47), *Hecla* (9), *Humber* (71), *Inconstant*, *Inflexible*, *Northumberland*, *Sphinx*, *Thalia*, *Tyne*.

El-Teb-Tamaai 29th February and 13th March 1884

Authorized on 20th June 1884. This bar was awarded to all those who had taken part in both actions. It is unusual to find a medal with this as a single bar.

7th (17), 79th Foot (9); HMS *Briton* (19), *Dryad* (220), *Euryalus* (28); *Hecla* (23), *Humber* (3), *Sphinx* (12).

General Order No 97 of 1st September, 1885 authorized the award of a medal (undated) to troops who were on duty at Suakin between 26th March 1884 and 14th May 1885 provided they had not already received one.

The Nile 1884-85

Authorized on 1st September 1885. This bar was only awarded to those who served south of Assouan, on or before 7th March, 1885, in the expedition to relieve General Gordon in Khartoum.

Four camel regiments were formed for this campaign as follows:

Heavy Camel Regiment—Staff (4), approx. 2 officers and 43 other ranks from each of the following: 1, 2 Life Guards; Royal Horse Guards; 2, 4, 5 Dragoon Guards; 1, 2 Dragoons; 5, 16 Lancers.

Light Camel Regiment—Staff (3), approx 2 officers and 43 other ranks from each of the following: 3, 4, 7, 10, 11, 15, 18, 20, 21 Hussars.

Guards Camel Regiment—Staff (5), 2 officers and 43 other ranks from each of the following: 1, 2, 3 Grenadier Guards; 1, 2 Coldstream Guards; 1, 2 Scots Guards; and 4 officers and 102 other ranks Royal Marine Light Infantry.

Mounted Infantry Camel Regiment: Staff (5), 1/13, 19 (10), 1/21, 35, 38, 42, 46, 50, 52 (33), 56, 1, 2 and 3/60, 75, 94, 97 Foot and Rifle Brigade.

Regiments present: 19 Hussars; 1/1 Southern Div RA; 18 (647), 35, 38, 42, 46, 50, 56, 75, 79, 88 (27) Foot.

Medals are known with this bar to the Army Pay Department, Commissariat and Transport Corps and RE, 26th Co.

Naval Brigades (289) from HM ships *Albacore*, *Briton*, *Carysfort*, *Condor*, *Coquette*, *Cygnet*, *Dolphin*, *Falcon*, *Helicon*, *Humber*, *Iris*, *Monarch*, *Myrmidon*, *Rambler*, *Ranger*, *Sphinx*, *Starling*, *Turquoise*, *Tyne*,

Wye and *Woodlark*.

River gunboats: *Bordein, Saphia, Tewfikea, Tull-Howeija*.

Three hundred and ninety-two Canadian boatmen: Officers (8), Caughnawaga (56), Manitoba (88), Three River's (41), Ottawa (169), Peterborough (15), Sherbrooke (6), Sydney (1), Hospital Staff (1), Wheelmen (8).

Abu Klea 17th January 1885

Authorized on 1st September 1885. Awarded to those troops who took part in the action at Abu Klea on 17th January 1885 under Major General Sir H. Stewart, KCB.

This bar, of which 1581 were issued is never found singly but always with that for 'The Nile 1884-85'.

Regiments present: 1 (39), 2 Life Guards (38); Royal Horse Guards (46); 2 (40), 4 (41), 5 Dragoon Guards (32); 1 (38), 2 Dragoons (39); 4 Hussars (2); 5 (35), 16 Lancers (40); 19 Hussars (135); 1 (40), 2 (44), 3 Grenadiers Guards (36); 2 Coldstream Guards (90); Scots Guards (84); 1 Som LI (21); Rl Scot Fusiliers (22); 2 DCLI (28); 1 Rl Sussex (282); 1 S Staffs (24); 2 Essex (22); Rl Highlanders (23); 1 (28), 2 Rl W Kent (21); 1 (13), 2 (28), 3 KRRC (25); Gordon Highlanders (32); 2 Connaught Rangers (24); Rifle Brigade (38); 1/1 S Div RA (46); 26 Coy RE; Commissariat and Transport Corps; RMLI (92).

A Naval Brigade of four officers and fifty-five men under Lord Charles Beresford.

Kirbekan 10th February, 1885

Authorized on 1st September 1885. Awarded to those troops who took part in the action at Kirbekan on 10th February 1885 under Major General W. Earle, CB, CSI.

This bar of which 1,200 were issued is never found singly but always in conjunction with that for 'The Nile 1884-85'.

Regiments present: One squadron 19 Hussars (95); 1 South Staffs; 1 Black Watch; D Company 1 Gordon Highlanders (97). Also known to the 2 Essex Regiment, RE and Commissariat and Transport Corps.

A Maxim Gun Detachment from HMS *Wye* was present and also 45 Canadian Boatmen who receive this bar and 'The Nile 1884-85'— Officers (1), Caughnawaga (3); Manitoba (14); Three Rivers (1); Ottawa (24); Peterborough (1); Sydney (1).

Suakin 1885 1st March-14th May 1885

Authorized on 1st September 1885. Awarded to troops who took part in operations at Suakin between the above dates.

This was the first occasion that Australian units were sent overseas and fought with Imperial troops. 720 qualified for the bar.

Regiments present: 5 Lancers (102); 19, 20 (82) Hussars; 'G/B Brigade RHA'; 5 and 6 Batteries 1 Brigade Scottish Division RA; One Field Battery New South Wales Artillery; 9 Bengal Cavalry; 10, 17, 24, 26 Companies RE; 3 Grenadier Guards; 1 Coldstream Guards; 2 Scots Guards; 18 (42), 1/19 (51 plus 10x2 bars), 1/42, 49, 53, 68, 70, 79 (2), 86 (14) Foot; New South Wales Infantry* (500); NSW Artillery (205); NSW Ambulance Corps (22); NSW Band (14); Australian Chaplains (2); Artillery, Ambulance Corps Staff; 3rd and 7th Company C and TC Indian Brigade; 11, 15 Sikhs; 17 Bengal Infantry; 128 Pioneers; 2 Queen's Own Sappers and Miners; Bombay Comm Department; Ind Transport Department.

Naval Brigade from HM ships: *Alexandra, Carysfort* (32), *Condor* (122), *Coquette* (64), *Cygnet* (84), *Dee* (35), *Dolphin* (115), *Humber* (100), *Northumberland, Sphinx* (185), *Tourmaline, Tyne* (125), and *Starling* (59), Government Launch *Foscolmetto* (1), HM Tug *Prompt* (1).

Tofrek 22nd March 1885

Authorized on 1st September 1885. Awarded to troops present at the action at Tofrek on 22nd March 1885.

The bar is found only in conjunction with that for 'Suakin 1885' and,

---

*The citizens of Sydney presented 800 medals, 28mm diameter, to the members of this contingent. They bore the Arms of the Corporation on the obverse; on the reverse was the inscription, 'PRESENTED BY THE CITIZENS OF SYDNEY. T. PLAYFAIR, MAYOR, 1885'.

owing to the small size of the force engaged, it is quite rare to British troops.

Regiments present: One squadron 5 Lancers (102); One squadron 20 Hussars (82); 6 Battery 1 Brigade Scottish Division RA; 24 Company RE; 1 Royal Berks; Indian Brigade; 11, 15 Sikhs; 17 Bengal Infantry; 128 Pioneers; 2 Queen's Own Sappers and Miners. Medals are known to the 1/DLI.

Naval Brigade from HM ships *Alexandra, Carysfort* (12), *Condor* (7), *Coquette* (2), *Dolphin* (12), *Sphinx* (13), *Starling* (3), and a Royal Marine Br (542).

For their distinguished conduct at this battle, the Berkshire Regiment gained the prefix 'Royal'.

General Order No 68 dated 1st June, 1886 stated that troops who served to the south of Wadi Halfa between 30th November, 1885 and 11th January, 1886 were entitled to the Egypt Medal (undated), without bar, provided they had not previously received one. On 30th December 1885, the Battle of Ginnis was fought.

Regiments present: 1 Cameron Highlanders; 1 Rl Berkshire; 1 Rl W Kent; 2 DLI; Egyptian Army; Sudanese Army.

Gemaizah 1888 20th December 1888

Authorized in January 1890. Granted to all troops who were landed at Suakin before the action at Gemaizah on 20th December 1888 and who were there on that date.

Regiments present: 20 Hussars (147); 17 members of the 24 Company RE; 2/25, 41, 86 (34) Foot; Egyptian Native Troops.

Naval detachments from HMS *Starling* (medal and bar 39, bar only 22: total 61), *Racer* (medal and bar 91, bar only 30: total 121), Khedive's *Noor-El-Bahr* (medal and bar 11, bar only 1: total 12).

The Egypt Medal without bar was also authorized in January 1890 to all troops employed on the Nile, at and south of Korosko on 3rd August 1889.

Toski 1889 3rd August 1889

Authorized in January 1890. Awarded to all troops present at the action at Toski on 3rd August 1889.

Regiments present: 20 Hussars (98); 83 Foot (29); Egyptian troops.

Only Lieutenant H. Wiltshire and sixteen men of 20 Hussars received Toski as a single bar; four officers and seventy-seven men received it with the bar for Gemaizah. Private A Brooks, 19th Hussars, received these two bars and that for Suakin 1885; this is probably unique. Sergeants H. W. Yates and T. H. Lane and one other NCO, Rl Irish Rifles, each received a medal with this single bar. They were attached to the Army Medical Corps at the time.

The Egyptian Campaigns 1882-9

Egypt 1882

After the opening of the Suez Canal on 16th November 1869, the affairs of Egypt took on an international aspect, because whoever controlled the country controlled the canal, the use of which was to be free to all nations. At the same time the canal was vital to British trade routes to the East.

In 1863, Ismail Pasha succeeded Said Pasha as Viceroy of Egypt and in 1867 he was given the title of 'Khedive' by the Sultan of Turkey.

His efforts toward autonomy, westernisation and the speedy economic development of Egypt coupled with an ambitious programme of territorial expansion ultimately brought financial ruin to his country. With Egypt impoverished he sold his shares in the Suez Canal to Britain in 1875. In the following year he was forced to accept British and French control over Egyptian finances. Finally in 1879 he was deposed by the Sultan of Turkey and replaced as Khedive by his son, Tewfik.

The increase in foreign intervention during Ismail's reign was generally resented and coupled with the deteriorating state of affairs led to the growth of a nationalist movement.

On 1st February 1881 the Egyptian Army mutinied in favour of Arabi Pasha and other military leaders. The Khedive was powerless to resist the strength of the nationalists and early in 1882 they formed a government with Arabi as Minister of War.

With both influence and nationals in Egypt at risk, British and French naval squadrons were despatched, arriving off Alexandria in May 1882. On 11th June serious riots broke out, directed against foreigners and Christians.

Admiral Sir Beauchamp Seymour commanding the British squadron at Alexandria was given orders to prevent any attempt to fortify the port. In spite of protests, work on the fortifications progressed. On the 9th July, Admiral Seymour threatened to bombard the city if work on the forts was not halted. On the 10th he demanded the surrender of the batteries on Ras-el-Tin. On the same day the French squadron left harbour, refusing to co-operate with the British and taking no part in the forthcoming action.

At 7am on the 11th July 1882 the bombardment of the fortifications began and continued until 5.30pm when the squadron withdrew. During the night fires were started throughout the city by incendiaries and murder and pillage became rife.

The next morning, the white flag having been hoisted, a force of Marines was landed. Arabi Pasha, together with the Egyptian army, now no longer loyal to the Khedive, had withdrawn and Tewfik emerged from Ramleh and took up residence under the protection of British guns. The period 13th-17th was occupied in landing marines and occupying the important places in the city. On the 17th Major-General Sir Archibald Alison arrived with military reinforcements.

The Khedive, now free to dismiss Arabi passed the matter of the restoration of law and order to Britain. The French failed to assist.

An expeditionary force of 25,000 men was organised under the command of Sir Garnet Wolseley, who landed at Alexandria on 15th August.

The first task was to seize the Suez Canal and Port Said. Captain Fairfax of HMS *Monarch* occupied Port Said, Captain Fitzroy of HMS *Orion* took Ismailia, while Commander Edwards of HMS *Ready* seized all the canal barges and dredgers and occupied the telegraph station at Kantara. At the same time, Admiral Hewett took control of the canal at Suez. With the ports and means of landing a force under British control, the next consideration was to ensure the safety of the water supply, which depended on the fresh water canal between Ismailia and Cairo. It was reported that the rebels were damming this at Magfar (or Mukfar), so they were attacked and driven off on 24th August. They withdrew towards Tel-el-Mahuta and Kassassin, which latter was attacked and captured on the 26th. On the 27th August, Mustapha Fehmy, Arabi's second-in-command was captured whilst he was reconnoitring British positions. On the 28th August and 9th September the Egyptians attacked British positions at Kassassin, but were repulsed. British forces were in the meantime gathering at Kassassin in preparation for an attack on Arabi's positions at Tel-el-Kebir. Wolseley personally reconnoitring the Egyptian positions on the 12th launched an attack with two divisions in the early hours of the 13th August. The brunt of the fighting was borne by the Highland Brigade under Sir Archibald Alison. The Egyptians were driven from their positions and pursued so effectively that Cairo was entered on the 14th September. Out of 38,000 Egyptians, 2,000 were killed and over 500 wounded; British losses numbered 57 killed, 382 wounded and 30 missing from approximately 17,000 present.

Arabi and the remainder of his army surrendered unconditionally. After his trial he was banished to Ceylon in December 1882; he was pardoned in 1901.

Soon after the entry into Cairo the Khedive dissolved his army and appointed Sir Evelyn Wood, VC, the commander of a new one. In 1883 (authorized by His Imperial Majesty the Sultan of Turkey) the Khedive signified his desire to express his appreciation of the services rendered by the British Army and Navy by awarding a bronze star. (See No. 107).

Three Victoria Crosses were awarded for the Egyptian War of 1882. These being to Gunner I. Harding, HMS *Alexandra;* Private F. Corbett, 3rd Battalion, 60th KRRC, and Lieutenant W. M. M. Edwards, 74th Foot.

Sudan 1884

In July 1881, Sheik Mahomed Ahmed of Dongola proclaimed himself the Mahdi, the Guided by God or Directed One. He quickly gathered thousands of fanatical religious followers (Dervishes) and led them in a revolt against Egypt. After several clashes with Egyptian troops in 1881-1883 they annihilated an Egyptian force under William Hicks Pasha at Kashgil near El Obeid, Kordofan on 3rd-5th November 1883.

On the 1st February 1884, led by Osman Digna, they destroyed another Egyptian army under Valentine Baker Pasha at El Teb near Tokar.

After this success Osman Digna placed the port of Suakin, on the Red Sea, in a state of siege; but the prompt action of Admiral Sir William Hewett, who landed a Naval Brigade from HM ships *Decoy, Euryalus, Ranger* and *Sphinx*, saved it from capture. Reinforcements were sent from Aden and Egypt, which disembarked at Trinkitat on 23rd February, 1884. Under Major General Sir Gerald Graham, VC, KCB, Osman Digna was defeated at El Teb on the 29th February losing 1,500 men killed, the British 34 killed and 155 wounded. Digna was defeated again, at Tamaai on 13th March with losses approaching 2,000; the British suffering 109 killed and 104 wounded.

Following his two defeats, Osman Digna was located at Tamanieb and attacked on 27th March. After this he left the district. The army re-embarked and returned to Egypt, leaving a garrison of Marines at Suakin, which was continually attacked though guarded by a ring of landmines.

After all this bloodshed, trouble and expense the British Government decided to abandon the Sudan, save for a small garrison at Suakin, men and ships were withdrawn, leaving Osman Digna, the Mahdi and dervishes uncaptured, unrepentant and very much unsubdued.

Four Victoria Crosses were awarded for the Sudan war of 1884, these being to Captain A. K. Wilson, RN; Quartermaster-Sergeant W. T. Marshall, 19th Hussars; Private T. Edwards, 42nd Foot, and Lieutenant P. S. Marling, 60th Foot.

The Nile Expedition 1884-85

In January 1884, General Charles Gordon was sent by the British Government to Khartoum to supervise the withdrawal of Egyptian and Sudanese forces from the area. However, with the main British forces positioned far to the north and those to the east having been withdrawn, the Mahdi's forces were able to invest Khartoum without interference. Gordon made repeated and successful sallies but could never hope to raise the siege without external help. With Gordon's position inseparably connected with British prestige, an expedition for the relief of Khartoum was, at length, determined upon.

In August, 1884 (five months after the investment started) preparations were made for his relief. Two expeditions, under the joint command of Sir Garnet Wolseley, were to advance towards Khartoum. One, accompanied by Sir Garnet, advanced up the Nile; the second operated from Suakin. When the Nile column reached Korti on 26th December, 1884, Major-General Sir Herbert Stewart was ordered to take the Camel Corps and a naval brigade under Captain Lord Charles Beresford and cross the desert to Metemmeh to join up with the Nile steamers sent by Gordon from Khartoum. On the way, wells at Gakdul and Abu Klea would have to be captured. The first was found to be unoccupied, so that the force was watered and then continued the advance on 16th January, 1885. Later in the day the scouts of the 19th Hussars reported that the wells at Abu Klea were being held. On the 17th an action was fought at Abu Klea. The British force, 1,500 strong formed a square in the face of a fierce attack by 10,000 dervishes. Through lack of homogeneity the square was broken at its rear left corner, but when order was restored the dervishes were driven off leaving over 1,000 dead. In the desperate fighting, 74 British were killed and 94 wounded.

The wounded were left with a guard at Abu Klea and the remainder continued towards the Nile. Near Metemmeh, General Stewart was mortally wounded and was succeeded in command by Colonel Sir Charles Wilson. Fighting their way to the Nile the force established a defensive position at Gubat. An advance towards Arab held Metemmeh was made on the 21st January but the attack was cancelled. However, the same day the four small steamers (*Bordein, Tull-Howeija, Safia* and *Tewfikea*) despatched by Gordon arrived.

It was found that Gordon's steamers required a certain amount of repair. This was carried out and on the 22nd January they were ready to make the dash for Khartoum. However, instead of sending them off at once, Colonel Wilson wasted valuable time by having them bombard Shendy under Captain Beresford. It was not until the morning of the 24th that Colonel Wilson seemed to remember the object of the whole expedition and left for Khartoum with the *Bordein* and *Tull-Howeija*, together with about twenty men of the Sussex Regiment and about two hundred and eighty Sudanese.

The next that was heard of this party was on 1st February, when Lieutenant Stuart-Wortley returned to Gubat with the news that

Khartoum had fallen and Gordon had been murdered on 26th January, and that the two steamers were wrecked about half a mile or so below Khartoum. Sir Charles Wilson and his men were reported to be on an island about thirty miles upstream and in danger of attack by several thousand Sudanese who were holding an earthwork almost opposite them.

Lord Beresford selected a crew for the *Safia* from his Naval Brigade and a few picked shots from the mounted infantry, together with crews for two Gardner guns, and left on 2nd February. He reached the earthwork the next morning, but when trying to get past it his ship received a shot in the boiler which necessitated running her ashore on the opposite bank. The chief engineer, Mr Benbow, by a magnificent effort made a plate to cover the hole and got the engine working again in about ten hours. In the meantime Sir Charles Wilson had placed his wounded in a nuggar to drift down the stream, whilst he and the remainder of his party retired down the right bank of the river.

The expedition had failed in its purpose, and once again the sickening order to retire—with no useful purpose having been served—was issued. Lord Wolseley sent General Redvers Buller, VC, to Gubat to superintend the withdrawal of the force back to Korti.

Few military forces have deserved more credit than that which left Korti on 26th December, 1884, and returned on 7th March, 1885, after having traversed four hundred miles of desert. No praise could be too high for the members of the Naval Brigade, who acted as gunners, infantry, sailors and vets with conspicuous valour and success.

Whilst Stewarts' column was cutting across the desert towards Metemmeh, the bulk of the army under Major General W. Earle followed the course of the Nile upstream. When the news of Gordon's death was received the column halted for a few days. When the advance continued the Sudanese were found to be holding a position in front of Kirbekan, from which they were driven on 10th February. General Earle was killed, otherwise the casualties were slight. On the 25th orders were received to withdraw to Korti, where on or about 28th March fever broke out before the return of the whole force to Cairo.

To support the river and desert operations (above) it was decided in early February 1885 to mount an expedition from Suakin. The aim was that this force should build a railway from Suakin to Berber on the Nile, a distance of about two hundred and eighty miles and break the power of Osman Digna. Troops were assembled at Suakin from Britain, India and Australia under the command of Major General Sir Gerald Graham VC.

Moving inland, Graham defeated the Sudanese at Hasheen on the 20th March, 1885. On the 22nd, a detachment under General McNeill was surprised and attacked at Tofrek and only after heavy fighting were the Sudanese driven off. Sudanese losses numbered over 1,500; British and Indian casualties numbered 100 killed, 142 wounded and 71 missing. Operations inland continued into May when the enterprise was abandoned and the bulk of the troops were withdrawn.

Egypt and Sudan 1885-1891

The Mahdi died of smallpox in June, 1885 and was succeeded by Khalifa Abdullah el Taashi.

Following the withdrawal of the Nile expedition, there was considerable fighting on the Sudan/Egypt border. On 30th December 1885, Sir Frederick Stevenson with a force of 4,500 British and Egyptian troops defeated 6,000 Sudanese at Ginnis.

Fighting between Osman Digna and tribes opposed to the Khalifa occurred during 1886-87 in the eastern Sudan. In 1888 he again threatened Suakin. General Sir Francis Grenfell arrived from Cairo with British and Egyptian reinforcements. On the 20th December he made a sortie from Suakin and defeated the dervishes at Gemaizah. British and Egyptian casualties were minor. With the danger removed, the troops at Suakin were again withdrawn, except for a small garrison.

Following the Battle of Ginnis, border raids by the dervishes continued. In 1889 a major attempt to conquer Egypt was made by the Emir, Wad en Nejumi, who crossed the frontier in June with 14,000 men. Part of this force was defeated by the Egyptians under Colonel Wodehouse, RA at Argin on 2nd July. On the 3rd August the dervish army was heavily defeated at Toski by General Grenfell, the Sirdar or Commander-in-Chief of the Egyptian Army. With the defeat, the serious dervish threat to Egypt ended and the border area stabilized.

In January 1891 Osman Digna again became a threat in east Sudan. An army, principally of Egyptians, under Colonel Holland-Smith defeated Digna at Afafit on 19th February and then occupied Tokar. With this defeat the dervish threat to Suakin was removed. [The Egypt Medal 1882-9 was not awarded for the Tokar campaign; the Khedive awarded an undated bronze star and bar (or bar only to those already in possession of one of the three previous issues of star.)]

A Victoria Cross was awarded for this campaign, this being to Gunner A. Smith, RA.

107   *Egypt, Khedive's Stars* 1882-1891

General	Five pointed star
Obverse	In the centre is the Sphinx with the three Great Pyramids in the background. Around this is a raised band, on the upper part of which is embossed 'EGYPT' followed by a date or dates, the fourth type is undated. On the lower part of the band in Arabic is embossed, 'KHEDIVE OF EGYPT' plus the appropriate date A.H.
Reverse	The Khedive's monogram 'T.M.' surmounted by a crown within a raised band
Size	The maximum width of the star is 48mm.
Metal	Bronze
Ribbon	Plain dark blue, 39mm. wide
Suspension	A small ring is attached to the piece between the two uppermost rays of the star. To this ring is attached a straight laureated bar (43mm. x 5mm.) in the centre of which is a crescent and a small five pointed star
Manufacturer	Messrs Henry Jenkins & Sons of Birmingham
Naming	All the stars were issued unnamed. Most of the 1882 issue awarded to members of the Guards regiments bear the recipient's regimental number and the initials of his regiment impressed upon the reverse, eg. G.G., C.G. or S.G. Also found in various impressed and engraved styles
Bars issued	One, for Tokar

The stars were authorized by the Sultan of Turkey and conferred by the Khedive of Egypt, Tewfik Mahommed, to all those involved in the suppression of the Egyptian rebellion of 1882 and for the campaigns in Egypt and Sudan between 1884 and 1889. All recipients of the British medal for Egypt received an appropriate star.

There were four issues of the star to correspond with the different campaigns:

Star dated 1882, for the Campaign between 16th July and 14th September, 1882.

Star dated 1884, for the Campaign between 19th February and 26th March, 1884.

Star dated 1884-6, for the Campaigns between 26th March, 1884, and 7th October, 1886.

Star undated for the Campaign near Suakin in 1887 and on the Nile in 1889.*

All these stars, no two of which, except by mistake, were given to one man, could be worn in uniform. In 1893 the Khedive made a further issue of the undated stars to commemorate the action at Tokar on 19th February, 1891. Those present who had not already received a star were awarded one bearing the bar with the Arabic inscription 'TOKAR 1308H'. Previous recipients of the stars received the bar only. By the time the last star was issued, most men had already received one of the earlier ones, so that the undated star with the bar for Tokar is somewhat rare. As there was no British issue to commemorate Tokar, permission was granted for the bronze star and bar to be worn by those entitled to it though they may not have also received the silver medal for services between 1882 and 1889.

British Officers serving with the Egyptian Army at Tokar received the star and/or bar, as did officers and men of HMS *Dolphin* and *Sandfly* who were on transport duties.

---

*The undated stars are to be found with the word 'EGYPT' very crudely embossed.

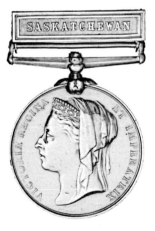

108 *North West Canada Medal* 1885

Obverse	The diademed and veiled head of Queen Victoria with the legend 'VICTORIA REGINA ET IMPERATRIX'
Reverse	Within a maple wreath the words 'NORTH WEST CANADA' with the date '1885' in the centre
Size	36mm. diameter
Metal	Silver
Ribbon	33mm. wide. Blue-grey with a red stripe near each edge
Suspension	By a straight swivelling suspender
Designers	Obverse: L. C. Wyon; Reverse: T. Brock
Naming	The medals were issued unnamed but a considerable number of them were named locally, individual units having their own particular style. Medals to the RCA, NWMP and the steamer Northcote were impressed in bold upright letters.
	Many of the medals are named in an abbreviated manner, eg '9e V.Q' for Neuvieme Voltigeurs de Quebec, 'P.A.V' for Prince Albert Volunteers
Bars issued	One, Saskatchewan

The medal was authorized by the Canadian Government on 18th September 1885 after consultation between the Governer General of Canada and the Secretary of State for the Colonies. It was awarded to all those serving west of Thunder Bay, who took part in the suppression of Riel's (Second) Rebellion of 1885.

Approximately 6,000 medals were issued to Canadian units. Except for seventeen British officers who were on the staff in Canada at the time no British troops were engaged.

British officers present: Maj Gen Melgand; Lieut A. J. Anson, HLI; Lieut L. G. Russell, RB; Lieut C. R. Hunter, RB; Maj E. C. Milner; Col A. Le Cocq, RA; Lieut H. B. Strange, RA; Asst Comm Gen F. Shortt; St Paymstr F. F. Tereday; Lieut H. Streatfield, Gren Gds; Lt Gen Lord Russell, Bt; Lt Col R. B. Lane, RB; Col W. Black; Capt R. Nagle; Col C. S. Akers, RE; Asst Comm Ordnance W. Booth and Dep Surgn Gen W. Cattell.

Some of the Canadian Units known to have been awarded medals: A Bty Regt Cdn Art; A Troop Cavalry School Corps; Alberta Mtd Rifles; B Bty Regt Cdn Art; Battleford Rifle Coy; Boulton's Mtd Inf; Birtle Coy Inf; C Coy Inf Corps School; DLS Intelligence Corps; French's Scouts; GG Body Guard; Halifax Prov Batt; Inf Btn Wpg (95th); Light Inf Bn Wpg; Montreal Bde Gar Art; Midland Bn; Moose Mountain Scouts; Medical Staff; Northcote Steamer (34 medals with bars); North West Mounted Police; Ottawa Sharpshooters; Rocky Mountain Rangers; Steele's Scouts; Staff; Transport Officers, Scouts; Winnipeg Fld Bty; Winnipeg Troop Cavalry; Yorkton Co Inf; York & Simcoe Prov Bn; 2nd Bn QOR; 7th Bn Fusiliers; 9th Bn Que Volt; 10th Bn Royal Grenadiers; 65th Bn Mt Royal Rifles; 90th Bn Wpg Rifles.

Saskatchewan

The bar Saskatchewan was awarded to all who had taken part in any or all of the three main encounters during the rebellion; these being along the Saskatchewan and Fish rivers and the Battle of Batoche.

Approximately 1760 recipients of the medal received the bar.

Medals are, from time to time, found with unofficial bars for Batoche, Bartouche and Fish Creek.

The campaign came about through the Canadian Government's decision to open up the North-West Territory to new settlers; a decision resented by the local Indians and others. Seizing upon this discontent Louis Riel (leader of the 1869-70 revolt) styling himself leader of a provisional government led an uprising, calling upon the Indians and other malcontents to support his cause.

The rising called out practically all of the Canadian forces. The main responsibility for suppressing the revolt fell upon General Frederick D. Middleton, who with consummate skill organized his forces into three columns. In operations which lasted from 24th April to 28th May, 1885, the rebels were completely defeated. Riel was captured and was tried and hanged for treason.

109 *Royal Niger Company's Medal* 1886-1897

Obverse	Head of Queen Victoria, crowned, veiled and wearing a wreath of laurel, with the legend, 'VICTORIA. REGINA. ET. IMPERATRIX.' Originals had 'SPINK & SON LOND.' below the bust. In 1933 the obverse die was renewed with 'SPINK & SON LTD' below the bust
Reverse	Shield with the words 'PAX, JUS, ARS' arranged in the form of a letter Y with a trophy of arms and flags behind the shield. The whole is surrounded by a wreath of laurel
Size	38mm. diameter
Metal	Issued in silver and in bronze
Ribbon	31mm. wide with three equal width stripes of yellow, black and white (The Company's colours)
Suspension	Straight suspender
Designer	The medals were designed and made by Messrs Spink & Son, London
Naming	Silver medals impressed in bold capitals, several engraved medals are known. Bronze medals are unnamed but bear instead a number between 1 and 2,361. Unnumbered medals are known
Bars issued	One bar reading 'Nigeria 1886-97' on the silver medal, one reading 'Nigeria' on the bronze

The National African Company was incorporated in 1882. In 1886 it was chartered as the Royal Niger Company, with Lord Aberdare as Chairman. On 9th August, 1899, the charter was revoked and the territory was taken over by the Imperial Government.

There were numerous expeditions in the Company's territory between 1886 and 1897, but there were also some which involved considerable fighting in 1898 and 1899, such as the expedition which operated in June, 1898, against the Lapai and Argeyes tribes.

Specimens of this medal were either struck with heavy gauge blanks or with 'S' of 'Son' obliterated and 'copy' stamped on the rim.

Silver medals to Europeans and bronze medals to natives were awarded by the Company in 1899 for services in various punitive expeditions in the Company's territory between 1886 and 1897. Only those expeditions in which casualties were sustained counted towards th award. Silver medals bore a bar, 'NIGERIA 1886-97', irrespective of th date the service was rendered. Bronze medals were issued with the undated bar 'NIGERIA'. Those natives who had taken part in appropriate expeditions but who were no longer in the Company's service at the time of issue were not awarded the medal. Neither were medals given to the next-of-kin of men who would otherwise have been eligible had they lived. An exception to this was the medal to

Lieutenant R. H. McCorquodale, 3 Dragoon Guards, 1870-1896.

As originally proposed, the silver medal was to have been issued with two bars, 'NIGERIA 1886-97' and 'NIGERIA 1898-99'. The later bar was not proceeded with, the actions being covered by the East & West Africa Medal. However, for civilians in the employ of the Company, all designated actions between 1886 and 1899 counted for the award of the medal; five civilians are known to have only served in expeditions of 1898/1899.

One hundred silver medals with the bar 'NIGERIA 1886-97' and one thousand bronze medals with the bar 'NIGERIA' were originally produced by Spink and Son Ltd.

Recipients: Silver medal: HM Forces, Officers and NCOs (49); Royal Niger Company, Officers (38); Royal Niger Constabulary (10).

110 *Imperial British East Africa Co Medal* 1888-95

Obverse	The arms of the Company, being a crowned rayed sun with a scroll below bearing the motto 'LIGHT AND LIBERTY' with an Arabic inscription below translated as 'The Reward of Bravery.' A scroll partly encloses the centre with the inscription, 'THE IMPERIAL BRITISH EAST AFRICA COMPANY'
Reverse	Plain except for a wreath of lotus flowers
Size	40mm. diameter
Metal	Silver
Ribbon	Plain blue
Suspension	A swivelling scroll suspender or a ring suspender
Naming	Engraved on the edge or the reverse
Bars issued	Nil

The Company received its charter on 3 September 1888 and was wound up on 30 October 1895.

Medals are believed to have been initially awarded for bravery; after the demise of the Company claims were then made on the basis of campaign service.

The following campaigns were in the Company's jurisdiction: Against the Sultan of Witu 1890, for which the bar on the East and West Africa Medal was given. 150 IBEA Company Police served with Royal Naval and Sultan of Zanzibar's forces. The Company steamers *Juba* and *Henry Wright* were also used.

Uganda Religious Wars 1891-92. Endemic conflict between (a) Christian and Moslem, (b) Catholic and Protestant continued during the Company's tenure. The Company taking the part of the Christian/Protestant faction.

There is no roll listing the awards authorized during the years of the Company's existence. A provisional roll (Macfarlane, Miscellany of Honours 1980) based on known medals and post 1895 authorizations lists 29 names:

Maj A. F. E. Smith, LG; Capt F. J. D. Lugard, Norfolk R; Capt J. R. L. MacDonald, RE; Capt J. W. Pringle, RE; Capt A. S. Rogers, Punjab Police; Capt W. H. Williams, RA; Dr W. H. B. MacDonald; Dr J. S. Macpherson; Mr J. Ainsworth; Mr. S. S. Bagge; Mr F. G. Foaker; Mr W. Grant; Mr F. J. Jackson; Mr K. MacDougall; Mr J. Martin; Mr C. Palmer; Mr J. P. Wilson.

(Native Officer) Billal Effendi; Sgt Ferej Yusuf; Cpl Seyd Amir; L/Cpl Yusuf Seyd; L/Cpl Ferej Mahomed Witu; Pte Seyd Dinkawe; Pte Ferej Nasor; Pte Seyd Mahomed Aden; Pte Abdulla Ramathani; Sgt Surur Adam; Pte Bilal Abdalla; Pte Merjan Hicks.

111 *East and West Africa Medal* 1887-1900

Obverse	The diademed and veiled head of Queen Victoria with the legend, 'VICTORIA REGINA'.
Reverse	A scene of bush fighting around a tree between British soldiers and natives (as for the Ashantee Medal, 1873 and Central Africa Medal, 1891.)
Size	36mm diameter. The gauge is slightly thinner than that of the very similar Ashantee Medal, 1873.
Metal	Silver and bronze
Ribbon	33mm wide. Yellow with black borders and two thin black stripes down the centre.
Suspension	By a swivelling straight bar suspender.
Designers	Obverse: L. C. Wyon. Reverse: Sir Edward Poynter, RA.
Naming	Often seen engraved to British officers. In engraved capitals to some colonial units. Impressed block capitals to British and some colonial units. Naval medals generally with larger impressed naming.
Bars issued	Twenty, possibly twenty-two: 1887-8, Witu 1890, 1891-2, 1892, Witu August 1893, Liwondi 1893, Juba River 1893, Lake Nyassa 1893, 1893-94, Gambia 1894, Benin River 1894, Brass River 1895, 1896-97 (?), 1896-98, Niger 1897, Benin 1897, Dawkita 1897, 1897-98, Sierra Leone 1898-99, 1896-99 (?), 1899, 1900.

Those who had received the Ashantee Medal, 1873, either with or without the bar for Coomassie, were only awarded the appropriate bar(s) for further service in East and West Africa.

The first issue was authorized on 1st November 1892, and altogether over twenty bars were awarded. For the M'wele Campaign in 1895-96 no bar was issued, but the name and date were engraved round the rim.

The greatest number of bars seen on this medal is seven, but this may not be the maximum, because all those seen were dated between 1890 and 1894.

1887-8 13th November 1887-2nd January 1888

Army Order 212 of 1892 authorized a medal and bar for operations against the Yonnie Tribe from 13th November to 2nd January 1888, both dates inclusive. A punitive expedition under the command of Colonel W. de Winton was raised to punish the Yonnie Tribe whose villages were located deep in Sierra Leone.

Although a relatively short expedition, progress was slow and extremely arduous due to the dense forests through which the force had to cut a passage. The situation was not helped by the constant threat of ambush; the Yonnie method of attack was to erect barricades along the route to halt the force and, from concealed position, fire with great effect their ancient muzzle loading rifles.

The rebel towns of Robari and Rorreto were taken and destroyed. The rebel chiefs surrendered in December, following which the troops returned to the coast and the naval party to their ships.

Regiment present: 1 West India Regiment (298); Political Officers (19); Sierra Leone Frontier and Civil Police (45); Navy: HMS *Acorn* (14), *Icarus* (8), *Rifleman* (17).

Witu 1890 17th-27th October 1890

This bar was awarded to members of the expedition under Vice-Admiral Sir Edmund Freemantle against the Sultan Fumo Bakari of Witu who had countenanced the murder of several Germans. This area of present day Kenya, formerly under the control of the German East Africa Company, had been transferred to the British under the Anglo-German Agreement of 1890.

Once Witu was reached by the main force, the Sultan's forces were dispersed.

(See also the Imperial British East Africa Medal, 1888-95).

Units present: Indian Police of the IBEA Company (150); Sultan of Zanzibar's troops (200).

HM Ships : *Boadicea* (327), *Brisk* (90), *Conquest* (190), *Cossack* (79), *Humber* (20), *Kingfisher* (96), *Pigeon* (10), *Redbreast* (47), *Turquoise* (131). In addition 281 were awarded to Seedies attached to ships.

Hired transport: *Somali*, IBEA Company's *SS Juba* and *Henry Wright*.

1891-2 29th December 1891-5th February 1892

The bar was issued for a series of expeditions in Gambia against Chief Fodeh Cabbah. In early 1891 he had attacked and wounded several members of an Anglo-French Boundary Commission who were passing through his country. The resulting punitive expeditions were not entirely successful.

Regiments present: 2 West India Regiment (168); Gambia Police (31); Royal Engineers.

HM Ships: *Alecto* (7), *Racer* (91), *Sparrow* (44), *Thrush* (44), *Widgeon* (53).

Colonial Steamer: *Lily*.

Duplicates (14) were issued to Ord. J. Bishop, AB H. Rogers of HMS *Sparrow*; AB J. Connell, Ord E. P. Hawton, Sto R. Hensey, AB, J. Holland, Ord. H. Lee, Ord. E. M. Pratt, AB W. J. Sparks, Blksm J. Stephens of HMS *Racer*; SB Att I. Davis, Pte E. Welch of HMS *Thrush*; AB E. King, Ord H. Lake of HMS *Widgeon*

1892 8th March-25th May 1892

This bar was awarded for expeditions against:
1 Tambi, in Sierra Leone (8th March-11th April, 1892)
2 Toniataba, in Sierra Leone (12th March-30th April 1892)
3 The Jebus in Nigeria (12th-25th May 1892)

1 Tambi expedition
Regiments present: 1 West India Regiment (531); West Indian Fortress Company RE (7); Sierra Leone Frontier Police (163).
  HM Ships: *Alecto, Racer, Sparrow, Thrush* and *Widgeon*.
  Sierra Leone Colonial Steamer: *SS Countess of Derby* (23)

2 Toniataba expedition
Regiments present: 1 West India Regiment (349); Gambia Police (9).
  HM Ships: *Alecto, Racer, Sparrow, Thrush* and *Widgeon*.

3 The Jebu (Ijebu) expedition
Regiments present: 1 West India Regiment (61); Gold Coast Constabulary (150); Lagos Hausas (169).
  A Victoria Cross was awarded for this expedition to L/Cpl W. J. Gordon, 1st Battalion West India Regt.

Witu August 1893 7th-15th August 1893

The bar was authorized on 30th August 1895 for the Pumwani and Jongeni August 1893 Campaign.

The bar was awarded to members of the expedition under Captain G. R. Lindley RN, against Sultan Fumo Omari of Witu (Fumo Bakari's brother, see 'Witu 1890').

HM Ships: *Blanche* (69), *Sparrow* (35), *Swallow* (56).

In addition to the above, medals were given to a Captain in the service of the Imperial East Africa Company, the Consul General for East Africa, the Consul to Zanzibar and the Commander of the Zanzibar forces.

Liwondi 1893 February-March 1893

The bar was authorized on 30th August 1895 for an expedition along the Upper Shire River (Malawi). In response to slave raids made by Yao Chief Liwondi, expeditions were mounted by Commissioner H. H. Johnston and Captain C. E. Johnston. That of Commissioner Johnston got into difficulties and had to be relieved by a Royal Naval and volunteer force under Lieutenant G. S. Q. Carr and Lieutenant C. H. Robertson. After effecting the commissioner's rescue, Liwondi was defeated.

This bar was issued to Royal Navy personnel only, whilst for other members of the expedition the Central Africa Medal was awarded.

HM Ships *Herald* (16), *Mosquito* (17).

C. Banks, a member of the Armourer's crew was issued with two duplicate medals (three in all).

Recipients:
Lieut George Shadwell Carr *Mosquito;* Surgeon Alexander Fleming Harper *Mosquito;* Lieut Charles Hope Robertson *Herald;* SBA G. R. Archer *Herald;* Armrs Cr C. Banks *Herald;* AB G. E. Bird *Mosquito;* Sto G. Blee *Mosquito;* AB W. Burstow *Herald;* AB A. Campbell

Mosquito; PO 1Cl J. Charlton *Mosquito;* PO 1Cl E. Coombs *Mosquito;* PO 1Cl W. Cornelius *Herald;* PO 1Cl P. Courtney *Herald;* AB W. Deeney *Herald;* Sto H. Esgate *Herald;* AB I. Gent *Herald;* AB W. Gilley *Herald;* AB C. Honeyball *Herald;* L Sto C. F. Letchford *Mosquito;* AB H. Mottley *Mosquito;* AB J. Nickels *Mosquito;* PO 1Cl T. Polhill *Mosquito;* AB J. E. Pownall *Mosquito;* AB C. Richards *Herald;* ERA A. Stanley *Mosquito;* AB G. Swinn *Mosquito;* AB W. C. Titmus *Mosquito;* CPO H. W. Walker *Mosquito;* AB S. White *Mosquito;* PO 1Cl C. Whitlock *Herald;* Cars Mte J. Wicks *Herald;* AB G. Wightman *Herald;* AB G. Wright *Herald.*

Juba River 1893 23rd-25th August 1893

The bar was authorized on the 30th August 1895 for an expedition against the Somalis of Jubaland.

Lieutenant P. Vaughan Lewes, RN, with forty naval volunteers from HMS *Blanche* and Count Lovatelli successfully carried out a small expedition to Gobwen to rescue Captain Tritton and Mr McDougall from the Somalis and some levies of the Hyderabad Contingent who had rebelled.

Twenty-one bars were issued to seamen who had previously been awarded the medal and bar for 'Witu August 1893'.

Recipients:
Gnr L. Barber; Lieut P. V. Lewes; Shpt J. Avery; AB W. Bellamy; CPO J. Bennett; Ch Wr A. Betts; AB T. J. Bridle; ERA 3Cl C. F. Carey; AB G. A. Clarke; AB C. Clift; LS T. J. Cole; Sto G. T. Cudlip; Ord A. Davey; AB J. Denham; Sto W. Easterbrooke; Sto W. Edmonds; AB C. F. Evans; AB C. Grant; 2 Yeo Sgls T. Harding; Act Ch Armr W. Henwood; AB A. Howard; PO 2Cl W. Jennings; Sh Std A. Johnson; AB H. R. Locke; AB C. Lyne; AB A Maddock; LS E. S. Maddock; Sh Cpl 2Cl H. C. Marsh; Cooper J. J. Millett; Sto H. Palmer; SB Att J. Pedley; PO 2Cl W. H. Potter; Cpl E. Reading; AB E. Richardson; Ord H. Singer; PO 1Cl H. Smith; PO 2Cl W. H. Taylor; LS S. Train; AB W. J. Ware; AB J. Weekes; L Sto A. J. White.

Lake Nyassa 1893 November 1893

This bar was authorized on the 30th of August 1895 for the second expedition against Chief Makanjira in Central Africa.

Twenty-eight single bars were awarded to naval European officers and men who manned the boats HMS *Adventure* (11) and HMS *Pioneer* (17). An additional thirty-two bars were awarded to Seedies.

The ships were built at Jarrow-on-Tyne, sent out to Africa in sections, and hauled over two hundred miles of virgin country to the edge of the lake where they were assembled.

The army personnel, consisting of a hundred and one Sikhs who accompanied the expedition, received the Central Africa Medal (see page 175).

Carpenter's Mate W. Maber and AB G. Powell, both from HMS *Pioneer*, received duplicate medals.

Recipients:
Gnr Joseph William De Matose *Pioneer;* Surgeon Alexander Fleming Harper *Adventure;* Surgn Elrington Francis McKay *Pioneer;* Lieut Charles Hope Robertson *Adventure;* Lieut Edward Cecil Villiers *Pioneer;* AB F. Alway *Pioneer;* PO 2Cl T. C. Baxter *Adventure;* L Sto J. Bramble *Pioneer;* L Sto W. Brown *Pioneer;* AB P. J. Caddy *Pioneer;* Act CPO G. Chaverton *Pioneer;* AB J. Coghlan *Adventure;* LS P. Dealey *Adventure;* PO 1Cl W. Drew *Pioneer;* L Sto C. Edney; *Pioneer;* L Sto E. S. Harris *Adventure;* ERA A. Hedgcock *Adventure;* ERA W. Henning *Adventure;* PO 1Cl H. Howard *Pioneer;* Car Mte W. Maber; *Pioneer;* AB G. Powell *Pioneer;* SS Asst C. M. Priscott *Adventure;* ERA J. Richardson *Pioneer;* ERA A. Sandy *Pioneer;* SBA A. Simmons *Pioneer;* AB J. Symes *Pioneer;* PO 1Cl A. Thomas *Adventure;* AB E. Toleman *Adventure.*

1893-94 26th November 1893-11th March 1894

The authorization of this bar covered two separate expeditions.
a) Operations against the Sofas in Sierra Leone from 26th November 1893, to 20th January 1894. An expedition under Colonel Ellis was dispatched to quell the Sofas who had been raiding from French Territory areas under British influence.

Regiments present: RE, ASC, AMS. etc; (33), 1/WIR (470); Sierra Leone Frontier Police (157); Navy: Colonial Steamer *Countess of Derby* (25).

b) Operations on the Gambia River from 22nd February 1894 to 11th March 1894. This bar was awarded for an expedition against Chief Fodeh Silah, who had been slave raiding and terrorising the district west of Cape St Mary and generally threatening the Colony of Gambia.

The Navy did not receive the bar for this action but qualified for 'Gambia 1894' which follows.

Regiments present: Sierra Leone Frontier Police (48); 1/WIR (380); RE (12); AMS (7); ASC (1).

Gambia 1894 23rd February-11th March 1894

This bar, authorized on 30th August 1895, was awarded to Naval personnel involved in the expedition up the Gambia river (See '1893-94' above).

In February a Naval Brigade, commanded by Captain Gamble, RN (HMS *Raleigh*), went inland to attack Chief Fodeh Silah. On its way back it was ambushed. Lieutenants W. H. Arnold, F. W. Hervey and Sub-Lieutenant F. W. Meister and fifteen men were killed. A further attack was made on a force commanded by Lieutenant-Colonel Corbet. Reinforcements were sent under Major S. G. Fairclough and Major G. C. Madden. Gunjur was bombarded by Rear-Admiral F. Bedford's squadron. Chief Silah surrendered to the French in Senegal.

HM Ships: *Alecto* (47), *Magpie* (41), *Raleigh* (349), *Satellite* (164).

Duplicates have been issued to: *Alecto,* J. Allen, *Magpie,* G. Huse, R. W. Jane and Tom Walker (Native). *Raleigh,* W. Aldred, R. Browning, T. Davis, G. Harrold, G. Heathfield, E. R. Lakey, H. L. Road, E. Tablock, W. F. White, H. Worth and Tom Lee (Native). *Satellite,* H. Bummage, W. Gatrell, C. H. Green, H. J. Pope, F. J. White, J. Wingard and G. W. Woodruff.

Benin River 1894 August-September 1894

Authorized on the 30th August 1895, this bar was awarded to members of the expedition that went up the Benin River to punish chief Nana of Brohemie who had been terrorizing the surrounding area. The expedition, chiefly of Naval personnel, was under the command of Rear Admiral Bedford.

Regiments present: Niger Coast Constabulary (157); Hausas.
HM Ships: *Alecto* (43), *Philomel* (165), *Phoebe* (190), *Widgeon* (4).

Brass River 1895 7th-26th February 1895

This bar was awarded to members of an expedition against King Koko who had attacked the River Niger Company's trading post at Akassa. Forty-three African captives were mutilated, butchered and eaten. Rear Admiral Sir Frederick Bedford in command of the Cape and West Africa Station, led the expedition against King Koko.

HM Ships: *Barrosa* (19), *St George* (23), *Thrush* (22), *Widgeon* (5).

Major A. G. Leonard, C and T. Corps, and Major Leishman, Border Regt. received this bar.

M'wele 1895-1896

No bar was issued for these operations, however the word 'Mwele' was impressed on the rim of the medal to the left of the claw and date '1895' or '1895-6', to the right.

Bronze medals were also issued for these operations.

East and West Africa Medals already issued for earlier campaigns were returned for the addition of 'M'wele' on the rim.

This medal was awarded for a series of actions against the Kenyan coastal Arabs under the rebel Mbaruk. A naval force under the command of Admiral Rawson was despatched to Mbaruk's stronghold at M'wele. Following its capture, Arab domination of the Kenyan coast was effectively ended.

Regiments present: Uganda Rifles (439); Bombay Rifles (500); 24, 26, Bombay Infantry; 1 Punjabis.

HM Ships: *Barrosa* (5), *Phoebe* (4), *Racoon* (70), *St George* (22), *Thrush* (4), *Widgeon* (1).

1896-97

This bar is reported to have been authorized but there is no evidence of it ever having been issued. (See bar '1896-99').

1896-98 27th November 1896-14th June 1898

Authorized in 1900, this bar was awarded for several minor expeditions in the Northern Territories of the Gold Coast. These became necessary following the 1895-96 Ashanti Campaign to counter growing French and German influence in the region.

Regiments present: 2 West India Regiment (200).

1896-99

This bar would seem to have been authorized but there is no evidence of it ever having been issued.

Army Order 250, December, 1901, states that all officers and men on military duty between the dates specified in Army Order 253 of 1900, at any place within the Northern Territories of the Gold Coast, or in the hinterland of Lagos, will be considered as entitled to the Medal and Clasp for operations in 1896-1899.

Niger 1897 6th January-25th February 1897

The bar was authorized in 1897 for operations to Egbon, Bida and Ilorin and for garrison duty at Fort Goldie and Lokoja. Major A. J. Arnold, 3 Hussars commanded the expedition.

Recipients: 24 British officers and 7 British NCOs attached to the Royal Niger Constabulary (RNC); 651 Natives of the RNC; 15 British civilian employees of the Royal Niger Company, including four medical officers.

Benin 1897 6th February-7th August 1897

This bar was awarded for an expedition to Benin City against Chief Overiami who had been indulging in human sacrifice and slave trading. Lieutenant-Colonel Bruce Hamilton commanded a force of Niger Coast Constabulary and Rear Admiral Rawson commanded the naval force.

Regiments present: Niger Coast Constabulary (500), British Army officers (6).

HM Ships: *Alecto* (76), *Barrosa* (31), *Forte* (320), *Magpie* (86), *Philomel* (337), *Phoebe* (258), *St George* (456), *Theseus* (551), *Widgeon* (79).

Naval Nurses (3), RN officers on SS *Malacca* (2).

This is one of the few instances where naval personnel who remained on board were entitled to the medal and bar.

Dawkita 1897 28th March 1897

Authorized in April 1898, this bar was awarded to the force under Lieutenant F. B. Henderson RN (Private Secretary and ADC to the Governor) for the defence of the town of Dawkita in the Gold Coast hinterland when it was attacked by the powerful Sofa slavers.

The bar was awarded to forty-two men of the Gold Coast Constabulary.

Royal Mint records indicate that an order was placed on 7th March, 1898 for forty-three medals and bars for Dawkita, forty-two were despatched on the 11th of March 1898. A further order was placed for fifty medals with this bar on the 3rd of June, 1909, and were delivered on the 1st of July 1909.

1897-98 September 1897-14th June 1898

This bar was authorized in 1900 for the expeditions in the hinterland of Lagos between September 1897 and 14th June, 1898.

Regiments present: 2 West India Regiment (559); 1 Bn N Nigeria Regt (149), 2 Bn N Nigeria Regt (99); Gold Coast Constabulary (847); Lagos Hausa Force (431); Royal Artillery (30).

Bars were also issued to British officers and civilians.

1898

This bar was authorized in 1900 for the undermentioned expeditions in Northern Nigeria:

(a) With a force under Lieut-Col. J. Willcocks in Borga before 14 June, 1898.

(b) In the Lapai Expedition under Lieut-Col. Pilcher from 8th to 27th June, 1898.

(c) In the expeditions known as Ibouza, Anam, Barua, Basema and Siama, Angiama, Illah, Dama, all in 1898.

Regiments present: Rifle Bde (13); Army Medical Corps (10); 2 West India Regiment (5); 1 Bn. N Nigeria Regt (68); 2 Bn N Nigeria Regt (2); Lagos Hausa Force (141); 1 Bn WAFF (348); 2 Bn WAFF (34).

Bars were also issued to British officers and civilians.

HM Ships *Heron* (10).

Sierra Leone 1898-99 18th February 1898-9th March 1899

This bar is deeper than any of the others awarded with this medal, as the inscription occupies two lines. Only medals issued with this bar were named in square block capitals.

This bar was authorized in 1900 and was awarded for services in the 'Hut Tax' War.

Regiments present: Army Medical Service (44); ASC (27); AOC (9); RE (56); RGA (85); 1 (1,123); 2 (594), 3 (159) West India Regiment; West Africa Regiment (895); Sierra Leone Volunteers (126); Sierra Leone Police (553); Waterloo Volunteer Corps (61).

Bars were also awarded to various British officers and civilians.

Naval Brigade from H. M. Ships: *Alecto* (54); *Blonde* (120); *Fox* (86); and Colonial Steamer *Countess of Derby* (19).

1899 February-May 1899

Authorized in 1900 for the Bula Expedition, the Central Division Expedition (February-March 1899) and the Benin Territory Expedition (April-May 1899).

These expeditions were under the command of Captain C. H. P. Carter and Captain R. Gabbett.

Regiments present: Niger Coast Protectorate Force (290); WAFF (282).

1900 4th January-9th May, 1900

This bar was granted in 1903 for the Munshi Expedition (4th January-19th March 1900) and the Kaduna Expedition (20th February-9th May 1900) in Northern Nigeria. These expeditions arose from the need to ensure the safe passage for caravans and the abolition of the slave trade.

Regiments present: RE (8); RAMC (3); 1 Bty N Nigeria Regt (41); 1 Bn (178), 2 Bn (499) N Nigeria Regt. Attached officers and NCOs (19).

112 *British South Africa Company's Medal* 1890-1897

Obverse	The crowned and veiled head of Queen Victoria with the legend 'VICTORIA REGINA'.
Reverse	A charging lion with an assegai sticking in its chest; in the background a Mimosa bush; and in the foreground a native shield and assegais. Above are the names and dates of the campaign for which the award was made (Matabeleland 1893, Rhodesia 1896, Mashonaland 1897). The Mashonaland 1890 Medal, sanctioned in 1926, has no details of the campaign. Below is the wording 'BRITISH SOUTH AFRICA COMPANY'.
Size	36mm diameter
Metal	Silver
Ribbon	35mm wide with four yellow/gold and three dark blue stripes.
Suspension	By a flat wide swivel suspender which is composed of representations of roses, shamrocks and thistles.
Designer	R. Caton Woodville
Manufacturer	Heaton and Company, Birmingham
Naming	Engraved in upright and sloping capitals. The medals for Matabeleland 1893 and Rhodesia 1896 are also found in indented capitals. The Mashonaland Medal 1890 was engraved in London and in Southern Rhodesia between 1928 and 1946, consequently several different styles are known, perhaps five.
Bars issued	Four; Mashonaland 1890, Matabeleland 1893, Rhodesia 1896 and Mashonaland 1897.

In 1896 the Queen sanctioned the medal for 'Matabeleland 1893'; in 1897 the medals for 'Rhodesia 1897' and 'Mashonaland 1897' were sanctioned. In 1926 the medal for services in Mashonaland 1897 was sanctioned.

112A *Mashonaland 1890 Medal* 1st June 1890-12th September 1890

This extremely rare medal was sanctioned by the Southern Rhodesia Government in Gazette Notice No 267 of 30th April 1926. As the reasons for the medal's existence are not generally known, the Southern Rhodesia Gazette is quoted:

'It is hereby notified that His Majesty the King has been graciously pleased to approve of a medal with clasp inscribed 'MASHONALAND 1890' being awarded to the Colonial Forces who were engaged in the expedition which marched into and occupied Mashonaland in September, 1890, on the following conditions:

(1) The medal, which will be designated the 'Mashonaland 1890, Medal', will be in silver, and similar to that sanctioned by Her Late Majesty Queen Victoria, to be granted by the British South Africa Company for military operations in Matabeleland, 1893, but with the superscription 'Matabeleland, 1893' omitted from the reverse.*

(2) The riband will be identical with that of the Matabeleland War Medal, 1893.

(3) Members of the Pioneer Corps and escort of British South Africa Company's Police who have already been awarded the medal granted for operations in Matabeleland 1893, or Rhodesia 1896, will surrender that medal and receive in lieu thereof the 'Mashonaland 1890, Medal' with clasp 'Mashonaland 1890' and 'Matabeleland 1893' or 'Rhodesia 1896' respectively. Those members who were not entitled to the medal granted for operations in Matabeleland 1893, or Rhodesia 1896, will receive the 'Mashonaland, 1890 Medal' with clasp 'Mashonaland 1890'.

(4) Provided claims are approved by the competent authorities, the medal with clasp will be granted to all officers, warrant officers, non-commissioned officers and other ranks who actually served on the establishment of the Pioneer Corps or British South Africa Company's Police and who entered Mashonaland between the 1st June and the 12th September, 1890.'

Of the six hundred and seventy-two names which were put forward for this medal, only two hundred were issued [British South Africa Co Police (110); Pioneer Column (90)]. Of the ten men entitled to this medal with four bars, Trooper M. E. Weales, BSA Co Police, is the only recipient known to have had one issued to him. Fifteen men were entitled to the medal with three bars and fifty-nine men are entitled to two bars. The remaining one hundred and twenty-five men were entitled to the single clasp Mashonaland 1890.

Those who had been issued with one of the three earlier medals and bars, and in 1927 claimed the bar for Mashonaland 1890, were expected to hand their original medal in for exchange, although a number did not do so.

On 29th October, 1889, a charter was granted to the British South Africa Company to develop the district between the Lower and Central Zambesi on the north and Transvaal border on the south. The Portuguese sent an exploring expedition under Lieutenant Cordon, into the same territory and claimed the province of Zumbo on 7th November, 1889. Protests were made to the Portuguese Government by the Marquis of Salisbury, who referred them to the agreements made with King Lobengula of Mashona and Makalakaland in 1888 and to those made with other tribes. The Portuguese Foreign Minister, Senor Barros Gomez, replied that Portugal maintained her claims as a result of exploration and prior occupation of the territory. This attitude was followed up by the sending of a force of about 4,000 men, under Major Serpo Pinto, to form a camp in the Makolo country. He displeased the natives and demanded that British settlers should submit to Portuguese authority. Lord Salisbury insisted that British subjects should not be attacked, but he received a reply to the effect that the Portuguese action was justified owing to the disturbed state of the country. Lord Salisbury then suggested that the matter be referred to a conference of the Powers in accordance with the Treaty of Berlin (1878), and in the meanwhile demanded the immediate withdrawal of the Portuguese troops. Senor Gomez reported that this had been done but, on 9th January, 1890, Lord Salisbury learnt that not only had the force not been withdrawn but, what is more, they were treating Nyasaland as a Portuguese colony. He then demanded the withdrawal to take place by 10pm 11th January, 1890. He further informed the Portuguese Government that if this was not done, HMS *Enchantress* would enter The Tagus and embark the personnel of the British Legation and all British subjects in Lisbon. This had the desired effect and the demands were complied with, though the complete evacuation did not take place until March, prior to which a survey party under Mr Selous had entered the territory and had not been molested.

In July it was considered advisable to send a column into Mashonaland—not with any hostile intentions, yet prepared to use force if necessary.

This column, under the command of Lieutenant-Colonel E. G.

Pennefather, was composed of the company's policemen and enlisted pioneers totalling about 700 men.

On the 11th September as a result of a report received from a scouting party that Mount Hampden had been sighted, Colonel Pennefather with his second-in-command and the Chief Scout rode forward to reconnoitre. The three of them followed the south bank of the strongly flowing Makabusi River until they reached a kopje (then known as Harare Kopje after a local native chief and shortly to be renamed Salisbury Kopje). In the vicinity of the Kopje they crossed the river and headed northwards in the direction of Mount Hampden.

A survey of Mount Hampden area revealed there was insufficient water for a settlement of any size. Colonel Pennefather then decided on the site in the vicinity of Harare Kopje and the Makabusi River. The Chief Scout was sent back to the Column with instructions to take them to this area. The Column reached the area where the Anglican Cathedral now stands about midday on the 12th September. The site is about 12 miles south-east of Mount Hampden. A parade was held at 10.00am the following morning and the Union Flag hoisted.

Major Johnson, in his Orders of the Day, announced that the place where the Column had halted should be called Fort Salisbury after Lord Salisbury, the Prime Minister of Great Britain. The Pioneer Corps did not dismiss until the 30th September, when they held their last parade. Mount Hampden had been named by F. C. Selous on one of his earlier hunting expeditions 'after that good Englishman who gave his life in the defence of the liberties of his country'.

As it turned out, this bar, or medal, was not awarded for combatant service. Though in view of what had been going on in the territory, nobody knew what might have happened.

Matabeleland 1893 16th October-24th December, 1893

In July, 1893, the Matabeles raided the Mashonas, and then they invaded the British settlement at Fort Victoria; but it is doubtful whether it was at the instigation of King Lobengula, who was peacefully inclined but lacked control over his subordinates. Be that as it may, it was necessary to defend the settlers and punish the Matabeles, so three mounted columns were organised; one at Tuli, one at Salisbury, and the third at Fort Victoria.

When all was ready the Salisbury and Fort Victoria columns moved off and joined at Intaba Zimbi (Iron Mine Hill) on 16th October. They were attacked on the Shangi river on 24th October and on the Mbembesi (M'Bembezu) on 1st November. It transpired later that Lobengula had sent envoys for peace but that they had been shot at Tati by mistake on or about 23rd October, so the advance to Bulawayo was undertaken with the object of capturing Lobengula, who, however, had fled by the time his kraal was entered on 4th November. Messages were sent to him offering him a safe conduct, but as no answer was received a force under Major Forbes was sent off on the 14th to capture

---

*Both the obverse and reverse of this medal have milled borders.

him. On the 3rd December the Shangani river was reached and a small party of about thirty men under Major Allan Wilson was sent across the river to arrest him. Whilst these men were on the other bank the river rose rapidly in flood, so that they were cut off. They were attacked by an overwhelming force of Matabeles. The epic stand they made forms one of the bright pages of history.

The Matabele chiefs surrendered on 14th January. Lobengula died of fever on the 23rd.

Army Order 202 of December, 1896, authorized the award of a medal to all officers, non-commissioned officers and men of the Regular Forces, Bechuanaland Police, and British South Africa Company's Forces who were employed in connection with the operations in Matabeland within the country west of Iron Mine Hill, north of Palla Camp and east of the boundary of the German possessions in South-West Africa, between the 16th October and 24th December, 1893. The grant of the medal to officers of the Regular Forces was limited to those who had official sanction to be present.

The name and date of this campaign are on the medal. Those who received one of the undated medals were awarded a bar.

Of the 1,596 medals awarded only 88 were issued to Imperial Troops.

Regiments present: Imperial Troops—3 Dragoon Guards (3); 20 Hussars (1); RA (1); RE (1); Coldstream Guards (1); Grenadier Guards (1); DLI (1); KOYLI (1); N Staffs Regt (1); 1 Rl Highlanders (Black Watch) (18); 2 W Riding Regt (54); 2 Yorks and Lancs Regt (3); 3 Yorks and Lancs Regt (1); MSC (1).

Colonial Troops—Bechuanaland Border Police (558); Cape Mounted Rifles (37); Cape Police (3); Civilians (11); Native Commissioner's Dept (1); Raaff's Column (249); Salisbury Horse (262); Victoria Column (358); Unattached Troops (1).

Rhodesia 1896 24th March—31st December, 1896

In 1895 the territories subject to the British South Africa Company were named Rhodesia after Cecil Rhodes. Rhodesia was divided into Northern Rhodesia (which in turn was subdivided into North Eastern and North Western Rhodesia, or Barotseland) and Southern Rhodesia. North Eastern Rhodesia was administered from Fort Jameson; North Western Rhodesia from Kalomo; and Southern Rhodesia from Salisbury, in Mashonaland.

In March, 1896, the Matabeles, under Chief Olimo, revolted and were joined by the native police in the Insega and Filibusi districts. They massacred some settlers, including Constable Bentley and Assistant Native Commissioners Graham and Handley. Relief forces were formed which took the names of the Bulawayo Field Force, the Matabeleland Relief Force, and others as mentioned later on.

Several small encounters took place, including those in the Shiloh district between 4th and 8th April; the attack on Captain Brand's patrol on the Tuli Road, 10th April; the action on the Umgusa River on 22nd April and the two actions at Gwelo on 1st May and 6th June.

In June the Mashonas also rose in revolt, so that martial law was proclaimed in Salisbury. Commissioner Graham was murdered at Inyati; the mission station at Ingwengwesi River was destroyed, and severe fighting took place at Umfuli on 22nd June. Chief Olimo was killed during the fighting in the Matoppo Hills and a heavy defeat inflicted on the rebels at Thbas-I-M'hamba on 5th July. Chief Secombo's stronghold in the Matoppos was stormed by Colonel Plumer's force; Colonel Alderson captured Chief Makoni's kraal in August, and the chief himself was captured in September near Umtali and shot, as was Chief Aweenya. Chief Mtigeza surrendered together with other chiefs in September. Finally a conference was held between Mr Rhodes and the native chiefs, during which peace terms were agreed upon on 20th September, though peace was not declared until 13th October.

Army Order 96 of July 1897 authorized the award of a medal to all those who were employed in connection with the operations in the provinces of Matabeland and Mashonaland, known as Southern Rhodesia, between the 24th March and the 31st December 1896 both dates inclusive.

The medal was of exactly the same design as that previously issued for Matabeland 1893, except that it bore the inscription 'Rhodesia 1896' instead of 'Matabeleland 1893' on the reverse.

Those who had been awarded the medal for Matabeland, or subsequently received the undated medal received a bar inscribed 'Rhodesia 1896'.

Regiments present and number of Rhodesia 1896 medals and bars issued:

IMPERIAL TROOPS

Commandant General's Staff (4); Headquarters Staff Corps (25); Infantry Brigade (3); Army Medical Staff (35); Army Ordnance Corps (6); Army Service Corps (10); Army Veterinary Department (1); Derbyshire Regiment (Sherwood Foresters) (7); Dragoons 1 Royal (1); Dragoon Guards 3 Battalion (2), 6 Battalion (1); Hampshire Regiment 2 Battalion (25); 7 Hussars (228); King's Royal Rifle Corps 2 Battalion (2), 3 Battalion (28), 4 Battalion (32); Leicestershire Regiment 1 Battalion (2); Medical Staff Corps (59); Norfolk Regiment 2 Battalion (31); Rifle Brigade 2 Battalion (31), 4 Battalion (31); Royal Artillery (2), 10 Mountain Battery (49), 24 Coy Western Division (8), 25 and 26 Coys Western Division (6); Royal Dublin Fusiliers 1 Battalion (33); Royal Engineers (3), 43 Coy (42); Royal Highlanders (1); Royal Irish Fusiliers 2 Battalion (27); Royal Irish Regiment 1 Battalion (30); Royal Irish Rifles 1 Battalion (28); Royal Welsh Fusiliers 2 Battalion (2); Royal West Kent Regiment 2 Battalion (2); South Wales Borderers (1), 1 Battalion (2); West Riding Regiment 2 Battalion (270); West Yorkshire Regiment Depot (1); Wiltshire Regiment 2 Battalion (1); Yorks and Lancaster Regiment 1 Battalion (1), 2 Battalion (156); Yorkshire Light Infantry 1 Battalion (1).

COLONIAL AND LOCALLY RAISED TROOPS

Africander Corps (20), 'A' Troop (110), 'B' Troop (106); Artillery Troop Corps (78); Belingwe Column Corps Staff (13), 'A' Troop (23), 'B' Troop (23), 'C' Troop (22), 'D' Troop including Cape Boys (55), 'E' Troop (36), Maxim Troop (30), Scouts (7); British South Africa Police (782); Bulawayo Field Force Corps (126), Staff (33), Ambulance Corps (4), Artillery Troop (141), Band (18); Bulawayo Field Force Corps: Commissariat Department (24), Remount Depot (29), Swansons Volunteers (43); Transport Department (29), 'C' Troop (88), 'D' Troop (95), 'E' Troop (132), 'F' Troop (102), 'G' Troop (180), 'H' Troop (109), 'K' Troop (71), 'L' Troop (112), 'M' Troop (14); Charter Garrison Corps (28); Colenbrander's Cape Boys Corps (395); Engineer Corps (58); Enkeldoorn Garrison Corps (57); Gifford's Horse (171); Grey's Scouts Corps (63); Gwelo Burghers Corps (63); Gwelo District Volunteers (4); Gwelo Volunteers Corps (319); Honey's Scouts (15); Mangwe Field Force Corps (120); Mashonaland Field Force Corps, Headquarters Staff (4); Mashonaland Mounted Police Corps (127), Ambulance Troop Corps (12), Artillery Troop (14), 'A' Troop (28), 'B' Troop (46), 'C' Troop (42), 'D' Troop (43), 'E' Troop (25), 'F' Troop (41); Matabeleland Relief Force Corps (1075); Mounted Infantry Staff (1); Municipal Police (51); Natal Troop Volunteer Corps (65); Native Commissioner's Department (6); Native Contingent (1); Post and Telegraph Staff Corps (12); Rhodesia Horse Volunteers Dismounted Troop (41), Mounted Troop (102); Robertson's Cape Boy Corps (187); Salisbury Field Force (734); Salisbury Rifle Corps Chisawasha Garrison (17); Salisbury Volunteer Corps (14), Umtali Artillery (25); Umtali Burghers (143); Umtali Volunteer Corps (198); Victoria Rifles Corps (154); Victoria Transport Convoy Corps (2); Volunteer Defence Corps (28).

Summary:	1896 bars	1896 medals	Total awards
Imperial Troops	22	1208	1230
Colonial and locally raised troops	832	6354	7186
Sundry awards	5	89	91
	859	7651	8510

Mashonaland 1897 24th March, 1896-31st October, 1897

On 19th October, 1896, Gatze's kraal was taken by Major F. S. Evans; Lieutenant-Colonel Baden-Powell captured eight more kraals between the 16th and 28th and burnt that of Chief Dango on the 30th; Colonel Paget dispersed the rebels in the Thaba Insimba Hills on 20th November; Major Gosling captured Seka's kraal on 15th January, 1897. Many more kraals were captured in February. Marandella's kraal was stormed and captured on 26th May; heavy fighting broke out in July on the Umyami and near Fort Charter; more kraals, including that of Chief Matshayongombi, were taken on the same day.

The troubles may be considered to have stopped in September, though the final surrender of all the Mashona chiefs did not take place until 29th October.

Government Notice No 168, from the Secretary's Office, Salisbury, notified the grant of the medal for operations in Rhodesia between the 24th March and 31st December 1896 being extended to those employed in the subsequent operations in Mashonaland up to the 31st October 1897 inclusive. The medals awarded to those who only served in Mashonaland in 1897 were to have the inscription 'Mashonaland 1897' on the reverse. Those who had received any of the previous medals were awarded a bar inscribed 'Mashonaland 1897'.

Regiments present: Imperial troops—3 Dragoon Guards (2); 7 (201); 15 (1) Hussars; 2 Hamps (25); 1 Leicester (1); Rl Irish Fus (1); W Riding (1); RA 10 Mtn Bty (1); Mounted Infantry (16); RAMC (3);

ASC (1); Commandant General's Staff (4).

Colonial units—BSAP (688); Umtali Volunteers (211); Mount Darwin Volunteers (82); Garrison Volunteers (174); Native Commissioner's Department (12); Rhodesia Horse Volunteers (175).

Only four Matabeleland medals were awarded with the single bar for 'Mashonaland 1897'. The recipients were Captain C. D. L. Monro, Maj Sadler, Cpl T. Gardner and 1972 Tpr A. Knight, Bechuanaland Border Police.

Three Victoria Crosses were awarded for Matabeleland, these being to Tpr H. S. Henderson, Bulawayo Field Force; Tpr F. W. Baxter, Bulawayo Field Force and Capt R. C. Nesbitt, Mashonaland Mounted Police.

113 *Hunza Nagar Badge* 1891

General	Rectangular, slightly concave badge.
Obverse	An officer and two sepoys storming a fort in the hills. In the bottom right hand corner is the inscription 'HUNZA NAGAR 1891'
Reverse	Plain, with two loops for a split pin. In the centre is impressed, 'GURNEY & SON. LONDON, WOODSTOCK STREET'.
Size	53 x 26mm
Metal	Bronze
Ribbon	45mm. wide. The stripes run diagonally from top right to bottom left and have serrated edges. The centre stripe is white, 6mm wide; this is flanked by two maroon stripes 11mm wide; the top left- and bottom right-hand corners are green.
Suspension	See text below
Designer	The badges were made by Messrs. Gurney & Son, London; it is not known if they designed them as well.
Naming	The badges were issued unnamed
Bars issued	Nil

The badge was given by the Maharajah of Jummoo and Kashmir to his Imperial Service troops who took part in the Hunza-Nagar Expedition. These were additional awards, as Army Order No. 168 of 1st September, 1892 authorized the award of the India General Service Medal of 1854 with the bar for Hunza 1891 to all soldiers of the Kashmir Army who served in the expedition. See page 124.

As originally issued, the badge was intended to be worn as a brooch at the neck. It was later decided that they could be worn as medals and some of the badges had the original fittings altered to more easily accommodate the ribbon.

114 *Central Africa Medal* 1891-1898

*One is known with the bar 'CENTRAL AFRICA 1894-98' awarded to a native of the 2nd British Central African Rifles, which was named in script followed by the words 'PRESENTED BY THE KING'.

Obverse	The diademed and veiled head of Queen Victoria with the legend, 'VICTORIA REGINA'
Reverse	A scene of bush fighting around a tree between British soldiers and natives.
Size	36mm diameter
Metal	Silver and bronze
Ribbon	33mm wide. Three colours of equal width, reading from left to right facing the wearer; black, white and terracotta. The colours are symbolic of the troops who took part, namely African, British and Indian.
Suspension	By means of a small swivelling ring through which the ribbon passes, those issued with a bar had a plain straight suspender.
Designers	Obverse—L. C. Wyon; Reverse—Sir Edward J. Poynter.
Naming	Medals are found unnamed, engraved in script or impressed in capitals*
Bars issued	One: Central Africa 1894-98.

Care must be taken to distinguish this medal from the Ashantee Medal 1873 and East and West Africa Medals due to the general similarity between them.

The medal was issued on two occasions, firstly in 1895 to commemorate ten small campaigns in Central Africa between 1891 and 1894, and again in 1899, for several more in the same area.

On the first occasion, the piece was suspended by a swivel ring and no bar was awarded. On the second occasion a bar inscribed 'Central Africa 1894-98' was given, and the piece was fitted with a plain straight suspender. A few were issued in bronze.

The medal without bar was authorized on 1st April 1895 and awarded for various expeditions against native chiefs and slave raiders in the general vicinity of Lake Nyassa in present day Malawi, formerly British Central Africa/Nyasaland. Two exceptions were the expeditions to Unyoro and Mruli which took place in Uganda.

1 Expedition to Mlanje July-August, 1891
Expedition under Captain C. M. MacGuire against the Yao slaver Chimkumbu in the area of the Mlanje Mountains.

2 Expedition against Makanjira October-November, 1891
Expedition under Commissioner H. H. Johnston and Captain MacGuire against the Yao Slaver Makanjira on Lake Nyassa. Also against the Yao Chief Mponda.

3 Expedition against Kawinga November, 1891
Expedition under Captain MacGuire against Chief Kawinga of the Yaos.

4 Expedition against Zarafi January-February, 1892
Expedition against Yao Chief Zarafi by Commissioner H. H. Johnston.

5 Expedition along the Upper Shire January-February, 1893
In response to slave raids made by Yao Chief Liwondi, expeditions were mounted by Commissioner H. H. Johnston and Captain C. E. Johnston. That of Commissioner Johnston got into difficulties and had to be relieved by a Royal Navy and volunteer force under Lieutenant G. S. Q. Carr and Lieutenant C. H. Robertson. After effecting the commissioner's rescue, Liwondi was defeated.

For this expedition, the Royal Navy personnel drawn from HM Ships *Herald* and *Mosquito* received the East and West Africa Medal with bar 'Liwondi 1893'; the land forces including volunteers received the Central Africa Medal.

6 Expedition to Mlanje August-October, 1893
Expedition under Lieutenant C. A. Edwards against Chief Nyassera of the Yaos. After defeating Nyassera, Edwards defeated Mkanda another troublesome chief in the Mlanje area.

7 Expedition against Makanjira November 1893-January 1894
Captain Johnston and Lieutenant Edwards with over one hundred men defeated Chiwauru, an associate of Makanjira to the east of Lake Nyassa and released many slaves. Then together with the gunboats *Pioneer* and *Adventure* captured the lakeside stronghold of Kalunda, Makanjira's mother. Makanjira's settlement was then captured and Makanjira defeated in battle.

For this series of actions the army received the Central Africa Medal; Navy personnel received the East and West Africa Medal with bar 'Lake Nyassa 1893'

8 Expedition against Chirandzulu December, 1893
Commanded by Capt. C. E. Johnston.

9 Expedition to Unyoro (Uganda) December, 1893-February, 1894
A series of expeditions against King Kaberega of the Bunyoro who was defeated.

10 Expedition to Mruli (Uganda) April-June, 1894
Further expeditions against King Kaberega who was again defeated.

Recipients of medals without bars: 1 (7), 2 (10), 3 (5) Lancers (Hyderabad Contingent); 1 Sikh Lancers (23); 23 (26), 32 (23) Bengal Pioneers; 15 (14), 22 (6), 24 (14), 26 (5), 28 (19), 30 (13), 31 (14), 35 (15), 36 (26), 45 (17) Bengal Infantry; 1 Sikh Regt. (15); IMS (2);

British Central Africa Rifles; Volunteers (23); Uganda Rifles (Uganda Expeditions)
Also to Lieut. Chaworth-Masters, 3rd Hussars.

Central Africa 1894-98

For fixing this bar, the ring was removed and replaced by a straight bar suspender.

The bar, authorized in August 1899 was awarded for several small expeditions in the region of Lake Nyassa with the exception of that against Mpezeni which took place in Zambia, formerly Northern Rhodesia.

1 Operations around Fort Johnston January, 1894

2 Expedition against Kawinga March, 1895
Expedition against Chief Kawinga of the Yaos.

3-6 Expeditions against Chiefs Zarafi, Mponda, Matapwiri and Makanjira September-November, 1895
A series of expeditions against Yao Chiefs resulting in the pacificiation of the land about the southern end of Lake Nyassa.

7-8 Expeditions against Mlozi and Mwazi December, 1895
Expeditions mounted against slavers around the nothern region of Lake Nyassa.

9 Expedition against Tambola January, 1896
Expedition under Lieutenant C. A. Edwards against Chief Tambola of the Angonis. The Angonis, of Zulu stock, occupied an area west of Lake Nyassa.

10 Expeditions against Odeti and Mkoma October, 1896
Expedition under Captain Manning against Chewa Chief Odeti who was harbouring the fugitive Tambola.

11 Expedition against Chikusi October, 1896
Expedition under Captains Manning and Stewart against Angoni Chief Chikusi.

12 Expedition to Chilwa August, 1897
Expedition under Captain Manning against Chief Serumba of the Anguru, south of Lake Chilwa.

13 Expedition against Mpezeni (Zambia) January-February, 1898
Expedition under Captain H. E. J. Brake defeated Angoni Chief Mpezeni and his son Singu in operations about the Luangwa Valley (Zambia).

14 Expedition to South Angoniland April, 1898
Expedition under Captain F. B. Pearce and Lieutenant J. S. Brogden against Angoni raiders.

Recipients of medals with the bar 'Central Africa 1894-98': 2 (5), 4 (5) Mountain Battery PFF; 1 (8) Punjab Infantry; 2 (10), 4 (10) Sikh Infantry; 14 (1), 15 (11), 19 (3), 21 (1), 22 (1), 24 (11), 25 (9), 26 (10), 27 (10), 28 (11), 29 (10), 30 (6), 31 (12), 35 (50), 36 (10), 45 (19) Bengal Infantry; 11 Bengal Lancers (1), 1 (629), 2 (90) British Central African Rifles; Volunteers (21); IMS; Royal Navy (20).

115 *The Hong Kong Plague Medal* 1894

Obverse   A soldier warding off the Angel of Death, who is aiming his spear at a plague-stricken Chinese man laid on a table. A female, symbolic of Charity, has her right hand over the patient's heart, and in her left has a medicine bottle. On the ground a brush and pail. To the left the words 'HONG KONG', in Chinese characters. In exergue, on wavy ground, a scroll, '1894'. To the left, in the exergue, F. BOUCHER, DES.

Reverse   Within a circle, 'FOR SERVICES RENDERED DURING THE PLAGUE OF 1894.' Around on a raised beaded border, 'PRESENTED BY THE HONG KONG COMMUNITY.'

Size   36mm diameter

Metal   Gold and silver

Ribbon   32mm wide. Red with yellow edges and two additional thin yellow stripes down the centre.

Suspension   A loop is soldered on to the top of the piece, through which passes a 11mm. diameter ring.

Designer   Designed by Frank Boucher and struck by A. Wyon, FSA

Naming   In thin well-spaced indented capitals giving recipient's rank, name and regiment but not number.

Bars issued   Nil

This medal was given by the Hong Kong Community to three hundred men of the Shropshire Light Infantry and fifty members of the Royal Navy and Royal Engineers, also to members in the local police. Approximately 40 medals were given in gold to officers, nursing sisters (9) and a few civilian officials.

Gold medals are known to Maj W. Machaughlin; Maj A. F. A. Lyle; Capt G. H. L. Buchanan; Capt H. B. Welman; Capt E. Howell; Capt J. G. Forbes; Capt G. C. Vesey; Lieut R. A. A. Y. Jordan; Lieut J. A. Strick; Lieut E. B. Luard; 2nd Lieut W. J. Robinson; 2nd Lieut R. T. Carreg and Atr Mastr J. C. Wilson.

One officer and six men lost their lives in endeavouring to stamp out the deadly bubonic plague which lasted from 5th May to 3rd September 1894.

As this was not considered a service medal permission to wear this medal in uniform was refused.

116 *India Medal* 1895-1902

Obverse	*1st issue.* The crowned and veiled head of Queen Victoria and legend, 'VICTORIA REGINA ET IMPERATRIX'
	2nd issue. Bust of King Edward VII in Field Marshal's uniform with the legend 'EDWARDVS VII REX IMPERATOR'.
Reverse	*1st issue.* A British and Indian soldier both supporting the same standard. On the left is the word 'INDIA' and on the right the date '1895'.
	2nd issue. As above with '1895' date deleted.
Size	36mm diameter. The 2nd (Edward VII) issue was struck having a thinner gauge.
Metal	Silver and bronze.
Ribbon	32mm wide. Crimson with two dark green stripes down the centre.
Suspension	By means of a floreated swivelling suspender.
Designer	Obverse: *1st issue,* T. Brock; *2nd issue,* G. W. de Saulles; reverse: G. W. de Saulles.
Naming	Running script unless otherwise stated.
Bars issued	Seven: Defence of Chitral 1895, Relief of Chitral 1895, Punjab Frontier 1897-98, Malakand 1897, Samana 1897, Tirah 1897-98, Waziristan 1901-2.

Army Order dated 1st April 1896 approved of the 'India Medal 1895' with two bars Defence of Chitral 1895 and Relief of Chitral 1895.

North West Frontier Operations 1895-1902

Chitral is a small state on the North West Frontier of India. On 30th August, 1892, the Mehtar of Chitral was assassinated. His son Afzul-ul-Mulk, who seized the throne, was promptly murdered by his uncle, who in turn was defeated and displaced by Nizam-ul-Mulk. This concluded with the recognition of Nizam-ul-Mulk by the British, who sent Surgeon-Major Robertson as Political Agent into the district in January, 1893. The Nizam was murdered by his brother Amir-ul-Mulk on 10th January, 1893, and soon after the state was invaded by Umra Khan. Dr. Robertson returned to Chitral and formally but temporarily recognised Amir-ul-Mulk as Mehtar in January, 1895. In March he did the same to Shujah-ul-Mulk and put Amir-ul-Mulk under surveillance. In the same month Umra Khan was joined by Sher Afzul from Cabul. The British then proclaimed against Umra Khan, who started operations without delay, resulting in many engagements with the tribesmen. Lieutenant Edwardes and Fowler were besieged in Reshun and their relief force attacked in the defile at Karagh on 8th March. The small British force accompanying the Agent, Dr. Robertson, was besieged in Chitral until relieved by Lieutenant-Colonel J. G. Kelly. An expeditionary force under Major-General Sir Robert Low crossed the Malakand Pass to the Jandol Valley, and eventually Umra Khan was driven out of Chitral.

On 26th July, 1897, a fanatical rising broke out in the Swat Valley, where the Mullah's followers attacked the garrisons in the Malakand Pass, Chakdara and the Shabkadr Fort on 7th August. The Swatis, Mohmands and Afridis united in rebellion against British rule on the North West Frontier.

The bar for Malakand was awarded for service against the Swatis, the Tirah bar for service against the Afridis, and the Punjab Frontier bar for all services along the North West Frontier.

Brigadier-General W. Meiklejohn was attacked in the Malakand Pass by the Swatis; Lieutenant Rattray was besieged in the fort at Chakdara and thousands of Afghans and Mohmands attacked the fort at Shabkadr.

An expeditionary force of one division known as the Malakand Field Force was mobilized under Major-General Sir Bindon Blood, whilst another was prepared under Major-General E. R. Elles.

The campaign against the Swatis did not take long, so that General Blood was able to attack the Mohmands in conjuction with General Elles's division. These two divisions then jointly formed the Mohmand Field Force.

Whilst these operations were going on trouble broke out on the Samana Ridge, where a force under Major-General Yeatman-Biggs was occupied with the joint predatory efforts of the Afridis and Orakzais, who attacked the forts with great vigour.

The many tribes along the Northern Frontier then united in rebellion against British rule which resulted in the mobilization of the Tirah Field Force under General Sir William Lockhart. Many actions took place between October 1897 and April 1898 before the situation was calmed.

In 1901 the Mahsuds and Waziris ambushed a column in the Gomal Pass resulting in further fighting.

Defence of Chitral 1895 3rd March-19th April 1895

The bar was authorized along with the medal on 1st April 1896.

This bar was awarded to the garrison under Brevet-Major C. V. F. Townsend CB. The garrison was composed of the following troops: 14th Sikhs (88); 4th Kashmir Rifles (300); Punyalis—local levies (medals are named 'Gilgit Levy') (100); Camp followers (40)—who received a bronze medal.

In addition to the above, four Syces present received a bronze medal: Sepoy Sujen Singh, Bhisti Ami Chand, Bhisti Khim Singh, Bhisti Ala Vaux.

See also Jummoo and Kashmir Medal page 179.

A Victoria Cross was awarded to Surgeon Captain H. F. Whitchurch, IMS, for the Defence of Chitral.

Casualties of the Garrison from 3 March to 20 April 1895
14th Sikhs
Killed
1442 L/Naik Bakhtawar Singh; 829 Naik Mota Singh; 1950 Sepoy Sawan Singh; 1666 Sepoy Jiwan Singh; 1295 Sepoy Narain Singh
Wounded
1932 Sepoy Attar Singh; 1501 Sepoy Bhola Singh; 739 Sepoy Fouja Singh; 772 Sepoy Garja Singh; 1510 Sepoy Harnam Singh; 1540 Sepoy Harnam Singh; 1436 Sepoy Keher Singh; 511 Havdr Mal Singh; 1252 Sepoy Partap Singh; 1804 Sepoy Partap Singh; 1633 Sepoy Thamman Singh

4th Raghunath Kashmir Light Infantry
Killed
Sepoy Beli Ram; Sepoy Dewi; Sepoy Doolo; Naik Dhanbahadur; Sepoy Debi Singh; Sepoy Gopal Singh; Sepoy Gurkoo; Sepoy Hushiara; Sepoy Jebe (748); Sepoy Jagbir; Sepoy Kaloo; L/Naik Kishen Singh; Sepoy Kalbir; Sepoy Kesar Singh; Sepoy Kakir; Sepoy Lachman; Sepoy Lachhman; Sepoy Madan Singh; Sepoy Mukti Ram; Sepoy Mool Singh (907); Sepoy Mian Singh; Sepoy Ram Ratan; Sepoy Rubela; Sepoy Sundar; L/Naik Sri Man
Wounded
Sepoy Amar Singh; Sepoy Arjan; Sepoy Abhad Singh; Sepoy Bhogma; Sepoy Beli Ram; Sepoy Chandarbir; L/Naik Chanda Singh; Sepoy Chait Singh; Sepoy Dhani Ram; Sepoy Deedo; Havdr Dhani; H/Mjr Durga Singh (18); K/Havr Gulaboo; Sepoy Gobind Ram (984); Sepoy Hari Singh; Sepoy Hiroo; Sepoy Jagat Deo; Sepoy Jot Jaman; Sepoy Jita; Sepoy Jamoher; Sepoy Kashi Nath; Sepoy Ilahi Baksh; Sepoy Kirpa; Sepoy Khushia; Sepoy Khyali; Sepoy Kalu Raj; Sepoy Kakir; Sepoy Karkbir; Sepoy Kharak Singh; Naik Nain Singh; Sepoy Pyar Singh; Sepoy Parti Mun; Sepoy Prem Singh; Sepoy Raghubir; Sepoy Santoo; Sepoy Sono; Sepoy Santbir; Sepoy Sant Ram; L/Naik Sundar; Sepoy Singbir

Various Casualties
General Baz Singh, Kashmir State Forces, Killed; Major Bhikam Singh, Kashmir State Forces, Killed; Captain Baird, J. McD., 24th Punjab Infantry, Died of Wounds; Captain Campbell, C. P., Central India Horse, Wounded; Sgn/Maj Robertson, G. S., CSI, Wounded; Jemadar Rab Nawaz Khan, 15th Bengal Cavalry, Wounded; 3rd Grade Hospital Assistant Bhawani Dass, Indian Medical Service, Wounded; Sowar Mahmood, Central India Horse, Wounded; Sepoy Sultan Shah, Gilgit & Hunza Levies, Wounded; Sepoy Rajab, Gilgit & Hunza Levies, Wounded; Syce Habibullah, Private Servant, Wounded; Sher (Pakali), Private Servant, Wounded; Driver Gokal, Follower, Wounded; Barber Labboo, Follower, Wounded; Bhisti Ami Chand, Follower, Wounded; Bhisti Roda, Follower, Killed; Bhista Hukma Singh, Follower, Killed; Kahar Dewi, Follower (14th Sikhs), Killed; Kahar Mohamdoo, Follower, Killed.

Relief of Chitral 1895 7th March-15th August 1895
This bar was authorized on 1st April 1896.
This bar was awarded for service under:
1 Lieutenant-General Sir R. C. Low, GCB, between 2nd April and 15th August, 1895.
2 Brevet-Colonel J. G. Kelly, CB, ADC, between 26th March and 20th April, 1895.
3 Captain F. J. Moberley, DSO, 37th Bengal Infantry, at Mastuj.
4 Lieutenant S. M. Edwardes, DSO, 2nd Bombay Infantry, at Reshan.
5 Captain C. R. Ross, 14th Bengal Infantry, who left Mastuj on the 7th March to give assistance to Lieutenant Edwardes at Reshan.

Regiments present: Colonel Kelly's Force: Two guns of 1st Kashmir Mountain Battery; 32 Pioneers (400); Kashmir Infantry (100); Kashmir Sappers and Miners (34); Hunza and Punnial Levies (100). Lieutenant-General Sir Robert Low's Force: 1st Brigade—Guides Cavalry; 3 Mountain Battery RA; 4th D Gds (7); 5th Lancers (3); 11 (12), 18 (16), 19 (6) Hussars; 1 Royal Scots (13); Buffs (3rd Foot); Devons (15); East Surrey's (21); 1 Bedfords; 1 Northampton Regt.; 1 Royal West Kents (9); 1 King's Royal Rifle Corps; 15 Sikhs; 37 Dogras. 2nd Brigade—Guides Cavalry; 2 KOSB; 1 Gordons; Machine Gun Section of 1 Devons; Guides Infantry; 4 Sikhs; 11, 15 Bengal Infantry. 3rd Brigade—8 Mountain Battery RA; No 2 (Derajat) Mountain Battery; 1,

4, 6 Companies Bengal Sappers and Miners; 1 Buffs; 2 Seaforth; 25 Punjabis; 2/4 Gurkhas. Lines of Communication troops: 11 Bengal Lancers; Guides Cavalry; 1 East Lancs; 23 Pioneers; 13 Rajputs; 30 Punjab Infantry. Also present: 9 Bengal Lancers; 15 Field Battery RA; 8 Mountain Battery RA; 1 Kashmir, Mountain Battery; No 4 (Hazara) Mountain Battery; No 7 (Bengal) Mountain Battery; 6 Company Bengal Sappers and Miners; 1 PWO Sappers and Miners; RE and Indian Medical Service; 4 Sikhs; 26, 29, 30 Punjab Infantry; 34 Pioneers; 2/1, 2/3, 2/5 Gurkhas; Gwalior and Jodhpore Carrier Corps; Kurram and Border Military Police.
Medals are known to the 2 Royal Irish and Dorset Regiments.

Punjab Frontier 1897-98 10th June 1897-6th April 1898
This bar was authorized in June 1898.
Medals with this bar to the Highland Light Infantry are named in block capitals.
This bar was awarded to the defenders of Shabkadr Fort on 7th August 1897, and to the members of the Mohmand Field Force under Major-General E. R. Elles, CB., which operated from 15th September to 4th October 1897. It was also given to the Tirah Expeditionary Force under Lieutenant-General Sir W. S. A. Lockhart, KCB, KCSI, which operated between 2nd October 1897, and 6th April 1898.
Mohmand Field Force (Major-General E. R. Elles, CB). 1st Brigade—Somerset LI; 2/1 Gurkhas; 20 Bengal Infantry. 2nd Brigade—11, 13 Bengal Lancers; 5 (Bombay) Mountain Battery; 8 (Bengal) Mountain Battery; 3 Mountain Battery RA; 4 and 5 Companies Bengal Sappers and Miners; North'd Fusiliers; 1 DCLI; 2 KOSB; Devon Regt; Norfolk Regt; Argyll and Sutherland Highlanders; 2 Ox and Bucks LI; QO Corps of Guides; 27 Bengal Infantry; 9 Gurkhas. 3rd Brigade—two squadrons 4 Dragoon Guards; 5th Lancers (14); 11 Hussars, two squadrons (283); 11 Bengal Lancers; 1 Sikh Inf (100); 'K' Battery RHA; 1 Mountain Battery RA; 3 Company Bengal Sappers and Miners; 2 Queen's; 2 HLI; 1 Connaught Rangers (15); Argyll and Sutherland Highlanders; 22, 39 Bengal Infantry.
Unbrigaded troops: Corps of Guides; 24 Bengal Infantry; C. T. Dept. 1 Royal West Kents are also known to have been present.
Lieutenant R. Gordon, Queensland Mounted Infantry, received a medal with this bar and that for Tirah 1897-98 and so did members of the 19th Hussars (6) and 16th Lancers (48).
Eleven Victoria Crosses were awarded for the Punjab Frontier expeditions.

Malakand 1897 26th July-2nd August 1897
This bar was authorized in June 1898.
This bar was awarded to those who took part in the Defence and Relief of Chakdara and Malakand. The garrisons were commanded by Colonel W. H. Meiklejohn, CB, CMG, and were drawn from: 11 Bengal Lancers; No 8 Mountain Battery; No 5 Company Madras Sappers and Miners: 45 Sikhs; 24, 31 Punjab NI.
The relief force, known as the Malakand Field Force, was commanded by Major-General Sir Bindon Blood, KCB, and was composed as follows: 1st Brigade—1 RW Kent (3); 45 Sikhs; 24, 31 Punjab Infantry. 2nd Brigade—11 Bengal Lancers; No 5 Company Bengal Sappers and Miners; 1 Buffs; Guides Infantry; 35 Sikhs; 38 Dogras. 3rd Brigade— 1 Queen's; 38 Bengal Infantry; 39 Garhwals; 22 Punjab Infantry. Divisional troops; One squadron each of 10, 11 Bengal Lancers; Guides Cavalry; 10 Field Battery RFA; Nos 1 and 7 Mountain Batteries RA; No 8 (Bengal) Mountain Battery; No 3 (Bombay), 4 (Bengal), 5 (Madras) Sappers and Miners; 21 Punjab Infantry. Lines of communication troops; 2 Highland Light Infantry.

Samana 1897 2nd August-2nd October 1897
This bar was authorized in June 1898.
This bar, which is never found singly, was awarded to the garrisons beyond Kohat. The medals to the 36th Sikhs who defended Fort Gulistan, the gateway to the Afridi Hills, deserve special notice. The rare tribute of a special memorial at Amritsar was paid to the gallant defenders of Saragarhi, which consisted of a native officer and twenty Sikhs, who were all killed. The troops under Major-General Yeatman-Biggs, RA, which formed the garrisons, as under, joined the Tirah Field Force on 2nd October, 1897.

12, 18 Bengal Lancers; two squadrons 3 Punjab Cavalry; 1, 2 Central Indian Horse; 3, 9, Field Batteries RA; No 9 Mountain Battery RA; No 2 (Derajat) Mountain Battery; No 4 Company Bombay Sappers and Miners; 2 Royal Irish Regiment; 2 R. Scots Fusiliers; 5th North'd Fusiliers; 1/ Northampton Regt, Norfolk Regt; 1 DCLI; 2, 5 Punjab Infantry; 3, 15, 36 Sikhs; 21 Madras Pioneers; 1/2, 1/3, 5 Gurkhas; Kurram Militia.

A medal is known to Pte W. Reidy, 1 Royal Irish Regiment and Pte J. Blundell; 1 Royal West Kent Regiment.

Tirah 1897-98 2nd October 1897-6th April 1898

This bar was authorized in June 1898. Medals with this bar to the HLI are named in block capitals.

This bar, never awarded singly, was awarded to the Tirah Expeditionary Force, which included the Kurram Column, Peshawur Column, and the Rawal Pindi Brigade. The troops on the lines of communication and those in the Swat Valley also received the award.

Tirah Field Force (Lieutenant-General Sir W. S. A. Lockhart, KCB, KCSI). 1st Division: 1st Brigade—1 Devon; 2 Notts and Derbys; 1 Queen's; 2 Green Howards; 20 Bengal (Punjab) Infantry; 2/1 Gurkhas; No 6 Brigade and 34 Native Field Hospital. 2nd Brigade—1 Queen's; 2 Green Howards; 3 Sikhs; 2/4 Gurkhas; 28 Bombay Pioneers; Kapurthala Imperial Service Infantry; Nos 8 and 14 British and 51 Native Field Hospitals. 1st Divisional troops: Two squadrons 18 Bengal Cavalry; No 1 Mountain Battery RA; No 1 (Kohat) Mountain Battery; No 2 (Derajat) Mountain Battery; 3, 4 Companies Bombay Sappers and Miners; Maler Sappers and Miners; 28 Bombay Infantry (Pioneers); Nabha Imperial Service Infantry; No 13 British and 63 Native Field Hospitals.

2nd Division: 3rd Brigade—1 Dorsets; 1 Gordons; 1 Connaught Rangers (11); 15 Bengal (Sikh) Infantry; 1/2 Gurkhas; 24 British and 44 Native Field Hospitals. 4th Brigade—2 KOSB; 1 Northamptons; 36 Bengal (Sikh) Infantry; 1/3 Gurkhas; sections of No 9 and 23 British and No 48 Native Field Hospitals. 2nd Divisional troops: Machine Gun Detachment of 16 Lancers; two squadrons 18 Bengal Lancers; 8, 9 Mountain Batteries RA; 5 (Bombay) Mountain Battery; Rocket Det 5 Company W Div RGA; 4 Company Madras Sappers and Miners; Sirmoor Sappers and Miners; 21 Madras Pioneers, Jhind Imperial Service Infantry; 13 British and 42 Native Field Hospitals.

Kurram Column (Colonel W. Hill); 6 Bengal Cavalry; 38, 39 Central India Horse; one troop of 3 Field Battery RA; 12 (Khelat) Bengal Infantry; 1/5 Gurkhas; Karpurthala Infantry; Nabha Infantry; 'D' section of No 46 British and all No 62 Native Field Hospital.

Peshawur Column (Brigadier-General A. G. Hammond, VC, CB, DSO, ADC): 9 Bengal Cavalry; 57 Field Battery RA; No 3 Mountain Battery RA; No 5 Company Bengal Sappers and Miners; 2 Ox and Bucks LI; 2 R. Inniskilling Fusiliers; 45 Sikhs; 9 Gurkhas; No 5 British and No 45 Native Field Hospitals.

Rawal Pindi Brigade (in reserve) (Brigadier General C. R. Macgregor, DSO); Jodhpur Imperial Service Lancers; 1 DCLI; 2 KOYLI; 27 Bombay Infantry; 2 Hyderabad Infantry; No 12 British and No 53 Native Field Hospitals.

Lines of communication troops (Lieutenant General Sir A. P. Palmer, KCB); 3, 18 Bengal Cavalry; 9 Field Battery RA; No 1 (Kashmir) Mountain Battery; No 1 Company Bengal Sappers and Miners; 39 Bengal Infantry; 2, 22 Punjab Infantry; 2/2 Gurkhas; Jodhpore and Gwalior Transport Corps; Ordnance, Engineer and Veterinary Services; Nos 11, 25 British and 42, 47, 53, 64 Native Field Hospitals.

Swat Valley: 2 Royal Sussex Regiment.

Also present: 1, 2 Royal Scots Fusiliers, 2 Durham Light Infantry (4 officers, 10 ORs) 11 (12), 19 Hussars (6), 2 Suffolks (1), 1 Royal West Kents (7).

Waziristan 1901-2 23rd November 1901-10th March 1902

This bar was authorized in March 1903 to those engaged in the Mahsud and Waziri districts.

All single bar 'Waziristan 1901-2' medals were issued with the Edward VII obverse.

There was no expedition in the usually accepted term, but mobile columns were formed, as sort of counter-raids, against the Mahsuds in the Kabul Khel country. Major General C. C. Egerton CB, formed four columns of all arms drawn from the following troops:

1, 2, 5 Punjab Cavalry; No 2 (Derajat), 7 (Gujerat) (Bengal) Mountain Batteries; 1, 2, 9, 27, 28, 29 Punjab Infantry; 3, 4, 35, 45 Sikhs; 17 Bengal Infantry; 9, 23, 24 Bombay Infantry; 38 Dogras; 23, 32 Pioneers; 13 Rajputs; 3 Gurkhas; North and South Waziri Militia, 43 Native Field Hospital; 1 Battalion Cheshire Regiment (4) 2 Battalion Suffolk Regiment (7), 1 Battalion Wiltshire Regiment (2), 1 Battalion Yorkshire Regiment (1), 1 Battalion Middlesex Regiment (1) on HQ Staff; RE officers (8).

Medals are known to the 8th Mule Corps, 5th Punjab Infantry, 11th Rajputs, Murree Mountain Battery and the Supply and Transport Corps.

It is believed that single bar medals to men on the HQ Staff were officially renamed.

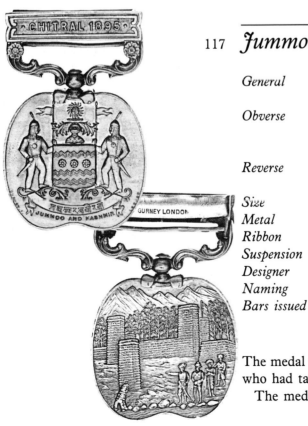

117 *Jummoo and Kashmir Medal* 1895

General	The medal is kidney-shaped, being recessed at the centre of the top and bottom.
Obverse	A coat of arms supported by two native soldiers below which is a scroll with an inscription in Hindustani, beneath this are the words, 'JUMMOO AND KASHMIR'.
Reverse	A large fortress having mountains and trees in the background and an officer and three native soldiers in the foreground.
Size	39mm wide, 34mm from top to bottom at its narrowest part.
Metal	Bronze
Ribbon	32mm wide. Equal stripes of red, white, green, white, red.
Suspension	By the same type of suspender as the India General Service Medals.
Designer	Manufactured and possibly designed by Messrs Gurney & Son, London
Naming	Found either unnamed or very crudely impressed in block letters.
Bars issued	One—Chitral 1895. The bar is of the same pattern as those of the India General Service Medals. The reverse of the bar is stamped, 'GURNEY, LONDON'.

The medal was given by the Maharajah of Jummoo and Kashmir to his native troops who had taken part in the Defence of Chitral in 1895, and its subsequent relief.

The medal was not given without the bar.

118 *Ashanti Star* 7th December 1895-17th January 1896

General	In the shape of a four-pointed star with a St Andrew's Cross between the arms.
Obverse	In the centre is the Imperial Crown surrounded by a raised band on which is the word 'ASHANTI' above and the date '1896' below.
Reverse	In raised lettering are the words 'FROM THE QUEEN'
Size	38mm diameter
Metal	Bronze
Ribbon	31mm wide. Yellow with two black stripes.
Suspension	By means of a ring attached to the top of the uppermost point.
Designer	Reputed to have been designed by Princess Henry of Battenberg, whose husband died of fever during the campaign.
Naming	All the stars were issued unnamed, but the Colonel of the 2nd Battalion The West Yorkshire Regiment had those awarded to his battalion engraved at his own expense.
Bars issued	Nil

The star was awarded in 1896 to members of Major General Sir Francis C. Scott's expedition against the Ashantis under King Prempeh (Kwaka Dua III).

The expedition became necessary to enforce the demand made that the Ashanti Kingdom became a British Protectorate. The non-payment of the indemnity of the 1874 treaty and claims of human sacrifice provided further grounds for action.

The Ashantis made no effort to resist the expedition and on the 17th January 1896 the capital Kumassi was entered. On the 20th, Prempeh made his submission to Scott and Governor Sir William Maxwell, following which, the King and his chief adherents were arrested and deported and a Protectorate established.

Regiments present:
Detachments of RA; RHA; RE; ASC; AMC (including three Nursing Sisters); AOC; APD; 2 West Yorkshire Regiment was the only complete battalion present (420). A composite battalion was formed of approximately twenty men each from 2/1 Guards (18); 2/2 Guards (16); 1/3 Guards (19); 1/5 (26); 2/11 (26); 51 (1); 3/60 (26); 4/60 (1); 80 (26); 85 (26); 89 (26); 100 (26); 2 Rifle Brigade (26); 2/WIR (403); Hausa Force (837); Gold Coast Constabulary (18).

119 *Queen's Sudan Medal* 1896-98

Obverse	Half length figure of Queen Victoria wearing a small crown and veil, holding a sceptre in her right hand, with the legend, 'VICTORIA REGINA ET IMPERATRIX'.
Reverse	A figure of Victory, who is seated, holding a palm branch in her right hand and laurel wreath in her left. At her feet is the word 'SUDAN' on a plaque supported by three lilies. Behind her and on either side are the British and Egyptian flags.
Size	36.5mm diameter
Metal	Silver and bronze
Ribbon	32mm wide. Half yellow, half black with a thin dividing red stripe.
Suspension	A straight swivelling suspension bar
Designer	G. W. de Saulles
Naming	Engraved in sloping or upright capitals. To Indian troops engraved in script. To Egyptian/Sudanese troops engraved in Arabic.
Bars issued	Nil

The medal was authorized in March 1899 for award to all British, Indian and Egyptian forces and native allies engaged in the reconquest of Sudan, ie to those who took part in any of the first six actions for which bars to the Khedive's Sudan Medal were issued:
Firket 7th June 1896; Hafir 19th-26th September 1896
Abu Hamed 7th July 1897; Sudan 1897 15th July-6th November 1897
The Atbara 8th April 1898; Khartoum 2nd September 1898—Battle of Omdurman.

The Queen's Sudan Medal was awarded to 17 officers and men of the Royal Navy, and 27 officers and men of the Royal Marines who saw service afloat in the gunboats of the Nile Flotilla, or on shore whilst attached to the Army during the reconquest of the Sudan between 1896-98.

Those officers and men who were later landed for service in the Sudan in 1899 did not receive the Queen's Sudan Medal. Their service was commemorated by the award of the Khedive's Sudan Medal with bar 'Sudan 1899'.

The Queen's Sudan Medal was also awarded to 13 locally recruited 'Seedies' who were employed with the Naval forces. The medal was also granted to 25 civil Marine Engineers who were employed to operate the River gunboats and supply transport vessels. The Medal Roll indicates that all of these medals were returned to the Principal Ordnance Officer Woolwich Arsenal on 10 January 1900. A number of these medals are, however, known to be in private collections and museums.

Five Victoria Crosses were awarded for the Sudan campaign, being to Capt. P. A. Kenna, 21st Lancers; The Hon Lieutenant R. H. L. J. De Montmorency, 21st Lancers; Pte T. Byrne, 21st Lancers; Captain N. M. Smyth, 2nd Dragoon Guards; The Hon Captain A. G. A. Hore-Ruthven, 3rd Battalion HLI.

120 *Khedive's Sudan Medal* 1896-1908

Obverse	An Arabic inscription which reads 'ABBAS HILMI THE SECOND' dated 1314 AH (1897 AD)
Reverse	An oval shield bearing three stars and crescents in the centre and surrounded by lances and flags. The whole is superimposed on two crossed rifles and cannons with a pyramid of six cannon balls. Beneath the whole is the Arabic inscription 'THE RECONQUEST OF THE SUDAN, 1314'.
Size	39mm diameter
Metal	Silver and bronze
Ribbon	39mm wide. Yellow with a broad blue stripe down the centre symbolic of the Nile flowing through the desert.
Suspension	By a plain, straight swivelling suspension bar
Designer	G. W. de Saulles.
Naming	Those issued to British troops are named in sloping capitals though some are impressed; those to Indian troops are mostly in script, whilst those to native troops are named in Arabic. Most of the later issues were unnamed.
Bars issued	Fifteen. They were named in English and Arabic: Firket, Hafir, Abu Hamed, Sudan 1897, The Atbara, Khartoum, Gedaref, Gedid, Sudan 1899, Bahr-el-Ghazal 1900-02, Jerok, Nyam-Nyam, Talodi, Katfia, Nyima.

This medal was authorized under Special Army Order Cairo 12th February 1897 to commemorate the military operations in connection with the reconquest of the Dongola Province.

The medal to British troops is rare with more than two bars (ie those for Atbara and Khartoum) however, Lieutenant S. K. Flint, Royal Irish Rifles, was awarded the medal with 10 bars—Firket, Hafir, Abu Hamed, Sudan 1897, The Atbara, Khartoum, Gedaref, Gedid, Sudan 1899, Nyam-Nyam.

No bar medals

Those who served at and south of Sarras between 30th March and 23rd September, 1896, or in Brigadier-General Egerton's Force at Suakin, between the same dates, received the silver medal without a bar, as did the crews of HMS *Melita* (139) and *Scout* (149), a few Nile steamers and 'G' Company Royal Dublin Fusiliers.

Brigadier-General Egerton's force (approx 4,000 men) 1 Bombay Lancers, 26, 35 Bengal Infantry, 2 Maxim Guns, 5 Bombay Mountain Battery, Sappers and Miners.

Other no bar medals are known: Northumberland Fusiliers (60).

Firket 7th June 1896

The first phase of the reconquest of the Sudan was the occupation of Dongola. On 2nd June 1896, headquarters were established at Akasha, from which the advance was continued on 5th June towards Firket, where, on 7th June 1896, the Emir Osman Azraq was defeated.

Regiments present: Egyptian Cavalry, Camel Corps; 2 Company RE; 1 N Staffs (18);† Connaught Rangers (7);† 2, 3, 4, 7, 8 Egyptian Infantry; 9, 10, 11, 12, 13 Sudanese Infantry.

Hafir 19th-26th September 1896

After the Battle of Firket the advance continued and reached Kerma on 19th September, Merowe on 26th September, and Dongola on 15th October 1896. Hafir is on the west bank of the Nile opposite Kerma,

†Only the machine-gun sections of these two regiments were present.

and it was here that the battle was fought. The bar was awarded to those who had taken part in the operations south of Fareig on 19th September 1896.

Regiments present: Egyptian Artillery; Egyptian Cavalry; RE; RAMC (20); 1 N Staffs (588); 1 Connaught Rangers (6); 1, 2, 3, 4, 5, 7, 8, 15 Egyptian Infantry; 9, 10, 11, 12, 13 Sudanese Infantry, also Capt B. Y. McMahon, 1st R Dgns.

HM gunboats: *Abu Klea, El Teb, Matemmeh, Tamaai, Zafir.* Approx 16 bars to the RN and RM.

Abu Hamed 7th July 1897

This bar was awarded to members of Major-General A Hunter's Force which set out from Kassingar to capture Abu Hamed, which it did on 7th July 1897.

Regiments present: 1 Troop Egyptian Cavalry; No 2 Field Battery Egyptian Artillery; 3 Egyptian Infantry; 9, 10, 11 Sudanese Infantry; Madras Sappers and Miners.

Sudan 1897 15th July-6th November 1897

This bar was not awarded for any particular action, but was given to those who had already received the medal and were south of Kerma and south of No 6 Station between the 15th July and 6th November 1897.

Regiments present: RE; Camel Corps; No 2 Field Battery Egyptian Artillery; 3, 8 Egyptian Infantry; 9, 10, 11, 13 Sudanese Infantry.

HM Gunboats: *Abu Klea, El Teb, Fateh, Matemmeh, Nazir, Tamaai* and *Zafir.* Royal Navy and Royal Marines (12).

The Atbara 8th April 1898

This bar, which it is rare to find singly, was awarded for the Battle of The Atbara fought against the Dervish army commanded by Emir Mahmoud.

Regiments present: Egyptian Cavalry and Camel Corps; 1 R Warwicks; 1 Lincolnshire Regiment; 1 Seaforth; 1 Camerons; Det 16 Company Eastern Division RGA; ASC; 1, 2, 4, 5 Batteries Egyptian Artillery; 2, 3, 4, 7, 8 Egyptian Infantry; 9, 10, 11, 12, 13, 14 Sudanese Infantry. HSH Prince Francis of Teck, 1st Rl Dgns received the medal with bars Hafir and Khartoum. Royal Navy (6).

Khartoum 2nd September 1898

This bar was awarded for the Battle of Omdurman. Though the entry into Khartoum followed immediately, it is unusual to find a bar inscribed differently from the battle for which it was awarded. A similar case occurred after the Ashantee campaign of 1873, when a bar inscribed 'Coomassie' was awarded for the action at Amoaful.

Regiments present: Four squadrons 21 Lancers; Egyptian Cavalry and Camel Corps; 32 (159); 37 (71) Field Batteries RA, detachment from 16 Company Eastern Division RA; ASC; 1, 2, 3, 4, 5 Field Batteries Egyptian Artillery; No 2 Company RE (14); 1 Grenadier Guards; 1 R Northumberland Fusiliers; 1 R Warwicks; 1 Lincolnshire Regiment; 2 Lancashire Fusiliers; 1 Seaforth Highlanders; 1 Cameron Highlanders; 2 Rifle Brigade; and a machine-gun detachment of the Royal Irish Fusiliers (102); 1, 3, 4, part of 5, 7, 8, 15, 17, 18 Egyptian Infantry; 9, 10, 11, 12, 13, 14 Sudanese Infantry.

HM Gunboats: *Fateh, Melik, Nazir, Sheikh, Sultan, Tamaai.*
Royal Navy and Royal Marines (33).

21st Lancers list of awards and casualties for the Battle of Omdurman

There is no known roll listing members of the 21st Lancers who 'charged' at Omdurman. However, of the 449 officers and men entitled to the Khartoum bar only 320 were known to have participated in the charge. Confirmation of a 'charger' can therefore only be proven if he received the Victoria Cross, Distinguished Conduct Medal, a wound, mortal or otherwise, or through contemporary documentary evidence.

Capt P. A. Kenna, VC; Lieut R. H. De Montmorency, VC; Lieut A. M. Pirie, wounded; 2/Lieut C. S. Nesham, wounded; Lieut J. Vaughan, KIA (att 7th Hussars); Lieut J. C. Brinton, wounded (att 2nd L Gds); Lieut R. H. Molyneux, wounded (att RH Gds); 2792 Sgt R. Allen, KIA; 3464 Pte B. H. Ayton, DCM; 4064 Pte G. Baker, wounded

r arm; 3026 L/Cpl G. Borthwick, KIA; 4022 Pte H. Bradshaw, KIA; 3850 Pte W. Brown, DCM, wounded l shoulder and r hip; 3231 Pte E. Bushell, wounded r shoulder; 3710 Pte W. Bushell, DCM; 2998 Pte T. Byrne, VC, wounded r arm and breast; 3052 L/Sgt E. Carter, KIA; 2518 L/Sgt W. Chalmers, DCM; 3494 Pte C. Cook, sword wound l hand; 3064 Pte H. Edmunds, spear wound r arm; 3615 L/Cpl F. W. S. Elliott, KIA; 2105 SSM A. English, wounded; 4054 Pte W. Etherington, KIA; 3593 Pte E. Farndell, wounded severely, hand; 2820 Sgt G. Freeman, sword wound, face; 3362 Pte W. Freeman, spear wound, back; 3304 Pte C. Gardiner, wounded, thigh; 2910 Sgt A. Grantham, KIA; 3730 Pte W. Hadley, died of severe spear wound r arm; 4108 Pte T. Hannah, KIA; 3801 Pte E. Harpley, wounded, back, r elbow and r hand; 3444 Cpl SS W. Harris, wounded, l knee; 3940 Pte E. Hatter, KIA; 2833 Sgt H. Hawken, sword wound l arm; 3135 SS A. Head, sword wound r hand; 3947 Sgt A. Higgs, wounded r hand; 3952 Pte T. Honeysett, wounded r hand; 3345 Pte J. Hope, wounded r hand; 2579 Sgt T. Hotchkiss, wounded r hand; 3569 Pte H. Hunt, KIA; 3727 Pte F. J. Kelly, KIA; 1724 Cpl. T. King, contusion to shoulder; 1917 Sgt T. Laurence, spear wound, r arm and l shoulder; 3371 Pte C. Lodge, crushed under horse; 4014 Pte T. Miles, KIA; 2672 Pte F. Morhall, KIA; 3080 Pte F. Pedder, DCM; 3613 L/Cpl H. D. Penn, DCM; 3512 Pte F. Porch, wounded r clavicle; 3061 Sdlr Cpl F. Pothecary, wounded l arm; 3934 Pte J. Quigley, spear wounds, l forearm and chin; 2305 Cpl J. Range, wounded; 3413 Pte F. Rawle, KIA; 3209 L/Cpl E. Raynor, spear wound r side; 3268 Pte J. Redferne, wounded r arm; 3897 Pte J. Reynolds, wounded r arm; 3299 Pte G. Rice, wounded, shoulder; 3351 Pte A. Roberts, KIA; 3133 Tptr G. Robinson, spear wound r hand; 3205 Pte H. Rowlett, wounded both arms; 2701 L/Cpl A. Sadler, spear wound r elbow; 3523 Pte J. Scattergood, KIA; 1980 SS Farr T. Scholes, wounded; 3526 SS P. Skelton, sword wound l hand; 3881 Pte T. Stevens, spear wound, chest; 3460 Cpl F. W. Swarbrick, DCM; 3766 Pte J. Thompson, wounded over r eye; 3965 Pte J. Varley, wounded; 2266 SSM G. Veysey, spear wound, l chest; 3325 L/Cpl J. Weller, KIA; 3853 Pte G. Western, sword wound, l wrist; 3582 L/Cpl W. Wilson, sword wound, l side and r shoulder; 3645 L/Cpl I. Wood, KIA; 3810 Pte F. Woodside, wounded r arm; 3626 L/Cpl C. Wright, KIA.

Gedaref 7th September-26th December 1898

This bar was awarded to those who took part in the fighting in the Eastern Sudan against Ahmed Fedil, who had established himself at Gedaref. The operations lasted from 7th September 1898, when Colonel Parsons left Kassala to occupy Gedaref, until 26th December 1898, when Ahmed Fedil escaped by crossing the White Nile near Kosti.

Regiments present: Camel Corps; 16 Egyptian Infantry; 9, 10, 12, 14 Sudanese Infantry; Royal Irish Fusiliers with two machine-guns (20); RA (3); Medical Corps (2) and 495 Irregulars under 3 Sheikhs.

HM gunboats: *Abu Klea, Dal, Fateh, Nazir, Sultan.* RMA (9).

Gedid 22nd November 1899

Ahmed Fedil, after his escape from Gedaref, rejoined the Khalifa, who had been routed at the Battle of Omdurman. Though attempts had been made to bring these two to action they proved too elusive and it was not until 12th November 1899, that they were again encountered. On this day the Khalifa attacked the gunboat *Sultan* opposite Aba Island. Sir Reginald Wingate, with 2,300 men, was sent out to catch him. On 22nd November 1899, the enemy was defeated at Gedid. The Khalifa and Ahmed Fedil were both killed and the reconquest of the Sudan completed.

Regiments present: Two sqdns Egyptian Cavalry; Camel Corps; 2 Field Battery Egyptian Artillery; 9, 14 Sudanese Infantry; one company of 2 Battalion Egyptian Infantry. Royal Navy (1), Royal Marines (4).

Sudan 1899

This bar was awarded to all who served on the Blue and White Niles south of Khartoum during 1899, including six to the RN, one being to Cmdr H. Escombe.

Bahr-el-Ghazal 1900-02 13th December 1900-28th April 1902

This bar was awarded to five British and eleven native officers together with three hundred and fifty native troops for policing operations under Sparkes Bey. The bar was also awarded to Lieutenant Fell, RN, and a few Naval ratings for services during November and December, 1900. All these operations took place in the Bahr-el-Ghazal Province.

Lieutenant-Colonel H. Gordon, CB, CMG, received this bar and that for Nyam-Nyam. Royal Marines (2).

Jerok January-March 1904

This bar was awarded to the force under the command of Miralai Gorringe Bey, CMG, DSO, which attacked the slave trader Ibrahim Wad Mahmud at Gebel Jerok on 11th February, 1904, and finally captured him on 3rd March 1904. The force consisted of about eight hundred Sudanese Infantry, together with a machine-gun section. These operations took place on the Blue Nile near the Abyssinian border.

Nyam-Nyam January-May, 1905

This bar was awarded for the suppression of further trouble in the Bahr-el-Ghazal province, on the Belgian Congo border. On this occasion it was caused by the Nyam-Nyam tribe. A force under Boulnois Bey, composed of eighteen British and thirty native officers and about seven hundred men with five machine-guns, was sent to restore order. It was organised in January and withdrawn in May.

Talodi 2nd-15th June, 1905

This bar was awarded for the suppression of the Abu Rufas Rising in the Nuba Mountains. Miralai O'Connell Bey, together with three hundred and eighty camelry and one hundred and fifty men of the 12th Sudanese Infantry, left El Obeid on 2nd June and reached Talodi on the 12th and finally stamped out the rising at Eliri on the 15th.

Katfia April 1908

This bar was awarded for the suppression of the rebellion led by Mohammed Wad Habuba, who had styled himself Prophet Isa and avowed his intention of opposing British authority. After treacherously murdering officials who went to interview him, a small force was sent to round him up. He was captured and hanged.

Nyima 1st-21st November, 1908

This bar was awarded to members of the force under Kaimakam Lempriere Bey which undertook a punitive expedition in the Nyima Hills. The force was drawn from the Camel Corps and the 10th and 15th Sudanese Infantry.

121 *General Gordon's Khartoum Star*

Obverse	A star of seven points with seven crescents and stars in the angles, in the centre a Grenade, surrounded by a Turkish inscription, 'The Siege of Khartoum' and the year of the Hegira '1301 (AD 1884)'
Reverse	Plain and convex
Size	60mm (variable)
Metal	Silver-gilt, silver and pewter
Ribbon	Magenta
Suspension	By a crescent and star loop suspension
Designer	General Gordon
Manufacturer	The Goldsmith 'Bishara Abdel Molak'

During the Siege of Khartoum, General Gordon designed and had cast by the goldsmith Bishara Abdel Molak these decorations which were copies of the Turkish Order of Medjidie. They were issued in three classes:

a) silver-gilt to Officers of the rank of Bimb and upwards, to merchants, notables and civilian employees (about forty). Each notable or merchant was charged at first £10 for the decoration, the money being distributed amongst the poor. Every notable was allowed to order his badge through Bishara Abdel Molak;

b) silver to all Officers of the rank of Mulazem up to Sagh only;

c) pewter to all NCOs and men, female servants of the troops, and the students of the school. These are very similar to the silver examples but poorer in quality and finish.

Although women received the decoration, there is no evidence to suggest it was any different from the men's award, although the 'War Medal Record' illustrates a smaller variation supposedly awarded to a lady.

122 *East and Central Africa Medal* 1897-1899

Obverse	The half-length figure of Queen Victoria wearing a small crown and veil, holding a sceptre in her right hand, and legend 'VICTORIA REGINA ET IMPERATRIX'
Reverse	The standing figure of Britannia holding a trident in her right hand. In her left hand, which is extended, she is holding an olive branch and a scroll. Behind her is a fine figure of the British Lion. In the right background is the rising sun, and in the exergue 'EAST & CENTRAL AFRICA'
Size	36mm diameter
Metal	Silver and bronze
Ribbon	32mm wide, half yellow (to the left facing wearer) and half red
Suspension	By a straight, plain suspender
Designer	G. W. de Saulles
Naming	The recipient's rank and name are in rather thin sloping or upright capitals
Bars issued	Four: Lubwa's, Uganda 1897-98, 1898, and Uganda 1899

The medal was authorized in February 1899 and was initially granted to the forces employed in military operations in the Uganda Protectorate during the years 1897-98.

A few men were awarded the medal without a bar, including Armr Sgt A. W. Strong, Ord Corps and Sgt T. Scott, R Scots Fus.

Mainly awarded in silver but a few were issued in bronze to camp followers.

Lubwa's 23rd September 1897-24th February 1898

Granted to all HM forces and allies who took part in operations against the Sudanese mutineers. This bar is usually found in conjunction with that for Uganda 1897-98.

Disaffected Sudanese troops refused to go on an exploratory mission. They marched to Fort Lubwas on Lake Victoria and were joined by the garrison and members of the Buganda tribe bringing their numbers to approximately eight hundred. Major J. R. L. MacDonald with a scratch force of three hundred and forty Swahilis and a few Europeans and Sikhs arrived at the fort on 18th October. His ill-trained force was attacked and the mutineers were driven off only after a prolonged fight.

The mutineers eventually evacuated Lubwas and crossed the Nile. They were pursued by Major MacDonald who had received reinforcements and were defeated at Kijembo, Kabagambi and Masindi.

Regiments present: Uganda Rifles (55); East Africa Rifles; 27 Baluch Light Infantry (88); 14, 15 Sikhs. Awarded to a few women who nursed the sick. Also to civilians of the administration, church etc.

Uganda 1897-98 20th July 1897-19th March 1898

Granted to all HM forces and allies who took part in operations in Uganda, other than those against the mutineers, or who reached Uganda within the above dates.

Awarded for an expedition under Lt Col W. A. Broome into the Tieta country.

Regiments present: 1 Uganda Rifles (1074); East Africa Rifles; 27

Baluch Light Infantry (536); 27 Bombay Light Infantry (339); 14, 15 Sikhs. Awarded to seven women who nursed the sick. Also to civilians of the administration, church etc.

Sgt R. Thompson, Seaforth Highlanders received this bar as did Mr S. D. Shaw, J. D. Wilson, S. Ormsby and W. Grant.

1898 12th April-3rd October 1898

The bar was authorized in July 1899 and awarded to forces operating against the rebellious Ogaden Somalis under Sultan Ahmad bin Marghan. The force was commanded by Major W. Quentin.

Regiments present: 4 Bombay Rifles (777); 27 Baluch Light Infantry (163); 1 Uganda Rifles; East African Rifles; 46 Native Field Hospital.

Uganda 1899 21st March-2nd May 1899

This bar was authorized in December 1900 and awarded to members of the forces under Major G. C. Martyr and Colonel J. T. Evatt which advanced down the Nile and then defeated and captured both Kabarega and Mwanga in the Uganda Protectorate and then continued on to Nandi.

Regiments present: 27 Baluch Light Infantry (344); 1 Uganda Rifles.

Medals were also awarded to Lieutenant C. de Vere Beauclerk, KRRC, and Sgt S. W. Bone, South Lancs Regiment, and a bronze medal to Bhisti Len Singh, 4th Bombay Rifles.

A total of eighty-one medals were issued with this bar to civilians.

123 *The British North Borneo Company's Medal* 1897-1916

Obverse	The shield of the Company supported by a native on either side. Above the shield, two arms one clothed the other naked supporting the Company's flag. Below the shield is the motto 'PERGO ET PERAGO'
Reverse	The British Lion facing left, standing in front of a bush. Between the two is a flagstaff from which flies the Company's flag. Around the top is the inscription 'BRITISH NORTH BORNEO'. There is an unusually large exergue, in the centre of which is a wreath. At the top left of the exergue is 'SPINK & SON' and top right 'LONDON'
Size	38mm in diameter, 5mm thick
Metal	Issued in silver and bronze
Ribbon	The original issue was a watered golden colour 32mm wide. In 1917 this was altered to one of the same width, having maroon edges, two yellow stripes with a dark blue band down the centre. The ribbon was of a heavier material than usual
Suspension	By a floreated clasp of the IGS Medal pattern
Naming	Medals with the bar Punitive Expedition or Punitive Expeditions were issued unnamed, some were then engraved locally (see text)
Bars issued	Three: Punitive Expedition, Punitive Expeditions, Rundum. The bars are 36mm long and 8mm wide, being of the IGS Medal pattern

The medal was manufactured by Spink & Son. Specimens of the medal have either been made in a heavy gauge, or with 'S' of 'SON' stamped out in the reverse exergue and 'COPY' stamped on the rim. All medals were issued with a bar; only two recipients of the medal are known to have been authorized a second bar (see Rundum).

Punitive Expedition 1897

The medal and bar was given for a small expedition against Mat Saleh conducted by Mr Hewett the Resident of Labuan, together with a few police officers, thirty-eight Sikhs, some Sugat policemen and a 7 pdr gun. The main action took place in December 1897, though there had been two smaller clashes in July and August.

Extant unofficial Spink records indicate that thirteen silver and seventy-five bronze medals were initially produced. Awarded in silver to officers (twelve issued) and in bronze to NCOs and men (seventy-four issued). Supplied unnamed, some were then engraved locally. In 1905/06, recipients of the bronze medal were able to make the exchange for a silver one. The number that did so is unknown, however unofficial Spink records list twenty-four impressed named silver 'Punitive Expedition' medals supplied in 1905. A further ten unnamed silver medals were supplied in 1906 and another twelve in 1909.

Punitive Expeditions 1898

In January 1898 Mat Saleh caused further trouble which necessitated another expedition, this time under Captain C. H. Harrington.

Extant unofficial Spink records indicate that eighteen silver and one hundred bronze medals were initially produced. Awarded in silver to officers (five issued) and bronze to NCOs and men (forty-seven issued). Supplied unnamed, some were then engraved locally. Bronze medals could be exchanged for silver in 1905/06. Whilst the number making the exchange is unknown, unofficial Spink records list nine silver 'Punitive Expeditions' medals with impressed naming being supplied in 1905. A further twelve unnamed silver medals were supplied in 1909.

A participant of both 1897 and 1898 expeditions received and was allowed to wear both medals.

Rundum 1915-16

The medal with this bar was awarded to a small force under Mr A. W. L. Bunbury, consisting of three white men and some one hundred and ten Sikhs and natives. This contingent relieved the village of Rundum which was besieged by hostile natives.

The medal and bar in silver was issued to all participants, no bronze medals were produced. Unofficial Spink records list a total of ninety-eight recipients. Those in possession of either of the previous medals or the medal with the Tambunan bar (see no. 124) received the bar only. Records indicate that two bars were awarded, to Jemadar Akbar Khan who held the replacement silver medal for Punitive Expeditions and to Sergeant Major 223 Allah Singh who held the replacement silver medal for Punitive Expedition.

124 *The British North Borneo Company's Medal* 1899-1900

Obverse	The Company's shield, above which are the words 'BRITISH NORTH BORNEO', and below, the date '1900'
Reverse	In the centre one clothed and one naked arm supporting the Company's flag surrounded by a wreath. Around the whole is the motto 'PERGO ET PERAGO'. At the bottom in very small lettering 'SPINK & SON LONDON'
Size	38mm in diameter. The silver medal is 5mm thick, the bronze medal 4mm
Ribbon	31mm wide. Yellow with a green stripe 10mm wide down the centre
Suspension	By a plain straight suspender, as used on the Queen's South Africa Medal
Naming	Engraved (see text)
Bars issued	One—Tambunan. The bar is of the same pattern as for the IGS Medals.

The medal was manufactured by Spink & Son. Specimens of the medal have either been made in a heavy gauge or with the 'S' of 'Son' stamped out on the reverse and 'COPY' stamped on the rim.

All medals were issued with the bar.

> The medal was awarded for another expedition led by Captain C. H. Harrington against Mat Saleh, who was killed.
> Unofficial Spink records list seven silver medals being engraved to officers, with one hundred and sixteen bronze medals engraved and numbered to other ranks. Bronze medals could be exchanged for silver in 1905/06. Of the one hundred and sixteen named bronze medal recipients, thirty-six received a replacement silver medal with impressed naming. Spink records additionally note ten unnamed silver medals supplied in 1906 and another twelve unnamed medals supplied in 1909.

125 *The Sultan of Zanzibar's Medal* 1896

Obverse	An almost full-face bust of the Sultan, surrounded by an Arabic inscription which reads, 'EL SEYYID HAMDI BIN THWAIN, SULTAN OF ZANZIBAR, 1313'
Reverse	The same inscription in four lines occupying the whole field. Below in small letters, 'J. & S.B.'
Size	36mm diameter
Metal	Silver
Ribbon	32mm wide, plain bright scarlet
Suspension	By a straight, swivelling suspender
Naming	In crudely impressed block capitals, engraved or unnamed
Bars issued	Four were issued for Pumwani, Jongeni, Takaungu and Mwele. The wording is in Arabic.

Awarded to Indian troops for services in East Africa. The expedition(s) for which the Sultan made the award cannot be identified.

Awarded to the force raised by Lieutenant Lloyd-Mathew, RN, under the Sultan. The Naval Lieutenant was promoted to Brigadier General which is probably a record regarding promotion.

Medals are known to have been awarded to 3 King's African Rifles and Indian Contingent.

The Boer Wars

There are no British campaign medals for the 1st Boer War, 1880-81, or earlier conflicts with the Boers. However, such medals the British participants possessed become enhanced from the point of view of historical interest and value because of the recipients' connections with these unrewarded actions. This is especially true if the participant was noteworthy or a casualty.

The original Dutch Cape settlements were twice seized by Britain during the course of the Napoleonic Wars (1795 and 1806). With the Treaty of Paris, 1814, the Cape Colony was ceded to Britain. Friction between the British and the Dutch (Boer) settlers soon resulted in intermittent armed clashes; most notable the Slagter Nek Rebellion 1815.

The Great Trek 1835-37: Increasing British domination finally prompted a migration of Boer pioneer families, seeking land to the north and the east free from British authority. Boer settlements were established north of the Orange and Vaal Rivers and in Natal. Under Pretorius, the Boer Republic of Natal was proclaimed 1839. Tacit British acknowledgement of this was given by the withdrawal of the garrison from the settlement of Port Natal (Durban). However, on 4th May 1842, British troops re-occupied the port, thereby provoking Boer resistance. The garrison was defeated in an action outside Port Natal (23rd May 1842), then under siege, the garrison barely held out until the arrival of reinforcements (24th June 1842). By August 1843 British sovereignty in Natal was established. In March 1848 the land between the Orange and Vaal Rivers was annexed by Britain. In response, a revolt under Pretorius resulted in a battle at Boomplatz (29th August). Sir Harry Smith, Governor of the Cape Colonies, with 800 men, defeated Pretorius with 500 who then retreated across the Vaal. In 1852 the Sand River Convention confirmed the Independence of the Transvaal. In 1854 the Blomfontein Convention restored the Independence of the Transorangia: the Orange Free State. With the discovery of diamonds along the Orange River the Hopetown region of the Orange Free State was re-annexed in 1871. On 12th April 1877 the annexation of Transvaal was announced by Britain, partly for its resources, and partly because of its instability. The Transvaal Boers soon began to show signs of disaffection. In response to increasing threats of armed rebellion redoubts were built and garrisoned at various strategic points of the Transvaal.

The 1st Boer War (Boer: 1st War of Independence), well prepared for by the Boers, was touched off at Potchefstroom where, following a dispute over taxation, the British garrison was attacked (16th December 1880). A detachment of the 94th Foot en route to Pretoria was attacked with heavy loss at Bronkhorst Spruit (20th December). Elsewhere, British garrisons were placed under siege and their lines of communication cut. The Governor of Natal, Sir George Colley, intending to rectify the situation, entirely underestimated Boer capabilities. Advancing with an inadequate force he was defeated by Joubert at Laing's Nek (28th January 1881) and Ingogo River (8th February), sustaining heavy casualties. Making another attempt to break through, he was defeated and killed at Majuba Hill (27th February). Following these reverses, Britain gave up the contest and decided upon peace and withdrawal from the Transvaal.

The discovery of gold in the Transvaal (1886) drew a large number of outsiders (Uitlanders) whose presence posed a threat to Boer supremacy. A threat made more dangerous with Britain claiming to represent Uitlander interests. Hoping to utilize Uitlander support and bring about a British takeover, a Transvaal revolt was planned with the backing of Cape Prime Minister Cecil Rhodes. In an ill-conceived venture, Dr Jameson with a force of 520 men, mainly Mashonaland Mounted Police and Bechuanaland Border Police, rode towards Johannesburg (29th December 1895) counting on a general Uitlander uprising. No such uprising occurred and Jameson and his men were rounded up near Krugersdorp (2nd January 1896).

However, the Uitlander problem remained unsolved and it was upon this foundation that the 2nd Boer War was built.

Boomplatz 29th August 1848
2 Cos 45th, 2 Cos 91st Foot, 2 Cos 1/Rifle Bde, det Cape Mounted Rifles, dets RA and RE.

Laing's Nek 28th January 1881
58th Foot, 5 Cos 3/60th Rifles, Naval Brigade, AHC, Improvised Cavalry Force: 1st Dragoon Guards, Natal Mounted Police, 21st, 58th Foot, 3/60th Rifles, ASC etc.

Ingogo 8th February 1881
Cavalry force (38) 3 Cos 58th Foot, 5 Cos 3/60th Rifles, RA.

Majuba Hill 27th February 1881
15th Hussars, 2 Cos 58th Foot, 2 Cos 3/60th Rifles, 3 Cos 92nd Hldrs, 94th Foot (4), Naval Brigade, RE, AHC.

Six Victoria Crosses were awarded during the First Boer War (1880-1881), these being to L/Cpl J. Murray, 94th Foot; Pte J. Danaher, Nourse's Horse (later 94th Foot); Pte J. Osborne, 2 Bn 58th Foot; Lieut A. R. Hill, 58th Foot; Pte J. Doogan, 1st Dragoon Gds; Cpl J. J. Farmer, AHC.

126 *Queen's South Africa Medal* 11th October 1899-31st May 1902

Obverse	The crowned and veiled head of Queen Victoria and legend 'VICTORIA REGINA ET IMPERATRIX'
Reverse	*Type 1:* Britannia with a flag in her left hand holding out a laurel wreath towards an advancing party of soldiers. In the background are two warships. The wreath in Britannia's hand points to the letter 'R' in the word 'AFRICA'. Below the wreath, in two lines, appear the dates '1899-1900' in relief. Around the top are the words 'South Africa'.
	Type 1a Same as type 1 except that the dates '1899-1900' have been removed.
	Type 2 same as type 1a (ie without dates) except the wreath in Britannia's hand points to the letter 'F' in the word 'Africa'.
Size	36mm diameter
Metal	Silver and Bronze
Ribbon	32mm wide. Red with two dark blue stripes and a broad orange central stripe.
Suspension	By a straight swivel suspension.
Designer	G. W. de Saulles.
Naming	Generally impressed in block or sloping capitals. Those to officers and to some units were engraved.
Bars issued	Twenty-six: Cape Colony, Natal, Rhodesia, Defence of Kimberley, Elandslaagte, Defence of Mafeking, Talana, Defence of Ladysmith, Belmont, Modder River, Relief of Ladysmith, Tugela Heights, Relief of Kimberley, Paardeberg, Orange Free State, Driefontein, Wepener, Relief of Mafeking, Transvaal, Johannesburg, Laing's Nek, Diamond Hill, Wittebergen, Belfast, South Africa 1901, South Africa 1902.

The probable duration of the war was grossly underestimated, because the first issues bore the dates 1899-1900 on the reverse in raised figures. Lord Strathcona's Horse was the only unit to receive a limited number of these dated medals with digits in relief. They returned home to Canada via London as a complete unit before the war ended and approximately fifty medals with raised dates were awarded by Edward VII at Buckingham Palace. These fifty medals were issued without bars, the bars were sent out to Canada at a later date and affixed privately. Subsequently the dates were erased but on many medals 'ghost' dates can still be seen. A medal with raised dates has also been seen to the Royal Engineers.

In total, approximately 177,000 medals were struck.

The maximum number of bars to any one medal is nine to the Army and eight to the Navy; this excludes the two later bars; 'South Africa 1901' and 'South Africa 1902'.

Five 'State' bars were awarded, namely: Cape Colony, Natal, Rhodesia, Orange Free State, and Transvaal. These were given for service in the various states in which so many small actions were fought that it would have been impossible to have recognized each with a bar.

The bars for Cape Colony and Natal could not both be gained by one recipient. Those who received bars for Defence of Kimberley, Relief of Kimberley, Defence of Mafeking or Relief of Mafeking would not be entitled to the bars for Cape Colony or Natal.

Seventy-eight Victoria Crosses were awarded for this campaign.

Table showing the relative rarity of the Single Bar Queen's South Africa Medal

(Please note that this table has no bearing whatsoever on multiple bar medals)

Bar	Imperial Units (including Dominions other than South Africa)					South African Units				
	Common	Scarce	Rare	Extremely Rare	Unknown	Common	Scarce	Rare	Extremely Rare	Unknown
Cape Colony	●					●				
Natal		●							●	
Rhodesia				●					●	
Relief of Mafeking					●				●	
Defence of Kimberley				●			●			
Talana		●							●	
Elandslaagte				●						●
Defence of Ladysmith		●							●	
Belmont		●								●
Modder River			●							●
Tugela Heights	Impossible as a single bar									
Relief of Kimberley				●					●	
Paardeberg				●					●	
Orange Free State		●						●		
Relief of Ladysmith		●						●		
Driefontein				●						●
Wepener				●					●	
Defence of Mafeking				●				●		
Transvaal	●						●			
Johannesburg				●					●	
Laing's Nek			●							●
Diamond Hill			●						●	
Wittebergen		●							●	
Belfast			●							●
South Africa 1901		●						●		
South Africa 1902		●						●		

List extracted from a paper presented to the second South African Numismatic Convention by M. G. Hibbard at Cape Town, 7th January 1964.

Bronze Medals

Although the issuance of bronze medals is unclear, it would appear that they were awarded to some local natives, Indian troops and members of the West India Regiments. Non-attested men of whatever nationality were also eligible, these would have included a relatively small number of Europeans who acted as servants. Earlier editions of 'British Battles and Medals' have implied that these Europeans were mercenaries, it is clear however that this is not the case.

Cape Colony 11th October 1899-31st May 1902

Issued to all troops in Cape Colony at any time between 11th October, 1899 and 31st May, 1902, who received no bars for other actions in the Cape Colony, nor the 'Natal' bar.

Regiments present: 1, 2 Life Guards; Royal Horse Guards; 1, 2, 3, 6, 7 Dragoon Guards; 1 Royal Dragoons; 2, 6 Dragoons; 4, 7, 8, 10, 14, 19 Hussars; 5, 9, 16, 17 Lancers; RA; 1, 2, 3 Foot Guards; 1, 2, 3, 4, 5, 6, 7, 8, 9, 10, 12, 13, 14, 15, 16, 17, 18, 19, 20, 22, 23, 24, 25, 26, 27, 28, 29, 30, 31, 32, 33, 34, 35, 37, 38, 39, 40, 41, 43, 44, 45, 47, 57, 58, 60, 62, 63, 65, 66, 67, 68, 71, 73, 75, 78, 79, 83, 85, 87, 88, 91, 97, 100, 101 (1991), 102 (2,476) Foot; Rifle Brigade, City Imperial Volunteers; Approx 2,670 to Canadian units. *New South Wales Units:* 'A' Bty R. Australian Art; Imperial Bushmen; 3rd Imperial Bushmen. *S. Australian Units:* 1st and 2nd MR Contg; 3rd Bushmen Contg; 4th Imp Bushmen; 5th and 6th Imp Bushmen; 2nd Bn Aust Comm Horse. *Western Australian Units:* 1st and 2nd Mounted Inf Contgs; 3rd Bushmen Contg. *Tasmanian Units:* 2nd Tasmanian Contg; 2nd Tasmanian Bushmen; 1st Tasmanian Imp Contg; 2nd Imp Bushmen. *Queensland Units:* 1st, 2nd and 3rd Queensland Mtd Infy; 4th and 5th Queensland Imp Bushmen. *Victoria Units:* 2nd Victoria Mtd Rifles; 3rd Bushmen Contg; 4th Imp Contg; 5th Victorian Mtd Rifles. *New Zealand:* 1, 2, 3, 4, 5, 6, 7 and 8th Contingents.

Royal Navy.

Natal 11th October 1899-17th May 1900

Granted to all troops in Natal at any time between 11th October, 1899 and 11th June, 1900, both dates inclusive, who received no bar for an action in Natal nor the Cape Colony bar as already specified.

Regiments present: 5 Dragoon Guards; 5, 9 Lancers; 14 Hussars (HQ B and C Squadrons); 2, 11, 17, 20 (50); 27, 28, 31, 63, 88, 102 (25), 103 (111) Foot; Durham RGA; Strathcona's Horse; 5th and 6th W. Australian Mtd Infantry.
Royal Navy.

Rhodesia 11th October 1899-17th May 1900

Authorized for all troops under the command of Lt Gen Sir F. Carrington and Col Plumer in Rhodesia, between 11th October, 1899 and 17th May, 1900, both dates inclusive.

Regiments present: 1 (NZ) Bty RFA; 'C' Bty Royal Canadian Artillery; Rhodesia Regiment; Southern Rhodesian Volunteers; 65th (Leicestershire) Company 17th Battalion Imperial Yeomanry; British South African Police; New Zealand Mounted Rifles, 1, 3, 4, 5 and 7th New Zealand Contingents; 18 Imperial Yeomanry; Umvoti Volunteers, Menne's Scouts and Canadian Units. NSW Citizen Bushmen; NSW Imp Bushmen; 3rd S. Australian Bushmen; 4th S. Australian Imp Bushmen; 3rd W Australian Bushmen; 2nd Tasmanian Bushmen; 3rd Queensland Mtd Inf; 4th Queensland Imp Bushmen; 3rd Victoria Bushmen Contg; 4th Victorian Imp Contg.

Defence of Kimberley 15th October 1899-15th February 1900

Issued to all troops in the garrison of Kimberley between 14th October, 1899 and 15th February, 1900, both dates inclusive.

Regiments present: Cape Mounted Police (488); Kimberley Light Horse (427); Loyal North Lancs Mounted Infantry (22); 23rd Company Western Division RA (94); RE (51); ASC (9); Loyal North Lancs Regiment (422); Kimberley Town Guard (1,439); Diamond Field Volunteers (84); Diamond Field Artillery; Kimberley Regiment and about 1,000 members of neighbouring Town Guards—88 Officers (13 British and 75 Colonial) were awarded the bar. No women received the bar. The rarest combination of bars is probably Defence of Kimberley and Paardeberg (110).
Royal Navy.

Elandslaagte 21st October 1899

Issued to all troops at Elandslaagte on 21st October, 1899 who were on the right bank of the Sunday river and north of an east and west line through Buys Farm.

Regiments present: 5 Dragoon Guards; 5 Lancers; 21, 42 RFA; 1/11, 63, 92 Foot, Imperial Light Horse.

Defence of Mafeking 13th October 1899-17th May 1900

Issued to all troops in the garrison of Mafeking under Baden-Powell between 13th October, 1899 and 17th May, 1900, both dates inclusive. Approx 1,300 present although some were unclaimed making a nett figure of approx 1,150 issued, this being the rarest of all QSA bars.

Regiments present: S. African Constabulary (14); Mafeking Town Guard (513); Mafeking Railway Vols (26); Mafeking Cadet Corps (38); Protectorate Regiment Frontier Force (424); Bechuanaland Rifles (125); Cape Police District No. 1 (43); Cape Police District No 2 (54); Special Police Contingent, Mafeking (5); BSA Police BP Division (92); 1st Life Guards (1); Barkly West Town Guard (2); Border Horse (1); Border Scouts (1); 1 Brabant's Horse (1); 2 Brabant's Horse (2); Bushveld Carbineers (1); Cape Medical Staff Corps (4); Colonial Defence Force (1); Commander-in-Chief's Bodyguard (9); Diamond Fields Artillery (2); Driscoll's Scouts (4); 2nd Duke of Edinburgh's Own Rifles (1); French's Scouts (1); Gorringe's Flying Column (2); 1st Imperial Light Horse (1); Imperial Military Railway (2); Johannesburg Mounted Rifles (1); Kaffrarian Rifles (2); Kimberley Volunteer Regiment (7); 1st Kitchener's Fighting Scouts (3); Marshall's Horse (1); Nesbitt's Horse (3); Prince Alfred's Own Cape Artillery (1); Queenstown Rifle Volunteers (1); Railway Pioneer Regiment (2); Robert's Horse (2); Scott's Railway

Guards (1); Steinaecker's Horse (6); Transkei Mounted Rifles (1); Vryburg Town Guard (5); Western Province Mounted Rifles (2).

Queen Victoria personally presented Mother Mary Joseph with the Royal Red Cross for her devoted work during the siege.

Talana 20th October 1899

Granted to all troops under Lt Gen Sir W. Penn Symon's command on 20th October, 1899, who were north of an east and west line drawn through Waschbank Station. These bars are very rare to S. African units.

Regiments present: 18 Hussars; 13, 67, 69 RFA; 1/17, 1/60, 87, 103 (855) Foot, Dundee Town Guard, Dundee Rifle Assoc, Natal Police.

Defence of Ladysmith 3rd November 1899-28th February 1900

Authorized for all troops in Ladysmith between 3rd November, 1899 and 28th February, 1900, both dates inclusive.

Regiments present: 5 Dragoon Guards; 5 Lancers; 11 (Pte W. S. Wolfe); 18, 19 Hussars; Natal Carbineers; Natal Mounted Police; Natal Mounted Rifles; Border Mounted Rifles; Imperial Light Horse; 13, 21, 42, 53, 67, 69 RFA; RHA; No 10 Mountain Battery; 2 guns Natal Hotchkiss Detachment; 8, 11, 16 (24), 17, 28 (½ Bn), 1/60, 2/60, 63, 87 (½ Bn), 92, 2nd Bn, The Rifle Brigade; R Dublin Fus (45); 23rd Field Company RE; A Balloon and Telegraph Section RE; Army Service Corps and Army Ordnance Department; about 250 members of the Ladysmith Town Guard.
Royal Navy.

Belmont 23rd November, 1899

Awarded to all troops under Lt Gen Lord Methuen's command who were north of Witteputs, on 23rd November, 1899. The bar is rare to S. African units.

Regiments present: 9 Lancers; 18, 75 RFA; New South Wales Lancers; 2nd S. Australian Mtd R; 2nd W. Australian Mtd Infantry; 1st Tasmanian Contg; 1st Queensland Mtd Infantry; 1, 2, 3 Foot Guards; 1/5, 47, 58, 85, 101 (239), 105 Foot; Rimington's Guides, Kitcheners FS, Cape Medical Staff Corps, Imperial Light Horse, DEOVR.
Royal Navy.

Modder River 28th November 1899

Granted to all troops under Lt Gen Lord Methuen's command who were north of Honey Nest Kloof, and south of the Magersfontein ridge on 28th November, 1899.

Regiments present: 9 Lancers: 18, 62, 75 RFA; 1, 2, 3 Foot Guards; 5, 47, 58, 71, 85, 91, 101 (75), 105 Foot; NSW Lancers; 1st Australian Horse, Damant's Horse, Rimington's Guides, Kitchener's FS, Cape Medical Staff Corps, Imperial Light Horse, DEOVR.
Royal Navy.

Relief of Ladysmith 15th December 1899-28th February 1900

Granted to all troops in Natal north of and including Estcourt between 15th December, 1899 and 28th February, 1900, both dates inclusive.

Regiments present: The Royal Dragoons; 13, 14 Hussars; 2, 4, 7, 8, 2/11, 13, 14, 18, 20, 21, 23, 26, 27, 31, 33, 34, 40, 54, 60, 65, 68, 77, 87, 89, 101, 103 Foot (1,882); The Rifle Brigade.
Royal Navy.

Tugela Heights 14th-27th February 1900

Granted to all troops of the Natal Field Force, exclusive of the Ladysmith garrison, employed in the operations north of an east and west line through Chieveley Station between 14th and 27th February, 1900, both dates inclusive.

Regiments present: 1 The Royal Dragoons; 13, 14 Hussars; 2, 4, 7, 11, 14, 18, 20, 21, 23, 26, 27, 31, 34, 39, 40, 57, 60, 65, 68, 87, 88,

89, 101, 103 Foot (1,262); The Rifle Brigade; 'D' Coy, 6th Mounted Infantry.
Royal Navy.

Relief of Kimberley 15th February 1900

Issued to all troops in the relief column under Lt Gen French who marched from Klip Drift on 15th February, 1900, and all the 6th Division under Lt Gen Kelly-Kenny who were within 7,000 yds of Klip Drift on 15th February. Rare as a single bar to S. African units.
Regiments present: 1, 2 Life Guards; Royal Horse Guards; 3, 6 Dragoon Guards; 2 Dragoons; 9, 12, 16 Lancers; 10 Hussars; B Squadron 14 Hussars; 3, 9, 18 (139), 19, 22, 28, 33, 41, 43, 44, 58, 102 (32) Foot; 'D' Coy 6th Mounted Infantry; NSW Lancers; 1st Australian Horse; 1st Queensland Mtd Inf; New Zealand Mounted Rifles, Cape Medical SC, Cape GA, Damant's Horse, DEOVR, Field Int Dept, French's Scouts, Kimberley Regt, Kimberley Lt Horse, Kitchener's Horse, Robert's Horse, Scott's Railway Guards, SAC.
Royal Navy.

Paardeberg 17th-26th February 1900

Awarded to all troops within 7,000 yds of General Cronje's final laager between midnight of 17th February and midnight of 26th February, 1900, and to all troops within 7,000 yds of Koodoe's Rand Drift between those dates.
Regiments present: 1, 2 Life Guards; Royal Horse Guards; 3, 6 Dragoon Guards; 2 Dragoons; 9, 12, 16 Lancers; 10 Hussars; 1, 2, 3 Foot Guards; 3, 9 (4 offrs & 164 ORs), 10, 18 (138), 19, 22, 25, 28, 30, 33, 41, 43, 44, 46, 47, 67, 68, 71, 73, 75, 78, 85, 91, 102 (35) Foot; 1st Australian Horse; 1st NSW Mounted Rifles; 1st Queensland Mounted Infantry; No 1 Contingent, New Zealand; 2nd (Special Service) Bn, Rl Canadian R; Cape Medical Staff Corps, Commander-in-Chief's Bodyguard, Damant's Horse, DEOVR, FID, French's Scouts, Imp Lt Horse, Kimberley Lt Horse, Kimberley Vol Regt, Kitchener's Horse, Nesbitt's Horse, Rand Rifles, Robert's Horse, Scott's RG, SAC, Tucker's Scouts.
Royal Navy.

Orange Free State 28th February 1900-31st May 1902

Issued to all troops in the Orange River Colony at any time between 28th February, 1900 and 31st May, 1902, who received no bars for other actions in the Orange River Colony. Scarce as a single bar.
Regiments present: 1, 2, 3, 5, 6, 7 Dragoon Guards; 1 Royal Dragoons; 2, 6 Dragoons; 3, 4, 7, 8, 13, 14, 18, 19, 20 Hussars; 5, 9, 12, 16, 17 Lancers; RA; 1, 2, 3 Foot Guards; 1, 2, 3, 4, 5, 6, 7, 8, 9, 10, 11, 12, 13, 14, 15, 16, 18, 19, 20, 21, 22, 23, 24, 25, 26, 27, 28, 29, 30, 31, 32, 33, 34, 35, 38, 40, 41, 43, 44, 45, 46, 47, 54, 57, 58, 60, 62, 63, 65, 66, 67, 68, 71, 73, 75, 78, 79, 83, 85, 87, 88, 91, 96, 97, 98, 101 (3,131), 104, 105 Foot; The Rifle Brigade; CIV. *NSW Units:* 'A' Bty RAA; Imperial Bushmen; 3rd Mtd Rifles; 3rd Imp Bushmen; 1st Australian Comm Horse. *S. Australian Units:* 1st and 2nd Mounted Rifles Contg, 3rd Bushmen Contg; 4th Imp Bushmen; 5th and 6th Imp Contg; 2nd Bn Australian Comm Horse. *Western Australian Units:* 1st and 2nd Mtd Inf Contg; 3rd Bushmen Contg; 4th, 5th and 6th Mtd Inf Contg. *Tasmanian Units:* 2nd Tasmanian Bushmen; 3rd Tasmanian Contg; 4th Imperial Bushmen. *Queensland Units:* 1st, 2nd and 3rd Mtd Inf; 4th and 5th Imp Bushmen. *Victoria Units:* 2nd Mtd Rifles; 3rd Bushmen; 4th Imp Contg; 5th Mtd Rifles; 2, 3, 4, 6, 7 and 9th New Zealand Contingents.
Royal Navy.

Driefontein 10th March 1900

Awarded to all troops with Army Headquarters and Lt Gen French's column—ie, the left and centre columns, which advanced from Popular Grove on 10th March, 1900.
Regiments present: 1, 2 Life Guards; Royal Horse Guards; 6 Dragoon Guards; 2 Dragoons; 10 Hussars; 12 Lancers; 1, 2, 3 Foot Guards; 3, 18 (33), 19, 22, 24, 28, 32, 33 (500), 41, 43, 44, 73, 75, 78, 85, 91, 102

(36) Foot; NSW Lancers; 1st and 2nd Queensland Mounted Infantry; New Zealand Contingent.
Royal Navy.

Wepener 9th-25th April 1900

Awarded to all troops engaged in the defence of that place between 9th April, 1900 and 25th April, 1900, both days inclusive.
Regiments present. Kaffrarian Rifles; 1st Imperial Lt Horse (1); 2nd Imperial Lt Horse (2); Cape Medical Staff Corps (1); Johannesburg Mounted Rifles (2); 1st R Scots (83); R Engineers (11); S. African Constabulary; Driscoll's Scouts; Cape Mounted Rifles; 2nd Kitchener's Fighting Scouts (8); Prince of Wales Lt Horse (9); 1st Scottish Horse (7); 2nd Scottish Horse (2); 1st Brabant's Horse; 2nd Brabant's Horse.
Although 18 were originally issued to HMS *Doris* they were all recalled with one exception.

Relief of Mafeking 17th May 1900

Issued to all troops under the command of Colonel Mahon, who marched from Barkly West on 4th May, 1900, and to all troops who were under Colonel Plumber's command between 11th October, 1899 and 17th May, 1900, both dates inclusive, and who were south of an east and west line drawn through Palachwe.
Regiments present: Kimberley Light Horse; Imperial Light Horse; Damant's Horse; 2 sections of 'M' Battery RHA; 'F' section (pom-poms) and 'C' battery R Can Art; Rhodesia Regiment; Kimberley Mounted Corps; South Rhodesian Volunteers; 100 men from Barton's Fusilier Brigade (composed of men from the 2 Royal Fusiliers, 2 R Scots Fusiliers, 1 R Welch Fusiliers and 2 R Irish Fusiliers); NSW Citizen Bushmen; 3rd Queensland Mtd Infantry.

Transvaal 24th May 1900-31st May 1902

Issued to all troops in the Transvaal at any time between 24th May, 1900 and 31st May, 1902, who received no other bars for actions in the Transvaal.
Regiments present: 1, 2, 3, 5, 6, 7 Dragoon Guards; 1 Royal Dragoons; 2, 6 Dragoons; 5, 12 Lancers; 3, 4, 7, 8, 10, 13, 14, 19, 20 Hussars; 1, 2, 3 Foot Guards; 1, 2, 3, 4, 5, 6, 7, 8, 9, 10, 12, 13, 14, 15, 16, 17, 19, 20, 21, 22, 23, 24, 25, 26, 27, 28, 29, 30, 31, 33, 34, 38, 40, 41, 43, 44, 45, 46, 47, 49, 51, 54, 57, 58, 60, 62, 63, 65, 67, 68, 71, 73, 78, 79, 83, 85, 87, 88, 91, 97, 98, 100, 101, 102 (2,789), 105 Foot; The Rifle Brigade, CIV. *NSW Units:* 'A' Bty RAA; NSW Citizens Bushmen; 2nd and 3rd NSW Mtd Rifles; 3rd NSW Imp Bushmen; 1st Australian Comm Horse. *S. Australian Units:* 1st and 2nd Mtd Rifle Contgs; 3rd Bushmen Contg; 4th Imp Bushmen; 2nd Australian Comm Horse. *W. Australian Units:* 1st and 2nd Mtd Infantry; 3rd Bushmen; 4th, 5th and 6th Mtd Infantry. *Tasmanian Units:* 2nd Bushmen; 3rd Contg; 1st Australian Comm Horse. *Queensland Units:* 2nd Mtd Infantry; 4th and 5th Imp Bushmen; 1st and 3rd Australian Comm Horse. *Victoria Units:* 2nd Mtd Rifles; 3rd Bushmen Contg; 4th Imp Contg; 5th Mtd Rifles; 1, 4, 5, 6, 7, 8 and 9th New Zealand Contingents.
Royal Navy.

Johannesburg 31st May 1900

Awarded to all troops who, on 31st May, 1900, were north of an east and west line through Klip River Station (exclusive) and east of a north and south line through Krugersdorp Station (inclusive).
Regiments present: 1, 2 Life Guards; Royal Horse Guards; 6, 7 Dragoon Guards; 2, 6 Dragoons; 8, 10, 14 Hussars; 9, 12, 16, 17 Lancers; 1, 2, 3 Foot Guards; 6, 9, 10, 18 (104), 19, 22, 24, 25, 30, 35, 41, 44, 45, 46, 67, 68, 75, 79, 85, 102 (30) Foot: CIV. Canadian units; 'D' Co 6th MI; 1st NSW Australian Horse; 1st NSW Mounted Rifles; 1st and 2nd S. Australian Mounted Rifles; 1st and 2nd W. Australian Mounted Inf Contg; 1st Tasmanian Contg; 2nd Queensland Mounted Infantry; 1, 2 and 3rd New Zealand Contingents.
Royal Navy.

Laing's Nek 2nd-9th June 1900

Issued to all troops of the Natal Field Force employed in the operations, and north of an east and west line through Newcastle between 2nd and 9th June, 1900, both dates inclusive.

Regiments present: The Royal Dragoons; 3 Dragoon Guards; 13, 18 Hussars; 2, 4, 8, 11, 13, 14, 17, 18, 20, 26, 31, 40, 41, 60, 63, 65, 68, 77, 89, 92, 102 (735) Foot: The Rifle Brigade.

Royal Navy.

Diamond Hill 11th-12th June 1900

Awarded to all troops who, on 11th or 12th June, 1900, were east of a north and south line drawn through Silverton Siding and north of an east and west line through Vlakfontein.

Regiments present: 1, 2 Life Guards; 6, 7 Dragoon Guards; 2, 6 Dragoons; 8, 10, 14 Hussars; 9, 12, 16, 17 Lancers; 1, 2, 3 Foot Guards; 1, 2, 3, 6, 16, 18 (74), 19, 35, 41, 44, 45, 79, 102 (29) Foot CIV. Canadian Units, *NSW Units:* NSW Lancers; 1st Australian Horse; 1st Mounted Rifles. *S. Australian Units:* 1st and 2nd Mounted Rifles. *W. Australian Units:* 1st, 2nd and 6th Mounted Infantry. *Tasmanian Units:* 1st Tasmanian Contg. *Queensland Units:* 1st and 2nd Mounted Infantry. *Victoria Units:* 2nd Victoria Mounted Rifles; 1 and 3rd New Zealand Contingents.

Royal Navy.

Wittebergen 1st-29th July 1900

Granted to all troops who were inside a line drawn from Harrismith to Bethlehem, thence to Senekal and Clocolan, along the Basuto border, and back to Harrismith, between 1st and 29th July, 1900, both dates inclusive.

Regiments present: 1, 2 Life Guards; Royal Horse Guards; 9, 12, 16, 17 Lancers; 10 Hussars; RA; 1, 3 Foot Guards; 13, 15, 16, 18, 26, 29, 35, 38, 47, 62, 63, 71, 73, 78, 79, 96, 97, 99, 100, 101 (762), 102 (24), 105 Foot; 1st NSW Mounted Rifles; Imperial Bushmen; 1st, 2nd, 4th and 6th W. Australian Mounted Infantry; 3rd Tasmanian Contg; 1st New Zealand Contingent.

Royal Marines serving with the Army (7).

Belfast 26th-27th August 1900

Granted to all troops who, on 26th or 27th August, 1900, were east of a north and south line drawn through Wonderfontein (the garrison and troops quartered at Wonderfontein on those dates did not receive this bar), and west of a north and south line through Dalmanutha Station, and north of an east and west line through Carolina.

Regiments present: 3, 6, 7 Dragoon Guards; 2, 6 Dragoons; 5, 9, 12, 17 Lancers; 8, 10, 14, 18 Hussars; 1, 2, 3 Foot Guards; 1, 6, 8, 11, 17, 18, 19, 27, 41, 44, 60, 63, 75, 92 Foot; The Rifle Brigade. Canadian Units; 1st NSW Australian Horse and probably a few New Zealand troops.

Royal Navy.

South Africa 1901

This bar was awarded to those who were not eligible for the King's Medal, though they had served at the front between 1st January and 31st December, 1901.

Royal Navy.

South Africa 1902

This bar was awarded to those who were not eligible for the King's Medal, though they had served at the front between 1st January and 31st May, 1902.

Royal Navy.

Other units present, entitled to the medal with or without bar:

ARTILLERY

Royal Horse Artillery Batteries: 'A', 'G', 'I', 'J', 'M', 'O', 'P', 'Q', 'R', 'T', 'U'.

Royal Field Artillery Batteries: 2, 4, 5, 7, 8, 9, 13, 14, 17, 18, 19, 20, 21, 28, 37, 38, 39, 42, 43, 44, 53, 61, 62, 63, 64, 65, 66, 67, 68, 69, 73, 74, 75, 76, 77, 78, 79, 81, 82, 83, 84, 85, 86, 87, 88.

Royal Garrison Artillery Companies: Eastern Division—5, 6, 10; Western Division—2, 6, 10, 14, 15, 17, 23; Southern Division—14, 15, 16, 36.

Pom-pom Sections: A, B, C, D, E, F, G, H, J, K, L, M, N, O, P. Q, R, S, V, X, Z, A/A, B/B, C/C, D/D, E/E, F/F, G/G, H/H, J/J, K/K, L/L.

Mountain Batteries: 4, 10.

Additional Artillery: Cape Garrison; Cape Mounted Rifles; Diamond Fields Horse; Duke of Edinburgh's Own Volunteer; Elswick Volunteer Battery; Honourable Artillery Company (1 Battery); Natal Naval, Natal Volunteer; New South Wales; New Zealand; Prince Alfred's Own Cape Art; Queensland; Rhodesian; Royal Canadian; South Australian; Tasmanian; Victoria; Western Australia.

CORPS AND MEDICAL PERSONNEL

Royal Engineers; Army Service Corps; Royal Army Medical Corps; Ordnance Corps; Veterinary and Pay Corps; St John Ambulance Bde; Imperial Bearer Coy.

MISCELLANEOUS

Irish Guards (30).

Mounted units: Almost every county in the British Isles supplied yeomanry units, and many of them cyclist battalions as well.

In addition to the above, there were the City Imperial Volunteers, 5,363 strong, which included two companies of cyclists.

It must be remembered that small numbers of volunteers were called for from the infantry regiments of the Regular Army to form mounted units, which accounts for the appearance of such titles as the Loyal North Lancs Mounted Infantry, to give only one example; medals to these units are scarce.

90 silver medals to officers of the Indian Army, some with bars; 817 bronze medals to ORs Indian Army, all with no bars; 215 silver medals to S & T Corps; 3,500 bronze medals to S & T Corps.

The medal was awarded without bars to troops who guarded Boer prisoners on the island of St. Helena, nurses, members of St. John Ambulance Brigade, some naval personnel, and civilians whose work furthered the war efforts, though they took no part in the fighting.

The following units were raised in the UK: Duke of Cambridge's Own Yeomanry (raised by Lord Donoughmore); Lovat's Scouts (raised by Lord Lovat); Paget's Horse (raised by Mr George Paget); The Roughriders (raised by Lord Latham).

United States Hospital Ship—*Maine;* supplied and fitted out by the United States by public subscription.

IMPERIAL YEOMANRY

Medals to those on the Staff of the battalions formed were named with the battalion number and the word 'Staff'. Some other units may be found named to 'Base Coy' etc. Medals were named with the man's company number after his name or the battalion number. Medals with just 'Imperial Yeomanry' after the man's name are late issues.

The bars won by the Imperial Yeomanry are for the most part 'State' bars: Cape Colony, Orange Free State, Transvaal, and the two dated bars: South Africa 1901 and South Africa 1902. The bars for Rhodesia and Wittebergen may also be found.

Some Officers and Non-Commissioned Officers of the Imperial Yeomanry are credited with some of the 'battle' bars; these were won whilst serving with other units.

The Imperial Yeomanry in South Africa

Coy. No.	County of the Yeomanry Cavalry Regiment	Btn No.	Orig. Contg	Second Contg	Bars awarded other than Cape Colony, Orange Free State and Transvaal
1	Wiltshire	1	105		Wittebergen for OFS, SA 1901 (61)
				140	SA 1901 (112); SA 1902 (110)
2	Wiltshire	1	120		Wittebergen for OFS, SA 1901 (80)
				150	SA 1901 (140); SA 1902 (140)
3	Gloucestershire	1	120		Wittebergen for OFS, SA 1901 (80)
				140	SA 1901 (140); SA 1902 (130)
4	Glamorganshire	1	118		Wittebergen for OFS Combined with 2nd draft
				160	Roll for SA 1901 (150); SA 1902 (150)
63	Wiltshire	1		135	Not Transvaal, SA 1901 (115); SA 1902 (115)
5	Warwickshire	2	137		SA 1901 (82)
				146	SA 1901 (130); SA 1902 (120)
21	Cheshire	2	135		Not Transvaal, SA 1901 (65)
				154	SA 1901 (150); SA 1902 (115)
22	Cheshire	2	125		Not Transvaal, SA 1901 (70)
				155	Few had Transvaal, SA 1901 (125); SA 1902 (100)
32	Lancashire	2	144		Cape Colony (a few had OFS) SA 1901 (90)
				130	SA 1901 (115); SA 1902 (98)
103	Warwickshire	2	158		SA 1901 (130); SA 1902 (100)
110	Northumberland	2	130		SA 1901 (130); SA 1902 (75)
Gun Sec	No County given	3	13		SA 1901 (10); SA 1902 (1)
9	Yorkshire (Doncaster)	3	165		6 men had Wittebergen, SA 1901 (85); SA 1902 (9)
				180	SA 1901 (175); SA 1902 (150)
10	Sherwood Rangers	3	135		SA 1901 (60)
				135	Only half had OFS, SA 1901 (120); SA 1902 (97)
11	Yorkshire	3	131		SA 1901 (75); SA 1902 (72)
				175	SA 1901 (150); SA 1902 (140)
12	South Nottingham	3	120		SA 1901 (60)
				160	Half had only CC, a quarter had CC and OFS. The rest had the 3 bars and SA 1901 (150); SA 1902 (125)
109	Yorkshire Hussars	3	175		SA 1901 (175); SA 1902 (140)
66	Yorkshire	3	150		SA 1901 (150); SA 1902 (150)
111	Yorkshire Dragoons	3	120		SA 1901 (120); SA 1902 (95)
6	Staffordshire	4	120		Wittebergen for OFS, SA 1901 (90); SA 1902 (1)
				170	SA 1901 (140); SA 1902 (?)

Coy. No.	County of the Yeomanry Cavalry Regiment	Btn No.	Orig. Contg	Second Contg	Bars awarded other than Cape Colony, Orange Free State *and* Transvaal
7	Leicestershire	4	135		Wittebergen for OFS, SA 1901 (100)
				140	Few had Wittebergen, SA 1901 (135); SA 1902 (105)
8	Derbyshire	4	120		About two-thirds had Wittebergen for OFS, SA 1901 (65)
				170	SA 1901 (170); SA 1902 (155)
28	Bedfordshire	4	130		Johannesburg for Transvaal, SA 1901 (1)
				160	SA 1901 (155); SA 1902 (100)
41	Hampshire	4	140		SA 1901 (135); SA 1902 (130)
104	Derbyshire	4	114		Most did not have OFS and Transvaal. SA 1901 (100); SA 1902 (80)
15	Northumberland	5	176		SA 1901 (155); SA 1902 (140)
16	Worcestershire	5	135		SA 1901 (75)
				175	SA 1901 (140); SA 1902 (110)
55	Northumberland	5	110		30 of this Coy had CC only, SA 1901 (70); SA 1902 (60)
100	Northumberland	5	125		SA 1901 (90); SA 1902 (80)
101	Northumberland	5	150		SA 1901 (150); SA 1902 (150)
102	Worcestershire	5	115		SA 1901 (100); SA 1902 (100)
17	Ayrshire	6	115		Wittebergen for OFS, SA 1901 (95); SA 1902 (1)
18	Queen's Own Royal Glasgow & Lower Ward of Lanark	6	120		Wittebergen for OFS, SA 1901 (80); SA 1902 (1)
19	Lothian and Berwickshire	6	120		Three only had Wittebergen, SA 1901 (?); SA 1902 (?)
	Colt Gun 17/18/19		17	450	17 SA 1901 (120); SA 1902 (100) 18 SA 1901 (140); SA 1902 (110) 19 SA 1901 (110); SA 1902 (24)
19	Lothian			70	SA included in above
20	Fife and Forfar Light Horse	6	135		40 had CC and Transvaal only. SA 1901 (80)
				200	SA 1902 (150)
107	Lanarkshire	6	170		CC and Wittebergen, SA 1901 (170); SA 1902 (130)
108	Royal Glasgow	6	270		SA 1901 (190); SA 1902 (135)
25	West Somerset	7	92		Johannesburg, Diamond Hill, CC, OFS, SA 1901 (62)
				173	102 had single Transvaal. SA 1901 (162); SA 1902 (150)
26	Dorsetshire	7	175		Joh, D. Hill, CC, OFS, SA 1901 (135); SA 1902 (2)
				160	150 had Transvaal only, others as Orig Coy, SA 1901 (160); SA 1902 (130)

Coy. No.	County of the Yeomanry Cavalry Regiment	Btn No.	Orig. Contg	Second Contg	Bars awarded other than Cape Colony, Orange Free State *and* Transvaal
27	Devonshire	7	200		105 had D. Hill, CC, OFS. The rest had the usual three, SA 1901 (65)
				145	32 had the three bars. The rest single Transvaal, SA 1901 (145); SA 1902 (95)
48	North Somerset	7	120		Joh, D. Hill, CC, OFS, SA 1901 (68); SA 1902 (2)
				170	Single Transvaal 5 or 6 with CC and OFS, SA 1901 (155); SA 1902 (110)
69	Sussex	7	140		CC, Transvaal, few with OFS, SA 1901 (140); SA 1902 (95). An Officer of this Company had Defence of Mafeking.
23	Lancashire	8	150		Only about a quarter had the three bars. Usual CC and OFS, SA 1901 (120); SA 1902 (2)
				180	Mostly three bars. SA 1901 (170); SA 1902 (130)
24	Westmorland and Cumberland	8	140		SA 1901 (95); SA 1902 (10)
74	Dublin	8	165		SA 1901 (145); SA 1902 (110)
				255	SA 1901 (230); SA 1902 (190)
77	Manchester	8	120		SA 1901 (80)
				140	SA 1901 (140); SA 1902 (90)
99	Irish	8	120		Single bar CC. Only 12 had the three bars, SA 1901 (17); SA 1902 (6)
105	Manchester	8	170		SA 1901 (160)
29	Denbighshire	9	125		Bars CC and OFS, SA 1901 (100); SA 1902 (3)
			20		CC, OFS and Transvaal, SA 1901 (19); SA 1902 (6)
				140	SA 1901 (140); SA 1902 (120)
30	Pembrokeshire	9	112		CC and OFS
			17		CC, OFS and Transvaal, SA 1901 (90); SA 1902 (3)
				140	Half had CC and OFS only SA 1901 (125)
31	Montgomeryshire	9	120		CC and OFS only SA 1901 (130)
			50		CC, OFS and Transvaal, SA 1902 (10)
31	Montgomeryshire	9		120	OFS only ⎤
				100	CC only ⎥ SA 1901 (120);
				71	CC and Trans ⎬ SA 1902 (100)
				5	CC, OFS and Transvaal ⎦
49	Montgomeryshire	9	130		Usual three bars, SA 1901 (80); SA 1902 (2)
				167	Usual three bars (CC & OFS 2) SA 1901 (153); SA 1902 (126)
88	Welsh Yeomanry	9	1		Bronze to Indian Servant
			130		CC only, SA 1901 (130); SA 1902 (110)

Coy. No.	County of the Yeomanry Cavalry Regiment	Btn No.	Orig. Contg	Second Contg	Bars awarded other than Cape Colony, Orange Free State *and* Transvaal
89	Montgomeryshire	9	18		Usual three bars. Joined at Mafeking SA 1901
			120		Date bars only shown, SA 1901 (120); SA 1902 (90)
37	Buckinghamshire	10	125		No note of date bars.
				100	SA 1901 (110); SA 1902 (100)
38	Buckinghamshire	10	120		SA 1901 (75)
				120	SA 1901 (120); SA 1902 (100)
39	Berkshire	10	93		Usual three bars, SA 1901 (87); SA 1902 (3)
			37		Wittebergen for OFS
				140	SA 1901 (140); SA 1902 (110)
40	Oxfordshire	10	11		Wittebergen for OFS with Knox's Column
			120		Usual three bars, SA 1901 (80)
				165	SA 1901 (149); SA 1902 (111)
33	Royal East Kent	11	131		6 CC, Witt and Trans; 25 CC, OFS and Trans; rest CC and Wittebergen, SA 1901 (85); SA 1902 (2)
				225	SA 1901 (155); SA 1902 (105)
34	Middlesex	11	120		Wittebergen for OFS, SA 1901 (65)
				160	SA 1901 (140); SA 1902 (110)
35	Middlesex	11	120		Wittebergen for OFS, SA 1901 (67)
				150	SA 1901 shows (305) and SA 1902 (255). This hardly seems possible!
36	West Kent	11	120		Wittebergen for OFS, SA 1901 (81)
				170	SA 1901 (150); SA 1902, (135)
55	Northumberland	11	140		Wittebergen for OFS. No note of date bars
62	Middlesex	11	150		Wittebergen for OFS, SA 1901 (120)
112	Middlesex	11		170	SA 1901 (150); SA 1902 (80)
41	Hampshire	12	140		Wittebergen for OFS, SA 1901 (80); SA 1902 (1)
42	Hertfordshire	12	120		Wittebergen for OFS, SA 1901 (55); SA 1902 (3)
				170	SA 1901 (140); SA 1902 (120)
43	Suffolk	12	120		SA 1901 (70); SA 1902 (3)
44	Suffolk	12	150		Wittebergen for OFS, SA 1901 (70)
				160	SA 1901 (160); SA 1902 (122)
46	Belfast	12	155		CC and OFS only
			54		Usual three bars, SA 1901 (170); SA 1902 (135)
51	Paget's Horse	12	145		Usual three bars
			85		CC and Transvaal
53	Royal East Kent	12	15		SA 1901 (160); SA 1902 (160)
45	Dublin	13	100		SA 1901 (40); SA 1902 (2)
46	Belfast	13	130		CC and OFS only, SA 1901 (65); SA 1902 (1)

Coy. No.	County of the Yeomanry Cavalry Regiment	Btn No.	Orig. Contg	Second Contg	Bars awarded other than Cape Colony, Orange Free State *and* Transvaal
47	Duke of Cambridge's Own or Lord Donoughmore's	13	140		SA 1901 (7)
54	Belfast	13	130		CC and OFS, a few Transvaal, SA 1901 (48); SA 1902 (1)
53	Royal East Kent	14	120		Wittebergen for OFS, SA 1901 (75); *See 12th Bn*
55	Northumberland	14	120		SA 1901 (80); SA 1902 (4)
62	Middlesex	14	130		Wittebergen for OFS, SA 1901 (20); SA 1902 (1)
69	Sussex	14	125		Joh, D. Hill, CC and OFS, SA 1901 (75)
56	Buckinghamshire	15	160	160	SA 1901 (85) / SA 1901 (140)
57	Buckinghamshire	15	65 / 75	130	Wittebergen for OFS / Usual three bars / SA 1901 (130); SA 1902 (125)
58	Berkshire	15	140	120	A few had Witt for OFS, SA 1901 (85) / SA 1901 (115); SA 1902 (110)
59	Oxfordshire	15	130	185	SA 1901 (65) / SA 1901 (185); SA 1902 (170)
63	Wiltshire	16	90		Wittebergen for OFS, SA 1901 (75)
66	Yorkshire	16	160		Wittebergen for OFS, SA 1901 (80)
74	Dublin	16	100		SA (1901) 75. Some CC only
50	Hampshire	17	120	140	Usual three bars plus Rhodesia, SA 1901 (85) / Usual three bars only. SA 1901 (140); SA 1902 (120)
60	North Irish Horse (Belfast)	17	70	60 / 150	Usually CC, OFS and Rhodesia. A few Transvaal / CC, OFS and Rhodesia, SA 1901 (combined 95) / Usual three bars. SA 1901 (150); SA 1902 (120)
61	South Irish Horse (Dublin)	17	150 / 15	160	CC, OFS Trans and Rhodesia Single Transvaal, SA 1901 (90); SA 1902 (3) / CC and OFS only, SA 1901 (145); SA 1902 (120)
65	Leicestershire	17	120	145	SA 1901 (100); SA 1902 (2) / SA 1901 (145); SA 1902 (80)
67	Sharpshooters	18	120	160	Usual three bars and Rhodesia, SA 1901 (80) / CC and OFS usual, a few Trans, SA 1901 (155); SA 1902 (110)
70	Sharpshooters	18	115	150	CC, OFS and Rhodesia, SA 1901 (110) / CC and OFS; a few Trans, SA 1901 (150)

Coy. No.	County of the Yeomanry Cavalry Regiment	Btn No.	Orig. Contg	Second Contg	Bars awarded other than Cape Colony, Orange Free State and Transvaal
70/71	Sharpshooters	18	20		CC and OFS, SA 1901 (?)
71	Sharpshooters	18	130	155	Usual three bars, plus Rhodesia. A few single Rhodesia, SA 1901 (90) CC and OFS and few Rhodesia, SA 1901 (155); SA 1902 (120)
75	Sharpshooters	18	120	155	Usual three bars, plus Rhodesia, SA 1901 (100) CC and OFS only. SA 1901 (155); SA 1902 (135)
57	Buckinghamshire	19	4		CC and OFS only
68	Paget's Horse	19	2		CC and OFS only
73	Paget's Horse	19	1		CC, OFS and Transvaal
—		19	54		CC and Transvaal
51	Paget's Horse	19	105		CC and Trans and a few OFS, SA 1901 (70)
52	Paget's Horse	19	100		CC and Transvaal
68	Paget's Horse	19	115		CC and Transvaal, SA 1901 (80); SA 1902 (1)
73	Paget's Horse	19	85 91 5		Usual three bars CC and Trans, SA 1901 (85) Gun Section
72 76 78 79	Rough Riders Rough Riders Rough Riders Rough Riders	20	529		All Companies are mixed together, usual three bars SA 1901 (340). Rough extract of numbered entries: 72 (79); 76: (98); 78 (96); 79 (83); no Company numbers (156)
80	Sharpshooters	21	125		SA 1901 (125); SA 1902 (100)
81	Sharpshooters	21	125		SA 1901 (130), this includes a few of other Companies, SA 1902 (115)
82	Sharpshooters	21	135		SA 1901 (130); SA 1902 (100)
83	Sharpshooters	21	110		SA 1901 (110); SA 1902 (80)
78	Rough Riders	22	60		SA 1901 (120), this must take in Company (76); SA 1902 (30)
76	Rough Riders	22	135		SA 1901 (2); SA 1902 (1)
84	Rough Riders	22	150		CC and OFS only SA 1901 (110)
85	Rough Riders	22	115		SA 1901 (115); SA 1902 (95)
86	Rough Riders	22	120		SA 1901 (120); SA 1902 (90, CC and OFS only)
87	Rough Riders	22	120		SA 1901 (120); SA 1902 (100, CC and OFS only, two had Transvaal added later)
90	Sharpshooters	23	140		40 had CC and OFS only. SA 1901 (135); SA 1902 (120)

Coy. No.	County of the Yeomanry Cavalry Regiment	Btn No.	Orig. Contg	Second Contg	Bars awarded other than Cape Colony, Orange Free State *and* Transvaal
91	Sharpshooters	23	110		CC and OFS only SA 1901 (105); SA 1902 (85)
92	Sharpshooters	23	120		Usual three bars. SA 1901 (110); SA 1902 (100)
93	Sharpshooters	23	120		Usual three bars. SA 1901 (120); SA 1902 (100)
94	Metropolitan Mounted Rifles	24	150		Usual three bars. SA 1901 (130); SA 1902 (75)
95	Metropolitan Mounted Rifles	24	140		SA 1901 (140); SA 1902 (100)
96	Metroplitan Mounted Rifles	24	120		SA 1901 (115); SA 1902 (90)
97	Metropolitan Mounted Rifles	24	115		SA 1901 (115); SA 1902 (90)
115	Sharpshooters	25	1		Usual three bars
117	Sharpshooters	25	1		Usual three bars
118	Sharpshooters	25	3		Usual three bars
120	Younghusband's Horse	26	25		CC and SA 1901, SA 1901 (140); SA 1902 (140). Claims for medal on other lists.
		27	417		CC, SA 1901 and SA 1902, Regt Nos up to 44575
127	Westminster Dragoons	28	100		CC and SA 1902
128	Westminster Dragoons	28	90		CC and SA 1902
129	Westminster Dragoons	28	130		CC and SA 1902
130	Westminster Dragoons	28	100		CC and SA 1902
131	Irish Horse	29	120		CC and SA 1902
132	Irish Horse	29	100		CC and SA 1902
133	Irish Horse	29	130		CC and SA 1902
134	Irish Horse	29	120		CC and SA 1902
Gun Sect.	Irish Horse	29	16		CC and SA 1902
175	Irish Horse	29	120		CC and SA 1902
176	Irish Horse	29	105		CC and SA 1902
—		30	70		CC and SA 1902
			38		Bar only, SA 1902
135		30	105		CC and SA 1902
137		30	95		CC and SA 1902
138		30	95		CC and SA 1902
139	Fincastle's Horse	31	100		CC and SA 1902
140	Fincastle's Horse	31	102		CC and SA 1902
141	Fincastle's Horse	31	105		CC and SA 1902
142	Fincastle's Horse	31	100		CC and SA 1902
143		32	95		CC and SA 1902
145		32	90		CC and SA 1902
146		32	100		CC and SA 1902

See 'The Canadians' by G. A. Roncetti and E. E. Denby

CANADIAN UNITS
Approximately 3,750 medals with 'erased' reverse dates were awarded to Canadians.

List of Canadian units and bars awarded:

Royal Canadian Regt of Infantry	Cape Colony; Relief of Mafeking (scarce); Paardeburg; Orange Free State (scarce); Driefontein; Transvaal (scarce); Johannesburg; South Africa 1902 (scarce)
1st Canadian Mounted Rifles	Cape Colony; Orange Free State; Transvaal (scarce); Johannesburg; Diamond Hill; Belfast; South Africa 1902 (scarce)

2nd Canadian Mounted Rifles	Cape Colony; Transvaal; South Africa 1902 (scarce)
Royal Canadian Dragoons	Cape Colony; Relief of Kimberley (scarce); Orange Free State; Transvaal; Johannesburg; Diamond Hill; Belfast, South Africa 1902 (scarce)
Royal Canadian Field Artillery	Cape Colony; Rhodesia (scarce); Relief of Mafeking (scarce); Orange Free State; Transvaal; Belfast (scarce)
Lord Strathcona's Horse	Cape Colony (scarce); Natal; Orange Free State; Transvaal (scarce); Belfast; South Africa 1901; South Africa 1902 (scarce)

All the undermentioned bars are scarce to these units:

Medical Staff	Cape Colony; Orange Free State; Johannesburg
10th Field Hosp	Cape Colony; Johannesburg; Transvaal; South Africa 1902
Can Postal Corps	Cape Colony; Orange Free State; Transvaal
Can Staff	Cape Colony; Orange Free State

AUSTRALIAN UNITS
Approx strength of the 57 Australian Units in South Africa which comprised 15,500 ORs and 840 officers:

New South Wales
NSW Lancers (170); 1st Australian Horse (1st Contingent) (34); 1st Australian Horse (2nd Contingent) (107); 'A' Battery Royal Australian Artillery (177); 1st NSW MR (405); NSW Citizen Bushmen (525); Imperial Bushmen (762); 2nd NSW MR (995); 3rd NSW MR (997); 3rd NSW Imp Bushmen (this unit was formed in South Africa, 230 men plus 200 Riverma Bushmen); 1st Australian Comm Horse (375); 3rd Australian Comm Horse. (No active service) (371); 5th Australian Comm Horse; NSW Army Medical Corps (1st Contingent) (86); (2nd Contingent) (94); (Imperial Draft Contingent) (53).

South Australia
1st MR Contingent (126); 2nd MR Contingent (119); 3rd Bushmens Contingent (99); 4th Imperial Bushmen Contingent (234); 5th Imperial Contingent (316); 6th Imperial Contingent (316); 2nd Battalion Australian Comm Horse (171); 4th Battalion Australian Comm Horse. (No active service) (120); 8th Battalion Australian Comm Horse (245).

West Australia
1st Mounted Infantry Contingent (130); 2nd Mounted Infantry Contingent (103); 3rd Bushmen Contingent (116); 4th Mounted Infantry Contingent (127); 5th Mounted Infantry Contingent (221); 6th Mounted Infantry Contingent (228); 2nd Battalion Australian Comm Horse (60); 4th Battalion Australian Comm Horse (120); 8th Battalion Australian Comm Horse (120).

Tasmania
1st Tasmanian Contingent (80); 1st Tasmanian Contingent (Draft) (47); 2nd Tasmanian Bushmen (54); 3rd (First Tasmanian Imp Contingent) (122); 4th (2nd Imp Bushmen) (253); 1st Battalion Australian Comm Horse (Tasmanian ½ Unit) (62); 3rd Battalion Australian Comm Horse (Tasmanian Unit) (121); 8th Battalion Australian Comm Horse (Tasmanian Unit) (120).

Queensland
1st Queensland Mounted Infantry (262); 2nd Queensland Mounted Infantry (154); 3rd Queensland Mounted Infantry (316); 4th Queensland Imp Bushmen (384); 5th Queensland Imp Bushmen (529); 6th Queensland Imp Bushmen (401), Draft (78), Draft (21); 1st Australian Comm Horse (Queensland Unit) (123); 3rd Australian Comm Horse (122); 7th Australian Comm Horse (490).

Victoria
1st Victoria Mounted Infantry Co (252); 2nd Victoria Mounted Rifles (265); 3rd Bushmens Contingent (251); 4th Imperial Contingent (629); 5th Mounted Rifles Contingent (1,037); 2nd Battalion Australian Comm Horse (372); 6th Battalion Australian Comm Horse (489).

NEW ZEALAND UNITS
1st Contingent (215); 2nd Contingent (258); 3rd Contingent (264); 4th Contingent (466); 5th Contingent (595); 6th Contingent (578); 7th Contingent (600); 8th Contingent (1,196); 9th Contingent (1,076); 10th Contingent (1,168).

SOUTH AFRICAN UNITS

TOWN GUARD UNITS
The numbers claimed are shown in brackets but it would appear likely that a fairly large percentage was later returned to the issuing authorities.

Aberdeen (50); Adelaide (70); Albany (50); Alexandria (25); Alice (60); Alicedale (170); Aliwal North (70); Barberton (140); Barkly East (50); Barkly West (85); Beaconsfield; Beaufort West; Bedford (1,350); Bethulie (43); Bluecliff and Glenconnor (12); Boshof (18); Brandfort (22); Britstown (35); Burgersdorp (205); Cala (120); Campbell (30); Carnarvon (29); Cathcart (80); Ceres (80); Clanwilliam (35); Colesberg (130); Cookhouse (100); Cradock (440); Cyphergat (75); Danielskuil (26); Darling (11); De-Aar (5); Dordrecht (85); Douglas (50); Dundee (195); Durban Road (23); East London; Edenberg (55); Farmer; Fauresmith (10); Fort Beaufort (59); Fraserberg (26); Fraserberg Road; George (110); Graaf Reinet (266); 1st Grahamstown (41); 2nd Grahamstown (127); Griquatown (37); Hanover (54); Hopetown (29); Hoppesia; Humansdorp (68); Indwe (137); Jagersfontein (77); Jamestown (40); Jansenville; Kimberley (2,594); Keindes (4); Kenhardt (50); King Williams Town (329); Klerksdorp (118); Klipdam (11); Kynsna (154); Kokstad (145); Komgha (32); Kuruman (21); Ladybrand (8); Ladygrey (108); Ladysmith; Laingsberg; Mafeking (513); Malmesbury; Maraisberg (17); Middleburg (100); Middleton (36); Molteno (74); Montagu (32); Mossel Bay (118); Naauwpoort (129); Namaqualand (240); Newcastle (243); Niger River (75); Oudtshoorn (233); Oumbu; Paarl (27); Pearston (14); Petrusville (52); Pietersburg (12); Piquetberg (23); Port Elizabeth (562); Port Nolloth (22); Potchef Stroom (63); Prieska (56); Prince Albert (45); Prince Albert Road; Queenstown (331); Richmond (70); Riversdale (68); Robertson; Rosmead (38); Salt River Works; Sandflats; Somerset East (186); Springbokfontein (12); Starkstroom; Steynsburg (68); Steytlerville (100); Stormburg; Sutherland (26); Swallendam (55); Swallendam Railway (35); Tarkastad (134); Touws River; Tsome (15); Towfre (137); Uitenhage (893); Upington (4); Victoria West (42); Vryburg (212); Warrenton (55); Wellington (106); Willowmore (109); Windsorton and Wedburg (74); Worcester (153); Zeerust (46).

DISTRICT MOUNTED TROOPS (DMT)
Aberdeen (100); Adelaide (90); Albany (480, including a few Cape Colony bars); Alexandria; Aliwal North (5); Baca (42); Beaufort West; Bedford (135); Burgersdorp (90); Cala (30); Caledon (62); Carnarvon (60); Cathcart (190); Christiana (30); Colesberg (75); East London (300); Elsies River Troop (14); Fort Beaufort (106); Fraserberg (26); Fraserberg Road (20); Graaf Reinet (145); Green River (29); Harrismith (99); Hawick (30); Hay (11); Hex River (23); Highland (15); Hopefield (46); Houw Hoek (26); Humandsdorp (107); Indwe (19); Jansenville (200); Karkloop (15); Kei Road (36); King William Town (135); Koffy (30); Komgha; Krom River (18); Kruisfontein (1); Kynsna (36); Ladysmith (47); Laingsberg; Lidgetton (25); Mafeking (66); Malmesbury (89); Malmesbury Police (12); Malbon (22); Matjesfontein (46); Melmoth (17); Middleburg (18); Modder River (3); Montagu (27); Mosita Squadron (59); Mossel Bay (40); Mtshate (14); Naauwpoort (128); New Hudson (20); Nottingham Road (41); Oudtshoorn (140); Paarl (278); Peddie (251); Piquetsberg (22); Port Elizabeth (80); Prince Albert (60); Prince Albert Road; Queenstown (230); Riversdale (46); Robertson (67); Sandflats (66); Sir Lowry's Pass (15); Somerset East (197); Stellenbosch (84); Steytlerville (117); Storkensheim (76); Stutterheim; Sutherland (38); Swallendam (42); Uitenhage (264); Uniondale (37); Victoria East (139); Warhburg (72); Warrenton (50); Wellington (91); Willowmore (64); Windsorton and Wedburg (105); Worcester (99).

ADDITIONAL SOUTH AFRICAN UNITS AND OTHERS
Ashburner's Light Horse; Bayly's Horse; Bechuanaland Rifles; Beddy's Scouts; Bethune's Mounted Infantry; Border Horse; Border Mounted Police; Border Mounted Rifles; Border Scouts; Brabant's Horse (1st and 2nd); British South Africa Police; Burma Mounted Infantry; Bushmen Borderers; Bushveld Rifles; Cameron's Scouts; Canadian Contingent; Cape Cavalry Brigade; Cape Colony Cyclist Corps; Cape Medical Staff Corps; Cape Mounted Police; Cape Mounted Rifles; Cape Police; Cape Railway Sharpshooters; Cape Special Police; Cape Town Highlanders; Cape Volunteer Bearer Company; Ceylon Contingent; Ceylon Mounted Infantry; Clifford's Scouts; Colesburg Mounted Rifle Club; Colonial

Defence Force; Colonial Light Horse; Colonial Scouts; Colonial Volunteer Corps; Composite Regiment Mounted Infantry (mostly men from home mounted infantry units); Commander-in-Chief's Bodyguard; Cullinan's Horse; Damant's Horse (formerly Rimington's Guides); Dennison's Scouts; Diamond Fields Horse; District Military Police (these took the name of their districts); District Mounted Troops (these took the name of their districts, such as Modder River District Mounted Rifles, Vryburg Mounted Rifles, etc); Divisional Scouting Corps; Driscoll's Scouts; Duke of Edinburgh's Own Volunteer Rifles; Durban Light Infantry; East Griqualand Mounted Rifle Volunteers; Eastern Province Horse; Eastern Transvaal Scouts (these were native scouts in Colonel Benson's Column); Engcobo Mounted Rifle Club; French's Scouts; Frontier Light Horse; Frontier Mounted Rifles; Gatacre's Scouts; Gorringe's Fighting Scouts; Gough's Mounted Infantry; Grahamstown (1st City) Volunteers; Griqualand Mounted Rifle Volunteers; Harrismith Light Horse; Heidelburg Volunteers; Heidelburg Scouts; Herschel Mounted Volunteers; Herschel Native Police; Imperial Bushmen; Imperial Light Horse (1st and 2nd); Imperial Light Infantry; Imperial Railway Volunteer Corps; Imperial Yeomanry Scouts; Johannesburg Mounted Rifles; Kaffrarian Rifles; Kenny's Scouts; Kimberley Regiment; Kimberley Light Horse; Kimberley Mounted Corps; Kimberley Mounted Rifles; Kimberley Volunteers (or Kimberley Volunteer Regiment); Kitchener's Fighting Scouts (1st and 2nd); Kitchener's Horse; Komgha Mounted Volunteers; Knysna Rangers; Le Gros Scouts; Loch's Horse; Loxton's Horse; Loyal Farmers' Light Horse; Lumsden's Horse (250); Maclean's Scouts; Malta Mounted Infantry; Maritzani Mounted Irregulars; Marshall's Horse; Matatiele District Defence Force; Menné's Scouts; Midland Mounted Rifles; Montmorency's Scouts; Morley's Scouts; Mounted Pioneers; Murray's Horse; Namaqualand Border Scouts (natives); Natal Bridge Guards; Natal Carbineers; Natal Guides; Natal Hotchkiss Detachment; Natal Police (mounted and dismounted); Natal Mounted Rifles; Natal Royal Rifles; Natal Naval Volunteers; Natal Composite Regiment; National Scouts; Nesbitt's Horse; New England Mounted Rifles; New Zealand Contingent; Orange River Colony Volunteers; Orpen's Horse; Pietersburg Light Horse (formerly Bushveld Rifles); Prince Alfred's Own Volunteer Guards; Prince of Wales's Light Horse; Protectorate Regiment; Queensland Contingent; Queenstown Rifle Volunteers; Railway Pioneers Regiment; Rand Rifles; Rhodesian Field Force; Rhodesian Regiment; Rimington's Guides (subsequently Damant's Horse); Roberts's Horse (originally Warren's, then 2nd South Africa Light Horse); Royal Canadian Regiment; Royal Horse Artillery Mounted Rifles (in the latter stages of the war the artillery was reduced, and the men thus released were formed into mounted riflemen. A few colonials were included); Rundle's Scouts; Scottish Horse; Scott's Railway Guards; South African Constabulary; South African Mounted Irregular Forces; South African Light Horse; South African Mounted Infantry; South Rhodesian Volunteers; Steinaecker's Horse; Stellenbosch Mounted Infantry (a unit of the South African Light Horse); Strathcone's Horse; Struben's Scouts; Swaziland Police; Swellendam Mounted Infantry; Tembuland Mounted Rifle Club; Tempest's Scouts; Thorneycroft's Mounted Infantry; Transkei Mounted Rifles; Transvaal Mounted Infantry; Tucker's Scouts; Uitenhage Mounted Infantry; Uitenhage Volunteer Rifles; Umvoti Mounted Rifles; Utrecht Mounted Rifles; Utrecht-Vryheid Mounted Police; Victorian Contingent (which included Mounted Infantry and Bushmen); Vryburg Mounted Rifles; Warren's Light Horse (which later became 2nd South Africa Light Horse, which became Robert's Horse); Warren's Mounted Infantry; Warren's Scouts; Warwick's Scouts; Western Light Horse; Western Province Mounted Rifles; Wodehouse Yeomanry; Xalanga Mounted Rifles; Younghusband's Horse.

Summary of QSA bars Tables Courtesy of Fevyer and Wilson 'The Queen's South Africa Medal to the Royal Navy and the Royal Marines'

Ship/Unit	Belmont	Modder River	Paardeberg	Driefontein	Johannesburg	Diamond Hill	Belfast	Wittebergen	Relief of Kimberley	Cape Colony	Orange Free State	Transvaal	Rhodesia	Tugela Heights	Defence of Ladysmith	Relief of Ladysmith	Laing's Nek	Natal	South Africa 1901	South Africa 1902	TOTAL
Barracouta										55									25	50	130
Barrosa			25	24						56		17									122
Beagle										17									17		34
Blanche										18									13		31
Doris	129	109	152	149	44	54	50		13	222	13	46		1		1	1	14	6	1	1005
Dwarf																					0
Fearless																					0
Forte										2	25	28		32		37	28	120		2	274
Gibraltar										4											4
Magicienne										3								3			6
Magpie										14									1		15
Monarch	116	100	170	168	120	118	107	1	27	146	8	1		5		5	1	1	2	0	1096
Naiad										117									117		234
Niobe										129		1								1	131

Summary of QSA bars Tables Courtesy of Fevyer and Wilson 'The Queen's South Africa Medal to the Royal Navy and the Royal Marines'

Ship/Unit	Belmont	Modder River	Paardeberg	Driefontein	Johannesburg	Diamond Hill	Belfast	Wittebergen	Relief of Kimberley	Cape Colony	Orange Free State	Transvaal	Rhodesia	Tugela Heights	Defence of Ladysmith	Relief of Ladysmith	Laing's Nek	Natal	South Africa 1901	South Africa 1902	TOTAL
Partridge										6			5						3		14
Pearl										14										14	28
Pelorus										1								13	1		15
Philomel			2	1	2	2	2			2	27	30		41		41	30	30	1		211
Powerful	110	79	71	69	21	20	18		21	5	1			3	275	3					696
Racoon																		2			2
Rambler																					0
Rattler																					0
Redbreast																					0
Sappho										1									1		2
Sybille										85									4	1	90
Tartar						4	5			47	20	19		26		29	20	18	1		189
Terpsichore										137									137		274
Terrible										45	2	1		274	1	292	1	223			839
Thetis										1								101	1		103
Thrush										15									15		30
Widgeon																		72			72
Cape & Transport Staff										12									2	1	15
Marines serving with Army								7		18	10	11	2					5			53
Royal Indian Marine																		8			8
Natal Naval Volunteers										1	28	30		52	64	53	33	8			269
TOTAL	355	288	420	411	187	198	182	8	61	1173	134	183	8	434	340	461	114	618	347	70	5992

ROYAL NAVY units present: **Summary of QSA medals and bars**

Ship/Unit	Number of Bars										Total	Returned	Entitled
	0	1	2	3	4	5	6	7	8	Unknown			
Barracouta	262	1	36	19							339	21	318
Barrosa	102	31	1	7	17						194	36	158
Beagle	110	0	17								139	12	127
Blanche	155	5	13								216	43	173
Doris	346	183	28	31	67	16	9	33	5		804	86	718
Dwarf	176										286	110	176
Fearless	145										151	6	145
Forte	415	122	9	1	4	23					683	109	574
Gibraltar	617	4									673	52	621
Magicienne	230	6									256	20	236
Magpie	75	13	1								95	6	89
Monarch	812	58	37	31	18	18	50	39	17	11	1262	171	1091
Naiad	133	0	117								274	24	250
Niobe	530	129	1								755	95	660
Partridge	150	8	3								174	13	161
Pearl	189	0	14								230	27	203
Pelorus	215	13	1								249	20	229
Philomel	152	30	17	3	3	24	1				269	39	230
Powerful	415	308	13	5	28	19	2	16	2		898	90	808
Racoon	176	2									208	30	178
Rambler	110										145	35	110
Rattler	76										86	10	76
Redbreast	83										87	4	83
Sappho	254	0	1								274	19	**255**
Sybille	187	80	5								312	40	272
Tartar	103	59	9	4	1	18	1				237	42	195
Terpsichore	136	0	137								313	40	273
Terrible	538	273	261	13	0	1					1147	61	1086
Thetis	183	101	1								297	12	285
Thrush	65	0	15								116	36	80
Widgeon	19	72									112	21	91
Cape & Transport Staff	35	10	1	1							47	0	47
Marines serving with Army	9	8	3	9	3						32	0	32
Royal Indian Marine	34	8									42	0	42
Natal Naval Volunteers	0	68	25	6	2	25					135	9	126
TOTAL	7237	1592	766	130	143	144	63	88	24	11	11537	1339	10198

127 *Queen's Mediterranean Medal* 1899-1902

Obverse	The crowned and veiled head of Queen Victoria and the legend, 'VICTORIA REGINA ET IMPERATRIX'
Reverse	Britannia with a flag in her left hand and holding out a laurel wreath in her right towards an advancing party of soldiers. In the background are two warships. With the legend, 'MEDITERRANEAN'
Size	36mm diameter
Metal	Silver
Ribbon	As for the Queen's South Africa Medal, 1899: red with two dark blue stripes and a broad orange stripe down the centre
Suspension	By a straight suspender
Designer	G. W. de Saulles
Naming	Indented block capitals
Bars issued	Nil

The medal was awarded to garrisons in the Mediterranean who guarded Boer prisoners of war. The third battalions of the following Regiments received it:
Royal Northumberland Fusiliers (574); Royal Fusiliers; West Yorks (721); Loyal North Lancs (202); Royal West Kent; King's Own Yorkshire Light Infantry (775); Seaforth Highlanders (784); Royal Munster Fusiliers (498).

128 *King's South Africa Medal* 1901-1902

Obverse	The bust of King Edward VII and legend 'EDWARDVS VII REX IMPERATOR.'
Reverse	As for the second issue of the Queen's South Africa Medal
Size	36mm diameter
Metal	Silver
Ribbon	32mm wide. Green, white and yellow in equal widths
Suspension	By a plain, straight swivelling suspender
Designer	G. W. de Saulles
Naming	Impressed in block capitals, some officer's medals engraved
Bars issued	Two—South Africa 1901 and South Africa 1902

Queen Victoria having died during the South African War, King Edward VII authorized this medal to be given to all who were serving in South Africa on or after 1st January, 1902, and who would complete eighteen months' service before 1st June, 1902.

Only thirty-one of these medals were awarded to the Navy, as the Naval Brigades returned to their ships in 1901, and men who did not see service ashore were not awarded it (1 to HMS *Doris,* 11 to RM, and 19 to miscellaneous RN personnel). 160 were awarded to Canadians.

This medal was never issued alone, but always in conjunction with the Queen's Medal, and neither was it issued without a bar, except to nursing sisters, to whom 587 were awarded. This medal was occasionally given with the single bar 'South Africa 1902'. A man who missed qualifying for the 1901 bar because of wounds etc, but who returned after January 1902 and completed a total of 18 months before 31st May, 1902, could qualify for just the 1902 bar.

129 *St John Ambulance Brigade Medal for South Africa* 1899-1902

Obverse	Bust of King Edward VII facing left, wearing the badge of the Order of St John at the neck; with the legend, 'EDWARDVS VII. D.G. BRITT. REX. F.D. IND. IMP.' Beneath the truncation, 'FUCHS 1901'
Reverse	In the centre, resting on the badge of the Order, a shield bearing the cross of St George having in alternate quarters a lion or unicorn. On each side of the badge is a sprig of St John's Wort. Above the badge, 'SOUTH AFRICA 1899 1902'. Below the badge on a scroll, 'PRO FIDE PRO UTILITATE HOMINUM'. The whole enclosed by the legend, 'MAGNUS PRIORATUS ORDINIS HOSPITALIS SANCTI JOHANNIS JERUSALEM IN ANGLIA
Size	38mm diameter
Metal	Bronze
Ribbon	32mm wide. Black with white edges
Suspension	By a plain straight swivelling suspender
Designer	Emil Fuchs MVO
Naming	Engraved in upright capitals
Bars issued	Nil

The medal was awarded to members of the St John Ambulance Brigade who went overseas and served in the South Africa War of 1899-1902 or who were involved in mobilisation, training, despatch of medical stores etc, within the period.

Permission to wear the medal in uniform was given in January 1904.

A total of fourteen brigade members who travelled from South Africa to China aboard the USS *Maine* were awarded the China Medal, 1900 in addition to the above medal.

A total of 1,871 medals were issued.

130 *Kimberley Star* 1899-1900

General	A six-pointed star with a ball on each point
Obverse	At the centre, the coat-of-arms of Kimberley with the motto, 'SPERO MELIORA.' The whole enclosed by a band having the name 'KIMBERLEY' above and the dates '1899-1900' below
Reverse	Plain except for the words, 'MAYOR'S SIEGE MEDAL 1900' in three lines, in raised capitals. Below this is the Birmingham hallmark of an anchor and lion followed by the date letter 'a' (see text below) below this is the manufacturer's mark 'AHD'
Size	46mm diagonal diameter
Metal	Silver and gold
Ribbon	26mm wide. In the centre, equal stripes of red, white and blue, a band of black to the left, a band of yellow to the right. The ribbon is worn with the black band nearest to the centre of the chest
Suspension	By means of an ornate straight bar suspension attached to the uppermost ball of the star by a ring. Sometimes the straight bar is dispensed with and the ribbon is threaded directly through the ring. The star is hung from a plain buckle
Designer	Unknown, manufactured by A. H. Darby
Naming	Issued unnamed
Bars issued	Nil

Issued by the Mayor of Kimberley to all members of the garrison or their next-of-kin who served ninety days in the siege between 1st October 1899 and 28th February 1900.

The medals are generally found with the hallmark date letter 'a' for 1900 though some were produced later and have a date letter 'b' or 'c'.

It would appear that some 5,000 silver stars were produced.

Two gold stars were issued to Mayor H. A. Oliver, JP and Mr R. Archibald of De Beers Co. The gold stars which differ slightly from the silver version were produced by a jeweller in Kimberley.

The Star could not be worn in uniform.

131 *Kimberley Medal* 1899-1900

Obverse	The winged figure of Victory holding laurel wreaths and a palm with the legend, 'SOUTH AFRICA'. Below the figure is Kimberley Town Hall. In the exergue the dates '1899-1900'
Reverse	In the centre are two shields, on one is the wording, 'INVESTED 15 OCT 1899' on the other, 'RELIEVED 15 FEB 1900'. Above the shields is an Imperial crown and below is a monogram 'VRI'. The whole is partly enclosed by the legend, 'TO THE GALLANT DEFENDERS OF KIMBERLEY'
Size	38.5mm diameter
Metal	Silver
Ribbon	As for the Kimberley Star
Suspension	The ribbon passes through a ring which is attached to the medal by means of a claw and loop
Designer	Unknown
Naming	Issued unnamed
Bars issued	Nil

The medal was struck as a commemorative for the defence of Kimberley. No authorization was given for the issue of this medal and the quantity produced is unknown.

132 *Yorkshire Imperial Yeomanry Medal* 1900-1902

Obverse	In the centre the rose of York with a coronet above, partly enclosed by the legend, 'A TRIBUTE FROM YORKSHIRE' around the circumference is a laurel wreath
Reverse	*Type (a)* Prince of Wales feathers with the motto 'ICH DIEN'. Below, the numeral '3' about which is a scroll having the inscription, 'IMPERIAL YORKSHIRE YEOMANRY' below this the legend, '1900. SOUTH AFRICA 1901'
	Type (b) As type (a) except the lower legend reads '1901 SOUTH AFRICA 1902'
	Type (c) As type (a) except the numeral is '66'
Size	39mm diameter
Metal	Silver
Ribbon	Usually worn from the plain yellow Imperial Yeomanry LS Medal ribbon
Suspension	Claw and swivelling ring
Designer	Mr Bradshaw, manufactured by Spink & Son Ltd
Naming	Impressed in upright capitals
Bars issued	Nil

This medal is a Boer War 'tribute' medal given to the men of Yorkshire for service in South Africa with the 3rd Battalion and 66th Company, 16th Battalion Imperial Yeomanry. The medal being unofficial was not permitted to be worn in uniform.

Numbers produced,	Type (a) 3rd Bn, 1900-01	470
based on Spink estimates:	Type (b) 3rd Bn, 1901-02	700
	Type (c) 66th Co, 1900-01	160

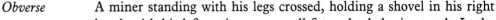

133 *The Cape Copper Company Ltd, Medal for the Defence of Ookiep* 4th April-4th May 1902

Obverse	A miner standing with his legs crossed, holding a shovel in his right hand, with his left resting on a small four-wheeled mine truck. In the background is a hill, behind which the sun is rising. The whole is surrounded by the inscription, 'THE CAPE COPPER COMPANY LIMITED'. In the centre, at the bottom, is the date '1888'
Reverse	The whole of the reverse is taken up by the following inscription which occupies thirteen lines of capital lettering: 'PRESENTED TO THE OFFICERS, NON-COMMISSIONED OFFICERS AND MEN OF THE GARRISON OF OOKIEP IN RECOGNITION OF THEIR GALLANT DEFENCE OF THE TOWN UNDER LT. COL. SHELTON, D.S.O., AGAINST A GREATLY SUPERIOR FORCE OF BOERS APRIL 4TH TO MAY 4TH 1902'. The medal has a raised rim as found on the Long Service Medals awarded during the reign of Queen Victoria
Size	36.5mm diameter
Metal	Silver and bronze
Ribbon	37.5mm wide. Dark brown with a central green stripe, 12.5mm wide
Suspension	By means of a floreated suspender identical to those fitted to India General Service Medals. The pin on which the suspender swivels is fixed direct to the piece ie there are no claws over the raised rim
Designer	Designer and manufacturer unknown
Naming	In indented capitals
Bars issued	Nil

The medal was awarded in silver to officers (very rare) and in bronze to other ranks. It was probably allowed to be worn in uniform. In Forsyth's roll, eighteen recipients of the silver medal are listed including one to Pay Sgt H. Rodda, apparently the only other rank to receive a silver medal. The roll indicates that 537 men may have qualified for the bronze medal.

It is possible that medals were only awarded to Company employees in the Namaqualand Town Guard (formed by the amalgamation of the Ookiep TG, Concordia TG and Port Nolloth TG in October 1901) and Ookiep Volunteers. However a silver medal to Captain A. Borcherds, Cape Garrison Artillery is known.

Ookiep, in Namaqualand, lay about seventy-five miles inland on a light railway from Port Nolloth and was the centre of the Cape Copper Mining Company. Lieutenant-Colonel Shelton, 3rd West Surrey Regiment, was in command of all the forces in the district with his HQ in Ookiep and small garrisons at Concordia, Nababeep and Springbok. When Smuts invaded the district the garrison at Nababeep retired on Ookiep; that at Concordia surrendered without offering any opposition to him, whilst that at Springbok surrendered to Maritz.

Major Dean, the Company's manager, prepared the town for defence and erected a perimeter of blockhouses. The garrison consisted of 661 half-castes, 206 European miners, 44 men of the 5th Warwickshire Militia and 12 men of the Cape Garrison Artillery who manned the

9-pdr and Maxim gun. The total strength was 923 officers and men.

Major Edwards was placed in command of the outer, whilst Major Dean commanded the inner defences; Captain Freeland was CRA; Captain Macdonald, Intelligence Officer, with Lieutenant Meyrick looking after the plate-layers and half-castes.

The garrison was relieved by a force dispatched by sea from Cape Town under the Command of Colonel Cooper, though the immediate relief was carried out by a column of this force composed of 5th Lancers (109) 116th and 118th Companies Imperial Yeomanry (170); one squadron Cape Police and two guns of the 44th Battalion, all under command of Colonel Callwell.

134 *China War Medal* 10th June-31st December 1900

Obverse	The crowned and veiled head of Queen Victoria and legend, 'VICTORIA REGINA ET IMPERATRIX'
Reverse	A collection of war trophies, with an oval shield with the Royal Arms in the centre, all positioned under a palm tree. Above is the legend, 'ARMIS EXPOSCERE PACEM'. In the exergue is, 'CHINA 1900'
Size	36mm diameter
Metal	Silver and bronze
Ribbon	32mm wide. Crimson with yellow edges
Suspension	By a plain, straight swivelling suspender
Designer	Obverse—G. W. de Saulles. Reverse—W. Wyon
Naming	Indented in thin block capitals, and engraved in running script. Medals to the Navy impressed in slightly larger block capitals
Bars issued	Three: Taku Forts, Defence of Legations, Relief of Pekin. The maximum number of bars on any medal is two

The China War of 1900-01 is more commonly referred to as the 'Boxer Rebellion'. The Boxers formed a Chinese secret society known as the I-ho-ch'uan—the Society of Righteous and Harmonious Fists (hence 'Boxers'). The aim of the Boxers and other similar societies was to eradicate all foreigners and Christians from China; the government under Dowager Empress Tzu Hsi secretly supported these fanatical organisations.

Violence directed against foreigners and Christians mounted throughout 1899 and into 1900. Finally, with the foreign community in Pekin becoming increasingly at risk and with the unwillingness of the Chinese government to halt the growing anarchy, a small international force was landed on 10th June 1900 under Admiral E. H. Seymour. The force, some 2,000 strong attempted to relieve Pekin proceeding there by rail from Tientsin. Successful actions were fought at Lang-fan but at length they were compelled to retreat in the face of vastly superior numbers of Boxers and Chinese regulars. Retreating towards Tientsin, they captured the arsenal of Hsi-ku on 22nd June and held it until relieved on 26th June.

The Taku Forts were captured on the 17th June by the allied naval force and on the 14th July Tientsin was taken after considerable fighting.

Following the capture of the Taku Forts, the situation in Pekin worsened, the Empress ordered that all foreigners be killed and on 19th June the German Minister Baron Klemens von Kettler was murdered. The foreign and Christian community of Pekin then found themselves under siege centred upon the British Legation compound and the Pei-Tang Cathedral. The Legation guard consisted of 27 officers, 392 regulars and 125 volunteer civilians under the command of British Ambassador Sir Claude MacDonald.

Throughout the NE provinces, chiefly Shanxi, Jilin and Manchuria the slaughter of missionaries and thousands of Chinese Christians took place, one such being Roman Catholic Bishop Guillon who was burnt alive in Mukden.

By early August the allied force in Tientsin numbered some 20,000 and consisted of contingents from Great Britain, America, Austria, France, Germany, Italy, Japan and Russia. On 4th August the advance from Tientsin to Pekin was begun and on 5th August a Chinese force was defeated at Peit-sang.

Reaching Pekin on the 13th August the city was attacked and entered on the 14th and the defenders of the cathedral and legations who had been under incessant attack since 20th June were relieved. The next day the Imperial City was attacked and later occupied.

Punitive actions continued into 1901 and not until September 1901 was a protocol signed, ending hostilities.

Taku Forts 17th June 1900

Naval units, see table.

Defence of Legations 20th June-14th August 1900

Defence of Legations Medal Roll
British Legation:
R. E. Bredon, Depty Insp Gen Chinese Customs; Edwd Wyon, Supt Chinese Mint at Canton; Sir C. M. MacDonald, Minister; F. G. Poole, Capt; Wordsworth Poole, Doctor; H. G. M. Dening, 2nd Secretary; H. Cockburn, Chinese Secretary; W. P. Ker, Vice Consul; B. G. Towers, Asst Consular Service; W. P. M. Russell, Student Consular Service; D. Oliphant, Asst Consular Service; I. G. Hancock, Student Consular Service; A. J. Flaherty, Student Consular Service; H. G. Bristow, Student Consular Service; C. C. A. Kirke, Student Consular Service; H. Porter, Student Consular Service; W. N. Hewlett, Student Consular Service; C. A. W. Rose, Student Consular Service; R. D. Drury, Student Consular Service; L. H. R. Boron (?), Student Consular Service; L. Giles, Student Consular Service; W. E. Townsend, Student Consular Service; Sgt R. D. Hewing; T. B. Clarke Thornhill; W. Cowan, Office of Works; I. R. Brazier, Chinese Customs; C. H. Brewitt Taylor, Chinese Customs; I. H. Macoum, Chinese Customs; B. L. Simpson, Chinese Customs; A. G. Bethill, Chinese Customs; L. Sandercock, Chinese Customs; I. H. Smyth, Chinese Customs; C. Mears, Chinese Customs; A. F. Wintour, Chinese Customs; R. B. de Courcy, Chinese Customs; I. H. Richardson, Chinese Customs; W. S. Duprce, Chinese Customs; M. Honiton, Imperial China Bank; N.

Oliphant; I. K. Tweed; A. W. Brent; H. B. Bristow; G. E. Morrison; Capt P. Smith; Rev. F. Norris; Rev. R. Allen; A. Peel; G. B. Peachey; G. Backhouse; H. Warrin; Lt Col A. G. Churchill; I. Allardyce; P. Turner; S. M. Russell; Rev. T. Biggin; J. Baillie; Rev. J. Stonehouse.

Royal Navy and Royal Marines: Pte A. Alexander; L/Cpl T. R. Allin; L/Cpl W. G. Angel; Pte C. Baker; Pte W. Betts; Pte J. Buckler; Pte W. Cheshire; Pte F. J. Cresswell; Pte G. Davis; Pte J. Dean; Pte A. Dunkley; Pte W. Edney; Pte W. Ford; 2/SBStd R. G. Fuller; Pte G. Goddard; Cpl D. J. Gowney; Pte H. Grainger; Pte H. J. Green; Cpl W. Gregory; Pte S. W. Haden; Capt (RMLI) L. S. T. Halliday; Pte W. R. Harding; Pte J. W. Heap; Pte R. Hendicott; Pte D. Hill; Pte W. Horne; Pte J. G. Howard; Pte W. J. Hunt; Pte C. Johnson; Cpl J. Johnson; Pte A. Jones; L/Cpl A. Jones; Pte G. T. Jones; Pte K. King; Pte A. J. Layton; Pte G. Lister; Pte J. Marriott; Pte J. Masters; Pte A. G. Mayo; Pte J. Mears; Pte S. Mellows; Sgt J. Murphy; Pte J. Murray; Pte J. D. Newland; Pte J. Ormiston; Pte C. W. Phillips; Pte J. F. Pitts;. Pte E. E. Powell; Sgt J. E. Preston; Pte A. S. Roberts; Pte W. G. Roe; Pte P. A. Rose; Pte J. Rumble; L/Cpl H. J. Salvin; Pte H. Sands; Sgt A. E. Saunders; Pte A. G. Sawyer; Pte A. Scadding; Cpl G. Sheppard; Pte G. Shilliam; Pte F. G. Smith; Pte W. Smith; L/Cpl W. J. Sparkes; Capt (RMLI) B. M. Strouts; L/Sig H. Swannell; Pte F. Tanner; Pte W. A. Taylor; Arm J. T. Thomas; Pte A. J. Tickner; Pte W. Turner; Pte W. Viney; Pte J. W. Walker; Bugler A. F. Webb; Pte E. Webb; Pte H. A. Webster; Pte A. E. Westbrook; Pte W. T. Woodward; Capt (RMLI) E. Wray.

Duplicate medals: Pte G. T. Jones; Pte J. Mears; Pte G. Forrester; Pte J. Greenfield; Pte J. A. Myers; Pte E. G. O'Neill.

Relief of Pekin 10th June-14th August 1900

Royal Navy: see table.

Army units present: 12 Battery RFA; R/7 Ammunition Column; 2, 4 Batteries Hong Kong/Singapore Bn RGA (2 guns, 4 maxims); Royal Engineers; RMLI (300); Royal Welsh Fusiliers (300); 1 Bengal Lancers (400); 7 Bengal Infantry (500); 24 Punjab Infantry (300); 1 Sikhs (500); Hong Kong Regiment (100); Chinese Regiment (100).

In addition, Royal Irish Rifles (4), Royal Warwickshire Regt (7), and men from several regiments from India for duty as telegraphists and hospital orderlies.

Medals to J. Shepherd, Hampshire Regt and Sgt Sims, 2 Bn Border Regiment are known.

Other units present: (bar entitlement unknown)

Cavalry: 1, 16 Bengal Lancers; 3 Bombay Cavalry; 1 Jodhpur Lancers. Artillery: B. Batt RHA (153); R/2, Ammunition Column (5); 1, 2, 3, (43), 4 (45), 5 (45) Maxim Gun Sections; Vickers Maxim Battery (131); 15 Siege Train Western Division RGA (97); 62 Co (194), 91 Co (218) 92 Co RGA; Royal Engineers, Sappers and Miners.

British Infantry: Norfolk Regiment (24), Beds and Herts (11-no bar), Cheshire Regiment (12), 2 Royal Welsh Fusiliers (530), Rifle Brigade (7).

Native Infantry: 4, 14, 20, 24 Sikhs; 3, 28, 31 Madras Infantry; 2, 6, 7, 9, 26 Bengal Infantry; 4, 20, 24 Punjab Infantry; 22, 26, 30 Bombay Infantry; Alwar and Bikanir Infantry; 1/4 Gurkhas; 26 Baluchistan Infantry; 4 Bengal, 2 Bombay, 3 Madras Cos Sappers and Miners; Maler Kotla Sappers and Miners; 1 Madras, 34 Punjab Pioneers; 8 Mule Corps; Shanghai Volunteers; Wei Hai Wei Volunteers (31); Teintsin Volunteers (65); Newchang Volunteers (34); 1 Chinese Regiment; Hong Kong Volunteer Corps (37).

Civilians: Doctors; lady nurses (15—without bar); native servants (bronze medal); St John Ambulance Brigade serving aboard the American hospital ship *Maine* (14).

Two Victoria Crosses were awarded for this campaign, these being to Capt L. S. T. Halliday, RMLI; and Midshipman B. J. D. Guy, HMS *Barfleur*, RN.

The former for the Defence of Legations and the latter for the attack on Tientsin.

Name of Ship or unit	Defence of Legations	Taku Forts and Relief of Pekin	Taku Forts	Relief of Pekin	No bar	Total
HMS *Alacrity*		42	8	1	87	138
HMS *Algerine*		9	94	1	9	113
HMS *Arethusa*					306	306
HMS *Aurora*		46	10	258	231	545
HMS *Barfleur*		70	22	272	398	762
HMS *Bonaventure*					342	342
HMS *Centurion*		20	8	390	332	750
HMS *Daphne*					136	136
HMS *Dido*					460	460
HMS *Endymion*		25	10	280	288	603
HMS *Esk*					95	95
HMS *Fame*		3	58	1	3	65
HMS *Goliath*		1		1	760	762
HMS *Hart*					56	56
HMS *Hermione*		1			332	333
HMS *Humber*					103	103
HMS *Isis*					432	432
HMS *Linnet*					95	95
HMS *Marathon*					226	226
HMS *Orlando*		81	35	194	220	530
HMS *Peacock*		1			81	82
HMS *Phoenix*				13	102	115
HMS *Pigmy*					74	74
HMS *Pique*					289	289
HMS *Plover*					74	74
HMS *Redpole*					72	72
HMS *Rosario*					109	109
HMS *Snipe*					20	20
HMS *Terrible*				263	706	969
HMS *Undaunted*					512	512
HMS *Wallaroo*					219	219
HMS *Waterwitch*					80	80
HMS *Whiting*				55	9	64
HMS *Woodcock*					44	44
HMS *Woodlark*					37	37
Legation Guard	78					78
NW Fort, Taku					194	194
Naval Depot, Wei-Hai-Wei				72	99	171
New South Wales Naval Defence Force					250	250
South Australian Naval Defence Force					102	102
Victorian Naval Defence Force					197	197
RIMS *Canning*					143	143
RIMS *Clive*					185	185
RIMS *Dalhousie*					118	118
RIM Ship not specified				10	14	24
Miscellaneous				3	5	8
Total	78	299	245	1814	8646	11082

135   *Transport Medal* 1899-1902

Obverse	Bust of King Edward VII in Naval uniform and legend, 'EDWARDVS VII REX IMPERATOR'
Reverse	HMT *Ophir,* above which is part of the map of the world and the Latin inscription 'OB PATRIAM MILITIBUS PER MARE TRANSVECTIS ADJUTAM'. (For services rendered in transporting troops by sea.)
Size	36mm diameter
Metal	Silver
Ribbon	32mm wide. Red with two blue stripes. On the ribbon the stripes are nearer the edges than on the I.G.S. 1854 Medal, otherwise the colours are the same.
Suspension	By a plain, straight, swivelling suspender.
Designer	Obverse—G. W. de Saulles; Reverse—The design was supplied by the Admiralty.
Naming	Impressed in block letters. Only the recipient's name is given; neither his rank nor the ship on which he served is mentioned. There are, however, official rolls in existence for the purposes of verification.
Bars issued	Two—S. Africa 1899-1902 and China 1900.

This medal was sanctioned on 8th November, 1903, for award to the Master, 1st, 2nd and 3rd Officers, 1st, 2nd and 3rd Engineers, Pursers and Surgeons of merchant vessels employed in the Transport Service which took troops to the South African War and to the Boxer Rebellion in China. One hundred and seventeen transports and eleven hospital ships were used in the above two campaigns.

Medals Received	S. Africa	China	S. Africa & China	Total
Masters	122	38	34	194
Officers	515	145	71	731
Engineers	475	135	66	676
Surgeons	68	4	1	73
Pursers	39	0	6	45
TOTALS	1219	322	178	1719

Table by courtesy of W. H. Fevyer.

A total of 118 medals were returned to the Royal Mint being unclaimed.

The medal was to have been issued in future wars to officers of the Mercantile Marine serving in transports. However this intention was not proceeded with and for the Great War the Mercantile Marine Medal was issued to both officers and men.

Men from the following ships were awarded medals.

Algeria, America, American, Antillian, Arawa, Ariosto, Armenian, Ashruf, Assaye, Atlantian, Aurania, Austral, Avoca, Ballaarat, Bavarian, Booldana, Britannic, British Prince, British Princess, Canada, Canning, Carthage, Carthaginian, Catalonia, Cavour, Cepalonia, Cestrian, Cheshire, Chicago, Chingtu, City of Cambridge, City of London, City of Rome, City of Vienna, Clavering, Colombian, Custodian, Cymric, Dictator, Dilwara, Dominion, Duke of Portland, Dunera, Ellora, Englishman, Fazilka, Formosa, Formosa, Fultala, Glengyle, Golconda, Gwalior, Haiching, Harlech Castle, Hawarden Castle, Henzada, Hilarious, Hinsang, Idaho, India, Ionian, Islanda, Itaura, Itinda, Itola, Itria, Jamaican, Jelunga, Kaifong, Kent, Kildonan Castle, Lake Erie, Lake Manitoba, Lalpoora, Landaura, Laurentian, Lawada, Lindula, Lismore Castle, Loodiana, Mahratta, Maine, Majestic, Malta, Manchester Corporation, Manchester Merchant, Manchester Port, Manhattan, Manila, Maplemore, Matiana,
Milwaukee, Mohawk, Mombassa, Mongolian, Monteagle, Monterey, Montfort, Montrose, Muttra, Nairung, Nankin, Narrung, Nawab, Nerbudda, Nevasa, Nile, Nizam, Norseman, Nowshera, Nubia, Nuddea, Nurani, Orcana, Orient, Orissa, Orotava, Ortona, Palamcotta, Palawan, Palitana, Pavonia, Pekin, Pentakota, Persia, Pindari, Pinemore, Plassy, Pomeranian, Princess of Wales, Pundua, Purnea, Putiala, Rajah, Ranee, Rapidan, Rewa, Roslin Castle, St. Andrew, Salamis, Sardinia, Secundra, Servia, Shengking, Siberian, Sicilia, Sicilian, Simla, Sirsa, Soudan, Spartan, Staffordshire, Sumatra, Sunda, Sutlej, Syria, Tagua, Taisang, Templemore, Trojan, Uganda, Ujina, Ula, Ulstermore, Umbria, Umta, Upada, Urlana, Urmston Grange, Vadala, Victorian, Virawa, Wakool, Wardha, Warora, Winifredian, Winkfield, Yorkshire, Zamania, Zayathla, Zibenghla.

136 *Ashanti Medal* 31st March-25th December 1900

Obverse	Bust of King Edward VII facing left, with the legend, 'EDWARDVS VII REX IMPERATOR'.
Reverse	The British Lion standing on a rock looking left towards the rising sun; below are a native shield and two assegais, and a scroll bearing the word 'ASHANTI'.
Size	36mm in diameter
Metal	Issued in silver and bronze
Ribbon	33mm wide. Black with two dark green stripes 9mm wide.
Suspension	By a straight suspender
Designer	G. W. de Saulles
Naming	Impressed in rather small square capitals, officer's medals are also seen engraved in script.
Bars issued	One—for Kumassi

This medal, the first awarded in the reign of Edward VII, was sanctioned in October 1901, to be awarded to all who had participated in the suppression of the Ashanti rising between 31st March and 25th December, 1900.

The medals, issued in silver and bronze, are to be found in both high and low relief. Those in low relief bear the designer's initials, 'DeS' on the obverse.

After the expedition of 1895-96 (for which the Ashanti Star was awarded) there had been comparative peace but no lack of ill-feeling. The 'Golden Stool', was regarded by the natives as the soul of the Ashanti nation, whilst to most Europeans, including the Governor, Sir Frederic Hodgson it was regarded as a symbol of authority and rallying point of Ashanti discontent. To remove the threat it was decided, therefore, that this Stool should be captured and Captain Armitage set off with a small force to locate it. However, the natives, getting wind of this, attacked the force and rose in rebellion.

They besieged the Governor and his wife, Sir Frederic and Lady Hodgson, in Kumassi. Captain Middlemist, with a force of one hundred and seven men, broke through on the 18th of April and Captain Aplin, with another force of two hundred and forty-five, broke through on the 29th. Major Morris, with two hundred and thirty-six reinforcements got through on the 15th of May, by which time the situation in Kumassi had become very serious because of starvation, disease and casualties.

On the 23rd of June, Sir Frederic and Lady Hodgson, with a force of six hundred under Major Morris, and over a thousand non-combatants, left Kumassi. Captains Bishop and Ralph were left behind with a garrison of about a hundred men.

A relief force under Brigadier-General Sir W. J. Willcocks, KCMG, relieved the town on the 15th of July. Leaving a small garrison, he took the worst of the sick and wounded back to Bekwai. A further relief force, under Colonel A. P. Burroughs, relieved Kumassi on the 5th of August.

The fighting continued until the chiefs surrendered in December.

The Boer War was at its height at this time, so that no European troops could be spared. There were, of course, European officers and NCOs; medals to the latter are found named with their parent units.

The nature of the fighting and the general conditions involved in this little-known campaign are well illustrated in the casualty returns. These show a total of fifty-eight British officers, ten British NCOs, and nine hundred natives during the nine months.

Two Victoria Crosses where awarded for this campaign these being to Sergeant John Mackenzie, DCM, 2nd Battalion 78th Highlanders (later Captain Royal Scots) and Captain Charles J. Melliss, ISC.

Units present: The HQ staff consisted of British officers, civilian doctors and political officers. The fighting troops were as follows: Four 75mm guns WAFF; four 7 pdr guns WIR; four Companies each of 1 and 2 WAFF; 2 Companies Southern Nigeria Regt; 6 Companies West Africa Regt; half Bn each of 1 and 2 Central African Regt (title altered to King's African Rifles on the 1st of January, 1902); Northern Nigeria Regt; Gold Coast Constabulary (700); Lagos Constabulary (300); Sierra Leone Frontier Police (50); Lagos Hausa Force and elements of the Indian Army (80).

The Munster Fusiliers received one single bar and eight no bar medals.

Thirty-six doctors received the medal, though not members of the forces at the time.

A medal with bar was awarded to the 45th Sikhs. The recipient was serving with the Central African Rifles at the time. Sixty Sikhs took part in the campaign, but the naming details are unknown.

A total of one hundred and eighty-three European officers, eighty NCOs, one hundred and thirty-one European civilians, three native officers and some four thousand native other ranks received the silver medal.

About nine hundred carriers were employed, all of whom were entitled to the bronze medal. There were also numerous levies who may have got them too.

Kumassi 31st March-15th July 1900

This bar was awarded to all who had garrisoned Kumassi at any time between 31st March and 15th July, and to those who were members of either of the relieving columns under Brigadier-General Willcocks or Colonel Burroughs.

137 *Africa General Service Medal* 1902-1956

Obverse	*1st issue:* King Edward VII in uniform, facing left, and legend: 'EDWARDVS VII REX IMPERATOR'. *2nd issue:* King George V in military uniform, facing left, and legend: 'GEORGIVS V BRITT: OMN: REX ET IND: IMP:' *3rd issue:* Queen Elizabeth II, facing right and legend: 'ELIZABETH·II·DEI·GRATIA·REGINA·F: D: +.'
Reverse	The standing figure of Britannia holding a trident in her right hand. In her left hand, which is extended, she holds an olive branch and a scroll. Behind her stands a lion and in the right background is the rising sun. In the exergue is the word 'AFRICA'.
Size	36mm diameter
Metal	Silver and bronze
Ribbon	32mm wide. Yellow edged with black and with two green stripes towards the centre.
Suspension	By a plain straight swivelling suspender. The exception being the medal with the bar 'Somaliland 1920' which has a non-swivelling suspender.
Designer	Reverse: G. W. de Saulles. Obverse: 1st issue G. W. de Saulles, 2nd issue unknown, 3rd issue Mrs Mary Gillick CBE.
Naming	In various impressed block capitals and script. Some locally named medals are to be found in irregular impressed capitals.
Bars issued	A total of forty-five bars issued. Thirty-four with the Edward VII obverse, ten with the George V obverse and one with that of Elizabeth II. *Edward VII:* N. Nigeria, N. Nigeria 1902, N. Nigeria 1903, N. Nigeria 1903-04, N. Nigeria 1904, N. Nigeria 1906, S. Nigeria, S. Nigeria 1902, S. Nigeria 1902-03, S. Nigeria 1903, S. Nigeria 1903-04, S. Nigeria 1904, S. Nigeria 1904-05, S. Nigeria 1905, S. Nigeria 1905-06, East Africa 1902, East Africa 1904, East Africa 1905, East Africa 1906, West Africa 1906, West Africa 1908, West Africa 1909-10, Somaliland 1901, Somaliland 1902-04, Somaliland 1908-10, Jidballi, Uganda 1900, BCA 1899-1900, Jubaland, Gambia, Aro 1901-02, Lango 1901, Kissi 1905, Nandi 1905-06. *George V:* Shimber Berris 1914-15, Nyasaland 1915, East Africa 1913, East Africa 1913-14, East Africa 1914, East Africa 1915, East Africa 1918, Jubaland 1917-18, Nigeria 1918, Somaliland 1920. *Elizabeth II:* Kenya.

This silver medal (occasionally issued in bronze) was sanctioned in 1902 to replace the East and West Africa Medal to which twenty-two bars had been awarded. The medal was never issued without a bar and medals are known with seven or more. The 1st issue medal was struck in high and low relief. The pieces of the second issue are thinner than those of the first.

Troops which took part in operations for which the Africa General Service Medal was awarded during the period of the First World War were not entitled to receive any 1914-18 war medals. However troops eligible for the Africa General Service Medal could also be entitled to 1914-18 war medals, having passed though a designated First World War theatre of war (see p. 230).

There are genuine medals in existence to Indian units that cannot be traced as having been present. It is suggested therefore, that there must have been occasions when the medal was impressed with the name of the unit that the man was serving with before he left India, or after his return.

Indians selected from several units of the Indian Army were employed with the African regiments.

On 1st January, 1902, the various local East African forces were amalgamated into the King's African Rifles. The following list gives the former title of the battalions:

1st Bn KAR, formerly the 1st Bn Central Africa Rifles.
2nd Bn KAR, formerly the 2nd Bn Central Africa Rifles.
3rd Bn KAR, formerly the East Africa Rifles.
4th Bn KAR, formerly the 1st Bn. Uganda Rifles.
5th Bn KAR, formerly the 2nd Bn Uganda Rifles.
6th Bn KAR, formerly the various local forces in the Somaliland Protectorate. In 1909 this battalion was disbanded and was replaced by the Somaliland Camel Constabulary, which was later renamed the Somaliland Camel Corps.

The above change in title was not strictly adhered to and medals may be found which have the pre-1902 designation.

N. Nigeria July 1900-September 1901

A total of 365 of these bars, which bear no date, were awarded to members of the Northern Nigeria Regiment for service in any of the following operations:
a) Operations against the forces of Bida and Kontagora under Major W. H. O'Neill, RA, from July to December, 1900; or under Major G. V. Kemball, RA, from 19th January 1900 to 17th February 1901.
b) The expedition against the Chief of Tawaria under Major A. W. Cole, Royal Welch Fusiliers, from 6th to 8th December 1900.
c) Operations against the Emir of Yola under Lieutenant-Colonel T. L. N. Morland, KRRC, in August and September 1901.

N. Nigeria 1902 1st February-16th May and 15th June-30th November 1902

A total of 535 of these bars were awarded to members of a further expedition under Lieutenant-Colonel T. L. N. Morland, KRRC, to Bornu which lasted from 1st February to 16th May 1902, and also to members of the Kontagora Force, which operated between 12th and 20th February 1902.
Army Order No. 4 of 1905 sanctioned the award of this bar to those under the command of Captain G. C. Merrick, RA, at Argungu and on French convoy duty between 15th June and 30th November 1902.
The 1st and 2nd Northern Nigeria Regiment composed most of the forces.

N. Nigeria 1903 29th January-27th July 1903

In October 1903, sanction was granted for the award of 734 bars to members of an expedition to Kano and Sokoto, under General Kemball, between 29th January and 15th March 1903. In April 1905, it was decided that all who had operated between Sokoto and Birni between 15th April and 27th July 1903, should also be awarded this bar.
The recipients were as follows: twenty-four British officers; twelve British NCOs; and natives of the 1st and 2nd Northern Nigeria Regiments, S. Nigeria Regiment and 4th (Lagos) Bn. West African Frontier Force.
A Victoria Cross was awarded for this expedition that being to Lieutenant Wallace D. Wright, Queens Regt.

N. Nigeria 1903-04 23rd December 1903-12th March 1904

Three hundred silver and four hundred bronze medals were awarded to members of the Bassa Expedition under Captain G. C. Merrick, RA, between 23rd December 1903, and 12th March 1904. Members of the 2nd Northern Nigeria Regiment received over two hundred silver medals. Four hundred bronze medals were awarded to native carriers. The Northern Nigeria Constabulary received the silver medal.

N. Nigeria 1904 March-October 1904

This bar was awarded for the following expeditions:
a) Under the command of Lieutenant S. B. B. Dyer, DSO, 2nd Life Guards, in the Dakka Kerri country in March 1904.
(b) Under the command of Lieutenant (local Captain) P. M. Short, Gloucestershire Regiment, against the pagan tribes who occupied the country north of Wase on the high road from the Bauchi between 25th March and 18th April 1904.
(c) Under the command of Captain G. C. Merrick, DSO, Royal Artillery, against the people of Semolika in October 1904.
(d) Under the command of Lieutenant I. G. Sewell, Royal Fusiliers, against the Kilba tribe north of Yola in July 1904.
The recipients consisted of British officers and NCOs and members of the 1st and 2nd Northern Nigeria Regiments.

N. Nigeria 1906 14th February-24th April 1906

This bar was awarded for the following expeditions:
(a) Under the command of Lieutenant F. E. Blackwood, East Surrey

Regiment and Captain R. H. Goodwin, Royal Artillery who took part in the operations against the Satiru rebels near Sokoto from 14th February to 11th March 1906.
(b) Under the command of Colonel A. W. G. Lowry Cole, DSO, Northern Nigerian Regiment West African Frontier Force, who took part in the operations against the Emir of Hadeija from the 16th to 24th April 1906.
In the Sokoto campaign the recipients consisted of British officers and NCOs and members of the 1st and 2nd Northern Nigeria Regiments.
In the Hadeija campaign recipients consisted of British officers and NCOs and the 1st, 2nd and 3rd Northern Nigeria Regiments.

S. Nigeria March-May 1901

This bar was awarded to members of the Southern Nigeria Regiments who took part in the Ishan and Ulia Expeditions under Captain W. C. G. Heneker, Connaught Rangers, between March and May 1901.
Recipients consisted of British officers and NCOs and the Southern Nigeria Regiment.

S. Nigeria 1902 15th June-30th December 1902

This bar was awarded for the following expeditions:
a) Under the command of Capt. P. K. Carre, Royal Warwickshire Regiment, in the Ngor country in July 1902.
b) Under the command of Capt. A. J. Campbell, DSO, 19th Hussars, in the Ebeku country in September 1902.
c) Under the command of Capt. A. D. G. Grayson, Royal Artillery, in the Ikwe country in October, 1902.
d) Under the command of Brevet Lieut-Colonel W. C. G. Heneker, DSO, Connaught Rangers, in the Ibeku Olokoro country between the 26th October and 8th December 1902.
e) Under the command of Captain and Brevet-Major I. G. Hogg. DSO, 4th Hussars, in the Ibekwe country in October 1902.
f) Under the command of Captain and Brevet-Major W. J. Venour, DSO, Royal Dublin Fusiliers, in the Nsit country in December, 1902.
g) Under the command of Captain and Brevet-Major H. C. Moorhouse, Royal Artillery, in the Asaba hinterland in December 1902.
Recipients consisted of British officers and NCOs and members of the Southern Nigeria Regiment.

S. Nigeria 1902-03 7th July 1902-8th June 1903

This bar was awarded to members of the Southern Nigeria Regiment for service under Colonel A. F. Montanaro, CB, RA, against the Uris and the people of Omonoha and Ebima between 7th July 1902 and 8th June 1903. It was also awarded for operations under Lieutenant-Colonel W. C. G. Heneker, DSO, Connaught Rangers, against Chief Adukukaiku of Igarra and further operations in the Afikpo district in December 1902, and January 1903.
Medals were also awarded to six civilians and four doctors.

S. Nigeria 1903 4th February-5th December 1903

This bar was awarded to members of the Southern Nigeria Regiment for the following expeditions:
a) Under Brevet-Colonel A. F. Montanaro, CB, RA, on the Nun river in September and October.
b) Under Brevet-Major A. M. N. Mackenzie, RA in the Eket district between 16th and 25th September.
c) Under Brevet-Major A. M. N. Mackenzie, RA, in the Mkpani country from the 1st to the 5th December.
Army Order No. 40 of 1906 extended the award of this bar to include the following operations:
d) Under Captain H. H. Sproule, 4th Cavalry, in the Ebegga country in February.
e) Under Captain E. L. Roddy, Cheshire Regiment, in the country west of Anan in March.
Medals were also awarded to doctors and civilians in the political service.

S. Nigeria 1903-04 24th December 1903-15th January 1904

his bar was awarded to members of the Southern Nigeria Regiment for the expediton, under Brevet-Major I. G. Hogg, DSO, 4th Hussars, to the towns of Osea, Oriri and N'doto.

S. Nigeria 1904 12th January-3rd June 1904

his bar was awarded for the following expeditions:
a) Under the command of Brevet-Colonel A. F. Montanaro, CB, Royal Artillery, and Captain H. C. MacDonald, Argyll and Sutherland Highlanders, in the Northern Ibibio district between 12th January and the 31st March, 1904.
b) Under the command of Brevet-Major I. G. Hogg, DSO, 4th Hussars, against the natives of the Asaba hinterland between the 17th January and 25th April 1904.
c) Under the command of Brevet-Major I. G. Hogg, DSO, 4th Hussars, in the Kwale country between 21st March and 24th April.
d) Under the command of Brevet-Major H. M. Trenchard, Royal Scots Fusiliers, in the Owerri district on the right bank of the Imo River, in March 1904.
e) Under the command of Captain H. H. Sproule, 4th Cavalry, and Lieutenant R. D. Whigham, Lancashire Fusiliers at Obokum and the patrol under Brevet-Major H. M. Trenchard, Royal Scots Fusiliers, between 3rd February and 3rd June 1904.
   Medals were awarded to British officers and NCOs and members of the Southern Nigeria Regiment.

S. Nigeria 1904-05 15th November 1904-27th February 1905

This bar was awarded to the Southern Nigeria Regiment for operations under Brevet-Major H. M. Trenchard, Royal Scots Fusiliers, through the Ibibio and Kwa country.
   Medals were also awarded to British officers and NCOs and civilians.

S. Nigeria 1905 10th-18th October 1905

This bar was awarded to members of the Southern Nigeria Regiment for operations in the Kwale district, under Brevet Major Maclear.
   Recipients of the bar were not entitled to the S. Nigeria 1905-06 bar.
   Only twelve single bar medals were issued, a further sixty-six bars are found in multiple bar combinations.

S. Nigeria 1905-06

Army Order No. 277 of 1906, which authorized the issue of this bar, does not state the inclusive dates of the operations for which it was awarded. The award was for officers and men of the columns which concentrated at Bende and Oka under Brevet-Major H. M. Trenchard, Royal Scots Fusiliers, and Captain G. T. Mair, RFA, and took part in the Bende-Onitsha Hinterland Expedition.
   Medals were issued to British officers and NCOs, doctors and political officers and members of the Southern Nigeria Regiment.

East Africa 1902 4th September-25th October 1902

This bar was awarded for the Maruka Patrol under Lieutenant F. W. O. Maycock, Suffolk Regiment, against the Kikuyu tribe.
   A total of 78 bars were awarded to British officers, political officers (5), 3rd KAR and East Africa Police.

East Africa 1904 13th February-17th March 1904

This scarce bar was awarded to members of the Iraini Patrol under Captain F. A. Dickinson, DCLI, which operated between 13th February and 17th March 1904.
   Bars were awarded to British officers, political officers, 3rd KAR and East Africa Police.

East Africa 1905 31st May-9th October 1905

This bar was awarded to members of two expeditions; the first, under Major L. R. H. Pope-Hennessy, DSO, Oxford and Bucks Light Infantry, to Sotik between 31st May and 12th July, 1905; the second under Captain E. V. Jenkins, DSO, The Duke of Wellington's Regiment, to Kissi between 1st September and 9th October, 1905.
   Bars were awarded to officers, political officers, 3rd KAR, East Africa Police, medical and transport staff.

East Africa 1906 18th June-19th July 1906

This bar was awarded to members of the 3rd King's African Rifles and East African Police who accompanied Lieutenant F. W. O. Maycock, DSO, to the Embu Territory between 18th June and 19th July, 1906.
   Bars were also awarded to British officers and political officers.

West Africa 1906 9th June 1906-17th February 1907

This bar was awarded to members of the punitive expedition, under Captain W. C. E. Rudkin, DSO, RFA, which operated in the Owa Territory between 9th June and 3rd August 1906.
   It was also awarded for two other small expeditions under Lieutenants P. Chapman and E. J. Worsley, which operated between 12th November 1906, and 17th February 1907.
   The recipients were members of the Southern Nigeria Regiment and 2nd Northern Nigeria Regiment.

West Africa 1908 11th-31st December 1908

This bar was awarded to members of the Southern Nigeria Regiment who operated in the Sonkwala district between 11th and 31st December 1908, under Lieutenant-Colonel G. F. A. Whitlock, RE.
   Bars were also awarded to British officers, NCOs and political officers. Forty-three medals were awarded to German Colonial troops from the Cameroons who assisted in the operations.

West Africa 1909-10 2nd November 1909-27th May 1910

This bar was awarded to members of the Southern Nigeria Regiment and Southern Nigeria Police for operations in the Ogwashi-Oku country under Major G. N. Sheffield, 3rd Bn. Essex Regiment, between 2nd November and 18th December 1909 and between 6th January and 24th April 1910, and for a further expedition under Major G. L. Bruce between 4th and 27th May 1910.
   Bars were also issued to British officers, NCOs, political officers and medical personnel.

Somaliland 1901 22nd May-30th July 1901

This bar was awarded for the first expedition against the 'Mad Mullah' Mohammed Abdullah, which lasted from 22nd May to 30th July, 1901. It was commanded by Colonel E. J. E. Swayne, who had under his command twenty-one British officers, fifty Punjabis and about 1,500 Somali levies.
   This is a very rare bar which the Somali levies received in silver or bronze according to whether they fulfilled a combatant or non-combatant role.
   Mohammed Abdullah, claiming to be the Mahdi, first began to wage his religious war against the British in 1899.

Somaliland 1902-04 18th January 1902-11th May 1904

Between 18th January 1902 and 11th May 1904, there were three more expeditions against the 'Mad Mullah' for which both silver and bronze medals were awarded.
   The bar was also granted to those officers and men accompanying Colonel A. N. Rochfort, CB, CMG, with the Abyssinian forces: Royal Navy, King's Liverpool Regiment (14).

Those who took part in the Battle of Jidballi or who acted as baggage guard on the 10th January 1904 received an additional bar 'Jidballi'.

Second Expedition (8th February to 17th October 1902, under Colonel E. J. E. Swayne): British Staff Officers (12): 1 King's African Rifles (Sikhs) (60); 2 King's African Rifles (Yaos) (300); 6 King's African Rifles (Somalis) (500); Mounted Infantry (450) and Camelry; 1 and 2 Bombay Grenadiers.

Third Expedition (4th November 1902, to 3rd July 1903): 4 King's Royal Rifle Corps (147); Mounted Infantry; Somaliland Burgher Corps; Punjab Mounted Infantry; 8 or 28 (Lahore) Mountain Battery (65); King's African Rifles Camel Battery (45); Telegraph Section RE (58); Bikanir Camel Corps; 107 Bombay Pioneers (737); 1 (Sikhs), 2 (Yaos), 3 (Sudanese), 5 (Sikhs) 6 (Somalis), King's African Rifles; 23 Bombay Rifles (400); 2 (later renumbered 52) Sikhs; 15 British and 58, 65, 69 Native Field Hospitals; 15 Company, ASC.

Fourth Expedition (26th October 1903 to 25th April 1904): All the above troops were present and the following additional ones: 1 Bn Hampshire Regiment (326); R. Warwicks (Lieutenant G. D. Martin, 1 Sgt, 1 Cpl and 25 Ptes); Essex Regiment (45); 17 and 19 Companies Bombay Sappers and Miners; 27 Punjabis.

This bar is also found to the Yorkshire Regiment and a few others including 2nd R. Dgns (2), King's Liverpool Regiment (14) and Norfolk Regiment (28—1 to an Officer & 27 to other ranks). A medal is known named to the corps of Military Staff Clerks.

Naval medals were awarded to those engaged in Somaliland between 18th January 1902 and 11th May 1904, and to those who accompanied Colonel A. N. Rochfort, CB, CMG, with the Abyssinian forces. The award to the Navy included all those serving on HM ships employed in connection with the operations within the limits of a sphere comprising the Somaliland coast from Berbera to Mogadishu and including Aden, but excluded those serving in torpedo boats.

HMS Cossack (215), Dryad (137), Fox (404), Harrier (153), Highflyer (536), Hussar (145), Hyacinth (553), Merlin (143), Mohawk (205), Naiad (285), Perseus (329), Pomone (310), Porpoise (237), Redbreast (81). Royal Indian Marine ships: Canning, Dalhousie, Mayo. Hospital ship: Hardinge. Royal Italian Navy (2: Capt E. Finzi and Cmdr L. Stanisla)

Naval medals were also awarded to locally recruited crewmen (seedies and native interpreters).

Eighty-seven medals were authorized with bars Somaliland 1902-04 and Somaliland 1908-10.

Five Victoria Crosses were awarded for this expedition: Capt Act Lt-Col Alexander S. Cobbe, DSO, IA; Capt John E. Gough, Rifle Brigade; Lieut Clement L. Smith, 2 Bn, DCLI; Capt William G. Walker, IA; and Capt George M. Rolland, IA.

Jidballi 10th January 1904

This bar was awarded to those who took part in the engagement and to those who formed part of the guard left behind during it in charge of the baggage under the command of Major W. B. Mullins, 27th Punjabis.

Those who received it also received the bar 'Somaliland 1902-04', so that this bar is not found singly. The units that follow would be entitled to both bars.

Regiments present: Poona, Umballa and 5 Indian Mounted Infantry; Gadabursi Horse; Bikanir Camel Corps; 8 or 28 (Lahore) Mountain Battery (65); King's African Rifles Camel Battery (45); 19 Company Bombay Sappers and Miners; 1 Hants (259); sections of the Royal Warwickshire Regiment (12); Liverpool Regiment (14); Norfolk Regiment, Essex Regiment, York and Lancs Regiment, Yorkshire Regiment, 2 Middlesex Regiment, 4 KRRC (105), and the Rifle Brigade; 1, 2, 3 King's African Rifles; 27 Punjabis; 2 Sikhs (later renumbered 52); Arab Police Corps.

Medals bearing this bar are to be found to NCOs of regiments not given above. They were instructors to the King's African Rifles or in charge of some of the native labour and carrier units.

The only Naval recipient of this bar was Commander E. S. Carey, of HMS Naiad.

A Victoria Cross to Lieutenant H. A. Carter, Indian Army, was awarded for this action.

Somaliland 1908-10 19th August 1908-31st January 1910

This bar was awarded for further services, under Colonel J. E. Gough, VC, CMG, against the rebellious Somalis.

Regiments present: 1, 3, 4, 6 King's African Rifles; 66 Punjab Infantry; 127 Baluch Light Infantry and 129 Baluchis (The medals so named were awarded to men who served with the 127th Regiment during the campaign) Wilde's Rifles; Sikh FF.

Ships of the Mediterranean Fleet and East Indies Squadron were employed in the blockade of the Somali coast in connection with the operations. The bar was granted to all who took part in the patrolling, or at Aden between 19th August 1908, and 31st January 1910. Occasional visits did not, however, count for the award.

HMS Barham (210), Diana (411), Fox (350), Hyacinth (532), Philomel (482), Prosperine (457). Royal Indian Marine ship Hardinge.

Uganda 1900 3rd July-October 1900

This bar was awarded for operations in the Nandi Country, under Lieutenant-Colonel J. T. Evatt, DSO, Indian Staff Corps. The recipients were fifty-five officers and NCOs and eight hundred and eighteen members of the 4th KAR.

B.C.A. 1899-1900 August 1899-December 1900

This bar, for British Central Africa, was awarded for services in any of the following operations:
(a) Operations against Nkwamba from August to October, 1899, under Captain F. B. Pearce, West Yorks.
(b) Operations in North Eastern Rhodesia against Kazembe from September to November 1899.
(c) Operations in central Angoniland, against Kalulu in December 1900, under Captain R. Bright, The Buffs.

Regiments present: 24 Punjab Infantry; 34, 45 Sikhs; 1 King's African Rifles, Central African Rifles. Also present were British officers, volunteers, staff and medical personnel.

Jubaland 16th November 1900-30th April 1901

This bar was awarded for service under Colonel T. Ternan, against the Ogaden Somalis, including military forces at Kismayu and to officers and men of the Royal Navy and Marines who landed to supplement the garrison at Kismayu between 16th November 1900, and 30th April 1901. The number of medals awarded to Indian troops were about four hundred and sixty-five silver and twenty-six bronze. The medals to African troops were usually marked with the recipient's number and name only.

Regiments present: One section of No. 9 (Murree) Mountain Battery (93); 16 Bombay Infantry; King's African Rifles; Aden Camel Corps; Supply and Transport Corps (the only medals that are known have been of bronze).

HMS Magicienne (172), Scout (15), and Terpsichore (15).

Gambia January-March 1901

This bar was awarded to those who took part in the operations under Lieutenant-Colonel H. E. J. Brake, CB, DSO, RA. The Naval awards were limited to a few officers, petty officers and seamen who were under fire in the action at Dumbutu on 11th January 1901. Those engaged in patrolling rivers, or transporting troops, were not eligible, so that the crews of HMS Magicienne, Scout and Terpsichore, though present, were not rewarded.

Regiments present: RMLI (4); 2 King's African Rifles; 3 West Indian Regiment and District Commissioners who served with the Gambia Expeditionary Force received this bar.

HMS Forte (29); Thrush (49); Dwarf (2); Transport Service (2).

Aro 1901-1902 15th November 1901-23rd March 1902

The rather unusual dating of this bar should be noted, the second date being repeated in full. This bar was issued to fourteen British Military

Officers and 1,830 native soldiers in addition to the Naval personnel mentioned below. Eleven District Commissioners and officers of the Niger Police were also present, with the Aro Expeditionary Force under Lieutenant-Colonel A. F. Montanaro, RGA.

Regiments present: 4 (Lagos) and 5 Southern Nigeria Regiment; 1, 2 Northern Nigeria Regiment.

HMS *Thrush* (54); S. Nigerian Gunboat *Jackdaw* (29).

Lango 1901 24th April-24th August 1901

This bar was awarded to members of a punitive expedition under Major C. Delme-Radcliffe, Connaught Rangers, against Sudanese mutineers between 24th April and 24th August 1901. The only regiment to participate was the 4th Bn. King's African Rifles (381). Bars were also given to British officers and NCOs and the Buganda Levy.

Kissi 1905 27th March-28th June 1905

This rare bar was awarded to members of the Sierra Leone Bn of the West African Frontier Force (326) who operated in the Kissi Country under Captain C. E. Palmer, RA, between 27th March and 28th June, 1905.

Bars were also given to British officers and NCOs and members of the British Consulate at Monrovia.

Nandi 1905-06 18th October 1905-6th July 1906

This very rare bar was awarded for service in Nandi Country under Lieutenant-Colonel E. G. Harrison DSO, Reserve of Officers, Major Walker, Royal Fusiliers, and Capt Mackay, Seaforth Highlanders.

Regiments present: 1, 3 4 King's African Rifles; East African Police Force.

Medals are known to an officer whose unit is given as the Mombasa Defence Force, and another to Captain B. R. Graham, QO Corps of Guides.

Shimber Berris 1914-15 19th November 1914-9th February 1915

This bar was awarded for two small campaigns against the Dervishes from 19th to 25th November 1914, and again from 2nd to 9th February 1915, under Lieutenant-Colonel T. A. Cubitt, DSO, RA.

This is a rare bar, though the total number of officers and men who must have been entitled to silver medals was about eight hundred and twenty.

Regiments present: King's African Rifles (250); 23 Sikh Pioneers (30); Somaliland Camel Corps (450).

Nyasaland 1915 24th January-17th February 1915

This bar was awarded to a few members of the 1st King's African Rifles, a few of the Nyasaland Volunteer Reserve, and native policemen and others from Blantyre and Ncheu, who quelled a small rising in the Shire Highlands between 24th January and 17th February 1915.

East Africa 1913 17th June-7th August 1913

This bar was awarded for operations under Captain Brooks, DCLI, against the Dodingas between June and August 1913. The recipients were members of the 4th King's African Rifles (265).

East Africa 1913-14 15th December 1913-31st May 1914

This bar was awarded for operations under Lieutenant-Colonel B. R. Graham, 3 King's African Rifles, against the Merehan Tribe. The recipients were members of the 1, 3 and 4 King's African Rifles; 53 Silladar Camel Corps; Serenli Military Transport Company, E. A. Police; Commissioners and staff.

East Africa 1914 2nd April-7th July 1914

This bar was awarded for a punitive expedition under Captain R. H. Leeke, The Rifle Brigade; Lieutenant S. W. H. Silver, The Suffolk Regiment, and Lieutenant H. A. Lilley, The Yorkshire Regiment, against the Turkhana Tribe in the North Frontier District of British East Africa and the Uganda Borders West of Lake Rudolf. The recipients were the East Africa Police and 4 King's African Rifles (265).

East Africa 1915 4th February-28th May 1915

This bar was awarded for an expedition under Lieutenant-Colonel W. F. S. Edwards, DSO, against the Turkhanas between 4th February and 28th May 1915. Recipients were members of the Uganda Police (62). East African Police (198); 9th Sudanese Infantry (133).

Jubaland 1917-18 23rd July 1917-24th March 1918

This bar was awarded for services under Lieutenant-Colonel W. E. H. Barratt, King's African Rifles, Major E. G. M. Porcelli, DCLI, Captain J. F. Wolseley-Bourne, and Captain O. Martin, King's African Rifles, in the military operations against the Northern Aulihan tribe west of the Juba river, or north or east of a line Waregta—Lake Albeleni—Lorian Swamp—El Wak—Dolo.

The bar was awarded to 3, 5 and 6 King's African Rifles; No 9 (Murree) Mountain Battery, N. Frontier District Constabulary (150).

Twenty-six bronze medals were issued bearing this bar.

East Africa 1918 20th April-19th June 1918

This bar, sanctioned by Army Order No 51 of 1920, was awarded for services under Major R. F. White, The Essex Regiment; Major H. Rayne, MC, King's African Rifles; and Captain J. H. R. Yardley, DSO, Royal Inniskilling Fusiliers, in military operations against the Northern Turkhana, Marille, Donyiro and kindred tribes in the vicinity of the southern Sudan boundary and west of Lake Rudolf.

The bar was awarded to the East African Regiment, 2, 3 4, 5 and 6 King's Africa Rifles, Uganda Police.

Nigeria 1918 11th June-31st July 1918

This bar was awarded under Army Order No 460 of 1924, for services against the Egba tribe in the vicinity of the Nigerian Government Railway (main line) from Abeokuto in the north to Lagos in the south within the area bounded on the east by a line from Abeokuta through Ijebu—Ode to Lagos, and on the west by a line from Abeokuta to the Ilaro, thence through Igbessa to Lagos.

Approximately 1000 medals were awarded mainly to Nigerian military personnel.

Somaliland 1920 21st January-12th February 1920

The suspender on this medal does not swivel. This bar was awarded for the fifth and final expedition against the 'Mad Mullah'. The expedition was commanded by Major (temporary Colonel) G. H. Summers, CMG, Light Cavalry, Indian Army, under the general directions of the Governor and Commander in Chief of the Protectorate, Sir G. R. Archer, KCMG.

The bar was awarded to 2 and 6 King's African Rifles, Somaliland Camel Corps, Somaliland Police, 1/101 Bombay Grenadiers, Somaliland Levies. RAF, HM Ships *Ark Royal* (149), *Clio* (147), *Odin* (156). The Medals issued to *Clio* and *Odin* include respectively 30 and 36 awards to locally recuited 'Seedies'. Captain A. Gibb DSO, DCM, was the only European to take part in all five expeditions against the 'Mad Mullah'.

Kenya 21st October 1952-17th November 1956

The award of this bar was approved by Queen Elizabeth II in February 1955. Awarded for 91 days or more service against the Mau Mau within designated operational areas: Central or Southern Province of Kenya, in the Naivasha, Nakuru or Laikipia Districts of the Rift Valley Province, or the Nairobi extra-provincial District.

A state of emergency was declared in Kenya by the Governor, Sir Evelyn Baring in early October 1952 following the murder of Africans loyal to the Government by members of the Kikuyu Tribe. This was the start of the so called Mau Mau Rebellion. The causes of unrest were various and complicated but the main reason for the rising by the Kikuyu was the unlawful possession, as they saw it, by white settlers of prime agricultural land in the white Highlands. The settlers had understood in the early 1900s that they had made outright purchases of land while the Kikuyu had thought the white settlers were merely renting or leasing. The four year rebellion was notable for the incidence of violence and atrocities but was eventually put down by the Army and Police. The security Forces suffered a total of 590 killed of which only twelve were British soldiers. However, 11,500 Mau Mau were killed during the struggle, a figure indicative of the fanaticism engendered by the Mau Mau movement.

Awarded to the Royal Navy, Royal East African Navy, British Army including—East Kent Regiment; Northumberland Fusiliers; Devon Regiment; 1st Battalion Lancashire Fusiliers; Royal Inniskilling Fusiliers; Gloucester Regiment; King's Shropshire Light Infantry; King's Own Yorkshire Light Infantry; Black Watch; Royal Irish Fusiliers; Rifle Brigade; RA; WRAC; RAF 30, 152 and 208 Squadrons; WRAF; King's African Rifles; Kenya Regiment; East African Pioneer Corps; East African Rifles Camel Battery; East African Recce Squadron; East African Artillery; East African Independant Armoured Car Squadron; Kikuya Guard; Kenya Police and Reserve; Tribal Police and Reserve; Civil Prisons Service; Civil Administration Service including Provincial and District Commissioners, District and Executive Officers, Chiefs and Headmen; British Red Cross Society and the Order of St John; Women's Voluntary Services.

The award of this bar, thirty-five years after its predecessor is a remarkable comment on the medal's longevity; the longest of any British Campaign Medal.

138 *Tibet Medal* 13th December 1903-23rd September 1904

Obverse	The bust of King Edward VII and legend: 'EDWARDVS VII KAISAR-I-HIND'.
Reverse	A fine view, in rather shallow relief, of the fortress of Potala Lhassa with the words 'TIBET 1903-4'.
Size	36mm diameter
Metal	Silver and bronze.
Ribbon	32mm wide. Green with a white stripe either side of a central maroon band.
Suspension	By an ornamental scroll swivelling suspender as used for the IGS Medal.
Designers	Obverse—G. W. de Saulles; Reverse—E. G. Gillick.
Naming	In neat, rather thick, running script.
Bars issued	One—for Gyantse.

This medal was authorized on 1st February 1905, to be awarded to all who took part in the Tibet Mission and to the troops accompanying it who served at or beyond Silgari between 13th December 1903, and 23rd September 1904.

The medal was also issued in bronze, including the bar for Gyantse, when applicable, to the Peshawur Camel Corps, native camp followers, and others.

In July 1903, a trade Mission under Colonel Younghusband was sent by the Indian Government to meet the Tibet and Chinese officials in Gyantse. This Mission met with a hostile reception on the way and when it arrived at Tanu it was advised by the Tibetan general to return to Quatong to avoid bloodshed. This Colonel Younghusband refused to do, but ordered the Tibetan troops to be disarmed.

On 31st March 1904, the Tibetans fired on the column and suffered heavily for doing so. On the 8th April, the 32nd Sikh Pioneers stormed the Red Idol Gorge. A force under General Macdonald arrived at Gyantse after having had to fight its way there. The Dalai Lama refused to negotiate, so that it became obvious that the way would have to be cleared right through to Lhassa. Colonel Brander was sent from Gyantse with a force to clear the Karo Pass, which he did on 6th May.

The Tibetans surrounded Gyantse and repeatedly attacked it. Colonel Younghusband demanded that the Amban should go to Gyantse with a view to putting an end to the trouble, but this he refused to do. Eventually an expeditionary force, 4,600 strong, was employed. The Tibetans were heavily defeated outside Gyantse and a Lama was sent from Lhassa to sue for peace.

In July, Colonel Younghusband stated that the Mission would proceed to Lhassa to demand an apology. Preceded by General Macdonald's force, the Mission arrived on the 3rd August, and a treaty was signed in the Portala Lhassa (which is depicted on the reverse of the medal).

The Mission, after blessings and presents all round, including a golden image of Buddha to Colonel Younghusband, left Lhassa on 23rd September, 1904.

A Victoria Cross was awarded to Lieutenant J. D. Grant, Indian Army, for services in Tibet.

Regiments present: No 7 British Mountain Battery; one section from each of the 27 and 30 Mountain Batteries; 3 Bengal and 12 Madras Sappers and Miners; four companies of 1st Bn. Royal Fusiliers; a machine-gun section from the 1st Bn. Norfolk Regiment (18), King's Own R. Lancs. (8), Royal Irish Rifles (1) and 3rd Rifle Bde; 23, 32 Sikh Pioneers; 19 Punjab Infantry; 8 and machine-gun section of 9 Gurkhas; 55 Cokes Rifles; 40 Pathans; 5, 6, 9, 11, 12, 19, 24 and part of 26 Mule Corps; Peshawur Cooly Corps; Sikkim Cooly Corps; Supply and Transport Corps; Army Veterinary Department; Survey Department; Telegraph Department; a few volunteer officers; British Officers (160); NCOs and men (600); Indian Officers (60); NCOs and men (2,500).

Gyantse 3rd May-6th July 1904

This bar was awarded to members of the above mentioned units who took part in the operations around Gyantse between 3rd May and 6th July 1904.

---

139 *Natal Rebellion Medal* 8th February-3rd August 1906

Obverse	The coinage head of King Edward VII facing right, with the legend: 'EDWARDVS VII REX IMPERATOR'.
Reverse	In the centre are the figures of Britannia and Natalia. The former is holding an orb, surmounted by the figure of Peace in her left hand, and Natalia is holding a large sword in her right hand. In the background are some natives and a kraal. In the exergue is the word 'NATAL'.
Size	36mm diameter
Metal	Silver; but bronze trial strikings exist.
Ribbon	32mm wide. Crimson with black edges
Suspension	By a plain, straight suspender.
Designer	The medal was designed and manufactured by the Goldsmiths and Silversmiths Co., London.
Naming	Impressed in thin block capitals, a few are found unnamed. Officer's medals are engraved.
Bars issued	One—1906

On the 9th May, 1907, the Natal Government was authorized to issue a medal to those who had taken part in the suppression of the Zulu Rising in 1906. Approx. 10,000 medals issued, about 20% being without bar.

The reverse of this medal is particularly attractive, there is nothing depicting triumph, the attitude of the natives in the right background is so beautifully in keeping with the solicitous attitude of Britannia, who seems to be sympathizing with the figure of Natalia. It is such a breakaway from the usual not to see Britannia with her usual wreath of laurels. The design of the bar with its mottled background and the stop before and after the date is much more pleasing than any of the others which carry a single date, such as those on the medals for South Africa between 1877 and 1879, and the East and West Africa Medals.

The medal, which was only awarded in silver, was the first campaign medal to bear the Sovereign's head facing to the right.

It has been said that the Cameron Highlanders were awarded medals for service in the rebellion, but it is understood that they never left Pietermaritzburg. Furthermore, the Natal Government refused the help of Imperial troops.

The medal without the bar '1906' was awarded to those who served for a continuous period of twenty to forty-nine days, whilst those who served for fifty or more days received the bar.

The cause of the rebellion was the native refusal to pay hut taxes, followed by the murder of two Natal policemen on 8th February.

On the 10th Colonel Duncan Mackenzie, CB, CMG, raised a force with a view to a 'drive' in the Southern Natal with a further force under Colonel G. Leuchars, CMG. These two forces rounded up Chiefs Ngobizembe, Mskofeli and Gobizembe. At a parade at Mapumulo on the 10th March, Colonel Leuchars announced the fines, in cattle, to be imposed. This brought the first part of the rebellion to a close.

On the 3rd April, Chief Bambata incited the rebels in the Greytown District to revolt. They ambushed a police column and practically besieged Greytown, Melmoth and Eshowe. A large sum was offered for the capture of Bambata, who crossed the Tugela River into Zululand, where he was joined by Chiefs Sigananda and N'Dubi in the Nkandhla Forests. It was now decided to raise more forces and organize a drive through the forests. The Transvaal raised a force under Lieutenant-Colonel W. F. Barker and the Cape another, under Lieutenant-Colonel J. Dick. In addition to these State forces Colonel J. R. Royston raised a unit known as Royston's Horse. The Naval Corps, under Commander F. Hoare, was mobilized. Sir Abe Bailey raised a small unit from the Lancaster and York Association (Occasionally, in error, quoted as the York and Lancaster Regiment). The Natal Indian Congress raised a stretcher-bearer unit, the Sergeant-Major of which was a certain M. K. Gandhi.

As soon as these forces were ready the 'drive' started and the rebels were driven out of the forests into the mountains. On 16th June Chief Sigananda surrendered. On the 19th, a further outbreak was started by Chiefs Ndhlova and Messini. On the 8th July, the rebels were totally defeated at Izinsimba and both Chiefs surrendered.

Summary of Units, Medals and Clasps Awarded

Table courtesy of D. R. Forsyth.

Unit	With Bar	No Bar	Total
Amabomvu Levy	—	32	32
Amafunze Tribe	—	20	20
Border Mounted Rifles	213	38	251
Cape Mounted Riflemen	70	—	70
Chaplains	4	2	6
Civilian Employees	—	135	135
Doctors	—	4	4
Dundee Borough Reserves	—	35	35
Dundee District Reserves	—	62	62
Dunns Scouts	20	—	20
Durban Light Infantry	539	93	632
Durban Militia Reserves	—	194	194
Escourt Militia Reserves	105	13	118
Greytown Reserves (1st)	—	42	42
Greytown Reserves (2nd)	1	—	1
H. E. The Governor—Staff	2	1	3
Imperial Officers	—	4	4
Indian Stretcher Bearer Corps	—	20	20
Intelligence Service	17	34	51
Klipriver Reserves	-	62	62
Krantzkop Reserves	71	4	75
Lancashire & Yorkshire Contg	150	—	150
Lower Tugela Reserves	—	35	35
Melmouth Reserves	25	32	57
Militia Reserves Lower Tugela Div.	—	52	52
Militia Transport Service Corp.	45	28	73
Natal Carbineers	878	132	1010
Natal Field Arty 1st Bdge Staff	3	2	5
Natal Field Arty 'A' Battery	94	21	115
Natal Field Arty 'B' Battery	101	5	106
Natal Field Arty 'C' Battery	91	10	101
Natal Field Arty Pom Pom Section	24	—	24

Unit	With Bar	No Bar	Total
Natal Guides	4	—	4
Natal Medical Corps	104	19	123
Natal Militia Staff	30	1	31
Natal Mounted Rifles	424	38	462
Natal Police Gaolers	50	—	50
Natal Rangers	839	68	907
Natal Royal Regiment	225	33	258
Natal Service Corps	111	8	119
Natal Telegraph Corps	38	6	44
Natal Veterinary Corps	11	2	13
Newcastle Division Reserves	—	88	88
New Hanover Reserves	—	75	75
Nkandhla Town Guard	—	17	17
Northern Districts Mounted Rifles	233	6	239
Nurses	—	7	7
Royston's Horse	714	31	745
Royston's Horse 2nd	93	—	93
Searchlight Section	3	—	3
Sibindies Levies	1	—	1
Sundry Recipients	16	4	20
Transvaal Medical Staff Corps	9	—	9
Transvaal Mounted Rifles	489	46	535
Transvaal Volunteer Staff	3	—	3
Transvaal Volunteer Transport Corps	1	—	1
Umsinga Militia Reserves	6	40	46
Umvoti Division Reserves	61	27	88
Umvoti Mounted Rifles	327	98	425
Zululand Chiefs	—	15	15
Zululand Field Force	1	—	1
Zululand Mounted Rifles	124	31	155
Zululand Natives	—	33	33
Zululand Police	122	25	147
TOTAL	**8045**	**1934**	**9979**

140 *India General Service Medal* 1908-1935

Obverse	*1st issue*—Bust of King Edward VII in uniform and legend 'EDWARDVS VII KAISAR-I-HIND'. *2nd issue*—Crowned bust of King George V in robes, and legend 'GEORGIVS V KAISAR-I-HIND'. (This issue started with the medal given with the bar for Abor, 1911-12.) *3rd issue*—Crowned bust of King George V in robes and legend 'GEORGIVS·V·D·G·BRITT·OMN·REX·ET·INDIÆ·IMP.' (This issue started with the medal given with the bar for North West Frontier, 1930-31.)
Reverse	The fort at Jamrud (which commands the Khyber Pass eleven miles from Peshawur), with mountains in the background. Below, the word 'INDIA' between a branch of oak and olive, tied with a ribbon at the base.
Size	36mm diameter
Metal	Silver and bronze (see text)
Ribbon	32mm wide. Green with a central dark blue band.
Suspension	By a swivelling floral suspender, as used on previous India General Service Medals. The claws of the medals struck by the Calcutta Mint differ from those of the Royal Mint. Those of the former being a plain curved style, the latter being a more elaborate raised scroll type.
Designer	Richard Garbe
Naming	Impressed and engraved, details to be given under the relevant bar.
Bars issued	Twelve: North West Frontier 1908, Abor 1911-12, Afghanistan NWF 1919, Mahsud 1919-20, Waziristan 1919-21, Malabar 1921-22, Waziristan 1921-24, Waziristan 1925, North West Frontier 1930-31, Burma 1930-32, Mohmand 1933, North West Frontier 1935.

The institution of a new 'India' medal was approved by King Edward VII on 1st January 1909. The medal was always issued with a bar.

After the 11th August 1920, permission was given for those 'Mentioned in Despatches' to wear a bronze oak leaf emblem on their medal ribbon.

North West Frontier 1908 14th February-31st May 1908

Medals with this bar were awarded in silver and bronze.
Naming: In running script.
The bar was awarded to the following:
a) Those who formed part of the Bazar Valley Field Force, and proceeded under the orders of the General Officer commanding that Force from Ali Musjid into or towards the Bazar Valley between 14th February 1908, and the 1st March 1908.
Those who did not proceed beyond Ali Musjid are not entitled.
b) Those who served north of the Adinazai boat bridge between the 19th and 25th April 1908.
c) Those who were at Landi Kotal between the 2nd and 4th May, 1908.
d) Those who formed part of the Mohmand Field Force, and proceeded under the orders of the General Officer commanding that Force beyond Hafiz Kor between the 12th and 31st May, 1908.
   Regiments present: 10 Hussars; 19, 21, 37 Indian Cavalry; Guides Cavalry; 18, 80 Batteries RFA; RGA; 2, 3, 8, 22, 23, 28 Mountain Batteries; 1, 6 Companies Bengal and 9 Company Madras Sappers and Miners; 1 Northumberland Fusiliers; 1 Royal Warwicks; 1 West Yorks; 1 Seaforth; 2 Gordons; 1 Royal Munster Fusiliers; 19, 20, 21, 22, 25, 28, 29, 30, 33 Punjab Infantry; 15, 23, 34, 45, 53, 54, 55 Sikhs; 57, 59 Rifles; Khyber Rifles; Guides Infantry; 40 Pathans, 1, 4, 5, 6, 8 Gurkhas; 7, 16 Mule Corps.

Abor 1911-12 6th October 1911-20th April 1912

This was the first bar to be awarded with the second issue obverse. The medals with this bar were awarded in silver and bronze.
Naming: In running script.

This bar was awarded for services against the Abors under Major General Sir H. Bower, KCB, The expedition became necessary following a massacre of a party under Mr. Williamson. After little opposition the tribesmen responsible were captured, tried and sentenced and the Abor region pacified. There was also a considerable amount of survey work carried out.

Regiments present: Except for their British officers, this bar was only awarded to Indian troops.

Assam Valley Light Horse; 1 Company King George's Own Sappers and Miners; 1/2, 1/8 Gurkha Rifles; 32 Sikh Pioneers; 26 Mule Corps; 1, 2, 3, 4, 5 Naga Carrier Corps; 1, 2 Gurkhali Carrier Corps; Assam Military Police, Lakhimpur Military Police; Lushai Hills Bn; Supply and Transport Corps, Telegraph Dept, IMS, 31 Signal Co. MSC.

Medals also known to the 30 Lancers, 1/61 Pioneers, 114 Mahrattas, 1/3 Gurkhas, Survey of India.

Afghanistan NWF 1919 6th May-8th August 1919

No bronze medals were issued for this or any further bars to the India General Service Medal, 1908.
Naming: Impressed block capitals.

This bar was awarded for service in the Third Afghan War, under General Sir A. A. Barratt, GCB, KCSI, KCVO, ADC. The year '1919' occupies a second line on the bar of which 12,500 were struck for distribution.

This was the first occasion in which the Royal Air Force took part in the Indian campaigns. The previous service of the Royal Flying Corps which was in action during the Mohmand Blockade in 1916 was excluded.

Only one five bar medal and seven four bar medals were issued to the RAF.
Regiments present:
British Army
Cavalry:
1 King's Dragoon Guards.
Artillery:
'M' Battery RHA; 4, 38, 74, 77, 79, 89, 90, 101, 102, 1091, 1093, 1096, 1104, 1107 Batteries RFA; 1, 3, 4, 6, 8, 9 Mountain Batteries RGA; 60, 68 Heavy Batteries RGA.
Armoured Cars and MG Companies:
1, 2, 3, 4, 5, 6, 7, 8, 11 Armoured Motor Batteries; 15, 22, 24, MG Squadrons; 3, 15, 19, 22, 222, 260, 263, 270, 281, 285, 286 Machine-Gun Companies.
Infantry:
1/4 Royal West Surrey Regiment; 3 Buffs (115); 1/25 Royal Fusiliers; 2 Kings; 2 Somerset Light Infantry; 1 Yorkshire Regiment; 1 Duke of Wellington's Regiment; 2/4 Border Regiment; 1, 2/6 Royal Sussex; 1/5 Hants; 1 South Lancs; 1/1 Kent Regiment; 1/4 Royal West Kent Regiment; 2 North Staffs; 1 Durham Light Infantry; No 17 Special Service Bn; 15, 25 Bn The London Regiment; 1 Kent Cyclist Bn, East Yorks; DCLI; Seaforth Highlanders; HLI; Gordon Highlanders; Liverpool Regiment; Devon Regiment; Manchester Regiment; Lincoln Regiment; Prince of Wales Volunteers.
A few medals may be found to some of the above although the unit was not present as a whole.
Corps:
RAMC: QAMNSR: TFNS: IMS: RAVC: RASC.

Indian Army
Cavalry:
1, 13, 30, 31, 37 Lancers; 3 Horse; 4, 12, 17, 23, 25, 27, 40, 41, 42 Cavalry; 28, 33 Light Cavalry; Patiala, Alwar, Navanagar and Bhopal Lancers; 40th Mule Corps.
Artillery:
22, 23, 24, 27, 28, 30, 33, 35, 37, 38 Mountain Batteries; Frontier Garrison Artillery; 1, 2 Kashmir Mountain Batteries.
Signals:
6, 12 Cavalry Brigade Signals; 43, 44, 45, 46, 67, 68 Brigade *Signals:* Ind Tel Dept.

Sappers and Miners:
1, 7, 53, 55, 56, 57, 58 1st Sappers and Miners; 8, 11, 14, 15, 63, 64, 66, 67, 68, 69, 76, 2nd Sappers and Miners; 17, 24, 71, 73, 74, 3rd Sappers and Miners.
Infantry:
2/2, 1/11, 2/11, 16 Rajputs; 3 Guides Infantry; 2/3 Gaur Brahmins; 1/5 Light Infantry; 1/6, 2/10 Jats; 14, 1/15, 2/15, 1/35, 2/35, 2/54 Sikhs; 1/19, 1/22, 2/26, 2/27, 1/30, 2/30, 1/33, 2/33, 1/66, 2/67, 1/69, 2/69, 2/72, 1/76, 82, 2/89, 1/90, 2/90, 1/152, 1/153, 2/153 Punjabis; 37, 1/41, 2/41 Dogras; 3/39, 4/39 Garhwal Rifles; 40 Pathans; 1/55, 2/56, 1/57 Frontier Force; 1/97, 1/98, 1/109, 2/112, 2/113, 2/119, 120, 1/150, 3/150, 1/151, 2/151, 1/154 Infantry; 1/102, 2/102 Grenadiers; 1/103, 110 Mahratta Light Infantry; 1/124, 3/124, 126, 1/129, 2/129 Baluchis; Jind, Gwalior, Patiala, Karpurthala, Nabha, 1st and 2nd Kashmir Rifles of Imperial Service Infantry, and the 2nd Rifle Regiment (Nepalese); Chitral Scouts.
Pioneers:
1/12, 2/12, 2/23, 2/34, 3/34, 1/61, 2/61, 1/81, 2/81, 1/107.
Gurkhas:
2/1, 3/1, 2/2, 3/2, 4/3, 1/4, 3/5, 3/6, 2/7, 3/7, 2/8, 1/9, 2/9, 3/9, 2/10, 1/11, 2/11, 3/11.

RAF:
52nd Wing; composed of 20, 31, 48, 114 Squadrons. (Approx 850 bars.)
A Victoria Cross was awarded to Captain H. J. Andrews, MBE, IMS for this campaign.

Mahsud 1919-20 27th November 1919-7th May 1920

Naming: Impressed in thin block capitals.
Army Order No 361 of 1921 sanctioned the award of this bar to all who served under Major-General A. Skeen, west of and including Jandola between 18th December 1919 and 8th April 1920. Army Order No 347 of 1922 also granted the award of this bar to all who served under the GOC Waziristan Force on the Takki Zam Line north of and including Jandola between 18th December 1919 and 8th April 1920. The bar for Waziristan 1919-21 next mentioned should be consulted for units present, as this bar is nearly always found on the same medal as that for Warizistan 1919-21, as the Mahsud territory is enclosed by Northern and Southern Waziristan. Medals with this single bar are known to the Royal West Kent Regiment and to the 2nd Queen Victoria's Own Sappers and Miners.
RAF (175).

Waziristan 1919-21 6th May 1919-January 1921

Naming: Thin impressed block capitals.
This bar was awarded for punitive operations against the Tochi and Wana Wazirs and Mahsuds, who had caused considerable depredations since the end of the Third Afghan War. The operations were under Major-General A. Skeen, C.M.G., I.A.
Distribution of troops in Waziristan 6th May, 1919:
BANNU AREA
Bannu
31 DCO Lancers (less one squadron); one section 33 Indian Mountain Battery; 1/103 Mahratta Light Infantry; 3/6 Gurkha Rifles.
Dardoni
One Squadron 31 DCO Lancers; one section 33 Indian Mountain Battery; 55 Field Company Sappers and Miners; 1/41 Dogras; 2/112 Infantry. Also Northern Waziri Militia and Frontier Constabulary.

DERAJAT AREA
Dera Ismail Khan
27 Cavalry (less one Squadron); 27 Indian Mountain Battery; 1/76 Punjabis; 2/2 Gurkha Rifles; No 7 Armoured Motor Battery.
Monzai
76 Field Company Sappes and Miners; 1/66 Punjabis. Also Southern Waziri Militia and Frontier Constabulary.

COMPOSITION OF THE THREE ECHELONS OF THE TOCHI COLUMN ON 13th NOVEMBER 1919
No 1 Echelon
One and a half Squadrons DCO Lancers; 35 Indian Mountain Battery;

55 Field Company Sappers and Miners; 2/61 Pioneers; Northern Waziri Militia; 1/55 Coke's Rifles; 1/103 Mahratta Light Infantry; 104 Wellesley's Rifles; 2/112 Infantry; 2/21 Punjabis; 2/76 Punjabis (later transferred).
No 2 Echelon
74 Field Company Sappers and Miners; 3/34 Pioneers; 2/152 Punjabis; No 6 Armoured Motor Battery.
No 3 Echelon
One Squadron DCO Lancers; 33 Indian Mountain Battery, 4/39 Garhwal Rifles; 57 Wilde's Rifles; 82 Punjabis.

STRIKING FORCE—TOCHI AND DERAJAT COLUMNS
Cavalry:
Two Squadrons DCO Lancers; one Squadron 21 PAVO Cavalry.
Artillery:
One section 4.5 Howitzers RFA; No 6 Mountain Battery RGA; Nos 27, 33, 35 Indian Mounted Batteries.
Sappers and Miners:
55, 74 Field Companies.
Infantry:
43rd Brigade—4/39 Garhwal Rifles; 57 Wilde's Rifles; 82 Punjabis. 67th Brigade—1/55 Coke's Rifles; 1/103 Mahrattas, 104 Wellesley's Rifles; 2/112 Infantry.
Pioneers:
3/34 Sikh; 2/61 Pioneers.

LINES OF COMMUNICATION—FIGHTING TROOPS
TOCHI
No 1 Section Bannu L of C
Cavalry:
31 DCO Lancers (less two Squadrons).
Artillery:
One section 33 Indian Mountain Battery; 15-pdr and 6.3in Frontier GA.
Machine Gun Corps:
No 5 Armoured Motor Battery.
Infantry:
45th Brigade—2/4 Rajputs; 2/25 Punjabis; 1/150, 2/154 Infantry.

No 2 Section Bannu L of C
Cavalry:
Two Squadrons DCO Lancers.
Artillery:
No 33 Indian Mountain Battery; one section RGA.
Sappers and Miners:
No 74 Field Company
Infantry:
47th Brigade—2/21, 2/69, 3/151, 3/152 Punjabis.

DERAJAT
No 1 Section Tank L of C
Cavalry:
16th Cavalry; 21 PAVO Cavalry; 27 Light Cavalry.
Artillery:
One section 35 Indian Mountain Battery; one section RGA.
Machine Gun Corps:
No 6, 7 Armoured Motor Batteries.
Infantry:
62nd Brigade—2/90 Punjabis 2/102 Grenadiers; 2/94, 2/113, 2/150 Infantry, 2/127 Baluchis, Southern Waziri Militia.

No 2 Section Tank L of C
Cavalry:
One troop 21 PAVO Cavalry.
Artillery:
No 35 Indian Mountain Battery.
Sappers and Miners:
75 Field Company.
Infantry:
68th Brigade—3rd Guides; 2/19, 2/76 Punjabis; 109 Infantry.

Note:
The 2/19, 82 Punjabis, 1/103 Mahratta Light Infantry and 2/112 Infantry were transferred to the Line of Communication and replaced by the 4/3, 2/5, 2/9, 3/11 Gurkha Rifles

RAF:
5, 20, 27, 28, 31, 60 and one flight each of 97 and 99 Squadrons (approx. 600 bars).
The following regiments which took part in the later stages of the campaign also received the award: The Queen's, 2 Norfolks, RW Fusiliers, Border Regiment, W. Yorks.
Medals are also known to MGC, IMS, ANC.
A Victoria Cross was awarded to Lieutenant W. D. Kenny, Indian Army for the campaign. A further VC was awarded to Sepoy Ishar Singh, Indian Army near Haidari Kach (Waziristan) 10·4·21.

Malabar 1921-22 20th August 1921-25th February 1922

Naming: In thin impressed block capitals.
Army Order 50 of 1924 sanctioned the award of this bar to all who took part in the suppression of the Moplah Rebellion in Malabar within the area bounded as follows: On the west by the sea, on the south by the Ponnani river, on the east by a north-and-south line from Gudalur to the Ponnani river, on the north by an east-and-west line from Gudalur to the sea.
Regiments present: One squadron of Queen's Bays: one section 67 Battery RFA; 10 Mtn Bty RGA; RA; 1 Suffolk Regiment (less 'C' Company); 2 Dorsetshire Regiment; 1 Leinster Regiment (332); Royal Tank Corps; Madras Sappers and Miners (1 platoon); 64 Pioneers (detachment); 3 Madras Regiment: 83 Wallajabad Light Infantry; 1/39 Royal Garhwal Rifles; 3/70 Burma Rifles; Malabar Territorial Infantry; 2/8, 2/9 Gurkhas and Special Police.

Waziristan 1921-24 21st December 1921-31st March 1924

Naming: In thin impressed block capitals.
Army Order 177 of 1926 authorized the issue of this bar to all who served in North and South Waziristan, Bannu, the Dera Ismail Khan Civil Districts and that part of the Mianwali District which lies west of the River Indus, also the military posts of Mari Indus and Darya Khan east of the River Indus between 21st December 1921, and 31st March 1924.
As a large number of troops were employed in small garrisons over a wide area it would be almost impossible to give the names of every unit from which one or more men served in the campaign. Included in the following list are the names of those regiments present as a whole and those to whom medals are known.
Regiments present:
Cavalry:
7, 16, 17, 21, 27, 28 Regiments.
Artillery:
6, 11, 12, RA, 21, 27, 33, 35 Indian Artillery, 10, 13, 47, 128 Medium Howitzer Batteries, RGA; 101, 103, 106, 107, 108, 112, 114, 115, 119, 121 Batteries Pack; 5, 16 Armoured Motor Batteries.
Corps:
Rl Tank Corps, RASC, R Signals, RAMC.
Armoured Car Companies:
7, 9, 10.
Sappers and Miners:
5, 12, 13, 14, 19, 20, 21, 94, 96, 113 Companies.
Pioneers:
1/1, 2/1 Madras; 1/3, 2/3, 3/3, 21, 32, 34 Sikh; 1/4 Hazara; 48, 2/61, 1/12 Pioneers.
Infantry European:
2 Queen's; 1 Royal Welch Fusiliers; 1 Border Regiment; 1 Welch Regiment; Sherwood Foresters; Royal Berks, KOSB.
Indian:
2/1, 4/1, 2/2, 1/19, 2/21, 2/25, 1/26, 1/28, 1/30, 1/69, 2/69, 82 Punjabis; 1/3 Brahmans; 1/4, 2/4, 1/7, 16 Rajputs; 3/5 Mahratta Light Infantry; 1/6, 2/6, 4/6, 5/6 Rajputana Rifles; 1/9, 2/9, 3/9 Jat Regiment; 4/10, 5/10 Baluch Regiment; 1/12, 2/12, 3/12 Frontier Force Regiment; 2/13, 4/13, 5/13 Frontier Force Rifles; 1/17, 37, 2/41 Dogras; 2/18, 1/109, 2/113; 1/119 Infantry; 36 Sikhs; 4/39 Garhwal Rifles; 2/50 Kumaon Rifles; 1/73 Carnatic Infantry; 2/101, 2/102 Grenadiers; 104 Wellesley's Rifles; 2/1, 2/2, 1/3, 2/3, 4/3, 1/4, 1/5, 2/6, 2/8, 1/9, 3/11 Gurkhas; North West Militia; South Waziri Militia; Tochi Scouts; 112 Labour Corps; 3, 9 Mule Corps; 43 Camel Corps; Indian ASC; Indian Medical Service.

RAF:
5, 27, 28, 31, 60 Squadrons (approx 600 bars).

Waziristan 1925 9th March-1st May 1925

Naming: In thin impressed block capitals.
This bar, awarded for service under Wing Commander R. C. M. Pink, CB, RAF, against the Waziris, was only awarded to the RAF. This was the first occasion in which the RAF was used independently of the Army.
Those who had already qualified for the bar 'Waziristan 1921-24' and who also took part in these operations were given the option of receiving the earlier bar **or** that for 'Waziristan 1925'.
Recipients:
At Tank Headquarters: Five officers and twenty airmen. No 5 (AC) Squadron Bristol Fighters—ten planes—fourteen officers; sixty-nine airmen.
At Miramshah: No 27 (B) Squadron DH9A—eight planes—fifteen officers, fifty-eight airmen. No 60 Squadron DH9A—eight planes—thirteen officers, sixty-seven airmen.
Other personnel included one army officer and one civilian.

North West Frontier 1930-31 23rd April 1930-22nd March 1931

This was the first bar to be awarded with the third issue obverse.
Naming: In thin impressed block capitals.
This bar was awarded for services in Kohat, Waziristan and the Peshawur District between 23rd April and 30th September, 1930, and also for services between 1st October 1930, and 22nd March 1931, in the area bounded as follows: *North:* Bazar river, Khyber river to the bridge on the Peshawur Jamrud road seven and a half miles from Peshawur. *East:* From the road from the above bridge to Narai Khwan Post, thence to Frontier Road to Bara Fort-Malaimi. *South and West:* From a line from Aimal Chabutra to Point 2498, thence to the Afghan Frontier.
Awarded for the Afridi and Red Shirt Rebellions. The rebel organization known as Redshirts under Abdul Ghaffar, had been causing trouble along the Mohmand Frontier and in the border villages, so that it became necessary to establish a blockade line and an improved system of roads. A few minor actions were fought, but most of the period was spent in making roads and building posts, except for a small expedition into Tirah.

Regiments present: 15/19 Hussars; Poona Horse; 20th Lancers; Guides Cavalry; E Bty RHA; 31, 58 Field Batteries RFA; 17 Light Battery RA; 1, 2, 4, 8, 16 Mountain Batteries; 3, 4, 5 Companies Bengal Sappers and Miners; 2 Bombay Pioneers; 1 Light Tank Company RTC; 2 Border Regiment; Royal Sussex; South Lancs; 2 Essex; 2 KOYLI; 1 KSLI; 2 DLI; 2 Seaforth, 1/1, 2/1, 3/1, 5/2, 1/8, 2/8, 3/8, 1/15, 1/16 det of 4/16 Punjab Regiment; 2/6 Rajputana Rifles; 1/7, 2/7, 4/7 Rajput Regiment, 2/9 Jat Regiment; 1/10, 2/10, 3/10, 4/10, 5/10 Baluch Regiment; 1/11, 2/11, 3/11, 4/11 Sikh Regiment; 2/12, 4/12, 5/12, det of 3/12 Frontier Force Regiment; 2/13, 4/13, 5/13, 6/13 Frontier Force Rifles; 2/17, 3/17 Dogra Regiment; 2/18, 3/18 Royal Garhwal Rifles; 1/19 Hyderabad Regiment; 1/1, 1/3, 2/4, 1/5, 2/5, 1/6 Gurkhas; 21 DTT; Animal Transport Companies; Police Department.

RAF: 5, 11, 20, 27, 28, 39, 60 Squadrons. (Approx. 1,350 bars.)

Burma 1930-32 22nd December 1930-25th March 1932

Naming: In small block capitals.
The bar was sanctioned by Army Order 94 of 1933 for award to all who were dispatched from India and actually served in Burma between 22nd December 1930, and 25th March 1932. It was also awarded for service in Shwebo, Bassein, Toungo, Meiktila, Sahaingu, Myaungmya, Tharrawaddy, Pegu, Pakokku, Lower Chindwin, Prome, Insein, Mimbu, Kyaukse, Pyapon, Hanthawaddy, Thayetmyo, Myingyan, Mandalay, Maubin, Henzada, Magwe and Yamethin.
Regiments present: 7 Mtn Bty; RE; one company of Madras Sappers and Miners; 1 Buffs; 2 Ox and Bucks LI; 2 Manchesters; 2/5 Mahratta

LI; 3/6 Rajputana Rifles; 3/10 Baluch Regt; 2/15, 3/16 Punjab Regt; 1/17 Dogra Regt, 2/20, 3/20 Burma Rifles; Burma Military Police; 18 Mule Transport Company.

RAF: 36 (Torpedo Bomber) and 205 (Flying Boat) Squadrons. Total of 14 bars to the RAF.

Mohmand 1933 28th July-3rd October 1933

Naming: In thin block capitals.
The Mohmand Column operated against the Upper Mohmands and was commanded by Brigadier C. J. E. Auchinleck, DSO, OBE.
Regiments present:
Mohmand Column: 18 (KEO) Cavalry; 2 (Derajat) Mountain Battery; 4 (Hazara) Mountain Battery; 10 (Abbottabad) Mountain Battery; 22 Mountain Brigade Signals; 1/7 Rajputs; 5/10 Baluch Regiment; 3/14 Punjab Regiment; 5/12 Frontier Force; QVO Corps of Guides; Nos 2, 3 (KGO) Bengal Sappers and Miners; 2 Field Ambulance; 30, 34, 37, 39 Animal Transport Companies.
L of C Troops: 1/11 Sikhs; 3/2 Punjab Regiment; 5/12 Frontier Force; 1, 32 Animal Transport Companies.
Mohmand Blockhouse Line Force: 58 Field Battery RA; 6 Armoured Car Company.
Reserve Force: 2 (Derajat) Mountain Battery; Frontier Force; 3/11 Sikh Regiment. Medals to the Royal Tank Corps; Gordon Highlanders, 3/10 Baluch Regiment; 1/1 Hyderabad Regiment; 21 DTT Company are also known.
RAF: No 20 Squadron only (180).

North West Frontier 1935 12th January-3rd November 1935

Naming: In thin impressed block capitals.
Mohmand Force
18 (KEO) Cavalry; 4 Field Brigade RA; 13, 22 Mountain Batteries; 15 Medium Battery, RA; detachment of 8 AA Battery, RA; 3, 5 Field Companies KGO Bengal Sappers and Miners; 2 Light Tank Company and one section 8 Armoured Car Company RTC; 4/15 Punjab Regiment; 2/1 Gurkhas.
2 officers, 1 sergeant and 8 men of 2 Welch Regiment were attached to Force Headquarters.
Peshawur Brigade
2 HLI; 5/1 Punjab Regiment; 1/4 Bombay Grenadiers; 5/10 Baluch Regiment.
Nowshera Brigade
2 Duke of Wellington's Regiment; 3/2, 2/15 Punjab Regiment; 5/12 Frontier Force (QVO Guides).
Rawalpindi Brigade
1 Hampshire Regiment; 2/2, 1/15 Punjab Regiment; 3/11 Sikhs (Rattray's).
Jhelum Brigade
2 Argyll and Sutherland Highlanders; 1/14, 4/16 Punjab Regiment.
RAF
No 20 Squadron only.
Medals are also known to the Royal Northumberland Fusiliers and 21 DTT Company.
A Victoria Cross was awarded to Captain G. Meynell, Indian Army, for this campaign.

141 *Khedive's Sudan Medal* 1910-1922

Obverse	An Arabic inscription which reads 'ABBAS HILMI THE SECOND', with the Mohammedan year 1328 for the issues from 1910 to 1917, those from 1918-1922 contained a new cypher
Reverse	A lion partly standing on a plinth, which is inscribed with the word 'SUDAN' in English. Behind the lion is the River Nile, on the far bank of which are two clumps of palm trees. In the background is the rising sun with spreading rays. In the exergue is a shield with crossed spears. The initials 'R.G.' appear to the right of the right-hand spear
Size	36mm.
Metal	Silver and bronze
Ribbon	32mm. wide. A black watered centre with a thin green and red stripe on either side. These colours are said to symbolize the Sudan, guarded by Egypt (the green) and Britain (the red)
Suspension	A straight, swivelling suspender for the first issue, the second issue is non-swivelling
Designer	Richard Garbe
Naming	Issued unnamed, but medals to Royal Warwicks are found impressed
Bars issued	Sixteen, each of which is inscribed in English and Arabic: Atwot, S. Kordofan 1910, Sudan 1912, Zeraf 1913-14, Mandal, Miri, Mongalla 1915-16, Darfur 1916, Fasher, Lau Nuer, Nyima 1917-18, Atwot 1918, Garjak Nuer, Aliab Dinka, Nyala, Darfur 1921

On 12th June, 1911, His Highness the Khedive authorized the issue of a new medal to replace that which was first issued in 1897. The greatest number of bars issued with this medal is five. Bronze medals were issued without bars.

Atwot February-April, 1910

This bar was awarded for an expedition against the Atwot Dinkas between 9th February and 17th March, 1910, and another in the Aliab District of the Mongalla Province between 29th March and 4th April, 1910. The troops taking part were drawn from the 13th Sudanese Infantry and were commanded by El Kaimakam Harvey Bey. The crews of the Nile steamers which took part received silver medals. Camp followers and syces received bronze medals.

S. Kordofan 1910 10th November-19th December, 1910

This bar was awarded for two expeditions to the Kordofan District, which is about two hundred miles to the South-West of Khartoum. The first lasted from 10th to 19th November, and the second from 27th November to 19th December, 1910. The first expedition, commanded by El Lewa Asser Pasha, was composed of cavalry, camelry, artillery and the 10th and 12th Sudanese Infantry. It operated in the Eastern Gebels district. The second expedition consisted of a patrol under El Kaimakam Conry Bey, DSO, which operated in the Dilling district.

Sudan 1912 March, 1912

This bar was awarded to thirteen British officers seconded to the Egyptian Army and twenty-one native officers and four hundred and seven men of the 13th Sudanese Infantry, under Major Leveson, DSO for

operations against the Adonga Anuak. Two British and three native officers, together with forty-two other ranks, were killed in these operations, which ended on the Abyssinian border.

Zeraf 1913-14 December, 1913-June, 1914

This bar was awarded to members of a patrol under Captain D. A. Fairbairn, West Riding Regiment, and detachments from the 9th and 12th Sudanese Infantry, and a few mounted infantry, which operated in the Zeraf District. Owing to the swampy nature of the country it was very difficult to gain and maintain contact with the elusive Gaweir Nuer, so that the operations, which started in December, 1913, were continued for several months.

Mandal March, 1914

In March, 1914, a patrol of camelry under Captain Romilly, DSO, Scots Guards, was dispatched to punish the Nubas for cattle-thieving. As punishment for their depredations the unusual idea of a fine of rifles was imposed.

Miri April, 1915

In March, 1915, it was learned that Fiki Ali, with his followers in the Miri Hills, intended to attack the District Headquarters at Kadugli.

Reinforcements consisting of cavalry, camelry, and four companies of infantry were sent to reinforce the garrison and then Fiki Ali was attacked. The active operations lasted from 15th to 21st April.

Mongalla 1915-16 December, 1915-14th March, 1916

In December, 1915, it became necessary to undertake active operations in the Imatong and Lafite Mountains. A patrol, consisting of three companies of the Equatorial Battalion under Major D. C. Percy Smith, DSO, operated in the Imatongs, where they were joined by another patrol under Captain Hobbs composed of men of the 9th Sudanese Infantry and later by some artillery. The combined force then operated in the Lafite Mountains until the 14th March, 1916.

Darfur 1916 March-23rd May, 1916

This bar was awarded for operations in Darfur against Sultan Ali Dinar, who, encouraged by Enver Pasha and the Senussi, appeared likely to join the Turks in operations against the British. A force, commanded by Lieutenant-Colonel P. V. Kelly, 3rd Hussars, and composed of sixty mounted infantrymen, four companies of camelry, and eight companies of infantry, together with eight guns and two machine-guns, was assembled at Nahud. Moving westwards, Meleit was occupied on 18th May, and the Sultan's army, about three thousand five hundred strong, was found to be holding a strong position north of Fasher. Fasher was occupied on 23rd May, but Dinar had escaped. Some Royal Flying Corps and Army Service Corps personnel also received the medals with this bar. Some recipients: Capt E. Bannatyne, Lieut J. C. Slessor, Lieut J. K. Maurice, MC, RASC, Pte J. E. Clark, R Warwick Regt, and Capt G. D. Hall, R West Kent Regt, Capt F. Bellamy, MC, RFC, received this bar and that for Fasher.

Fasher 1st September-23 November, 1916

On 1st September, 1916, a force commanded by Major W. H. McCowan, Cameron Highlanders, and composed of four British and fourteen native officers and four hundred and sixty-eight other ranks, left Fasher on patrol to find Sultan Ali Dinar. On 1st November, Major H. J. Huddleston, Dorset Regiment, with three British officers and about three hundred other ranks, left Dibbis on the same errand. On the 6th November, Ali Dinar was surprised in his camp at Guiba. After a short fight, his troops stampeded and his body was found near the camp. His son, Zakaria, escaped, but surrendered to Major Huddleston on 23rd November, 1916. Three members of the RFC, and ASC personnel received the medal with this bar.

Lau Nuer March-May, 1917

As a result of persistent raids by the Lau Nuer against the Dinkas in the Bor district of Mongalla and other depredations, it was decided to send out a punitive patrol under Major E. A. T. Bayly, DSO, Royal Welch Fusiliers. The patrol, which was composed of Sudanese Infantry, combed the Lau country during March, April and May, and after establishing a post at Nyerol under Captain C. C. Goodwin, The Yorkshire Regiment, the patrol was withdrawn.

Nyima 1917-18 2nd November, 1917-February, 1918

On 16th January, 1917, Chief Agabna, of the Nubas, who lived in the Nyima Hills, raided Kasha and caused other disturbances which necessitated the sending out of a strong force as soon as the rainy season ended. In November, 1917, a force consisting of thirty-one British officers, one hundred and five native officers and 2,875 other ranks was placed under the command of Lieutenant-Colonel L. K. Smith, DSO, Royal Scots, with orders to clear the area. At the end of February, Agabna was captured together with over 2,000 troublesome natives.

Atwot 1918 1st January-26th May, 1918

Once again the Atwot Dinkas caused trouble, this time under the leadership of Malwal Matiang. A patrol consisting of four companies of infantry and one company of mounted infantry with two machine guns was sent out in January, 1918, and operated until the 26th May, when Matiang surrendered. So as not to confuse this bar with that awarded for similar operations in February-April, 1910, the year 1918 was added to the title.

Garjak Nuer December 1919-April 1920

The Garjak Nuer are a tribe which live in the Eastern Nuer District of the Upper Nile. In December, 1919, they raided their neighbours, the Burun, who were quite peacefully inclined. To prevent the troubles from spreading to the Lau Nuer two strong columns were sent out, the Northern commanded by Major G. C. Cobden, 9th Lancers, and the Southern commanded by Major C. R. K. Bacon, OBE, The Queen's Royal Regiment. Operations continued until the end of April, 1920.
RAF (approx. 30).

Aliab Dinka 8th November, 1919-May, 1920

This bar was awarded for service against the Aliab Dinka, Bor Dinka, and Mandari tribes, who rose unexpectedly and attacked the post at Menkamon. Two columns commanded by Major R. F. White, Essex Regiment, and Major F. C. Roberts, VC, DSO, MC, Worcestershire Regiment, were dispatched. The latter column was surprised by the Dinka, and, owing to the stampeding of its carriers, was forced to return to Tombe, which it reached on 13th December, 1919. In March, 1920, a further force under Lieutenant-Colonel R. H. Darwall, DSO, Royal Marines, composed of mounted infanty, camelry, and Sudanese infantry, established itself at Pap and gradually cleared the country.

Nyala 26th September, 1921-20th January, 1922

It should be noted that this bar comes before that for Darfur, 1921, though the period of service for which it was awarded continued on much later. In September, 1921, Fiki Abdullahi el Suheina proclaimed himself to be the Prophet Isa and obtained a considerable following in Southern Darfur. On 26th September he attacked the District Headquarters at Nyala, but was driven off and killed; but this did not put an end to the troubles, which lasted for a further four months. This bar was awarded to forty mounted infantrymen, forty police and a few friendlies for the defence of Nyala, and also to members of the column under Major S. T. Grigg, DSO, MC, West Yorkshire Regiment, which operated south of Nyala until 20th January, 1922.

Darfur 1921 26th September-22nd November, 1921

It should be noted that this bar follows that for Nyala in spite of the fact that the period for which it was awarded was completed first.

This bar was awarded to those who served at, or west of, Kereinik between 26th September and 22nd November, 1921. It was also awarded for services against Fiki Abdullahi and his followers (see Nyala above), to those who did not qualify for Nyala.

142 *1914 Star* 5th August-22nd November, 1914

General	A four pointed star having the uppermost point replaced by a crown and suspension ring. The star, crown and ring are stamped out together as a solid piece. Across the face are two crossed swords, the points and handles of which protrude between the points of the star
Obverse	In the centre on a scroll is the date '1914'; on two further scrolls, one above and one below the date are the months 'AUG' and 'NOV'. The three scrolls are surrounded by an oak wreath, on the bottom of which is superscribed a 'G' which encloses a 'V'
Reverse	Perfectly flat and plain except for the stamping of the recipient's number, rank, name and regiment
Size	Height including suspension ring, 62mm; width, 44.5mm
Metal	Bronze
Ribbon	32mm wide. A watered ribbon of red merging into white which merges into blue
Suspension	Ring suspension (see above)
Designer	W. H. J. Blakemore
Naming	The recipient's number, rank, initials, name, and unit are stamped in block capitals on the reverse in three lines for officers and other ranks
Bars issued	One: '5th Aug.-22nd Nov. 1914'

The 1914 Star was authorized in April, 1917, to be awarded to those who served in France or Belgium on the strength of a unit, or service in either of those two countries between 5th August and midnight on 22nd/23rd November, 1914.

In October, 1919, the King sanctioned the award of a bar to this star to all who had been *under fire* in France or Belgium during, or between the above dates.

The bar is of bronze 31mm x 5mm and has small holes at each corner enabling it to be sewn on to the ribbon. Recipients of the bar were entitled to wear a small silver rose on the ribbon when the star itself was not worn.

The Star and bar are often incorrectly referred to as the 'Mons Star' or 'Mons bar'.

Recipients of the 1914 Star always received the British War Medal and Victory Medal.

Groups are to be found, which include this star, and also the Mercantile Marine Medal. The recipients probably transferred to the Merchant Service subsequent to serving ashore during the qualifying period.

Personnel of the Royal Navy were awarded the 1914-15 Star, except for the few who served at Antwerp prior to midnight, 22nd/23rd November, 1914.

378,000 Stars were issued but it is not known how many of these were awarded with the bar.

160 Stars without bars were awarded to Canadians.

1914 Stars issued to medical units:

Ambulance Manners (8); Florence Fiennes Hospital (12); Womens Hosp Corps Wimereux (20); Millicent Sutherland Ambulance (21); Lady Doctors Hosp, Claridges Hotel Paris (22); Aux Hosp Unit Antwerp (36 approx.); Haden Guest Unit (42); QAIMNS (173); QAIMNSR (175); TFNS (61); Civil Hosp Res (370).

143 *1914-1915 Star* 5th August 1914-31st December 1915

General	A four pointed star having the uppermost point replaced by a crown and suspension ring. The star, crown and ring are stamped out together as a solid piece. Across the face are two crossed swords, the points and handles of which protrude between the points of the star
Obverse	In the centre on a scroll is the date '1914-15', this is surrounded by an oak wreath, on the bottom of which is superscribed a 'G' which encloses a 'V'
Reverse	Perfectly flat and plain except for the stamping of the recipient's number, rank, name and regiment
Size	Height including suspension ring, 62mm; width, 44.5mm
Metal	Bronze
Ribbon	32mm wide. A watered ribbon of red merging into white which merges into blue
Suspension	Ring suspension (see above)
Designer	W. H. J. Blakemore
Naming	The recipient's number, rank, initials, name and unit are stamped in block capitals on the reverse in three lines for officers and other ranks. Stars to New Zealand naval recipients have the ship's name in place of the RN, RNR, RNVR, etc.
Bars issued	Nil

The star was authorized in 1918 and was awarded to those who saw service between 5th August 1914 and 31st December 1915. Those eligible for the 1914 Star were not eligible for the 1914-15 Star.

Naval personnel qualifying for the Star consisted of officers and men of the Royal Navy, Royal Marines, Royal Naval Reserve, Royal Naval Volunteer Reserve, Royal Naval Air Service, Indian and Dominion forces who were mobilized and served at sea or served on land within a theatre of war within the above dates. Also to members of the RNAS employed in flying from naval air stations on overseas patrols. Also to Mercantile Marine personnel serving under special naval engagements and canteen staff employed on naval warships at sea within the approved dates.

Army personnel eligible consisted of officers and men of British, Dominion, Indian and Colonial forces and medical personnel serving in military hospitals within a theatre of war within the above dates.

Theatres of War

1 **West European:** Operations in France and Belgium from midnight 22nd-23rd November, 1914.

2 **East European:** Operations in Greece, Macedonia, Serbia and Bulgaria from 5th October, 1915. Gallipoli and Aegean Islands from 25th April, 1915. Operations at Seddul Bahr and Kum Kale, 4th March, 1915.

3 **Egyptian:** Operations against Turkish forces from 5th November, 1914. Operations against Senussite forces in Western Egypt and on the borders of Cyrenaica from 3rd November, 1915.

4 **African:** Operations in British East Africa, German East Africa, Rhodesia, Nyasaland and Uganda and on the African lakes from 20th August, 1914. German SW Africa and adjoining areas of the Union of South Africa from 20th August, 1914 to 9th July, 1915. Cameroon and Nigerian frontiers from 24th August, 1914. Togoland from 7th August, 1914 to 26th August, 1914.

5 **Asiatic:** Operations in Mesopotamia from 6th November, 1914. Tsing-Tau from 23rd September to 7th November, 1914. At Shaik Said in SW Arabia on 10th November, 1914. Operations by the Aden Field Force from 3rd July, 1915. Operations in Muscat under Colonel S. M. Edwardes in January 1915. In Seistan under Lieutenant Colonel J. M. Wilkeley during 1915. In the Tochi Valley and Derajat from 28th November, 1914 to 27th March, 1915. Against the Mohmands and Swatis as follows:
(i) Under Major General C. F. G. Young, near Hafiz Kor in April 1915. (ii) Under Brigadier General N. G. Woodyatt in August 1915. (iii) Under Brigadier General W. G. L. Benyon on the Landakai Ridge, August 1915. (iv) Under Major General F. Campbell near Hafiz Kor and Shabkadar from August to October 1915. (v) Operations by the Malakand Moveable Column, 1915.

6 **Pacific:** Operations in New Britain, 11th-21st September, 1914. New Ireland, 16th September-18th October, 1914. Kaiser Wilhelmland, 18th September, 1914. Admiralty Islands, 21st November, 1914. Nauru 6th November, 1914. Operations in German Samoa, 29th August, 1914.

The 1914-15 Star was not awarded for service which qualified for the Africa General Service Medal or the Sudan Medal 1910.

Recipients of the 1914-15 Star always received the British War Medal and Victory Medal.

Approximately 2,366,000 stars were issued (283,500 to the Royal Navy and 71,500 to Canadian units).

A 'Gallipoli Star' was at one time proposed and although the medal was cancelled in favour of the more general 1914-15 Star, ribbon for the award was produced. Ribbon for the proposed Gallipoli Star consisted of equal bands of yellow, blue and grey with a red stripe either side of the blue.

144 *British War Medal* 1914-20

Obverse	The coinage head of King George V with the legend 'GEORGIVS V BRITT: OMN: REX ET IND: IMP:'
Reverse	Naked figure of St. George on horseback facing right. The horse is trampling on an eagle shield representing the Central Powers and on a skull and crossbones symbolic of death; above the horse's head is the sun, symbolic of victory. Around the edge are the dates, '1914' and '1918'
Size	36mm diameter
Metal	Silver and bronze
Ribbon	32mm wide. A broad orange watered band down the centre, bordered with white, black and blue stripes
Suspension	By a plain, straight non-swivelling suspender. Calcutta Mint issues have a more substantial suspension claw
Designer	W. McMillan
Naming	Various styles of rather faint indented block capitals
Bars issued	Nil (see text)

This medal commemorates some of the most terrible battles the world has ever known. The military war dead of the British Empire totalled over 900,000.

The medal was instituted by George V in 1919 to mark the end of the Great War and record the service given.

The conditions of award were as follows:

ROYAL NAVY
The medal was granted to the undermentioned who performed twenty-eight days' mobilized service, or lost their lives in active operations before completing that period, between August 5th, 1914, and November 11th, 1918.
a) Officers and men of the Royal Navy, Royal Marines, Royal Naval Air Service, Royal Indian Marine, Royal Naval Reserve (including Trawler and Fishery Sections), Royal Naval Volunteer Reserve and Dominion and Colonial Naval Forces
b) Mercantile Marine officers and men serving in HM commissioned ships and auxiliaries under Special Naval Engagements
c) Officers and enrolled members of the Women's Royal Naval Service who proceeded and served overseas.
d) Members of Queen Alexandra's Royal Naval Nursing Service and Royal Naval Nursing Service Reserve and other recognized official nursing organisations, who served in a hospital ship at sea or proceeded overseas and served in a hospital abroad
e) Canteen staffs serving in a ship of war at sea
f) Non-nursing members of medical units, eg, dispensers, store-keepers, clerks, wardmaids, etc, who served in a hospital ship at sea or proceeded overseas and served in a naval hospital abroad

ARMY
The medal was granted to the undermentioned who either entered a theatre of war on duty or who left their places of residence and rendered approved service overseas, other than the waters dividing the different parts of the United Kingdom, between August 5th, 1914, and November 11th, 1918.
a) Officers and men of the British, Dominion, Colonial and Indian military forces
b) Members of women's formations who were enrolled under a direct contract of service for service with His Majesty's Imperial forces
c) All who served on the staffs of military hospitals, and all members of recognized organisations who actually handled the sick and wounded
d) Members of duly recognized or authorized organisations
e) Enrolled and attested followers on the establishment of units of the Indian Army

ROYAL AIR FORCE
a) Officers and men of the Royal Naval Air Service, Royal Flying Corps or Royal Air Force
b) Members of women's formations employed under a direct contract of service with the Royal Air Force Medical Service
c) Members of duly recognized or authorized organisations
The medal was also granted to all officers and men of the Royal Naval Air Service, Royal Flying Corps and Royal Air Force who—
i) were actively engaged in the air against the enemy whilst borne on the strength of an operational unit in Great Britain
ii) were employed in flying new aircraft to France
iii) Formed part of the complement of an aircraft-carrying ship

The qualification period was later extended to cover post-war mine clearance and service in Russia during 1919 and 1920.

The question of giving bars for certain battles and theatres of operations was raised; sixty-eight were suggested for Naval recipients and seventy-nine for the Army, however, the idea was dropped in 1923 because of the expense involved. The Naval bars were actually authorized in August 1920 but no further action was taken. No full-size bars were issued but the relevant Naval bars are often seen on miniature War Medals. Occasionally privately made full-size bars for Army and Navy service are seen fitted to the medal.

List of Naval bars authorized in 1920.

General actions at sea
Heligoland 8 Aug 1914; Falkland Islands 8 Dec 1914; Dogger Bank 24 Jan 1915; Jutland 31 May 1916

Single ship actions
Cap Trafalgar 14 Sept 1914; Emden 9 Nov 1914; Konigsberg July 1915; Leopard 16 March 1917; 21 April 1917

Fighting at sea in particular areas (year date up to '1918' in each case)
North Sea 1914; Narrow Seas 1914; Home Seas 1914; Arctic 1914; Baltic 1914; Mediterranean 1914

Special Services not in Particular Areas
Minesweeping; Minelaying; 'Q' Ships; Submarines; Baltic S/Ms;
Heligoland Bight S/Ms; Marmora S/Ms

Actions with Enemy's Land Forces
Belgian Coast; Dardanelles; Gallipoli Landing; Gallipoli; Tsingtau; Suez
Canal; Zeebrugge, Ostend; Ostend 10 May 1918

Operations with Land Forces
Mesopotamia; Red Sea; German East Africa; German SW Africa; Pacific
Islands; Cameroons

Services in Serbia and Russia, and Post Armistice Operations
Eastern Baltic 1918-19; Mine Clearance 1918-19; North Russia 1918-19;
Serbia; Serbia 1918-19; Russia; Black Sea; Caspian

Approximately 6,500,000 silver and 110,000 bronze medals were issued.
   It was issued in bronze to Chinese, Maltese, Indian and other native
Labour Corps and also to other native personnel who were mobilized

for war service and received pay at military rates.
   The naming detail given on the medal differs according to rank and
unit. Medals to Army officers do not give the regiment, those to officers
of the RN, RNR, RNVR, RM and RAF have the appropriate letters
after their name. Medals to Army 'other ranks' have the recipient's
number, rank, name and regiment, those to the Navy give the number,
rating and name followed by the relevant letters, RN, RNR, etc. With
the exception of medals to New Zealanders, no ship name is given.
Medals having the recipient's name only would be awarded to personnel
on war service though not in one of the recognized military services:
Merchant Navy, civilian nurses, press, etc.
   This medal was issued singly without the Allied Victory Medal to
certain regular and mobilized personnel who did not see any fighting.
   Recipients of a Mention in Despatches who did not qualify for the
Allied Victory Medal wore a bronze oak leaf on the ribbon of this
medal.
   A total of six hundred and thirty-three Victoria Crosses were awarded
between 1914-1919 including two awards for the NW Frontier of India
in 1915 and five for Russia in 1919.

145 *Mercantile Marine War Medal* 1914-18

Obverse	The coinage head of King George V with legend 'GEORGIVS V BRITT. OMN: REX ET IND: IMP:'
Reverse	Within a border of laurel, a merchant steamship is shown in a heavy sea. In the right background is a sailing ship, in the middle distance to the right is a sinking submarine.
	In the exergue in three lines is the wording 'FOR WAR SERVICE MERCANTILE MARINE 1914-1918'.
Size	36mm diameter
Metal	Bronze
Ribbon	32mm wide. Watered green and red divided by a thin white stripe. When worn, the red should be nearest the left shoulder. The colours of the ribbon represent the colours of ship's lights.
Suspension	By a straight, non-swivelling suspender.
Designer	Harold Stabler
Naming	The medals were named in indented block capitals or unnamed.
Bars issued	Nil

This bronze medal, issued by the Board of Trade, was awarded to members of the
Mercantile Marine, as the Merchant Navy was then called, who served on one or more
voyages through a danger zone. It was given in bronze to officers and men alike as opposed
to the earlier Transport Medal which was awarded to ship's officers only.

A few members of the Royal Navy were seconded for service with the
Mercantile Marine to man the defensive weapons between 4th August
1914, and 31st December 1915. These men received the appropriate
Star, the British War Medal and the Victory Medal, as well as the
Mercantile Marine Medal.
   Certain members of the Mercantile Marine joined the Royal Navy
between the above dates. They also received the four medals.
   Those who completed the whole of their service at sea with the
Mercantile Marine, no matter for how long or between which dates,
were awarded only the Mercantile Marine Medal and the British War
Medal.
   It was, of course, possible for a man who did not qualify for one of
the stars to get only three medals—namely, the British War Medal,
Mercantile Marine Medal, and the Victory Medal—providing he had not
less than six months' service at sea.
   Those who served this period at sea in pilot and/or lighthouse vessels,
Government cable ships or as fishermen also qualified.
   A total of 133,135 medals were issued, approximately 100 were to
Canadians.

146 *Victory Medal* 1914-19

Obverse	The winged, full-length figure of Victory, with her arm extended and holding a palm branch in her right hand.
Reverse	The inscription 'THE GREAT WAR FOR CIVILIZATION, 1914-1919' surrounded by a wreath.
Size	36mm diameter
Metal	Bronze
Ribbon	37mm wide. Watered, reading from the centre outwards, the colours are red, yellow, green, blue and violet merged into a rainbow pattern.
Suspension	The ribbon is threaded through a 14mm diameter ring, which passes through a loop fixed to the top of the piece.
Designer	W. McMillan
Naming	In faint impressed block capitals. Details of naming, as for the British War Medal.
Bars issued	Nil

The medal was authorized in 1919 to commemorate the victory of the Allies over the Central Powers. It was resolved that each of the Allies should issue a 'Victory Medal' to their own nationals so to prevent a mass exchange of commemorative awards between the nations. It was further resolved that all the issues would have as a common feature the figure of Victory upon the obverse. The issue of the Victory Medal was optional and in the event the following countries issued medals: Great Britain, Belgium, Brazil, Cuba, Czechoslovakia, France, Greece, Italy, Japan, Portugal, Roumania, Thailand, Union of South Africa and United States of America.

Eligibility for the British Victory Medal was as follows:
ROYAL NAVY
The medal was granted to the undermentioned who were mobilized and gave service at sea between midnight 4th-5th August 1914 and midnight 11th-12th November 1918 or who were on the establishment of a unit within a theatre of operations (see below).
a) Officers and men of the Royal Navy, Royal Marines, Royal Naval Air Service, Royal Indian Marine, Royal Naval Reserve, Royal Naval Volunteer Reserve, Royal Naval Auxilliary Sick Berth Reserve and all Dominion and Colonial Naval Forces.
   Members of the RNAS employed in actual flying from Naval Air Stations at home on overseas missions were also eligible.
b) Mercantile Marine officers and men serving in HM commissioned ships and auxiliaries under Special Naval Engagements.
c) Officers and enrolled members of the Women's Royal Naval Service.
d) Members of Queen Alexandra's Royal Naval Nursing Service and the Royal Naval Nursing Service Reserves.
e) Canteen staffs who served in a ship of war at sea.

ARMY
The medal was granted to the undermentioned who actually served on the establishment of a unit within a theatre of war within the specified dates.
a) Officers and men of the British, Dominion, Colonial and Indian Forces.
b) Members of women's formations who were enrolled under a direct contract of service for service with HM Imperial forces.
c) All who served on the staffs of military hospitals and all members of recognized organisations who handled the sick and wounded.

ROYAL AIR FORCE
The medal was granted to the undermentioned officers and men.
a) Those who served in a unit within a theatre of war within specificed dates.
b) Those who served with an operational unit in the British Isles or overseas and who were actively engaged in the air against the enemy.

c) Those who flew new planes from Britain to France.
d) Those who formed part of the complement of an aircraft-carrying ship.

Theatre of Operations:
1 Western European Theatre
a) France and Belgium, between midnight August 4th-5th 1914, and midnight November 11th-12th 1918.
b) Italy, between midnight April 17th-18th 1917, and midnight November 4th-5th 1918.

2 Balkan Theatre
a) Greek Macedonia, Serbia, Bulgaria and European Turkey, between midnight October 4th-5th 1915, and November 11th-12th 1918.
b) Gallipoli and Islands of Aegean Sea, between midnight April 24th-25th 1915, and midnight January 9th-10th 1916.

3 Russian Theatre. All operations in Russia from midnight August 4th-5th 1914.

4 Egyptian Theatre
a) In Egypt, between midnight November 4th-5th 1914, and midnight March 18th-19th 1916. (Excluding operations for which the Sultan's Sudan Medal was awarded.)
b) Conducted by the Egyptian Expeditionary Force, between midnight March 18th-19th 1916, and midnight October 31st-November 1st 1918. (Excluding operations for which the Sultan's Sudan Medal was awarded.)

5 African Theatre. All operations except local military operations against native tribes or rebels for which the Africa General Service Medal was awarded.
a) In British, German and Portuguese East Africa, Nyasaland and Northern Rhodesia, between midnight August 19th-20th 1914, and midnight November 25th-26th 1918.
b) In German South-West Africa and on the adjacent borders of the

Union of South Africa, between midnight August 19th-20th 1914, and midnight July 9th-10th 1915.

c) In the Cameroons and on the Eastern and Northern Frontiers of Nigeria, between midnight August 23rd-24th 1914, and midnight February 18th-19th 1916.

d) In Nigeria, between midnight January 4th-5th 1917, and midnight May 15th-16th 1917.

e) In Togoland, between midnight August 6th-7th 1914, and midnight August 26th-27th 1914.

6 Asiatic Theatre

a) In Hedjaz, between midnight November 4th-5th 1914, and midnight January 13th-14th 1919.

b) In Mesopotamia, from midnight November 5th-6th 1914.

c) In Persia and the Persian Gulf, from midnight November 5th-6th 1914.

d) In Trans-Caspia, from midnight July 18th-19th 1918.

e) At Shaik Said (South-West Arabia), on November 10th and 11th 1914; and at Perim, on June 14th and 15th 1915.

f) Conducted by the Aden Field Force, between midnight July 2nd-3rd 1915, and midnight January 13th-14th 1919.

g) In the frontier regions of India, carried out by forces which actually took the field between August 5th 1914, and October 31st 1918.

h) At Tsing-Tau, between midnight September 22nd-23rd 1914, and midnight November 7th-8th 1914.

7 Australasian Theatre. All operations against the German Pacific Dependencies.

a) New Britain, from midnight September 10th-11th 1914, to midnight September 21st-22nd 1914.

b) New Ireland, from midnight September 15th-16th 1914, to midnight October 18th-19th 1914.

c) Kaiser Wilhelmland, on September 24th 1914.

d) Admiralty Islands on November 21st 1914.

e) Nauru, on November 6th 1914.

f) German Samoa, on August 29th 1914.

Approximately 5,725,000 British Victory Medals were issued.

All recipients of the British Victory Medal received the War Medal; all recipients of the 1914 and 1914-15 Stars received the War and Victory Medals. Recipients of the War Medal were not automatically entitled to the Victory Medal.

Those who were mentioned in despatches between 4th August 1914, and 10th August 1920, were allowed to wear an oak leaf on the ribbon. The leaf worn on the ribbon with the medal is slightly larger than that worn on the riband bar when the medal is not worn. In the rare cases when the recipient of a 'Mention in Despatches' did not receive a Victory Medal, or the British War Medal, the emblem is worn on the jacket. Only one emblem could be worn no matter how many times a person was mentioned in despatches.

---

147 *South Africa Victory Medal* 1914-19

Obverse	The winged full-length figure of Victory, with her left arm extended and holding a palm branch in her right hand.
Reverse	The inscription in seven lines in English and Afrikaans, 'THE GREAT WAR FOR CIVILISATION DE GROTE OORLOG VOOR DE BESCHAVING 1914-1919', surrounded by a wreath.
Size	36mm diameter
Metal	Bronze
Ribbon	37mm wide. Watered, reading from the centre outwards, the colours are red, yellow, green, blue and violet merged into a rainbow pattern.
Suspension	The ribbon is threaded through a 14mm. diameter ring, which passes through a loop fixed to the top of the piece.
Designer	W. McMillan
Naming	In impressed block capitals

148 *Territorial Force War Medal* 1914-19

Obverse	The coinage head of King George V with legend 'GEORGIVS V BRITT. OMN: REX ET IND: IMP:'
Reverse	The legend 'TERRITORIAL WAR MEDAL' around the top. Inside a wreath is the inscription 'FOR VOLUNTARY SERVICE OVERSEAS 1914-19'.
Size	36mm diameter
Metal	Bronze
Ribbon	32mm wide. Watered, yellow with two green stripes.
Suspension	By a plain, non-swivelling suspender.
Designer	As the reverse only bears an inscription, no designer was employed.
Naming	The medals were named in impressed block capitals.
Bars issued	Nil

This bronze medal was awarded to all members of the Territorial Force including Nursing Sisters, who were members of the service on 4th August 1914, and to those who had completed four years' service before 4th August 1914, providing that they had rejoined on, or prior to, 30th September 1914. In addition to the above, to be eligible for the award members must have: a) undertaken on, or before, 30th September 1914, to serve outside the United Kingdom; b) served outside the United Kingdom between 4th August 1914 and midnight 11/12th November 1918; c) been ineligible for either the 1914 or 1914-15 Star.

The medal is worn immediately after the Allied Victory Medal and before all subsequently awarded war medals, and, of course, before Long Service and Meritorious Service Medals.

The dates on the reverse should be noted. As eligibility terminated on 11th November 1918, it is difficult to see why the date 1919 was put on the medal.

A total of 33,944 medals were issued.

149 *HMAS Sydney—SMS Emden Medal* 1914

On the outbreak of the First World War on 4th August 1914, a few German warships were away from their home ports. The most individually famous of these was the light cruiser *Emden,* which by brilliant tactical handling and clever camouflage and that modicum of luck which is seldom denied a bold commander, enabled Captain von Muller to enter Penang Roads, on 30th September, sink the old Russian gunboat *Jemchug,* shell the shore installations and then escape. For some while after this her whereabouts were unknown.

About seven hundred miles to the south-west of Sumatra is a small group of islands known as the Cocos or Keeling Islands. On one of these lone British possessions there was a wireless station. The *Emden* anchored offshore and sent a landing party to demolish the transmitter, but the chief operator had his suspicions aroused and managed to get off a message before the party arrived. This message was picked up by HMAS *Sydney,* which immediately altered course and steamed at full speed for the islands. On arrival her 6in. guns soon reduced the *Emden* to a shambles and forced her to surrender.

When she was boarded by the crew of the *Sydney* a quantity of Mexican silver dollars were found.

1,000 of these dollars were mounted as medals and given to the crew of HMAS *Sydney* to commemorate the engagement whilst 996 were sold to the general public to defray the cost of this free distribution. The medal consists, therefore, of a Mexican dollar piece on which a Crown has been fitted and the words '9th NOV., 1914, HMAS SYDNEY—SMS EMDEN' added. In addition Capt. J. T. Glossop of HMAS *Sydney* was given a $20 US gold piece, another being kept at the Navy Office in Melbourne.

These medals, which were really only mementoes, were not allowed to be worn in uniform.

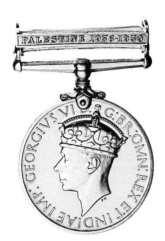

150 *Naval General Service Medal* 1915-1962

Obverse   *1st issue* bears the bust of King George V in Naval uniform with the legend 'GEORGIVS V BRITT: OMN: REX ET IND: IMP:'
2nd issue (1936-1949) has the crowned coinage head of King George VI and bears the legend 'GEORGIVS VI G: BR: OMN: REX ET INDIAE IMP:'
3rd issue (1949-1952) has the crowned head of George VI and the legend 'GEORGIVS VI DEI: GRA: BRITT: OMN: REX F.D.DEF +.'
4th issue has the crowned bust of Queen Elizabeth II facing right and the legend 'ELIZABETH II D: G: BR: OMN: REGINA F:D.'
5th issue (1953-1962) has the crowned bust of Elizabeth II and the legend 'ELIZABETH II DEI. GRATIA REGINA F.D. +.'

Reverse   Britannia on two sea horses, with her left hand resting on the Union Shield, and her right holding a trident

Size   36mm diameter

Metal   Silver

Ribbon   32mm wide. Crimson with three white stripes

Suspension   By a plain straight suspender. The first issue, George V and fifth issue, Elizabeth II have swivel suspensions; all others have a fixed suspension

Designer   Miss Margaret Winser

Naming   The first issue is named in large impressed block capitals which give the recipient's number, name, rank, and ship. The second issue is named in very small impressed block capitals, and the name of the recipient's ship is not given, only the initials 'R.N.' or 'R.M.' after the name. The same applies to the later issues

Bars issued   Sixteen: Persian Gulf 1909-1914, Iraq 1919-1920, NW Persia 1919-20, NW Persia 1920, Palestine 1936-1939, SE Asia 1945-46, Minesweeping 1945-51, Palestine 1945-48, Bomb and Mine Clearance 1945-53, Malaya, Yangtze 1949, Bomb and Mine Clearance Mediterranean, Cyprus, Near East, Arabian Peninsula, Brunei

The medal was instituted on 6th August 1915 for service in minor Naval war-like operations. This medal could not be issued without a bar.

Permission was granted to recipients of a Mention in Despatches during any of the operations for which this medal was awarded after 11th August, 1920, to wear a bronze oak leaf emblem on the ribbon.

Persian Gulf 1909-1914 19th October, 1909-1st August, 1914

The bar was instituted on 10th August, 1915 and was awarded to the officers and Men of HM Ships who were employed in the operations for the suppression of the arms traffic in the Arabian Sea or Persian Gulf, North of Latitude 22°N, and West of Longitude 64°E, between the 19th October 1909 and the 1st August 1914. The award was extended to the officers and men of the RM co-operating with the RN in a Naval sense, but not to those on Transport work only. This grant included RIMS *Minto*, the RIM ranks and ratings in the Armed Launches and the staffs of the Coal Depots at Basian and Heniam.

HMS: *Alert* (332); *Dartmouth* (383); *Espiegle* (237); *Fox* (1001); *Harold* (33); *Highflyer* (518); *Hyacinth* (434); *Karanja* (29); *Lapwing* (24); *Mashona* (44); *Minor* (28); *Musbee* (13); *Odin* (353); *Panther* (4); *Pelorus* (254); *Perseus* (505); *Philomel* (505); *Proserpine* (447); *Redbreast* (60); *Sheik Berhkud* (17); *Sphinx* (163), *Swiftsure* (702); *Tamil* (18).
Ships of the Royal Indian Marine: *Lawrence* (336); *Minto* (480); *Palinurus* (178).
Basian Coal Depot Staff (40); Heniam Coal Depot Staff (19).

The following officers also received the medal with this bar:
Major H. H. Austin, R.E., Naval Intelligence Staff; Major C. C. R. Murphy, I.A., Naval Intelligence Staff; Captain G. S. G. Crauford, Naval Intelligence Staff; Captain J. J. Eadie, I.A., attached Naval Staff; Captain R. F. Woodward, attached Naval Staff; E. G. Gregson, Indian Police, attached Naval Staff; Lieutenant-Colonel F. A. Smith, 2 Rajputs, HMS *Pelorus;* Captain R. T. Arundell, 2 Rajputs, HMS *Pelorus;* Captain L. Birdwood, I.A., 2 Rajputs, HMS *Pelorus;* Captain W. R. C. Griffiths, 2 Rajputs, HMS *Pelorus;* Lieutenant C D. Noyes, 2 Rajputs, HMS *Pelorus;* Major J. Stewart, I.A., HMS *Perseus;* Captain W. L. Watson, Indian Medical Service, HMS *Philomel;* Lieutenant C. M. Maltby, 95th Russell's Infantry, HMS *Fox;* Lieutenant G. Rawson, RIM; Lieutenant H. B. Livesey, RIM; Lieutenant R. C. P. Price, RIM.

A consignment of these medals was despatched from London on 18th December 1915 on board the SS *Persia.* Unfortunately on the 30th December she was torpedoed and sunk by the U.38 and the medals together with 334 of the 501 passengers and crew, were lost. This is possibly the reason why Persian Gulf medals are occasionally seen impressed in a smaller type of lettering; these being the later replacements of those lost.

Iraq 1919-1920 1st July-17th November 1920

This award was granted to officers and men who served in River Gun-Boats within the boundaries of Iraq between 1st July and 17th November 1920. In view of this it is difficult to see why the bar is dated 1919-1920.

Medals issued with this single bar have a fixed suspension. These awards are believed to have been awarded after 1935.

A total of nine officers and one hundred and nineteen ratings from the following ships received the award.

HMS *Clio, Espiegle, Triad.*

Seven ratings previously issued with the medal received the bar only. W. A. Rapley RN. HMS *Clio*, was one of eight who received this bar and the 'Somaliland 1920' bar on the Africa General Service Medal.

NW Persia 1919-20

Those qualifying for the bar NW Persia 1920 were originally issued with the bar NW Persia 1919-20. This bar was later withdrawn and those who had received it were then expected to return it for an exchange.

NW Persia 1920 10th August-31st December 1920

This bar was awarded to the Officers and Men who served in the Naval Mission under Commodore D. T. Norris, CB, CMG, RN, in North West Persia between 10th August 1920 and 31st December 1920.

Recipients: Commodore D. T. Norris, CB, CMG, RN; Paymaster Lieutenant H. G. Pertwee, DSO, RN; Chief Petty Officer H. Dickason and Able Seaman C. B. Haig.

In September 1918 Commodore Norris commanded a flotilla with Russian support and attacked the Turkish port of Baku on the Caspian Sea. However by the end of the year the flotilla was menaced by the growing Bolshevik presence. This resulted in Commodore Norris attacking and defeating the Bolshevik ships. Control of the Caspian Sea was returned to the Russian Navy when Commodore Norris withdrew in 1920.

Palestine 1936-1939 19th April 1936-3rd September, 1939

This bar was awarded for service in connection with military operations along, and off, the coast of Palestine between 19th April 1936 and 3rd September 1939. Entitlement was earned merely by being present. Some ships served only days whilst others were actively engaged for many months in anti-gun running operations, or gave close inshore artillery support to the army on shore. This was the first bar to be awarded with the second issue obverse of the medal.

A total of 79 naval ships were engaged in the 3½ years of conflict which was temporarily interrupted by the start of the Second World War. The crews of numerous small inshore craft and auxilliary vessels, as well as requisitioned merchant vessels, became eligible for the medal. A total of 13,600 medals/bars were issued.

HMS: *Aberdeen, Active, Adventure, Agate, Ajax, Amethyst, Antelope, Arethusa, Beagle, Blanche, Boadicea, Boreas, Brazen, Brigand, Brilliant, Bulldog, Cedar, Clyde, Cornelian, Cyclops, Delhi, Despatch, Douglas, Durban, Emerald, Galatea, Gallant, Garland, Gipsy, Glowworm, Grafton, Grenade, Greyhound, Griffin, Hardy, Hasty, Havock, Hawthorn, Hereward, Hero, Holly, Hotspur, Icarus, Ilex, Imogen, Imperial, Impulsive, Inglefield, Intrepid, Isis, Ivanhoe, Jasper, Keith, Laurel, Lilac, Maine, Magnolia, Malaya, Narwhal, Pangbourne, Pearl, Porpoise, Protector, Reliant, Repulse, Ross, Ruby, Sapphire, Severn, Sussex, Sutton, Syringe, Thames, Topaze, Tourmaline, Turquoise, Valiant, Weston, Willow.*

SE Asia 1945-46

To qualify for this award a member of the Naval Forces must have served a total of twenty-eight days afloat within five miles of the operational areas given below and within the specified periods. These areas and dates are the same as those which enabled the Army and the Royal Air Force to qualify for the General Service Medal (see page 240).

Naval personnel who served on operational duty ashore qualified under Army rules. The qualifying period for official visits and inspections was one week. Naval air crews qualified if they had performed one operational sortie over any of the land operational areas.

Recipients of a King's Commendation, Mention in Despatches or any British honour for service rendered in any of the specified areas and within the specified dates were eligible for the award, though they may not have completed the full twenty-eight days' service.

Curtailment of the specified period through death or by evacuation on account of wounds or disability caused by service did not debar eligibility.

The qualifying areas and dates are:
1) Java and Sumatra from 3rd September, 1945, to 30th November, 1946, both dates inclusive.
2) French Indo-China from 3rd September, 1945, to 28th January, 1946, both dates inclusive.

Approximately 2,000 medals/bars were awarded.

Minesweeping 1945-51 3rd September 1945-30th September 1951

This was the first bar to be awarded with the third issue obverse.

The qualifying period for this award was six months' Naval minesweeping service afloat after 3rd September, 1945.

The grant of a King's Commendation, Mention in Despatches or other British honour for minesweeping service within the qualifying zones and dates qualified the recipient for the award, though he may not have completed the full six months' service.

If the qualifying service was ended by death or curtailed by reason of wounds or any disability due to service, the reduced period of service was considered sufficient to gain the award.

The minesweeping zones and terminal dates of the operations were: East Indies, South West Pacific and China Coast; 30th December 1946 Mediterranean (except Greek waters) and approaches to Gibraltar; 15th August, 1947
North West Europe and British Isles, including the North Sea; 30th October, 1947 (except for the Thames Estuary)
Red Sea; 15th April, 1948
Greek Waters; 30th September, 1951
Approximately 4,750 medals/bars were awarded.

Palestine 1945-48 27th September 1945-30th June 1948

The qualifying period was given as (1) twenty-eight days afloat in ships employed on the Palestine Patrol against illegal immigration, or (2) in close support of the defined Army Forces, which meant service within three miles of any qualifying land area.

Naval personnel who served ashore and Naval air crews came under the same qualifications as those for the Army. Service which was curtailed through death, or other causes due to service, would qualify for the award. Men of the Merchant Navy employed in transporting illegal immigrants from Haifa to Cyprus or employed on Merchant or Royal Fleet Auxiliary ships in attendance on the ships of the fleet, also qualified.

The British mandate in Palestine ended at midnight, 14th May 1948.

Approximately 7,900 medals/bars were issued.

HMS *Ajax, Aurora, Bigbury Bay, Brissenden, Chequers, Charity, Cheviot, Childers, Chieftain, Chevron, Chaplet, Chivalrous, Cardigan Bay, Espiegle, Enard Bay, Fierce, Haydon, Hascosay, Liverpool, Lookout, Mauritius, Milne, Matchless, Moon, Magpie, Mermaid, Orion, Octavia, Phoebe, Providence, Peacock, Pelican, Rowena, Sirius, Superb, Saumarez, Stevenstone, Skipjack, Seabear, Stormcloud, St Austell Bay, St Brides Bay, Troubridge, Talybont, Truelove, Venus, Virago, Volage, Verulam, Veryan Bay, Welfare, Whitesand Bay, Widemouth Bay, M.F.V. 55, M.F.V. 101.*

Bomb and Mine Clearance 1945-53

This was awarded on the medal with either the fourth or fifth issue obverse.

This bar was awarded for six months' consecutive work (including Australian units) in the disposal of bombs and mines in different parts of the world. The terminal dates varied from 16th December, 1946, around Hong Kong to 28th April, 1953, for clearances off the Solomon Islands, New Guinea and Papua.

A total of 145 medals/bars were issued (28 bars and 117 medals with bar), nine medals were awarded posthumously.

Malaya 16th June 1948-31st July 1960

The bar was awarded on the medal with either the third, fourth or fifth issue obverse.

The qualifying service afloat was 28 days after 16th June 1948 in ships or craft patrolling off the Malayan Coast in support of operations against bandits, or one journey in a harbour defence launch, motor launch, or other small craft up a river or creek, in the Federation of Malaya, in close support of operations against bandits.

The qualifying period on shore was one day on duty in the Federation of Malaya, attached to 3-Commando Brigade, Royal Marines, or other eligible forces or Police. Naval air crews were required to make one sortie over the operational area. The Commonwealth Naval Forces, and its Reserves, qualified in the same manner as the Royal Navy.

Naval inspecting officers and visitors had to be present for a period of thirty days to qualify.

Approximately 7,800 medals/bars were issued.

Yangtze 1949 20th April-31st July 1949

With the third issue obverse.

This bar was awarded to members of all three Services for operations in the Yangtze river against the Chinese Communist Forces.

It should be especially noted that personnel of the Army and the Royal Air Force were awarded a Naval medal.

The qualifications for the award were as follows:

ROYAL NAVY
It was awarded to members of His Majesty's ships for service on, or between, the dates mentioned:

HMS *Amethyst*, 20th April-31st July, 1949
HMS *Black Swan*, 21st April, 1949
HMS *Consort*, 20th April, 1949
HMS *London*, 21st April, 1949.

It was also awarded to the officers who joined HMS *Amethyst* on the 21st or 22nd April, 1949, after being flown to the ship in a Sunderland aircraft of the Royal Air Force.

ARMY
It was awarded to personnel who flew to HMS *Amethyst* on the 21st or 22nd April, 1949, in the Sunderland aircraft of the Royal Air Force.

ROYAL AIR FORCE
It was awarded to the crew of the Sunderland aircraft which flew to HMS *Amethyst* on 21st or 22nd April, and to Flight Lieutenant M. E. Fearnley, who remained on board the warship as medical officer.

Approx. 1,450 medals/bars were awarded for the incident which originated about 140 miles up the Yangtze river during the fighting between the Chinese Communists and Nationalist forces, the former of whom held the north bank and the latter the south.

HMS *Amethyst* was ordered up to Nanking to relieve HMS *Consort* and to take up supplies to the British community. On 20th April, whilst on her way up, she was heavily shelled by the Communist forces and driven ashore, suffering seventeen killed and ten wounded casualties, among the latter being the commanding officer, Lieutenant-Commander B. M. Skinner, RN. HMS *Consort* hurried down to her relief, but could not stop and reached Kiangyin with twelve casualties.

When the perilous plight of the *Amethyst* became apparent, the cruiser HMS *London* (Captain P. G. L. Cazalet, RN) and the frigate *Black Swan* (Captain A. D. H. Jay, DSO, DSC, RN) were ordered to proceed up the river to assist her. The attempt was made on 21st April, but the fire from the Communist-held shore was so severe that the two ships had to return. HMS *London* received thirty-two casualties (fifteen killed, seventeen wounded), and the *Black Swan* had five men wounded.

Whilst these rescue attempts were being made, the Royal Air Force flew a British and an American doctor to the *Amethyst,* which had succeeded in moving to a more sheltered position upstream and Lieutenant-Commander J. S. Kerans assumed command.

Negotiations concerning the release of the ship became protracted and the supplies of food and fuel were running short, so Lieutenant-Commander Kerans decided that the ship should escape, and the necessary preparations were made.

By an extraordinary blend of good preparation, good discipline, good seamanship and the good fortune which invariably favours the brave, the ship rejoined the fleet on 30th July.

She eventually reached England on 1st November, 1949, where the Commander-in-Chief, Plymouth, notified the ship's company that their conduct was 'up to standard', which, when compared with the many other Naval occasions mentioned in this book, is a particularly apt description.

HMS Amethyst-Yangtze 1949

Nominal Roll of Officers, Petty Officers and Seamen
The roll given below shows all those officers and men who served aboard HMS *Amethyst* during the period 20 April-31 July 1949. It has been possible to identify those who remained in the *Amethyst* after the evacuations at Rose Island on 20 April, and the Hsiao Ho on 21 April, their names being shown in bold type.

OFFICERS
Alderton, J. M., Surgn Lieut, MB, RN   Killed. Posthumous MID
Berger, P. E. C., Lieut (ND), RN   Wounded. Awarded DSC
Fearnley, M. E., Flt-Lieut, RAF   Awarded DSC. Joined from Sunderland flying boat, 21 April as Medical Officer
Hett, K. S., Lieut, RN   MID
Kerans, J. S., Lieut-Comdr, RN   Awarded DSO. Joined on 22 April to take command of HMS *Amethyst* from Lieut Weston, DSC
Mirehouse, H. R. M., Lieut, RN   Wounded
Monaghan, E., RN
Skinner, B. M., Lieut-Comdr, RN, Capt of HMS *Amethyst* Died of wounds. Posthumous MID
Strain, G. B., Lieut-Comdr (L), RN   Awarded MBE
Weston, G. L., Lieut, DSC, RN   Severely wounded. Awarded bar to DSC.
Assumed temporary command of the ship when Lieut-Comdr Skinner was wounded
Wilkinson, E. G., Lieut, (E), RN   Wounded

CIVILIANS
Macnamara, J. J. S., Canteen Manager, NAAFI

PETTY OFFICERS & SEAMEN
Aldridge, Thomas James, Able Seaman D/SSX 819105   Aberdeen
Anderson, Thomas, Stoker Mechanic P/SKX 803062   Glasgow Wounded
Ashford, John Rayston, Able Seaman D/SSX 778094   Bristol
Aubrey, Owen Frederick Charles, CPO Stoker Mechanic P/KX 80496 Wimborne   Killed
Augustyns, Denis Charles, Leading Stoker Mechanic D/KX 97531   Hull

Bailey, Ronald Owen, Ordinary Seaman D/JX 836014   Tavistock
Baker, Thomas Owen, Sick Berth Attendant D/SMX 817098 Port Talbot   Killed
Bannister, Samuel J., Stoker Mechanic D/SKX 833816   Belfast Wounded
Barnbrook, Maurice John Edwin, Boy First Class D/JX 836255 Birmingham   Killed
Barrow, William, Stoker Mechanic P/SKX 790306   Manchester   Killed
Battams, Charles William, Ordinary Seaman D/SSX 837992   Barnet Killed
Bell, David, Able Seaman D/SSX 795674   Birmingham
Blomley, Hugh Edmond, Electrician, PO D/MX 844298   Oxford
Bowles, George Arthur, Petty Officer D/JX 146751   Plymouth
Brown, Arthur Thomas, Stoker Mechanic D/SKX 770296   Walsall
Bryson, James MacFarlane, Able Seaman D/SSX 831629   Gallashiels

Calcott, Raymond, Able Seaman D/SSX 818675   Coventry
Canning, Leonard Gordon Madden, Stoker Mechanic D/SKX 831991 Bristol   Wounded
Cavill, George D. R., Cook (S) D/MX 814944   Teignmouth
Chare, Lionel Harry, Electrical Artificer 4th Class   Pittenweem   MID

Clarkson, Lawrence H., Yeo of Signals C/JX 155179   Chesterfield
Connor, Leonard James, Petty Officer Stoker Mechanic D/KX 96160
  Haydock
Cook, Derek Arthur, Telegraphist D/JX 660534   New Earswick
Crann, Leslie, Stoker Mechanic D/KX 93630   London   Killed
Crighton, Arthur Baker, Leading Seaman D/JX 152789   Bournemouth
  Wounded
Crocker, William Samuel, Leading Telegraphist D/JX 166578   Leigh

Davies, Ames William John, Able Seaman D/SSX 815834   Newport
  Wounded
Davies, Ronald Thomas, Able Seaman D/SSX 818663   Wolverhampton
Davis, Dennis, Cook (S) D/MX 848033   Birmingham   Wounded
Dawson, Kenneth, Able Seaman P/SSX 747859   Stockport
Day, Jack Allan, Able Seaman D/SSX 837670   Hatfield
Delve, Kenneth, Ordinary Seaman D/SSX 855437   Liverpool
Donaldson, William Joseph, Able Seaman P/SSX 819199   South Shields
Donnelly, Malachy, Electrician's Mate 1st Class D/MX 802818
  Uddingston
Driscoll, Albert Edgar, Ordinary Seaman D/SSX 815835   Torquay
  Killed

Eddleston, Ronald Hargreaves, Able Seaman D/SSX 818718   Blackburn

Fellows, Albert Edwin, Stoker Mechanic D/KX 811006   West Bromwich
Ferrett, Joseph Harold, Leading Signalman P/JX 163032   Wimborne
Ferrier, David Ferguson, Able Seaman D/JX 419503   Glasgow
Fletcher, Ronald, Stoker Mechanic D/KX 145165   Oldham   Wounded
Frank, Leslie, Petty Officer D/JX 667520   Plymouth   Awarded DSM
Freeman, William Henry, Petty Officer D/JX 149820   New
  Brighton   MID
French, Jack Leonard, Telegraphist D/JX 671532   Ashburton
  Awarded DSM

Garfitt, William, Leading Seaman D/JX 254252   Sheffield
Garns, Albert, Petty Officer Stoker Mechanic D/KX 92134   Manchester
Gibson, Robert, Stoker Mechanic D/SKX 770304   Irvine
Gill, Donald Clifford, Able Seaman D/SSX 818   Harrogate
Graham, Gerald Charles Gaffney, Engine Room Artificer 3rd Cl.
  D/MX 59026   Newcastle-upon-Tyne
Grazier, Bernard, Ordinary Seaman D/JX 820368   Leicester
Griffiths, Dennis James, Ordinary Seaman D/SSX 855416   Wirrall
  Killed
Griffiths, George, Petty Officer Cook (S) D/MX 80750   Hednesford

Hackman, Clive, Boy 1st Class D/JX 836234   Loughborough
Harratt, Norman Arthur, Able Seaman D/JX 661155   Leicester
Harris, Henry, Ordinary Seaman D/SSX 855417   Arradoul
Hartness, George Joseph, Leading Seaman D/JX 286570   West Kirby
Haveron, Hugh, Able Seaman D/SSX 818679   Belfast
Hawkins, Charles Arthur, Stoker Mechanic P/SKX 771189   Cambridge
Heath, David Graham, Petty Officer D/JX 164027   Dartmouth
Heighway, Percy Cyril, Joiner 3rd Class D/MX 510381   Liverpool
Hicks, Sydney Powell, Electrician's Mate 1st Cl. D/MX 802832
  Manchester   Killed
Higgins, Stewart, Stoker Mechanic D/SKX 779600   Edinburgh
Hiles, Norman, Ordinary Seaman D/SSX 855418   Stockport
Holloway, Eric Pearson, Mechanic 1st Cl. D/KX 117597
  Wellingborough
Horton, Sydney Stephen, Boy 1st Class D/JX 836291   Plymstock
Howell, Brynley, Stores Assistant D/MX 122427   Haverfordwest
  Wounded
Hutchinson, Roland Leslie, Able Seaman D/SSX 661144   Wallsend

Irwin, Vernon Edward, Electrician P/MX 745767   Weymouth

Johnston, James Foster, Able Seaman, D/SSX 818642   Bangor
Jones, Donald Reginald, Able Seaman D/SSX 848096   Gloucester
Jones, John, Ordinary Seaman D/SSX 855419   Liverpool
Jones, Peter, Ordinary Seaman D/JX 854289   Wallasey

Kay, Raymond, Able Seaman D/JX 661157   Rochdale
Keicher, Charles Augustus, Able Seaman D/SSX 847007   Glencraig

Lees, Leslie William, Ordinary Seaman D/JX 836005   Shrewsbury
Logan, George Ronald, PO Stoker Mechanic D/KX 105115   Liverpool
Loving, Bryan Albert, Stoker Mechanic D/KX 854572   Fairford
  Wounded

Macdonald, Duncan, Leading Stoker Mechanic C/KX 94342   Pitcaple
Maddocks, George, Stoker Mechanic D/SKX 854929   Liverpool
  Wounded
Marsh, Samuel Robert, Boy 1st Class D/JX 836294   Honiton   Wounded
Martin, Keith Cantrill, Boy 1st Class D/JX 836190   Leicester
  Wounded, MID
Maskell, Victor Douglas, Stoker Mechanic C/KX 118897   Oakham
  Killed
McCarthy, John Justin, Stores Petty Officer D/MX 57988   Larne   MID
McCullough, Raymond Charles, Able Seaman D/SSX 661212   Belfast
McGlashen, Ian, Engineroom Artificer 2nd Class D/MX 62026
  Glyn Ceiriog
McLean, James, Able Seaman D/SSX 660776   Belfast
Mewse, Leonard Charles, Petty Officer Telegraphist D/JX 160004
  Campletown
Mitchell, Robert Monteith, Able Seaman D/SSX 847014   Glasgow
Morgan, Dennis Harry, Stoker Mechanic D/SKX 770391   Birmingham
  Killed
Morrey, Frederick William, Stoker Mechanic P/SKX 770848   Elliswell
  Wounded
Morrison, George, Ordinary Seaman D/JX 830720   Granton-on-Spey
Mortimer, Ernest James, Electrician's Mate 1st Class C/MX 844681
  Bradford
Morton, John Kenneth, Boy 1st Class D/JX 836312   Newton Abbot
Muldoon, Patrick, Stoker Mechanic D/SKX 833831   Burnley   Killed
Mulley, Kenneth D. W., Able Seaman C/JX 170643   Welling
Mullins, Thomas Stanislaus, Leading Seaman D/JX 129448   Queenstown
Munson, Ernest William, Ordinary Seaman D/JX 836297   Dunster
Murphy, Jeramiah, CPO Stoker Mechanic D/KX 86633   Timoleague
Murphy, John, Ordinary Seaman D/SSX 847015   Cookstown
Mustoe, Eric Ernest, Able Seaman D/SSX 815353   Birmingham

Nicholls, Rosslyn, Petty Officer D/JX 154157   Plymouth   Wounded
Nolan, James, Ordinary Seaman D/SSX 855760   Dublin

Ormrod, Thomas, Leading Stoker Mechanic D/KX 93158   Keyham
Osbourne, Alfred, Able Seaman D/SSX 837928   Gillingham

Parish, Colin Edward John, Boy 1st Class D/JX 856269   Teignmouth
Parnell, Wilfred Douglas, Boy 1st Class D/JX 836292   Liskeard
Paul, George Ernest, Electrician's Mate 1st Class D/MX 509752
  Milton of Campsie
Pearce, Albert Henry Richard, Stoker Mechanic D/KX 853391
  Cirencester
Pitman, Horace William, Able Seaman D/SSX 818524   Birmingham
Porter, Donald, Able Seaman D/SSX 815788   Worcester
Potter, Ronald Charles, Able Seaman D/SSX 837604   Greenford
  Wounded

Quinn, John Thomas, Ordinary Seaman D/SSX 847599   Walsall

Ray, John Frederick, Ordinary Seaman D/SSX 837800   Lewisham
Redman, Donald Raymond, Able Seaman D/JX 760454   Bridgwater
  Wounded
Rees, Trevor Leighton Clay Thomas, Ordance Artificer 4th Cl. D/MX
  102469   Treorchy
Richards, Ronald George, Able Seaman D/SSX 818884   Birmingham
  Wounded
Rimmington, Albert, Able Seaman D/SSX 815944   Tunstall   Wounded
Roberts, Brian, Ordinary Seaman D/JX 836189   Sheffield   Wounded
Roberts, Dennis, Ordinary Seaman D/JX 836256   Plymouth
Roberts, Dennis Wynne, Signalman D/JX 611646   Deintolen   Wounded
Roblin, Stanley Thomas, Chief Engineroom Artificer D/MX 49524
  Wellington Quay   Wounded
Rutter, Jack, L/REM D/SMX 770424   Thurnscoe East

Sampson, Arnold, Able Seaman D/SSX 815327   Warrington
Saunders, Eric Noble, Able Seaman D/SSX 815328   Liverpool
Shaw, Bernard, Boy 1st Class D/JX 836173   Ilkeston

Silvey, Anthony Frederick, Stores Assistant D/SMX 856193   Camberwell
    Wounded
Sinnott, Patrick Joseph, Ordinary Seaman D/SSX 815697   Dublin   Killed
Smith, William Russell, A/Shipwt. 4th Class D/SMX 758980   Glasgow
Stapleton, Albert Norman, Stoker Mechanic D/SKX 526232   Truro
Stevens, Gwilyn Leslie, Leading Seaman D/SSX 28257   Newport
    Wounded
Stone, Robert Ernest, Telegraphist D/JX 760459   Torquay

Tattersall, Edmund, Probationary Writer D/SMX 815173   Edinburgh
    Killed
Tetler, Maurice Peter, Able Seaman D/SSX 815664   Manchester
    Wounded
Thomas, David Glyn, Ordinary Seaman D/SSX 855432   Swansea   Killed
Thomas, James Edward, Signalman D/JX 572884   Breedon-on-the-Hill
Todd, Matthew Joseph, Able Seaman D/JX 535132   Derby
Townsend, Thomas John, Able Seaman D/JX 660853   Cefn Hengoed
Traylor, Bruce Charles Owen, Able Seaman D/JX 161426   Barry
Turner, Robert Anthony, Able Seaman D/SSX 815239   Manchester

Venton, William R. T., Petty Officer Stoker Mechanic D/KX 81516
    Plymouth
Vincent, Albert Anthony J., Able Seaman D/JX 162775   Newport   Killed

Wakeham, Brian Edward, Able Seaman D/JX 661171   Torquay
Walker, Jack, Able Seaman D/JX 198562   Birmingham
Warwick, Walter John, Ordnance Artificer 2nd Class D/MX 55305
    Plymstock
Watson, Thomas, Leading Seaman D/JX 157248   Bolton
Webb, John Ernest, Petty Officer D/JX 152870   Manchester
Wells, Richard, Able Seaman D/SSX 815174   West Hartlepool
Wharton, Douglas Henry, Signalman D/SSX 661314   Birmingham
    Wounded
White, Alfred, Petty Officer D/J 105373   Tottenham
Williams, Albert, Ordinary Seaman D/SSX 855455   Pendeen
Williams, Cyril, Leading Seaman D/JX 180671   Blaenau Festiniog
    Wounded
Williams, Edward James, Able Seaman D/SSX 815067   Liverpool
    Wounded
Williams, Leonard William, Engineroom Artificer 2nd Class D/MX 55557
    Felixstowe   Awarded DSM
Williams, William Thomas, Able Seaman D/JX 660859   Hengoed
Williscroft, Kenneth Peter, Ordinary Seaman D/SSX 855456   Rugeley
    Wounded
Wilson, Denis, Able Seaman D/SSX 841405   Barrow-in-Furness
Winfield, Kenneth Alfred, Stoker Mechanic D/KX 782557   Chesham
Winter, George, Ordinary Seaman D/SSX 818706   Blackpool
    Died of wounds
Wright, Gordon Albert, Able Seaman D/SSX 818530   Coventy
Wright, Reginald Jack, Ordinary Seaman D/SSX 831955   Plymouth
    Killed, Posthumous MID

In addition to the above there were a certain number of Chinese ratings
employed as stewards and cooks, together with civilian tradesmen, such as
tailors and laundrymen, allowed on board for such trade as they could make.
It is generally believed that these numbered approximately fourteen.

B & M Clearance, Mediterranean 1st January 1953-
31st December 1960

The bar was sanctioned in Admiralty Fleet Order 1943 dated 27th July
1956 which states that the Mediterranean Fleet Clearance Diving Team
has, since 1st July 1955, been engaged in further bomb and mine disposal
operations as arduous and dangerous as those which earned the earlier bar,
'Bomb & Mine Clearance 1945-53'.
    Qualifying service would be the same as that stated for the earlier award.
The majority of the work centred around Malta and, in particular, the Main
Harbour of Valletta where large quantities of Bombs were recovered from a
number of merchant vessels that had been sunk by air attack, such as the
motor vessels, *Talbot* and *Pampas*. Because of the rigid adherence to the
rules governing eligibility, only a small number of officers and men
qualified. There is general belief that those who qualified were all divers,
however, this is incorrect as a number of men of the seamen branch were
employed in small craft in the movement of the recovered bombs to a safe
place and in their final disposal.
    60 medals/bars are estimated to have been awarded.

Cyprus 1st April 1955-18th April 1959

This bar was sanctioned by Admiralty Fleet Order 1512 dated 15th June
1957. It was awarded in recognition of service in the suppression of acts of
terrorism during the emergency in Cyprus, with special regard to the
hardships and dangers which accompanied duty there. The qualifying
period for the RN and RM was four months (120 days) either on shore in
Cyprus or in ships of the Cyprus Patrol based on Cyprus ports, or on patrol
within 20 miles of the coast. Members of the Royal Fleet Auxiliary qualified
as did the crews of ships chartered to the Ministry of Transport, Civil
Aviation and crews of Tank Landing Ships.
    Approximately 4,300 medals/bars were awarded, a large proportion being
to Royal Marines.

Near East 31st October-22nd December 1956

This bar was sanctioned in Admiralty Fleet Order 400 dated 14th February
1958, in recognition of services in the Middle East in the period 31st
October to 22nd December 1956. The qualifying period for naval personnel
was one day, or part day, spent in a ship operationally employed off the
Egyptian Coast, either in the Mediterranean, or Red Sea. Naval aircrew
qualified by taking part in one sortie over the operational zone. 64 major
warships were employed, as well as 38 lesser vessels, such as LSTs, LCAs,
LCTs, tugs, salvage vessels, dockyard craft, etc. The fleet train consisted of
25 Royal Fleet Auxiliaries. In addition, a further 34 merchant vessels had
been requisitioned. The total number of ships employed is estimated to
have been in excess of 170 for an action that was virtually over in three days.
This was the first major action in which the Royal Navy operated
helicopters which flew from HMS *Ocean* and *Theseus*. The carriers *Albion*,
Bulwark, and *Eagle,* flew fixed wing strikes which, along with the RAF
squadrons, destroyed the major part of the Egyptian Air Force whilst still
on the ground. HMS *Newfoundland* (Light Cruiser) was the only ship
engaged in a traditional role when she sank, in a few minutes, the frigate
Domiat in the Red Sea.
    An estimated 17,800 medals/bars were issued to naval personnel for
operation 'Musketeer'.

Arabian Peninsula 1st January 1957-30th June 1960

This bar was sanctioned by Admiralty Fleet Order 323 dated 10th February
1961, in recognition of service for operations against dissidents and to
counter border raids in the Arabian Peninsula.
    The qualifying period was 30 days between 1st January 1957 and 30th
June 1960. Officers and men of the Royal Navy could not qualify by service
on shore. Naval personnel qualified by service afloat with a naval unit,
specifically sailed or diverted for operations in direct support of the Army in
the Arabian Peninsula, or by participation in a joint operation which
culminated in the landing of an armed force by sea, for operations against
the rebels. Naval air crew qualified by five sorties over land specifically
ordered in support of army operations.
    An estimated 1,200 medals/bars were awarded, a significant proportion
being awarded to Royal Marines.

Brunei 8th-23rd December 1962

This bar was sanctioned by Admiralty Fleet Order 2283 dated 6th
December 1963 in recognition of services in the Brunei operations.
Qualifying service was one day or more between 8th and 23rd December
1962 on the posted or attached strength of a unit or formation which took
part in the operations in the State of Brunei or in North Borneo, qualifying
service being restricted to service on shore, or on ships operating on the
rivers.
    As entire ships' companies were not eligible for the award, commanding
officers had to submit nominal lists of officers and men who had fulfilled the
qualification. Naval air crew operating helicopters from HMS *Albion* in
direct support of the operations qualified, as did 42nd Royal Marine
Commandos who were heavily engaged on shore. An estimated 900 medals
and bars, and 450 separate bars, were issued. A significant proportion were
awarded to Royal Marines serving with 42nd Commando.

151 *General Service Medal* 1918-1962

Obverse	*1st issue 1914-1934*—The coinage head of King George V facing left and legend 'GEORGIVS V BRITT : OMN : REX ET IND : IMP'. *2nd issue 1934-1936*—The crowned head of King George V in robes and the legend 'GEORGIVS V . D . G . BRITT . OMN . REX . ET . INDIAE . IMP'. *3rd issue 1936-1949*—The crowned head of King George VI and the legend 'GEORGIVS VI D : G : BR : OMN : REX ET INDIAE IMP :' *4th issue 1949-1952*—The crowned head of King George VI and the legend 'GEORGIVS VI DEI GRA : BRITT : OMN : REX FID : DEF+' *5th issue 1952-1953*—The crowned bust of Elizabeth II and the legend 'ELIZABETH II D : G : BR : OMN : REGINA F. D.' *6th issue 1953-1964*—The crowned bust of Elizabeth II and the legend 'ELIZABETH II DEI GRATIA REGINA F. D.'
Reverse	The standing winged figure of Victory, who is placing a wreath on the emblems of the two Services. In her left hand she is holding a trident.
Size	36mm diameter
Metal	Silver
Ribbon	32mm wide. Purple with a green stripe down the centre.
Suspension	An ornamental suspender, which does not swivel in the case of the first, second and third issues.
Designer	E. Carter Preston
Naming	In thin impressed block capitals; engraved to the RAF
Bars issued	Sixteen: S. Persia; Kurdistan; Iraq; N.W. Persia; Southern Desert, Iraq; Northern Kurdistan; Palestine; Bomb and Mine Clearance 1945-49; Bomb and Mine Clearance 1945-56; Palestine 1945-48; Malaya; S.E. Asia 1945-46; Cyprus; Near East; Arabian Peninsula; Brunei.

This medal was instituted by Army Order No. 4 dated 19th January, 1923, as a contemporary of the Naval General Service Medal instituted in 1915.

It was awarded for services other than those on the adjacent frontiers of India, and East, West and Central Africa.

The medal was issued with four different obverse effigies and several different legends.

The medal was never issued without a bar.

Permission was granted to recipients of a Mention in Despatches during any of the campaigns or expeditions for which this medal was awarded after 11th August, 1920, to wear a bronze oak leaf emblem on the ribbon.

S. Persia 12th November 1918-22nd June 1919

This bar was awarded for services under *(a)* Major-General J. A. Douglas, CMG, CIE, and Brigadier-General A. M. S. Elsmie, CMG, at or near Bushire between 12th November 1918, and 22nd June 1919, *(b)* Major-General Sir P. Sykes, KCIE, CMG, or Lieutenant-Colonel E. F. Orton at or near Bandar Abbas between 12th November 1918, and 3rd June, 1919. Only Indian units were employed, the complete names of which are not available. There were a few European recipients apart from the officers, such as Sergeant A. Prangle 1st Bn. The Royal Hampshire Regiment.

Regiments present: 81 Pioneers; 1/55 Coke's Rifles Frontier Force; 1/127 Baluchis; 2, 6 Gurkhas; South Persia Rifles; 1 Kent Cyclist Bn.

RAF: 30 Squadron only.

Kurdistan 23rd May 1919-6th December 1919 and 19th March-18th June 1923

This bar was originally awarded for services as follows: *(a)* At Kirkuk or north of a line east and west through Kirkuk between 23rd May and 31st July 1919; *(b)* at Dohok or north of a line east and west through Dohok between 14th July and 7th October 1919 *(c)* north of the advanced bases near Akra and Amadia between 7th November and 6th December 1919.

Army Order 387 of 1924 and Army Instruction (India) No. 132 of 1925 extended the award to cover operations in Kurdistan in 1923 as follows: *(a)* Operations under Air Marshal Sir J. M. Salmond, KCB, CMG, DSO, or Colonel Commandant B. Vincent, CB, CMG, from 19th March to 18th June, 1923; *(b)* operations under Commandant H. T. Dobbin, DSO, from 27th March to 28th April 1923.

During these operations troops were moved by air. This is the first occasion on which aeroplanes were used as troop carriers in military operations, so that the date, 21st February 1923, is worth noting. The troops moved consisted of two companies of the 1/11th Sikhs.

The operations in 1919 were against Kurdish chief Sheik Mahmoud. Regiments present included:

1 *Southern Kurdistan:* 1/5th East Surreys; 6/LN Lancs (L of C); 85th Burma Rifles; 1/87th Punjabis; 1/116th Mahrattas; 1/10th Gurkha Rifles; 1/3rd Gurkha Rifles, 3/9th Bhopal Inf.; 8th and 14th Light Armoured Motor Brigade, MGC; 32nd Lancers; 1/8th Rajputs (2 Coys); 239th and 207th Coys, 18th (Ind) Bn, MGC; Guides Cavalry (1 Squad); 1st Sappers and Miners (2 Coys); B and D Batteries 336th Bde, RFA; 25th Mtn Bty; 50th Mtn Bty (1 section); A Flight , 63rd Squadron, RAF.

2 *Central Kurdistan:* 1/39th Garhwal Rifles; 1/52nd Sikhs, F.F.; 1/7th Gurkha Rifles; 1/8th Rajputs; 1/128th Pioneers; 1/113th Inf; 1/126th Baluchis; 11th Lancers (3 Squad); D Troop 1st Australian Wireless Sq (4 Pack Stn); C Bty, 336th Bde, RFA; 34th Mtn Bty; 49th Mtn Bty; 238th Coy, MGC (1 section); 1st Sappers and Miners (2 sections); Sappers and Miners (1 Coy); A Flight, 63rd Sq, RAF; Assyrian Bn.

Other units represented include South Wales Borderers; 51st Sikhs; 26, 34 Mtn Bty.

The operations in 1923 were against the Kurdish, chief Sheik Mahmoud, who, assisted by a small Turkish force at Rowanduz, had installed himself at Salaimaniyah, in the north-east corner of Iraq. Two columns were formed as under:

Koicol (Colonel Vincent):
120th Pack Battery RA; 2nd Bn The West Yorkshire Regiment; 2nd Bn The Cameronians; 63rd Company Madras Sappers and Miners; 1/11, 2/11 and 14 Sikhs; 1/13 Frontier Force Rifles; 3/16 Punjab Regiment; Iraq Troops; Signal Section; Field Ambulance; Mobile Veterinary Section; Pack Train.

Frontier Col (Commandant Dobbin):
Assyrian Levies only.
RAF: 6, 30, 63 Squadrons.

Mosul Col:
34th Mountain Bty; 52nd Sikhs; 39th Garhwal Rifles; 7th Gurkhas; 8th Co Sappers and Miners. Possibly 55th Burma Rifles.

Iraq 10th December 1919-17th November 1920

This bar was awarded to: *(a)* Those who served at Ramadi or north of a line east and west through Ramadi between 10th December 1919, and 13th June 1920, and *(b)* Those who were present on the strength of an establishment within the boundaries of Iraq between 1st July and 17th November 1920.

6th DIVISION
74th Brigade:
2/7 Rajputs; 1/15 Sikhs; 3/123 Outram's Rifles.
75th Brigade:
2/96 Infantry; 2/116 Mahrattas; 3/70 Burma Rifles.
76th Brigade:
3/23 Sikh Pioneers; 2/89 Punjabis; 2/117 Mahrattas.
Divisional Troops:
F Battery RHA; 17th Brigade RFA (10, 26, 92 (Howitzer) Batteries) 11, 63, 69 Companies 2nd Sappers and Miners; 1/12 Pioneers; 8th Machine-Gun Battalion.

Additional Troops:
2 East Yorks; 2 DCLI: 1 KOYLI, 3/153 Rifles; 2/5, 2/11 Gurkhas, Kapurthala Light Infantry.

17th DIVISION
34th Brigade:
2 Royal Irish Rifles; 1/99 Deccan Infantry; 108 Infantry; 114 Mahrattas
51st Brigade:
2 York and Lancs; 2/6 Jat Light Infantry; 1/80 Carnatic Infantry; 1/10 Gurkhas.
52nd Brigade:
4 Royal Fusiliers; 45 Sikhs; 1/94 Russell's Regiment; 1/113 Infantry.
Divisional Troops:
19th Brigade RFA (39, 96, 97, 131 (Howitzer) Batteries); 13 Pack Artillery Brigade (13 (British), 31, 45, 49 Indian Batteries); 17th Divisional Signal Company; 9, 61, 64, 67 Field Companies; 2nd Sappers and Miners; 1/32 Sikh Pioneers; 6, 7 Light Armoured Motor Bty; 17th Machine-Gun Battalion; 5th Cavalry and 32, 37 Lancers.

18th DIVISION
53rd Brigade:
2 Manchester Regiment; 8 Rajputs; 86 Carnatic Infantry; 1/87 Punjabis.
54th Brigade:
2 Royal Northumberland Fusiliers; 1/39 Garhwal Rifles; 52 Sikhs; 1/7 Gurkhas.
55th Brigade:
1 Rifle Brigade; 3/9 Bhopal Infantry; 13 Rajputs; 1/116 Mahrattas; 1/3 Gurkhas.
Divisional Troops:
13 Brigade RFA (2, 8, 44, 160 (Howitzer) Batteries); 2 Pack Artillery Brigade (14 (British), 25, 34, 40, 50 Indian Batteries); 18 Division Signals Company; 2, 6, 8 Field Companies; 1st Sappers and Miners; 106 Hazara Pioneers; 17 Machine-Gun Battalion; 11 Lancers; 35 Scinde Horse; 8, 14 Light Armoured Motor Batteries.
7th Cavalry Brigade:
1, 7 Dragoon Guards; 16 Machine Gun Squadron; 8 Field Troop 2nd Sappers and Miners.
Army Troops:
5th Battery RGA; 9th Company 2nd Sappers and Miners; 132, 133, 138 Railway Construction Companies; 7th Light Armoured Motor Battery; 1 Railway Armoured Battery.
Baghdad Garrison:
2/9 Delhi Regiment; 2/119 Infantry.
Lines of Communication Troops:
Sam Browne's Cavalry (two squadrons); 37 Lancers; 35 Scinde Horse; Royal Irish Fusiliers; 83 Wallajabad Light Infantry; 2/125 Napier Rifles; 2/129 Baluchis; 124, 134, 140 Railway Construction Companies.
RAF:
6, 30, 55, 63, 84 Squadrons.
Medals are also found to the 8th Hussars, Leicestershire Regiment and R. Berkshire Regt (153 and also 73 with NW Persia.)

A Victoria Cross was won by Captain G. S. Henderson, Manchester Regt near Hillah, Mesopotamia on 24th July 1920.

N.W. Persia 10th August-31st December 1920

This bar was awarded to members of Noperforce (North Persia Force) and those on the lines of communication, under Brigadier-General H. F. Bateman-Champain, CMG, which consisted of the 36th (Indian) Mixed Brigade:

'A Battery RHA; 19 Company 3 Sappers and Miners; Royal Northumberland Fusiliers; 1 Royal Berks (624 and 73 with Iraq); 2 York and Lancs; 1 Royal Irish Fusiliers; 1/42 Deoli Regiment; 1/67 Punjabis; 122 Rajputana Infantry; 1/2 Gurkhas; 48th Division Signals. Lines of communication troops: Guides Cavalry, 2/26 Punjabis; 64 Pioneers; 79 Carnatic Infantry; 7, 52, 65 Companies Sappers and Miners.

RAF: 6, 30, 63 Squadrons.

Southern Desert: Iraq 8th January-3rd June 1928

This bar was mainly awarded to the RAF for services against the Akhwan in the Southern Desert, under Air-Commodore T. C. R.

Higgins, CB, CMG, between 8th and 22nd January 1928, or under Wing-Commander E. R. C. Nanson, CBE, DSC, AFC, between 22nd January and 3rd June 1928.

RAF: 30, 55, 70, 84 Squadrons. A few British officers including Capt C. L. M. Voutes, 10/5 Maharatta LI with the Indian and Iraqi armies. 25 to Indians and over 550 to native personnel with the Iraq Army.

Northern Kurdistan 15th March-21st June 1932

Issued with the crowned Geo. V. obverse.

No British troops were engaged in these operations against Sheik Admed of Barzan in the area Diana—Erbil—Aqra—Suri due north to the Turkish Frontier.

RAF: 30, 55, 70 Squadrons, together with ground support staff, a total of sixty-six officers and two hundred and seventy-nine airmen.

Iraq Levies, and a few British officers.

Palestine 19th April 1936-3rd September 1939

The medals with this and the next five bars bear the crowned coinage head of King George VI and have a small raised rim.

Regiments present: The Royals; Scots Greys; 4/7 R. Dragoon Guards; 8, 11 Hussars; B, O and M/P Bty RHA; 25/26, 27/28 Med. Bty, det. 19 Hvy Bty RA (plus others); Royal Tank Corps RE; RCS: RASC: RAMC: RAOC: Coldstream Guards; Scots Guards; Irish Guards; Royal Scots; 2 Queen's; 1, 2 Buffs; King's Own; 1, 2 R Northumberland Fusiliers; 2 R Lincolnshire Regiment; 2 West Yorkshire Regiment; 2 East Yorkshire Regiment; 1, 2 Bedfordshire and Hertfordshire Regiment; 2 Leicestershire Regiment; Green Howards; 1 R Scots Fusiliers; 2 Cheshire Regiment; 2 South Wales Borderers; 1 King's Own Scottish Borderers; 1 Worcestershire Regiment; Border Regiment; 1 R Sussex Regiment; 1 R Hampshire Regiment; South Staffordshire Regiment; 1 Welch Regiment; Black Watch; 1 Essex Regiment; Foresters; 1 Loyal Regiment; 2 Dorsetshire Regiment; 2 Wiltshire Regiment; Manchester Regiment; 1 York and Lancaster Regiment; 2 R Berkshire Regiment; 2 Hampshire Regiment; 2 Highland Light Infantry; 1 Seaforth Highlanders; 2 Cameron Highlanders; R Ulster Rifles; 1 R. Irish Fusiliers; 2 R W Kents; 2 N Staffordshire Regiment; 1 King's Royal Rifle Corps; 1 Argyll and Sutherland Highlanders; Rifle Brigade; The Palestine Police.

RAF: 6, 14, 33, 80, 208, 211, 216 Squadrons.

S. E. Asia 1945-46

Naming to Indian units: It appears that these medals were issued after the partition of India by the respective governments of India and Pakistan. Medals to those who went to the Indian Army or were living in India after 1947 are impressed in rounded capitals. Unit shown is the recipient's 1945-46 unit (which in some cases was allotted to Pakistan). It is believed that those issued by Pakistan were un-named.

British troops were involved throughout S.E. Asia after the Japanese Surrender on 15 August 1945 in restoring the pre-war status quo, guarding thousands of Japanese prisoners of war, and maintaining law and order. British troops landed in Java in September 1945 and freed 200,000 Dutch prisoners of war. They re-occupied Malaya, Burma and Singapore and took over the adminstration of the southern half of what had formerly been French Indo-China on 12 September 1945. The Chinese administered the northern half of the country. The whole of Indo-China was returned to French colonial rule in September 1946. It was a complicated and sensitive time during which British troops were given little thanks for reinstating unpopular Dutch and French colonial regimes in Indonesia and Indo-China. Burma however was granted its independence by the British in 1948 and Singapore, British Borneo and Malaya were guided more slowly towards eventual independence in 1957. By November 1946 British troops had handed over their responsibilities to the British and French Colonial authorities.

Units present:
JAVA AND SUMATRA
5th Indian Division:
Divisional Troops: 3/2 Punjab Regt; MG Bn, Dogra Regt.
9th Ind Bde: 2 W Yorks; 3rd Bn Jat Regt (to 49 Bde).

123rd Ind Bde: 2/1 Punjab Regt; 1st Bn Dogra; 3/9 GR.
161st Ind Bde: 1/1 Punjab Regt (to Batavia); 4th Bn Rajput Regt.
23rd Indian Division:
Divisional Troops: 2nd Bn Kumaon Regt.
1st Ind. Bde: 1/16 Punjab Regt; 1st Patiala Inf SF; 1st Seaforths.
37th Ind Bde: 3/3 GR; 3/10 GR; 3/5 GR.
49th Ind Bde: 4th Bn Mahratta Regt; 6th Bn Mahratta Regt (to Batavia); 5th Bn Rajputana Rifles.
26th Indian Division:
Divisional Troops: MG Bn F F Regt.
4th Ind Bde: 6th S Wales Borderers; 2/13 F F Rifles; 2nd Bn Rajput Regt.
36th Ind Bde: 8/13th F F Rifles; 1/8 GR.
71st Ind Bde: R Lincs Regt; 8/8 Punjab Regt; 1st Bn R Garhwal Rifles.
Other troops: 6th Bn Rajputana Rifles; MG Bn 13th F F Rifles; 2nd Patiala Inf S F; 146 RAC; 3/4 GR (from July 1946); 4/8GR (from 7th Ind Div); 11th Cavalry; 2nd Bn Indian Grenadiers; (2nd Buffs, 178th Assault RA, mentioned in 'The Regiments Depart'

INDO-CHINA
20th Indian Division
Divisonal Troops: MG Bn Jat Regt; 2/8 Punjab Regt; 9/12 FF Regt.
32nd Ind Bde: 9/14 Punjab Regt; 3/8 GR; 4/2 GR.
80th Ind Bde: 4th Bn Dogra Regt; 1st Bn Kumaon Regt; 3/1 GR.
100th Ind Bde: 1/1 GR; 14/13 FF Rifles; 4/10 GR.
Additional troops: 16th Light Cavalry; 23rd Mountain Regt.

GEOGRAPHICAL LOCATION UNCERTAIN
KOSB; Green Howards; Camerons; AAC: RAOC: RA: Bengal Engineer Group, Bombay Engineer Group, RIE; 5/8 Punjab Regt; IEME.

ARMY
The qualifications for the Army is quoted as entry into one of the areas mentioned below.

For official visits and inspections the time qualification was one week. (The meaning of the wording is not clear, as it would appear that a member of a unit had only to enter one of the areas, even for a day, to qualify, whereas an inspecting officer had to remain the minimum period of a week.)

The areas referred to are:
1 Java and Sumatra from 3rd September 1945 to 30th November 1946, both dates inclusive.
2 French Indo-China from 3rd September 1945, to 28th January 1946, both dates inclusive.

ROYAL AIR FORCE
The qualifications may be summarized as follows:
1 One operational sortie over the areas mentioned for the Army.
2 One sortie in connection with the removal of prisoners of war and internees in South-East Asia between 3rd September 1945, and 4th October 1945, whether the squadron was based within the area mentioned for the Army or not. This service included Java, Sumatra, Malaya, Siam, French Indo-China and the Andaman Islands.
3 Non-aircrew personnel who served in the areas and between the dates given for the Army qualified for the award as well as those who were members of any squadron which carried out operational sorties as mentioned in the last paragraph, providing that they served for a minimum period of one month with such a squadron.
4 For official visits and inspections the qualifying period was one week.
5 The recipient of a King's Commendation, whether non-aircrew or non-operational, was eligible, even though he may not have completed the necessary qualifying period.
6 A reduced period of service caused by death or evacuation due to disability caused by service was considered as sufficient qualification in the case of non-operational personnel.

The following units were concerned in the operations referred to above. It should be noted that some of them are mentioned more than once. This is accounted for by the fact that they operated over more than one area and were also engaged in the removal of internees and prisoners of war.
1 Units operating over Java and Sumatra between 3rd September 1945, and 30th November 1946, both dates inclusive: 27, 47, 62, 89, 96, 117, 136, 194, 215/48 Squadrons; also ACSEA and Malaya Communication Squadrons and 224 Group.

2 Units operating over French Indo-China between 3rd September 1945 and 28th January 1946, both dates inclusive: 62, 96, 117, 159, 194, 215/48, 233, 357, 358 Squadrons.

3 Units engaged in removal by air of internees and prisoners of war in South East Asia to Singapore or other ports for onward shipment between 3rd September and 4th October 1945, both dates inclusive: 8, 27, 31, 47, 48, 62, 89, 96, 99, 117, 136, 159, 160, 194, 203, 215, 233, 321, 355, 356, 357, 358 Squadrons; also ACSEA and Malaya Communication Squadrons and 224 Group.

No 1341 Special Flight was also employed, as were the following units of the Royal Australian Air Force: 12, 23, 25, Squadrons and No. 200 Flight.

No 321 Squadron was a Dutch squadron, and only British personnel employed with it, if any, were eligible for the award.

Bomb and Mine Clearance 1945-49
Bomb and Mine Clearance 1945-56

With the third or fourth obverse issues.

The qualification for this award was originally an aggregate of 180 days' active engagement in the clearance of bombs and mines in the United Kingdom and Northern Ireland between 9th May 1945, and 31st December 1949. In May 1956, the Queen approved the extension of the period of eligibility to 1st January 1955, for service in the Mediterranean.

Any member of the Royal Navy and Royal Air Force employed on this work on land qualified under the same conditions as those for the Army.

The term 'active engagement' must be translated as meaning the process of digging down to a bomb or its removal and final disposal. In the case of mines it means the entering of the perimeter of live minefields, disarming the mines or acting as a water jet operator.

It should be noted that being a member of a unit so employed did not, in itself, count as a qualification. To be eligible the recipient must have been personally engaged in one or all of the processes from the reaching to the final disposal of the bombs or mines.

Death or the curtailment of the qualifying period through wounds or disability due to service did not debar eligibility, and those who received a King's Commendation or a Mention in Despatches also qualified, even though they may not have completed the necessary 180 days' aggregate service.

Palestine 1945-48 27th September 1945-30th June 1948

After the British Army, with the help of indigenous Arabs, had ejected the Turks from Palestine in 1917, the League of Nations granted Britain a mandate to rule Palestine. The League supported the British proposal, which had been first stated in the Balfour Declaration of November 1917, to establish in Palestine 'a National Home for the Jews'. The suggestion was anathema to the Arabs who rebelled in 1936. Although by 1939 this rebellion was put down by the British Army, part of the resulting settlement was the imposition of a Quota System on Jewish immigration into Palestine. This so enraged the Jews that they engaged in guerrilla warfare against the British from 1940-1948*. Towards the end of this period British soldiers could only look on helplessly as Jew and Arab fought each other for control of Palestine. By this time the British Government had decided to wash its hands of the whole affair. Britain's responsibility for Palestine ended on 14 May 1948 when the State of Israel was born.

The medal with this bar was awarded with the third or fourth type obverse.

This bar was awarded to officers and other ranks (including women) of the British Commonwealth and Colonial Forces, also British personnel of the Palestine Police, Palestine Civil Service and various other civilian services on the strength of a unit in Palestine for one or more days between 27th September 1945 and 30th June 1948. Service in Transjordan did not qualify. For official visits and inspections the qualifying period was thirty days.

Medals to the following Indian units have been seen: Scinde Horse; Jodhpur Lancers; ISF; 7th Sikh Regiment.

RAF: The following operational squadrons were based in Palestine for

*Hostilities until 1945 were seen as part of World War II hostilities.

various periods between the qualifying dates: 6, 13, 27 (detachment), 32, 37, 38, 70, 113, 178, 208, 213, 214, 256, 620, 621, 644, 651 (detachment), 680 (detachment) Squadrons.

It should be noted that, in addition to these, a few aircraft of certain squadrons based outside the area visited Palestine from time to time on official duty, and there were also numerous ground units of the Royal Air Force in Palestine during the qualifying period, all of whom qualified for the medal and bar.

Cyprus 1st April 1955-18th April 1959

Cyprus was ceded to Britain in 1878 by Turkey. It remained a colony of relatively little importance, even during the Second World War. The island became militarily important for Britain in 1954 when HQ Middle East was sited there and even more so when it was used as the main launching point for the Suez operations in 1956. It was exactly at this juncture that the movement for union with Greece or Enosis began under the political leadership of Archbishop Makarios and military leadership of General George Grivas the latter leading the guerrilla organisation EOKA against the British Army. The campaign was at times a bloody one. Grivas tied down 40,000 British troops over four years and killed 99. In the wider sense he achieved very little, though he perhaps brought colonial rule to an end a few years earlier than would otherwise have been the case.

The qualifications for this award were:
ARMY
Four months' (or 120 days') service with a unit stationed in Cyprus. The service need not be continuous.
ROYAL AIR FORCE
As for the Army, with the addition of the air-crews of Nos. 37 and 38 Maritime Reconnaissance Squadrons based on Malta who have flown ten or more sorties over Cyprus waters.
POLICE AND FIRE BRIGADE
A total of 120 days' service in the case of regular members of the above, and a total of 822 hours of duty in the case of Special Constables.
CIVILIAN CATEGORIES
All members of the Church and welfare organisations.
GENERAL
Those recommended for a decoration of any kind, a Mention in Despatches, or a Queen's Commendation qualify irrespective of their length of service.

Some of the units involved were: Royal Horse Guards; RA; RE; Royal Scots; 1 Royal Warwickshire Regt; 1 Royal Norfolks; Suffolk Regt; 1 Royal Leicestershire Regt; 2 Green Howards; 2 Royal Inniskilling Fusiliers; 1 Oxfordshire and Buckinghamshire Light Infantry; 1 King's Own Yorkshire Light Infantry; Wiltshire Regt; Duke of Wellington's Regt; Welch Regt; 1 Middlesex Regt; Gordon Highlanders; Royal Ulster Rifles; 1, 2, 3 Parachute Regt; RAF.

Malaya 16th June 1948-31st July 1960 (Colony of Singapore 16th June 1948-31st January 1959)

The Communist Malayan People's Anti-Japanese Army was, by 1945, 7,000 strong. By 1948 it had been reconstituted as the Malayan People's Anti-British Army. Though they had fought, at the Soviet Union's request, alongside the British during the war, they now sought to force the British from Malaya and to initiate a communist revolution. It took twelve years to defeat the communist insurgents. The Director of Operations in 1950 and 1951 was Lt General Sir Harold Briggs. It was he, and later General Sir Gerald Templer, who, as High Commissioner and Director of Operations, together were mainly responsible for breaking the back of the enemy offensive by co-ordinating a series of novel anti-guerrilla measures over the years. The British Army ultimately defeated the Chinese Communist terrorists because they were prepared, by living and fighting in the jungle for long periods to take on and beat the insurgents at their own game.

A hundred thousand British soldiers served in Malaya from 1948-60 and most were National Servicemen.

The medal with this bar was issued with the third, fourth or fifth type obverse.

The qualifications for the award of the bar are as follows:

ARMY

One or more days' service on the strength of a unit in the Federation of Malaya or the Colony of Singapore since the first qualifying date inclusive.

ROYAL AIR FORCE

The qualifications are the same as for the Army. Service with detached squadrons normally based elsewhere, or with detachments of squadrons based elsewhere (such as that of No 45 Squadron) also qualified.

LOCAL FORCES

Members of all the Local Forces, providing they had completed their training, qualified in exactly the same way as the corresponding Regular Force to which they were attached individually or as a complete unit.

CIVIL POLICE FORCES

The period of qualification was three months full-time service.

CIVILIANS

All the various members of the organizations that supplied everything from 'beer to beauty' qualified in the same way as Army personnel, except members of Ferret Force, the Civil Liaison Corps, and Dyaks recruited in Sarawak, whose qualifying period was twenty-eight days.

Regiments present: 1 King's Dragoon Guards; 4 Queen's Own Hussars; 11 Hussars; 12 Royal Lancers; 13/18 Royal Hussars; 15/19 The King's R Hussars; 2, 25, 26, 48 Field Regt RA; 1 Singapore Regt RA; 100, 101, 105 Field Bn RAA; 11 Indep Field Squadron RE; 50 Gurkha Field Engineer Regt RE; 51 Field Engineer Regt RE; 74 Field Park RE; 410 Indep Plant Troop RE; 3 Grenadier Gds; 2 Coldstream Gds; 2 Scots Gds; 40, 42, 45 Commando Royal Marines; 1 Bn Queen's Royal Regt; 1 Bn Royal Lincolnshire; 1 Bn Devonshire Regt; 1 Bn The Suffolk Regt; 1 Bn The Somerset Lt Inf; 1 Bn The West Yorkshire Regt; 1 Bn The East Yorkshire Regt; 1 Bn The Green Howards; 1 Bn The Royal Scots Fusiliers; 1 Bn The Cheshire Regt; 1 Bn The Royal Welch Fusiliers; 1 Bn The South Wales Borderers; 1 Bn The Cameronians; 1 Bn The Royal Inniskilling Fus; 1 Bn The Worcestershire Regt; 1 Bn The Royal Hampshire Regt; 1 Bn The Sherwood Foresters; 1 Bn The Loyal Regt; 1 Bn 3rd East Anglian Regt (16/44 Foot); 1 Bn QOR West Kent; 1 Bn KO Yorkshire Lt Inf; 1 Bn The Wiltshire Regt; 1 Bn The Manchester Regt; 1 Bn Seaforth Highlanders; 1 Bn Gordon Highlanders; 1 Bn The Rifle Brigade; 22 Special Air Service Regt; The Indep Para Squadron; 17th (Gurkha) Signal Regt; 208 (Commonwealth) Signal Squadron; Malaya Command Signal Squadron; 1/2, 2/2 King Edward VII's Own Gurkha Rifles; 1/6, 2/6 Queen Elizabeth's Own Gurkha Rifles; 1/7, 2/7 Duke of Edinburgh's Own Gurkha Rifles; 1/10, 2/10 Princess Mary's Own Gurkha Rifles; Gurkha Military Police; Gurkha ASC; 1, 3 Bn The King's African Rifles; 1 Bn The Northern Rhodesia Regt; 1 Bn The Fiji Infantry Regt; 1 Singapore Regt; 1, 2, 3 Bn The Australian Regt; 1, 2 Bn The New Zealand Regt; The New Zealand Squadron (Special Air Service); The Rhodesia Squadron (Special Air Service who were awarded 120 medals of the 3rd issue); 1st Bn Rhodesian African Rifles (who were awarded 894 of the 4th issue.)

Near East 31st October-22nd December 1956

In the summer of 1956 both Britain and the United States decided not to make a loan to Egypt to finance the Aswan Dam Project, mainly because they doubted Egypt's ability to repay the loan. Days later the Soviet Union denied publicly that they had ever offered to finance the building of the dam. For the Egyptians that left only one other possible source of revenue: the Suez Canal. The last British troops had left Egypt in June. There was nothing to stop President Nasser nationalising the Suez Canal Company. This he did on 26 July. Nasser had also been at loggerheads with the Israelis since September 1954 when he ordered an Israeli ship passing through the canal to be seized. There had also been clashes in the Gaza strip. On 29 October 1956 the Israelis launched an assault on Egyptian Forces in the Sinai. The British and French had meanwhile been preparing to seize the canal by force. A vast armada set out from Malta and air attacks from Cyprus commenced on 31 October. The airborne assault on the Port Said area followed on 5 November and the seaborne landing on 6 November. French and British troops successfully captured all their initial objectives and

pushed out some 25 miles beyond Port Said. Then, at midnight on the 6th, international pressure and threats of nuclear retaliation against London and Paris by the Soviet Union forced the British and French Governments to agree to a United Nations request for a ceasefire. The last British and French troops were evacuated on 22 December and were replaced by United Nations troops.

British casualties in Operation Musketeer were 22 killed and 97 wounded. The French lost 10 killed and 33 wounded. Egyptian casualties in the Port Said area were 750 killed and 2,350 wounded. Though the adventure was a political disaster, the operation was a military success. It involved 45,000 British soldiers, 300 aircraft and 100 warships. (French figures were 34,000, 200 and 30 respectively).

The qualifications were:

ARMY

One day's service, or part thereof, ashore in Egypt or off the Egyptian coast.

ROYAL AIR FORCE

As for the Army or the participation in one or more operational sorties over the area of operations from their bases in Cyprus.

CIVILIAN CATEGORIES

Accredited War Correspondents and certain officially appointed advisers.

GENERAL

For visits and inspections one day in the operational area was required.

This is the first award for which part of a day's service is mentioned in the official qualifications.

In these days of prompt evacuation of the wounded it should be remembered that a man could land on a hostile shore, be wounded, and evacuated to many miles away all in the space of a few hours.

Units present: 1, 2, 3* Bn The Parachute Regt supported by the 33rd Parachute Lt Regt RA; 31, LAA Bty RA; 1, 6 Royal Tank Regt; 1 Royal Scots; 1 Royal Fusiliers; 1 Royal West Kent Regt; West Yorkshire Regt; 1 York and Lanc Regt; Argyll & Sutherland Highlanders, RE; Royal Signals, etc.

Disposition of British Air Units:

Base	Squadron	Aircraft
Luqa/Hal Far	9	Canberra B6
	12	Canberra B6
	15	Canberra B2
	37	Shackleton MR2
	101	Canberra B6
	109	Canberra B6
	138	Valiant B1
	139	Canberra B6
	148	Valiant B1
	207	Valiant B1
	214	Valiant B1
Nicosia	1	Hunter F5
	10	Canberra B2
	15	Canberra B2
	18	Canberra B2
	27	Canberra B2
	30	Valetta C1
	34	Hunter F5
	35	Canberra B2
	44	Canberra B2
	61	Canberra B2
	70	Hastings C1/2
	84	Valetta C1
	99	Hastings C1/2
	114	Valetta C1
	115	Canberra B2
	511	Hastings C1/2
Akrotiri	6	Venom FB4
	13	Canberra PR7
	32	Venom FB4
	39	Meteor NF13
	73	Venom FB4
	249	Venom FB4
	543	Valiant B(PR)1
	1903 Flight	Auster AOP6

*This unit made the initial airborne landing and were heavily engaged.

Aircraft Carrier	Squadron	Aircraft
HMS *Eagle*	830	Wyvern S4
	831	Wyvern S4
	849 A Flt	Skyraider AEW 1
	891	Sea Venom FAW 21
	893	Sea Venom FAW 21
	899	Sea Hawk
HMS *Albion*	800	Sea Hawk FGA 4
	802	Sea Hawk FGA 3
	809	Sea Venom FAW 22
	810	Sea Hawk FGA 6
	849 B Flt	Skyraider AEW 1
	894	Sea Venom FAW 21
	895	Sea Venom FAW 21
HMS *Bulwark*	804	Sea Hawk FGA 4
	897	Sea Hawk FGA 4
HMS *Theseus*	845	Whirlwind HAS 22
HMS *Ocean*	JEHU	Whirlwind, Sycamore

Arabian Peninsula 1st January 1957-30th June 1960

British involvement in Muscat dates from the early days of the East India Company in the seventeenth century. This involvement largely came about due to the co-operation between the British and the Sultan of Muscat to suppress piracy. By the Treaty of 1852 Britain recognized the independance of the Sultan though he was able to call on British help in time of trouble.

Due to disagreement over oil and land rights, the Imam of Oman, who enjoyed a large measure or autonomy, rebelled against the Sultan of Muscat. The Sultan's forces suffered major setbacks and in July 1955 he appealed for British military assistance. The rebels were forced into the Jebel Akhdar mountains whence it was virtually impossible to dislodge them with the forces available. It was not until elements of 22 SAS under Major John Watts (later Major General and Commander of the Sultan of Oman's Land Forces) were deployed, supported by small numbers of British soldiers from several supporting arms, that the rebels were driven out of their mountain stronghold and soundly defeated. It was a very small operation involving only 250 British soldiers but it was brilliantly successful.

This bar was authorized by Army Order 9 dated 22nd February 1961, for award to those who had served 30 days in the Aden Colony or Protectorate and the Sultanates of Muscat and Oman, or any of the adjacent Gulf States.

In addition to members of the Army and Royal Air Force it was also awarded to those who served with the NAAFI, WVS, British Red Cross and the Soldiers' and Airmen's Scripture Readers' Association.

A truly bewildering number of Tribal Guards, Police Forces and The TOS (Trucial Oman Scouts) now the Union Defence Force of the United Arab Emirates were also eligible under the same conditions as the Army and Royal Air Force, though the period mentioned does not apply to them in all cases.

Those who were withdrawn from Cyprus for service in any of the above mentioned territories before completion of the necessary service to qualify for the 'Cyprus' bar were granted it and should wear that for the 'Arabian Peninsula' immediately after (ie above) that for 'Cyprus'.

Those awarded a Mention-in-Despatches or a Queen's Commendation are entitled to wear the emblem on the ribbon. Recipients of either of these, whose service was curtailed through no fault of their own, are entitled to the bar irrespective of their length of service.

Some of the units present: Life Guards; 13/18 Hussars; 15/19 Hussars; Cameronians; SAS; REME; Royal Corps of Signals; RAMC; RAF; Trucial Oman Scouts.

Brunei 8th-23rd December 1962

Approximately three-quarters of the island of Borneo forms part of the Republic of Indonesia whilst the remaining quarter along the northern coast of the island was in 1962 under British colonial rule or protection. In the north east was the colony of north Borneo or Sabah, to the west lay the Sultanate of Brunei and stretching along the remainder of the northern coast was the colony of Sarawak. Indonesia had gained its independence from the Dutch in 1949. President Sukarno's main desire was to create a Greater Indonesia including the whole of British North Borneo and the newly independant Malaya. He was opposed by Tunku Abdul Rahman, Prime Minister of Malaya, who in 1961 attempted to form a Federation consisting of Malaya, Singapore, the North Borneo states and the Sultanate of Brunei. The Sultan hesitated and it was here in Brunei that Sukarno saw his opportunity to foment trouble in December 1962. The so-called North Kalimantan National Army rose in revolt against the Sultan of Brunei who immediately requested help from the British Government. A force of British and Gurkha troops were quickly dispatched by air and sea from bases in Singapore. Some eight days later, on 16 December, British Far Eastern Command stated that all major centres in Brunei were clear of rebel forces though it was not until May 1963 that the last of the rebels were eliminated.

This bar was authorized by AO 44/1963 for award to members of all the Services of the British, Australian and New Zealand forces who served for a period of one day in the operational areas in the State of Brunei and/or North Borneo and Sarawak between the dates, both inclusive, mentioned.

Units present: 12 Bty, det 20 Bty RA; Queen's Own Highlanders; 1/2, 2/10 Gurkha Regiment; Gurkha Engineers; 69 Gurkha Ind Field Squadron, det of 248 Gurkha Signals; 31 Co Gurkha ASC; Gurkha Military Police; North Borneo and Sarawak Police Forces.

In addition to the above it was also awarded to those who served in various ancilliary services: Soldiers, Sailors and Airmen's Families Association; Nursing Service; British Red Cross Society Welfare Service; Women's Voluntary Service; Soldier's and Airmen's Scripture Readers Association; Ministry of Defence Fire Service, etc.

152 *India General Service Medal* 1936-39

Obverse	The crowned coinage head of King George VI and legend 'GEORGIVS VI D: G: OMN: REX ET INDIAE IMP:'
Reverse	A tiger, with raised right front paw, head turned back almost meeting its long tail which is curled over its back, standing astride mountains. The word 'INDIA' is above
Size	36mm diameter
Metal	Silver
Ribbon	32mm wide. A grey sandy-coloured central band flanked by red and green stripes
Suspension	By a swivelling floral suspender as used on previous India General Service Medals. The claws of the medals struck by the Calcutta Mint differ from those of the Royal Mint. Those of the former being a plain curved style, the latter being a more elaborate raised scroll type
Designer	H. Wilson Parker
Naming	In thin impressed block capitals
Bars issued	Two—North West Frontier, 1936-37, and North West Frontier, 1937-39

Instituted on 3rd August, 1938 to replace the India General Service Medal of 1908.

As indicated above there are two different strikings of the medal. The English striking has artistic shoulders to the claw, whereas the Calcutta striking is quite plain. The relief work on the reverse of the Indian striking is distinctly crude, there being practically none on the neck and fore-paws of the tiger. The Calcutta Medals are slightly thicker than those struck by the Royal Mint.

The bar North West Frontier 1937-39 and the medal governing this period was not issued in England until after the war, this type does not swivel.

The medal was never issued without a bar.

Permission was granted to recipients of a Mention in Despatches during any of the campaigns for which this medal was awarded to wear a bronze oak leaf emblem on the ribbon.

North West Frontier 1936-37 24th November 1936-16th/17th January 1937 and 16th/17th January 1937-15th/16th December 1937

Regiments present: 8th Light Cavalry; Probyn's Horse; 14th Scinde Horse; RIASC; IMS; 2 (Derajat) 3, 4, 5, 7 (Bengal), 8, 12, 13 (Dardoni), 15 (Jhelum), 17, 19 (Maymyo) Mountain Batteries; 1 Royal Norfolk Regiment; 1 Leicestershire Regiment; 1 East Yorkshire Regiment (about twenty men); 2 Green Howards; 1 South Wales Borderers; Duke of Wellington's Regiment; Hampshire Regiment; 1 Northamptonshire Regiment; 2 Argyll and Sutherland Highlanders; 2/1, 3/1, 5/1, 2/2, 2/8, 4/8, 6/13, 1/14, 2/14, 3/15, 1/16, 3/16, 4/16 Punjab Regiment; 2/4 Bombay Grenadiers; 2/6, 3/6, 4/6 Rajputana Rifles; 2/7, 3/7 Rajput Regiment; 3/9 Jat Regiment; 1/11, 2/11 Sikh Regiment; 3/12, 5/12 Frontier Force Regiment; 1/13, 2/13, 6/13 Frontier Force Rifles; 1/17, 2/17 Dogra Regiment; 2/1, 1/2, 1/3, 2/4, 1/5, 2/5, 1/6, 2/6, 1/9 Gurkhas; 2, 12 Company QO Madras Sappers and Miners; South Waziri and Tochi Scouts; 2 Native Road Construction Battalion; Animal Transport Corps.
RAF: 5, 11, 20, 27, 28, 31, 39, 60, 70 (BT) Squadrons.

North West Frontier 1937-39 15th/16th December 1937-31st December/1st January, 1939; 15th/16th June, 1938-1st/2nd November, 1938; 31st December, 1938-31st January, 1939; 31st December, 1939-1st January, 1940

This bar was sanctioned by Army Order 217 of 1940 to be awarded for operations in Waziristan between midnight 15th/16th December, 1937, and midnight, 31st December, 1939/1st January, 1940. The operations were conducted by General Sir John F. S. D. Coleridge, KCB, CMG, DSO, ADC, who was the GOC in C of the Northern Command (India). The two divisions employed were commanded by Major-General E. de Burgh, CB, DSO, OBE, and Major-General A. F. Hartley, CB, DSO.

Below, is the list of complete units present but, as for all Indian campaigns, medals are to be found to individuals from several regiments which were not present as a whole.

Regiments present:

Cavalry:
Skinner's Horse (1 Duke of York's Own); Probyn's Horse (5th King Edward's Own); 8 (King George's Own); a detachment of the Scinde Horse (14 Prince of Wales's Own)

Artillery:
4, 7, 63, 66, 80, 81 Field Batteries
2, 3, 9 Light Batteries
Section each of 20/21 and 26 Medium Batteries
2, 3, 4, 5, 7, 8, 12, 13, 15, 17, 18, 19 Batteries and one section of 20 Mountain Battery

Sappers and Miners:
2, 3, 4, 5, 6, 9, 12, 14, 15, 19, 20, 22 Companies

Royal Tank Corps:
1, 6, 7, 8, 9, 11 Tank Companies

European Infantry:
1 R. Warwicks; 1 Norfolks; 2 Suffolks; 1 Leicesters;* 2 Green Howards; 1 South Wales Borderers; 1 Hants;* R Ulster Rifles; 1 Northamptons

Indian†
2/1 Punjab Regiment; 3/1 Punjab Regiment; 1/2, 2/2 Punjab Regiment; 2/4 Bombay Grenadiers; 1/5 Mahratta Light Infantry; 2/6, 3/6, 4/6 Rajputana Rifles; 2/7, 3/7 Rajput Regiment; 2/8, 3/8, 4/8, 5/8 Punjab Regiment; 3/9 Jat Regiment; 1/10, 3/10 Baluch Regiment; 1/11, 2/11 Sikhs; 1/12, 3/12, 5/12 Frontier Force Regiment; 1/13, 4/13, 6/13 Frontier Force Rifles; 1/14, 2/14, 3/14 Punjab Regiment; 3/15 Punjab Regiment; 1/16, 3/16, 4/16 Punjab Regiment; 1/17, 2/17, 3/17 Dogras; 1/18 Royal Garhwal Rifles; 1/1, 2/1, 1/2, 1/3, 2/3, 1/4, 2/4, 1/5, 2/5, 1/6, 2/6, 2/8, 1/9 Gurkhas.
Road Construction Battalions: 1, 2, 4, 5

RAF:
5 (AC), 11 (B), 20 (AC), 27 (B), 28 (AC), 31 (AC), 39 (B), 60 (B), one flight of 70 (BT) Squadrons

---

* The title 'Royal' was granted in November, 1946.
† The regiments are given in their numerical order, which was not that of their seniority in the Indian Army.

153   *The British North Borneo Company's General Service Medal* 1937-41

Obverse	The shield of the Company supported on either side by a native. Above the shield are two arms, one clothed, the other naked, supporting the Company's flag. Below the shield is the motto, 'PERGO ET PERAGO'
Reverse	The seated figure of Britannia facing left, holding a trident in her left hand, her right hand resting on a shield which bears the Union Flag. Around the circumference, above the exergue, is the inscription, 'NORTH BORNEO GENERAL SERVICE MEDAL.' In the exergue is a branch with eleven leaves
Size	38mm diameter, 3mm gauge
Metal	Silver
Ribbon	For specially valuable or long and meritorious service: 35mm wide, half dark green, half yellow. For gallantry: 35mm wide, half dark green, half yellow with a thin 1.5mm red stripe in the centre
Suspension	By means of a ring which is attached to the piece by an ornate claw
Bars issued	Nil

The medal was manufactured by Spink & Son. Specimens of the medal have in the reverse exergue the top of the end leaf stamped out and in addition, 'Copy' is stamped on the rims of those produced since 1955.

This medal was sanctioned by the Company's Official Gazette (Extraordinary) No 9, dated 6th April, 1937, the first five paragraphs of which read:

1 The Court of Directors have been pleased to approve the creation of a medal to be designated 'The North Borneo General Service Medal'

2 This medal will be granted for
   a) Specially valuable services to North Borneo
   b) Long and meritorious service of not less than eighteen years in any capacity in North Borneo, irrespective of whether such service has been rendered in the service of the Chartered Company or not
   c) Acts of exceptional courage in North Borneo

3 After publication of the first list, recommendations for the award of the medal under Regulation 2 *(a)* and *(b)* above shall be submitted by the Governor to the Court of Directors annually on the 1st of July; and awards will be published annually in the *North Borneo Gazette* on the 1st of November (Charter Day). Recommendations for the award of the medal under Regulation 2 *(c)* may be made by the Governor at any time

4 The medal shall consist of a circular medal in silver, having on the obverse a representation of Britannia within the cirle and the words 'NORTH BORNEO GENERAL SERVICE MEDAL', and on the reverse the arms of the Chartered Company, and shall be worn on the left side suspended by a ring to a riband of dark green and

yellow in equal proportions of one inch and three-eighths of an inch in width, with the addition in the case of recipients under Regulation 2 *(c)* above of a central red stripe of about one-sixteenth of an inch
5 Recipients who are British subjects are not permitted to wear this medal except in North Borneo

From the above paragraphs it can be seen that it is not a campaign medal pure and simple.

The word 'General' in its title is apt as recipients were members of the Legislative Council, railway executives, clergy, district officers, rubber planters, members of the local constabulary, native chiefs etc. The following is a list of the forty-four recipients taken from the Journal of the Orders and Medals Research Society. Except where stated, all are for long and meritorious service.

Gazette of 6 April 1937/The British North Borneo Herald of 1 June 1937
1 Ernest Bateson; 2 James Beatty, for specially valuable services; 3 Percival Alfred Dingle, CBE; 4 Richard Knox Hardwick; 5 Kahhar, Orang Kaya Kaya; 6 192 Sergeant Karam Lai; 7 Li Tet Phui; 8 Charles Frederick Cunningham Macaskie; 9 Charles Darke Martyn; 10 The Venerable Bernard Mercer; 11 186 Sergeant-Major Ojajar Singh; 12 Captain Charles Henry Campbell Pearson; 13 Frederick Walter Pinnock; 14 483 Sergeant Sagunting; 15 Saman, Orang Kaya Kaya Awang Mohammed; 16 John Owen Shircore, CMG, for specially valuable services; 17 Charles Robert Smith; 18 The Very Revd Monsignor Augustine Wachter; 19 Herbert James Walker; 20 Samuel Willie.

Gazette of 3 August 1937
21 Douglas James Jardine, CMG, OBE, for very valuable services.

Gazette of 2 November 1937/The British North Borneo Herald of 2 November 1937
22 The Reverand Mother Mary Alban; 23 Herbert James Rust Beckett; 24 Frank Reginald Hallowell Carew; 25 Horace Alabone Dabell; 26 Chief Inspector Dualis; 27 Arthur Nicholas Melville Garry; 28 Jemadar Gulam Rasul; 29 Mrs Douglas James Jardine, for specially valuable services; 30 Lajungah, Orang Kaya Kaya; 31 Louis Lai Phan; 32 Eric Walter Skinner.

Gazette of 11 May 1938/The British North Borneo Herald of 16 May 1938
33 Mrs C. D. Martyn, for specially valuable services.

Gazette of 2 November 1938
34 Jose Agama; 35 Anik bin Patek; 36 Daud bin Mat Jappar; 37 Li Chi On.

Gazette of 3 August 1939/The British North Borneo Herald of 17 July 1939
38 Leong Yew Pong, for an act of exceptional courage.

Gazette of 2 November 1939
39 Harry Arthur Byron; 40 Alexander Archibald Keasberry.

The British North Borneo Herald of 18 November 1940
41 Mrs C. Boyer; 42 G. C. Woolley.

Gazette of 3 November 1941/The British North Borneo Herald of 17 November 1941
43 Subedar Dewa Singh; 44 Yahya bin Abdul Rahman, Orang Kaya Kaya

---

Second World War Stars 1939-1945

General	Six pointed star
Obverse	In the centre the Royal cypher 'GRI' with 'VI' below. The cypher is surmounted by a crown superimposed on a circlet which bears the title of the star
Reverse	Plain
Size	43mm diameter
Metal	Bronze
Ribbons	These were designed by His Majesty King George VI and vary with each star. The colours are given in the text below. They are all 32mm wide
Suspension	The ribbon passes through a ring attached to the uppermost point of the star
Designer	The stars were designed by the Royal Mint engravers
Naming	All issued unnamed by the British Government. Some Commonwealth countries had their stars named in impressed lettering prior to issue. Stars may be found privately engraved
Bars issued	A total of nine which are sewn on to the appropriate ribbon

Those who wish to obtain the full particulars of the awards made for the World War, 1939-45, should consult the pamphlet issued by the Committee on the grant of Honours, Decorations and Medals, and published by HM Stationery Office in June, 1946, and subsequent publications.

It was decided by the Honours Committee, after due deliberation, that the campaign stars and medals awarded to Imperial troops for service during the 1939-45 War would not be stamped with particulars of the name and unit of the recipients at Government expense, but that they could be added under private arrangement. Not only does this lower the intrinsic value of all these stars and medals, but it will necessitate a careful scrutiny of the recipient's Record of Service to verify the authenticity of any group.

No one person could receive more than five campaign stars and the two medals, as the following will show:
1939-45 Star
Atlantic (or Air Crew Europe or France and Germany Star)
Africa Star
Pacific Star (or Burma Star)
Italy Star
Defence Medal
War Medal

No individual was awarded more than one bar or emblem to any one campaign star, nor was he entitled to wear more than one emblem on any one of the star ribbons when the ribbon only was worn.

General remarks concerning the 1939-45 Campaign Stars

1 Service in ships making occasional visits to the scenes of operations for refuelling would not necessarily be a qualification.

2 The expression 'entry into operational service' in the case of the Atlantic and Air Crew Europe Star was subject to the qualification that six or two months' operational service must already have been rendered. For awards to the Royal Navy and the Merchant Navy of the Pacific, Burma and Italy Stars a similar prior time qualification of six months also applied. There were, however, certain exceptions to these rules which have been enumerated in the appropriate text.

3 A recipient of the 1939-45 Star who qualified for it by less than the six or two months' service respectively had to complete the requisite period before he could begin to qualify for the Atlantic or Air Crew Europe Stars respectively. In the case of the Royal Navy and Merchant Navy, the applicable qualifying period had to be completed before they could begin to qualify for the Pacific, Burma and Italy Stars.

4 For the Atlantic or Air Crew Europe Stars in the Armed Forces or Merchant Navy, or for the Pacific, Burma or Italy Stars in the Royal Navy or Merchant Navy, operational service for a period less than six or two months as the case may be, which was brought to an end by death, wounds or other disability due to service; or, alternatively, the grant for service in operations of an Honour, Decoration, Mention in Despatches, King's Commendation for brave conduct or King's Commendation for valuable service in the air, was a qualification for award, without regard to the prior service requirement. The restrictions concerning the alternative awards of the stars still applied.

5 Time spent as a prisoner of war would count towards the 1939-45 Star, but it would not be counted towards earning any of the other stars unless the full qualifying periods for the 1939-45 Star had been completed before capture. If, however, the candidate had completed his requisite period for the 1939-45 Star and was captured during the period he was qualifying for one of the other stars, then the period spent in captivity would count. In the case of the Merchant Navy, at least one voyage must have been completed in the necessary qualifying area since the completion of the service necessary to qualify for the 1939-45 Star.

6 Service spent in qualifying for one star could not run concurrently with service qualifying for another, except that an individual who had completed the six or two months' operational service required for the award of the 1939-45 Star was not required to complete this period of qualifying service a second time in order to begin to qualify for the other. A similar arrangement applied to the prior service qualification for awards in the Royal Navy and the Merchant Navy of the Pacific, Burma and Italy Stars. An exception was made to this rule in the case of the Merchant Navy as regards the Atlantic Star which is mentioned in the text referring to it.

7 No individual was awarded more than one bar to any one star.

8 The 1939-45 and Africa Stars were awarded to crews of transport aircraft that flew over certain specified routes. The same applies to crews of the Royal Air Force Transport Command that did similar duties.

9 Personnel of the Royal Navy and Merchant Navy who were on operational service on 8th May, 1945, or during the six months immediately preceding it were granted the Italy Star by virtue of entry into a theatre of operations, and the prior six months' service requirement did not apply. A similar waiving of the prior service requirement extended to the Atlantic Star. The actual requirement for the Atlantic Star was thus reduced in that period until it consisted merely of entry into operational service.

10 Personnel of the Royal Navy and the Merchant Navy who were in operational service on 2nd September, 1945, received the Pacific or Burma Star, as the case might be, by virtue of entry into a theatre of operations, and the prior six months' service requirement did not apply. In such cases only one star was awarded for service at sea during the last six months in the Atlantic, Italy, Pacific and Burma areas. The star awarded was the one appropriate to the last area in which service was rendered. The 1939-45 Star was not awarded in cases where the operational service amounted to less than the necessary six or two months respectively.

11 Civilians who performed not less than twenty-eight days' operational service (a) under the Council of Voluntary War Work, (b) as recognised Press Correspondents in an operational command, (c) as a member of a civil air transport crew which flew over certain specified areas, or (d) officers who performed meteorological work, RAF education, works service, in uniform, in the area of Army operational commands were eligible for the Campaign Stars and the War Medal.

154 *The 1939-45 Star* 3rd September, 1939-2nd September, 1945

Obverse	Within a circlet are the words, 'THE 1939-1945 STAR'
Ribbon	The colours of the ribbon are, reading from the left when facing the wearer, equal bands of dark blue, red and light blue. They symbolize the Royal Navy and Merchant Navy, the Army and the Royal Air Force
Bars issued	One: Battle of Britain

This star was awarded for service in the Second World War between 3rd September, 1939 and 2nd September, 1945. (First announced as the 1939-43 Star).

Qualifications for the star were as follows:

NAVY
Six months* service afloat in areas of active operations. Members of the Fleet Air Arm could qualify for the Star, either by six months service afloat or under any of the qualifications applicable to the Royal Air Force.

ARMY
Six months service in an operational command. Airborne troops qualified if they had participated in any airborne operations and had completed two months service in a fully operational unit.

RAF
Operations against the enemy providing that two months service had been completed in an operational unit. Non-aircrew personnel had to complete six months service in an area of an operational army command.

MERCHANT NAVY
Personnel who completed six months' service afloat qualified, providing that at least one voyage was made through an operational area. Service

---

* As the period of a month will often be mentioned in connection with the 1939-45 awards it is as well to call attention to the official duration of such a period. A month is 30 days; two months are 60 days; four months are 120 days; six months are 180 days. The difference between these periods and the corresponding calendar should be noted.

performed during the evacuation of Dunkirk also qualified. Service in fishing vessels and in coastal craft was also included.

GENERAL

Time spent as a prisoner of war was allowed to count towards the award.

Operational service brought to an end through death, disability or wound qualified for the award, irrespective of the length of service.

A recipient of an honour, decoration, Mention in Despatches or King's Commendation in respect of operational service qualified for the award, again irrespective of the length of service.

Service in areas where troops were evacuated such as Dunkirk, Norway, Greece, Crete, etc. or who were engaged in Commando raids to Dieppe, St Nazaire, etc. or who saw service in certain other specified areas, were also eligible, entry into the zone of operation being the only qualification.

Recipients of the Star for less than the full qualifying periods of six months', or two months', service had to complete the remainder of their qualifying period in any theatre of operations before being allowed to count service for the Atlantic or Air Crew Europe Star.

In the case of the Royal Navy and the Merchant Navy, a full period of six months' operational service must have been rendered before eligibility for the Pacific, Burma or Italy Stars began.

Members of the women's Naval, Military and Air Force organizations were eligible for the Star on the same basis as the male members of the services to which they belonged.

Battle of Britain

Members of the crews of fighter aircraft who took part in the Battle of Britain between 10th July and 31st October, 1940, were awarded the bar, 'Battle of Britain' to be affixed on to the ribbon when the 1939-45 Star was worn. When the ribbon was worn alone, a silver-gilt rose emblem was fixed upon it to denote the bar.

It should be noted that combat in the air during the qualifying period did not in itself constitute a qualification no matter in what type of aircraft the combat took place. The squadrons that qualified were: Nos 1, 17, 19, 23, 25, 29, 32, 41, 43, 46, 54, 56, 64, 65, 66, 72, 73, 74, 79, 85, 89, 92, 111, 141, 145, 151, 152, 213, 219, 222, 229, 234, 235, 236, 238, 242, 248, 249, 253, 257, 264, 266, 302, 303, 310, 312, 401 (No 1 RCAF Squadron), 501, 504, 600, 601, 602, 603, 604, 605, 607, 609, 610, 611, 615, 616 and the Fighter Interception Unit.

155 *The Atlantic Star* 3rd September, 1939-8th May, 1945

Obverse	Within a circlet are the words, 'THE ATLANTIC STAR'
Ribbon	The ribbon is of the shaded and watered type of dark blue, white and sea-green symbolic of the Atlantic. The dark blue is worn to the left when facing the wearer
Bars issued	Two: Air Crew Europe and France and Germany

The star was awarded to commemorate the Battle of the Atlantic within the period 3rd September, 1939 to 8th May, 1945. It was designed primarily to reward those serving in convoys, fast merchant ships, escorts and anti-submarine forces. The 1939-45 Star must have been earned by six or, in the case of the air crews, two months' service in operations before the qualifying period for the Atlantic Star began.

The qualifications within the above period were as follows:

NAVY

Six months service afloat in the Atlantic or Home waters. Service with convoys to North Russia and service in the South Atlantic west of longitude 20°E also counted.

The period of qualification for the France and Germany Star could not run concurrently with that for the Atlantic Star.

Prisoners of war were entitled to the star, providing that they had already completed the qualifying period for the 1939-45 Star and had begun to earn the Atlantic Star at the time of capture.

MERCHANT NAVY

Awarded under the same conditions as the Navy (above) except that six months' service anywhere at sea will qualify provided that one or more voyages were made in the defined area.

For the Merchant Navy, when calculating the second six months' service at sea, no deduction was made of time spent in other operational areas which entitled the person to another star.

Service afloat in fishing vessels and certain coastal craft was excluded from the award of this star, though recognized for the 1939-45 Star.

Prisoners of war were entitled to the star, providing they had already completed the qualifying period for the 1939-45 Star and had began to earn the Atlantic Star including at least one voyage in the defined area.

RAF

Members of air crews who had taken part in active operations within the specified area, providing that they completed two months' service in an operational unit after earning the 1939-45 Star.

Four months' service as a member of an air crew in an operational unit was also considered as a qualification for the star, providing that any two of them qualified for this star.

Time spent as a prisoner of war was not counted, unless the period necessary to earn the 1939-45 Star had been completed at the time of capture.

ARMY AND RAF

Army and Air Force personnel who served with the Navy or Merchant Navy qualified in the same way as members of the service with which they served.

GENERAL

This star could not be earned unless the qualification to earn the 1939-45 Star had been fulfilled.

Service for the Atlantic Star brought to an end by death, wounds or disability qualified as did service marked by an award, mention in despatches, etc irrespective of the time served.

In the last six months of operational service up to the 8th May, 1945, persons who entered operational service for the last two or six months (depending on the service) qualified for the Atlantic Star provided they did not serve subsequently in another operational area. In these cases the 1939-45 Star was not awarded.

Bars and Emblems

Those who qualified for the Atlantic Star and who in addition qualified for the Air Crew Europe and/or France and Germany Star, were entitled to wear one bar denoting service for which the second star would have been awarded. When the ribbon alone was worn, a silver rose emblem was fixed upon it to denote the award of a bar. Only one bar could be awarded to the Atlantic Star.

156 *The Air Crew Europe Star* 3rd September 1939-5th June 1944

Obverse   Within a circlet are the words 'THE AIR CREW EUROPE STAR'

Ribbon   The ribbon is light blue with black edges and two yellow stripes, representing continuous service by day and by night

Bars issued   Two: Atlantic and France and Germany

This star was awarded for operational flying from United Kingdom bases over Europe between the dates mentioned.

The qualifications within the above period were as follows:

RAF

The time qualification was two months service as air crew. The 1939-45 Star had to be earned before a person could begin to qualify for the Air Crew Europe Star. Four months service as air crew in an operational unit, any two of which qualified for the Air Crew Europe Star, was regarded as a qualification for that Star.

ARMY

Army personnel qualified for this star if they had served on aircrew duties for four months with the RAF operational unit providing that two months of this period was employed on operational flying over Europe and at least one operational sortie was made.

GENERAL

Time spent as a prisoner of war was not counted, unless the qualifying period for the 1939-45 Star had been completed before capture.

Service curtailed by death, or disability due to service, would qualify, as would any service during which an award or a Mention in Despatches was gained.

Bars and Emblems

Those who qualified for the Air Crew Europe Star and who in addition qualified for the Atlantic and/or France and Germany Star, were entitled to wear one bar denoting service for which the second star would have been awarded. A silver rose emblem indicating the award of a bar was attached to the ribbon when the ribbon alone was worn.

157 *The Africa Star* 10th June 1940-12th May 1943

Obverse   Within a circlet are the words 'THE AFRICA STAR'

Ribbon   The colours of the ribbon are pale buff with a central red stripe and two narrow stripes, one of dark blue and the other of light blue. The dark blue stripe is worn innermost, *ie* to the left when facing the wearer

These colours are symbolic of the desert, the Royal Navy, the Army and the Royal Air Force

Bars issued   Three: 8th Army, 1st Army, North Africa 1942-43

This star was awarded for one or more days' service in North Africa between 10th June, 1940, and 12th May, 1943, both dates inclusive.

The qualifications for the Star were:

NAVY AND MERCHANT NAVY

Any service at sea in the Mediterranean between 10th June, 1940, and 12th May, 1943, and/or service in support of the campaigns in Abyssinia, Somaliland and Eritrea between 10th June, 1940 and 27th November, 1941.

Naval service ashore in the same areas as the Army would also qualify. Members of the Merchant Navy who took part in the operations off the coast of Morocco between 8th November, 1942, and 12th May, 1943, would also qualify.

ARMY

The qualification is the entry into North Africa on the establishment of an operational unit.

Service in Abyssinia, The Somalilands, Eritrea, Sudan and Malta was included, but not that in West Africa.

RAF

The qualification was to have landed in, or flown over, any of the areas previously mentioned (except West Africa), or territory occupied by the enemy.

GENERAL

Visits, inspections, etc. did not qualify unless they amounted to thirty days and were specially approved.

The conditions governing the award of this star are in no way connected with those for the 1939-45 Star.

Bars and Emblems

NAVY

Personnel who served inshore or on escort duty off the North African coast between 23rd October, 1942, and 12th May, 1943, were entitled to wear a silver rose emblem on the ribbon to denote entitlement to the bar 'North Africa 1942-43.' Those who served with either the Eighth or First Armies were granted a silver emblem of the Arabic figure '8' or '1' according to the army with which they served.

ARMY

Three emblems were awarded to the Army, which consisted of (1) a numeral '8', (2) a numeral '1', or (3) a silver rose emblem to denote the award of the bar 'North Africa 1942-43'. Only one could be worn. The qualifications were:
1) The numeral '8' representing the '8th Army' bar was awarded for

service in the Eighth Army between 23rd October, 1942, the date of the Battle of El Alamein, and 12th May, 1943.

2) The numeral '1' representing the '1st Army' bar was awarded for service in the First Army in a unit or formation in Tunis or Algeria between 8th November and 31st December, 1942, or thereafter between 1st January and 12th May, 1943, in any unit under the command of the First Army.

3) The silver rose emblem was awarded to personnel of the Headquarters of the 18th Army Group who did not qualify for either of the numerals. Members of the Union Defence Force attached to the South African Air Force Squadrons, which qualified for the rose emblem, also qualified for it.

RAF

A silver rose emblem denoting award of the bar 'North Africa 1942-43' was awarded to those who served under the command of the AOC Western Desert, ACNW African Forces, AOC Malta, or any others who operated against the Germans or Italians between 23rd October, 1942, and 12th May, 1943.

MERCHANT NAVY

Inshore service on the North African coast between 23rd October, 1942, and 12th May, 1943, and participation in the landings on the Moroccan coast between 8th November, 1942, and 12th May, 1943, qualified for the bar 'North Africa 1942-43'.

Service in any vessel in support of the operations in North Africa, during the period 23rd October, 1942, to 12th May, 1943, qualified for the bar 'North Africa 1942-43.'

GENERAL

Only one bar, or emblem, was awarded to any one individual in conjunction with this star. If, however, an individual qualified for all three bars, then the one to which he first became entitled was awarded.

When the star is worn, then the appropriate bar inscribed with the title '8th Army', '1st Army' or 'North Africa 1942-43' is worn attached to the ribbon.

158 *The Pacific Star* 8th December 1941-2nd September 1945

Obverse   Within a circlet are the words, 'THE PACIFIC STAR'

Ribbon   The ribbon is dark green with red edges with a central yellow stripe, also a thin one of dark blue and another of light blue. The dark blue stripe should be worn furthest from a left shoulder, *ie* to the left when facing the wearer. The green and yellow symbolize the forests and beaches; the dark blue represents the Navy, the red the Army, and the light blue the Royal Air Force

Bars issued   One: Burma

This star was awarded for service in the Pacific theatre of operations between 8th December 1941, and 2nd September 1945, both dates inclusive.

The qualifications were:

ROYAL NAVY AND MERCHANT NAVY

Service in the Pacific Ocean, South China Sea and the Indian Ocean east of a line running approximately south of Singapore.

The 1939-45 Star must have been earned by six months' service before qualification for the Pacific Star could commence, except in the case of those who served in the Pacific zone for less than six months after 2nd March 1945. Persons who entered operational service during the last six months qualified for the star if they did not serve subsequently in another operational area. In this case the prior time qualification of six months did not apply. The 1939-45 Star was not awarded in such cases where the total operational service amounted to less than six months.

Naval personnel who served ashore qualified under the same rules as those pertaining to the Army.

ARMY

Qualifying service for the Army was restricted to the territories which had been subjected to enemy or allied invasions. Service in Burma was, however, excluded. Service in China and Malaya between 8th December 1941 and 15th February 1942, was included.

In the case of the Army there was no prior time qualification required.

RAF

RAF crews must have completed at least one operational sortie over the appropriate land or sea area to qualify.

GENERAL

Official visits under the authority of the Commanders of the Military or Air Forces engaged did not qualify unless they exceeded thirty days in duration.

Bar and emblem

Those who qualified for both the Pacific and Burma Stars were awarded the star that was earned first and a bar to denote the second. When the ribbon alone was worn a silver rose emblem was fixed on the ribbon to denote the award of a bar.

159 *The Burma Star* 11th December 1941-2nd September 1945

Obverse   Within a circlet are the words, 'THE BURMA STAR
Ribbon   The ribbon is dark blue with a wide red stripe down the centre. The blue edges each have a central orange stripe. The red symbolizes the British Commonwealth Forces and the orange the sun
Bars issued One: Pacific

This star was awarded for service in the Burma Campaign between 11th December 1941 and 2nd September 1945, both dates inclusive.

The qualifications for the different Services are as follows:

ROYAL NAVY AND MERCHANT NAVY
The area is restricted to the Bay of Bengal, enclosed by a line running from the southernmost point of Ceylon for a distance of 300 miles south, thence to a point 300 miles west of the southernmost point of Sumatra, and continuing east to the western side of the Sunda Strait. The Malacca Straits are included.

The 1939-45 Star must have been earned by six months' service in operations before eligibility for the Burma Star could begin.

Persons who entered operational service during the last six months qualified for the star if they did not serve subsequently in another operational area. In this case the prior time qualification of six months did not apply. The 1939-45 Star was not awarded in such cases where the total operational service amounted to less than six months.

Naval personnel who served ashore qualified under the same rules as the Army.

ARMY
Service in any part of Burma between 11th December 1941 and 2nd September 1945, qualified for the award, as did that in the provinces of Bengal and Assam between 1st May 1942 and 31st December 1943, and in the same provinces between 1st January 1944 and 2nd September 1945. Service in China and Malaya between 16th February 1942 and 2nd September 1945, was also included.

RAF
One operational sortie qualified. Non-aircrew qualified under the same rules as for the Army.

GENERAL
Visits and inspections which were approved by any of the Commanders-in-Chief would qualify, providing that they were of over thirty days' duration.

Bar and emblem
Those who qualified for both the Burma and Pacific Stars were awarded a silver rose emblem to be worn on the ribbon of the star first earned when the ribbons alone are worn. When the Burma Star itself is being worn the recipient is entitled to wear a bar with the title 'Pacific' attached to the ribbon.

160 *The Italy Star* 11th June 1943-8th May 1945

Obverse   Within a circlet are the words, 'THE ITALY STAR'
Ribbon   The Italian colours are represented on the ribbon by equal stripes of red, white, green, white, red
Bars issued Nil

This star was awarded for operational service in Sicily or Italy, from the date of the capture of the island of Pantellaria on 11th June 1943 to 8th May 1945.

The qualifications were:

ROYAL NAVY AND MERCHANT NAVY
The 1939-45 Star must have been earned by six months' service in operations before the qualifying period for the Italy Star could commence. Service in the Mediterranean and the Aegean Seas and operations in and around the Dodecanese, Corsica, Greece, Sardinia and Yugoslavia after 11th June 1943, would qualify.

Persons who entered operational service during the last six months qualified for the star if they did not serve subsequently in another operational area. In this case the prior time qualification of six months did not apply. The 1939-45 Star was not awarded in such cases where the total operational service amounted to less than six months.

Naval personnel who served ashore qualified under the same rules as the Army.

ARMY
There was no prior time qualification for the Army.

Operational service in the Aegean, Dodecanese, Corsica, Greece, Sardinia, Yugoslavia and Elba between 11th June 1943 and 8th May 1945, qualified.

Service in Sicily after 17th August 1943, in Sardinia after 19th September 1943, and in Corsica after 4th October 1943, did not qualify.

RAF
There was no prior time qualification for the RAF. Qualification consisted of participation in aircrew service within the Mediterranean theatre, including sorties from the Mediterranean area over Europe.

GENERAL
Entry into Austrian Territory during the last few days of the war qualified for this star, not for the France and Germany Star.

Visits of over thirty days' duration qualified for the award, providing that they were undertaken under the authority of one of the Commanders-in-Chief.

The star was awarded in addition to the other stars, so that no clasps were awarded to it.

161 *The France and Germany Star* 6th June 1944-8th May 1945

Obverse	Within a circlet are the words 'THE FRANCE AND GERMANY STAR'
Ribbon	The colours of the ribbon are blue, white, red, white, blue in equal width stripes which are symbolic of the Union flag and those of France and the Netherlands. It will be noted that Belgium is not represented in these colours
Bars issued	One: Atlantic

This star was awarded for service in France, Belgium, Holland or Germany between D Day and the German surrender—that is for the period 6th June, 1944 to 8th May 1945.

The qualifications were:

ROYAL NAVY AND MERCHANT NAVY
There was no prior time qualification.

Qualification consisted of service afloat in direct support of land operations in France, Belgium, Holland, Germany, etc in the North Sea south of a line from the Firth of Forth to Kristiansand, in the English Channel or the Bay of Biscay east of longitude 6°W.

Service off the South of France did not qualify for this star but for the Italy Star.

Service ashore in any of the areas of land operations also qualified.

ARMY
The only qualification necessary was the participation in any operation on land in any of the above countries.

RAF
Any service over Europe between the above dates constituted a qualification, except those which started from the Mediterranean area, which would qualify for the Italy Star.

Non-aircrew personnel qualified under the same conditions as the Army.

GENERAL
Visits of an official nature which lasted over thirty days would qualify, provided they were approved.

Bars and emblems

The France and Germany Star was not awarded in addition to the Atlantic or Air Crew Europe Star.

Those who qualified for the Atlantic, Air Crew Europe or France and Germany Star, or two of them, were awarded only the star for which they qualified first, and received a bar for the second. A second bar was not awarded to those who qualified for all three stars.

Those who qualified for the France and Germany Star followed by the Atlantic were awarded the bar 'Atlantic' to be worn on the ribbon. When the ribbon alone was worn, a silver rose emblem was fixed on the ribbon to denote the award of a bar.

A bar for 'Air Crew Europe' was not awarded with this star.

162 *The Defence Medal* 3rd September 1939-2nd September 1945

Obverse	The uncrowned head of King George VI and legend 'GEORGIVS VI D: BR: OMN: REX F: D: IND: IMP:'
Reverse	The Royal Crown resting on the stump of an oak tree and flanked by two lions. On the top left is the date 1939, and on the top right the date 1945. In the exergue, is the wording 'THE DEFENCE MEDAL'
Size	36mm diameter
Metal	Cupro-nickel although the Canadian version was in .800 fine silver
Ribbon	32mm wide, flame coloured with green edges, symbolic of the enemy attacks on our green land. The black-out is commemorated by two thin black stripes down the centre of the green ones
Suspension	By a plain, straight, non-swivelling suspender
Designers	Obverse—T. H. Paget; Reverse—H. Wilson Parker
Naming	Issued unnamed
Bars issued	Nil

The qualifications for the award were:
1 Service in the Forces in non-operational areas subjected to air attack or closely threatened, providing such service lasted for three or more years.
2 Non-operational service in the Forces overseas or outside the country of residence, providing that such service lasted for one year, except in

territories threatened by the enemy or subject to bomb attacks, in which case it was six months.

3 Civil Defence or other similar service in military operational areas providing the civil category was not eligible for campaign stars.

4 The qualifying period of service in Mine and Bomb Disposal Units was three months.

5 Those who were awarded Campaign Stars could also, providing they fulfilled the necessary conditions, be awarded this medal.

6 Service in the United Kingdom Forces in West Africa, Palestine and India would count for the award of this medal, as well as by Dominion Forces, other than operational air crews, in non-operational areas outside their own countries.

7 Part-time service in the Malta Home Guard also counted.

8 The closing date for those in the Forces was extended to 2nd September 1945, for those serving overseas.

9 Members of any of the civilian services that were entitled to wear chevrons for their war service were eligible for this medal.

10 Members of the Home Guard resident in the United Kingdom qualified for the medal by rendering three years' service (or three months in the case of those who served in a bomb and mine disposal unit). British citizens from overseas qualified with six months' service or three months in the bomb and mine disposal units.

11 Service curtailed by death due to enemy action or service wounds was considered eligible. Those who received a personal award conferred by the King were also eligible irrespective of their length of service providing they were serving in a category that qualified for the medal.

12 Recipients of the George Cross, or George Medal, were eligible for the Defence Medal whether they were serving in a category eligible for the medal or not, providing that the decorations were gained for service in Civil Defence.

GENERAL

The plastic oval badge granted to civilians who were awarded a King's Commendation for brave conduct was replaced, except in the Merchant Navy, by an emblem of silver laurel leaves to be worn on the ribbon of the Defence Medal. When the Defence Medal was not granted, or the award was for services after the war, the emblem was to be worn directly on the coat, after any ribbons or alone. Approval was given for a small oval badge to be awarded to those civilians who were granted a King's Commendation for valuable service in the air. This badge was to be worn on the coat immediately under any medal ribbons, or in civil air-line uniform on the panel of the left breast pocket.

163 *The War Medal* 3rd September 1939-2nd September 1945

Obverse	The crowned head of King George VI surrounded by the legend 'GEORGIVS VI D: G: BR: OM: REX ET INDIAE IMP:'
Reverse	A lion standing on a dragon with two heads, above are the dates 1939 and 1945
Size	36mm diameter
Metal	Cupro-nickel although the Canadian version was in .800 fine silver
Ribbon	This embodies the red, white and blue of the Union Flag. It has a narrow red stripe down the centre with a narrow white stripe on both sides of it. The remainder of the sides of the ribbon are equally divided into blue and red stripes with the blue ones next to the white
Suspension	By a plain, straight, non-swivelling suspender
Designer	E. Carter Preston
Naming	Issued unnamed
Bars issued	Nil

This medal was awarded to all full-time personnel of the Armed Forces wherever their service during the war was rendered. Operational and non-operational service counted, providing that it was of twenty-eight days' or more duration. In the Merchant Navy there was the requirement that the twenty-eight days should have been served at sea.

Operational service that was terminated by death, wounds or a disability due to service, capture or the cessation of hostilities which qualified for one of the Campaign Stars also qualified the recipient for the War Medal even though the total service did not amount to twenty-eight days. This proviso did not, however, apply to those who were not awarded one of the Campaign Stars. If one of the Campaign Stars were awarded for service of less than twenty-eight days, the War Medal was granted in addition.

When issued by Canada to a next-of-kin a silver memorial bar engraved with the name and date of death is attached to the ribbon (40,000 issued). 700,000 silver medals were issued to Canadians, including 4,450 to the Canadian Merchant Marine.

A total of 182 Victoria Crosses were awarded between 1939-45.

164 *India Service Medal* 3rd September 1939-2nd September 1945

Obverse	Crowned head of King George VI surrounded by the legend, 'GEORGIVS VI D:G: BR: OMN: REX ET INDIAE IMP:'
Reverse	Map of India with the legend, 'INDIA 1939-45'
Size	36mm diameter
Metal	Cupro-nickel
Ribbon	Light blue with two central dark blue stripes and dark blue edges. The light blue represents the Order of the Star of India, the dark blue that of the Order of the Indian Empire
Suspension	Plain, straight, non-swivelling suspender
Naming	Issued unnamed
Bars issued	Nil

On 6th June 1946, it was announced in Parliament that the King had sanctioned the award of this medal to Indian Forces for three years' non-operational service in India or elsewhere between 3rd September 1939, and 2nd September 1945. It was not to be awarded to those who qualified for the Defence Medal. The award was additional to the War Medal and the Campaign Stars and takes precedence immediately after the War Medal.

The following were eligible for this medal:
1 British officers resident in India, Viceroy Commissioned officers, British other ranks and Indian personnel of the Indian Army.
2 Members of the Indian Territorial and Auxiliary Forces who were called up for service, Indian State Forces which were embodied and the Indian Women's Services.
3 Non-combatants in military employ who performed duties with a military formation.
4 British personnel who served with the British or Indian Armies providing that they resided in India prior to 3rd September 1939.
5 Indians and Europeans who resided in India prior to 3rd September 1939, who served with the British Forces in India, or elsewhere, who were not eligible for the Defence Medal.

Those who were serving with the United Kingdom Forces in India during the war, whether stationed there prior to 3rd September 1939, or not, and those who were recruited from outside India but served with the Indian Army, were *not* eligible. Approximately 222,000 issued.

165 *Canadian Volunteer Service Medal*
2nd September 1939-1st March 1947

Obverse	Seven marching figures representing the three fighting services, male and female, together with the Nursing Service. Around the circumference is the inscription '1939 CANADA 1945' at the top and 'VOLUNTARY SERVICE VOLONTAIRE' around the bottom. The last three words are separated by maple leaves
Reverse	The Canadian Coat of Arms
Size	36mm diameter
Metal	Silver
Ribbon	32mm wide. Dark blue central band with a stripe of scarlet and green at each side, the green being on the edge
Suspension	There is a small ring fitted to the top of the piece through which passes a loose ring, which also passes through a hole in the centre of a straight, non-swivelling suspender of a unique design
Designer	The obverse was designed by the Canadian Army war artist, Major C. F. Comfort
Naming	It was decided that the medals should not be named
Bars issued	There are no bars to commemorate any particular action or theatre of service, but there is a straight bar with a maple leaf in the centre to denote service outside the Dominion.

The award of this silver medal was sanctioned by an order of the King's Privy Council for Canada No. PC 8160 of 1943, to which amendments were made in the three following years.

Members of the fighting services and the Nursing Service were eligible for the award, providing that they had completed eighteen months' voluntary service or had been honourably discharged before the full period was completed. Those whose total overseas service amounted to not less than six days, not necessarily continuous ones, were awarded the bar already described. The bar is worn on the ribbon. When the medal is not worn the recipients wear a small maple leaf in the centre of the ribbon. Those who volunteered and were serving on 2nd September 1939, though under eighteen years of age, were also eligible. Prior service in any of His Majesty's Forces, or those of the United States, also counted towards the award. Posthumous awards were made.

The qualifying period was from 2nd September 1939 to 1st March 1947. Those who were serving on voluntary active service on 1st September 1945, would qualify upon completion of eighteen months' continuous active service, but the service of those appointed, or enlisted, after 1st September 1945, would not constitute qualifying service.

The medal follows after all the Campaign Stars and the Defence Medal, but precedes the 1939-45 War Medal.

650,000 medals were issued of which 525,500 were issued with the bar.

166 *The Africa Service Medal* 1939-1945

Obverse	The map of Africa, with the inscription 'AFRICA SERVICE MEDAL' around the left half of the circumference and 'AFRIKADIENS-MEDALJE' around the right half
Reverse	A leaping springbok facing right
Size	36mm diameter
Metal	Silver
Ribbon	32mm wide. Central band of orange flanked by stripes in the springbok colours of gold and green, the green stripes being at the edges
Suspension	By a straight suspender
Designers	The designs of the obverse and reverse were suggested by the Prime Minister and Minister of Defence of the Union of South Africa and sketched by a member of the South African Mint
Naming	In indented block capitals. The prefix 'N' indicates a Native whilst 'C' indicates a Coloured recipient
Bars issued	Nil

The award of this silver medal was approved by His Majesty the King on 16th November 1943, and gazetted in the *Union Government's Gazette* No 3407, dated 27th October 1944.

The qualifications for the award were:
1 The signing of the Africa Oath acknowledging liability for service with the Union Defence Forces anywhere in Africa, and/or
2 The signing of the General Service Oath acknowledging liability for service with the Union Defence Forces in any theatre of war.

The following also qualified:
1 Personnel of the Union Defence Forces who served in a full- or part-time capacity.
2 Personnel of other uniformed services, male or female, who performed full-time service with their respective units. These services include membership of the South African Police, Essential Services Protection Corps, South African Military Nursing Services, VAD officers and members, and women's services.

In the case of full-time service the qualifying period was thirty days. The part-time qualifying period was eighteen hours' non-continuous training. Approximately 192,000 struck.

Issued with a Protea leaf in bronze which is attached to the ribbon to denote a mention in despatches or a King's commendation.

167 *The Australia Service Medal* 3rd September 1939-2nd September 1945

Obverse	The crowned head of King George VI, with the legend, 'GEORGIVS VI D: G: BR: OMN: REX ET INDIAE IMP:'
Reverse	The Coat of Arms of the Commonwealth of Australia, with the legend 'THE AUSTRALIA SERVICE MEDAL 1939-1945'
Size	36mm diameter
Metal	Nickel-silver
Ribbon	32mm wide. Dark blue, khaki and light blue with intervening stripes of red. The first three colours represent the Navy, the Army and the Air Force respectively. The red stripes represent the Australian Mercantile Marine
Suspension	By a straight suspender
Naming	With the regimental or service number (when applicable), initials and surname in impressed capitals. The number may be prefixed by a letter indicating the parent 'state' or enrollment depot
Bars issued	Nil

The King's approval of the award of this medal to all members of the Australian armed forces and the Australian Mercantile Marine who served overseas for at least eighteen months between the dates mentioned was announced by the Prime Minister of Australia on 1st December 1949.

The qualifications are as follows:
1 Honourable discharge and the completion of a period of continuous training on full-time service of not less than eighteen months or part-time service of three years. Eligibility will include those who served both full- and part-time service. In this case full-time service will count double towards the qualifying period of three years with the proviso that defence duty was performed on not less than sixty days during the service.
2 Members of the Australian Mercantile Marine must have served eighteen months at sea.
3 In addition to the Australian armed forces and the Australian Mercantile Marine, the following are also eligible: Civilian members of the RAAF Reserve who flew over operational zones, official Press representatives, official photographers and all who served in uniform on full-time duty attached to the armed forces.
4 Civil aircrew personnel must have made three or more flights over, or three landings in, zones of military operations unless para. 5 is applicable to their case.
5 Service, whether full- or part-time, which was terminated by death, wounds or any disability due to service will qualify.
Approximately 177,000 issued.

168 *The New Zealand War Service Medal*
3rd September 1939-2nd September 1945

Obverse	The uncrowned head of George VI, with the legend 'GEORGIVS VI D:G: BR: OMN: REX F:D: IND: IMP.'
Reverse	The inscription 'FOR SERVICE TO NEW ZEALAND 1939/45' above a frond of fern
Size	36mm diameter
Metal	Cupro-nickel
Ribbon	32mm wide. Black, watered and edged with white stripes
Suspension	The suspender is composed of two fern leaves joined at the stalk end to form a 'U'. The tips of the leaves are joined by a thin bar to take the ribbon
Naming	Issued unnamed
Bars issued	Nil

The qualifications are as follows:
1 Personnel of the RNZ Navy, the NZ Army (including the National Military Reserve) and the RNZ Air Force (including commissioned ranks of the Air Training Corps) who completed an aggregate of at least 28 days' full-time service or six months' part-time service either at home

or abroad between 3rd September 1939 and 2nd September 1945, will qualify for the award provided that the recipient, if not still serving, has been honourably discharged.

2 Similar periods of service in the Home Guard between 16th August 1940 and 1st January 1944, and in the Naval Auxiliary Patrol Service between 31st December 1941 and 31st July 1944, will qualify.

3 Members of the NZ Merchant Navy and of the Civil Air Lines registered in New Zealand who rendered service beyond New Zealand will qualify for the award under certain conditions.

4 Full-time uniformed civilians who served as members of the NZ Armed Forces will qualify in the same way as full-time members of such Forces.

5 'Part-time service' is defined as service rendered by a member of the Armed Forces who was not fully mobilized but was liable to render service by the performance from time to time of short periods of training or other duties and did in fact carry out such training or duties.

6 The qualifying service, whether part-time or full-time, need not necessarily have been performed in the one service. Short periods of service may be aggregated. In such cases seven days' part-time service is to be taken as equivalent to one of full-time service, and vice versa.

7 If the service was terminated by capture by the enemy, the recipient must have been free from blame.

8 Service brought to an end by death on duty, or due to wounds or injuries sustained on duty, or honourable discharge as a direct result of injuries sustained whilst on duty will qualify for the medal, even though the service may not have amounted to 28 days or six months as the case may be.

Approximately 238,000 struck.

169 *The South African Medal for War Services*
6th September 1939-15th February 1946

Obverse	The Union Coat of Arms
Reverse	A wreath of Protea enclosing the figures '1939-1945', the design being circumscribed by the words 'SOUTH AFRICA SUID—AFRIKA FOR WAR SERVICES. VIR OORLOGDIENSTE.'
Size	36mm diameter
Metal	Silver
Ribbon	32mm wide. Equally divided into three vertical stripes of orange, white and blue
Suspension	By a straight suspender
Naming	Unnamed
Bars issued	Nil

This medal was instituted by a Royal Warrant dated 29th December 1946, countersigned and sealed at Cape Town on 6th February 1946, for award to both sexes, whether British subjects or not.

The qualifications were:

1 A minimum of two years' service, one at least of which was continuous, rendered voluntarily and without pay, within or without the Union, in one or more of the officially recognized voluntary organizations, providing that five or more hours were worked every week.

2 Service counting towards the African Service Medal could not be included.

Approximately 17,500 issued.

Issued with a Protea leaf in bronze which is attached to the ribbon to denote a mention in despatches or a King's commendation.

170 *The Southern Rhodesia War Service Medal* 1939-45

Obverse	Crowned head of George VI with the legend 'GEORGIVS VI D: G: BR: OMN: REX ET INDIAE IMP:'
Reverse	Arms of S. Rhodesia surrounded by 'FOR SERVICE IN SOUTHERN RHODESIA 1939-1945'.
Size	36mm diameter
Metal	Cupro-nickel
Ribbon	32mm wide. Dark green with narrow black and red stripes at each edge.
Suspension	Straight bar
Naming	Issued unnamed
Bars issued	Nil

Awarded to those who served in South Rhodesia. Not issued to anyone qualifying for the campaign stars and medals. As many Rhodesians served overseas only 1,700 medals were issued.

171 *Newfoundland Volunteer War Service Medal* 1939-1945

Obverse   The Crown of King George VI, surmounted by a Newfoundland stag caribou, baying, is centred over the Royal Cypher 'G.R.VI'. The motif is surrounded on the outside rim by the words 'NEWFOUNDLAND VOLUNTEER SERVICE MEDAL 1939-1945'.

Reverse   The central figure of Britannia representing the mother country of the Commonwealth is shown being stalked by beasts of prey represented by two male lions symbolic of the threat of the enemy. Britannia is protected by a stylised scallop shell suggesting Newfoundland's heritage and contribution to the final victory.

Size   36mm. diameter

Metal   Silver

Ribbon   32mm wide. The middle two-thirds of the ribbon appear in deep claret trimmed on the outer edges with a narrow band of dark blue followed progressively by equal bands of white and red; this latter colour forming the outer edges of the ribbon. The claret in the ribbon is the regimental colour of the Royal Newfoundland Regiment, whilst the red, white and blue, indicates the connection with Britain.

Suspension   Claw and straight bar

Designer   Ian Stewart

Naming   Issued unnamed

Number Struck 7,500 by the Royal Mint

During the 1939-45 War, volunteers from Newfoundland joined the Royal Navy and Royal Air Force and those joining the Army formed the 166th Regiment and 57th Heavy Regiment Royal Artillery. Many others joined the various Canadian Forces. Those who were in the Canadian Forces were entitled to the CVSM. Recently, the Provincial Government saw fit to establish a Volunteer Service Medal for those who served with the British Imperial Forces.

The Volunteer War Service Medal Act; Chapter 33 of the 1981 Statutes of Newfoundland states:

2 b)   'Veteran' means every person in the province who volunteered to serve in the British Imperial Forces during the Second World War.

3 (1) Subject to subsection (2), the Government of the Province shall award the medal to:
a) every veteran who:
(i) served overseas during the Second World War in any of the British Imperial Forces, and
(ii) ineligible for or has not received a volunteer service medal from any other country: and
b) every veteran who for various reasons did not participate in overseas duty.

(2) Every veteran is eligible to receive a medal if his place of domicile was in the Province prior to his enlistment in the British Imperial Forces.

4   Where a veteran did not participate in overseas duty, he shall by oath or affirmation certify in such a manner as may be prescribed by the Lieutenant-Governor in Council by regulation that he volunteered to serve in the British Imperial Forces.

5   Where a veteran who would be eligible to receive a medal under this Act was killed during the Second World War or has died since the end of that War, a medal may be awarded to a relative of that veteran as may be prescribed by the Lieutenant-Governor in Council by regulation.

6   The Lieutenant-Governor in Council may make regulations for carrying out the purposes and provisions of this Act.

172 *Korea Medal* 2nd July 1950-27th July 1953

Obverse	The laureated bust of Queen Elizabeth II facing right surrounded by the legend: *1st type* 'ELIZABETH II DEI GRA : BRITT : OMN : REGINA F:D+'. *2nd type* 'ELIZABETH II : DEI : GRATIA : REGINA F:D:+' *3rd type* 'ELIZABETH II DEI GRATIA REGINA' with 'CANADA' below the bust.
Reverse	Hercules, armed with a dagger, and his left arm out horizontally holding Hydra, which he is also holding off with his left leg. The word 'KOREA' is in the exergue.
Size	36mm diameter
Metal	British issue in cupro-nickel. Canadian issue in silver.
Ribbon	32mm wide. Yellow with two blue stripes.
Suspension	By a plain, straight, non-swivelling suspender.
Designers	Obverse—Mrs. Mary Gillick, CBE; Reverse—E. Carter Preston
Naming	British medals: impressed in thin capitals. Australian, Canadian and New Zealand medals impressed in larger capitals, with number and name only.
Bars issued	Nil

The medal was sanctioned by King George VI in 1951.

The qualifications were as follows:

NAVY
Twenty-eight days afloat in the operational areas of the Yellow Sea and Sea of Japan, or one or more days of shore duty.
ARMY
Service of at least one day on the strength of a unit serving in Korea.

RAF
1 One operational sortie over Korea or Korean waters
2 Service of one or more days on land.
3 Service of twenty-eight days afloat in the areas mentioned for the Navy.

GENERAL
Visits of an official nature lasting thirty days qualified for the award of a medal.
   Those unable to complete the required period of service due to sickness, wounds or death were also eligible.
   Authority was given to the wearing of a bronze oak leaf emblem by those who were Mentioned in Despatches.

ARMY
The following regiments were recognized by the Battles and Nomenclature Committee as being eligible to claim battle honours for the 'Korean Campaign 1950-53':
5th Royal Inniskilling Dragoon Guards, 8th King's Royal Irish Hussars, Royal Tank Regiment, Royal Scots, Royal Northumberland Fusiliers, Royal Fusiliers, King's Liverpool Regiment, Royal Norfolk Regiment, Royal Leicestershire Regiment, King's Own Scottish Borderers, Gloucestershire Regiment, Duke of Wellington's Regiment, Welch Regiment, Black Watch, King's Shropshire Light Infantry, Middlesex Regiment, Durham Light Infantry, Royal Ulster Rifles, Argyll and Sutherland Highlanders.
   Other units present include: Royal Artillery, Royal Engineers, Royal Army Chaplain's Department, Royal Army Medical Corps, Royal Army Catering Corps, Royal Army Service Corps, Royal Army Ordnance Corps, Army Physical Training Corps, Royal Signals, Royal Electrical and Mechanical Engineers, Royal Armoured Corps, Buffs, Queen's Royal Regiment, Royal Warwickshire Regiment.
   A large number of medals were named to regiments that were not present in Korea as a whole. These men sent as reinforcements to units in Korea received medals named to their parent unit.

Canadian units: Lord Strathcona's Horse (2nd Armoured Regt.), Royal Canadian Dragoons (1st Armoured Regt.), Artillery, Engineers, Signals, Royal Canadian Regiment, Princess Patricia's Canadian LI, Royal 22ᵉ Régiment, Black Watch, Queen's Own Rifles, Canadian Guards, RCASC, Medical and other ancillary units.
   Australian units: 1st, 2nd, 3rd Bn Royal Australian Regiment.

NAVY
The following Commonwealth warships were present but the list is not complete as it does not include ancillary craft.
Royal Navy:
Aircraft-carriers, *Glory, Ocean, Thesus, Triumph*
Aircraft Maintenance Carrier, *Unicorn*
Cruisers, *Belfast, Birmingham, Ceylon, Jamaica, Kenya, Newcastle*
Destroyers, *Cockade, Comus, Consort, Cossack*
Frigates, *Alacrity, Amethyst, Black Swan, Cardigan Bay, Hart*
Headquarter Ship, *Ladybird*
Depot ship, *Tyne*
Hospital ship, *Maine*
   Medals were also issued to the Royal Marines.
Royal Canadian Navy:

Athabaskan, Cayuga, Huron, Sioux, Haida, Nootka, Iroquois, Crusader
Royal Australian Navy:
Anzac, Bataan, Condamine, Culgoa, Murchison, Shoalhaven, Sydney,
Tobruk, Warramunga and 805, 808, 817 Squadrons Fleet Air Arm
Royal New Zealand Navy:
Hawera, Kanierg, Pukaki, Roboit, Taupo and *Tutira*

AIR FORCE

RAF fighter pilots flew in Sabre aircraft of the United States Air Force and some photographic interpreters also served with the Reconnaissance Wing of the same forces.

Nos 88, 205 and 207 Flying Boat Squadrons, which, based at Seletar, formed the Far East Flying Boat Wing, flew Sunderlands from Iwakuni (Japan) on operational sorties over Korean waters. Also 30, 152, 208, 801 and 810 Squadrons.

Royal Australian Air Force: 36 Squadron (Dakota) and 77 Squadron (Mustang and Meteor).

Royal Canadian Air Force.

At the end of the 1939-45 War the peninsula of Korea was divided into two countries. The northern part was ruled by a puppet government under Russian control whilst the southern one was under United States supervision. The supervisory powers supposedly withdrew from their spheres of influence in 1948/49, leaving the north with military superiority.

On 25th June 1950, the North Koreans attacked the South Koreans who appealed to the United Nations for military support. In the absence of the USSR veto, military support was forthcoming chiefly from the USA but with British and Commonwealth support.

The first British troops to arrive in Korea were the 1st Battalions of the Argyll and Sutherland Highlanders and Middlesex Regiments who landed at Pusan on 29th August 1950.

One outstanding British action during the war was at Hill 235 where 750 men of the 1st Bn Gloucester Regiment gallantly fought off repeated enemy attacks until overwhelmed by weight of numbers (25th April 1951).

After a succession of attacks and counter-attacks by both sides, resulting in great loss of life, an armistice was signed on 27th July 1953. The then existing battle lines forming the boundary between North and South Korea.

Four Victoria Crosses were awarded: Major K. Muir, A&SH; Lieutenant Colonel J. P. Carne, Glos. R; Lieutenant P. K. E. Curtis, DCLI attached Glos R; Pte W. Speakman, BW attached KOSB.

173 *South African Korean Medal* 19th September 1950-27th July 1953

Obverse	Maps of the Union of SA and Korea in relief joined by an arrow with the sea as a background. The whole design partly surrounded by laurel and 'KOREA' 'VRYWILLIGERS VOLUNTEERS' 'U VAN SA U OF SA'.
Reverse	Union coat of arms and the Royal Cypher.
Size	38mm diameter
Metal	Silver
Ribbon	33mm wide. Sky blue centre with stripes of dark blue and orange.
Suspension	Ring and claw
Naming	Impressed block capitals
Bars issued	Nil

Instituted by Royal Warrant and signed by Queen Elizabeth in 1953.

Qualifications:
1) Service of at least one day on the strength of an active unit.
2) Thirty days service for those engaged in inspections, official tours, etc.

Recipients: Ten army officers attached to the Commonwealth Division. No 2 Squadron SA Air Force. A total of 800 medals were issued in all.

174 *Campaign Service Medal* 1962–

Obverse	The crowned bust of Queen Elizabeth II with the legend 'ELIZABETH II DEI GRATIA REGINA F. D.'
Reverse	A wreath of oak surrounding the words 'FOR CAMPAIGN SERVICE' with crown above.
Size	36mm diameter
Metal	Cupro-nickel
Ribbon	32mm wide. Purple with green edges.
Suspension	By an ornamental swivelling suspender.
Designer	T. H. Paget, OBE
Naming	Impressed in small thin block capitals.
Bars issued	Eight (to date) Borneo, Radfan, South Arabia, Malay Peninsula, South Vietnam, Northern Ireland, Dhofar, Lebanon

This medal instituted under Ministry of Defence Order No. 61 dated 6th October, 1964, supersedes both the Naval General Service Medal 1915 and the General Service Medal 1918 (Army and RAF).

The order of wearing the bars is that of the date of the periods of service for which the bars are awarded, not the dates of the relevant Army Orders (ie if an earlier period of service qualified for 'Radfan' followed by a period which qualified for 'Borneo', the 'Radfan' bar would normally have been issued with the medal and the 'Borneo' bar issued would then be placed above the 'Radfan')

Borneo 24th December 1962-11th August 1966

Following the defeat of the Brunei rebellion at the end of 1962, the Indonesian Foreign Minister announced a policy of 'confrontation' against Malaysia. The public justification for Indonesian expansion was that Malaysia was the accomplice of 'neo-colonialist and neo-imperialist forces pursuing a policy hostile towards Indonesia'. Simultaneously Indonesian 'volunteers' started to infiltrate across the border into Sarawak and Sabah. The Indonesian Government broke off diplomatic relations with Malaysia and a mob of 10,000 burned the British Embassy in Jakarta.

There were no British bases in Borneo. There were no stockpiles of military equipment, few motorable roads, only one deep sea port at Labuan and Singapore was 900 miles away. When General Walter Walker arrived in Borneo in December 1962 he faced immense problems but it was not many months before he had created the necessary military infrastructure to fight a jungle war. He also established an impressive British and Commonwealth force which was able to dominate the border area and defeat persistent border incursions by Indonesian regular and irregular forces. Total Commonwealth losses were 114 killed and 180 wounded. The official Indonesian losses were put at 600 killed but they were almost certainly larger.

This bar was authorized by Ministry of Defence AO 2/64 dated 6th October 1967, for service against the rebels on what was previously known as North Borneo (now Sabah, Sarawak or Brunei) between 24th December 1962 and 11th August 1966.
The qualifications are:

NAVY AND ROYAL MARINES
1) Service afloat for an aggregate of 30 days in ships or craft operating on the waters of Sabah, Sarawak, or Brunei, or off the coasts in support of shore operations.
2) One sortie, or more, as a member of an aircraft crew in support of operations ashore.
3) Service of 30 days, or more, ashore when posted to units operating in the above areas.

ARMY
Thirty days, or more, service, not necessarily continuous, in the above areas.

ROYAL AIR FORCE
1) Thirty days or more, not necessarily continuous in the areas mentioned whether serving with the RAF or any unit of HM Forces.
2) One sortie, or more, over the areas mentioned when in the direct support of operations. (Approximately 11,000 were awarded to the RAF)

AUSTRALIAN NAVY AND AIR FORCE
ROYAL NEW ZEALAND AIR FORCE
Only members of No. 41 Squadron, based in Singapore, have qualified by one, or more, sorties under the same conditions as the RAF.

GENERAL
Those who were awarded a decoration or whose service was curtailed by no fault of their own were eligible for the award.

The recipient of a Mention-in-Despatches may wear a bronze emblem on the ribbon, but a rosette may never be worn.

Some of the units present:
Royal Navy, 845 Squadron Fleet Air Arm, Royal Marine Commandos, Royal Artillery, Royal Engineers, Scots Guards, Queen's Own Buffs, 1st Battalion Royal Leicestershire Regiment, King's Own Scottish Borderers, 2/3rd Green Jackets, Durham Light Infantry, Gordon Highlanders, Argyll & Sutherland Highlanders, 2nd Parachute Regiment, SAS (including Australian and New Zealand SAS squadrons), 1/2nd, 2/2nd, 1/6th, 2/6th, 1/7th, 2/7th, 1/10th, 2/10th Gurkha Regiments, Gurkha Engineers, Gurkha Signals, Gurkha Transport, Gurkha Military Police, Gurkha Indep Parachute Co, 3rd Royal Malay Regiment, Border Scouts recruited from the indigenous tribes of the Dyak, Sea Dyak, Kenyan, Kcyan and others. Royal Air Force.

In addition to the above Services, members of the Royal Fleet Auxiliary Service, Army Fire Service, Women's Voluntary Service, members of the Meteorological Office serving with the RAF, Class 'C.C.' Commissions, etc., also qualified.

A Victoria Cross was won by L/Cpl Rambahadur Limbu, 2/10th PMO Gurkha Rifles at Sarawak, 21st Nov 1965.

Radfan 25th April-31st July 1964

The Radfan mountains were some 60 miles north of Aden which was formerly a dependency of the Government of India and became a Crown Colony in 1937. The emirates and sheikhdoms in the hinterland of Aden had accepted British protection since the Turkish invasion of Yemen and surrounding territories in the 1870s. Since 1955 however it had been necessary to station British troops in Aden in order to control inter-tribal rivalries and unrest. By 1964 the situation had grown considerably worse. The new Republican government in neighbouring Yemen, backed by Abdul Nasser of Egypt, was actively fomenting trouble among the tribesmen of the Sultanate of Upper Yafa, one of the Western Aden Protectorate states, that was refusing to join the Federation of South Arabia. The creation of the Federation by the British was an effort to form the disparate sheikhdoms into some sort of cohesive force prior to independence.

By December 1963 it was clear that an insurgency campaign was being waged against the Federation, prosecuted mainly by the tribes of the hinterland, in particular the tribesmen of the Radfan who were offered arms and cash promised by the Yemen and Egyptian agents if they closed the main road from Aden to the Yemen's frontier town of Dhala. The Radfan tribesmen were able to raise about 7,500 fighting men in the inaccessible mountains adjacent to the Dhala road. The campaign against them was short, intensive and highly effective. The tribesmen were defeated by a Brigade sized force of British troops backed by two Federal Regular Army battalions and RAF support.

This bar was authorized by AO 36/65 for award to all members of the United Kingdom Forces and those of the Federal Forces of Arabia who served for a continuous period of 14 days in the South Arabian Federation. The single bar is more often seen than the combination Radfan and South Arabia.

The rules concerning the granting of awards and curtailment of service apply as do those concerning the granting of medals to civilians who wore their prescribed uniform and who were attached to the Federal and/or National Guard of South Arabia for a qualifying period of 30 or more days from 1st August.

However three years later the bar was authorized for all troops who took part in these operations including those in a supporting roll in Aden itself.

Some of the units present:
16/5th Queen's Royal Lancers, 1st Bn The East Anglian Regt, 1st Bn The King's Own Scottish Borderers, 3rd Bn The Parachute Regiment, 45 Royal Marine Commando, 4th Royal Tank Regiment, J Battery 3 RHA, 170 Battery 7 RHA, Royal Engineers, 653 Squadron AAC, 22 SAS, 43 and 200 Sqns RAF (approx 5,000 bars), Federal Regular Army

Civilians who wore the approved uniform of their respective organisations also qualified, such as those of the following:
Soldiers' and Airmen's Scripture Readers Association, Nursing Service, British Red Cross Society Welfare Service, Women's Voluntary Service.

South Arabia 1st August 1964-30th November 1967

The campaign in Aden from 1964-67 cannot be separated from the Radfan Campaign which had been successfully concluded by the British in July 1964. Both were Egyptian inspired and both were designed to eject the British from Aden and destroy the embryo Federal Government. Although the British Government announced in 1964 that South Arabia would be granted its independence not later than 1968, the intention at this stage was to maintain a British military base in Aden. The terrorist campaign from 1964-67 was first an internecine affair between rival nationalist groups vying for control after independence and second a campaign to ensure the British did not retain a military presence after independence. The ensuing three years saw an exceptionally bloody campaign including numerous particularly shocking terrorist outrages against both military and civilian targets. The price paid by the British Army in Radfan and Aden was 90 killed and 510 wounded.

This bar was authorized in AO 40/66 being awarded for continuous service of 30 days or more between 1st August 1964 and 30th November 1967 in the Federation of South Arabia.

The rules concerning the granting of awards and curtailment of service applied.

Some units present:
The Queen's Dragoon Guards, The Queen's Own Hussars, 2nd Bn The Coldstream Guards, The Royal Sussex Regt, The Prince of Wales Own Regt of Yorkshire, The South Wales Borderers, 3rd Bn The Royal Anglian Regt, The Royal Northumberland Fusiliers, The Cameronians, The King's Own Border Regt, The Argyll and Sutherland Highlanders, The Lancashire Regt, 1st Bn The Parachute Regt, 42 Royal Marine Commando, 45 Royal Marine Commando, 31 Bty 45 Lt Regiment, RA, Royal Engineers, RAF (15,000 bars).

Malay Peninsula 17th August 1964-11th August 1966

The Malay Peninsula Campaign of 1964-66 was an extension of the Campaign in Borneo where British and Malaysian troops were operating against Indonesian insurgents. In 1964 President Sukarno of Indonesia decided to take the war to the Malayan mainland. Parachute landings were made near Labis in Johore while other groups managed to slip undetected across the Malacca Straits from Indonesian Sumatra and land on the west coast of the Malayan Peninsula. It was for operations in the jungles of the Malayan mainland against Indonesian infiltrators, as opposed to the concurrent operations in Borneo, that the Malay Peninsula bar to the CSM was awarded.

The bar was authorized in October 1967.

The qualifications are:

a) ASHORE Service of 30 days or more, not necessarily continuous, on land in the Malay Peninsula/Singapore between 17th August 1964 and 12th June 1965 (both dates inclusive) whilst on the posted or attached strength of any unit or formation in these areas.

b) AFLOAT Service of 30 days or more afloat, while in any Royal Navy, Royal Australian Navy, Royal New Zealand Navy or Army Department vessel on duty in the waters surrounding the Malay Peninsula/Singapore between 17th August, 1964 and 12th June, 1965 (both dates inclusive). Service in any Royal Navy, Royal Australian Navy, Royal New Zealand Navy vessel on sea patrol duties between 13th June 1965 and 11th August 1966 (both dates inclusive) may also reckon as qualifying service. This service may be aggregated with qualifying service on land as in (a) above to complete the required period of 30 days.

c) FLYING Completion of 30 or more sorties by aircraft crews of HM Forces engaged on operational patrols over the waters surrounding the Malay Peninsula/Singapore between 13th June 1965 and 11th August 1966 (both dates inclusive) may also reckon as qualifying service; each patrol may count as one day's qualifying service and may be aggregated with qualifying service on land and sea as in (a) and (b) above to complete the required period of 30 days.

SHORT SERVICE
If qualifying service was brought to an end before the completion of 30 days on account of death, or evacuation owing to wounds or other disability due to service, the reduced period of service will be sufficient qualification for the award.

The grant to individuals for gallantry in the operations on a specific occasion during the uncompleted qualifying period, not amounting to 30 days of a British Honour, Decoration or Medal of the status of a British Empire Medal or above or a Queen's Commendation or a Mention-in-Despatches will qualify the recipient for the above mentioned Medal and/or Bar.

SHORE ESTABLISHMENTS
RN and RM personnel who served for 30 days or more in HMS *Terror* or other shore establishment in the area between 17th August, 1964 and 12th June, 1965 are eligible.

PERSONNEL ON LOAN TO RMN
RN and RM personnel who served on loan with the Royal Malaysian Navy are eligible for the award under the terms of sub-paragraph a) above. Consideration will also be given to applications from those who cannot qualify under a) but would qualify under b) if this applied to RMN as well.

RFA PERSONNEL
Provided they wore uniform of their organization, Royal Fleet Auxilliary personnel will qualify for the award on the same terms as RN and RM

personnel as in paragraphs a), b) and c) above.

Units present:

HM Ships: Royal Navy Ships (approx 20,000 awards): *Agincourt, Aisne, Albion, Ajax, Barbain, Barfoil, Barrosa, Berwick, Brighton, Bulwark, Caesar, Camberford, Cambrian, Carysfort, Cassandra, Centaur, Chawton, Chichester, Corunna, Dampier, Dartington, Dido, Eagle, Eurayalus, Falmouth, Fiskerton, Greatford, Hampshire, Hartland Point, Houghton, Hubberston, Ickford, Invermoriston, Kent, Kildarton, Lincoln, Loch Fada, Loch Killisport, Loch Lomond, London, Lullington, Manxman, Maryton, Mull of Kintyre, Picton, Plymouth, Puncheston, Salisbury, Sheraton, Thankerton, Tilford, Triumph, Victorious, Whitby, Wilkieston, Woolaston, West*

Royal Navy Submarines: *Alliance, Ambush, Amphion, Anchorite, Andrew, Oberon.*

Royal Australian Navy Ships (approx 1,200 awards): *Curlew, Derwent, Duchess, Gull, Hawk, Ibis, Melbourne, Parramatta, Snipe, Supply, Teal, Vampire Vendetta, Yarra*

Royal New Zealand Navy Ships (approx 300 awards): *Hickleton, Otago, Santon*

The following HM Ships served in the Malay Peninsula/Singapore area but not for a sufficient period to qualify for the award. Personnel who served in these ships would need to aggregate their service with that in other ships or ashore to qualify for the award unless the short service provisions apply:

RN Ships: *Blackpool, Bossington, Cavendish, Londonderry, Lowestoft, Nubian, Penston, Rhyl.*

Royal New Zealand Navy Ships: *Royalist, Taranaki.*

Army: Gurkha units present: 2/2, 2/6, 1/7, 1/10 Gurkha Regiments, Gurkha Engineers, Gurkha Signals, Gurkha Transport, Gurkha Indep. Parachute Co, Gurkha Military Police. Medals were also issued to detachments from the following units: 1/2, 1/6, 2/7 and 2/10 Gurkha Regiment.

RAF: Approximately 6,500 awards.

South Vietnam 24th December 1962-29th May 1964

Authorized by Royal Warrant 8th June 1968 for award to Australian troops only. Qualifications are: 30 days service in ships employed in operations on inland waters and/or off the coast of Vietnam, one day or more on the posted strength of a unit on land, one operational sortie, or 30 days for official visits etc. The usual concession is made regarding termination of service by death, wounds or an award of a gallantry decoration. (The Australian Vietnam Medal with the Queen's effigy was awarded to Australian and New Zealand forces for services after the 29th May 1964.) 68 bars awarded, all to members of the Australian Army Training Team. Permission has also been granted to wear the South Vietnamese Government Medal with the Campaign Service Medal.

Northern Ireland 14th August 1969—

Awarded in recognition of service in Northern Ireland from 14th August, 1969 inclusive to a date to be decided in due course, with special regard to the hardships and dangers which have accompanied duty there. Personnel who have already received the Campaign Service Medal 1962 will receive the bar only.

The qualifications are:

a) Service of 30 days or more, not necessarily continuous, in Northern Ireland between 14th August 1969 and a date to be decided in the future, while on the posted or attached strength or any Regular Naval Military or Air Force unit of formation in that area, excluding recruits and junior soldiers under training.

b) Service of 30 days or more, not necessarily continuous, in Northern Ireland between 14th August 1969 and a date to be decided in the future, as a member of the Ulster Defence Regiment or Services Reserve Forces, on call out for permanent or emergency service in that area.

c) Service of 30 days or more afloat, not necessarily continuous, whilst in a Royal Navy or Army Department vessel on duty in the waters adjacent to Northern Ireland in support of the Land Forces between 14th August 1969 and a date to be decided in the future. Such service may, if necessary, be aggregated with service on land to complete the required period of 30 days.

SHORT SERVICE

If the qualifying service is brought to an end before the completion of 30 days on account of death, or evacuation, owing to wounds or other disability due to service, the reduced period of service will be sufficient qualification for the award.

The grant to individuals for gallantry in the operations on a specific occasion during the qualifying period, not amounting to 30 days, of a British Honour Decoration or Medal of the status of the British Empire Medal, or above, or a Queen's Commendation, or a Mention-in-Despatches will qualify the recipient for the above mentioned medal and/or bar.

Consideration may be given to the award of the Medal and/or bar to personnel who have been engaged in special hazardous operations of comparatively short duration.

CIVILIAN CATAGORIES

a) Members of the Royal Fleet Auxiliary will be eligible under the same terms as Royal Navy personnel provided that they wore the approved uniform of their organisation.

b) Members of the following organizations and any other organizations as may hereafter be determined who served with Forces in Northern Ireland will be eligible under the 30 day rules provided that they wore the approved uniform of their organisation:

HM Forces Fire Services
Ministry of Defence Police

Dhofar 1st October 1969-30th September 1976

In 1965 the mountain tribesmen of Dhofar (Oman) rose in revolt against the oppressive regime of Sultan Sa'ib bin Taimur. The revolt worsened in 1967 when the British left the neighbouring State of Aden. The new communist Government in what was now the People's Democratic Republic of Yemen provided a secure sanctuary and source of supply for the rebels. By 1970 it was clear that the Sultan would lose the war in Dhofar unless some fairly drastic steps were taken. On 23 July a bloodless palace coup planned and executed by the Sultan's son and heir Qaboos provided the change of direction that was needed. Some of the worst excesses of his father's regime were removed immediately, the Sultan's Armed Forces were expanded and Britain was asked for help. The SAS provided advisory teams to train local forces, the Royal Engineers completed substantial military and civil projects, and RAF pilots formed the backbone of the Sultan's Air Force. As well as this direct British involvement, many British officers were seconded to the Sultan of Oman's Armed Forces (SAF). In addition to this substantial British Military contribution, both Jordan and Iran provided troops. Total casualties during the 1969-76 period were 187 killed and 557 wounded of which 24 and 55 respectively were British. The British contribution to the defeat of communist insurgency in Dhofar was limited but vital. It is surprising how little is known about the crucial part played by British soldiers in securing peace and prosperity for this strategically important Arab state.

Awarded in recognition of service in the Dhofar Province of Oman from 1st October 1969 to 30th September 1976 (both dates inclusive) with special regard to the hardships and dangers which have accompanied duty there. Personnel who have already been awarded the Campaign Service Medal (1962) will receive the bar only.

The qualifications are:

a) Service of 30 days or more, not necessarily continuous, in the Dhofar Province of Oman between 1st October 1969 and 30th September 1976 while on the posted or attached strength of a unit or a formation of HM Forces in that area.

b) Thirty or more flights into Salalah airfield in support of operations at a rate of not more than one landing per day during the qualifying period as members of British Service transports or detachments.

c) Service of 30 days or more afloat, not necessarily continuous, while posted to a British Service vessel operating in Oman territorial waters, adjacent to the province of Dhofar in direct support of operations in the Dhofar campaign between 1st October 1969 and 30th September 1976. Such service may, if necessary, be aggregated with service on land to complete the required period of 30 days.

SHORT SERVICE

If the qualifying service is brought to an end before the completion of 30 days on account of death, or evacuation, owing to wounds or other disability due to service, the reduced period of service will be sufficient qualification for the award.

The grant to individuals for gallantry in the operations on a specific occasion during the qualifying period, not amounting to 30 days, of a British Honour, Decoration or Medal of the status of the Queen's Gallantry Medal, or above, or a Mention-in-Despatches will qualify the recipient for the above mentioned Medal and/or bar.

PERSONNEL ON LOAN

Personnel on loan or under contract to the Sultan's Armed Forces (SAF) will not qualify for the award of the Campaign Service Medal under these conditions while so serving.

CIVILIAN CATEGORIES

Members of the Royal Fleet Auxiliary Service will be eligible under the same terms as Royal Navy personnel provided that they wore the approved uniform of their organisation and served directly with units or formations of HM Forces in the qualifying area.

Lebanon 7th February 1983-9th March 1984

The Israeli invasion of Lebanon in 1982 was the direct result of Jordan's war against the PLO in 1970. King Hussein used his Bedouin Army to drive out the PLO when its terrorist activities threatened his Crown. Because Egypt and Syria had already imposed restrictions on terrorist activity from their territory, the PLO moved into Lebanon to establish a base for its operations against Israel. Anyway many Palestinians already lived there and the PLO already had some bases there. By 1982 the Israelis had had enough of the constant attacks mounted by the PLO from the Lebanon and determined to destroy PLO bases in Lebanon. They struck north to Beirut where they became embroiled in the complexities of Lebanese politics. It was at this stage in October 1982 at the instigation of the US, that a multi-national peace-keeping force was sent into Beirut. It was made up of marines from the USA, paratroops and Foreign Legionnaires from France, San Marco marines and other troops from Italy and 100 men from the Blues and Royals with Ferret Armoured Cars from Britain. Though the other three contingents all suffered casualties (the Americans 241 marines in one suicide attack alone, the French 58 paratroopers in a similar attack, and the Italians 2) the British carried out their task with great professionalism with no loss of life. Since it was becoming clear that the soldiers of the peace-keeping force were achieving little, being merely targets for the next shell, rocket or bomb attack they were withdrawn in February/March 1984.

The qualifications are:

a) MILITARY CATEGORIES

Accumulated service of 30 days or more, not necessarily continuous, within the territory of Lebanon and its territorial waters, between 7th February, 1983 and 9th March 1984, while on the posted or attached strength of any Regular Military, Naval or Air Force Unit or formation in that area, supporting the Multinational Force. In addition, aircrew who, as a member of a constituted crew, have carried out at least three operational sorties landing in or overflying Lebanese territory will qualify.

b) CIVILIAN CATEGORIES

i) United Kingdom based members of the Ministry of Defence who served with the United Kingdom Armed Forces in Lebanon whilst on the attached or posted strength of a unit.
ii) Members of the following organisations who served directly with or in support of the United Kingdom Armed Forces in Lebanon.
1 The Royal Fleet Auxiliary Service
2 The Navy, Army and Air Force Institutes
3 The Merchant Navy

c) SHORT SERVICE

i) If qualifying service is brought to an end before the completion of 30 days, on account of death, or evacuation owing to wounds or other disability due to service, the reduced period of service will be sufficient qualification for the award.
ii) The grant to individuals for gallantry in the operations on a specific occasion during the qualifying period, not amounting to 30 days, of a British Honour, Decoration or Medal of the status of British Empire Medal or above, or a Queen's Commendation, or a Mention-in-Despatches, will qualify the recipient for the above mentioned medal and/or bar. Consideration may be given to the award of the medal and/or bar to personnel who have been engaged in special hazardous operations of comparatively short duration.

Units known to have been present: Blues and Royals, Queen's Dragoon Guards, Royal Irish Rangers (2), Royal Welch Fusiliers (2), Royal Navy, Royal Marines, Royal Fleet Auxiliary, Royal Air Force. 700 bars were issued.

175 *Vietnam Medal* 1964

Obverse	Crowned bust of Queen Elizabeth II and the legend 'ELIZABETH II DEI GRATIA REGINA F.D.'
Reverse	Nude figure of a man separating two spheres, symbolic of two ideologies.
Size	36mm diameter
Metal	Cupro-nickel
Ribbon	32mm wide, on the left edge a dark blue stripe (Navy), on the right edge a light blue stripe (Air Force). Inside of these two stripes are 3mm wide red stripes (Army). The central band is yellow with three very narrow stripes of red in the centre, these being the colours of the National Flag of South Vietnam.
Suspension	Ornate swivel bar
Designer	Andor Meszaros; being the first operational medal to be designed and produced in Australia.
Naming	Australian Forces: Large impressed Roman capitals. New Zealand Forces: Small fine impressed Roman capitals.
Numbers	Approximately 18,000 issued to Australian Forces and 4,000 to New Zealand.

Vietnam was partitioned in 1954 after the end of the Indo-China War. The US at this stage determined to halt the spread of communism south of the demarcation line. By 1961 they had 700 military advisers supporting the South Vietnamese Army in its operations against regular units of the North Vietnamese Army that had infiltrated into the south and indigenous Viet Cong guerrillas. By 1964 US strength in South Vietnam was 20,000 and by August of that year the US Air Force was bombing military targets in North Vietnam.

Australian troops were first committed to South Vietnam in June 1965. The Australian Government had felt impelled to establish a presence in an area of such vital concern to its own interests and to the security of South East Asia as a member of SEATO. As a member of SEATO and being a signatory of the ANZUS Treaty New Zealand followed suit. The Australian commitment to the Vietnam War was a maximum at any one time of some 4500 troops and for the most part rather less than this. The New Zealand contribution was much smaller. Together they constituted a small but expert contribution to the

American war effort in Vietnam. US forces were withdrawn from Vietnam in 1973 and North Vietnam finally defeated the South in 1975. The Australian Task Force was withdrawn in late 1971 and all Australian combat forces and military advisors by June 1972.

Qualifications:
Medal awarded to Australian and New Zealand Armed Forces serving in South Vietnam after 28th May 1964. Awarded for twenty-eight days service on board ships, one day's service on land or for thirty days on official visits. Medal available to both Armed Forces and accredited relief Societies.

For those meeting the requirements, unrestricted 'permission to wear' was given for the South Vietnam Campaign Medal.

During the course of the war four Victoria Crosses were awarded: WO2 K. A. Wheatley, Major P. J. Badcoe, WO2 R. S. Simpson DCM, WO2 K. Payne.

176 *South Vietnam Campaign Medal* 1964

Obverse	Six pointed white enamel star with gilt rays between the points, a green enamel centre with a gilt map of Vietnam being consumed by red enamel flames
Reverse	Plain reverse having at its centre the inscription: 'VIET-NAM, CHIEN-DICH BOI-TINH'
Size	41mm diameter
Metal	Gilt plated base metal
Ribbon	36mm wide, mid-green ribbon with three white stripes
Suspension	Ring and trough shaped suspender
Naming	Originally unnamed; later Australian manufactured medals engraved on reverse
Bars issued	One, a white metal bar dated '1960'

Awarded for six months campaign service.

Originally recipients were expected to purchase the awards from the Government of South Vietnam, but as those were of inferior quality, the Australian and US Governments produced their own medals.

177 *Rhodesia Medal* 1st December 1979-20th March 1980

Obverse	The crowned effigy of the Queen (Jubilee head designed by David Wynne), with the legend, 'ELIZABETH II DEI GRATIA REGINA FID. DEF.'
Reverse	A sable antelope surrounded by the inscription 'THE RHODESIA MEDAL 1980'
Size	36mm diameter
Metal	Cupro-nickel, rhodium plated
Ribbon	32mm wide. Sky-blue with three central narrow stripes of red, white and blue
Suspension	By means of a fixed plain, straight suspender
Naming	Issued unnamed by the Royal Mint

This cupro-nickel medal was awarded to people in the Services, the Police and to civilians (including The Governor, the Election Commissioner and members of their staffs and to MOD sponsored personnel) of the small multi-national force on 'Operation Agila' who kept the peace between 22,000 guerillas and the Rhodesian forces during the ceasefire run-up period to the elections. The medal was also made available to the Governments of Australia, New Zealand, Fiji and Kenya whose forces took part.

The operation was described by the then Defence Secretary, Mr Francis Pym, as 'a superb job that did much to further constitutional progress in Rhodesia.'

Fourteen days' service in Rhodesia is the basic qualification for the medal, but there are variations to this for RAF aircrew, those granted awards equal to or higher than the Queen's Gallantry Medal or a Queen's Commendation for gallantry, and for casualties.

Approximately 2,500 medals were issued.

Recipients of this medal also received the Zimbabwe Independence Medal (numbered) in either silver or bronze.

178 *South Atlantic Medal* 2nd April 1982-12th July 1982

Obverse	Crowned head of the Queen facing right (Jubilee Head). 'ELIZABETH II DEI GRATIA REGINA FID. DEF.'
Reverse	Armorial bearings of the Crown Colony of the Falkland Islands and its Dependencies, encompassed by the legend, 'SOUTH ATLANTIC MEDAL' and sprigs of laurel.
Size	36mm diameter
Metal	Cupro-nickel
Ribbon	32mm wide, shaded and watered bands of blue, white, green, white, blue.
Suspension	Swivel straight bar, with riveted claw attachment.
Designer	Mr R. Lowe
Naming	Upright non-serif capitals impressed upon the rim, being slightly larger and less deeply impressed for Merchant Navy recipients.
Bars issued	None, see following text concerning rosette.

This medal was awarded for service during the Anglo-Argentine war of 1982.

Authorized under the terms of Command Paper 8601, dated 13 July of that year, the medal was intended as a 'recognition of service in the South Atlantic with special regard to the hardships and dangers which have accompanied duty there'. The operational area which determined entitlement to the award was one of the largest for which any British campaign medal has ever been authorized. It covered the vast tract of ocean stretching down from just below the Equator to the vicinity of the Antarctic Circle. It included the islands within that area and, for a limited number of personnel, it included active service on the mainland of Latin America.

Production of the medal was in several respects unusual. The design was determined by two primary requirements: economy and speed. Cupro-nickel was chosen in preference to silver on the grounds of cost. Then there was the question of bars. In the extraordinary circumstances of this campaign, and following the precedents set in earlier campaigns, it might have been fitting if four variants of the medal could have been awarded: with a 'Defence of Stanley' bar for the defence of East Falkland by the Royal Marines of Naval Party 8901 on 2 April; with a 'Defence of S Georgia' bar for the battle fought by the Royal Marines Detachment from HMS *Endurance* on 3 April; with a 'Falklands' bar for the recovery of the main islands in May and June; and 'without bar' for service north of latitude 35 degrees South and on Ascension Island.

In the event, economic restraint and the requirement to produce a swift popular token of the nation's gratitude resulted in a design which was uncomplicated and of modest cost. The staff of the Royal Mint succeeded in achieving full production of the new medal within six weeks of publication of the Command Paper. The first batch was delivered in late August to the Army Medal Office, Droitwich, for individual naming and despatch to recipients.

It was initially estimated that more than 30,000 would be required. The Army Medal Office was accustomed to a normal monthly work-load of approximately 5000 medals and decorations of all types, so the new medal represented a significant increase. New machinery was purchased and additional staff recruited to meet the call for speed. As had been the case with all campaign medals issued since 1919, the South Atlantic Medal was machine-stamped with the recipient's particulars at Droitwich and despatched from there to the Services concerned.

The design of the ribbon is attributed to HM the Queen. Following the precedent set by her father, King George VI, whose ideas formed the basis for the design of the Second World War campaign ribbons, she prepared a pastel sketch which was passed to the firm of Toye, Kenning & Spencer Limited. This company overcame numerous technical difficulties to manufacture 14,000 metres of ribbon and to deliver it to the Royal Mint in record time. The combination of white, five different shades of green, and seven shades of blue, was simply the reverse order of the Atlantic Star of 1939-1945 vintage, but the modern use of polyester fibres in place of traditional silks created obstacles in achieving the desired 'shaded and watered' effect.

The medal was unique in that personnel who served ashore or afloat below 35 degrees South, or who flew operationally below Ascension Island, were entitled to wear a small white metal rosette sewn to the ribbon. This ruling applied even when the recipient was wearing the full medal and not just the riband bar. There is no precedent in British medallic history for such a device. Adopted as an alternative to the award of bars, it cannot be regarded as an attractive innovation. These rosettes also were manufactured by Toye, Kenning & Spencer Limited, a stock of 35,100 being delivered to The Royal Mint at short notice.

The total number of persons awarded the South Atlantic Medal is stated to be 29,712, of which the majority were entitled also to the rosette. The first examples to be seen in public were worn by men and women taking part in the Victory Parade through the City of London on 12 October, only thirteen weeks after the award was first authorized. The task of naming and despatching the medals was completed in the following February. It is unlikely that any other British medallic award has ever been conceived, designed, manufactured, named, and distributed, with such a strong sense of urgency.

Civilians played an important part in the campaign, and provision was made in the Command Paper for the medal to be granted to those who had served afloat or ashore while posted to, or attached to, or serving under the orders of, units of HM Armed Forces. This ruling encompassed a wide range of recipients, the most numerous being men and women of the Merchant Navy and the Royal Fleet Auxiliary Service. It included also the NAAFI personnel and Hong Kong Chinese laundrymen serving in RN and RFA ships.

Additional provision was made for the award to 'personnel who have been engaged in specially hazardous operations of comparatively short duration'. It might be thought that this clause would apply to certain other civilians who took an active role in the campaign: Mr Richard Baker, Chief Secretary to the Falkland Islands Government, who risked his life to negotiate the surrender of Port Stanley on 2 April; Mr Stephen Martin, the Magistrate on South Georgia, who attempted on 3 April to deter the Argentine invasion while under fire; some of his British Antarctic Survey colleagues who maintained a hazardous coast watch during and after the invasion; Captain Stewart Lawrence and the crew of the RRS *Bransfield*, which provided an important radio link in April; and certain Falkland Islanders who rendered valuable and hazardous services. Despite representations to the Foreign Secretary, none of these people received the medal. The only concession was that it should be given to Governor Rex Hunt in his capacity as local Commander-in-Chief, and to the thirty-six men of the Falkland Islands Defence Force who reported for duty on the evening of 1 April and who performed guard duties during the night of the invasion.

By contrast, it may be noted that the medal was given to Ministry of Defence civilian personnel employed in public relations and technical roles on Ascension Island. There were fifteen such awards, these being 'without rosette'.

Forty-eight medals 'with rosette' were awarded to civilians who went south with the Task Force and who shared the hardships of the campaign as journalists, television camera crews, press photographers, and as solitary lady war artist.

Qualifications: With Rosette: Service of one day in the Falkland Islands or their Dependencies or in the South Atlantic, south of 35 degrees South and north of 60 degrees South, or in any operational aircraft sortie south of Ascension Island, between 2 April and 14 June 1982, both inclusive.

Without Rosette: Service of 30 days or more in the South Atlantic, south of 7 degrees South and north of 60 degrees South, not necessarily continuous but commencing between 2 April and 12 July 1982, both dates inclusive, and completing not later than 12 July 1982.

The significance of 14 June is that this was the day on which Argentine forces on East Falkland agreed to cease fire. The formal surrender document was signed by the senior officer of the invading forces, General Mario Menendez, in the presence of the British land forces commander, Major General Jeremy Moore CB, MC, RM, on the following day.

Recovery of the islands of South Georgia, East and West Falkland and Thule was a unique long-distance amphibious operation, and it is not surprising that the largest numbers of awards were to the sailors who spear-headed the Task Force and to the mariners who sustained it over eight thousand miles of seaway. According to the Ministry of Defence, the main categories of recipient were: Royal Navy 12,927 medals, Royal Marines 3,729, Army 6,968, Royal Air Force 2,008, Royal Fleet Auxiliary Service 1,960, Merchant Navy, Royal Maritime Auxiliary Service and other civilians 2,010, and NAAFI personnel not serving afloat 80.

Two Victoria Crosses were awarded for the campaign, both posthumously: Lieutenant Colonel H. Jones OBE, 2nd Bn The Parachute Regiment, and Sergeant I. J. McKay, 3rd Bn The Parachute Regiment.

Ships and personnel from the following ships and units qualified for the medal.

ROYAL NAVY

Aircraft carriers: *Hermes* (flagship) and *Invincible*. Destroyers: *Antrim, Brilliant, Bristol, Broadsword, Cardiff, Coventry* (sunk), *Glamorgan* and *Sheffield* (sunk). Frigates: *Active, Alacrity, Ambuscade, Andromeda, Antelope* (sunk), *Ardent* (sunk), *Argonaut, Arrow, Avenger, Minerva, Penelope, Plymouth* and *Yarmouth*. Amphibious Warfare Vessels: *Fearless* and *Intrepid*. Ocean Survey Vessels (modified as Casualty Evacuation Ships): *Hecla, Herald* and *Hydra*. Offshore Patrol Vessels: *Leeds Castle* and *Dumbarton Castle*. Ice Patrol Ship: *Endurance*. Submarines: *Conqueror, Courageous, Onyx, Spartan, Splendid* and *Valiant*.

FLEET AIR ARM

Personnel from the following Naval Air Squadrons received the medal, either as a result of their services aboard Royal Navy ships (Ship's Flights), or while embarked in other ships, or while operating from shore bases.
Sea Harrier FRSl: 800, 801, 809 and 899 Squadrons. Wessex HAS3: 737 Squadron. Wessex HU5: 845, 847 and 848 Squadrons. Sea King HAS5: 820 and 826 Squadrons. Sea King HAS2: 824 and 825 Squadrons. Sea King HC4: 846 Squadron. Lynx HAS2: 815 Squadron. Wasp HAS1: 829 Squadron.

ROYAL MARINES

40, 42 and 45 Commandos. Commando Logistics Regt RM. Signals Squadron RM. Commando Brigade Air Squadron. Commando Forces Band. 2 and 6 Special Boat Squadron RM. Raiding Squadron RM. Mountain and Arctic Warfare Cadre RM. Various Ships' Detachments and Naval Parties.

ROYAL FLEET AUXILIARY SERVICE

Tankers: *Appleleaf, Bayleaf, Blue Rover, Brambleleaf, Olmeda, Olna, Pearleaf, Plumleaf, Tidepool* and *Tidespring*. Stores and Replenishment Ships: *Fort Austin, Fort Grange, Regent, Resource* and *Stromness*. Logistic Landing Ships: *Sir Bedivere, Sir Galahad* (sunk), *Sir Geraint, Sir Lancelot, Sir Percivale* and *Sir Tristram*. Helicopter Support Ship: *Engadine*.

ROYAL MARITIME AUXILIARY SERVICE

Mooring, Salvage and Boom Vessel: *Goosander*. Ocean Tug: *Typhoon*.

REQUISITIONED HULL TRAWLERS

Five trawlers were commissioned temporarily into the Royal Navy and served as 11th Mine Countermeasures Squadron: *Cordella, Farnella, Junella, Northella* and *Pict*.

SHIPS TAKEN UP FROM TRADE (STUFT)

Forty-three vessels of various types were either chartered or requisitioned from Merchant Navy sources during the period of the conflict, but not all of them entered the qualifying operational area for the requisite period of time. The following are those known to have qualified: *Alvega, Anco Charger, Atlantic Causeway, Antlantic Conveyor* (sunk), *Avalona Star, Balder London, Baltic Ferry, British Avon, British Dart, British Enterprise III, British Esk, British Tamar, British Tay, British Test, British Trent, British Wye, Canberra, Contender Bezant, Eburna, Elk, Europic Ferry, Fort Toronto, Geestport, Hercules, Iris, Irishman, Lycaon, Nordic Ferry, Norland, Queen Elizabeth II, St Edmund, Salvageman, Saxonia, Scottish Eagle, Stena Seaspread, Tor Caledonia, Uganda, Wimpey Seahorse* and *Yorkshireman*. NB the Motor Cargo Ship *Monsunen* was one of two small coastal ships operated by the Falkland Islands Company. Commandeered by the Argentines in April, she was salvaged by the Royal Navy on 4 June and deployed with a Navy ship's company under the command of an officer from HMS *Fearless*. It is thought that the medals subsequently awarded to RN personnel who served in this ship were impressed with the name of the parent ship, not *Monsunen*.

ARMY

2 Troops, B Squadron, The Blues and Royals. 29 Commando Regt RA, and numerous other Royal Artillery units. 2nd Bn Scots Guards. 1st Bn Welsh Guards. 2nd and 3rd Bns The Parachute Regt. 1/7th Duke of Edinburgh's Own Gurkha Rifles. 59 Independent Commando Squadron RE, and various other Royal Engineers units. D and G Squadrons, Special Air Service Regt. Detachments and sub-units from 30 Signal Regt RS, 17 Port Regt RCT, 47 Air Despatch Squadron RCT, 16 Field Ambulance RAMC, 81 Ordnance Company RAOC, and other specialist Corps troops.

ARMY AIR CORPS
Gazelle AH1 and Scout AH1: 656 Squadron

ROYAL AIR FORCE
Harrier GR3; 1(F) Squadron. Phantom FGR2: 29(F) Squadron.
VC-10C1: 10 Squadron. Hercules C1/C3: 24, 30, 47 and 70 Squadrons.

Nimrod MR1: 42(TB) Squadron. Nimrod R1: 51 Squadron. Nimrod
MR2: 120, 201 and 206 Squadrons. Vulcan B2: 44, 50 and 101
Squadrons. Victor K2: 55 and 57 Squadrons. Chinook HC1: 18
Squadron. Sea King HAR3: 202 Squadron. Blindfire Rapier: 63
Squadron RAF Regiment.

---

179 *Arctic Medal* 1818-55

General	Octagonal medal
Obverse	Queen Victoria wearing a small tiara instead of the usual coronet. The hair at the back comes down lower than on the India General Service Medals. The rim is lined with a beaded edge. The word 'VICTORIA' appears on the left of the head and 'REGINA' on the right.
Reverse	A three-masted sailing ship, with icebergs in the background and a sledging party in the foreground; in the exergue are dates '1818-1855'. Around the top is written 'FOR ARCTIC DISCOVERIES'.
Size	33mm diameter
Metal	Silver
Ribbon	38mm wide, watered white
Suspension	Affixed to the top of the octagonal piece is a small claw above which is a star (symbolic of the Pole Star) which has five large points with five smaller ones between them. On the topmost large point is a swivel ring suspension, 15mm in diameter.
Designer	L. C. Wyon
Naming	The medals were issued unnamed, though many are found unofficially named.
Bars issued	Nil

The medal was instituted on 30th January 1857

The following ships took part in voyages to the Arctic regions and their crews were eligible for the medal, of which a total of 1,486 were issued: 1,106 were awarded to the Royal Navy, the remainder were issued to crews of private vessels. Sgt John Ross, RA took part in the third expedition 1833-35 under Sir Geo Black.

Arctic Advance, Alexander, Assistance, Blossom, Breadalbane, Dorothea, Enterprise, Erebus, Felix, Fox, Fury, Griper, Hecla, Herald, Investigator, Isabella, Lady Franklin, Nancy Dawson, North Star, Phoenix, Pioneer, Plover, Prince Albert, Rattlesnake, Rescue, Resolute, Sophia, Terror, Trent, Victory.

Details and dates of the various expeditions are as follows:

Expedition	No Medals Issued
Officers and men of the Royal Navy 1818-55	1,106
First expedition to the shores of the Polar Seas under the command of Sir George Black. 1819-22	—
Second expedition under the command of Sir George Black. 1825-27	—
Third expedition under the command of Sir George Black. 1833-35	5
Expedition for survey of the shores of the Arctic Seas under the command of Lieut. afterwards R. Admiral Sir John Franklin. 1821	2
Expedition under the command of Captain John Franklin. 1826	—
Detachment from Sir J. Franklin's expedition in 1826 commanded by Dr John Richardson, MD, Surgeon RM Chatham Division	1
Private ship *Victory*, 1829-33	6
Searching expedition under command of Sir John Richardson, MD, CB, Inspector of Haslar Hospital. 1848	9
Detachment from Sir John Richardson's expedition under the command of John Rae Esq, to search Wollaston Sound in 1849	—
Nancy Dawson, 1849	1
Private ship *Lady Franklin*, 1850-51	19
Private ship *Sophia*, 1850-51	10

Expedition	No Medals Issued
Felix, 18th May, 1850-11th October, 1851	11
Prince Albert, first voyage 1850—fitted out by Lady Franklin	7
Prince Albert, second voyage 1851-52—fitted out by Lady Franklin	5
Expedition to the Arctic Seas in search of Sir John Franklin under the command of Lieut De Haven, United States Navy. 1850-51	33
Brig *Advance* (16 medals) and Brig *Rescue* (17 medals)	33
Isabel, 1852	5
Breadalbane, 8th May 1853-21st August 1853	5
Expedition to the Arctic Seas in search of Asst Surgeon E. K. Kane under the command of Lieut Hy I. Hartstein, United States Navy. 1855. Bark *Rescue* (26 medals) and Propeller *Arctic* (21 medals). Asst Surgeon E. K. Kane and Party (16 medals)	63
Fox, commanded by Captain F. L. M. McClintock, RN Final expedition fitted out by Lady Franklin, 1857-59	11
Hudson's Bay Company	187
Total	1,486

180 *Arctic Medal* 1875-76

General	Circular medal with a milled edge.
Obverse	The crowned and veiled bust of Queen Victoria, and legend, 'VICTORIA REGINA 1876'.
Reverse	An ice-bound ship with clouds above.
Size	36mm diameter
Metal	Silver
Ribbon	33mm wide, watered white
Suspension	Swivelling straight suspender.
Designer	Obverse—G. G. Adams; Reverse—L. C. Wyon.
Engraver	J. Pinches
Naming	In small block lettering.
Bars issued	Nil

The medal was sanctioned on the 28th November 1876, to be awarded to the crews of the *Alert* (63) (Captain Sir George Nares, KCB) and *Discovery* (57) (Captain H. F. Stevenson) for Arctic exploration between 17th July 1875, and 2nd November 1876. At the same time authority was given for it to be awarded to the crew of the private yacht *Pandora* (50), which voyaged in the Arctic regions, under the command of Captain Allen Young, between 25th June and 19th October 1875, and 3rd June and 2nd November 1876.

181 *Polar Medal* 1904—

General	Octagonal medal
Obverse	*1st type:* Bust of Edward VII facing left in admirals uniform, 'EDWARDVS VII REX IMPERATOR'.
	2nd type: Bust of George V facing left in admirals uniform, 'GEORGIVS V BRITT: OMN: REX ET IND: IMP'.
	3rd type: Crowned head and robed bust of George V facing left, 'GEORGIVS V. D. G. BRITT. OMN. REX ET INDAE IMP.'
	4th type: Coinage head of George V facing left, 'GEORGIVS V D. G. BRITT. OMN. REX ET INDAE IMP.'
	5th type: Coinage head of George VI facing left, 'GEORGIVS VI D: G: BR: OMN: REX: F: D: IND: IMP.'
	6th type: Coinage head of Elizabeth II facing right, 'ELIZABETH II DEI: GRA: BRITT: OMN: REGINA: F: D: +'.
	7th type: Coinage head of Elizabeth II facing right, 'ELIZABETH II DEI GRATIA REGINA F: D: +'.
Reverse	The *Discovery* with a sledging party of six in the foreground, and a heavily laden sledge with a square sail.
Size	33mm diameter
Metal	Silver and bronze
Ribbon	32mm diameter, plain white.
Suspension	By an ornamental swivelling suspender.
Designers	Obverse 1st type: G. W. Saulles; 2nd-4th types: Sir Bertram Mackennal; 5th type: Hugh Paget; 6th and 7th type: Mrs Mary Gillick. Reverse—E. G. Gillick
Naming	Impressed and engraved capitals.
Bars issued	All medals with the exception of the bronze 1902-04 issue were awarded with a bar (engraved or embossed) stating the period of service.

This is the current medal for Arctic and Antarctic exploration. It was instituted in 1904 by King Edward VII, and since then has been issued with the heads of King George V, King George VI and Elizabeth II. It has been awarded in silver and bronze, and those recipients who made further voyages were awarded bars to their medals. If, however, the original award was not of the same metal as that subsequently gained, then another medal was given.

The silver and bronze medals constitute two separate awards and may be worn at the same time.

Alfred Cheetham was awarded two bars to each of his silver and bronze medals. There were three other recipients of the two medals.

Frank Wild was awarded four bars to his silver medal.

Those who have been awarded either a silver or bronze Polar Medal may wear a rose emblem, of the same metal as the medal, on the ribbon to denote participation in subsequent expeditions for which an award was sanctioned. The wearing of one emblem denotes participation in two expeditions, the wearing of two emblems the participation in three expeditions, and so on.

King George V by a decree dated 16th October 1933 ordered that in future all Polar Medals were to be struck in silver; however bronze medals are known to have been issued bearing bars with dates up to 1939.

182   The United Nations Korea Service Medal
27th June 1950-27th July 1954

Obverse	The United Nations Emblem.
Reverse	Perfectly plain except for the inscription 'FOR SERVICE IN DEFENCE OF THE PRINCIPLES OF THE CHARTER OF THE UNITED NATIONS' in five lines.
Size	36mm diameter
Metal	Bronze
Ribbon	36mm wide, with nine blue and eight white stripes.
Suspension	By a straight, non-swivelling suspender
Naming	Awarded unnamed, except to Canadians whose medals are impressed
Bars issued	One—Korea

The suggestions for the awarding of this medal came from the Philippine delegation in December 1950. The authority for its award to United Kingdom and Commonwealth Forces was published on 6th November 1951.

The names of all units of the United Nations Forces eligible for the award of the bar 'KOREA' appear in General Orders published by the United Nations Commander-in-Chief and include all who rendered service whether combatant or non-combatant. The latter category includes the hospital units supplied by certain nations.

The regulations made by the different nations whose units qualified are not known, but those of the United Kingdom and Commonwealth Forces are as follows:

For all the Services the qualifying period was one day, except for visits of inspection which, either continuous or in aggregate, had to total thirty days.

Certain civilians whose organizations were certified by the Commander-in-Chief as having supported military operations were also eligible.

International Red Cross personnel engaged for service under the United Nations Commander-in-Chief with any United Nations relief team in Korea were, strange to say, *not* eligible for this medal.

It should be noted that the qualifications for this medal are not the same as those for the Queen's Korea Medal, as service in Korea after the armistice does not qualify.

The medal was struck in twelve languages: English, Amharic (Ethiopia), Dutch, French, Greek, Italian, Korean, Spanish (Columbia), Thai, Turkish, Tagalog (Philippines), Flemish (Belgium)—some of these differ slightly in design from the English version.

183 *United Nations Emergency Force Medal (UNEF)*
7th November 1956-10th June 1967

Obverse	The United Nations emblem with 'U.N.E.F.' above.
Reverse	Plain, with 'IN THE SERVICE OF PEACE' in two lines.
Size	36mm diameter
Metal	Bronze
Ribbon	37mm wide. Pale yellow with a central pale (UN) blue band with dark blue and dark green stripe to either side.
Suspension	Bead and ring
Naming	Awarded unnamed
Bars issued	Nil

Awarded for the UN patrol on the Israeli-Eygyptian border.

The medal was authorized on 7th November 1956, 'For award to any person belonging to the military services of a state serving under the Commander of the UNEF as a member of the national contingent or otherwise for a period of 90 days.

Over 47,000 of the medals were awarded to military and police personnel of the following countries: Brazil, Canada, Columbia, Denmark, Finland, Indonesia, India, Norway, Sweden, Yugoslavia.

184 *United Nations Medal* 1948 –

Obverse	The United Nations emblem with 'U.N.' above.
Reverse	Plain, with 'IN THE SERVICE OF PEACE' in two lines.
Size	36mm diameter
Metal	Bronze
Ribbon	(see below)
Suspension	Bead and ring
Naming	Awarded unnamed
Bars issued	One—Congo

This medal was instituted by the United Nations Secretary General on 30th July 1959. It was awarded for general peace-keeping operations. Each medal is issued with a specific ribbon representing the operation covered.

In 1979 it was announced that personnel then serving or in future serving with any of the UN missions, who had served more than one qualifying tour of duty with a specific mission, would qualify for a numerical emblem equal to the number of tours, to be worn on the ribbon. The emblem authorized would be an arabic numeral in silver metal.

UNTSO—United Nations Truce Supervisory Organisation, (1948-) for duties in zones between Israel and the arab countries, chiefly Egypt and Syria. Ribbon: blue with two narrow white stripes towards the edge.

UNOGIL—United Nations Observation Group in Lebanon (11th June 1958-9th December 1958) for duties along the Lebanon-Syria border. Ribbon: as UNTSO.

ONUC—Organisations des Nationes Unies du Congo (July 1960-1964). For duties in the Congo now Zaire. Ribbon—Originally worn from a blue and white ribbon as UNTSO. with a small bronze bar 'Congo'. In 1963 this was replaced by a new ribbon: green with white and blue edges.

UNTEA—United Nations Temporary Executive Authority (1962) For operations in Netherlands New Guinea. Ribbon—Blue with a central band of green, white, green.

UNMOGIP—United Nations Military Observer Group in India and Pakistan (1949-) For supervising the Kashmir cease fire on the India-Pakistan border. Ribbon—Varying shades of green with a white and pale blue border.

UNIPOM—United Nations India/Pakistan Observation Mission (September 1965-March 1966). Ribbon: as for UNMOGIP.

UNYOM—United Nations Yemen Observer Mission (13th June 1963-4th September 1964) to observe the ceasefire in the Yemen civil war. Ribbon—Brown centre merging into pale yellow with pale blue border.

UNFICYP—United Nations Force in Cyprus (March 1964-) To prevent fighting between the Greek and Turkish Cypriots. Ribbon—Pale blue with a central band of white bordered by a stripe of dark blue.

UNEF 2—United Nations Emergency Force (1973-) To observe the Israeli-Egyptian cease-fire. Ribbon—Pale blue with a central band of pale yellow which has in its centre two dark blue stripes.

UNDOF—United Nations Disengagement Observer Force (6th May 1974-) Operations along the Golan Heights. Ribbon—Burgundy with stripes of white, black, pale blue and red.

UNIFIL—United Nations Interim Force in Lebanon (March 1978-) Ribbon—Pale blue with a central dark green band edged in white, red and white stripes.

UN General Service—for service in HQ, New York. Ribbon—Pale blue.

25

27, 28, 37, 43, 44, 110

38, 41

46, 64, 75

31, 32, 34, 38, 40, 47,
51, 73, 78

50

52

54

56

58, 59, 60

61

62A, 63

65

67

68

69

70

72

74, 107

79

79 Proposed

80, 81, 82, 84, 85, 104

83

86

87

88

89

90

91

92

96

97

97 Variant

98

99

100

101, 111

102

103

105

106

108

109

112

113

114

115

116

117

118

119

120

122

123 1st type

123 2nd type

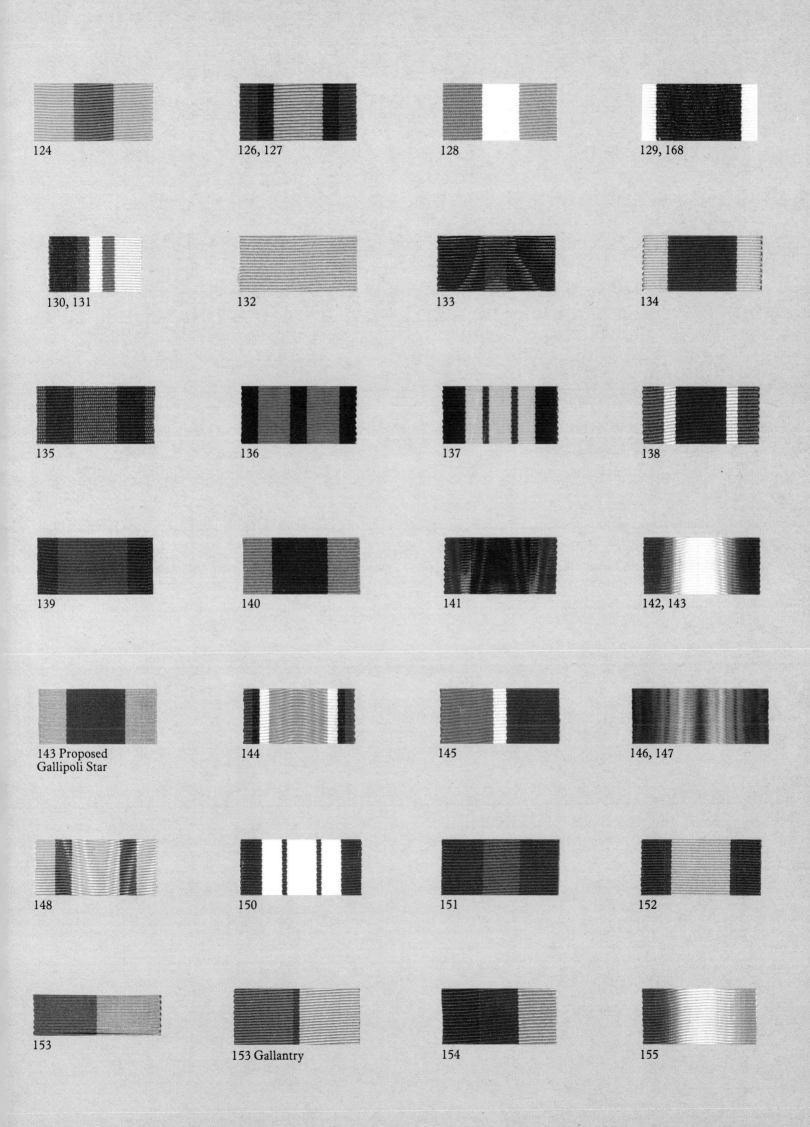

124

126, 127

128

129, 168

130, 131

132

133

134

135

136

137

138

139

140

141

142, 143

143 Proposed
Gallipoli Star

144

145

146, 147

148

150

151

152

153

153 Gallantry

154

155

156

157

158

159

160

161

162

163

164

165

166

167

169

170

171

172

173

174

175

176

177

178

179, 180

181

182

183

184 Cyprus

Indian Army Ranks and British Equivalents

One must preface these remarks with the reminder that they refer to the period prior to the 15th August, 1947.

Cavalry	Infantry
Risaldar Major	Subadar-Major
Risaldar	Subadar
Jemadar	Jemadar

The above were senior Indian officers to whom there were no British equivalents. They exercised command similar to a British captain or subaltern, but the most junior British officer ranked senior to them all.

Cavalry	Infantry	British Equivalent
Duffadar-Major	Havildar-Major	Regimental Sergeant-Major
Quartermaster Duffadar	Quartermaster Havildar	Regimental Quartermaster Sergeant
Duffadar	Havildar	Sergeant
Lance-Duffadar	Naik	Corporal
	Lance-Naik	Lance-Corporal
Sowar	Sepoy	Private

There were the ranks of Tindal and Khalassi (corrupted to Lascar) in the artillery.

The spellings of the Indian ranks altered with the years. In the official orders of about the 1790's one finds the words Soubadar, Jemidar, Naick, etc. When so many different spellings occur in official records, it is impossible in this space to list all variations.

In the British Infantry regiments stationed in India the head man of the followers was known as the Kotwal. The other followers, together with their duties, were:

Bhisti	Water carrier	Mehta	Sweeper
Dhobi	Washerman	Syce (or Sais)	Groom
Khidwatgar	Table servant		

The Indian regiments had another follower known as a Langri. He was a cook.

The word 'bearer' is, of course, connected with the palanquin or palke. This was a type of sedan chair or litter about 8 feet long, 4 feet wide, and 4 feet high, roofed in and fitted with blinds and furnished with cushions or a mattress. It was carried by four hammels, or bearers, two at each end, who held the handles or poles fitted to each side.

When the palanquins were abolished the term 'bearer' was retained, indicating a personal servant. The term 'hammal' was used in the Bombay Presidency to denote a personal servant.

The ambulances used dhoolies, or stretchers, and those who carried them were known as dhoolie-bearers. They, of course, were entitled to a campaign medal for active service so that there were different employments covered by the term 'bearer'.

List of Regiments and Corps 1987

Arranged alphabetically, listing Division and authorized abbreviations.

The Argyll and Sutherland Highlanders (Princess Louise's) *Scottish Division*	A and SH
Army Air Corps	AAC
Army Catering Corps	ACC
Army Legal Corps	ALC
Army Physical Training Corps	APTC
The Black Watch (Royal Highland Regiment) *Scottish Division*	BW
The Blues and Royals (Royal Horse Guards and 1st Dragoons) *Household Cavalry*	RHG/D
The Cheshire Regiment *Prince of Wales's Division*	CHESHIRE
Coldstream Guards *Guards Division*	COLDM GDS
Corps of Royal Electrical and Mechanical Engineers	REME
Corps of Royal Engineers	RE
Corps of Royal Military Police	RMP
The Devonshire and Dorset Regiment *Prince of Wales's Division*	D and D
The Duke of Edinburgh's Royal Regiment (Berkshire and Wiltshire) *Prince of Wales's Division*	DERR
The Duke of Wellington's Regiment (West Riding) *King's Division*	DWR
General Service Corps	GSC
The Gloucestershire Regiment *Prince of Wales's Division*	GLOSTERS
The Gordon Highlanders *Scottish Division*	GORDONS
The Green Howards (Alexandra Princess of Wales's Own Yorkshire Regiment) *King's Division*	GREEN HOWARDS
Grenadier Guards *Guards Division*	GREN GDS
2nd King Edward VIIs Own Gurkha Rifles (The Sirmoor Rifles) *Bde of Gurkhas*	2 GR
6th Queen Elizabeth's Own Gurkha Rifles *Bde of Gurkhas*	6 GR
7th Duke of Edinburgh's Own Gurkha Rifles *Bde of Gurkhas*	7 GR
10th Princess Mary's Own Gurkha Rifles *Bde of Gurkhas*	10 GR
Gurkha Transport Regiment *Bde of Gurkhas*	GTR
Intelligence Corps	INT CORPS
Irish Guards *Guards Division*	IG
14th/20th King's Hussars *RAC*	14/20 H
The King's Own Royal Border Regiment *King's Division*	KING'S OWN BORDER
The King's Own Scottish Borderers *Scottish Division*	KOSB
The King's Regiment *King's Division*	KINGS
15th/19th The King's Royal Hussars *RAC*	15/19 H
17th/21st Lancers *RAC*	17/21 L
The Life Guards *Household Cavalry*	LG
The Light Infantry *Light Division*	LI
Military Provost Staff Corps	MPSC
Officers Training Corps	OTC
The Parachute Regiment	PARA
The Prince of Wales's Own Regiment of Yorkshire *King's Division*	PWO
Queen Alexandra's Royal Army Nursing Corps	QARANC
1st The Queen's Dragoon Guards *RAC*	QDG
The Queen's Gurkha Engineers *Bde of Gurkhas*	QGE
Queen's Gurkha Signals *Bde of Gurkhas*	QG SIGNALS
Queen's Own Highlanders (Seaforth and Camerons) *Scottish Division*	QO HLDRS
The Queen's Lancashire Regiment *King's Division*	QLR
The Queen's Own Hussars *RAC*	QOH
The Queen's Regiment *Queen's Division*	QUEENS
The Queen's Royal Irish Hussars *RAC*	QRIH
16th/5th The Queen's Royal Lancers *RAC*	16/5 L
The Royal Anglian Regiment *Queen's Division*	R ANGLIAN
Royal Armoured Corps	RAC
Royal Army Chaplain's Department	RAChD
Royal Army Dental Corps	RADC
Royal Army Educational Corps	RAEC
Royal Army Medical Corps	RAMC
Royal Army Ordnance Corps	RAOC
Royal Army Pay Corps	RAPC
Royal Army Veterinary Corps	RAVC
Royal Corps of Signals	R SIGNALS

Royal Corps of Transport	RCT
4th/7th Royal Dragoon Guards *RAC*	4/7 DG
The Royal Green Jackets *Light Division*	RGJ
The Royal Hampshire Regiment *Prince of Wales's Division*	R HAMPS
The Royal Highland Fusiliers (Princess Margaret's Own Glasgow and Ayrshire Regiment) *Scottish Division*	RHF
Royal Horse Artillery	RHA
The Royal Hussars (Prince of Wales's Own) *RAC*	RH
13th/18th Royal Hussars (Queen Mary's Own) *RAC*	13/18 H
5th Royal Inniskilling Dragoon Guards *RAC*	5 INNIS DG

The Royal Irish Rangers (27th (Inniskilling) 83rd and 87th) *King's Division*	R IRISH
9th/12th Royal Lancers (Prince of Wales's) *RAC*	9/12th L
Royal Pioneer Corps	RPC
Royal Regiment of Artillery	RA
The Royal Regiment of Fusiliers *Queen's Division*	RRF
The Royal Regiment of Wales *Prince of Wales's Division*	RRW
The Royal Scots (The Royal Regiment) *Scottish Division*	RS
The Royal Scots Dragoon Guards (Carabiniers and Greys) *RAC*	SCOTS DG
Royal Tank Regiment *RAC*	RTR
The Royal Welch Fusiliers *Prince of Wales's Division*	RWF

Scots Guards *Guards Division*	SG
Small Arms School Corps	SASC
Special Air Service Regiment	SAS
The Staffordshire Regiment (The Prince of Wales's) *Prince of Wales's Division*	STAFFORDS
Welsh Guards *Guards Division*	WG
Women's Royal Army Corps	WRAC
The Worcestershire and Sherwood Foresters Regiment *Prince of Wales's Division*	WFR

T.A. Units Unit titles of which differ from those of Regular units.

Royal Monmouthshire Royal Engineers (Militia)	R MON RE (M)
The Honourable Artillery Company	HAC
The Royal Yeomanry *RAC*	RY
The Royal Wessex Yeomanry *RAC*	R WX Y
The Queen's Own Mercian Yeomanry *RAC*	QOMY
The Queen's Own Yeomanry	QOY
The Duke of Lancaster's Own Yeomanry *RAC*	DLOY
52nd Lowland Volunteers *Scottish Division*	52 LOWLAND
51st Highland Volunteers *Scottish Division*	51 HIGHLAND
The Yorkshire Volunteers *King's Division*	YORKS

The 4th (Volunteer) Battalion Royal Irish Rangers (27 (Inninskilling) 83rd and 87th (The North Irish Militia))	4 (V) R IRISH
Wessex Regiment *Prince of Wales's Division*	WESSEX
Mercian Volunteers *Prince of Wales's Division*	MERCIAN
Light Infantry Volunteers *Light Division*	LI (V)
The Ulster Defence Regiment	UDR

PRECEDENCE OF CORPS, ETC

1 The Life Guards and The Blues and Royals
2 Royal Horse Artillery
3 Royal Armoured Corps
4 Royal Regiment of Artillery (Royal Horse Artillery excepted)
5 Corps of Royal Engineers
6 Royal Corps of Signals
7 Regiments of Foot Guards
8 Regiments of Infantry
9 Special Air Service Regiment
10 Army Air Corps
11 Royal Army Chaplains Department
12 Royal Corps of Transport
13 Royal Army Medical Corps
14 Royal Army Ordnance Corps
15 Corps of Royal Electrical and Mechanical Engineers

16 Corps of Royal Military Police
17 Royal Army Pay Corps
18 Royal Army Veterinary Corps
19 Small Arms School Corps
20 Military Provost Staff Corps
21 Royal Army Educational Corps
22 Royal Army Dental Corps
23 Royal Pioneer Corps
24 Intelligence Corps
25 Army Physical Training Corps
26 Army Catering Corps
27 Army Legal Corps
28 General Service Corps
29 Queen Alexandra's Royal Army Nursing Corps
30 Women's Royal Army Corps
31 Royal Monmouthshire Royal Engineers (Militia) (Territorial Army)
32 The Honourable Artillery Company (Territorial Army)
33 Territorial Army (other than 31 and 32 above)
34 Ulster Defence Regiment

PRECEDENCE OF INFANTRY REGIMENTS

The Royal Scots (The Royal Regiment)
The Queen's Regiment
The King's Own Royal Border Regiment
The Royal Regiment of Fusiliers
The King's Regiment
The Royal Anglian Regiment
The Devonshire and Dorset Regiment
The Light Infantry
The Prince of Wales's Own Regiment of Yorkshire
The Green Howards (Alexandra Princess of Wales's Own Yorkshire Regiment)
The Royal Highland Fusiliers (Princess Margaret's Own Glasgow and Ayrshire Regiment)
The Cheshire Regiment
The Royal Welch Fusiliers
The Royal Regiment of Wales (24th/41st Foot)
The King's Own Scottish Borderers
The Royal Irish Rangers (27th (Inniskilling) 83rd and 87th)
The Gloucestershire Regiment
The Worcestershire and Sherwood Foresters Regiment (29th/45th Foot)
The Queen's Lancashire Regiment
The Duke of Wellington's Regiment (West Riding)
The Royal Hampshire Regiment
The Staffordshire Regiment (The Prince of Wales's)
The Black Watch (Royal Highland Regiment)
The Duke of Edinburgh's Royal Regiment (Berkshire and Wiltshire)
Queen's Own Highlanders (Seaforth and Camerons)
The Gordon Highlanders
The Argyll and Sutherland Highlanders (Princess Louise's)
The Parachute Regiment
The Brigade of Gurkhas
The Royal Green Jackets

Cavalry and Infantry Regiments of the British Army

Cavalry Regiments

Old Title (c 1900)	Present Title	Date of Formation	Notes
1st Life Guards 2nd Life Guards	} The Life Guards	1661	Originally composed of three troops: The King's Own, The Duke of York's and Duke of Albemarle's. The latter Duke, as Lord Monk, commanded the fleet at Dunkirk in 1666.
The Royal Horse Guards (The Blues)	The Blues and Royals (Royal Horse Guards and 1st Dragoons)	1661	Originally known as the Earl of Oxford's Regiment of Horse, later the Oxford Blues. Amalgamated in 1969 with the 1st Dragoons.
1st (The King's) Dragoon Guards	1st The Queen's Dragoon Guards	1685	Originally known as the Queen's Regiment of Horse or Second Horse. Amalgamated in 1959 with The Queen's Bays.
2nd Dragoon Guards (Queen's Bays)	1st The Queen's Dragoon Guards	1685	Originally raised by the Earl of Peterborough and styled the Third Horse. In 1921 became The Queen's Bays (2nd Dragoon Guards). Amalgamated in 1959 with the 1st Dragoon Guards
3rd (Prince of Wales's) Dragoon Guards	The Royal Scots Dragoon Guards (Carabiniers and Greys)	1685	Raised by the Earl of Plymouth and originally styled the Fourth Horse. Amalgamated in 1922 with the Carabiniers (6th Dragoon Guards) to form the 3rd/6th Dragoon Guards. Became the 3rd Carabiniers (Prince of Wales's) Dragoon Guards in 1928. Amalgamated in 1971 with the Royal Scots Greys (2nd Dragoons)
4th (Royal Irish) Dragoon Guards	4th/7th Royal Dragoon Guards	1685	Originally known as Arran's Cuirassiers, after their founder, later styled the Fifth Horse. Amalgamated in 1922 with the 7th Dragoon Guards
5th (Princess Charlotte of Wales's) Dragoon Guards	5th Royal Inniskilling Dragoon Guards	1685	Raised by the Earl of Shrewsbury and later styled the Sixth Horse. Fought at the Battle of the Boyne, 1st July 1690 as Coy's Horse. Amalgamated in 1922 with the Inniskillings (6th Dragoons) to form the 5th/6th Dragoons. Became the 5th Inniskilling Dragoon Guards in 1927, their present title dates from 1935.
6th Dragoon Guards (Carabiniers)	The Royal Scots Dragoon Guards (Carabiniers and Greys)	1685	Originally the Ninth Horse which, under Colonel Lumley, captured the Duke of Monmouth on 8th July 1685. Amalgamated in 1922 with the 3rd Dragoon Guards to form the 3rd/6th Dragoon Guards. Became the 3rd Carabiniers (Prince of Wales's) Dragoon Guards in 1928. Amalgamated in 1971 with The Royal Scots Greys (2nd Dragoons).
7th (The Princess Royal's) Dragoon Guards	4th/7th Royal Dragoon Guards	1688	Originally the Tenth Horse. Amalgamated with the 4th Dragoon Guards in 1922.
1st (Royal) Dragoons	The Blues and Royals (Royal Horse Guards and 1st Dragoons)	1661	Originally the Earl of Peterborough's Tangier Horse. Amalgamated in 1969 with The Royal Horse Guards.
2nd Dragoons (Royal Scots Greys)	The Royal Scots Dragoon Guards (Carabiniers and Greys)	1681	Styled in 1751 the 2nd Royal North British Dragoons. Amalgamated in 1971 with the 3rd Dragoon Guards
3rd (King's Own) Hussars	The Queen's Own Hussars	1685	Prior to 1861 they were known as the 3rd (King's Own) Light Dragoons. Amalgamated in 1958 with the 7th Queen's Own Hussars
4th (The Queen's Own) Hussars	The Queen's Royal Irish Hussars	1685	Raised originally as Princess Anne of Denmark's Dragoons on 17th July 1685. Became Light Dragoons in 1818 and Hussars in 1861. Amalgamated in 1958 with the 8th King's Royal Irish Hussars.
5th (Royal Irish) Lancers	16th/5th The Queen's Royal Lancers	1690	First constituted in 1690 as Dragoons and disbanded in 1798. Reconstituted in 1858. Amalgamated in 1922 with the 16th The Queen's Lancers.

Cavalry Regiments

Old Title (c 1900)	Present Title	Date of Formation	Notes
6th (Inniskilling) Dragoons	5th Inniskilling Dragoon Guards	1689	Amalgamated in 1922 with the 5th Dragoon Guards. Current title dates from 1935.
7th (Queen's Own) Hussars	The Queen's Own Hussars	1690	Originally Dragoons, becoming Light Dragoons in 1783 and Hussars in 1805. Amalgamated in 1958 with the 3rd Hussars.
8th (The King's Royal Irish) Hussars	The Queen's Royal Irish Hussars	1693	Raised from Irish Protestants by Colonel Henry Cunningham. Dragoons prior to 1822. Amalgamated in 1958 with the 4th (The Queen's Own) Hussars.
9th (Queen's Royal) Lancers	9th/12th Royal Lancers (Prince of Wales's)	1715	Originally styled Wynne's Dragoons. Became Lancers in 1816. Amalgamated in 1960 with the 12th Royal Lancers (Prince of Wales's)
10th (The Prince of Wales's Own Royal) Hussars	The Royal Hussars (Prince of Wales's Own)	1715	Originally known as Gore's Dragoons. It was first engaged at Falkirk, where the Young Pretender defeated the Royal Forces on 17th June 1746. Became Hussars in 1806. Amalgamated in 1969 with the 11th Hussars (Prince Albert's Own).
11th (Prince Albert's Own) Hussars	The Royal Hussars (Prince of Wales's Own)	1715	Originally known as Honeywood's Dragoons. Became Light Dragoons in 1783 and Hussars in 1840. Amalgamated in 1969 with the 10th Hussars (Prince of Wales Own)
12th (The Prince of Wales's Royal) Lancers	9th/12th Royal Lancers (Prince of Wales's)	1715	Originally known as Bowle's Dragoons. Became Light Dragoons in 1768 and Lancers in 1816. Amalgamated in 1960 with the 9th Queen's Royal Lancers
13th Hussars	13th/18th Royal Hussars (Queen Mary's Own)	1715	Originally raised in 1697, but disbanded soon afterwards. Originally Dragoons, they became Light Dragoons in 1783 and Hussars in 1861. Amalgamated in 1922 with the 18th Royal Hussars (Queen Mary's Own)
14th (King's) Hussars	14th/20th King's Hussars	1715	Originally Dragoons, became Light Dragoons in 1776 and Hussars in 1861. Amalgamated in 1922 with the 20th Hussars.
15th (King's) Hussars	15th/19th The King's Royal Hussars	1759	Originally Light Dragoons, became Hussars in 1806. Amalgamated with the 19th Royal Hussars (Queen Alexandra's Own) in 1922.
16th (The Queen's) Lancers	16th/5th The Queen's Royal Lancers	1759	Originally Light Dragoons, became Lancers in 1815. Amalgamated in 1922 with the 5th Royal Irish Lancers
17th Lancers (Duke of Cambridge's Own)	17th/21st Lancers	1759	The 'Death or Glory Boys' originated in Hertfordshire. Styled Light Dragoons until 1822. Amalgamated in 1922 with the 21st Lancers (Empress of India's)
18th Hussars	13th/18th Royal Hussars (Queen Mary's Own)	1759	Originally raised as Light Dragoons in Ireland by the Earl of Drogheda. Became Hussars in 1805 and were disbanded in 1822. Reformed in 1858 and in 1910 were styled 'Queen Mary's Own'. Amalgamated in 1922 with the 13th Hussars
19th Hussars	15th/19th The King's Royal Hussars	1759	Four regiments have been numbered as the 19th. (1) Formed in 1759, renumbered as 18th Light Dragoons in 1763 (see above). (2) 19th Light Dragoons 1779-1783. (3) 23rd Light Dragoons formed in 1781, renumbered the 19th in 1783, became Lancers in 1817, disbanded in 1822. (4) Originally 1st Bengal European Light Cavalry, 19th Hussars in 1861, 19th (Queen Alexandra's Own Royal) Hussars in 1908. Amalgamated in 1922 with the 15th The King's Hussars
20th Hussars	14th/20th King's Hussars	1759	Four regiments have been numbered as the 20th. (1) 20th Inniskilling Light Dragoons 1759-1763. (2) 20th Light Dragoons 1778-1783. (3) 20th Jamaica Light Dragoons 1791-1819. (4) Originally the 2nd Bengal European Light Cavalry, becoming the 20th Hussars in 1861. Amalgamated in 1922 with the 14th King's Hussars

Cavalry Regiments

Old Title (c 1900)	Present Title	Date of Formation	Notes
21st (Empress of India's) Lancers	17th/21st Lancers	1759	Four regiments have been numbered as the 21st. (1) 21st Light Dragoons, the Royal Windsor Foresters 1759-1763. (2) 21st Light Dragoons 1779-1783. (3) 21st Light Dragoons 1794-1819. (4) Originally the 3rd Bengal European Cavalry they became the 21st Hussars in 1861, 21st Lancers in 1897. In 1922 they amalgamated with the 17th Lancers (Duke of Cambridge's Own)

The following cavalry regiments have no present day representative.

Old Title (c 1900)	Present Title	Date of Formation	Notes
22nd Light Dragoons		1760	Four regiments have been numbered as the 22nd. (1) 1760-68. (2) 22nd or York Light Dragoons 1779-1783. (3) 1794-1802. (4) Originally the 25th Light Dragoons, formed in 1794, renumbered in 1802, disbanded in 1819
23rd Light Dragoons		1781	Three regiments have been numbered as the 23rd. (1) Formed in 1781 renumbered 19th in 1783 (see above). (2) 1794-1802. (3) Raised in 1794 as the 26th Light Dragoons, renumbered in 1802, became Lancers in 1816, disbanded in 1817
24th Light Dragoons		1794	Two regiments have been numbered as the 24th. (1) 1794-1802. (2) Raised in 1794 as the 27th Light Dragoons, renumbered in 1802, disbanded in 1818
25th Light Dragoons		1794	Two regiments have been numbered as the 25th. (1) Formed in 1794 and renumbered the 22nd in 1802. (2) Formed in 1794 as the 29th Light Dragoons, renumbered in 1802, disbanded in 1818

Brigade of Guards

Title	Date of Formation	Notes
1st Foot Guards, Grenadier Guards	1656	Title of Grenadiers granted 29th July 1815, after defeat of French Grenadiers at Waterloo. John Churchill, later Duke of Marlborough, was appointed to the Regiment about 1687. Originally raised by Lord Wentworth as escort to Charles II during his exile in Flanders in 1656. Amalgamated with Russell's Regiment and styled the King's Regiment of Foot Guards in 1665.
2nd Foot Guards, Coldstream Guards	1660	Lord Monk started from Coldstream when he marched to overthrow Parliament and reinstate the Monarchy. At the head of the Coldstreamers he entered London on 2nd February 1660. On the accession of Charles II the whole army was disbanded except the Lord General's Regiment, which paraded and laid down their arms for the Government and took them up again for the Sovereign. They were constituted The Queen's Regiment by Royal Warrant of March 1673, and to rank after the First Foot Guards.
3rd Foot Guards, Scots Guards	1660	Originally the Scot's Regiment of Guards, becoming in 1712 the 3rd Foot Guards, in 1831 The Scots Fusilier Guards and in 1877 the Scots Guards
4th Foot Guards, Irish Guards	1901	The regiment was raised by Queen Victoria, who appointed Lord Roberts to be their first Colonel
5th Foot Guards, Welsh Guards	1915	They were raised from Welshmen of the Brigade of Guards by King George V. Their first Colonel was the Prince of Wales.

Line Regiments

Pre-1881 Title	Other Bn No.	Post-1881 Title	Present Title	Date of Formation	Notes
1st (The Royal Scots)	—	1st and 2nd The Royal Scots (The Lothian Regiment)	The Royal Scots (The Royal Regiment)	1633	It is impossible to trace earlier authenticated history. Scots formed bodyguards to the Kings of Sweden and France in the ninth century. The Scots Brigade after the Battle of Nordlingen, 27th August 1634, appear to have joined up with John Hepburn's Scots and became known as Le Regiment de Douglas, then Dumbarton's Regiment, and they remained on the continent until 1661. The title of 'The Royal Regiment' was granted them by Charles II in 1684. Their first service in conjuction with English regiments was at Steenkerke on 24th July 1692. Present title dates from 1920.
2nd (The Queen's Own Royal)	—	1st and 2nd Bns. The Queen's (Royal West Surrey Regiment)	The Queen's Regiment	1661	Originally the Tangier Regiment, the title of the Queen's was granted in 1684, that of the Royal in 1703. Amalgamated in 1959 with The East Surrey Regiment to form The Queen's Royal Surrey Regiment. Amalgamated in 1966 with The Queen's Own Buffs The Royal Kent Regiment, The Royal Sussex Regiment and The Middlesex Regiment (Duke of Cambridge's Own).
3rd (East Kent) (The Buffs)	—	1st and 2nd Bns. The Buffs (East Kent Regiment)	The Queen's Regiment	1665	As the Regiment of Holland they saw much service in Holland before joining the Army establishment. They were later known as Prince George of Denmark's Regiment of Foot, and then Churchill's Regiment (the Duke of Marlborough's brother being their Colonel). The name Buff was derived from the colour of their facings. In 1935 became The Buffs (Royal East Kent Regt). Amalgamated in 1961 with The Queen's Own Royal West Kent Regiment to form The Queen's Own Buffs, The Royal Kent Regiment. Amalgamated in 1966 with the Queen's Royal Surrey Regiment, The Royal Sussex Regiment and The Middlesex Regiment (Duke of Cambridge's Own).
4th (The King's Own Royal)	—	1st and 2nd Bns The King's Own (Royal Lancaster Regiment)	The King's Own Royal Border Regiment	1680	In 1684 their title was Her Royal Highness the Duchess of York and Albany's Regiment, which was changed to that of The Queen's Regiment of Foot. At the capture of Gibraltar in 1704 they were acting as Marines. The title of the King's Own was given them by George I on parade at Windsor in 1715. Amalgamated in 1959 with the Border Regiment.
5th (Northumberland Fusiliers)	—	1st and 2nd Bns The Northumberland Fusiliers	The Royal Regiment of Fusiliers	1685	This was the date of their establishment, though it is possible to trace their existence before this as the Irish Regiment of the British Legion in Holland. Granted the title of 'Royal' in 1935. In 1968 amalgamated with The Royal Warwickshire Fusiliers, The Royal Fusiliers and The Lancashire Fusiliers.
6th (Royal Warwickshire)	—	1st and 2nd Bns The Royal Warwickshire Regiment	The Royal Regiment of Fusiliers	1685	They formed part of the forces in Holland before this date, being originally raised in 1673 for service with Sir Walter Vane. Became Fusiliers in 1963. Amalgamated in 1968 with The Royal Northumberland Fusiliers, The Royal Fusiliers and The Lacashire Fusiliers.
7th (Royal Fusiliers)	—	1st and 2nd Bns The Royal Fusiliers (City of London Regiment)	The Royal Regiment of Fusiliers	1685	It seems almost impossible to trace any organized forces which could be constituted as the forerunners of this regiment, which obtained its present title as the result of the amalgamation of several units then in existence. They formed part of the famous Fusilier Brigade at Albuhera, where Soult was defeated on 16th May 1811.

Line Regiments

Pre-1881 Title	Other Bn No.	Post-1881 Title	Present Title	Date of Formation	Notes
					Amalgamated in 1968 with The Royal Northumberland Fusiliers, The Royal Warwickshire Fusiliers and The Lancashire Fusiliers.
8th (The King's)	—	1st and 2nd Bns The King's (Liverpool Regiment)	The King's Regiment	1685	Their first title was The Princess Anne of Denmark's Regiment. It was not until after the Battle of Sheriff Muir, on 13th November 1715, that George I granted them the title of The King's and granted the Horse of Hanover as their badge. Amalgamated in 1958 with The Manchester Regiment to form The King's Regiment (Manchester and Liverpool). Present title dates from December 1968.
9th (East Norfolk)	—	1st and 2nd Bns The Norfolk Regiment	The Royal Anglian Regiment	1685	The regiment was originally raised in Gloucestershire. The original 2nd Bn was disbanded in 1815 and re-formed in 1858. Granted the title of 'Royal' in 1935. Amalgamated with The Suffolk Regiment in 1959 to form The 1st East Anglian Regiment (Royal Norfolk and Suffolk). Amalgamated in 1964 with The 2nd and 3rd East Anglian Regiments and The Royal Leicestershire Regiment.
10th (North Lincolnshire)	—	1st and 2nd Bns The Lincolnshire Regiment	The Royal Anglian Regiment	1685	They were originally formed from the garrison of Plymouth. Fought at Steenkerke 24th July 1692. Granted the title 'Royal' in 1946. Amalgamated in 1960 with The Northamptonshire Regiment to form The 2nd East Anglian Regiment (Duchess of Gloucester's Own Royal Lincolnshire and Northamptonshire). Amalgamated in 1964 with The 1st and 3rd East Anglian Regiments and The Royal Leicestershire Regiment.
11th (North Devonshire)	—	1st and 2nd Bns The Devonshire Regiment	The Devonshire and Dorset Regiment	1685	The second battalion was raised in 1756, later to become the 64th, which number was later turned over to the North Staffs Regiment. Amalgamated with The Dorset Regiment in 1958.
12th (East Suffolk)	—	1st and 2nd Bns The Suffolk Regiment	The Royal Anglian Regiment	1685	They were, before this, garrison troops at Windsor Castle. Amalgamated in 1959 with the Royal Norfolk Regiment to form The 1st East Anglian Regiment (Royal Norfolk and Suffolk). Amalgamated in 1964 with The 2nd and 3rd East Anglian Regiments and The Royal Leicestershire Regiment.
13th (1st Somersetshire) (Prince Albert's Light Infantry)	—	1st and 2nd Bns The Prince Albert's (Somersetshire Light Infantry)	The Light Infantry	1685	They fought at the Battle of the Boyne in 1690 and in Holland, under Marlborough, in 1701. Amalgamated in 1959 with The Duke of Cornwall's Light Infantry to form The Somerset and Cornwall Light Infantry. Amalgamated in 1968 with the King's Own Yorkshire, King's Shropshire and Durham Light Infantry.
14th (Buckinghamshire) (The Prince of Wales's Own)	—	1st and 2nd Bns The Prince of Wales's Own (West Yorkshire Regiment)	The Prince of Wales's Own Regiment of Yorkshire	1685	They were raised in the neighbourhood of Canterbury by Sir George Hales. In 1920 redesignated The West Yorkshire Regiment (The Prince of Wales's Own). Amalgamated in 1958 with The East Yorkshire Regiment (The Duke of York's Own).
15th (York East Riding)	—	1st and 2nd Bns The East Yorkshire Regiment	The Prince of Wales's Own Regiment of Yorkshire	1685	Originally raised in Nottinghamshire by Sir William Clifton. Amalgamated in 1958 with The West Yorkshire Regiment (The Prince of Wales Own).
16th (Bedfordshire)	—	1st and 2nd Bns The Bedfordshire Regiment	The Royal Anglian Regiment	1688	Their first service was at Walcourt, 25th August 1689. Became The Bedfordshire and Hertfordshire Regiment in 1919. Amalgamated in 1958 with

Line Regiments

Pre-1881 Title	Other Bn No.	Post-1881 Title	Present Title	Date of Formation	Notes
					The Essex Regiment to form the 3rd East Anglian Regiment (16th/44th Foot). Amalgamated in 1964 with the 1st and 2nd Anglian Regiments and The Royal Leicestershire Regiment.
17th (Leicestershire)	—	1st and 2nd Bns The Leicestershire Regiment	The Royal Anglian Regiment	1688	Granted the title 'Royal' in 1946. Amalgamated in 1964 with the 1st, 2nd and 3rd Anglian Regiments.
18th (The Royal Irish)	—	1st and 2nd Bns The Royal Irish Regiment		1684	They were disbanded on 31st July 1922.
19th (1st Yorkshire, North Riding Princess of Wales's Own)	—	1st and 2nd Bns The Princess of Wales's Own (Yorkshire) Regiment	The Green Howards (Alexandra, Princess of Wales's Own Yorkshire Regiment)	1688	Raised originally in Devonshire. At one time (about 1737) this regiment and the East Kent Regiment were both commanded by Colonels of the name of Howard. To distinguish them, the common practice being to call the regiment after its colonel, they were known as the Green Howards and the Buff Howards. Present title dates from 1921.
20th (East Devonshire)	—	1st and 2nd Bns The Lancashire Fusiliers	The Royal Regiment of Fusiliers	1688	They were garrison troops on St. Helena and supplied the funeral party for Napoleon on 5th May, 1821. Amalgamated in 1968 with The Royal Northumberland, Royal Warwickshire and Royal Fusiliers.
21st (Royal Scots Fusiliers)	—	1st and 2nd Bns The Royal Scots Fusiliers	The Royal Highland Fusiliers (Princess Margaret's Own Glasgow and Ayrshire Regiment)	1678	Originally the Earl of Mar's Regiment, they joined the establishment in 1688 as The Scots Fusiliers. Known as the 21st Royal North British Fusiliers during 1712-1877. Amalgamated in 1959 with The Highland Light Infantry (City of Glasgow Regiment).
22nd (The Cheshire)	—	1st and 2nd Bns The Cheshire Regiment	The Cheshire Regiment	1689	The regiment was raised by Henry, Duke of Norfolk, for service in Ireland.
23rd (Royal Welch Fusiliers)	—	1st and 2nd Bns The Royal Welsh Fusiliers	The Royal Welch Fusiliers	1689	Their first service was at the Battle of the Boyne, 1st July 1690. Current title dates from 1920.
24th (2nd Warwickshire)	—	1st and 2nd Bns The South Wales Borderers	The Royal Regiment of Wales (24th/41st Foot)	1689	The regiment was raised in Ireland, and was known as Dering's Regiment. Amalgamated in 1969 with The Welch Regiment.
25th (The King's Own Borderers)	—	1st and 2nd Bns The King's Own Borderers	The King's Own Scottish Borderers	1689	They were raised in Edinburgh by the Earl of Leven. The title 'Scottish' was not added until 1887.
26th (Cameronian)	90	1st Bn The Cameronians (Scottish Rifles)		1689	They were raised from Covenanters. Their first service was at Dunkeld, under Lord Angus. Disbanded in 1968.
27th (Inniskilling)	108	1st Bn The Royal Inniskilling Fusiliers	The Royal Irish Rangers (27th (Inniskilling) 83rd and 87th)	1689	Amalgamated in 1969 with The Royal Ulster Rifles and The Royal Irish Fusiliers.
28th (North Gloucestershire)	61	1st Bn The Gloucestershire Regiment	The Gloucestershire Regiment	1694	They first saw service in Holland, at Huy, in 1695.
29th (Worcestershire)	36	1st Bn The Worcestershire Regiment	The Worcestershire and Sherwood Foresters Regiment (29th/45th Foot)	1694	They were present at the Battle of the Glorious First of June and in 1909 were awarded a Naval crown superscribed 1st June 1794. Amalgamated in 1970 with The Sherwood Foresters (Nottinghamshire and Derbyshire Regiment).
30th (Cambridgeshire)	59	1st Bn The East Lancashire Regiment	The Queen's Lancashire Regiment	1702	Originally raised by Colonel Sanderson as Marines and served as such until 1814. Their first service was at the Capture of Gibraltar in 1704. Amalgamated in 1958 with The South Lancashire Regiment to form The Lancashire Regiment (Prince of Wales's Volunteers) and again in 1970 with The Loyal Regiment (North Lancashire).

Line Regiments

Pre-1881 Title	Other Bn No.	Post-1881 Title	Present Title	Date of Formation	Notes
31st (Huntingdonshire)	70	1st Bn The East Surrey Regiment	The Queen's Regiment	1702	They were originally raised by Colonel George Villiers as Marines and joined the establishement as infantry in 1715. Amalgamated in 1959 with The Queen's Royal Regiment (West Surrey) to form The Queen's Royal Surrey Regiment. Amalgamated in 1966 with The Queen's Own Buffs The Royal Kent Regiment, The Royal Sussex Regiment and The Middlesex Regiment (Duke of Cambridge's Own).
32nd (Cornwall) Light Infantry	46	1st Bn The Duke of Cornwall's Light Infantry	The Light Infantry	1702	They were originally raised as Marines. They became the Cornwall Regiment in 1782 and Light Infantry in 1858. Amalgamated in 1959 with The Somerset Light Infantry to form The Somerset and Cornwall Light Infantry. Amalgamated in 1968 with The King's Own Yorkshire Light Infantry, The King's Shropshire Light Infantry and The Durham Light Infantry.
33rd (Duke of Wellington's)	76	1st Bn The Duke of Wellington's (West Riding Regiment)	The Duke of Wellington's Regiment (West Riding)	1702	Became the 33rd 1st York West Riding Foot in 1782. Assumed the title 33rd (Duke of Wellington's) Foot in 1852 following the Duke's death.
34th (Cumberland)	55	1st Bn The Border Regiment	The King's Own Royal Border Regiment	1702	The regiment was originally raised in Essex and Norfolk. Amalgamated in 1959 with The King's Own Royal Regiment (Lancaster).
35th (Royal Sussex)	107	1st Bn The Royal Sussex Regiment	The Queen's Regiment	1701	Raised in Ireland by the Earl of Donegal. It was placed on the establishment in 1702 'for sea service'. In 1782 it became the 35th (Dorsetshire) Foot, changing to (Sussex) in 1805 and becoming 'Royal' in1832. Amalgamated in 1966 with The Queen's Royal Surrey Regiment, The Queen's Own Buffs The Royal Kent Regiment and The Middlesex Regiment (Duke of Cambridge's Own).
36th (Herefordshire)	29	2nd Bn The Worcestershire Regiment	The Worcestershire and Sherwood Foresters Regiment (29th/45th Foot)	1701	Originally raised in Ireland by Lord Charlemont, and served as Marines.
37th (North Hampshire)	67	1st Bn The Hampshire Regiment	The Royal Hampshire Regiment	1702	Their first service was at Schellengeberg under Marlborough. Styled 'Royal' in 1946.
38th (1st Staffordshire)	80	1st Bn The South Staffordshire Regiment	The Staffordshire Regiment (The Prince of Wales's)	1705	Raised in Lichfield and went to the West Indies in 1707, where it served for over fifty years. Amalgamated in 1959 with The North Staffordshire Regiment (The Prince of Wales's).
39th (Dorsetshire)	54	1st Bn The Dorsetshire Regiment	The Devonshire and Dorset Regiment	1702	Originally raised in Ireland. The only British regiment present at Plassey in 1757. Amalgamated in 1958 with The Devonshire Regiment.
40th (2nd Somersetshire)	82	1st Bn The Prince of Wales's Volunteers (South Lancashire Regiment)	The Queen's Lancashire Regiment	1717	They were formed from companies raised in the West Indies and America. Their first service was at Louisburg, 27th July, 1758. Amalgamated in 1958 with the East Lancashire Regiment to form The Lancashire Regiment (Prince of Wales's Volunteers). Amalgamated in 1970 with The Loyal Regiment (North Lancashire.)
41st (The Welsh)	69	1st Bn The Welsh Regiment	The Royal Regiment of Wales (24th/41st Foot)	1719	Their first title, The Regiment of Royal Invalids, is probably derived from the fact that they were originally formed from old veterans. They bear unique honours for Detroit and Miami on their Colours. They served in America throughout the Peninsular War. Redesignated The Welch Regiment in 1920. Amalgamated in 1969 with The South Wales Borderers.

Line Regiments

Pre-1881 Title	Other Bn No.	Post-1881 Title	Present Title	Date of Formation	Notes
42nd (The Royal Highland. The Black Watch)	73	1st Bn The Black Watch (Royal Highlanders)	The Black Watch (Royal Highland Regiment)	1725	Formed from independant companies of Highlanders. Their first foreign service was at Fontenoy, 30th April 1745. Current title dates from 1934.
43rd (Monmouthshire Light Infantry)	52	1st Bn The Oxfordshire Light Infantry	The Royal Green Jackets	1741	They first served overseas in Minorca in 1742, but their first active service was with General Wolfe at Quebec in 1759. They became Light Infantry in 1803. Became The Oxfordshire and Buckinghamshire Light Infantry in 1908. Redesignated as 1st Green Jackets (43rd and 52nd) in 1958. Amalgamated in 1966 with the 2nd and 3rd Green Jackets.
44th (The East Essex)	56	1st Bn The Essex Regiment	The Royal Anglian Regiment	1741	Their first active service was in America. Amalgamated in 1958 with The Bedfordshire and Hertfordshire Regiment to form The 3rd East Anglian Regiment (16th/44th Foot). Amalgamated in 1964 with The 1st East Anglian, 2nd East Anglian and Royal Leicestershire Regiments.
45th (Nottinghamshire)	95	1st Bn The Sherwood Foresters (Derbyshire Regiment)	The Worcestershire and Sherwood Foresters Regiment (29th/45th Foot)	1741	In 1902 their title changed to The Sherwood Foresters (Nottinghamshire and Derbyshire Regiment). In 1970 amalgamated with The Worcestershire Regiment.
46th (South Devonshire)	32	2nd Bn The Duke of Cornwall's Light Infantry	The Light Infantry	1741	This battalion was the old 57th, raised in 1741.
47th (Lancashire)	81	1st Bn The Loyal North Lancashire Regiment	The Queen's Lancashire Regiment	1740	Their first service was at Louisburg in 1758, then at Quebec 1759. In 1921 became The Loyal Regiment (North Lancashire). Amalgamated in 1970 with The Lancashire Regiment (Prince of Wales's Volunteers).
48th (Northamptonshire)	58	1st Bn The Northamptonshire Regiment	The Royal Anglian Regiment	1740	Amalgamated in 1960 with The Royal Lincolnshire Regiment to form The 2nd East Anglian Regiment (Duchess of Gloucester's Own Royal Lincolnshire and Northamptonshire). Amalgamated in 1964 with The 1st and 3rd East Anglian Regiments and The Royal Leicestershire Regiment.
49th (Princess Charlotte of Wales's)	66	1st Bn Princess Charlotte of Wales's (Berkshire Regiment)	The Duke of Edinburgh's Royal Regiment (Berkshire and Wiltshire)	1743	The regiment was formed from details of the 22nd Foot in the West Indies. They became the 49th in 1748. They served at Copenhagen in 1801 as Marines. Granted the title 'Royal' in 1885. Became The Royal Berkshire Regiment (Princess Charlotte of Wales's) in 1921. Amalgamated in 1959 with The Wiltshire Regiment (Duke of Edinburgh's).
50th (The Queen's Own)	97	1st Bn The Queen's Own (Royal West Kent Regiment)	The Queen's Regiment	1741	First known as the 7th Marines and disbanded in 1748. Re-formed in 1757. Their first service was at the attack on Rochefort, 20th September 1757. Became the 50th (West Kent) Foot in 1782. Amalgamated in 1961 with The Buffs (Royal East Kent Regiment) to form The Queen's Own Buffs, The Royal Kent Regiment. Amalgamated in 1966 with The Queen's Royal Surrey, The Royal Sussex and The Middlesex Regiments.
51st (2nd Yorkshire, West Riding Light Infantry)	105	1st Bn The King's Own Yorkshire Light Infantry	The Light Infantry	1755	Their first service was with General Mordaunt's expedition against Oleron and Rochefort in September 1757. Amalgamated in 1968 with The Somerset and Cornwall Light Infantry, The King's Shropshire Light Infantry and The Durham Light Infantry.

Line Regiments

Pre-1881 Title	Other Bn No.	Post-1881 Title	Present Title	Date of Formation	Notes
52nd (Oxfordshire Light Infantry)	43	2nd Bn The Oxfordshire Light Infantry	The Royal Green Jackets	1755	First saw service at Bunker's Hill on 17th June, 1775. On their return home in 1782 they were styled the Oxfordshire Regiment. Became the Oxfordshire and Buckinghamshire Light Infantry in 1908.
53rd (Shropshire)	85	1st Bn The King's Shropshire Light Infantry	The Light Infantry	1755	Their first foreign service was in Gibraltar and then in Canada. Amalgamated in 1968 with The Somerset and Cornwall Light Infantry, The King's Own Yorkshire Light Infantry and The Durham Light Infantry.
54th (West Norfolk)	39	2nd Bn The Dorsetshire Regiment	The Devonshire and Dorset Regiment	1755	Its first service was garrison duty in Gibraltar. It then served in America.
55th (Westmorland)	34	2nd Bn The Border Regiment	The King's Own Royal Border Regiment	1755	Its first service was in America.
56th (West Essex)	44	2nd Bn The Essex Regiment	The Royal Anglian Regiment	1755	Their first action was at Moro, in Cuba, on 30th July 1762. They are the only regiment to bear this battle honour.
57th (West Middlesex)	77	1st Bn The Duke of Cambridge's Own (Middlesex Regiment)	The Queen's Regiment	1755	Their first active service was at Brooklyn in 1776. They had previously done garrison duty in Gibraltar, the Balearic Islands and Ireland. Amalgamated in 1966 with The Queen's Royal Surrey Regiment, The Queen's Own Buffs The Royal Kent Regiment and The Royal Sussex Regiment.
58th (Rutlandshire)	48	2nd Bn The Northamptonshire Regiment	The Royal Anglian Regiment	1755	Their first service was at Louisburg in 1758, and then at Quebec in 1759.
59th (2nd Nottinghamshire)	30	2nd Bn The East Lancashire Regiment	The Queen's Lancashire Regiment	1755	Their first service was at Bunker's Hill, 17th June 1775.
60th (The King's Royal Rifle Corps)	—	1st, 2nd, 3rd and 4th Bns. The King's Royal Rifle Corps	The Royal Green Jackets	1755	Originally the 60th (Royal American) Foot. Their first service was at Charlestown, though their first Honour is for Louisburg, 1758. Became the 60th (Duke of York's Rifle Corps) in 1824 and the King's Royal Rifle Corps in 1830. In 1958 they became the 2nd Green Jackets (The King's Royal Rifle Corps). Amalgamated in 1966 with the 1st and 3rd Green Jackets.
61st (South Gloucestershire)	28	2nd Bn The Gloucestershire Regiment	The Gloucestershire Regiment	1756	They were formed from the 2nd Bn of the Buffs. Their first service was in Martinique.
62nd (Wiltshire)	99	1st Bn The Duke of Edinburgh's (Wiltshire Regiment)	The Duke of Edinburgh's Royal Regiment (Berkshire and Wiltshire)	1756	Their first service was as Marines under Admiral Boscawen when they arrived on 8th June 1758, at Jabaru's Bay to assist in the capture of Louisburg in 1758. Amalgamated in 1959 with The Royal Berkshire Regiment (Princess Charlotte of Wales's).
63rd (West Suffolk)	96	1st Bn The Manchester Regiment	The King's Regiment	1756	Raised from the 2nd Bn of the 8th Foot, they first served in Martinique in 1759. Amalgamated in 1958 with The King's Regiment (Manchester and Liverpool). Redesignated in 1968 The King's Regiment.
64th (2nd Staffordshire)	98	1st Bn The Prince of Wales's (North Staffordshire Regiment)	The Staffordshire Regiment (The Prince of Wales's)	1756	Raised from the 2nd Bn of the 11th Foot, it first saw active service in Martinque in 1762. It does not carry this battle honour. Amalgamated in 1959 with The South Staffordshire Regiment.
65th (2nd Yorkshire, North Riding)	84	1st Bn The York and Lancaster Regiment		1756	Originally the 2nd Bn of the 12th Foot, they first saw active service at Guadaloupe in 1759. Disbanded in 1968.

Line Regiments

Pre-1881 Title	Other Bn No.	Post-1881 Title	Present Title	Date of Formation	Notes
66th (Berkshire)	49	2nd Bn Princess Charlotte of Wales's (Berkshire Regiment)	The Duke of Edinburgh's Royal Regiment (Berkshire and Wiltshire)	1755	Originally the 2nd Bn 19th Foot, they became the 66th Foot in 1758. Their first foreign service was in Jamaica.
67th (South Hampshire)	37	2nd Bn. The Royal Hampshire Regiment	The Royal Hampshire Regiment	1756	Originally the 2nd Bn of the 20th Foot, they became the 67th in 1758
68th (Durham Light Infantry)	106	1st Bn The Durham Light Infantry	The Light Infantry	1756	Originally the 2nd Bn of the 23rd Royal Welsh Fusiliers, they became the 68th in 1758. Styled 68th (Durham) Foot in 1782 and Light Infantry in 1812. Amalgamated in 1968 with The Somerset and Cornwall Light Infantry, The King's Own Yorkshire Light Infantry and The King's Shropshire Light Infantry.
69th (South Lincolnshire)	41	2nd Bn The Welsh Regiment	The Royal Regiment of Wales (24th/41st Foot)	1756	Originally the 2nd Bn of the 24th Foot. Raised in Lincolnshire and first saw service in America. A detachment under Lieutenant Chas. Pierson served on HMS *Captain* with Nelson at St. Vincent.
70th (Surrey)	31	2nd Bn The East Surrey Regiment	The Queen's Regiment	1756	Originally the 2nd Bn of the 31st Foot. Styled the 70th (Glasgow Lowland) Regiment during the period 1812-25.
71st (Highland) Light Infantry	74	1st Bn The Highland Light Infantry (City of Glasgow Regiment)	The Royal Highland Fusiliers (Princess Margaret's Own Glasgow and Ayrshire Regiment)	1777	It was originally the 73rd Regiment, receiving its present number in 1786. First saw service in India in 1780. Amalgamated in 1959 with The Royal Scots Fusiliers
72nd (Duke of Albany's Own Highlanders)	78	1st Bn The Seaforth Highlanders (Ross-shire Buffs, The Duke of Albany's)	Queen's Own Highlanders (Seaforth and Camerons)	1778	Raised by Lord Seaforth. They first saw active service in India under General Stuart at the Siege of Cuddalore in 1783. Amalgamated in 1961 with The Queen's Own Cameron Highlanders.
73rd (Perthshire)	42	2nd Bn The Black Watch (Royal Highlanders)	The Black Watch Royal Highland Regiment	1780	Their first service was in India against Tippoo Hyder Ali and Tippoo Sahib.
74th (Highlanders)	71	2nd Bn The Highland Light Infantry (City of Glasgow Regiment)	The Royal Highland Fusiliers (Princess Margaret's Own Glasgow and Ayrshire Regiment)	1787	Their first service was against Tippoo Sahib in 1791.
75th (Stirlingshire)	92	1st Bn The Gordon Highlanders	The Gordon Highlanders	1787	Raised by Colonel Robert Abercromby and embodied at Stirling in June 1788. They first saw service in India, where they distinguished themselves at Seringapatam in 1799.
76th Foot	33	2nd Bn The Duke of Wellington's (West Riding Regiment)	The Duke of Wellington's Regiment (West Riding)	1787	Styled the 76th (Hindoostan) Foot until 1812.
77th (East Middlesex) (The Duke of Cambridge's Own)	57	2nd Bn The Duke of Cambridge's Own (Middlesex Regiment)	The Queen's Regiment	1787	This Battalion saw almost continuous service in India from 1788-1807.
78th (Highland) (Ross-shire Buffs)	72	2nd Bn The Seaforth Highlanders (Ross-shire Buffs, The Duke of Albany's)	Queen's Own Highlanders (Seaforth and Camerons)	1793	Raised by the Earl of Seaforth, their first active service was in the Netherlands in 1794.
79th (Queen's Own Cameron Highlanders)	—	1st Bn The Queen's Own Cameron Highlanders	Queen's Own Highlanders (Seaforth and Camerons)	1793	Founded by Sir Alan Cameron, the regiment first saw active service in Holland in 1799. A 2nd Battalion was formed in 1897. In 1961 it amalgamated with the Seaforth Highlanders (Ross-shire Buffs, Duke of Albany's).
80th (Staffordshire Volunteers)	38	2nd Bn The South Staffordshire Regiment	The Staffordshire Regiment (The Prince of Wales's)	1793	They first saw active service in the Netherlands under the Duke of York in 1794.

Line Regiments

Pre-1881 Title	Other Bn No.	Post-1881 Title	Present Title	Date of Formation	Notes
81st (Loyal Lincoln Volunteers)	47	2nd Bn The Loyal North Lancashire Regiment	The Queen's Lancashire Regiment	1793	This Battalion was raised in Lincoln and first saw active service in South Africa in 1799. Became the Loyal Regiment (North Lancashire) in 1921.
82nd (The Prince of Wales's Volunteers)	40	2nd Bn The Prince of Wales's Volunteers (South Lancashire Regiment)	The Queen's Lancashire Regiment	1793	They first saw service at St. Domingo and later at Copenhagen in the 1807 expedition.
83rd (County of Dublin)	86	1st Bn The Royal Irish Rifles	The Royal Irish Rangers	1793	They first saw service in the Maroon Rebellion on the island of Jamaica in 1795. In 1921 it was redesignated The Royal Ulster Rifles. Amalgamated in 1968 with The Royal Inniskilling Fusiliers and The Royal Irish Fusiliers.
84th (York and Lancaster)	65	2nd Bn The York and Lancaster Regiment		1793	They first served in India. On their return they took part in the Expedition to Flushing in 1809. Disbanded in 1968.
85th (Bucks Volunteers) (King's Light Infantry)	53	2nd Bn The King's Shropshire Light Infantry	The Light Infantry	1794	Fought in Holland in 1794 and 1799. Became Light Infantry in 1808 and fought in Walcheren in 1809.
86th (Royal County Down)	83	2nd Bn The Royal Irish Rifles	The Royal Irish Rangers	1793	They served as Marines 1795-96 and then went to the Cape of Good Hope. Their first active military service was in Egypt in 1801. Between 1809 and 1812 known as the 86th (The Leinster) Foot.
87th (Royal Irish Fusiliers)	89	1st Bn Princess Victoria's (The Royal Irish Fusiliers)	The Royal Irish Rangers	1793	Originally styled the 87th (The Prince of Wales's Irish) Foot. They fought at Montevideo on 3rd February 1807 and at Buenos Aires on 5th July 1807. Became The Royal Irish Fusiliers (Princess Victoria's) in 1920. In 1968 amalgamated with The Royal Inniskilling Fusiliers and The Royal Ulster Rifles.
88th (Connaught Rangers)	94	1st Bn The Connaught Rangers		1793	First saw active service at Alost in 1794. They were disbanded in 1922.
89th (Princess Victoria's)	87	2nd Bn Princess Victoria's (The Royal Irish Fusiliers)	The Royal Irish Rangers	1793	Their first service was in Holland. They were present in Ireland at Lake's defeat of the rebels at Vinegar Hill on 21st June 1798.
90th (Perthshire Volunteers Light Infantry)	26	2nd Bn The Cameronians (Scottish Rifles)		1794	They were raised by Mr. Thomas Graham. Their first service was at Isle de Dieu and Quiberon in 1795.
91st (Princess Louise's Argyllshire Highlanders)	93	1st Bn Princess Louise's (Argyll and Sutherland) Highlanders	The Argyll and Sutherland Highlanders (Princess Louise's)	1794	Their first service was at Cape Town in 1795. Their present title dates from 1920.
92nd (Gordon Highlanders)	75	2nd Bn The Gordon Highlanders	The Gordon Highlanders	1794	Raised by the Marquis of Huntly, later Duke of Gordon.
93rd (Sutherland Highlanders)	91	2nd Bn The Princess Louise's (Argyll and Sutherland) Highlanders	The Argyll and Sutherland Highlanders	1800	Originally known as the Sutherland Fencibles, they first served in Ireland and then at the Cape of Good Hope in 1806
94th Regiment of Foot	88	2nd Bn The Connaught Rangers		1823	The 94th (Scots Brigade) Foot was raised in 1803 and disbanded in 1818. The 94th Foot was reformed in 1823 and as the 2nd Bn. The Connaught Rangers was disbanded on 31st July 1922.
95th (Derbyshire)	45	2nd Bn The Sherwood Foresters (Derbyshire Regiment)	The Worcestershire and Sherwood Foresters Regiment (29th/45th Foot)	1824	This is the sixth Regiment to be so numbered. The fourth 95th was that which served in the Peninsular War, and is now the Rifle Brigade.

Line Regiments

Pre-1881 Title	Other Bn No.	Post-1881 Title	Present Title	Date of Formation	Notes
96th Regiment of Foot	63	2nd Bn The Manchester Regiment	The King's Regiment	1824	Their first active service was in New Zealand in 1845 after serving eleven years in America.
97th (The Earl of Ulster's)	50	2nd Bn The Queen's Own (Royal West Kent Regiment)	The Queen's Regiment	1824	This is the fifth regiment to bear this number. Its first active service was in the Crimean War.
98th (Prince of Wales's)	64	2nd Bn The Prince of Wales's (North Staffordshire Regiment)	The Staffordshire Regiment (The Prince of Wales's)	1824	They are the sixth regiment to bear this number. They served in South Africa and then in the China War of 1840-42.
99th (Duke of Edinburgh's) (Lanarkshire)	62	2nd Bn The Duke of Edinburgh's (Wiltshire Regiment)	The Duke of Edinburgh's Royal Regiment (Berkshire and Wiltshire)	1824	They ware raised in Scotland. Their first active service was in New Zealand in 1845.
100th (Prince of Wales's Royal Canadian)	109	1st Bn The Prince of Wales's Leinster Regiment (Royal Canadians)		1858	They were the sixth regiment to bear this number. The honour for Niagara was earned by the fourth: 100th Prince Regent's County of Dublin Foot. The Prince of Wales's Leinster Regiment was disbanded on 31st July 1922.
101st (Royal Bengal Fusiliers)	104	1st Bn The Royal Munster Fusiliers		1756	Before joining the Home establishment in 1861 their title had been the 1st Bengal Fusiliers. The Royal Munster Fusiliers were disbanded on 31st July 1922.
102nd (Royal Madras Fusiliers)	103	1st Bn The Royal Dublin Fusiliers		1748	Before joining the Home Establishment in 1861 their title had been the 1st Madras Fusiliers. The Royal Dublin Fusiliers were disbanded on 31st July 1922
103rd (Royal Bombay Fusiliers)	102	2nd Bn The Royal Dublin Fusiliers		1661	Known as the 1st Bombay Fusiliers before joining the Home Establishment in 1861. Disbanded on 31st July 1922.
104th (Bengal Fusiliers)	101	2nd Bn The Royal Munster Fusiliers		1839	Known as the 2nd Bengal Fusiliers before joining the Home Establishment in 1861. Disbanded on 31st July 1922.
105th (Madras Light Infantry)	51	2nd Bn The King's Own Yorkshire Light Infantry	The Light Infantry	1839	Known as the 2nd Madras Light Infantry before joining the Home Establishment in 1861.
106th (Bombay Light Infantry)	68	2nd Bn The Durham Light Infantry	The Light Infantry	1826	Styled the 2nd Bombay Light Infantry prior to joining the Home Establishment in 1861.
107th (Bengal Infantry)	35	2nd Bn The Royal Sussex Regiment	The Queen's Regiment	1854	Styled the 3rd Bengal Light Infantry prior to joining the Home Establishment in 1861.
108th (Madras Infantry)	27	2nd Bn The Royal Inniskilling Fusiliers.	The Royal Irish Rangers	1854	Known as the 3rd Madras Regiment before joining the Home Establishment in 1861.
109th (Bombay Infantry)	100	2nd Bn The Prince of Wales's Leinster Regiment (Royal Canadians)		1854	Styled the 3rd Bombay European Regiment before joining the Home Establishment in 1861. Disbanded on 31st July 1922.
The Prince Consort's Own Rifle Brigade	—	1st, 2nd, 3rd and 4th Bns The Prince Consort's Own (Rifle Brigade)	The Royal Green Jackets	1800	The Rifle Corps was formed in 1800 from details of the 21st, 23rd, 25th, 27th, 29th, 49th, 55th, 69th, 71st, 72nd, 79th, 85th and 92nd Regiments. Their title signifies their *raison d'être* in that they were formed to use the then newly introduced rifle. Known as the 95th Rifle Regiment in 1802, styled the Rifle Brigade in 1816. In 1920 their title was chaged to The Rifle Brigade (Prince Consort's Own). Redesignated the 3rd Green Jackets (Rifle Brigade) in 1958. Amalgamated in 1966 with the 1st and 2nd Green Jackets.

Bibliography

Ascoli D. *A Companion to the British Army, 1660-1983,* 1983

Biddulph, Major H. *Early Indian Campaigns and the Decorations Awarded for them* (1913)

Carter T. *War Medals of the British Army,* 1893

Chichester H. M. and Burgess-Short G. *Records and Badges of the British Army,* 1899

Dalton C. *The Waterloo Roll Call,* 1904

Dewar M. *Brush Fire Wars,* 1984

Douglas-Morris, Captain K. J. *The Naval General Service Medal Roll, 1793-1840,* 1982

Douglas-Morris, Captain K. J. *Naval Medals 1793-1856,* 1987

Dupuy R. E. and Dupuy T. N. *The Encyclopedia of Military History,* 1976

Everson G. R. *The South Africa 1853 Medal Roll,* 1978

Fevyer W. H. and Wilson J. W. *The China War Medal 1900 to the Royal Navy and the Royal Marines,* 1985

Fevyer W. H. and Wilson J. W. *The Queen's South Africa Medal to the Royal Navy and the Royal Marines,* 1983

Forsyth D. R. *Cape of Good Hope General Service Medal, The Medal Roll*

Forsyth D. R. *Medal for the Defence of Ookiep 4th April-4th May 1902*

Forsyth D. R. *Natal Native Rebellion 1906, The Medal Roll*

Forsyth D. R. *South African War Medal 1877-8-9, The Medal Roll*

Fortescue, The Hon J. W. *A History of the British Army,* 1899

Foster, Colonel Kingsley O. N. *The Military General Service Medal Roll, 1793-1814,* 1947

Gould R. W. and Douglas-Morris, Captain K. J. *The Army of India Medal Roll, 1799-1826,* 1974

Hailes, Colonel D. A. *Naval General Service Medal Roll 1793-1840*

Hastings Irwin D. *War Medals and Decorations,* 1910

Hawkins E. *Medallic Illustrations,* 1885

Hibbard M. G. *Boer War Tribute Medals,* 1982

James W. *The Naval History of Great Britain,* 1902

Jocelyn A. *Awards of Honour,* 1956

Mackinnon J. P. and Shadbolt S. H. *The South Africa Campaign of 1879,* 1882

Magor R. B. *African General Service Medals*

Maurice, Colonel J. F. *Military History of the Campaign of 1882 in Egypt,* 1887

Mayo J. H. *Medals and Decorations of the British Army and Navy,* 1897

Milford Haven, Admiral The Marquis of, *British Naval Medals,* 1919

Parritt, Colonel B. A. H. *Red with Two Blue Stripes,* 1974

Payne A. A. *A Handbook of British and Foreign Orders, War Medals and Decorations awarded to the Army and Navy,* 1911

Poulsom, Major N. *The White Ribbon,* 1968

Purves A. A. *The Medals, Decorations and Orders of the Great War 1914-18,* 1975

Roncetti G. A. and Denby E. E. *The Canadians*

Shadbolt S. H. *The Afghan Campaigns of 1878-80,* 1882

Siborne, Captain W. *History of the War in France and Belgium in 1815,* 1844

Tancred G. *Historical Record of Medals and Honorary Distinctions,* 1891

Taprell-Dorling H. *Ribbons and Medals, various editions*

Whitaker, Captain A. E. *British War Medals and Decorations,* 1890

The Army List

British Numismatic Journal

The London Gazette

The London Stamp Exchange Medal List

The Journal of the Orders and Medals Research Society

The Orders and Medals Research Society. The Miscellany of Honours

The Times History of the War in South Africa, 1899-1902, 1907

The War Medal Record 1896-1898

Journal of the Society of Army Historical Research.

Index of Medals

292

294

Index of Bars